EX·LIBRIS·SUNE·GREGERSEN

D1674279

Cyclical Change Continued

Linguistik Aktuell/Linguistics Today (LA)

ISSN 0166-0829

Linguistik Aktuell/Linguistics Today (LA) provides a platform for original monograph studies into synchronic and diachronic linguistics. Studies in LA confront empirical and theoretical problems as these are currently discussed in syntax, semantics, morphology, phonology, and systematic pragmatics with the aim to establish robust empirical generalizations within a universalistic perspective.

For an overview of all books published in this series, please see
http://benjamins.com/catalog/la

Founding Editor

Werner Abraham
Universität Wien / Ludwig Maximilian Universität München

General Editors

Werner Abraham
Universität Wien /
Ludwig Maximilian Universität München

Elly van Gelderen
Arizona State University

Advisory Editorial Board

Volume 227

Cyclical Change Continued
Edited by Elly van Gelderen

Cyclical Change Continued

Edited by

Elly van Gelderen

Arizona State University

John Benjamins Publishing Company

Amsterdam / Philadelphia

DOI 10.1075/la.227

Cataloging-in-Publication Data available from Library of Congress:
LCCN 2015044782 (PRINT) / 2016000409 (E-BOOK)

ISBN 978 90 272 5710 9 (HB)
ISBN 978 90 272 6743 6 (E-BOOK)

John Benjamins Publishing Company · https://benjamins.com

Table of contents

List of contributors

Johan van der Auwera
Department of Linguistics
University of Antwerp
2000 Antwerpen, Belgium
johan.vanderauwera@ua.ac.be

Mariana Bahtchevanova
School of International Letters and
Cultures
Arizona State University
Tempe, AZ 95287-0302
MarianaB@asu.edu

Elly van Gelderen
Department of English
Arizona State University
Tempe, AZ 95287-0302
ellyvangelderen@asu.edu

Remus Gergel
Department of English
University of Graz
Heinrichstr. 36
A-8010 Graz, Austria
remus.gergel@uni-graz.at

Tom Givón
Department of Linguistics
University of Oregon
Eugene, OR 97403-1290
tgivon@uoregon.edu

Łukasz Jędrzejowski
Universität Potsdam,
Germany
lukasz-jedrzejowski@daad-alumni.de

Robert LaBarge
Department of English
Arizona State University
Tempe, AZ 95287-0302
robert.labarge@gmail.com

John McWhorter
The Center for American Studies
Columbia University
New York, NY 10027
jm3156@columbia.edu

Marianne Mithun,
Department of Linguistics
University of Santa Barbara
Santa Barbara, California 93106-3100
mithun@linguistics.ucsb.edu

Clifton Pye
Department of Linguistics
University of Kansas
Lawrence, KS 66045
pyersqr@ku.edu

Benedikt Szmrecsanyi
Department of Linguistics
KU Leuven
Blijde-Inkomststraat 21
B-3000 Leuven, Belgium
Benedikt.Szmrecsanyi@kuleuven.be

Ljuba Veselinova
Department of Linguistics
Stockholm University
SE – 106 91 Stockholm, Sweden
ljuba@ling.su.se

Frens Vossen
Department of Linguistics
University of Antwerp
2000 Antwerpen, Belgium
famvossen@planet.nl

Johanna Wood
Aarhus University
Jens Chr. Skous Vej 4
DK-8000 Aarhus C, Denmark
engjw@dac.au.dk

PART I

Characteristics of cycles

Cyclical change continued

Introduction

Elly van Gelderen
Arizona State University

This introductory chapter outlines what a cycle is, what kinds of cycles are generally accepted, and how the contributions in this book fit the various cycles. Uncontroversial cycles are the negative, future, modal, and determiner cycles; these will be referred to as micro-cycles. More controversial are macro-cycles, i.e. cycles that shift a language from analytic to synthetic and from synthetic to analytic. These cycles are controversial partly because of the use of the terms analytic and synthetic, which will be discussed briefly. The introduction also includes a section on recent work, issues of debate, and on future directions.

1. What is the cycle?

The linguistic cycle is a name used to describe language change taking place in a systematic manner and direction. Cycles involve the disappearance of a particular word and its renewal by another. The most well-known cycle is the Negative Cycle where a new negative word may be added to an already negative construction for emphasis after which the earlier negative disappears. The new negative may be reinforced by another negative and may later disappear as well.

There are early advocates of the view that language change is cyclical. Robins (1967: 150–159) provides a useful overview of how, according to de Condillac (1746) and Tooke (1786–1805), abstract, grammatical vocabulary develops from earlier concrete vocabulary. Bopp (1816) similarly argues that affixes arise from earlier independent words. In the early twentieth century, work on cyclical change appears by von der Gabelentz (1901). Because new cycles are not identical to the old ones, one way of characterizing a cycle is as a spiral, as in the oft-cited passage in von der Gabelentz (1901: 256), which provides a very clear description of cyclical change.

(1)   "The history of language moves in the diagonal of two forces: the impulse toward comfort, which leads to the wearing down of sounds, and that toward clarity, which disallows this erosion and the destruction of the language. The affixes grind themselves down, disappear without a trace; their

DOI 10.1075/la.227.01gel

functions or similar ones, however, require new expression. They acquire this expression, by the method of isolating languages, through word order or clarifying words. The latter, in the course of time, undergo agglutination, erosion, and in the mean time renewal is prepared: periphrastic expressions are preferred ... always the same: the development curves back towards isolation, not in the old way, but in a parallel fashion. That's why I compare them to spirals"   (von der Gabelentz 1901: 256; my translation, EvG).

Meillet (1912: 140) also uses spiral as a term ("une sorte de développement en spirale") for what I will continue to refer to as a cycle.

In (1), von der Gabelentz states that languages may have affixes that then require a new expression after they are ground down. The new expression may be constructed "through word order or clarifying words". Von der Gabelentz argues that languages change from inflectional and agglutinative systems to isolating systems and then again develop into agglutinating ones. Meillet's (1912) work on language change as grammaticalization is an obvious source for ideas on cyclical change. For him, these changes come about because of a loss of expressivity and subsequent renewal. Meillet's examples of grammaticalization are many: the French verb *être* 'to be' going from lexical verb to auxiliary, *aller* 'to go' changing from a verb of motion to a future marker, and the Greek *thelô ina* 'I wish that' changing to a future marker that is much reduced in phonology, namely *tha*.

Hodge (1970) has done more than anyone to feed recent ideas on the cycle with his short article entitled 'The Linguistic Cycle' in which he examines the overall changes in the history of Egyptian. He uses lower and upper case to give a visual representation of full cycles from synthetic 'sM', i.e. a language with lots of inflectional morphology as indicated by the capital M and lower case s for less syntax, to analytic Sm, i.e. a language with a lot of syntax, indicated by the capital S, and less morphology, indicated by lower case m. By more or less syntax Hodge means the degree of reliance on function words and word order. His representation is provided in Table 1.

Table 1. Developments in Egyptian (from Hodge 1970: 5, *indicates a reconstructed stage)

Proto-Afroasiatic	Analytic	*Sm
Old Egyptian	Synthetic	sM
Late Egyptian	Analytic	Sm
Coptic	Synthetic	sM

Many of the early works on cyclical change analyze it as a change in the typological character of a language, e.g. from analytic to synthetic. This view, however, is currently not always accepted and there are challenges in defining the terms analytic and synthetic. Heine, Claudi, and Hünnemeyer (1991:245), basing themselves on the work of Givón (e.g. 1971, 1976), distinguish three kinds of cyclical change. The first only refers to "isolated instances of grammaticalization", when a lexical item grammaticalizes and is then replaced by a new lexeme. An example would be the lexical verb *go* (or *want)* being used as a future marker. Examples of this type of cyclical change are discussed in the present volume by Johanna Wood, Remus Gergel, Robert LaBarge, and Łukasz Jędrzejowski (Chapters 10 to 13). One could argue that these changes have wider implications and should therefore be counted as examples of the second type which refers to "subparts of language, for example, when the tense-aspect-mood system of a given language develops from a periphrastic into an inflexional pattern and back to a new periphrastic one" (Heine, Claudi & Hünnemeyer 1991:245) or when negatives change. Obvious examples of the second type of change are provided in the chapters by Marianne Mithun, Ljuba Veselinova, Johan van der Auwera and Frens Vossen, Clifton Pye, and Tom Givón (Chapters 2, 6, 7, 8, and 9). I refer to these two types as micro-cycles.

The third type of cyclical change that Heine et al. identify applies to entire languages and especially to language types and I therefore refer to these as macro-cycles. The descriptions by von der Gabelentz and Hodge, given above, fit this kind. Other examples of this change are discussed by John McWhorter, Benedikt Szmrecsanyi, and Mariana Bahtchevanova and Elly van Gelderen (Chapters 3 to 5).

Heine, Claudi, and Hünnemeyer (1991:246) argue that there is "more justification to apply the notion of a linguistic cycle to individual linguistic developments", e.g. the development of future markers, of negatives, and of tense, rather than to changes in typological character, as in the development from analytic to synthetic and back to analytic. Their reasons for caution about the third type of change, i.e. a cyclical change in a language's typology, is that we don't know enough about older stages of languages. This cautionary sentiment is reflected in the work of other linguists and, whereas most researchers are comfortable with cycles of the first and second kind, they are not with cycles of the third kind. Jespersen (1922; Chapter 21.9) criticizes the concept of cyclical change. His criticism is based on his views that languages move towards flexionless stages in a unidirectional manner and that they do not develop new morphology. Jespersen's views cannot be correct because languages and families such as Finnish, Altaic, and Athabascan increase in morphological complexity through a cyclical process (see van Gelderen 2011).

Because macro-cycles feature prominently in this volume, I briefly discuss some of the problems in characterizing a language as analytic or synthetic in the next section. It will of course be impossible to do justice to the vast literature on this topic. See Schwegler (1990) for more literature review.

2. Analytic and synthetic

Analytic languages have words with few morphemes, with the most analytic showing a one-to-one relationship between word and morpheme. Chinese is often cited as a good example of this, and I'll come back to this language below. Words in synthetic languages contain more than one morpheme. Languages with verbal agreement are synthetic. As is obvious from this description, it is relatively easy to decide on a purely analytic language but hard to decide on what counts as a synthetic language: is it having words that contain three morphemes or words with five morphemes? According to Schwegler (1990: 10), it was Du Ponceau who proposed a third type of language, namely polysynthetic, although von Humboldt (1836) may be more famous for it. As Sapir (1921: 128) puts it, polysynthetic languages are "more than ordinarily synthetic."

Another challenge, pointed out by Douglas Biber (p.c.), is that register plays a role in determining the analyticity of languages such as English. If, for instance, verbs are more inflected than nouns are and if verbs are more frequently used in a certain register, that would skew the results. Szmrecsanyi (Chapter 4) shows that this is in fact the case, making claims about this cycle very hard to evaluate.

Von Schlegel (1818) seems to be the first to use the terms analytic and synthetic where languages are concerned. As Schwegler (1990: 5) points out, from the beginning, the terms were not used in precise ways since they include gradations. Thus, the labels don't fit the Germanic languages very well in that, according to von Schlegel, these languages "penchent fortement vers les forms analytiques" ['lean strongly towards analytic forms'] and, at the same time, they have "une certaine puissance de synthèse" ['a certain power of synthesis']. Von Schlegel's reasons for postulating the terms may have been to distinguish the more 'perfect' synthetic languages from the less perfect ones. He sees the reason for change towards an analytic language to be "les conquérans barbares" ['the barbarian conquerors'] (1818: 24) who acquired Latin imperfectly. McWhorter (Chapter 3) engages this question of change towards analyticity in languages that are spoken by a majority of non-native speakers.

Apart from morphemes per word, a second distinction is made as to whether the morphemes in the synthetic languages are agglutinative, as in Inuktitut and Korean, or (in)flectional, as in English and Navajo. From a diachronic perspective, there is a cyclical relationship between these stages, for instance, as formulated by Crowley (1992: 170) and reproduced in Figure 1.

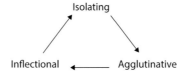

Figure 1. Attachment type

Thus, in the change from isolating to agglutinative, separate words are reanalyzed morphologically as a part of another word but with their own grammatical features connected to the morpheme. In the change from agglutinative to inflectional, the features of the two are combined. This last change increases the degree of syntheticity of a particular language. Bahtchevanova and van Gelderen examine the development of portmanteau morphemes in French which involves a change from agglutinative to inflectional but also an increase in degree of syntheticity.

How do we decide on the degree of analyticity or syntheticity? Greenberg (1960) provides a system where words are assigned values depending on their complexity. A completely analytic language (one word, one morpheme) would have the value 1.00, a mildly synthetic language would be 2.00 (two morphemes in a word), and a poly-synthetic language would average above 3.00. There are many drawbacks to this system and, as Schwegler (1990:22) points out, that may be the reason Greenberg stops pursuing it. Nichols (1992) is interested in where the synthesis occurs, on the head or the dependent and formulates a point system to determine how head-marking or dependent-marking a language is. She is less concerned how extreme a language is in its marking but more whether it is head-marking or dependent-marking consistently. Szmrecsanyi (2012; Chapter 4) defines analyticity as using "coding strategies that convey grammatical information via free grammatical markers" and syntheticity as "those coding strategies where grammatical information is signaled by bound grammatical markers" and proposes a measure in terms of number of free or bound morphemes per 1000.

Analytic and synthetic stages can co-occur in a language; languages can be in one stage for agreement and in another for TMA and negation. What conspires to make them super-synthetic or super-analytic is an open question. Chinese is analytic in that mood, negation, and aspect are expressed as separate words but might be becoming more synthetic because, for instance, the perfective marker -le in (2) cannot be on its own and has grammaticalized from the verb liao meaning 'to complete' among other meanings (Sun 1996:85; 178).

(2)   ta   ba wenjian-jia   qingqingde fang **zai le** zhuo shang Mandarin
      she BA document folder gently   put on PF table up
      'She put the documents gently on the table.'   (Hui-Ling Yang pc, from
                                                      ⟨yahoo.com.tw⟩

There are many other such words that can no longer be independent, e.g. the question marker ma and the object marker ba. LaBarge (Chapter 13) explores a change towards the synthetic as the Chinese word yào changes from a full verb meaning 'desire' to a future marker and is increasingly limited to occur before another verb. So, if we look carefully, highly analytic language are grammaticalizing as well (see Post 2007).

Synthetic languages such as Old English change into more analytic languages. For instance, verbs inflected for mood and aspect/tense come to be replaced by auxiliaries generated in positions just expressing mood and aspect/tense, originating in verbs. Modern English cannot, however, be characterized as a completely analytic language since modals, negatives, and *have* are merging into single words, as in (3a). It is even possible to see the first person *I* as an affix, always occurring before a verb and renewed by an oblique *me*, as in (3b).

(3) a. *I couldna done that*   Colloquial English
         'I could not have done that.'

     b. *Me, I couldna done that*

Not addressed very often is the question of derivational morphology. Especially since the 1500s, English has acquired many morphemes from loans (*trans-, anti-, micro-, ex-, -ion, -able, -ian, -ity*). Should that be included as well?

Modern French presents an interesting case for an analytic to synthetic stage as well. Tesnière (1932) points out that standard French is a synthetic language with an analytic orthography. With this, he means that the pronouns are written separately from the verb but are not in fact independent from these verbs. Bahtchevanova and van Gelderen (Chapter 5) show that the subject cycle has turned the pronouns into verbal agreement but that this has an effect on the preverbal object pronouns, which can be reanalyzed as agreement as well, turning the language into a really synthetic language. These developments show a macro-cycle in progress.

Concluding, it is very hard to give a precise definition of synthetic and analytic. A language with one (grammatical) morpheme per word is analytic and one with more than one per word is synthetic. A language where most arguments are marked on the verb and where nominals are optional is polysynthetic. As already mentioned, it is an open question what factors contribute to a language developing analyticity or syntheticity.

3.   Recent work and emerging questions

Although much work remains focused on the negative cycle, e.g. Larrivée & Ingham (2011), Vossen & van der Auwera (2014), and Willis et al. (2013), the edited volume that came out of the 2008 workshop on the linguistic cycle in Tempe, Arizona (van Gelderen 2009) contains chapters on the other cycles as well, namely the pronominal, demonstrative, copular, modal, and prepositional cycles. Other work includes Jäger (2012), Bacskai-Atkari (2014), Bácskai-Atkári & Dekány (2014), Egedi (2014), and Hegedüs (2014). Cyclical semantic change is getting more attention in the work of Regine Eckardt, Remus Gergel, and Ashwini Deo and it and phonological and pro-sodic change can also be thought of as cyclical, as in Bermúdez-Otero & Trousdale (2012) and Salmons & Zhuang (2014) respectively.

Looking at changes in a cyclical manner has brought up new questions. Some of the crucial descriptive questions in relation to the mechanisms of the linguistic cycle are summarized in (4).

(4)   Questions in relation to the linguistic cycle are:
    a.   Which cycles exist and why?
    b.   i   Which semantic and grammatical features participate in cycles?
        ii   What are the sources of renewal once a cycle has desemanticized a lexical item?
        iii   At what point in the cycle does the renewing element appear?
    c.   Are there typical steps in a cycle?
    d.   i.   Why are some changes frequent or infrequent?
        ii.   What structural factors interfere in this process?
    e.   What's the role of language contact?

Answering (4a) contributes to the 'definition' of the linguistic cycle. From a structural point of view, two main types of cycle occur: those where a full phrase strengthens the original lexical word, i.e. where doubling occurs, such as in the traditional negative cycle (Jespersen 1917; van der Auwera 2009), and those where a new word is used, without co-occurrence of the old and new, such as in Croft's Existential to Negative Cycle (Croft 1991; van Gelderen 2008). In the current volume, Veselinova (Chapter 6) discusses this cycle and many contributors comment on how 'their cycle' is a typical cycle or not, e.g. Mithun and Pye (Chapters 2 and 8).

Questions (4bi) and (4ii) are best answered by studying Heine and Kuteva (2002) who provide an incredibly helpful encyclopedia of grammaticalization. In it, they identify categories that are typically grammatical in languages of the world: time, space, cause, completion/telicity, intention, existence, negation, number, and person. The prevalence of certain cycles shows which of these categories are important for all languages and shed insight on the (human) cognitive faculty. Mithun's chapter adds the distributive cycle to the set of cycles, a rarer cycle, where verbal affixes cause the event/state to be spread in space, time, and participants.

Answers to question (4biii) remain controversial: will the old form first weaken phonologically or not? Although Meillet (1912:139) acknowledges the role of the weakening of pronunciation ("un affaiblissement de la pronunciation"), he believes that what provokes the start of the (negative) cycle is the need to speak forcefully ("le besoin de parler avec force"). Therefore, the loss in phonological content is not a necessary consequence of the loss of semantic content (see also Hoeksema 2009). Veselinova's contribution (Chapter 6) provides an interesting perspective on the question of when the renewing element appears and how long it stays around: stages with variation are quite stable. Likewise, Kiparsky (2011:19) argues "in the development of case, bleaching is not necessarily tied to morphological downgrading from postposition to clitic to suffix". The pronoun cycle shows different results in that a stage with just the affix is possible. Thus, there are estimates that only 30% of languages have pronouns (see Chapter 5).

As for question (4c), van der Auwera (2009) carefully lays out the typical steps of the negative cycle but also some variation in the stages. Van der Auwera and Vossen (Chapter 7) provide further evidence for solid Jespersen Cycles in two families of the Americas and one possible cycle that starts in a different position. Gergel (Chapter 11) compares English and German comparative temporal adverbs that acquire modal meanings and shows why they end up undergoing slightly different changes.

As for (4di), we have some sense what keeps the negative cycle going. As was mentioned above, because negatives are so important in language, pragmatic strengthening is frequent and this stimulates new forms next to pragmatically weaker ones (see also Meisner et al. 2014). Modal cycles are also omnipresent, as e.g. Nesselhauf (2012) has shown. Using Traugott and König's (1991) influential inferencing model, one can say that modals originate in verbs of motion, ability, volition, and intention that 'invite' certain inferences of futurity and possibility. A new modal is the result of the reanalysis of a pragmatic function into a grammatical category or feature.

The circumstances surrounding some of the other cycles are still mysterious, e.g. why subject pronoun cycles do not occur in East Asian languages. Chinese, Thai, Korean, and Indonesian (to name but a few) do not show tendencies to phonologically reduce the subject pronoun or to restrict its occurrence to a preverbal position. Subject pronouns themselves have been renewed through nouns in some of these languages (Thai and Indonesian) and, in these, there is a variety of pronouns to choose from but there has been no instance where the pronoun is reanalyzed as agreement marker.

Regarding (4dii), structural chance factors, such as word order and the particular position of the verb 'to be', may play a role, e.g. negatives are focused and therefore may be highlighted by 'be' and a combination of 'be' and the negative can become the new negative. Cycles may conflict and this structural conflict may constitute a slowing (or accelerating) factor, e.g. Croft's and Jespersen's cycles seem to work together (in Athabaskan and Ugric, see van Gelderen 2011), and subject and object pronoun cycles do interact (see Bahtchevanova and van Gelderen, Chapter 5). Copula verbs have many sources, demonstratives, adpositions, existence and motion verbs, and the choice of which of these emerges as the copula must be due to structural factors. English has a strong tendency to recruit verbs and that may be because it has a prominent T(ense) position; many Semitic languages and most creoles reanalyze demonstratives as copulas because these languages use topicalizations.

Regarding (4e), external reasons for accelerating or impeding the rate of change need to be studied. Heine and Kuteva (2005) have argued for accelerated grammaticalization due to language contact. In this volume, van der Auwera and Vossen's data show areal clusters in the stages of the negative cycle and Mithun suggests language contact as a potential contributor to cyclical change in the languages of Northern California because certain cycles appear in certain linguistic areas. She shows for Central Pomo, a Pomoan language, that directional prefixes on a verb are renewed through adverbs that are themselves being cliticized on a verb which is a feature present in the other languages as well. Szmrecsanyi's data show that something major happened in English around 1200; a contact explanation with Celtic or Old Norse would of course make sense (see e.g. Filppula et al. 2002 and Emonds & Faarlund 2014, respectively). McWhorter (2007, this volume) argues that languages with a lot of adult language learning may be stuck in one stage.

Related is the question of complexity and simplicity when the former is seen as due to social isolation and the latter as due to language contact (see Trudgill 2011). The linguistic cycle predicts that any language will accrue complexity when it changes from analytic to synthetic and lose this when it goes from synthetic to analytic again and the same with the other cycles. Modern English, with more non-native than native speakers is still accruing complexity, as shown in (3).

4.   Contributions to the cycle in this volume

Having given a brief idea of what micro- and macro-cycles are and of the questions we have regarding cycles, I discuss each contribution in terms of what it tells us about the big picture. The theoretical framework used by the various contributors varies because cyclical change can be examined from a variety of angles. To me, cycles are fascinating because of their systematicity. Systematicity in syntactic change, as Gianollo et al. (2015:4) put it, represents "an absolute novelty in the area of historical linguistics, where only sound change was considered to be subject to regularity". This systematicity provides a window on the universality of language or the language faculty, depending on one's theoretical disposition.

Marianne Mithun provides detailed examples of cycles in related languages that all proceed somewhat differently. She organizes them as due to phonological, semantic, or pragmatic change and chronicles reflexive, demonstrative, distributive, pronominal, and negative cycles in the Iroquoian languages. Each of the changes has its own local flavor. For instance, the cognate of a reconstructed reflexive is still present in many languages but was renewed through reduplication in all of the modern languages and the demonstrative cycle shows the classic change from demonstrative (still present in Cherokee) into one kind of article in Mohawk and another kind in Tuscarora, with a renewal through a locative in the latter. As mentioned, the chapter also considers the influence of contact and she concludes with what she sees driving this change, namely a "cognitive propensity for routinization" and a subsequent loss of salience in phonology, semantics, and pragmatics.

The chapters by John McWhorter, Benedikt Szmrecsanyi, and Mariana Bahtchevanova and Elly van Gelderen all address changes involving the status of a language (or family) as analytic or synthetic, i.e. macro-cyclical change. **McWhorter** asks why very analytic languages are mainly spoken in Southeast Asia and West Africa and argues that "radical analyticity is neither plausible nor documented as a stage that grammars reach amidst a cycle of inflectional growth and decay" but is "the result of widespread adult acquisition in the past". Most of the emphasis in the remainder of the chapter is devoted to showing that for the three sub-subfamilies of the Niger-Congo family, namely Gbe, Yoruba, and Nupoid, a scenario of second language acquisition makes sense.

Szmrecsanyi uses corpus-data from the history of English between 1100 and 1900 and argues that analyticity rises until the 17th century and then decreases; the opposite is true for syntheticity. So, after the 17th century, the trend is towards more syntheticity and less analyticity. Hence, Szmrecsanyi speaks of a spiral. His data also reveal that the text type makes a difference and that, by looking at which categories are responsible for the analytic or synthetic character of the stages, we arrive at a better sense of what we think of as analytic or synthetic. For instance, his results show that determiners and expletive *there* increase but that pronouns do not. This results in a much more complicated picture.

Bahtchevanova and van Gelderen discuss the status of French subject and object pronouns. If they are right, French is not only renewing its erstwhile synthetic subject agreement system but also moving towards more syntheticity in the object system. In their chapter, data is added that shows that in addition to first and second person singular subject pronouns, which are well on their way to being agreement, third person singular and plural pronouns are also changing. Some of them are skipping a stage in the cycle in that the agreement prefix is left out and the emphatic form serves as the regular pronoun. A second point to their chapter is to see if there are changes to preverbal object pronouns. They argue there are three kinds, namely a loss of the object pronoun, a reanalysis to agreement marker, and a change from pre- to postverbal position. These changes are to be expected because object clitics and inflectional subject affixes are mixed in preverbal position. The result is an accelerated object cycle. They also add an account for the changes in object pronouns that result from the changes in subject markers using a generative model with feature checking.

Negative cycles are discussed by Ljuba Veselinova, Johan van der Auwera and Frens Vossen, and Clifton Pye. **Veselinova** looks at the negative existential cycle in which negative existential verbs are reanalyzed as negative markers after which new existential verbs may arise. This cycle is also known as Croft's Cycle (Croft 1991 being one of the first to write about it). Using data from six families (Berber, Dravidian, Polynesian, Slavonic, Uralic, and Turkic), Veselinova raises the issue of the seemingly long time that it takes for this cycle to proceed, namely that it is "consistently of a lengthier kind".

Croft's Cycle predicts three stages, i.e. having the same negative for all verbs, having different negatives for existential and non-existential verbs, and having the negative existential used as the negative marker for all verbs (again). A wealth of data shows that the transitional periods in between these three stages are relatively long and stable. Concluding, she emphasizes that the difference between negation of actions and negation of existence must be so crucial to cognition that it keeps being renewed.

Van der Auwera and Vossen present data on negatives in 530 languages of the Americas. The negative precedes the verb in 48% of the languages surveyed and it follows the verb in 28% of languages and they find double marking in 20% of the languages in their sample. These percentage fit in a negative cycle picture if a doubling stage is followed by a new negative in final position. They then focus on three families of Central and South America, Mayan, Quechuan, and Maipurean, for the first two of which there is diachronic data. Their study reveals a clear negative cycle in Mayan from single to double negation to single marking again; it also shows an areal dimension to this change. The Quechuan languages show a very similar negative cycle with again an areal dimension, the central languages being the most progressive. Maipurean languages show more variation in the pre- and post-verbal negatives and the situation is much more complex. The authors provide a number of scenarios with one possibly showing a Jespersen Cycle 'in reverse' because the renewing element is on the left of the verb.

Pye reconstructs the history of negation marking in the Mayan languages and shows that one Mayan language exhibits the start of a typical Jespersen Cycle but that the majority of Mayan languages provide no evidence for a negation cycle that uses indefinite renewals. To strengthen the negative, the latter use adverbial clitics that are external to the clause. Pye attributes this to the "the unique syntactic organization of the Mayan languages". Pye adds that "French and the Germanic languages recruit words in the verb phrase to modify negation [and w]hen they become NPI they begin to interact more with negation than with the verb phrase, but still remain in the VP. The Mayan negation domain is independent of the VP and the verb complex. Its independence allows the languages to modify negation marking directly rather than reanalyzing a piece of the VP" (Pye, 22 November 2014 e-mail).

The last five chapters look at micro-cycles involving pronouns, quantifiers and modals. **Tom Givón** examines Ute clitic pronouns, contrasting them with other reference-coding devices, namely demonstratives, independent pronouns, zero anaphora, and flexible word-order. The conclusions he reaches are that most independent pronouns "are used in contexts of referential discontinuity" and most zero and clitic pronouns show "extreme referential continuity–a one-clause anaphoric gap". The fronting of pronouns and nominal groups is "strongly associated with referential or thematic discontinuity" whereas the post-posing of pronouns and nominals goes with referential continuity. This shows evidence of a typical cycle. His chapter also contributes to structural questions: why do pronouns cliticize to verbs and why in the particular position.

The DP Cycle is relatively well-known as a cycle where demonstratives are reanalyzed as articles which then in turn are reinforced by deictic element, e.g. adverbs or other demonstratives. **Johanna Wood** expands on this relatively well-known cycle by looking at changes in demonstratives in other parts of the DP, namely the Adjective Phrase. The demonstratives *this, that,* and *thus* have seen changes from manner to degree and Wood explores various paths of change and also renewals of erstwhile functions.

Remus Gergel illustrates cyclical semantic change in the domain of intensionality and degree marking. He looks at spirals involving the English adverb *rather* and its German counterpart *eher* ('sooner, earlier, rather'). *Rather* changes from a temporal comparative meaning of 'sooner' to a modally marked one, whereas *eher* retains the earlier temporal meaning and has more epistemic flavors. As Gergel puts it, the "difference lies in the fact that while *rather* appears to have grammaticalized to order propositions primarily with respect to desires, *eher* orders them primarily with respect to likelihood based on knowledge and evidence". The reason for the difference, he suggests, is because it fills a void in English, a void left by the loss of *leofer* 'preferably', where German retains this adverb in the form of *lieber*.

Łukasz Jędrzejowski looks at the relationship between three verbs in the history of German that now introduce or used to introduce negative complements and are therefore referred to as NPIs (Negative Polarity Items). The three verbs are *dürfen, bedürfen,* and *brauchen*, all having a basic meaning of 'need'. He shows a cyclical replacement of the one by the other and then by the third one. Big questions are what causes this cycle: is there a loss of features that sets it in motion or is there a position to which the verbs move and in which they are stuck.

Robert LaBarge discusses a change in the Chinese verb *yào* that resembles the one undergone by *will* in English, namely a change from verb of volition to future auxiliary and then the renewal of the older meaning by another verb of volition. He pays attention to the semantic features that change, the syntactic environment, and the position in the sentence in arguing that certain uses of *yào* are indeed auxiliary. The paper contributes to connecting cyclical change to structural positions and to discussions of layering in grammaticalization. It also provides an explanation for this change in terms of a relatively new approach in generative grammar: problems of labelling invite a reanalysis.

5.   Conclusion and future directions

In this introduction, I present the cycle and also the differences between micro- and macro-cycles. The reason for the distinction is the acceptance of the former but the unease many people have with the latter. I have also reviewed the contributions each of the chapters make. Enduring questions concern predicting the speed and the steps of a cycle.

Future directions can be theoretical and empirical. For instance, Chomsky (2013; 2015) suggests that certain configurations are unlabelable because they are both maximal projections or because their features clash. This idea provides an avenue to see if certain reanalyses can be predicted. Van Gelderen (2015) follows this up and looks at change involving phrases to heads, as occur in the Negative and Demonstrative Cycles, and LaBarge (Chapter 13) for head to head changes.

Another possible direction that might be fruitful to account for the absence of change is the one suggested in Bisang (2014). He compares the strength of morphological paradigms in highly analytic languages and notes that radical pro-drop is possible in East and mainland Southeast Asian languages but not in West African Niger-Congo languages. He argues that the ancestor languages of the latter had paradigms that "were strong enough to remain relevant in syntax after they got lost in morphology" (p. 24). This suggests covert features may be active in one language and drive renewal.

In short, cycles continue to provide an exciting window on the language faculty!

Acknowledgements

Many thanks to the participants in this volume for internal reviewing as well as to Werner Abraham, Douglas Biber, Gerrit Dimmendaal, Bonnie Fonseca-Greber, Jack Hoeksema, Agnes Jäger, Joe Salmons, Chaofen Sun, and David Willis for reviewing one or more chapters.

References

Bácskai-Atkári, Júlia. 2014. Cyclical change in Hungarian comparatives. *Diachronica* 31(4): 465–505. doi:10.1075/dia.31.4.01bac

Bácskai-Atkári, Júlia & Dékány, Éva. 2014. From non-finite to finite subordination. In Kiss (ed.), 148–223. doi:10.1093/acprof:oso/9780198709855.003.0006

Bermúdez-Otero, Ricardo & Trousdale, Graeme. 2012. Cycles and continua. In Nevalainen & Traugott (eds), 691–720.

Bisang, Walter. 2014. On the strength of morphological paradigms. In *Paradigm Change: In the Transeurasian Languages and Beyond* [Studies in Language Companion Series 161], Martine Robbeets & Walter Bisang (eds), 23–60. Amsterdam: John Benjamins. doi:10.1075/slcs.161.07bis

Bopp, Franz. 1816. *Über das Conjugationssystem der Sanskritsprache in Vergleichung mit jenem der griechischen, lateinischen, persischen und germanischen Sprachen*. Frankfurt-am-Main.

Chomsky, Noam. 2013. Problems of projection. *Lingua* 130: 33–49. doi:10.1016/j.lingua.2012.12.003

Chomsky, Noam. 2015. Problems of projection: Extensions. In *Structures, Strategies and Beyond: Studies in honour of Adriana Belletti* [Linguistik Aktuell/Linguistics Today 223], Elisa Di Domenico, Cornelia Hamann & Simona Matteini (eds), 3–16. Amsterdam: John Benjamins. doi:10.1075/la.223.01cho

de Condillac, Etienne Bonnot. 1746. *Essai sur l'origine des connaissances humaines*. Paris.

Croft, William. 1991. The evolution of negation. *Journal of Linguistics* 27: 1–27. doi:10.1017/S0022226700012391

Crowley, Terry. 1992. *An Introduction to Historical Linguistics*. Auckland: OUP.

Egedi, Barbara. 2014. The DP cycle in Hungarian. In Kiss (ed.), 56–82. doi:10.1093/acprof:oso/9780198709855.003.0003

Emonds, Joseph & Faarlund, Jan Terje. 2014. *English: The Language of the Vikings*. Olomouc: Olomouc Modern Language Monographs ⟨http://anglistika.upol.cz/vikings2014/⟩

Filppula, Markku, Klemola, Juhani & Pitkänen, Heli (eds). 2002. *The Celtic Roots of English*. Joensuu: University of Joensuu.

von der Gabelentz, Georg. 1891[1901]. *Die Sprachwissenshaft. Ihre Aufgaben, Methoden und bisherigen Ergebnisse*. Leipzig: Weigel. Reprint Tübingen: Narr, 1972.

van Gelderen, Elly. 2008. The negative cycles. *Linguistic Typology* 12(2): 195–243. doi:10.1515/LITY.2008.037

van Gelderen, Elly. (ed.) 2009. *Cyclical Change* [Linguistik Aktuell/Linguistics Today 146]. Amsterdam: John Benjamins. doi:10.1075/la.146

van Gelderen, Elly. 2011. *The Linguistic Cycle*. Oxford: OUP. doi:10.1093/acprof:oso/9780199756056.001.0001

van Gelderen, Elly. 2015. Problems of projection: The role of language change in labeling paradoxes. *Studio Linguistica*, published online: 28 October 2015. doi:10.1111/stul.12041

Gianollo, Chiara, Jäger, Agnes & Penka, Doris (eds). 2015. Language change at the syntax-semantics interface. Perspectives and challenges. In *Language Change at the Syntax-semantics Interface*, Chiara Gianollo, Agnes Jäger & Doris Penka (eds), 1–32. Berlin: De Gruyter.

Givón, Talmy. 1971. Historical syntax and synchronic morphology. *Chicago Linguistic Society Proceedings* 7: 394–415.

Givón, Talmy. 1976. Topic, pronoun, and grammatical agreement. In *Subject and Topic*, Charles N. Li (ed.), 151–188. New York NY: Academic Press.

Greenberg, Joseph. 1960. A quantitative approach to the morphological typology of language. *IJAL* 26: 178–194.

Hegedüs, Veronika. 2014. The cyclical development of Ps in Hungarian. In Kiss (ed.), 122–147. doi:10.1093/acprof:oso/9780198709855.003.0005

Heine, Bernd & Kuteva, Tania. 2002. *World Lexicon of Grammaticalization*. Cambridge: CUP. doi:10.1017/CBO9780511613463

Heine, Bernd, Claudi, Ulrike & Hünnemeyer, Friederike. 1991. *Grammaticalization: A Conceptual Framework*. Chicago, IL: University of Chicago Press.

Heine, Bernd & Kuteva, Tania. 2005. *Language Contact and Grammatical Change*. Cambridge: CUP. doi:10.1017/CBO9780511614132

Hodge, Carleton. 1970. The linguistic cycle. *Linguistic Sciences* 13: 1–7.

Hoeksema, Jack. 2009. Jespersen recycled. In van Gelderen (ed.), 15–34.

von Humboldt, Wilhelm. 1836. *Über die Verschiedenheit des menschlichen Sprachbaus und seinen Einfluss auf die geistige Entwicklung des Menschengeschlechts*. Berlin.

Jäger, Agnes. 2012. 'How' to become a comparison particle. DiGS 14 talk.

Jespersen, Otto. 1917[1966]. *Negation in English and other Languages*. Copenhagen: A.F. Høst.

Jespersen, Otto. 1922. *Language*. London: Allen & Unwin.

Kiparsky, Paul 2011. Grammaticalization as optimization. In *Grammatical Change Origins, Nature, Outcomes*, Dianne Jonas, John Whitman & Andrew Garrett (eds), 15–51. Oxford: OUP.

Kiss, Katalin É. (ed.). 2014. *The Evolution of Functional Left Peripheries in Hungarian Syntax.* Oxford: OUP. doi:10.1093/acprof:oso/9780198709855.001.0001

Larrivée, Pierre & Ingham, Richard. 2011. *The Evolution of Negation: Beyond the Jespersen Cycle.* Berlin: Mouton de Gruyter. doi:10.1515/9783110238617

McWhorter, John. 2007. *Language Interrupted.* Oxford: OUP. doi:10.1093/acprof:oso/9780195309805.001.0001

Meillet, Antoine. 1921[1912] L'évolution des formes grammaticales. In *Linguistique historique et linguistique générale*, Édouard Champion (ed.), 130–148. Paris: Librairie Ancienne Honoré Champion. Reprint 1958.

Meisner, Charlotte, Starke, Elisabeth & Völker, Harald (eds). 2014. Jespersen revisited: Negation in Romance and beyond. *Lingua* 147: 1–8. doi:10.1016/j.lingua.2014.05.014

Nesselhauf, Nadja. 2012. Mechanisms of language change in a functional system: The recent semantic evolution of English future time expressions. *Journal of Historical Linguistics* 2(1): 83–132. doi:10.1075/jhl.2.1.06nes

Nevalainen, Terttu & Traugott, Elizabeth Closs (eds). 2012. *Oxford Handbook on Historical English Linguistics.* Oxford: OUP. doi 10.1093/oxfordhb/9780199922765.001.0001

Nichols, Johanna. 1992. *Linguistic Diversity in Space and Time.* Chicago IL: University of Chicago Press. doi:10.7208/chicago/9780226580593.001.0001

Post, Mark. 2007. Grammaticalization and compounding in Thai and Chinese. *Studies in Language* 31(1): 117–175. doi:10.1075/sl.31.1.05pos

Robins, Robert H. 1967. *A Short History of Linguistics.* London: Longman.

Salmons, Joe & Zhuang, Huibin. 2014. East Asian prosodic templates: Change and Cyclicity. Ms.

Sapir, Edward. 1921. *Language.* New York NY: Harcourt, Brace and Company.

von Schlegel, August Wilhem. 1818. *Observations sur la langue et la literature provençales.* Paris.

Schwegler, Armin. 1990. *Analyticity and Syntheticity.* Berlin: Mouton de Gruyter. doi:10.1515/9783110872927

Sun, Chao Fen. 1996. *Word Order Change and Grammaticalization in the History of Chinese.* Stanford: Stanford University Press.

Szmrecsanyi, Benedikt. 2012. Analyticity and syntheticity in the history of English. In Nevalainen & Traugott (eds), 654–665.

Tesnière, Lucien. 1932. Synthétisme et Analytisme. *Charisteria Gvilelmo Mathesio Qvinqvagenario.* Prague Linguistic Circle.

Tooke, John Horne. 1786–1805. *The Diversion of Purley.* London.

Traugott, Elizabeth Closs & Ekkehard König. 1991. The semantics-pragmatics of grammaticalization revisited. In Elizabeth Closs Traugott & Bernd Heine (eds), *Approaches to Grammaticalization,* 1: Theoretical and Methodological Issues [Typological Studies in Language 19], 189–218. Amsterdam: John Benjamins. doi:10.1075/tsl.19.1.10clo

Trudgill, Peter. 2011. *Sociolinguistic Typology.* Oxford: OUP.

van der Auwera, Johan. 2009. The Jespersen cycles. In van Gelderen (ed.), 35–71.

Vossen, Frens & van der Auwera, Johan. 2014. The Jespersen cycles seen from Austronesian. In *The Diachrony of Negation* [Studies in Language Companion Series 160], Maj-Britt Mosegaard Hansen & Jacqueline Visconti (eds), 47–82. Amsterdam: John Benjamins. doi:10.1075/slcs.160.03vos

Willis, David, Lucas, Christopher & Breithbart, Anne (eds) 2013. *The History of Negation in the Languages of Europe and the Mediterranean,* Vol. I. Oxford: OUP. doi:10.1093/acprof:oso/9780199602537.001.0001

What cycles when and why?

Marianne Mithun
University of California

Certain kinds of grammatical markers show heightened propensities for turnover cross-linguistically. Some, like negatives, are widespread, while others, such as distributives, are rarer. Several factors might underlie these propensities. Most cycles involve two sets of processes: grammaticalization and renewal. Grammaticalization processes, which can result in phonological erosion, semantic generalization and abstraction, and pragmatic weakening, are generally driven by frequency. The resulting form/function mismatches can trigger renewal, stimulated by expressive need and the availability of resources for new markers. These factors are first investigated in negative, demonstrative, pronominal, reflexive, and distributive cycles from languages of the Iroquoian family, indigenous to eastern North America. Another potential factor, language contact, is then explored, with examples from languages indigenous to western North America.

It has long been recognized that rates of change are not constant across all parts of grammar. In her landmark 2011 volume *Cycles*, van Gelderen examines sets of grammatical markers with special propensities for accelerated turnover. The recurring patterns raise intriguing questions. Why do markers in certain domains cycle, and why do some of them cycle more frequently than others? Here some forces are explored which might trigger and propel them.

Most linguistic cycles involve two kinds of processes: grammaticalization and renewal. The first are often stimulated by a general cognitive phenomenon: the routinization of recurring series of tasks. For language, this can mean that frequently-used strings of words or morphemes come to be processed as chunks. The result is a loss of internal boundaries between elements: speaker consciousness of the individual components is reduced. This reduction is typically gradual, a progressive fading salience of the individual parts of the whole.

When elements of a recurring string are no longer processed individually, their phonological substance can erode. Separate words may lose their stress and ultimately become attached to adjacent words as clitics or affixes. They may then continue to erode and, in some cases, disappear entirely. There can also be semantic effects. When

DOI 10.1075/la.227.02mit

sequences of morphemes are processed as single lexical items, awareness of the individual semantic contributions of components can fade. There can also be other semantic changes. As a marker is extended to more contexts and uses, it can become more general and abstract in meaning. An oft-cited example is the English construction *be going to V*, as in *I'm going to eat*. The original construction denoted a concrete motion of displacement for a purpose, but its function has been extended to indicate intention and future tense. Finally, with increased use, constructions can lose their pragmatic force. English adverbs such as *awfully*, for example, are now nearly equivalent to the weak intensifier *very* (*It's awfully nice of you to ask*), which itself originally had a stronger meaning related to truth. Such phonological, semantic, and pragmatic effects often occur together, but they need not.

Once the form, meaning, and/or force of a marker has eroded, speakers may seek to renew the expression somehow. An additional marker may be added to reinforce the fading one, for example, or a new construction may be used with increasing frequency, perhaps ultimately replacing the original one entirely.

A sequence of phonological, semantic, and/or pragmatic weakening followed by renewal constitutes a linguistic cycle. But linguistic cycles are far from uniform. Most grammaticalization processes are driven by frequency of use, and constructions vary widely in their frequency in speech. Additional factors can affect rates of change as well. Phonological erosion can depend on patterns of stress and the position of a marker within the word, for example. Intensity is a more important aspect of some expressions than others. Rates of renewal also vary, depending on such factors as the utility of the distinction and likely sources for reinforcement. Of course no change has to happen. But the more we can learn about the kinds of changes that recur cross-linguistically, the closer we can come to understanding the cognitive forces which shape language.

1.   Routinization, phonological erosion, and semantic fading

When elements of a recurring string are no longer processed separately, their individual phonological and semantic contributions to the whole can recede from the consciousness of speakers. Separate words may lose their stress and ultimately become attached to adjacent words as clitics or affixes. Sequences of morphemes may fuse. Some markers may disappear entirely. An example of phonological erosion is in (1) from Seneca, an Iroquoian language spoken in Western New York State.

(1)   Proto-Northern-Iroquoian   >   Modern Seneca
      *ihraks   ia:s
       i-hra-k-s
      PROTHETIC-M.SG.AGENT-eat-HABITUAL
      'He eats it.'   'He eats it.'

The Seneca verb has lost most of the original masculine pronominal prefix *hra- 'he' and the entire verb root *-k 'eat': essentially the argument and predicate. What is left is a meaningless prothetic vowel *i-*, added to the beginning of verbs to ensure a site for penultimate stress, and the habitual aspect suffix *-s*. If words like these were processed morpheme by morpheme, such changes would be unlikely to occur.

Even after recurring sequences of morphemes have come to be processed as single lexical items, they can continue to evolve not only phonologically but also semantically, without regard to the identity of their components. As is well known, reflexives often develop into middle voice markers. A familiar example comes from French. The marker *se* functions as a reflexive in sentences like *Il s'est brulé* 'He burned **himself**'. It functions more as a middle voice marker in sentences like *Il s'est levé* 'He stood up'. Its semantic contribution is barely discernible in *Il s'est promené* 'He took a walk'. The boundary between reflexives and middles is not sharp. In essence, reflexives describe situations involving two separate roles, such as agent and patient, where both roles happen to be filled by the same referent: *He burned himself*. Middles blur the distinction between the two roles: *He stood (himself?) up.* Middles have a strong tendency to become lexicalized and develop idiosyncratic patterns. In German 'sit down' and 'lie down' are both expressed with middle forms: *sich hinsetzen* and *sich hinlegen*. German 'stand up' is not: *aufstehen*. As lexical items, middles often continue to develop semantically in various directions, to the point where the function of the reflexive/middle element is obscured. At this point, speakers may seek to reinforce the reflexive meaning with an analytic form, like English *self* or French *soi-même*. For this reason, cross-linguistically reflexive markers are often heavier than middle markers.

Languages of the Iroquoian family provide an interesting example of a reflexive cycle. A reflexive prefix *-at-* can be reconstructed for their common parent, Proto-Iroquoian. Cognates still occur in all languages of the family. Examples here are from Mohawk, a Northern Iroquoian language now spoken primarily in Quebec, Ontario, and New York State.

(2) Mohawk
     s-áhseht   'Hide (it)!'
     s-**at**-áhseht   'Hide **yourself**' = 'Hide!'

The same prefix now serves more often as a middle marker.

(3) Mohawk middles
     s-éta'   'Put it in!'
     s-**at**-íta'   'Get in!'

     s-kétsko   'Raise it!'
     s-**at**-kétsko   'Get up!'

     te-s-awénrie   'Stir it!'
     te-s-**at**-awénrie 'Travel around! Roam!'

Like their counterparts in other languages, Iroquoian middles appear in constructions indicating both direct and indirect effects on the single argument.

(4)   Mohawk middle
      s–e'serehtóhare   'Wash the car!'
      s-**at**-e'serehtóhare   'Wash your car!'

As noted, there is a strong tendency for boundaries between middle voice markers and verb roots to blur, for MIDDLE-ROOT sequences to lexicalize. The Mohawk verb stems in (5) all appear to contain an initial middle prefix.

(5)   Mohawk fading segmentation
      -ataweia't   'enter'   -atehen   'be embarrassed'
      -atek   'be burning'   -atenion   'stretch'
      -atetsh-   'be greedy'   -ate'kw   'escape'
      -atkahrit   'play'   -atkatston   'make soup'
      -atkennis   'assemble (INTR)'   -atikonhen   'put one's head down'
      -ato   'swell'   -atorishen   'rest'
      -athontat   'obey'   -atat   'talk'

For some of these stems, the effect of the event or state on the participant can still be imagined. In some, the root still occurs on its own: -at-o 'swell', -o 'be in water', and -at-hont-at 'obey', -hont- 'ear', -at 'stand' ('prick one's ears'). But for many, the verb root no longer occurs independently. It can be unclear whether a verb stem beginning with the sequence -at- is actually a middle formation or not. The verb root -atek 'burn', for example, is used intransitively and might have originally been a middle formation: io-atek-ha' NEUTER.PATIENT-burn-HABITUAL = iotékha' 'it is burning'. But there is no semantically-related root -ek. This could simply be a verb root beginning with a. Many Iroquoian verb stems containing a middle prefix are now idiomatic. One of the Mohawk verbs for 'sing', for example, contains a middle prefix, but the semantic contribution of the middle marker is not immediately obvious. A literal translation is enlightening.

(6)   Mohawk idiomaticity
      S**ate**rennó:ten!
      s-**ate**-renn-oten
      2SG.AGENT-**MIDDLE**-song-stand
      'Stand up (your own) song!' = 'Sing!'

The prefix *-at- is small. Already in Proto-Iroquoian, it never occurred at the beginning or end of a word, and it was usually unstressed. Several of the most common pronominal prefixes which precede it end in the vowel a, so its initial vowel disappears. The Proto-Iroquoian reflexive prefix already had an array of allomorphs. Reflexes of one allomorph, *-ar-, still appear in some old stems beginning in -a- in the modern languages. Reflexes of another, *-an- still occur before some stems beginning in -i-.

The basic prefix *-at- can now appear as simply -t-, -r- or -n-. The t/r/n alternation does not appear regularly elsewhere in the languages.

(7)   Mohawk middle prefix allomorphy
 a. Rarahsi'tóhares
  ra-ar-ahsi't-ohare-s
  M.SG.AGT-MIDDLE-foot-wash
  'He washes his feet.'
 b. Raníhtiaks.
  ra-an-ihtiak-s
  M.SG.AGENT-MIDDLE-put.around.neck-HABITUAL
  'He puts it around his neck.'

Thus already in Proto-Iroquoian, the reflexive prefix *-at- had lost both some semantic identity, because of its extension to use as a middle with a tendency toward lexicalization with the root, and some phonological substance.

The Iroquoian reflexive was renewed in an interesting way, through reduplication to *-atat-. The Iroquoian language family consists of two main branches, Southern Iroquoian, represented only by modern Cherokee, and Northern Iroquoian, with one sub-branch containing Tuscarora and Nottoway, and another consisting of Wendat, Wyandot, Seneca, Cayuga, Onondaga, Oneida, and Mohawk. Reflexes of the reduplicated reflexive appear in all of the modern languages in both branches.

(8)   Cherokee renewed reflexive: Montgomery-Anderson 2011: 344, 268, 355
 a. Taàwakhthoostóoʔi.
  Tee-aii-akahthoost-óʔi
  DISTR-1SG.PAT-look.at.INCOMPLETIVE-HAB
  'I look at [the trees].'

  Aàw-**ataa**-khthoósthánv.
  akw-**ataat**-akahthoósthán-vʔi
  1SG.PAT-**RFL**-look.at-EXPERIENCED.PAST
  'I looked at **myself**.'

 b. Ka-olihka > Kohlka. 'He knows, understands (it).'
  A-**àtaat**-olihka. 'He knows, recognizes **himself**.'

 c. Ji-kohwthíha. 'I see (it).'
  Aàkw-**ataa**-kohwthíha 'I see **myself**.'

(9)   Mohawk renewed reflexive
 a. Wa'kká:riʼ.
  wa'-k-kari-ʻ
  FACTUAL-1SG.AGT-bite-PFV
  'I bit (it).'

Wa'katatká:ri'.
wa'-k-**atat**-kari-'
FACTUAL-1SG.AGT-**RFL**-bite-PFV
'I bit **myself**.'

b.   Wa'tkáwe'ste'.   'I pricked (it), pierced (it).'
     Wa'tk-**atat**-áwe'ste'.   'I pricked **myself**.'

c.   Wa'kkòn:reke'.   'I hit (it) (as with a hammer).'
     Wa'k-**atat**-kòn:reke'.   'I hit **myself**.'

The reduplicated form is also used as a reciprocal with a dual or plural argument and as an intensifier contrasting with the middle.

(10)   Mohawk intensification
       S-**at**-konhs-óhare   S-**atat**-konhs-óhare
       2SG.AGENT-**MIDDLE**-face-wash   2SG.AGENT-**RFL**-face-wash
       'Wash your face!'   'Wash **your own** face.'

2.   Semantic generalization and abstraction

Semantic change drives another more common set of changes cross-linguistically: determiner cycles. In oft-cited work, Greenberg (1978) and Lyons (1999) noted the recurring shifts of demonstratives to articles and eventually class or case markers. Such changes are examined in closer detail in van Gelderen 2011, Chapter 6: The DP cycle. Parts of the cycle are familiar from European languages among many others, such as the development of Latin demonstratives *ille* and *illa* to modern French definite articles *le* and *la*.

The Southern Iroquoian language Cherokee contains a basic demonstrative *na(ʔ)* 'that/those'. It can occur on its own or in combination with another referring expression.

(11)   Cherokee demonstrative 'that/those': Montgomery-Anderson 2008: 153
       Náana   kato   úúst?
       na=na   kato   úúst-
       that=FOC what   something
       'What are **those**?'

(12)   Cherokee demonstrative 'that/those': Montgomery-Anderson 2008: 220
       Na askaya   tiitoonííski.
       na a-skaya   ti-a-atooniisk-i
       that 3SG.AGT-man   DISTR-3SG.AGT-conjure.INCOMPLETIVE.AGT-NMLZ
       '**That** man is a conjurer.'

Demonstratives with similar shapes can be seen in most of the Northern languages as well.

Diessel distinguishes various types of demonstratives, among them anaphoric demonstratives.

> Anaphoric demonstratives are coreferential with a noun or noun phrase in the previous discourse. Unlike exophoric demonstratives, which are primarily used to orient the hearer in the outside world, anaphoric demonstratives serve a language-internal function: they are used to track participants of the preceding discourse.   (Diessel 1999: 95–96)

Mohawk contains an anaphoric demonstrative *né:* 'that'. (All of the conversational material cited here was originally in Mohawk. Free translations are provided for material included for context.)

(13)   Mohawk anaphoric demonstrative
    A: 'That was my grandfather's second wife.
        She was my real grandmother's sister.'
    B: Ah.
    A: 'My grandmother's name was Wariá:nen.'
    B: 'Yes.'
    C: Ah.
    A: Wa'íheie' sok ki'   **né:**   sahotíniake'.
        she died so   then   **that one**   they remarried
        'She (Wariá:nen) died, so then he married **her**.'

In Mohawk, continuing topics are usually represented only by pronominal prefixes in the verb. Brand new referents are typically introduced with lexical nominals. The anaphoric demonstrative *né:* represents a referent that is already active in the discourse but not a continuing topic, just as described by Diessel.

Diessel also describes demonstratives of another type: discourse deictic demonstratives.

> Like anaphoric demonstratives, discourse deictic demonstratives refer to elements of the surrounding discourse.… Discourse deictic demonstratives are, however, not coreferential with a prior NP; rather, they refer to propositions.
>   (Diessel 1999: 100–101)

Mohawk *né:* serves this deictic function as well. This use can be seen below, where it refers to the entire speech the speaker would give to her children.

(14)   Mohawk discourse deictic
    ['A white man will lie to you. He'll say, "Oh, you're the only one I love. There is no one else. And he turns things around, he says things that aren't true.']
    Né: wa'khehró:ri nì:'i
    that I told them   myself
    '**That**'s what I told

ne   kheien'okòn:'a
the.aforementioned   I have them as offspring variously

shahontehiahrónnion.
as they have grown up variously

my children as they were growing up.'

In addition, Mohawk also contains an article *n(e)*, a proclitic which loses its vowel before another vowel in rapid speech.

(15)   Mohawk article *ne*
        'It was a log house. And at the end of the house

akwé:kon **onén:ia'.**
all   **stone**
it was all **stones.'**

'There they used to make the fire. There she would cook. And that's what we used to heat our house. And it gave us light. I remember how I used to like it before, when it was like that. Then at one point they changed it.'

Akwé:kon é:ren wahatihá:wihte' **n=onén:ia'.**
all   away they took away   **stone**
'They removed all **the stones** and took them away.'

In this example, *ne* appears to correspond to the English definite article *the* or the French *le/la*. Definite articles usually indicate that the speaker assumes the listener can identify a referent. For English and modern French, identifiability may come from previous mention as above, association with a previously-mentioned referent (*I saw a fox and a rabbit. The rabbit was scampering into his hole*), shared knowledge (*I washed the car*), cultural knowledge (*I stopped by the drugstore*), or uniqueness (*The moon is full tonight*). Mohawk *ne* signals identifiability only from previous mention or association with a previously-mentioned referent: 'the aforementioned'.

Unlike English and French articles, Mohawk *ne* appears with proper names, possessed nouns, generic nouns, kinship terms, pronouns, and subordinate clauses.

(16)   Mohawk article with kinship term
        Akhsotkénha'
        she was grandparent to me
        '**My late grandmother**

ken wahonwatinónhsani iatathróna.
here she house lent them   they two are married
rented a house to a couple here.'

[They moved upstairs. As soon as the wife would come home, they would fight upstairs. ... Almost as soon as the husband would take in the groceries, she'd throw them out, one by one ...']

Khare'   ó:nen ki'
and again   then   in fact

n=akhsótha   wa'akoterihonkóhten
the aforementioned=my grandmother it matter penetrated her
'Finally (**the**) **my grandmother** got fed up with

tsi niió:re' tsi sótsi sótsi ki: iáh ki'   tha'tehiatèn:rohs.
so it is far as   too   too   these not actually they two are friends
all their fighting.'

The previous mention of the referent need not be the same lexical item. In (17), 'his wife' was preceded by the article *ne* because the wife was identifiable from the incorporated noun *-hwatsir-* 'family' in the verb 'he has a family' used by the previous speaker.

(17)   Mohawk previous mention

A: Rahwatsí:raien'   kén?
     ra-**hwatsir**-a-ien-'   ken
     M.SG.AGT-**family**-LINKER-lie-STATIVE   Q
     'Does he have a **family**?'

B: Hén:,
     'Yes,

     nok tehonatekháhsion   ki'   **ne**   **ró:ne'.**
     but they have separated actually the aforementioned his spouse
     but he and (**the**) **his wife** are separated.'

The older Mohawk anaphoric/discourse demonstrative *né:* (with stress and vowel length) has developed into the modern article *ne* 'the aforementioned', though *né:* still survives in the language. This trajectory parallels a similar development from Latin to French. Classical Latin had no articles, but modern French has the definite articles *le* and *la*. The shift was not instantaneous, however, as described by Epstein.

> It is only in vulgar Latin that a definite article arose, documented as *le* in Old French. It was not used regularly for definite reference; rather it served to present participants that were identifiable from the context or co-text or else were prominent in discourse.   (Epstein 1993:111–34)

This is exactly the function of the modern Mohawk article.

It thus appears that a demonstrative perhaps related to Cherokee *na(ʔ)*, developed into the Mohawk anaphoric/discourse demonstrative *né:* and then into the Mohawk article *ne*, undergoing semantic abstraction from identifying referents by their location in concrete space to their location in discourse, accompanied by phonological reduction.

The possibility of identifying referents by concrete location has been renewed in Mohawk with new demonstratives, whose origins are still transparent.

(18) Mohawk demonstratives
    a. kí:ken, kí: 'this, these'
        <   ken'   í:ken
           ken'   i-ka-i
           here   PROTHETIC-NEUTER-be.STATIVE
           'Here it is.'
    b. thí:ken, thí: 'that, those'
        <   thó: í:ken
           tho: i-ka-i
           there   PROTHETIC-NEUTER-be.STATIVE
           'There it is.'

These demonstratives (unlike *né:*) are used to indicate concrete physical distance. They occur with or without a coreferential lexical nominal.

(19) Mohawk physical distance
    a. É:so   rohronkhà:'on   **kí:ken**   ranekénhteron.
        much   he.has.become.fluent   **this**   young.man
        '**This** man has become so fluent.'   (introducing man standing nearby)
    b. Ka'   non: iewahtsá:tonhs   **thí:ken?**
        which place it points there   **that**
        'Where is **that thing** pointing?'
                (gesturing toward ruler in listener's hand)

They have already been extended to indicate metaphorical distance as well.

(20) Mohawk temporal distance
    Nahò:ten' na'   **thí:ken,**
    what   guess that
    'What was **that**
    wà:kehre' enkehià:rake'.
    I thought I will remember
    that I meant to remember?'

(21) Mohawk discourse distance
    A: 'Did you know R?'
    B: 'That was S's husband.'
    A: 'No.'
    B: 'Oh. So it's not the same family?'
    A: Iah. Né: **kí:ken** roió'tehkwe'
        no   it.is **this**   he used to work
        tsi ionterihwahwaienstáhkhwa'.
        at   one makes people learn words with it
        'No, **this one** used to work at the school.'

The fact that these markers are the result of recent renewal is clear from their lack of match with counterparts elsewhere within Northern Iroquoian. Tuscarora has a completely different article *ha'*.

(22)   Tuscarora *ha'*

Tyahre'číhę kę:θ,   **uhséhare** wa'kkúhe'.
first   customarily ash   I went after
'First I would go after **ashes**.'

'I would prepare about four pounds.
And then I would put the kettle on, a kettle for boiling.
It would start to boil a little, it would just about boil.'

Ù:nę kę:θ   yahwa'kkę'né:ti'   hé'thu **ha'** uhséhare.
then customarily I poured into the kettle there the ash
'Then I would pour in **the ashes**.'

'I would stir it continuously.'

Wa'ktá'tawęht **ha' uhséhare**.
I dissolve it   the ash
'I would dissolve **the ashes**.'

Like Mohawk *ne*, Tuscarora *ha'* does not indicate general identifiability; it means 'the aforementioned'. In the passage below, *ha'* does not appear with the Bible, though the listeners certainly knew about the Bible from general shared knowledge. It does appear at the second mention of Abraham, however.

(23)   Tuscarora *ha'* 'the aforementioned'

Wa'ka'rihę́:tyę' **uhyatęhstatukéhti'**,
I word made   holy book
'I read in **(the) Bible**

urihwaká:kę' rayá:θęh   **Abraham**, rutyá:kę Sarah yeyá:θę,
old time   he is named Abraham his wife Sarah she is named
about a man named **Abraham**, in old times, his wife Sarah, ...

Há:ne:' hè:ní:kę: **ha' Abraham** wahrę́hrę:', " ..."
that one that   the Abraham he said
Then **the aforementioned Abraham** said, " ..."'

Like Mohawk *ne*, Tuscarora *ha'* also appears before previously mentioned ideas. Below it precedes the idea that the head man should make a sacrifice and give thanks.

(24)   Tuscarora aforementioned ideas: Elton Greene, speaker
Ù:nę **wahra'nyɛhwáhnę:'** hè:ní:kę:.
then he sacrificed   that one
'So then **he sacrificed**.

Ę̀:weh nęthrúhar,   hè:ní:kę:
where he has gotten it from that one
Where did he get it from

ha'   a:hra'nyè:wáhnę:',
the aforementioned he should sacrifice
the aforementioned that he should sacrifice

ha'   nyà:wę   a:hrę́hrę:'.
the aforementioned thank you he should say
the aforementioned that he should give thanks?'

The source of the Tuscarora article can still be discerned. It has developed from the anaphoric/discourse demonstrative *há:ne:'*, which still survives in the language.

(25)   Tuscarora demonstrative *há:ne:'*

Yahwa'kayehéhnara'.
they land reached
'They reached land.

Há:ne:' ha' kę́:ne: kyè:ní:kę: tyu'wna'kę́hra'r.
that   the here   this   point of land
'**That's** this point of land here.'

The cooccurrence of the demonstrative *há:ne:'* 'that' and the article *ha'* 'the aforementioned' confirms the fact that the article is now a separate marker. It is not clear whether *há:ne:'* is related to the Cherokee *na* or the Mohawk *né:'*, and if so, how. The forms are so short, and the consonant inventories of the languages so small, that resemblances could easily be due to chance. There are also no regular *a/e* correspondences between Southern Iroquoian (Cherokee) and Northern Iroquoian.

Finally, Tuscarora shows a renewal of demonstratives for expressing concrete spatial relations, just like Mohawk, though the forms used are slightly different.

(26)   Tuscarora demonstratives
   a.   kyè:ní:kę: 'this, these'
        <   kę́ne:' í:kę'
            kę́ne:' i-ka-i-'
            here   PROTHETIC-NEUTER-be-STATIVE
            'It is here.'
   b.   hè:ní:ke: 'that, those'
        <   hé'thu í:kę'
            hé'thu i-ka-i-'
            there PROTHETIC-NEUTER-be.STATIVE
            'It is there.'

As in Mohawk, the newer, more concrete Tuscarora demonstratives are already being extended beyond their function of specifying concrete location to indicating distance in time, empathy, and discourse.

The renewal of demonstratives in both languages through a locative adverb ('here', 'there') follows a recurring tendency noted by Brugè 1996 and cited in van Gelderen (2011:197).

3.   Pragmatic reinforcement

A number of cycles are set in motion by a weakening of pragmatic force. These cycles differ among themselves in their cross-linguistic frequency. Some are rare, while others are widespread.

3.1   Distributive cycles

One rarer cycle that can be seen in Iroquoian languages involves distributives, verbal suffixes which spread events and states over locations and sometimes, by extension, over times, participants, and/or kinds of participants. The Northern Iroquoian languages each have multiple distributive suffix forms which are lexically conditioned, learned with the stem.

(27)   Mohawk Distributives: -on, -hon, -(a)nion, -ton, -hson, -hseron, -'s

iotsinenà:rote'	'stump stands = stump'
iotsinenahró:t-**on**	'stump standing **here and there**' = 'lots of stumps'
teiotshà:kton	'it is bent'
teiotsha'kt-**ánion-'**	'it is bent **in several places**'
satè:sere	'Crawl!'
sate'seré-**hson**	'Crawl **around!**'
ia'khé:ken'	'I saw them there'
ia'khekén-**hseron-'**	'I saw them (**at various places**)'
wahikòn:reke'	'I hit him'
wahikonhrék-**hon-'**	'I beat him up'
senóhare	'Wash it!'
senoharé-**nion**	'Do the washing!'
seniión:ton	'Hang it up (as a curtain)!'
seniiontón-**nion**	'Hang **things** up, as ornaments on a Christmas tree'
raksa'táksen	'he is a bad child, bad boy'
ratiksa'táksen-**'s**	'they are bad children, **each in his own way**'

The markers were already relatively small suffixes, usually no more than a single syllable. (Mohawk orthographic ⟨on⟩ represents the nasalized vowel [ʉ], and ⟨i⟩ before a vowel represents a glide [j]. Thus what is spelled ⟨nion⟩ is [njʉ].) Since they were already suffixes, speakers could not add special prosody to emphasize the distributivity. (Mohawk stress is basically penultimate.) The language does show attempts at renewal, however. There are forms which consist transparently of combinations of the distributive suffixes: *-on-nion* and *-on-nion-'s*.

(28)   Mohawk compound distributive suffixes

káhere'	'it/they is/are sitting on something (as on a shelf)'
kahr-ón-nion-'	'they are sitting **here and there**'
iotshá:tare'	'there is a cloud'
iotshatar-ón-nion-'s	'there are clouds **here and there**'
káhere'	'it/they is/are sitting on something (as on a shelf)'
kahr-ón-nion-'	'they are sitting **here and there**'
iotshá:tare'	'there is a cloud'
iotshatar-ón-nion-'s	'there are clouds **here and there**'
káhere'	'it/they is/are sitting on something (as on a shelf)'
kahr-ón-nion-'	'they are sitting **here and there**'
iotshá:tare'	'there is a cloud'
iotshatar-ón-nion-'s	'there are clouds **here and there**'
saterennó:ton	'Sing!'
saterennot-ón-nion	'Sing **a variety of tunes!**'
sattsihkó:ten	'Button it!'
sattsihkot-ón-nion	'Button it all up, do up **all the** buttons!'

The compound distributive suffixes have now lost their added pragmatic force as well: they no longer have any more intensive meanings than single distributive suffixes. In some cases, doublets occur, stems with just one distributive suffix and stems with two, but there is no discernible difference in meaning.

(29)   Mohawk distributive doublets

ts(i)éntho	'Plant!'
ts(i)enthó-hseron	'Plant **a variety of things!**'
ts(i)enth-ón-nion	'Plant **a variety of things!**'

3.2   Pronominal cycles

A more frequent kind of cycle involves the development of independent pronouns into pronominal affixes or clitics and ultimately agreement affixes. Unstressed pronouns are easy targets for phonological reduction: they are small, they are frequent, and they often occur in a constant position adjacent to the verb. It is not surprising that they should show a propensity to lose independence and substance. Under typical circumstances, the erosion is not a pragmatic problem: pronouns usually represent given information, referents already identifiable from the linguistic or extra-linguistic context. Again well-known examples come from French, where unstressed pronouns have lost most of their prosodic independence in spontaneous speech: ʃtɛm 'I love you' (*je* 'I', *te* 'you').

The Iroquoian languages contain large paradigms of pronominal prefixes representing all core arguments. They distinguish three persons plus inclusive/exclusive first persons, three numbers, four genders, and two roles, grammatical agents and patients. They are obligatory on every verb, whether coreferential independent lexical nominals are present or not.

(30)   Mohawk pronominal prefix
    Thetèn:re   *wa**honwa**ia'tàta'*.
    thetèn:re   wa-honwa-ia't-at-'a-'
    yesterday   FACTUAL-**3MASC.PL/3MASC.SG**-body-be.in-INCH.PFV
    yesterday   **they** bodily inserted **him**
    '**They** buried **him** yesterday.'

The language also contains independent pronouns, which occur in addition to the pronominal prefixes, not in place of them.

(31)   Mohawk independent pronoun
    Wà:kehre'   **_ni:_**   *wáts*
    wa'-k-ehr-e'   ne=ì:'i watsik
    FACTUAL-**1SG.AGENT**-think-PFV   the-1 just
    '**I myself** thought that

    tóka' *nà:'a* *kí:,*   *na'teiotenonhianíhton.*
    toka' nà:'a kiken na'-te-io-ate-nonhi-ani-ht-on
    maybe guess this   PARTITIVE-DV-N.SG.PAT-MIDDLE-scary-BEN.
                            APPLIC-CAUS-STATIVE
    maybe something frightening had happened.'

The pronominal prefixes are fully referential in their own right, comparable in function to the unstressed pronouns of English. Speakers do not feel that anything is "missing" in sentences like (30) where referents are identified only by the prefixes.

The independent pronouns are relatively rare in speech. A 4000-clause sample of unscripted speech showed the occurrences in (32).

(32)   Independent pronouns in spontaneous speech.
    1.   Clauses with 1st person participants, any role   1086
            1st person free pronouns   95
            Percentage   **8.9%**

    2.   Clauses with 2nd person participants, any role   414
            2nd person free pronouns   14
            Percentage   **3.4%**

    3.   Third person free pronouns
            Vast majority of clauses include a 3rd person
            aónha 'it'   0
            akaónha 'she' 2
            raónha 'he'   7
            ronónha 'they' 5

The pronominal prefixes are demonstrably older than the independent pronouns. Nearly all can be reconstructed back to Proto-Northern-Iroquoian, most back still further to Proto-Iroquoian.

The independent pronouns are newer. Sources of the third person independent pronouns are still recoverable. They are not cognate across the two major sub-branches of Northern Iroquoian, represented here by Mohawk and Tuscarora.

(33)   Third person independent pronouns
       Mohawk   -onha   'alone' + patient pronominal prefix
       Tuscarora -ęru   'alone' + patient pronominal prefix

The independent pronouns are used in contexts where added salience is needed for focus, contrast, topic shifts, and a few other functions.

(34)   Mohawk contrastive focus
       A.   Hé,   tha'tesató:tat.
            hé: tha'-te-s-atotat
            hey   CONTR-DV-2SG.IMP.AGT-shut.up
            'Hey, keep quiet.'

       B   Í:se'   tha'tesató:tat
            í:se'   tha'-te-s-atotat
            2   CONTR-DV-2SG.IMP.AGT-shut.up
            '**You** keep quiet!'

(35)   Mohawk contrast
       A.   'What did you call that thing, the vacuum cleaner?'
       B.   Tewa'kenhrakwáhtha'.
            te-w-a'kenhr-a-kw-aht-ha'
            DV-NEUTER.AGT-dust-LK-pick.up-INST.APPL-HAB
            'It picks up dirt.'

            Ne:'   ki: ni'   kena'tónhkhwa'.
            nè:'e ki:ken   ne=ì:'i   ke-na'tonhkw-ha'
            that   this   the=1   1SG.AGT-call-HAB
            That's what I call it.' (Maybe other people call it something else.)

(36)   Mohawk topic shift
       A.   'He doesn't have a name yet.'
       B.   Ì:i'   ki'   enhihsén:non.
            ì:i'   ki'   en-hi-hsenn-on-'
            1   in.fact FUT-1SG>M.SG-name-give-PFV
            I'll give him a name.'

The pronominal prefixes were good candidates for grammaticalization: presumably small, unstressed, and in a constant position immediately before the verb. They became attached to verbs early in the development of the verbal morphology, and they still occur immediately before the verb stem. But over time, as additional prefixes became attached to verbs, the pronominal prefixes became less and less salient, no longer necessarily word-initial, usually unstressed, and not necessarily consisting of a full syllable. Their low formal salience is not incompatible with the function of maintaining reference to continuing referents, but it is at odds with marked discourse functions such as indicating focus, contrast, and topic shift. It is precisely in these contexts that we see renewal, the addition of the newer independent pronouns. (Further details are in Mithun 2013.)

3.3   Negative cycles

Perhaps the most-discussed cycles involve negation. These are often called Jespersen cycles because Otto Jespersen described them early on (1917), though Van der Auwera and De Vogelaer (2008), cited in van Gelderen (2011:192), credit Gardiner (1904) with first mention. More recent discussions are in van der Auwera 2009, van Gelderen 2011, and the papers in Hansen and Visconti 2014 among many others. The processes triggering negative cycles are much like those leading to pronoun cycles. Negation is very frequent in speech, which can lead to phonological erosion of the marker. Negative markers often occupy a fixed position adjacent to the verb, which can foster early attachment to it. Both effects can be seen in English *I wouldn't know*. But negation is usually a crucial element of the message. Its importance makes it prone to renewal when its salience is threatened. The renewal may involve various strategies. An additional negative marker might be added, such as a particle meaning 'no', itself often descended from a larger construction. Some kind of intensifier may be added, such as English *at all* or French *point*. If the intensifier did not have a negative sense before, it may acquire one by contamination from its presence in the negative construction. Over time, the original negative marker may disappear, leaving only the reinforcement. The reinforcement can then undergo the same kinds of processes as its predecessor: grammaticalization and renewal. An entirely new construction may replace the older one, such as one headed by a negative verb which, in turn, may erode to an auxiliary, then a particle, etc.

The Iroquoian languages provide examples of negative cycles involving a variety of renewal strategies. Nearly all of the languages show multiple coexisting negative constructions. Cherokee contains a prefix *kaa-* in the innermost prepronominal prefix position, immediately before the pronominal prefixes. This is the rarest of the Cherokee prepronominal prefixes.

(37)   Cherokee *kaa-* 'not since': Montgomery-Anderson 2008: 337
      Thla yiwikeétóʔa   talikwa
      thla yi-wi-ji-eétóʔa   talikwa
      NEG IRR-TRANSLOC-1SG.AGT-walk.around.PRS Tahlequah
      "I haven't returned to Tahlequah"

      kvvkintiinv́́ta   kahljoóte
      kaa-aki-natiinv́-ta   kahljoóte
      NEG-1SG.PAT-sell-PARTICIPIAL house
      (**not**) since my house was sold."

Another negative construction consists of an outer prepronominal prohibitive prefix *jii-* which is always word-initial, preceded by the prohibitive particle *thleesti/hleesti*. This construction is used for negative commands.

(38)   Cherokee prohibitive: Montgomery-Anderson 2008:532
       Hleesti   **jiiskinv`hī**
       hleesti   jii-ski-nv́hi
       PROHIBITIVE   PROHIBITIVE-2SG>1SG-call.IMM
       'Don't call me!'

The third negative construction is the usual unmarked one used for negative indicatives. It consists of the outer prepronominal irrealis prefix *yi-*, which is also always word-initial, preceded by the negative particle *thla*, usually pronounced *hla* in Oklahoma. This can be seen in the first line of (37) above and in (39) below.

(39)   Cherokee basic negative: Montgomery-Anderson 2008:297
       Thla yikooliika.
       thla yi-ji-oolihka
       NEG   IRR-1SG.AGT-understand.PRS
       'I don't understand it.'

The negative constructions represent different diachronic layers of development. Negative markers were apparently grammaticalized early in the development of the Iroquoian verbal morphology. All of the languages in both branches of the family contain a negative prefix in the innermost prepronominal position, immediately before the pronominal prefixes. The early prefixation of the negative is not surprising, for the reasons mentioned above. As noted, negation is frequent in speech and often expressed by a marker adjacent to the verb. Over time, additional prepronominal prefixes became attached to the verb, most of them still cognate across the Iroquoian family. But the prefixation of these markers compromised the salience of the internal negative markers. They were not only unstressed, they were also no longer guaranteed their prominent word-initial position. The lack of salience was at odds with the importance of the distinction for communication. Speakers of the different languages remedied the mismatch between form and function with different strategies, as can be seen by the fact that the negative constructions are not generally cognate across the family, with one exception.

The innermost Cherokee negative *kaa-* has an apparent cognate in a rare negative particle *kaǫ* in Cayuga, a Northern language. It is likely (though not firmly established) that the Iroquoian languages are remotely related to the Caddoan languages, which contain negative prefixes of the same shape: the Wichita negative prefix *ká:-* on nouns and indefinite pronouns (Rood 1976:157), the Pawnee verb prefix *ka-* (Parks 1976:235), and the Caddo prohibitive prefix *kaš-* 'don't' (Chafe p.c.). The Cherokee *kaa-* is now not only the innermost and rarest of the prepronominal prefixes, it also shows the most allomorphy, and it is confined to specific constructions like the 'not since' seen above and modal constructions meaning 'can't' and 'won't'.

This older Cherokee negative construction has been renewed with the construction seen in (39) above, the negative particle *thla/hla* with initial irrealis prefix *yi-* on the verb. Additional strategies for renewal can also be seen within Cherokee. Describing North Carolina Cherokee, King (1975:62) notes that emphatic negatives can be formed with the sequence *yi-vv-kaa-* IRREALIS-ITERATIVE-NEGATIVE-.

(40)   Cherokee emphatic negatives: King 1975:62
        Yvka-kvwahwthvhe:ʔi.   'I wouldn't have found you.'
        Yvka-kvliʔvvhnileeʔi.   'I wouldn't have whipped you.'
        Yvkv-hlstayvhvka.   'He won't eat.'
        Yvkv-niluʔki.   'They won't come.'

In nominalized verbs expressing inability, the older negative *kaa-* has been moved out of its innermost slot to word-initial position before the irrealis, and combined with the negative particle.

(41)   Cherokee inabilitative: Montgomery-Anderson 2008:340
        Hla khoúústi   **kaayuuntvʔvʔhnti**   yiki.
        hla kohúústi   kaa-yi-uunii-atcvˋhnt-i   yi-ki
        NEG something NEG-IRR-3PL.PAT-do.DEVERBAL.NOUN-NMZL IRR-be.PRS
        'They can't do anything.'

The Northern Iroquoian languages also show multiple renewal strategies. None of their negative markers are cognate with those in Cherokee (apart from the Cayuga relic). The basic innermost Iroquois negative prefix is *teʔ-*. In some of the languages, there has been a reshuffling, a movement of this inner prefix leftward across other prefixes toward the front of the word. In some, this inner prefix has been replaced with an outer, word-initial contrastive prefix *th-* if other prefixes are present. In most of the languages, the negative or contrastive prefix is now reinforced with an additional particle before the verb, though this word is not generally cognate even across the Northern languages. In Tuscarora, there is no inner negative prefix at all. (Further details are in Mithun 1995.)

The three kinds of cycles illustrated here, involving distributives, pronominals, and negatives, all appear to have been stimulated by a mismatch between form and function. All distinctions were expressed by small, generally unstressed affixes, in many cases trapped in word-internal position. But the frequency of distributive, pronominal, and negative cycles cross-linguistically is not the same. Distributive cycles are quite rare; pronominal cycles are more common; and negative cycles are pervasive.

Perhaps the most obvious difference among the three is the communicative importance of the distinction itself. The forceful expression of distributivity is rarely central to everyday conversation. Pronouns are prolific in speech in most (though not all) languages, and bound pronominal affixes are not uncommon. What is interesting is that in the Iroquoian languages, as in many other languages with pronominal affixes, renewed forms are used only for those pronouns with marked pragmatic functions such as focus, contrast, and topic shift. Finally, negation is a frequent, crucial distinction in speech. Negative expressions can show especially high turnover, and very many languages show the coexistence of older and newer negative constructions.

The cycles illustrated here also show that renewal can take a variety of forms. Here we saw the reinforcement of distributive suffixes by the addition of a second distributive suffix, the renewal of pronouns with forms meaning 's/he alone', and the renewal of negative constructions with the reordering of affixes, the repurposing of word-initial affixes, and the reinforcement of both with new negative particles.

4.   Contributions from contact

A less-discussed potential contributor to cyclic change is language contact. Contact can increase the frequency of expression of a particular distinction. Bilinguals accustomed to specifying certain distinctions in one of their languages easily transfer that frequency of mention to the other, exploiting native lexical resources. Over time, the added frequency can stimulate various grammaticalization processes in the second language, on its own or under continuing contact.

Likely effects of such processes can be seen in the expression of location and direction in languages indigenous to Northern California. Central Pomo, a language of the Pomoan family spoken north of present San Francisco, contains a set of directional suffixes on verbs.

(42)   Central Pomo directional suffixes on verbs
    -:qač' 'upward (changing place, as up a hill)'
    -č' 'up (as getting up)'
    -:la- 'downward'
    -:'w- 'here and there'
    -mli- 'around something'
    -:q 'by, on the level, southward'
    -mač' 'northward, upstream'
    -m 'on, across (as a creek or bridge)'
    -way 'against hither'

Some examples of their use can be seen in (43). (All verbs distinguish aspect. Perfective aspect is unmarked after a consonant, and *-w* after a vowel. Imperfective aspect is *-(a)n* for singulars and *(a)č'* for plurals.)

(43) Central Pomo verb *čá-* 'run' (one person)

čá-w	'run'
čá-:la-w	'run down' (drive down to Hopland)
čá-:qač'	'run up (as up a hill)'
čá-way	'run against hither'
čá-:'w-an	'run around here and there'
čá-mli-w	'run around something (a tree, rock, house, pole etc.)'
čá-mač'	'run northward'
čá-:q'	'run by, over (along on the level), southward'
čá-m	'run over, on, across something (as bridge)'

There are also some newer markers of location and direction, which generally precede verbs.

(44) Central Pomo locative adverbs

čáw	'in'
čal	'to inside'
čáwil	'towards inside'
qo:	'out'
qo:l	'outward'
da:	'outdoors'
da:l	'to outdoors'
dáwil	'towards outdoors'
yow	'below, place down'
yówil	'downward, southward'
'úyu:	'up, high'
'úyul	'to place up' (up onto a branch)
hal	'down'
dú:l	'away'
dúla:wal	'across'
qálil	'upward'
pʰdáqač'	'downstream'
danóqʰač'	'upstream'
'ě:y	'away'
béda	'here'
mída	'there'	etc.

Sources of some of these adverbs are still clear. Some contain clitics of their own.

(45)

čal	'inside'	
ča	'house'	
=l	'to'	

(46)

qálil	'upward'
qalí	'sky'

(47)

du:l	'away'
du:	'other'

(48) *qo:l*   'outward'
      qo: 'wilderness, the wild'

(49) *danóqʰač'*   'upstream'
      danó   'mountain'
      =qʰač'   'toward'

The adverbs can coccur with directional suffixes on verbs, but they are not required.

(50) *'úyu=:*   '*-né-m=la.*
      high   fingers-set.one-**on.level**=PERSONAL.AGENCY
      'I set it **up** there.'

(51) *Yów=il*   *wá-la-w.*
      below=toward one.go-**downward**-PFV
      '(S/he) walked **downhill**.'

(52) *Qalí=l*   *hlí-č'.*
      sky=toward   mutiple.move-**up**.PFV
      'They all got **up** (to go eat).'

(53) *Čá=w*   *čó-w=la.*
      house=in   place-PFV=PERSONAL.AGENCY
      'I put it (bread) **in** (the oven).'

(54) *Da=:*   *čó-:q-'=la.*
      outside=at place-**level**=PFV=PERSONAL.AGENCY
      'I took it **out**.'

(55) *Dúlu=:*   '*-né-w=la.*
      over=at   fingers-set.one-PFV=PERSONAL.AGENCY
      'I threw it **over**.'

(56) *Qó:=l*   '*-né-w=la.*
      out=to   fingers-set.one-PFV=PERSONAL.AGENCY
      'I threw it **away**.'

(57) *Dúla:wal*   '*i'-né-m=la.*
      across   fingers-set.one-**across**=PERSONAL.AGENCY
      'I threw it **across**.'

(58) *'úyu=l*   *pʰ-dí-:qač-'.*
      high=toward   soaring-one.move-**upward**-PFV
      'It flew **up** (onto a branch).'

(59) *Yá=ka*   *yów=il*   *hlá-la-w.*
      1PL.AGT=INFERENTIAL **below=toward** PL.go-**down**-PFV
      'Let's go **down** there.'

Some adverbs are now themselves undergoing grammaticalization to verbal proclitics.

(60) *Čáw=yo-m!*
      in=go-IMP.SG
      'Come in!'

(61) Wá:y   ʾa: sma   mṭí-č=da   ma   čál=yo-w   ʾe.
      already 1SG.AGT sleep SG-lie-INCH-as.DIFF 2SG.AGT **home**=go-PFV COP
      'I had already gone to bed when you got home.'

(62) Mu:l mída qó=yo-w,   ṭéṭe-:n='kʰe.
      that there **toward**=go-PFV tell-IPFV-INF
      'He came by to tell her.'

(63) Béda qó=yo-w-hi   čʰá:-č-im.
      here **toward**=go-PFV-IRR.SAME sit-INCH-IMP.SG
      'Come here and sit down.'

(64) Mu:l ʾdoma   dá:l=yo-w='kʰe.
      that HEARSAY   **out.to**=go-PFV=INF
      'He's going to go outside (to the toilet).'

(65) Ba: '=mú:ṭu   mi:=hṭow   qó:l   čadí-w   čʰó-w.
      someone COP=3SG.PAT there=from **out-to** chase-PFV not-PFV
      'Nobody from there chased her out.'

The grammaticalization is still in progress. Asked about *qó:l čadíw* in the last example, a speaker immediately translated it as 'order out', and said that it could be one word or two.

California is a strong linguistic area, characterized by longstanding contact among indigenous languages. Many communities have always been small, with considerable exogamy. There is significant genetic diversity among the languages, with twenty-two distinct families represented, but a number of grammatical parallelisms cross family boundaries. The elaboration of locative/directional suffixes stretches through Northern California, up into Oregon, and across Idaho. It is found in languages of the Pomoan, Shastan, and Palaihnihan families, and in Karuk, Yana, and Washo (all once grouped in a hypothesized "Hokan" superstock), as well as in the Maidun and Sahaptian families and in Klamath, (once grouped in a "Penutian" superstock.) The systems vary in the age of the markers, their substance, and their inventories. Klamath, for example, contains over 100 such suffixes (Barker 1963, 1964).

In addition to their locative/directional suffixes, all of these languages also contain independent words describing location and direction, just like Central Pomo. The Klamath suffixes have meanings such as 'away', 'along the back', 'into a container', 'around', 'out from underneath', between', 'taking home first', 'into the fire', 'to the limit, end', 'up high, hanging up', 'up against, to the shore', 'slitting open', 'across', 'over, above', 'up out of water', 'around, surrounding', down a hill', 'over a mountain', 'right beside', 'arriving', 'spread out, dispersed', 'into the mouth', 'on top of a full load', 'right up to', 'down off', 'from hand to hand', 'ending in a dead-end', 'stuck in a tight place', 'between', 'replacing', 'among', 'to the limit, end', 'in the sun', 'out of a tubular object', 'at, against, onto', 'up', 'downhill', 'over a mountain', 'back and forth', 'on a fire', 'in a narrow place', and more (Barker 1964:144–145). Examples of formations with the verb root *g-* 'go, move, are in (66). Many are lexicalized with meanings beyond the sum of their parts.

(66)   Klamath locative/directional suffixes with g- 'go': Barker 1963: 134–136

gaba:ta	'lands on, goes to shore'
gaba:yilg̱a	'goes to the end (of a canyon)'
gapč'a	'goes out of sight'
gatba	'arrives, comes home'
gak'ki:č'a	'turns around'
gak'i:m'a	'goes around the edge of'
gak'wa	'goes across'
galamna	'goes behind, at the back of'
galč'wi	'goes right up to'
gaLanc'a	'just went alongside, beside'
gal'a:l'a	'goes into a fire, visits someone when they are not at home'
gamni	'climbs, goes up'
gaqye:ta	'passes by close to'
gatq'apsa	'goes down from a height'
gattala	'goes from house to house'
gat'amsg̱a	'goes between'
gawasč'a	'travels from place to place, person to person'
gawal	'goes on top of'
gaw'a:Ya	'goes before and waits'
gaw'i:na	'goes among'
gayah?a	'hides'
gaya:tgo:la	'gets out of the way, avoids'
segatga	'part from each other, or make a treaty'
gelwi	'goes by a fire'
gelwipga	'visits'
geLo:la	'gets off a vehicle, horse'
geqa	'goes out, through'
geqwe:La	'goes down a slip'
get'le:g̱i	'goes over a mountain, into another room'
gewa	'goes into water, flat place'
gigog̱a	'goes into a container'
gičq'a	'goes onto and covers, pounces on, as a cougar does its prey'
giwba:ta	'goes up against, as a log drifts across the bow of a boat'
giwi:ga	'goes into a container, is satisfied'
goblanč'a	'just went downstream'
gotg̱i	'goes down a cliff, out of a tree'
goditgo:la	'goes out from underneath, has diarrhea'
godi:la	'goes under'
gog̱amna	'goes up'
gog̱a	'climbs'
golča	'comes apart, breaks easily'
golg̱i	'comes to with a purpose', 'attacks'
goli:na	'goes off the edge, leaves behind, beats in a game'

goLq'a	'goes off (feathers, hair)', sleet falls'
goLi:	'goes inside'
gone:ga	'goes down into a hole'
gosga	'comes off, as color, warts, etc.'
gota	'goes onto, attacks, as a disease'
gotq'aga	'goes up out of'
go:qi:wa	'goes out into a flat place, runs away from home'
goWasga	'goes away'
goygga	'goes up out of water'
goykaga	'escapes, runs off'
goyki:na	'goes out of fire, water'
gogo:lgi	'gather together'

Klamath also contains a substantial inventory of independent adverbs, some with suffixes of their own. They supply such meanings as 'here', 'there', 'beside, on one side', 'anyplace', 'on both sides, both ends', 'above, on top', 'near', 'far, deep, wide, tall', 'above, up high', 'down below', 'outside', 'neighboring', 'out behind, out back', 'the same place', 'half, middle, center', 'inside', etc. Example (67) contains the adverb *gida* 'here', with suffix *-l* 'toward' (longer form *dal'*). The verb also contains directional suffixes 'along' and 'toward'.

(67)   Klamath independent directional adverb: Barker 1964:287
        Gidal'   ho:t   gisč-ipg-a
        gida-l'   ho:t   gis-č-epg-a
        here-toward   that   walk-along-toward-INDICATIVE
        'He's walking this way.'

Example (68) contains the adverb *mona:* 'underneath' with directional suffix *-na*, and a verb with a directional suffix *-okang-* 'around'.

(68)   Klamath independent directional adverb: Barker 1964:282
        Mona:na   ho:t   wdomkanga.
        mona:-na   ho:t   wdom-kang-a
        underneath-around that   swim-around-INDICATIVE
        'He is swimming around down at the bottom.'

There is no philological record of the languages comparable to the corpora that exist for many European languages, but throughout the area, the individual systems show effects typical of grammaticalization and renewal. In Central Pomo, the older markers are now small suffixes, in some cases just a consonant. The newer markers are separate words, allowing greater specificity and in some cases the possibility of greater pragmatic force with heightened prosody. The diachronic layers of locative/directional markers across large swaths of geographical neighbors suggests that the cycles of grammaticalization and renewal are likely to have been stimulated by language contact (Mithun 2007).

5.   Conclusion

Recurring cycles provide glimpses of some of the kinds of processes that can drive language change. As a group, they suggest hypotheses about some of the cognitive, social, and communicative factors that might underlie them.

At their heart is a cognitive propensity for the routinization of frequently-recurring sequences of operations, in this case, the processing of sequences of morphemes and words as single chunks. This automation can result in the loss of salience of individual markers, with reduction in lexical autonomy, phonological substance, semantic specificity, and pragmatic force. All of these changes can lead to mismatches between form and function. At a certain point, speakers may seek to restore their fading expressive capacities with renewal: added forms for reinforcement or entirely new constructions to replace the old.

Various factors can lead to weakening. Frequency of use is often key: the more frequent a combination the more rapid the phonological, semantic, and pragmatic change may be. Other factors can enter in as well. Some kinds of semantic change recur over and over, for example, such as the development of reflexives into middles.

A number of factors can affect propensities for renewal as well. An important one is the communicative value of the fading distinction. Not surprisingly, negative cycles are pervasive cross-linguistically. Negation is highly frequent in speech, which leads to phonological erosion and potential loss of lexical autonomy, as well as pragmatic weakening. But negation is also a distinction that speakers always need to mark clearly and often emphatically. Pronominal cycles are only slightly less pervasive: reference to speech act participants and continuing topics is highly frequent in speech, so unstressed pronouns are good candidates for erosion to clitics and affixes. But speakers sometimes want to refer to given participants in pragmatically-marked focus, contrastive and topicalization constructions. It is in these constructions that we see renewed pronominal forms. Reflexives and middles are considerably less frequent in speech, and distributives even rarer. Form/function clashes involving them are much less common. Accordingly, reflexive and distributive cycles are noticeably rarer cross-linguistically. Another factor might play a role in renewal: the availability of resources. In just the cycles illustrated here we have seen not only reinforcement by the addition of words (the negative, pronominal, demonstrative, and locative cycles) but also the addition of a second suffix with similar function (the distributive cycle), the reduplication of an inner prefix (the reflexive cycle), the exploitation of an outer affix to replace an inner one (the negative cycle), and even the reordering of an inner prefix to a more prominent word-initial position (the negative cycle).

We are only beginning to appreciate the cross-linguistic distributions of different cycles and the factors which stimulate and propel them. The situation is complex, and there is much to be discovered.

References

Barker, M.A.R. 1963. *Klamath Dictionary*. University of California Publications in Linguistics 31. Berkeley, CA: University of California Press.

Barker, M.A.R. 1964. *Klamath Grammar*. University of California Publications in Linguistics 32. Berkeley, CA: University of California Press.

Brugè, Laura. 1996. Demonstrative movement in Spanish. *University of Venice Working Papers in Linguistics* 6(1): 1–53. http://dspace-unive.cilea.it/bitstream/10278/436/1/6.1.1.pdf

Diessel, Holger. 1999. *Demonstratives: Form, Function, and Grammaticalization*. Typological Studies in Language 42. Amsterdam: John Benjamins. doi:10.1075/tsl.42

Epstein, Richard. 1993. The definite article: Early stages of development. In *Historical Linguistics 1991*. [Current Issues in Linguistic Theory 107], Jaap van Marle (ed.), 111–134. Amsterdam: John Benjamins. doi:10.1075/cilt.107.10eps

Gardiner, Alan. 1904. The word. *Zeitschrift für Ägyptische Sprache und Altertumskunde* 41: 130–135.

van Gelderen, Elly. 2011. *The Linguistic Cycle: Language Change and the Language Faculty*. Oxford: OUP. doi:10.1093/acprof:oso/9780199756056.001.0001

Greenberg, Joseph. 1978. How does a language acquire gender markers? In *Universals of Human Language*, Vol. 3, Joseph Greenberg (ed.), 47–82. Stanford CA: Stanford University Press.

Hansen, Maj-Britt Mosegaard & Visconti, Jacqueline. 2014. *The Diachrony of Negation*. Amsterdam: John Benjamins. doi:10.1075/slcs.160

Jespersen, Otto. 1917. *Negation in English and Other Languages*. Copenhagen: Høst and Son.

King, Duane. 1975. A Grammar and Dictionary of the Cherokee Language. Ph.D. dissertation, University of Georgia.

Lyons, Christopher. 1999. *Definiteness*. Cambridge: CUP. doi:10.1017/CBO9780511605789

Mithun, Marianne. 1995. Affixation and morphological longevity. In *Yearbook of Morphology 1994*, Geert Booij & Jaap van Marle (eds), 73–97. Amsterdam: Kluwer.

Mithun, Marianne. 2007. Grammar, contact, and time. *Journal of Language Contact – Thema* 1: 133–155. ⟨www.jlc-journal.org⟩

Mithun, Marianne. 2013. Prosody and independence: Free and bound person marking. In *Language across Boundaries: Studies in Memory of Anna Siewierska*, Dik Bakker & Martin Haspelmath (eds), 291–312. Berlin: Mouton de Gruyter.

Mithun, Marianne. Forthcoming. Native North American languages. In *Cambridge Handbook of Linguistic Areas*, Raymond Hickey (ed.). Cambridge: CUP.

Montgomery-Anderson, Brad. 2007. *A Reference Grammar of Oklahoma Cherokee*. Ph.D. dissertation, University of Kansas.

Montgomery-Anderson, Brad. 2008. A Grammar of Oklahoma Cherokee. Ph.D. dissertation, University of Kansas.

Parks, Douglas. 1976. *A Grammar of Pawnee*. New York: Garland.

Rood, David. 1976. *Wichita Grammar*. New York: Garland.

van der Auwera, Johan. 2009. The Jespersen cycles. In *Cyclical Change* [Linguistik Aktuell/ Linguistics Today 146], Elly van Gelderen (ed.), 35–71. Amsterdam: John Benjamins. doi:10.1075/la.146.05auw

van der Auwera, Johan & De Vogelaer, Gunther. 2008. Negation and quantification. In *Syntactic Atlas of the Dutch Dialects*, Vol. 2, Sjef Barbier, Johan van der Auwera, Hans Bennis, Gunther De Vogelaer, Magda Devos & Margreet van der Ham (eds), 58–72. Amsterdam: Amsterdam University Press.

PART II

Macro-cycles

Is radical analyticity normal?

Implications of Niger-Congo and Southeast Asia for typology and diachronic theory*

John McWhorter
Columbia University

It is assumed among linguists that radical analyticity is a typological state that a language might develop into as the result of ordinary stepwise grammatical change. It is well-known that extensive second-language acquisition tends to make languages more, or even completely, analytic. Contact, however, is thought to be an *alternate* pathway towards analyticity. Diachronic theory has identified no mechanism via which a grammar would become completely analytic. While some affixes are worn away by phonetic erosion, inexorable processes of reconstitution operate at the same time, such as grammaticalization. The commonly cited case of Egyptian's inflectional "cycle" described by Hodge (1970) did not depict the language reaching anything approaching a completely analytic state. There is a growing awareness that the "natural" state of language, uninterrupted by adult acquisition, is one of heavy morphological complexity, while large-scale population movements often condition languages of a more moderate morphological complexity (McWhorter 2007; Trudgill 2011). Under this assumption, radically analytic languages are diachronically anomalous. In this presentation, I will propose a contact account for the radical analyticity of a certain few west African Niger-Congo languages and for the languages of Southeast Asia.

1. Introduction

1.1 The problem

The linguist is familiar with the fact that languages range from ones that allow a great many inflectional affixes to occur with a root, such as the Nilotic language Sabaot:

---

* The author would like to thank Jeff Good, Larry Hyman, and anonymous referees for invaluable feedback, including of the constructively trenchant kind, on this presentation.

DOI 10.1075/la.227.03mcw

(1)   Ká-   á-mnyáán-áá- té.
      PAST- I-be.sick-   STAT-DIR
      "I became sick while going away."   (Payne 1997:29)

to ones such as Yoruba (Niger-Congo), which all but lack inflectional affixation at all:

(2)   Mo mú ìwé   wá   fún   ẹ.
      I   take book come give you
      "I brought you a book."   (Stahlke 1970:63)

Linguists would seem to assume that these two states both represent possible outcomes of ordinary grammar-internal change. That is, the assumption is that the total absence of inflectional affixation is one trait out of many that a language may reach *via stepwise grammar-internal processes, while being transmitted completely across generations.*

In the meantime, it is also well known that incomplete transmission of a language also leads to degrees of analyticity. I intend analyticity as referring to: *paucity or absence of inflectional (as opposed to derivational) marking indicated by affixation, tone, or vowel changes in quality or length.* Pidginization and creolization are most noted for having this effect, while authors such as Kusters (2003), McWhorter (2007) and Trudgill (2011) have argued that especially widespread acquisition by adults, even if not having as extreme an effect as pidginization or creolization, has often rendered languages considerably more analytic than they once were, such as English, Mainland Scandinavian, Persian and Indonesian. Specialists in second language acquisition and in language contact concur that for adult acquirers, L2 inflectional morphology is especially subject to elimination (cf. Pienemann 1998; Plag 2008), as the result of factors of phonological and semantic transparency, of the same kind that condition hieracrchies of borrowability (cf. Thomason & Kaufman 1988; Matras 2099:153–7).

The causal link between second language acquisition and degrees of inflectional loss, then, is richly documented by the world's many pidgin and creole languages and vast empirical documentation of second language acquisition.

However, when it comes to what I will term *radical* analyticity – i.e. the near-total absence of inflectional morphology in Yoruba – the relationship between analyticity and ordinary grammar-internal change is much less apparent upon examination.

It must be noted that there is no claim that radically analytic languages do not express inflectional categories: they do so, of course, via isolated morphemes. However, the loss of the affixal means of indicating such categories remains more interesting than often thought. To wit, despite how readily specialists observe that a given language or group "lost" all of its inflectional affixation, *other than the intermediation of adult acquisition, diachronic linguistic theory includes no grammar-internal mechanism via which a grammar could lose its inflectional affixation entirely.*

The conventional term "drift" enshrining the concept since Sapir (1921) is descriptive rather than explanatory, as are approaches such as Lass' (1992:107) to English's loss of inflection as due to a "cumulative weighting of 'decisions'". It is appropriate that Lass puts *decision* in quotation marks: obviously, there were no actual "decisions," and as such, explanation remains elusive.

1.2 The proposal

Radically analytic languages are rather rare. Most linguists would be hard pressed to identify where such languages are to be found, other than some creoles, beyond Southeast Asia and one area of the west African coast where Niger-Congo languages of the subfamily formerly known as Kwa are spoken.

In fact, Donohue and Denham (2014), using the data in the *World Atlas of Language Structures* (Haspelmath, Dryer, Gil & Comrie 2005), identify radically analytic languages as limited to, indeed, Southeast Asia and the aforementioned area of West Africa, plus Indonesia and the island of New Guinea. In Indonesia the relevant cases include (1) colloquial Indonesian dialects; (2) various languages of Flores such as Keo, Ngadha, Lio, Ende, and Rongga; (3) ones of East Timor such as Tetun Dili, Tokodede, Mambai and Waimaha (cf. McWhorter 2011a: 223–60 for diachronic proposals on analyticity in Flores and Timor) and (4) cases on the northern coast of Papua cases including Abun, Tidore, Tobelo, Tehit, Moi, Meyah, Moskona, Ireres, Sogub, Hatam and Mpur (Paauw 2007).[1]

On Indonesia and New Guinea, increasing consensus among area specialists (e.g. Klamer 2012; Donohue & Denham 2014; cf. also McWhorter 2011: 223–60) attributes radical analyticity to adult acquisition, often amidst encounters between Austronesian speakers migrating eastward and encountering indigenous "Papuan" peoples. Meanwhile McWhorter (2005: 68–71) argues, in concurrence with work by previous analysts such as Grijns (1991), that highly analytic colloquial Malay/Indonesian varieties of that area such as Riau Indonesian classify as creoles, in that their structure is traceable to extensive second-language acquisition. That analysis is bolstered by the fact that scholars of these dialects have independently termed the ones of their specialty as "creoles," such as the Hokkien-influenced Baba Malay.

In this paper, I propose that the most economical approach to the world's other analytic languages be analogous. This proposal comes in the context of the now extensive literature arguing that the typical state of a human language is morphologically

---

1. Africanists are often aware that certain languages of the Khoi-San "family" have been described as analytic. It must be clear that these languages are not, however, *radically* analytic in the sense treated in this paper. Heine & König (2013) describe !Xun, for example, as "*fairly isolating-analytic*" (italics mine), with their description, as well as that of other Khoi-San languages such as Naro (Visser 2013), revealing grammars with much more inflectional affixation than in the languages I focus on in this paper.

elaborate, dense with irregularity, and highly challenging to second-language learners even at the basic level. The assumption is that this is because of inexorable processes of grammaticalization, rebracketing, semantic drift, phonetic erosion and other processes. What began as isolated statements such as Thurston (1987) has coalesced into a scholarly consensus represented by works such as Kusters (2003), Dahl (2004), McWhorter (2007), Wray & Grace (2007), Lupyan & Dale (2010), and Trudgill (2011).

Wray & Grace artfully describe what the "normal" language of "Early Man" was like, describing the time-traveller trying to learn a language but "impeded by the proliferation of difficult sound combinations, wayward form-meaning pairings (perceived as irregularities), and the impenetrable semantic representations that are characteristic of languages used for esoteric communication." By "esoteric" Wray & Grace mean languages used only within a given group, rather than as a lingua franca. This chapter will take the basic premise of the body of work they represent as confirmed. Crucially, to accept that premise leaves analyticity unconnected to second-language acquisition as a conundrum.

Specifically, in terms of an immediately plausible and well-researched mechanism via which a grammar loses *all* of its inflection, modern diachronic theory offers a single one: widespread second-language acquisition. As such, the proposal:

> The inevitable state of human language transmitted natively across generations over millennia is synthetic. Under ordinary conditions, grammar-internal change inevitably results in fusion of morphemes (and the consequences of morphophonemic stipulations and irregularity that this leads to).

> Therefore the radical analyticity in certain West Benue-Congo languages of Niger-Congo (Gbe, Yoruboid, Nupoid), and all Chinese, Tai-Kadai, and Hmong-Mien ones, most Austroasiatic ones and many Tibeto-Burman ones, is not a serendipitous homology that some languages happened to "drift" into.

> In both of these areas, logic suggests that radical analyticity is the result of widespread adult acquisition in the past, under which a group of people had reason to learn an inflected language rapidly under untutored circumstances. The linguistic evidence suggests that transmission of these languages was interrupted to a degree approaching, if not reaching, that traditionally termed pidginization.[2]

> Specifically, the Niger-Congo languages in question presumably became analytic as the result of widespread acquisition by adults resident in the areas those languages are now spoken in that a branch of earlier Niger-Congo moved to. The analyticity of the Southeast Asian families is presumably traceable to pidginization

---

2. *Pidginization* here refers to the classic definition of a pidgin: a rudimentary, non-native vehicle of communication with a limited lexicon and only moderately entrenched grammatical conventions; typical examples include Russenorsk and Chinook Jargon.

as the source of Proto-Sino-Tibetan, whose descendant Chinese varieties spread analyticity, in their migration southward, as an areal feature to erstwhile synthetic families in Southeast Asia.

This discussion is based on an important distinction in recent language contact literature between two types of language contact. Trudgill (2011) is most explicit in distinguishing between cases in which contact leads to structural *mixture* versus those in which contact leads to structural *abbreviation*. The former occurs amidst long-term natively acquired bilingualism, occasioning nothing most analysts would treat as simplification (cf. Dixon 1997 on linguistic equilibrium and Aikhenvald 2001). The latter occurs when a language undergoes especially vast acquisition by adults (Trudgill [57] suggests that the tipping point is likely when close to half of a language's acquirers are non-native), such that their rendition of the language is incomplete, and then passed down as a native variety to future generations. It is this kind of acquisition that I propose created radical analyticity in certain language groups.[3]

The overall goal of this thesis is theoretical economy. Currently, diachronic theory of morphosyntactic change posits that radical analyticity emerges either via incomplete acquisition, a well-documented and intuitively plausible mechanism, or an unexamined and counterintuitive one, under which a grammar mysteriously sheds all of its inflectional affixation as the result of something termed "drift." Yet it is difficult to see what diachronic theory gains from this latter notion. The survival of the "drift" idea seems due more to neglect than engagement.

I propose that the "drift" account of radical analyticity is implausible, outdated, and antithetical to scientific elegance, which requires that radical analyticity is nothing less than diagnostic of interrupted transmission.

1.3   Garden Path Number One: *Radical* analyticity

It must clear that the object of interest in this paper is the complete absence of inflectional marking via affixation or sound changes, not merely *relative* analyticity. Linguists are familiar with languages losing *some* of their inflectional morphology, through ordinary processes of sound change and levelling. French present-tense verbal inflection

---

3.   This thesis applies only to languages spread orally before widespread literacy. Languages such as Russian, spread amidst modern conditions through education and reinforced by media, do not undergo simplification because of the influence of prescriptive norms and print. However, even in antiquity, print often obscured spoken realities. Specialists increasingly assume that Middle English grammar was already spoken long before Old English stopped being used in print, just as for a long period Old Persian was used in writing by people who were speaking something much like Modern Persian (Schmitt 1989:60). Along the same lines, we can be sure that when Greek was a language of empire, its written forms masked an array of incomplete non-native renditions spoken by adults upon whom it was imposed.

is an example, resulting from the effects of vowel weakening in word-final, unstressed syllables:

Table 1. Latin and French present-tense verbal inflection

	Latin	French
I sing	[kanto]	[ʃãt]
you sing	[kantas]	[ʃãt]
he/she sings	[kantat]	[ʃãt]

Such processes occur to differing extents within languages by chance. Area specialists are familiar with certain languages in their group of specialty being less richly inflected than others. Crowley (2000) described the Oceanic close relatives Sye and Ura, the latter of which is less richly (and allomorphically) inflected than the former despite the two languages having had parallel histories with no widespread second language acquisition. Niger-Congo specialists often term many of the family's languages "analytic," but intended this in a relative sense, of languages with a fair amount of inflectional morphology nevertheless. Nurse (2007) refers to Niger-Congo as a family in which "most" languages (i.e. especially those beyond Narrow Bantu, Kordofanian, and certain Atlantic ones) are "analytic," even at one point singling out as "analytic" a language like the Gur subfamily's Supyire with its five noun classes and robust NP concord (Carlson 1994). Linguists often refer even to English as "analytic" compared to other Germanic languages.

However, Ura remains, overall, the well-inflected language typical of Oceanic ones; French remains a highly inflected language, including grammatical gender and inflection affix paradigms innovated since Latin, such as for the future and conditional. The question this paper will ask is why certain languages in a family would exhibit so *radically* analytic a state. Relative analyticity is often plausibly attributed to fortuitous results of various grammar-internal processes, or even to modest effects of language contact. However, linguistic theory has offered no explanation for how a language like Yoruba comes to have all but no inflectional affixation.

1.4   Garden Path Number Two: Cycles

A misinterpretation beckons: that radically analytic languages simply represent a stage in a cycle that languages go through. Hodge (1970) is often cited as showing that inflection cycles over time, such that Old Egyptian was well-inflected with prefixes that evanesced in later stages, while Late Egyptian and Demotic were "analytic" languages, after which Coptic developed a new battery of suffixes. This sketch version of Hodge's argument can be taken as suggesting that languages pass naturally through stages of Chinese-style analytic structure. However, Hodge actually documents a matter of degree.

While Late Egyptian was less synthetic than earlier stages, Hodge noted that "[a]t no stage do we have the isolating purely syntactic stage apparently envisaged by Bopp" (13). Late Egyptian was very much an inflected language, with suffixes marking tense, person, number and other categories. The analytic tendency was clear, but limited. For example, while Middle Egyptian tense suffixes on verbs were often replaced in Late Egyptian by auxiliaries, the latter continued to be themselves inflected. Similarly, grammatical gender suffixes fell away, but gender-distinct demonstrative/determiners remained (Junge 2001). Notably, a recent study (Kihm & Reintjes to appear) argues that even this degree of analyticity in Egyptian was due to adult acquisition by Greeks.

The idea of languages "cycling" through a stage of *complete analyticity*, then, fails, for two main reasons.

First, it is mechanistically implausible. Fusion is inexorable in language change, and historical linguistics has identified no mechanism that would block the grammaticalization of new inflections while certain other ones were wearing away elsewhere in the grammar. What would force the emergence of new affixes to "wait" for their "turn" in the cycle? Typical, instead are cases such as Romance, in which the erosion of Latin's future-marking suffixes was paralelled by the emergence of new ones from the grammaticalization of *habere* "to have" (as well as a new conditional-marking paradigm); the proliferation of declension-marking suffixes in the Kartvelian language Svan amidst its loss of Common Kartvelian's gender-marking suffixes (Harris 2004); and the grammaticalization of past-marking prefix *li-* from a locative verb in Swahili as the Common Bantu equivalent *a-* (Nurse 2008:257) wore away (McWhorter 1994:62–3).

The idea of a "drift" under which *all* inflectional affixes wear away while *no* new ones emerge in the meantime is a *post hoc* description, not an explanation. Cases where such a process can actually be documented would seem always to be ones involving non-native acquisition.

Second, the idea that linguistic diachrony regularly includes a stage of analyticity, even if not radical, is disconfirmed by the diachrony of the world's languages, of which Egyptian is only one. The process has only been even suggested – albeit via arguments often misinterpreted – in certain languages of Europe and the Middle East (Dahl 2004:261–88; McWhorter 2011: 38–9), while evidence that there is no such process worldwide is conclusive, including Hakulinen (1961:68) on Uralic, Poppe (1965:177–96) on Altaic; Dahl (2004:273–4) on Afroasiatic, and the sheer fact that specialists in Algonquian, Australian, Nakh-Dagestanian, Chadic, Arawakan, Slavic, Yeniseian – i.e. most of the world's languages – document no such cycles.

Therefore, radical analyticity is neither plausible nor documented as a stage that grammars reach amidst a cycle of inflectional growth and decay. To fully understand

this reveals the Niger-Congo and Southeast Asian cases as truly anomalous. Hodge (1970:9), then, dismissed the idea that the inflectional loss in Egyptian could be due to second-language acquisition:

> The hypothesis that Egyptian is a Mischsprache, arising from the confrontation of Semitic with some unknown African language is not considered here. It is irrelevant to our present thesis, unless one were to maintain that cycles were only characteristic of creoles, or that change as drastic as is evidenced could only occur with the intrusion of an alien element."

On the contrary, I am proposing that cases like this are due exactly to "intrusion of an alien element."

2.   West Africa

2.1   The languages, the problem

It is familiar to many linguists that many Niger-Congo languages spoken on the West African coast from Liberia eastward through Nigeria are analytic. However, this paper will require a more specific focus than what specialists once referred to as the Kwa languages, a term that has undergone a great deal of reassignment.

It is actually within three sub-subfamilies along this coast that we find languages maximally analytic to the degree that motivates the approach of this paper:

1. Gbe (comprising Ewe, Fon, and lesser-known dialects): Lefebvre and Brousseau (2002), in the most modern and comprehensive grammar of a Gbe language, describe Fongbe as lacking inflectional affixation, while Essegbey (2006:409) describes Ewe as having only a single inflectional affix (habitual -na).
2. Yoruboid: sources suggest that languages of the group other than Yoruba, such as Igala, Ede and Itsekiri, are of similar typology.
3. Nupe within Nupoid: Baker and Stewart (2002) treat Nupe as a language lacking inflectional affixation, with Kandybowicz (2008) usefully explicit in demonstrating this quality in the language. Other Nupoid languages are less analytic than Nupe, however (cf. 2.5.2.2).

Since Stewart (1989), modern specialists classify these languages not as "Kwa" but as members of the West Benue-Congo subfamily. However, that subfamily also includes Igboid, Edoid and other groups not *radically* analytic. For the purposes of exposition in this paper, the languages of interest will be referred to as GYN for Gbe-Yoruboid-Nupoid.

The key contrast is between a GYN language, offering the linguist no noun class system to describe at all other than scattered fossilizations, and the noun class system reconstructed for Bantu:

Table 2. Common Bantu noun class markers (Wald 1987: 1000–1)

1.	*mo-	2.	*ba-	human
3.	*mo-	4.	*me-	thin or extended objects, trees
5.	*de/i-	6.	*ma-	objects that tend to come in pairs or larger groups
7.	*ke-	8.	*bi-	instrument, manner
9.	*ne	10.	*di-ne-	miscellaneous, animals
11.	*do-	(6/10 plural)		
12.	*ka-	13.	*to-	diminutive
14.	*bo-			abstract nouns, qualities
15.	*ko-			body parts
16.	*pa-			place where
17.	*ko-			place around which, infinitive
18.	*mo-			place in which
19.	*pi-			diminutive

As Good (2012) notes, the general tendency in Niger-Congo is for these prefixes to be reorganized and reinterpreted in various ways rather than eliminated. While a Niger Congo language may lose some degree of the protolanguage's equipment, typically it remains an inflected language, such as many Northern Bantoid languages (Dimmendaal 2001: 379, 381). The utter absence of this material in the GYN languages becomes, therefore, a conundrum rather than an observation.[4]

Finally, despite the traditional focus on noun-class prefix loss in comparative work on Niger-Congo, in the GYN languages and beyond, loss of verbal extensions is just as vast, which includes some inflectional morphemes. The relevant comparison

---

4. The reorganization in question can include the transformation of affixes into tonal distinctions. This leaves some Bantu languages with significantly less *affixal* inflection than most. However, transformation is not elimination, and therefore languages of this kind do not constitute exceptions to my claim that the GYN languages are unique in their degree of inflectional loss. For example, in the Bantu language Nzadi, much of the typical Bantu affixation battery has been replaced by tonal distinctions (Crane, Hyman & Tukumu 2011), but in no sense is the language "uninflected."

is between a GYN language in which tense, aspect and valence are indicated with free morphemes and a Bantu language like Yao:

(3)   taam-uk- ul- igw- aasy- an- il- a
      sit- IMP- REV-PASS-CAUS-REC-APPL-V
      "to cause each other to be unseated for"   (Hyman 2004: 69)
                                              (IMP = impositive; REV = reversive)

It is one thing to refer to the difference between Yao and Yoruba in the abstract, as a descriptive matter. It is quite another thing to explain why ordinary grammar-internal change would eliminate such a vast battery of affixal material from both heads and dependents. This loss in its most radical degree occurs only in a very few contiguous groups within one subfamily. That some languages change into this direction while others change into the direction of a Fula with its 25 noun classes, retained over several millennia, surely requires explanation. A diachronic theory that simply classifies both of these outcomes as equally likely is at worst, incoherent, and at best, incomplete.[5]

2.2   A solution?

I propose that the radical analyticity of GYN is due to speakers of an early Niger-Congo language, or several, encountering speakers of other languages in the coastal region where these languages are spoken today. This early Niger-Congo would have been a typically synthetic language as are, today, Narrow Bantu languages and Kordofanian languages to the east, and many Atlantic languages to the west. The encounter between the speakers of this stage of Niger-Congo with speakers of unrelated languages on the coast entailed the latter acquiring the former's language imperfectly, but in such large numbers that this incompletely acquired form of the language conventionalized and eclipsed the original, fully transmitted version. The process would have been analogous to what happened to Old English after the Scandinavian invasions starting in the

---

5.   Grammarians differ on whether to analyze inflectional morphemes as free or bound. In older grammars, especially, the choice was often determined by criteria modern linguists would consider insufficient. Available sources do not allow me, of course, to determine whether inflectional morphemes are free or bound in hundreds of languages according to a consistent criterion. However, I submit that this does not invalidate venturing my thesis. I hazard, for example, that it is not accidental that the GYN languages and ones spoken near them have been so often transcribed analytically and been traditionally noted as especially analytic. It is reasonable to suspect a certain "wisdom of crowds" in operation: where are the grammars of southern Bantu languages where the grammarian was moved to transcribe the noun class markers and tense/aspect markers as free morphemes? Of course, a technique of analysis may emerge via which we learn that analyzing the GYN languages as analytic has been a mistake, and that they are actually as agglutinative as Bantu ones. However, I am wagering that this will not happen.

ninth century, AD, or the Mainland Scandinavian languages upon widespread acquisition by Low German speakers in the Middle Ages (Jahr 2001; Kusters 2003).

Within Niger-Congo, Blench (2006) estimates that Benue-Congo emerged around 3500 BC (ibid. 134–5), and classifies Volta-Niger as a subgroup of Benue-Congo that includes the GYN languages. As a subgroup of Benue-Congo, Volta-Niger would have arisen later than 3500 BC, and possibly before reaching the coast. At this writing, it is impossible to determine when, within this window of time, the proposed encounter would have been. However, I will argue that the linguistic data strongly suggest that the encounter occurred.

Crucially, the second-language learners of early Niger-Congo would not have had to speak analytic languages themselves. It is often forgotten that while it is possible for analyticity to transfer from one language to another, analyticity is, in the larger sense, a symptom of incomplete acquisition of a language *even by speakers of an inflected one*. Chinook Jargon developed into a creole on the Grand Ronde reservation in Oregon in the United States, and despite its source languages all being fearsomely inflected Native American languages of the Pacific Northwest, Chinook Jargon creole was as analytic as Chinese (Grant 1996). Highly analytic creoles such as Palenquero Creole Spanish and Guinea-Bissau Creole Portuguese were developed between speakers of well-inflected Ibero-Romance and equally well-inflected Niger-Congo languages (Kikongo for the former, Atlantic languages for the latter).

My approach to Niger-Congo is, ultimately, conservative. So striking is the difference between, e.g. Yoruba and Yao that it hardly surprises us that an early analyst such as Meinhof (1905, 1910) preliminarily assumed that languages like Gbe and Yoruba constituted a family-level group called Sudanic, distinct from the "Bantu" one. Thus I return to a perspective attractive to analysts as early as Lepsius (1880), who assumed that the analyticity of languages like Gbe and Yoruba was a latter-day rendition of an originally more synthetic state, analogous to English compared to Icelandic.

2.3   Evidence, Part One: Language spread

A necessary condition for GYN to have been impacted by non-native acquisition is that its originators are readily reconstructed as having encountered speakers of other languages, rather than being original inhabitants of their area.

This is unproblematic for the GYN languages. Archaeological research on West Africa is sparse at this writing, but has revealed evidence of Middle Stone Age hunter-gatherer populations. While there have been differing conclusions as to where Niger-Congo would have arisen, none have indicated the Bight of Benin where the GYN languages are spoken. All reconstructions are much further northward. Blench (2006: 123–5) surmises that with improving climate at the beginning of the Holocene, these populations began moving southward. Concrete evidence of this spread would include language isolates, as evidence of former occupants later largely replaced by newcomers, along the lines of isolated Khoi-San languages of Kenya and Tanzania after the Bantu spread, or the isolated Dravidian languages in northern India.

Along those lines, Blench proposes Jalaa in Nigeria as an isolate candidate amidst the Niger-Congo hegemony, and elsewhere Dompo and Mpra in Ghana (1999). Meanwhile, Dimmendaal's (2011:324) disinclusion of several groups (Mande, Ijoid, Dogon and Ubangian) from Niger-Congo, logical and overdue in my view, leaves many other languages that Niger-Congo speakers would have encountered. Contact with the large Mande family would have been especially significant, especially if this family once spread further to the south than currently. Ijoid, once treated as a "Kwa" language related to its westerly neighbors due to features such as SOV word order and an absence of even remnants of the Niger-Congo noun class markers, would be another remnant of the earlier inhabitants, surviving as the "Basque" of the area. The Dogon languages would qualify as further remnants of this kind.

2.4   Evidence, Part Two: GYN's difference from Proto-Niger-Congo parallels pidginization and creolization

2.4.1   *In syntax: Elimination of contextual rather than inherent morphology*
The difference between conservative Niger-Congo languages and GYN ones is not simply that GYN languages render the former's grammatical categories with free morphemes rather than affixes. In verbs, something close to this has occurred: a *make* verb recruited as a causative, a *give* verb as an applicative, etc. However, GYN did not replace noun class markers with free morphemes.

Yet as I have noted, languages can indeed encode noun classes with free morphemes. Relevant are numeral classifiers in East and Southeast Asian languages, free morphemes whose application to nouns is to a considerable extent unpredictable and is thus analogous to noun classes (cf. Grinevald & Seifart 2004). Crucially, many Niger-Congo languages have innovated actual free morpheme numeral classifiers (Kiessling 2013), and Wolof marks noun classes with determiner allomorphs. If the pathway to GYN was driven by a templatic restriction, we might expect at least one of these languages to retain noun class marking – i.e. inflection, albeit unbound – with a strategy like Wolof's that encodes the class marking beyond the root itself.

Instead, what determined which affixes GYN replaced appears to have been whether they were, in the terminology of Booij (1993), contextual or inherent inflection. Contextual inflection is linked to syntactic context, and includes structural case, concord and grammatical gender. Inherent inflection is (at least relatively) independent of syntactic context, and includes tense, aspect, and number markers. Roughly, inherent inflection has semantic content and "means something," whereas contextual inflection "does something." The verbal particles GYN languages have, equivalent in meaning to the pre- and postverbal affixes in synthetic Niger-Congo languages, are inherent morphology. Noun class marking and concord prefixes are contextual.

Yet there is no general diachronic tendency for contextual morphology to be more subject to extinction than inherent (cf. Nichols 1992:169 on head- and dependent-marking). Rather, the difference between GYN and its Niger-Congo relatives parallels a particular kind of language change: pidginization. To wit, contextual morphology, because its lack of semantics renders it less susceptible to conscious awareness and translation, is more fragile in contexts of second-language acquisition, not just change in general.

To the extent that any pidgins have inflection, be it bound or unbound, it is much less often contextual than inherent (Roberts & Bresnan 2008) – i.e. pidgins may have a tense or aspect marker, but almost never one marking case. Therefore creoles, as languages with degrees of pidginization in their history, tend to lack contextual inflection – bound or unbound – even though they tend strongly to have unbound inherent inflection (Plag 2008; Luís 2009). (Mufwene's proposal (e.g. 2001) that creoles result from mixture of features along the lines of population genetics, with pidginization and the effects of non-native acquisition of minimal import, is addressed comprehensively and critically in McWhorter (2012, 2013)).

2.4.2   In morphology: Grammatical simplification

The GYN languages also parallel creoles in that in comparison to their source grammars, subtraction predominated vastly over addition or substitution in terms of grammatical complexity in morphology and syntax. For example, in Egyptian, as Hodge documents, the "cycle" was one in which eventually, prefixes were replaced by suffixes. This has also been common in Niger-Congo, in which noun-class prefixes have often been replaced by noun-class suffixes over time, as chronicled by Greenberg (1978). The general tendency in Niger-Congo is, in general, for the noun-class and subject concord system to be reshuffled over time rather than to simply disappear (Mukarovsky 1977:32–5; Good 2012).[6]

---

6.   The tendency in question seems weaker if Mande, Ijo, and Dogon, in which noun classes are vestigial or absent, are included within Niger-Congo. However, among the many advantages of Dimmendaal's (2011) disinclusion of these groups from Niger-Congo, which I adopt, is that it vastly minimizes the volume of languages within Niger-Congo for which it is necessary to posit a mysterious loss of noun class markers. Niger-Congo specialists understandably process this loss as ordinary, but in the cross-linguistic sense it is actually a bizarre "drift" indeed. The only Indo-European language of Europe lacking grammatical gender is English, in which case the cause is largely agreed to have been non-native acquisition by Scandinavian invaders (cf. McWhorter 2005). Under ordinary conditions, over several millennia Indo-European languages have reorganized, but not eliminated, their gender markers.

This contrasts, then, with the disappearance of these affixes in GYN. More broadly, elsewhere in Niger-Congo, grammar-internal change tends to result in the development of new morphological apparatus as older apparatus wears away. Examples include: the prolific consonant mutations in Senegambian Atlantic that remained after noun class affixes wore away; the tonal and ablaut patterns marking tense and aspect in Nzadi in place of the affixes typical of Narrow Bantu, variant according to phonotactics and more (Crane, Hyman & Tukumu 2011:119–46), also present in a great many South Bantoid languages; the imperfective/neutral verb pairs in many Gur languages distinguished unpredictably by affixation, vowel length, tones, et al. (Naden 1989). These are traits demonstrate "reshuffling" of the kind chronicled by Mukharovsky and Good, with machinery less wearing away than transforming into other kinds of machinery.

The GYN languages overall give the appearance of abbreviations of the Niger-Congo inheritance rather than variations or elaborations on it, in the same way that despite certain innovations, English abbreviates the Proto-Germanic legacy more than any other Germanic language (McWhorter 2005:292–96). The noun classes are not transformed but fossilized into shards. Tense and aspect are indicated with free morphemes, while unlike in languages like Nzadi, the verb stem itself is tonally invariant. Elimination seems to have predominated over transformation.

Impressions, of course, can serve only as sparks for more precise argumentation – and as it happens, this impression of GYN is corroborated by quantitative analysis. Parkvall (2008) applies a complexity metric to 155 languages, based mainly on data from the *World Atlas of Language Structures* (Haspelmath, Dryer, Gil & Comrie 2005). The features mostly measure the marking of semantic categories, such as tense and aspect, degrees of distance in demonstratives, and degrees of number. Also included, however, are features such as overt marking of case.

In Parkvall's ranking – composed independently of any thesis such as mine about GYN – out of 155 languages in which the highest number represents the least complex grammar, Yoruba ranks down at 110 while Ewe, a Gbe variety, ranks at 127. Three observations are significant:

1. No Niger-Congo language other than Ewe occurs below Yoruba's 110. (Nupe was not included in the survey.)
2. Creole languages cluster in the realm of the ranking down beyond Ewe's 127.
3. These rankings are not a mere artifact of analyticity in general: analyticity and grammatical complexity of the kind specified above are hardly antithetical qualities. Analytic Sino-Tibetan Lahu ranks up at 64; despite its analyticity it includes evidential marking, numeral classifiers, modal and pragmatic particles as prolific as the famous ones in German, and serial verb constructions in which the encoding of grammatical relations varies according to person (cf. McWhorter 2005:53–7). For analogous reasons, largely analytic Fijian ranks at 79.

Surely the features included in such a survey would vary with each linguist who undertook the task. Yet, it is significant that according to the ones Parkvall happened to choose, the GYN languages fall where they do. Clearly, they are low on the kind of complexity that Parkvall's features focus on: the overt marking of semantic categories that many languages leave to context (*overspecification* in the terminology of McWhorter 2007). Widespread second language acquisition tends strongly to work against overspecification, as chronicled by Kusters (2003), Trudgill (2011) and others, and it follows that pidginization and creolization do so as well (McWhorter 2005: 38–71).

2.4.3   *In phonology: Monosyllabic template*

There has been one proposal, to my knowledge, of a grammar-internal diachronic mechanism that could create radical analyticity: Hyman (2004). He proposes that what caused the difference between verbs in the GYN languages, usually monosyllabic or at most disyllabic, and the heavily suffixed ones in Narrow Bantu languages was the development of a phonological template disallowing verbs of more than two syllables. I believe my proposal accounts for the phenomenon more economically for the following reasons.

1.   *Such a process is documented nowhere else.* Why, we must ask, did this template originate? Hyman's account is one of "drift," more descriptive than explanatory. It is hardly a cross-linguistic commonplace that languages permitting richly multisyllabic words gradually take on a "template" limiting words to one or two syllables, as an ordinary development alongside ones such as nasalization or resyllabification.

2.   *Languages resist letting phonological processes eliminate grammatical morphemes.* To be sure, Hyman posits various languages as cases intermediate between a Yao and a Yoruba, with Punu limiting verbs to four syllables, Basa to three, and Grassfields Bantu languages such as Mankon to two. However, it is hardly necessary that the entirety of this cline represents a sequential development. A certain degree of variation between syllabic templates (as well as phonological constraints of the kind Hyman describes in, for example, the language Tiene) is typical within a language family. However, Hyman's account requires that speakers of a language with a bisyllabic template "drifted" into a monosyllabic restriction *even on the pain of eliminating grammatically crucial affixes, replacing them with free morphemes –* despite linguists' well known findings that speakers resist phonological erosion when it threatens grammatical morphemes (cf. Guy 1991). Moreover, no speakers were aware of the "drift" or its direction: the very idea that the *directionality* of a templatic change could somehow be contained with the grammars of disparate speakers of dozens of languages is difficult to sustain.

3.   *Pidginization explains the data just as well.* The development Hyman describes seems rather peculiar, then, upon which it is relevant that the above described

process is perfectly explicable as *what happens in pidginization*. The reason words might become radically, as opposed to modestly, shorter in a language, to such a degree as to force a vast restructuring – as well as abbreviation – of the grammatical system, is the language's transformation by non-native acquirers less likely to master lengthier words (as well as grammatical features).

To the extent that the GYN languages restrict their verbs to a maximum of two syllables, it is relevant that, as pidgin specialist Mühlhäusler (1997: 140) puts it, "There appears to be a tendency in most stable Pidgins, whatever their sub- and superstrata languages and whatever their jargon predecessors, to favour open syllables and words of the canonical shape CVCV." Also, given Mühlhäusler's description of pidgins as favoring CV phonotactics, it is indicative that highly inflected Niger-Congo languages – under an analysis as conservative precursors of the GYN ones – often retain consonantal codas, such as languages of the Senegambian Atlantic group like Wolof and Fula.

Also, the continuum nature of the process Hyman proposes is equally explainable as the result of varying degrees of second-language acquisition in various locations. I hardly intend to argue that pidginization, to various degrees, has operated only in the GYN region, and am in agreement with Niger-Congo specialists who often hazard that degrees of second-language acquisition have affected the typologies of Niger-Congo languages.

Finally, these observations must be considered in light of the arguments in 2.4.1. and 2.4.2. already presented. In short, non-native acquisition provides a more economical explanation of GYN phonotactics than proposing that a monosyllabic template arose in a stepwise fashion apparently unparalleled in language change processes elsewhere in the world.

On three levels of grammar, the emergence of GYN entailed the same processes of grammatical transformation which linguists have identified as creating pidgin and creole languages. An orthodox response may be to suppose that this is simply an accident, but at the expense of scientific economy.

2.5   Evidence Part Three: Distribution of analyticity

The assumption that a grammar may become radically analytic via grammar-internal processes entails a prediction: that amidst Niger-Congo, radically analytic languages would be distributed randomly, with the map of Niger-Congo a patchwork of syntheticity and analyticity, with no especial pattern noticeable.

2.5.1   *Layers of analyticity*
As Niger-Congo specialists know, this is not the case. This becomes clearest using Dimmendaal's (2011: 323–4) revised conception of Niger-Congo, which omits Mande, Ubangian, Ijo, and Dogon as insufficiently demonstrated as relatives of the rest of

the family. GYN is a core of radical analyticity in a scientifically demonstrable Niger-Congo, surrounded by syntheticity increasing by degrees as one moves outward. This pattern is antithetical to any conception of analyticity as a mere matter of "drift" taking place in assorted languages to various degrees for no particular reason. The sheer existence of such a pattern in the distribution suggests that there was a factor at work beyond chance.

The most synthetic Niger-Congo languages occupy the outer edges, something well acknowledged in itself by specialists. Most westward are Atlantic languages, which include cases such as Fula and its 25 noun class suffixes and complex morphophonemic alternations that have developed as a result of them. In languages like Wolof and others, the noun classes are indicated by paradigms of free morphemes, but even these constitute, despite their unbound status, inflection. Atlantic is now thought to comprise three or more separate families, but all of these groups are synthetic and/or have unbound inflection paradigms, such as Fula and Wolof in the Senegambian group, Balanta and Bijago in the Bak group, Temne in the Mel group, and the Limba and Gola languages.

Eastward, the Kordofanian languages, although also now considered to likely represent several stocks, are notoriously synthetic, conserving noun classes traceable to Proto-Niger-Congo as well as various verbal extensions (e.g. Reh 1985). I am aware of no Kordofanian language documented as analytic to any considerable degree. Then, the "Narrow Bantu" languages covering most of sub-Saharan Africa are all inflected to some substantial degree (including via tone) on both the noun and the verb, with the only exceptions – i.e. analytic to a degree nearing GYN – being vehicular varieties born of adult usage such as Kituba and Lingala, often classified as pidgins or creoles.

Analyticity begins in subgroups inward of the aforementioned, but the discussion in the literature tends to imply that within this area, the analyticity is distributed in a uniformly scattered fashion – i.e. what we might expect of a trait that emerges as a mere result of "drift." However, leaving aside the question as to what would have retarded this "drift" so much in only the "outer ring" languages, the reality is that just as the conservative languages surround the moderately analytic ones, these in turn surround a core of radically analytic ones, the GYN trio. Even languages immediately adjacent to GYN, while often mentioned as if they and GYN were equally analytic, are in fact distinctly less so, although more so than languages further outward. Analytic "drift" in Niger-Congo is patterned, suggesting a causal agent beyond mere chance. The map in Figure 1 may be helpful.

2.5.2   *Analytic-lite: The Niger-Congo norm*

2.5.2.1   Syntheticity increases incrementally westward of GYN. *New Kwa.* New Kwa differs from GYN is that as a group, it is about as analytic as English – and in some cases vastly less so. Akan varieties retain a degree of concordial affixation within the

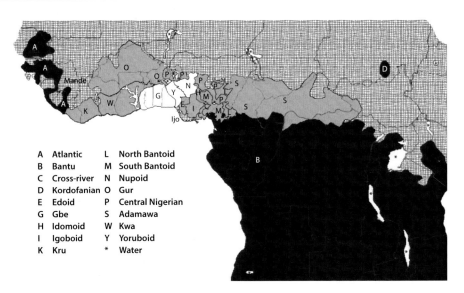

Figure 1. Map of relevant languages

noun phrase for animates, and subject pronominal, tense, aspect and mood prefixes, entrenched enough to be subject to morphophonological rules (Osam 2003). Akan's relatives within its Potou-Tano group such as Anyi-Baule, Nzema, Ahanta are even less analytic, with consonant mutations and verbal affixes that condition them, affixes for plural, and number concord (Nzema: ɣalɛ kɛnlɛma "fine child," mmalɛ ngɛnlɛma "fine children" (Dolphyne & Dakubu 1988:73). The facts are similar with the Guang languages (Gonja, Gichode, Nchumburu, Dwang), with remnants of number agreement and verbal affixes (ibid. 84).

The New Kwa branch comprised of Gã and Dangme has less nominal prefixation than the Potou-Tano languages, but Gã retains a degree of affixation for tense and aspect. Notably, Dangme, spoken eastward of Gã, displays less of this affixation, in a degree of analyticity intermediate between Gã and Gbe (Wilkie 1930; Dakubu 1988:104–5).

Meanwhile, the Central Togo languages retain an elaborate nominal concord system ("normal" Niger-Congo), and "six to twenty verbal conjugations" (Dakubu & Ford 1988:143).

Kru: In map view, syntheticity increases the further westward Niger-Congo occurs. According to Marchese (1989) and Williamson and Blench (2000:34), Kru languages include remnants of noun class along the lines of, e.g. Akan and Edo, as well as various verbal suffixes some of which are inflectional.

2.5.2.2   Syntheticity increases incrementally eastward of GYN. *Edoid.* In the best-known representative of this group just eastward of Yoruboid and Nupoid, Edo has vestiges of noun class marking, with a singular-plural distinction in animates

(Omoregbe & Aigbedo 2012), while on verbs, past tense (in the intransitive) is marked with a suffix in the intransitive and with high tone in the transitive (Ogie 2003). Other Edoid languages are often much less analytic, such as Oloma and Emhalhe's elaborate NP concord marking and Degema's robust noun class systems and subject-verb concord (Elugbe 1989; Kari 1995).

Igboid. These languages, the next subgroup eastward from Edoid, have rather elaborate verb suffixation. An extreme example is this Igbo sentence:

(4)   bi- kọ- rị- ta- tụ- wa- ra
      live-CONGREGATIV-BEN-DIR-'just slightly'-INCEPT-APP
      "begin to live together in one another advantage for someone"
                                                    (Ọnụkawa 1999:124)

It is thought that Igboid has innovated "most" of this post-verbal suffixation relatively recently (Williamson & Blench 2000:31), which implies that originally it had about as much verb suffixation as Edo or perhaps some more. This would be consonant with the general pattern in which syntheticity increases by degrees according to distance from GYN.

Cross-River. In these languages spoken eastward of Igboid, verbs can have various prefixes or suffixes (Williamson & Blench 2000:33), while noun class marking ranges from abundant to absent, although even the ones without it retain subject-verb concord (Faraclas 1989:391).

   It bears mentioning that the clinal nature of syntheticity in these languages eastward of GYN extends to the fact that within Nupoid, in contrast to radically analytic Nupe, the Gade language on the eastern edge has a full paradigm of noun class markers and a good deal of NP concord (Sterk 1978). It is also relevant that the other Nupoid languages, occurring eastward of Gbe and Yoruboid, depart slightly from radical analyticity in retaining a generalized plural prefix *a-* (Blench 1989:316).

2.5.2.3   Languages northward of GYN are more synthetic. *Idoma.* Noun class marking, with a singular/plural distinction, is reduced to one prefixal alternation, and verbal extensions are lost (Abraham 1951; Adejoh 2012). However, the language is inflected in other areas, such as some verb pairs that vary suppletively according to number (Adejoh 2012) and especially in object pronominal suffixation that conditions alterations of the preceding verb's vowel (*o ma* "he saw," *o mu-m* "he saw me" [Abraham 1951]).

Gur-Adamawa. The most conservative among these have many as six gender classes (Naden 1988; Miehe & Winkelmann 2007), and in the verb, some have imperfective/neutral pairs distinguished unpredictably by affixation, tone changes, vowel changes or lengthening, as well as other verbal inflections (Naden 1989). The Adamawa languages tend to have petrified but identifiable noun class suffixes and sometimes some NP concord (Williamson & Blench 2000:28; Dimmendaal 2001:379).

Central Nigerian. In these languages (including ones traditionally classified as Platoid and Jukunoid), "the drift in Niger-Congo in the direction of the simplification of the nominal classificational system" has often proceeded quite far (Gerhardt 1989:369), but not to the point of absence; there are also some verbal extensions.

North Bantoid. Fossilization and paucity of noun class prefixes (and suffixes) is common in these languages, sometimes possibly not even of Niger-Congo origin (Blench 2013). The Mambiloid languages are especially analytic in tendency, with only plural prefixes productive, and other affixes seemingly having become tones (Hedinger 1989).

South Bantoid other than Narrow Bantu: These languages, such as Tiv, Jarawan and the Grassfields languages, constitute the transitional zone between the relative analyticity described above and Narrow Bantu, with ample noun classes and verbal extensions of a kind that Bantuists experience as familiar, albeit less prolific than in Narrow Bantu.

2.6   What happened to Niger-Congo?

2.6.1   *From the inside out?*

Analyticity in Niger-Congo is not randomly distributed, nor is it randomly distributed even among the languages besides the peripheral synthetic ones. It is most extreme in a few contiguous languages along the Bight of Benin, and then exhibited beyond to incrementally lesser degrees.

On its face, this may not seem to present a challenge to theories of language change and contact. Many will see a manifestation of the well-known fact that within a language area, change often begins in the center and extends outward, leaving peripheral varieties more conservative. However, this account has two serious problems.

1.   Even if we presume that analyticity began with GYN and spread outward (which, below, I in fact will not), this schema is not useful for this particular change because it merely recasts the central question. The change here is not one in sound or word order, of a kind that regularly occurs amidst ordinary grammar-internal change. Rather, the change is a loss of not just some, but all inflectional morphology. As noted, there exists no account of how that would happen under normal conditions. Therefore, if GYN was the start of a trend, then the question this paper is posing remains: how did the trend even start in the first place?

This problem also applies to any account, such as Nurse's (2007), that Proto-Niger-Congo was analytic. Proto-Niger-Congo was a manifestation of human language which had existed, if we consider vastly earlier forms not even recognizable as what we now know as Niger-Congo, for tens of millennia previously. Via what process would it have developed the typological profile of Yoruba? Why would fusion not have occurred? "To propose an analytic structure for Niger-Congo," Nurse writes, "means that some mostly peripheral languages fused their structures, either independently or under the influence of neighbors. Fusion is natural and well-attested and only a small number of languages innovated this way." However, I would offer a correction: fusion is nearly a default process worldwide. As such, that "only a small number" of Niger-Congo languages would exhibit that fusion would be a conundrum.

2. Even putting aside the question as to how GYN would have become analytic in the first place, any general classification of Niger-Congo's analyticity as "areal" gives an impression of explanation that does not hold up to scrutiny. Even in the Southeast Asian case, it is debatable that what spread was analyticity as a feature, as opposed to the effects of non-native acquisition of originally synthetic languages, as I will argue in Section 3. However, even arguing for analyticity as a feature transferred in itself, in Southeast Asia we could point to aggressive and long-term migration by Han Chinese.

On the contrary, there is no evidence of general population movements outward from where GYN is spoken to regions westward, eastward and northward. All indications at present are that Niger-Congo began somewhere far northward of the Bight of Benin where GYN is spoken, with the decisive population movements being southwards towards that area.

Short of a migration account, we have to stipulate that analyticity spread ever further outward via bilingualism at the boundaries between languages. But this borders on unfalsifiability. There is no principled reason that the GYN languages' traits would spread outward to affect surrounding languages more robustly than the traits of the surrounding languages would affect the GYN languages. Would it surprise us if instead, due to this same kind of contact, it had been the GYN languages that had became more synthetic instead?

This, in fact, would be the more likely result. Worldwide, contact tends to lead languages to take on affixal categories (and sometimes the affixes themselves). Language contact transfer typically involves that which is present, not that which does not exist, as is amply documented in studies such as Heath (1978) on Australia, Aikhenvald (2001) and Seifart (2012) on South America. Positing that a mere three sub-subfamilies spread their analyticity through hundreds of languages east, north and south would be hopelessly *ad hoc*: no falsifiable account would be possible. To posit that in one part of Africa, amidst language contact over thousands of years, for some reason abbreviation vastly predominated over construction is, ultimately, to shrug the shoulders.

In contrast, recall that studies such as Kusters (2003), McWhorter (2007) and Trudgill (2011) have shown that grammatical simplification results, quite regularly, from adult acquisition, not simply language mixture in a general sense. As noted in 2.2, this simplification even occurs when all of the languages in the encounter are morphologically elaborate. In other words, we propose that subtraction predominated for exactly the reason that linguists would suppose: fundamental realities of how languages are acquired by adults.

2.6.2   *Niger-Congo analyticity as evidence of cycles of second-language acquisition*

I concur with the assumption of most Niger-Congo specialists that Proto-Niger-Congo would have been a synthetic language (and am more convinced by Hyman 2011 than Güldemann 2011 on the degree of that syntheticity). Along the lines of this paper, I assume that the "outer ring" languages of Niger-Congo, such as Atlantic, Kordofanian, and Narrow Bantu, reflect the protolanguage's typology – predictably so, in fact, as manifesting the normal state of language uninterrupted in its transmission: highly inflected.

What led to the analyticity in the rest of the subfamilies would have been encounters between Niger-Congo speakers migrating southward and other peoples, which to create such analyticity would have to have been of a kind that led to widespread rapid and incomplete acquisition of Niger-Congo. That is, I propose that the state of the moderately analytic "inner ring" of Niger-Congo represented by Kru, Gur-Adamawa, Potou-Tano, most of West Benue-Congo, Central Nigerian and "Bantoid" is *evidence that* widespread second-language acquisition occurred. That proposition is motivated by the fact that there is no mysterious analytic "drift" in language groups worldwide, suggesting that something intervened in the transmission of Niger-Congo.

Under this analysis, if Dimmendaal is correct that Mande is a separate language family, then contact with Mande could have had much to do with rendering Niger-Congo more analytic with movement southward. The Dogon languages, if not Niger-Congo, would have had a similar effect on languages in its area.

Then, the most economical account of the radical analyticity of the GYN languages is that they, on the Bight of Benin coast and thus representing one of the geographical end points of the migration, resulted from the incomplete acquisition of varieties which were themselves products of incomplete acquisition in the past – i.e. languages of today's intermediate "inner ring" varieties. The result was languages which, in comparison with Proto-Niger-Congo, were radically abbreviated in terms of grammatical elaboration: i.e. to the point of pidginization/creolization as described in 2.4. If Dimmendaal is correct that Ijoid is not Niger-Congo, then it would represent a survival of the populations that Niger-Congo-speaking migrants encountered when they reached the coast.

Under this cyclical account, it becomes predictable that Niger-Congo analyticity increases with proximity to the coast overall, not just where the GYN languages are spoken. The Kru and Potou-Tano languages westward of GYN, and the Edoid and Igboid ones eastward of GYN, are more analytic than ones further inland such as the Gur-Adamawa and Cross River languages. Notably, within this latter group, the Lower

Cross and Ogoni languages, spoken near the coast, are the most analytic (Faraclas 1989:391). Or, Idoma is more analytic than the Gur and Central Nigerian languages above it, while amidst Potou-Tano, the notably synthetic Central Togo languages are spoken inland of more analytic ones such as Gã and Dangme.

There are indeed some non-coastal Niger-Congo languages, as well, that show robust degrees of analyticity (although not reaching the state of the GYN languages), such as the Mambiloid languages of North Bantoid far inland in Cameroon. It would be unexpected that across such a vast territory the cline of analyticity I describe would be evidenced in perfect fashion among hundreds of languages with their various histories. Happenstances naturally played their part here and there; for example, the Mambiloid languages are considered relatively recent arrivals in their area, a range typically occupied by other families, suggesting that second-language acquisition had a significant impact upon them (Jeff Good, February 2014 p.c.). What is crucial is the general clinal tendency, a strong and readily apparent one, to which cases like Mambiloid qualify as predictable scattered exceptions.

Possibly, this analytic tendency towards the coast was due not only to multiple cycles of incomplete acquisition, but also to original populations there having been more numerous and/or difficult to subjugate than ones further inland. It is well-established in anthropological studies that coastal hunter gatherers tend to be more populous, sedentary and societally complex because of the richness of maritime resources (Keeley 1988; Ames 1994).

To be sure, Niger-Congo specialists propose contact accounts for analyticity in specific cases, such as Dimmendaal's (2001:381) speculation that, for example, Benue-Congo losses were due to contact with Chadic. My account simply attempts to apply this approach to a wider selection of data. Dimmendaal's surmises, for example, leave unexplained why GYN is so analytic when the languages are in contact only with other Niger-Congo ones.

2.6.3   *Cyclical second language acquisition: Parallels*

The language contact literature includes concrete demonstrations of the effects of cyclical second-language acquisition. An analagous case would be colloquial Indonesian varieties today, which parallel creole languages in terms of radically reduced morphological and syntactic features in comparison to Standard Indonesian. The strikingly telegraphic Riau Indonesian, described in the work of David Gil (e.g. 2001), is the best-known example among linguists today, but it is in fact one of many dialects of Indonesian with similar structure.

These varieties emerged via a two-step process of reduction. First, Standard Indonesian, i.e. Malay, is itself significantly less morphologically and syntactically complex than other Malayic languages such as Iban, Javanese, the Batak languages, and Tukang Besi (McWhorter 2007:197–251), as well as to its own ancestor Classical

Malay (cf. Cumming 1991). Described by Dalby (1998:391) as having "a more approachable structure than its relatives" because of its status as a lingua franca – i.e. having undergone widespread second-language acquisition in its use across Indonesia since early in the first millennium, A.D. – it strikingly reduces its ancestral battery of verbal morphology. Ross (2002:52–3) shows the difference between a typical such system in a reconstructed ancestor of languages of the Malay/Indonesian type and today's Standard Indonesian:

Table 3. Verb morphology in a hypothetical early Indonesian-type language and in Standard Indonesian

Early Indonesian:

	patient undergoer	location undergoer	circumstantial undergoer
ACTIVE			
neutral	maN-, -um-	maN-/-i, -um-, -i	maN-/-an
perfective	naN-	naN-/-i	naN-/-an
PASSIVE			
neutral	-ku	-i-ku	-an-ku
perfective	ku-, -in-/-ku	ku-/-i, -in-/-i-ku	ku-/-an, -in-/-an-ku

Modern Indonesian:

	patient object	location object	circumstantial object
ACTIVE	meN-	meN-/-i	meN-/-kan
PASSIVE	ku-	ku-/-i	ku-/-kan

Then, in the modern colloquial dialects, the morphology above is used either highly variably or barely at all, as the result of further second-language usage via its imposition across Indonesia (cf. Grijns 1991; McWhorter 2007:234–42); there are also syntactic rules that the colloquial varieties eschew. This example compares Standard Indonesian with the colloquial Indonesian of Java (David Gil, 2010 p.c.):

(5) (a) Anda **men**-cari buku yang sudah **di**-baca Ali.
         you   AO-search book REL   PAST   OO-read Ali

     (b) Lu   cari buku yang Ali udah baca.
         you look book that   Ali PAST read
         "You're looking for the book that Ali read."

(AO = agent-oriented, OO = object-oriented)

Another example of the cyclical effect of second-language acquisition is the development of Réunionnais Creole French (Baker & Corne 1982: 104–8; Cellier 1985). In the initial phase of the colonization of the island Réunion, when settlers and slaves co-existed in relatively equal numbers working alongside one another, slaves had enough contact with French to create a dialect that was slightly effected by second-language acquisition but hardly classifiable as something other than French. However, when sugar cultivation was inaugurated, slaves were imported in massive numbers rapidly. Exposed to this second-language variety of French and acquiring it as a second-language themselves, these slaves created a language much further from French in terms of morphological and syntactic elisions than the earlier variety – what is today known as the creole, in contrast to its predecessor, today processed as the "high" variety of creole.

2.7   Two questions, two answers

I propose that this account is compatible with the linguistic facts as well as the geographical ones, and that we take the next step of considering that the linguistic facts be treated as clues to historical ones rather than unworthy of engagement without them. As such, a question my account leaves is:

> *When Niger-Congo spread southward throughout the African continent, why did it remain as prolifically inflected as to yield the typical Bantu language, despite acquisition by Pygmy groups and Khoi-San speakers?*

Under the idea that languages can become analytic via stepwise grammar-internal development, that question is problematic for my account. However, we must recall (1) the mechanical implausibility of a language losing all of its inflectional affixes without gaining new ones, and (2) the fact that all *historically documented* cases of grammars undergoing such a process entail rampant non-native acquisition. This suggests that my account be taken as presenting not a description but an explanation. Namely, the linguistic facts can be taken as *evidence* that where Niger-Congo arose, population density and societal organization were greater than where it later spread southwards. It is also possible that Khoi-San languages persisted in especially unforgiving environments.

In the same way, my account could be read as leaving another question:

> *Why are a certain three language stocks along or near the Bight of Benin (GYN) so much more analytic than ones on or near the coasts westward and eastward?*

I suggest, similarly, that the linguistic nature of GYN can be taken as standing *evidence that* population density at the Bight of Benin and inland was especially dense – with the survival of Ijoid as a possible remnant of this. Future archaeological and sociohistorical research, alerted to this possibility by the linguistic data, could illuminate the facts more directly. The evidence can also be taken as suggesting that the area where GYN languages are spoken was the last area that Niger-Congo reached on the southern coast of the upper "Guinea" region of Africa, such that there, earlier Niger-Congo would have undergone the most cycles of second-language acquisition by original inhabitants.

The charge of circularity looms, but only via misunderstanding. The reasoning would be circular if we had a mechanism other than non-native acquisition to explain a language transforming from one like Fula to one like Fongbe. But we do not: it would appear that linguists have discovered that non-native acquisition is, in fact, the only way such a thing happens. I am simply seeking to apply that discovery to new data, in a quest to see whether this particular linguistic consensus allows us to discover new things.

3. Analyticity in the Sinosphere

Nevertheless, one might ask one more question: can we really treat radical analyticity as an anomaly when, while there are only a few such languages in Niger-Congo, there are at least a few hundred in East and Southeast Asia? One might reasonably suppose that their sheer number, spread across four families (Sino-Tibetan, Mon-Khmer, Tai-Kadai, and Hmong-Mien), shows that analyticity is indeed a state that a language can "drift" into via full transmission from one generation to another.

However, I submit that the analyticity of these hundreds of languages is due to what began with a mere single language losing all of its inflectional affixes.

3.1   Rolling back the tape

It would seem agreed that the analyticity so typical of East and Southeast Asia is an areal feature. Specifically, the area is considered what Matisoff (1991) terms a "Sinosphere," where the spread of Chinese left analyticity, among other traits, in its wake in a great many languages of various families. None venture the unscientific speculation that analyticity emerged in all of these languages just in this area by chance. None, either, would venture the equally unlikely notion that four contiguous *families* drifted into analyticity by chance, unless unaware of how rare analyticity is worldwide. Also, no scholar outside of China any longer classifies Tai-Kadai and Hmong-Mien as branches of Sino-Tibetan, which would allow the analyticity as an inherited family trait.

Rather, the areal analyticity is seen as sparked by Chinese. As late as the end of the first millennium, A.D., states such as the Bai and the Lolo still thrived alongside the Chinese (ibid. 486). Bellwood (2005: 223–7) chronicles, for example, that around

6000 BC, the Hmong-Mien were south of the middle Yangzi, speakers of what would become Austroasiatic were to the southwest, and speakers of what would become the Tai-Kadai family were southeast in the Guizhou, Guangxi and Guangdong provinces. But Chinese speakers began migrating southward in the final millennium, B.C. and continued doing so into the next millennium. Many of the groups they encountered were assimilated into Chinese culture and language, but others retreated to hill country (such as Hmong-Mien speakers) or migrated further southward (such as Tai-Kadai speakers).

The implication of these now well-known facts must be clear: in Southeast Asia analyticity traces to one language (group): Chinese. The corollary of this is that the families Chinese rendered analytic did not begin in that state. Rather, they began in the state that all languages, I claim, settle into under normal transmission: synthetic. If the Chinese had not migrated southward, we can presume that Southeast Asian language families would be like those almost everywhere else in the world: synthetic to various degrees, like even Austronesian, contiguous to all of them, is today.

As such, under a thesis that analyticity is not a normal state for language transmitted natively, Southeast Asia requires the explanation not of hundreds of languages, but solely of Chinese.

There are two mechanisms via which analyticity could have spread in this context:

1. Chinese speakers rendered the languages they encountered non-natively, yielding analytic structure.
2. Bilingual generations after the initial migration came to render their native languages analytically because of the influence of Chinese's structure, such that analyticity spread as a "feature" transferred into native languages along with tone, semantic patterns, etc.

Of course, the two scenarios could easily have operated in tandem, and the details would have differed from one place to another.

3.2 Language groups rendered analytic by Chinese migration

While details, to the extent that they are recoverable, remain to be found, all indications are compatible with a basic scenario under which the analyticity of one entity, Chinese, transformed families that were once synthetic.

Austroasiatic. The effect of Chinese is especially clear in this family, in which the westward Munda languages outside of Southeast Asia beyond the Chinese migration zone are synthetic, as are the southerly Aslian languages, spoken by isolated groups similarly distant from the Chinese migration (cf. Matisoff 2003). In general, Mon-Khmer languages are replete with largely fossilized remnants of erstwhile affixation. The absence of this in its best-known member, Vietnamese (and its close relatives) is an anomaly, traced by specialists to contact with Chinese (cf. Alves 2001). (Also relevant are the analytic Chamic languages, born of Austronesian deeply influenced by analytic Mon-Khmer; Chamic thus qualifies as rendered analytic by Chinese indirectly.)

Hmong-Mien. Ratliff (2006) notes conclusive evidence that Proto-Hmong-Mien had noun class prefix paradigms. Moreover, fossilized reflexes of the prefixes are more in evidence in Hmongic, which has had less Chinese influence than Mienic, and the prefixes are more common in fossilized expressions.

Starosta (2005:188) stated that Hmong-Mien already had isolating structure when the Han Chinese encountered it, but without demonstration. He perhaps assumed that the analyticity that resulted from contact between Sinitic and Hmong-Mien requires that both groups were analytic, and that if Hmong-Mien had been synthetic, Chinese there would have become more synthetic. However, as noted above (2.2.), contact between even highly synthetic languages can easily yield analytic contact languages. It is often assumed that syntheticity is, itself, more readily acquired by speakers of synthetic languages. But syntheticity that marks vastly different categories than a learner is accustomed to, with vastly unfamiliar phonetic forms, and subject to vastly different phonological rules, is presumably no less user-friendly to that speaker than to a speaker of an analytic language – especially given that the acquisition in these contexts would have been via oral transmission with minimal explicit instruction.

Tai-Kadai. The increasing consensus is that Tai-Kadai is a descendant of early Austronesian (Sagart 2004; Ostapirat 2005, although they differ on what stage of Austronesian is relevant). Austronesianists are united in reconstructing Proto-Austronesian (and earlier Austronesian in general) as inflected (cf. Table 3). Thus we can assume that the language that Tai-Kadai stemmed from was inflected, and that Tai-Kadai's analyticity is a later development.

Tibeto-Burman. The Sinosphere also includes languages of the larger of the two branches of Sino-Tibetan of which Sinitic (Chinese) is one, Tibeto-Burman. The radically analytic languages of this group are in the "Sinosphere" geographically and sociologically, including the Loloish, Karenic, Kachinic, and Bai subbranches (cf. Matisoff 1991). Meanwhile, other members of Tibeto-Burman, such as Tibetan and Burmese themselves, are synthetic languages.

Thus our question becomes: Whence the analyticity of the one language that sparked it in so many others?

3.3   Proto-Sino-Tibetan over Chinese

The actual answer to the question as to why Chinese is analytic is that its ancestor, Proto-Sino-Tibetan, is agreed to have been (e.g. LaPolla 2003), such that this is the language whose analyticity requires examination.

The main evidences for the analyticity of Proto-Sino-Tibetan are two. One is that unlike in the Niger-Congo case there is actual written evidence of a very early state of one of Sino-Tibetan's two branches, Sinitic: Old Chinese, which was a highly analytic language (see below). Evidence for grammatical structure becomes rich starting with material from the Late Zhou dynasty (475–221 B.C.).

Second is that the other of Sino-Tibetan's two branches, Tibeto-Burman, is also considered by many analysts to have been analytic itself. There are proposals otherwise, such as that the verbal subject agreement markers in many of the modern languages should be reconstructed in the protolanguage (Van Driem 1993; Delancey 2010). This has even been interpreted by some (e.g. Van Driem 2005) as part of a case that an inflected Proto-Tibeto-Burman be reconstructed as the family ancestor, with analytic Chinese as a branch under that.

However, I am convinced by LaPolla's (1992) reasoning that these Tibeto-Burman markers are innovations. LaPolla first notes that not even a majority of Tibeto-Burman languages have them, such that reconstructing them in the protolanguage requires positing that *most* of the modern languages mysteriously shed them, a proposition I find especially unlikely given my opening observations in this paper. LaPolla also shows that the suffixes tend to give evidence of recent grammaticalization, such as phonetic similarity to free pronouns and optional, pragmatically conditioned usage rather than obligatory, syntacticized usage.[7]

The scenario I will assume, then, is that Proto-Sino-Tibetan was analytic, and first branched off into two analytic descendants, Sinitic and Proto-Tibeto-Burman. Descendants of both branches have developed types of inflection since, ranging from Tibeto-Burman languages' affixal paradigms to Chinese numeral classifier "inflectional" morphemes and other morphemes verging on inflectional status. All of these languages, however, are helpful in making it clear how unusual it was that Proto-Sino-Tibetan and its immediate offshoots were as radically analytic as they were.

---

7.   This aspect of the Tibeto-Burman paradigm highlights a stipulation probably necessary in the presentation of this hypothesis. To the extent that *all or close to all* of the inflectional morphemes in a language are analyzable as clitics rather than affixes – e.g. under an analysis assuming that affixes are more subject to morphophonemic variation, create more semantically irregular combination with roots, are more tightly bound to a particular hosts than clitics, and are paradigmatically restricted in their occurrence with roots in terms of declension/conjugation classes – this can be taken as evidence of the intervention of non-native acquisition. This is because such a state implies a relatively recent state in which there were no inflectional affixes, which I propose would have only been possible after widespread non-native acquisition.

3.4   Old Chinese: Ordinarily transmitted grammar?

Chinese specialists often note that Sinitic is hardly as monosyllabic as often thought, including a certain amount of nascent affixation, and compounding as a norm in lexical formation (Kennedy 1951; Dai 1990). It is less known that Old Chinese actually was as monosyllabic as the modern languages are often thought to be.

    Lacking inflectional affixation was but one facet. It also lacked the numeral classifiers modern Sinitic has, as well as even free markers of tense and aspect. Nor were these features conveyed with tone – Old Chinese had none. Meanwhile, even the compounding so central to modern Sinitic lexicons was much less common in Old Chinese. (Data from Norman 1988; Pulleyblank 1995; and Herforth 2003.)

(6)   gjə tjits   njəjʔ C-rjək   ljajʔ   gjə k-ljuŋ pjəj njəjʔ C-rjək   ljajʔ
       its arrive you   strength PART its hit.on NEG you   strength PART
       "That you reach it is owing to your strength, but that you hit the mark is not
       owing to your strength."   (Herforth 2003:60; Baxter 1992)

The stark degree to which Old Chinese leaves meaning to context makes such a singular impression that Herforth (2003:60) notes:

> Readers will find that written [Late Zhou Chinese] seems in many ways a minimal linguistic system. Many obligatory distinctions made lexically and/ or morphologically and/or syntactically in modern European languages are simply not overt in [Late Zhou Chinese] text; rather, they must be construed compositionally from the immediate context or inferred from the larger context. Lest it be assumed that such minimality is entirely or even primarily an artifact of written [Late Zhou Chinese], interested readers may consult David Gil's description of Riau Indonesian, a spoken language in many ways as "underspecified" (Riddle & Stahlke 1992) as the written language analyzed here."

It is important that as we have seen in Section 2, Riau Indonesian itself is analyzed as having acquired its analyticity as the result of contact, not ordinary change.

    In assessing the plausibility that Old Chinese's grammar resulted from the ordinary transmission of a grammatical system, we must consider that the only languages as extremely telegraphic as Old Chinese are members of the creole class. Applying to Old Chinese Parkvall's (2008) complexity metric referred to above in 2.4.2., in which he finds that creole languages rank as among the least grammatically complex languages of the world, Old Chinese ranks as *less complex than all of the languages in the sample including the creoles*. Sango, a pidgin/creole of the Central African Republic, ranks .15, while Old Chinese tallies to .11.[8] Not a single language of the 155 that Parkvall treats is as low in complexity rating as Old Chinese.

---

8. Parkvall's (2008) features applied to Old Chinese:

Size of consonant inventory	.75
Size of vowel quality inventories	.5

It also bears mentioning that among the non-creole languages sharing space with creoles at the less-complex pole on Parkvall's continuum, all evidence salient grammatical complexities that happen not to have been covered in WALS and Parkvall's metric. None would evoke a comparison such as Herforth's to Riau Indonesian, nor have any elicited attention from writers investigating relative complexity between languages. Pirahã is richly inflected and has at least two phonemic tones. Maybrat of Papua New Guinea has a rich system of pronominal prefixes and numeral classifiers (Dol 2007). Kobon, also of Papua New Guinea, has an ample, fusional inflectional system (Davies 1981). Hmong has eight tones, dozens of numeral classifiers, and a full system of tense and aspect marking particles (Riddle 2008).

In contrast, in Old Chinese, it would be difficult to identify complexities that the WALS project happened not to cover, beyond occasional shards such as a case distinction between third-person pronominal forms. No linguist would find it unreasonable to at least speculate that this language was a product of incomplete transmission.

That Graham (1983) has perceived remnants of what could have been earlier tense-aspect affixes in Old Chinese should leave that speculation in place. These would be fossilizations, common in creoles as well – even pidginization and creolization

Phonemic vowel nasalization	0
Complexity of syllable structure	.5
Tone	0
Overt marking of direct object	0
Double marking of direct object	0
Possession by double marking	0
Overt possession marking	.5
Reduplication	1
Gender	0
Number of genders	0
Non-semantic gender assignment	0
Grammaticalized nominal plural	0
Definite articles	0
Indefinite articles	0
Inclusivity (in either pronouns or verb morphology)	0
Distance contrast in demonstratives	.25
Gender in pronouns	0
Politeness in pronouns	0
Person marking on adpositions	0
Comitative not instrumental	1
Ordinals exist as separate class beyond "first"	0
Obligatory numeral classifiers	0
Possessive classification	0
Conjunction 'and' is not adposition 'with'	.5
Difference between nominal and verbal conjunction	1
Grammaticalized perfective/imperfective	0
Grammaticalized past/non-past	0

preserve segmental fragments of grammatical processes in their source languages. An analyst of Mauritian Creole unaware of French might well reconstruct the rudiments of its determiner allomorphs and even partitive marking via fossilized remnants of them on nouns such as *lafwa* "faith" (< *la foi*), *lefwa* "liver" (< *le foie*), *lari* "street" (< *la rue*), and *diri* "rice" (< *du riz*).

3.5   Reading the data

Old Chinese was a language with essentially no inflectional morphology *either bound or free* and an overall degree of semantic underspecification surpassing that of even most languages known to be the product of non-native acquisition and usage, as well as even creoles.

There are languages in the world with no inflectional *affixation* or tone, but they reveal their status as products of ordinary grammar-internal development in their *unbound* inflection, in the form of tense and aspect particles, paradigms of numeral classifiers, and other features. In fact I am aware of such languages existing only in the Sinosphere and scattered in Indonesia and eastward. Crucially, the cases in Indonesia and eastward are, as mentioned, attributed by specialists to non-native acquisition as well.

Old Chinese's score in the Parkvall (2008) metric, then, is a quantitative demonstration of the fact that most linguists would be hard pressed to identify a language as

Remoteness distinctions of past	0
Morphological future	0
Grammaticalized perfect	0
Morphological imperative	0
Morphological optative	0
Grammaticalized evidentiality distinctions	0
Both indirect and direct evidentials	0
Non-neutral marking of full NPs	0
Non-neutral marking of pronouns	0
Subject marking as both free word and agreement	0
Passive	0
Antipassive	0
Applicative	0
Obligatory double negation	0
Asymmetric negation	0
Equative copula is not locative copula	0
Obligatorily overt equative copula	0
Demonstratives marked for number	0
Demonstratives marked for gender	0
Demonstratives marked for case	0
Total amount of verbal suppletion	0
Alienability distinctions	0
Number of pronominal numbers	0

strangely low on the features typical of ordinarily transmitted human language as Old Chinese. The only process known to linguistic science that predictably yields such a language, rendering such a grammar unremarkable, is non-native acquisition.

Given how rare radically analytic languages are worldwide, I propose that we take the nature of Old Chinese as evidence indeed – that Old Chinese grammar had a history in extensive acquisition by adults, and that its traits are an indication of precisely this. Properly, the comparative facts suggest that the language that underwent this process was Proto-Sino-Tibetan – i.e. Proto-Sino-Tibetan was a creole. And this means that the analyticity that this language spread throughout Southeast Asia was rooted in a diachronic anomaly.

3.6   Historical possibilities

As with the Niger-Congo case, historical evidence confirming this account is likely unavailable at this distance in time. The Bronze and Iron Ages knew no chroniclers of social history in the modern sense. What we can know from them is mere fragments in support of a story that requires filling in from other approaches. Archaeology is one; in this paper I propose that we treat linguistics as another.

Already, scholars such as Janhunen (1996:222) and Bellwood (2005:226), seeking to coordinate archaeology with linguistic deduction, place the birth of Sino-Tibetan amidst the Yangshao culture of 5000–3000 BC near the Yellow River. The first Chinese dynasty mentioned in writing is the Xia, likely represented archaeologically by the Erlitou culture and reigning from 2070 to 1600 B.C. (400 years before the first evidence of Old Chinese). The Erlitou culture is thought to have been a major state that expanded outward and ruled large territories (Bagley 1999:156), such that it is speculated that the Xia dynasty consisted of a small Chinese-speaking elite ruling over a non-Chinese speaking population (Pulleyblank 2002: IV-413). Skeletons of sacrificial victims are quite numerous in tombs from the succeeding Shang dynasty, and skulls from those of its Anyang culture are highly variegated racially (Chang 1976:55), suggesting elite dominance over people speaking other languages. If the Xia dynasty did similarly, perhaps the non-native populations created an abbreviated Sinitic grammar?

This could have yielded the peculiarity of Old Chinese, explaining therefore the analyticity that Chinese conditioned in the families its speakers encountered subsequently. It would have been too late to create a pidginized Proto-Sino-Tibetan, and thus a radically analytic Proto-Tibeto-Burman. The analyticity reconstructed for Proto-Sino-Tibetan itself, then, remains unexplained. However, I suggest two possible lines of investigation:

1. Perhaps conditions of this kind existed in the Yellow River valley before the Erlitou culture; Chinese archaeological discoveries are being made at such a fast clip as I write this that it is not impossible that evidence for this could be found.

2. Given how controversial the family tree of Sino-Tibetan remains, it could be worth investigating whether Tibeto-Burman branched off from an early stage of Sinitic, under which situation the conditions in the Erlitou civilization could have been the ones that created the analyticity of Sino-Tibetan in general.

Note that my proposal is that investigating these two possibilities is motivated by the *anomaly* of radical analyticity: a language like Old Chinese calls out for explanation. With the proper caution, it can even be seen as evidence in itself of sociological disruption in Bronze Age China, which archaeologists could be aware of in their investigations of the country's deep past.

4. If radical analyticity is so unnatural, why haven't these languages become synthetic?

There are two answers to this question.

First, my claim is that it is unnatural for a grammar to be radically analytic after tens of thousands of years, during which fusion would necessarily and ongoingly occur. This claim in no way necessitates that a language, once denuded of affixation, must regain the affixation within some small window of time. The claim is not that radical analyticity is somehow incompatible with human cognition. Like many, I assume that human language emerged in an isolating state, and as a creolist I could hardly suppose that a language without inflection is somehow incomplete. Affixation is, ultimately, the product of accident, due to rapid speech phenomena and attendant reanalysis and grammaticalization.

There is no reason to suppose that this accident happens quickly, however. English, for example, became a relatively analytic language in the 12th century, A.D., and since then, has developed very little new inflection in any dialect over almost a millennium and a half. As such, it is not a counterargument to my proposal that the languages I have treated have not become synthetic after a few thousands of years. Or: the fact that they have not become synthetic is logically independent from whether their radical analyticity resulted from ordinary grammar-internal development.

Second, the GYN languages and those of East and Southeast Asia do harbor the beginnings of inflectional affixation, just as we would expect. Inflectional affixation is an *inevitable* accident – i.e. linguistics knows no reason why it would *not* occur eventually in a language. In Mandarin Chinese various items are well on their way to inflectional status in the diachronic sense: e.g. *zi*, toneless and used often variably with nouns (*mào* [*zi*] "hat") in a future stage of the language could become a nominal affix. The change-of-state marker *le*, which occurs obligatorily after the verb it modifies, is also analyzable as inflectional. Also, numeral classifiers in Mandarin and most languages of the "Sinosphere" are typologically analogous to grammatical gender and noun class affixes (Grinevald & Seifart 2004). No element can intervene between the numeral and the classifier, and the classifiers' application is quite often as semantically arbitrary as Indo-European grammatical gender and Niger-Congo noun class marking; e.g. the application of Mandarin *tiáo* not only to elongated objects such as ropes and rivers, but also news and laws – while many elongated objects, such as arrows, take *zhī*.

Also, in Sinitic varieties other than Mandarin, there is even more incipient inflection. In Hakka, about 22 nouns have grammatical gender, in Jianyong Xiang, 28, and in both Cantonese and Anyi Gan, a handful (Lau 1999: 126–8). Southern Chinese varieties also have more numeral classifiers than Mandarin (Yue 2003: 85).

Languages without inflectional affixes can also mark inflectional categories via, for example, allomorphy as in Sino-Tibetan Tangut (extinct), where verbs, monosyllabic, occurred in alternate forms depending on agreement with third-person or non-third-person subjects: *dźjo²* "have," *dźjij²* "has" (Hwang-Cherng 2003: 609).

In GYN, Fongbe pronouns occur in pairs of clitic forms that vary according to case in the singular (Lefebvre & Brousseau 2002: 63) while Yoruba's pronouns vary according to case, negation and possession (Pulleyblank 1987: 982). In Fongbe, an imperfective marker *wè* has emerged, likely from a postposition, which in the modern language could be treated as an inflection:

(7) Kɔ́kú ɖò àsɔ́n ɔ́ ɖù wè.
     Koku be.at crab DEF eat POST
     "Koku is eating the crab."   (Lefebvre & Brousseau 2002: 96)

In terms of affixation in general, most of Fongbe's derivational affixes still correspond to free lexical reflexes, suggesting relatively recent emergence (ibid. 185). In Ewe, analysts differ as to how bound its grammatical morphemes are. This is partly because many of the experts wrote before modern linguistic analysis existed while modern specialists on the language are few and work from disparate analytical approaches. However, it may also indicate that there is a good deal of incipient, or even some present, inflectional affixation in Ewe at this point.

The above are developments my proposal would predict. My proposal neither predicts nor requires that these languages would now be heavily, or even moderately, inflected.

5.   Conclusion

The interruption in transmission that I propose to have led to the radical analyticity of these languages would have happened before recorded history. The evidence that would most engage the sociolinguist, for example, is forever lost. I propose, however, that we approach the linguistic data as *a source of insight into what is lost to history*. The GYN languages and Southeast Asia can be seen as offering linguists a challenge which the field is, at this point, well equipped to accept.

That is, a rigorous application of diachronic theory *requires* that we treat radical analyticity in any language as a concrete indication of widespread adult acquisition in the past. Rejecting vague appeals to drift, a linguistics orthodoxy that embraces this rigorous application of what we have learned about language change is poised to build ever more bridges with developments in archaeology and genetics in tracing the history of humanity.

Our question, therefore, is not "Is there sociohistorical and archaeological evidence that the GYN and Southeast Asian languages resulted from a break in ordinary language transmission?" The answer is "no." The question is: "Are there adequate *linguistic* arguments for presenting the GYN and Southeast Asian languages as evidence of a break in ordinary language transmission?" This article succeeds or fails on the basis of whether it succeeds in making this, and only this, case.

My proposal that radical analyticity be treated as a sign of non-native acquisition is based on four observations.

1. Radical analyticity is rare worldwide; that statement seems anomalous only in light of East and Southeast Asia, but as we have seen, the prevalence of radical analyticity there was sparked by one language, Chinese.
2. The only *known* process that creates radical analyticity is non-native acquisition.
3. Specific structural aspects of how radically analytic languages differ from their synthetic relatives are parallel with pidginization/creolization.
4. Conditions in all three places where radical analyticity is found are commensurate with a non-native acquisition account:
    a. In Indonesia and beyond, Austronesian migrants alternately overran or interbred with original inhabitants.
    b. In West Africa, radical analyticity is found only at a geographical limit to Niger-Congo's further spread (i.e. an oceanic coast) after what would have been multiple cycles of non-native acquisition by original populations encountered amidst the migration.
    c. In Southeast Asia, radical analyticity is agreed to have been sparked by Chinese, not to have reigned as an original trait.

On the basis of these facts, I propose that *radical analyticity be treated by linguists as a sign of non-native acquisition, and therefore of encounters between human populations.*

The methodology I espouse is, at heart, uniformitarian, under which linguists, like geologists, make the fundamental assumption that the processes they study were guided by the same laws in the past as they are today. Geologists treat cracked quartz as a sign of an occasion in the past of extreme heating, such as amidst volcanic eruption.

Its concentration in rocks at the boundary between the Mesozoic and Cenozoic eras is considered key evidence of volcanoes' role in the extinction of the dinosaurs. There is no speculation that quartz might *also* crack up for no particular reason. It is considered logical and economical to suppose that because quartz can be shown to crack under extreme heat in the present, the discovery of quartz which has cracked justifies reconstructing extreme heat in the past.

To be sure, historical linguistics does not allow experimentation and measurement as precise as geological science does. However, linguists have no account for radical analyticity as a happenstance, and countless examples of radical analyticity occurring as the result of non-native acquisition.

The logical conclusion would seem to be that we can let the facts in West Africa, Southeast Asia and Indonesia speak for themselves.

References

Abraham, Roy Clive. 1951. *The Idoma Language, Idoma Wordlists, Idoma Chrestomathy, Idoma Proverbs*. London: Lowe & Brydone.

Adejoh, M.O. 2012. Pluralisation in the Idoma language. *Journal of Igbo Language and Linguistics* 4: 37–42.

Aikhenvald, Alexandra Y. 2001. Areal diffusion, genetic inheritance, and problems of subgrouping: A North Arawak case study. In *Areal Diffusion and Genetic Inheritance*, Alexandra Y. Aikhenvald & Robert M.W. Dixon (eds), 167–94. Oxford: OUP.

Alves, Mark J. 2001. What's so Chinese about Vietnamese? In *Papers from the Ninth Annual Meeting of the Southeast Asian Linguistics Society*, Graham W. Thurgood (ed.), 221–242. Phoenix AZ: Arizona State University, Program for Southeast Asian Studies.

Ames, Kenneth. 1994. The Northwest Coast: Complex hunter-gatherers, ecology, and social evolution. *Annual Review of Anthropology* 23: 209–29.
doi:10.1146/annurev.an.23.100194.001233

Bagley, Robert. 1999. Shang archaeology. In *The Cambridge History of Ancient China*, Michael Loewe & Edward L. Shaughnessy (eds), 124–231. Cambridge: CUP.
doi:10.1017/CHOL9780521470308.005

Baker, Mark & Stewart, Osamuyimen T. 2002. A serial verb construction without constructions. Ms, Rutgers University.

Baker, Philip & Corne, Chris. 1982. *Isle de France Creole*. Ann Arbor MI: Karoma.

Baxter, William H. 1992. *A Handbook of Old Chinese Phonology*. Berlin: Mouton de Gruyter.
doi:10.1515/9783110857085

Bellwood, Peter. 2005. *First Farmers*. Malden MA: Blackwell.

Bendor-Samuel, John & Hartell, Rhonda (eds). 1989. *The Niger-Congo Languages*. Lanham MD: University Press of America.

Blench, Roger. 1989. Nupoid. In Bendor-Samuel & Hartell (eds), 305–322.

Blench, Roger. 1999. The languages of Africa: Macrophyla proposals and implications for archaeological interpretation. In *Archaeology and Language*, IV: *Language Change and Cultural Transformation*, Roger M. Blench & Matthew Spriggs (eds), 29–47. London: Routledge.
doi:10.4324/9780203208793_chapter_1

Blench, Roger. 2006. *Archaeology, Language and the African Past*. Lanham MD: Altamira Press.

Blench, Roger. 2013. The North Bantoid hypothesis. Author's website.

Booij, Geert. 1993. Against split morphology. In *Yearbook of Morphology 1993*, Geert Booij & Jaap van Marle (eds), 27–49. Dordrecht: Kluwer. doi:10.1007/978-94-017-3712-8_2

Carlson, Robert. 1994. *A Grammar of Supyire*. Berlin: Mouton de Gruyter. doi:10.1515/9783110883053

Cellier, Pierre. 1985. Description syntaxique de créole réunionnais: Essai de standardisation. Ph.D. dissertation, Université de Provence.

Chang, Kwang-Chih. 1976. *Early Chinese Civilization*. Cambridge MA: Harvard University Press.

Comrie, Bernard (ed.). 1987. *The World's Major Languages*. Oxford: OUP.

Crane, Thera Marie, Hyman, Larry & Tukumu, Simon Tsielanga SJ. 2011. *A Grammar of Nzadi* (B865). Berkeley CA: University of California Publications in Linguistics.

Crowley, Terry. 2000. Simplicity, complexity, emblematicity and grammatical change. In *Processes of Language Contact: Studies from Australia and the South Pacific*, Jeff Siegel (ed.), 175–93. Montreal: Fides.

Cumming, Susanna. 1991. *Functional Change: The Case of Malay Constituent Order*. Berlin: Mouton de Gruyter. doi:10.1515/9783110864540

Dahl, Östen. 2004. *The Growth and Maintenance of Linguistic Complexity* [Studies in Language Companion Series 71]. Amsterdam: John Benjamins. doi:10.1075/slcs.71

Dai, John Xiangling. 1990. Historical morphologization of syntactic structures: Evidence from derived verbs in Chinese. *Diachronica* 7: 9–46. doi:10.1075/dia.7.1.03xia

Dakubu, Mary Esther Kropp (ed.). 1988. *The Languages of Ghana*. London: Kegan Paul.

Dakubu, Mary Esther Kropp & Ford, Kevin C. 1988. The Central-Togo languages. In Dakubu, 119–154.

Dalby, Andrew. 1998. *Dictionary of Languages*. New York NY: Columbia University Press.

Davies, John. 1981. *Kobon*. Amsterdam: North Holland.

DeLancey, Scott. 2010. Towards a history of verb agreement in Tibeto-Burman. *Himalayan Linguistics* 9: 1–39.

Dimmendaal, Gerrit J. 2001. Areal diffusion versus genetic inheritance: An African perspective. In *Areal Diffusion and Genetic Inheritance*, Alexandra Y. Aikhenvald & Robert M.W. Dixon (eds), 358–392. Oxford: OUP.

Dimmendaal, Gerrit J. 2011. *Historical Linguistics and the Comparative Study of African Languages*. Amsterdam: John Benjamins. doi:10.1075/z.161

Dixon, Robert M.W. 1997. *The Rise and Fall of Languages*. Cambridge: CUP. doi:10.1017/CBO9780511612060

Dol, Philomena Hedwig. 2007. *A Grammar of Maybrat*. Canberra: Pacific Linguistics.

Dolphyne, Florence Abena & Kropp Dakubu, Mary Esther. 1988. The Volta-Camoé languages. In Dakubu (ed.), 50–90.

Donohue, Mark & Denham, Tim. To appear. Becoming Austronesian: Mechanisms of language dispersal across southern Island Southeast Asia. In *Austronesian Undressed*, David Gil & John McWhorter (eds).

Elugbe, Ben Ohi. 1989. *Edoid*. In Bendor-Samuel & Hartell (eds), 291–304.

Essegbey, James. 2006. *Ewe*. In *Concise Encyclopedia of Languages of the World*, Keith Brown & Sarah Ogilvie (eds), 408–409. Oxford: Elsevier.

Faraclas, Nicholas. 1989. *Cross River*. In Bendor-Samuel & Hartell (eds), 377–399.

Gerhardt, Ludwig. 1989. *Kainji and Platoid*. In Bendor-Samuel & Hartell (eds), 359–376.

Gil, David. 2001. Creoles, complexity, and Riau Indonesian. *Linguistic Typology* 2–3: 325–371.

Good, Jeff. 2012. How to become a "Kwa" noun. *Morphology* 22: 293–335. doi:10.1007/s11525-011-9197-2

Graham, Angus. 1983. Yún and Yuē as verbs and particles. *Acta Orientalia Havniensia* 44: 33–71.

Grant, Anthony. 1996. The evolution of functional categories in Grand Ronde Chinook Jargon: Ethnolinguistic and grammatical considerations. In *Changing Meanings, Changing Functions: Papers Relating to Grammaticalization in Contact Languages*, Philip Baker & Anand Syea (eds), 225–242. London: University of Westminster.

Greenberg, Joseph. 1978. How does a language acquire gender markers? In *Universals of Human Languages, III: Word Structure*, Joseph H. Greenberg (ed.), 47–82. Stanford CA: Stanford University Press.

Grijns, Cornelis D. 1991. *Jakarta Malay: A Multidimensional Approach to Spatial Variation*. Leiden: KITLV Press.

Grinevald, Collette & Seifart, Frank. 2004. Noun classes in African and Amazonian languages: Towards a comparison. *Linguistic Typology* 8: 243–285. doi:10.1515/lity.2004.007

Güldemann, Tom. 2011. Proto-Bantu and Proto-Niger-Congo: Macro-areal typology and linguistic reconstruction. In *Geographical Typology and Linguistic Areas. With Special Reference to Africa* [Tokyo University of Foreign Studies 2], Osamu Hieda, Christa König & Hiroshi Nakagawa (eds), 109–41. Amsterdam: John Benjamins. doi:10.1075/tufs.2.09gul

Guy, Gregory. 1991. Explanation in variable phonology: An exponential model of morphological constraints. *Language Variation and Change* 3: 1–22. doi:10.1017/S0954394500000429

Hakulinen, Lauri. 1961. *The Structure and Development of the Finnish Language*. The Hague: Mouton.

Harris, Alice. 2004. History in support of synchrony. In *Proceedings of the Berkeley Linguistics Society*, Charles Chang, Michael J. Houser, Yuni Kim, David Mortensen & Mischa Park-Doob (eds), 142–59. Berkeley CA: Berkeley Linguistics Society.

Haspelmath, Martin, Dryer, Matthew, Gil, David & Comrie, Bernard (eds). 2005. *World Atlas of Language Structures*. Oxford: OUP.

Heath, Jeffrey. 1978. *Linguistic Diffusion in Arnhem Land*. Canberra: Australian Institute of Aboriginal Studies.

Hedinger, Robert. 1989. *Northern Bantoid*. In Bendor-Samuel & Hartell (eds), 421–429.

Heine, Bernd & König, Krista. 2013. Northern Khoesan: !Xun. In Vossen (ed.), 293–325.

Herforth, Derek. 2003. A sketch of Late Zhou Chinese grammar. In Thurgood & LaPolla (eds), 59–71.

Hodge, Carleton. 1970. The linguistic cycle. *Language Sciences* 13: 1–7. Reprinted in *Afroasiatic linguistics, Semitics, and Egyptology: Selected Writings of Carleton T. Hodge*, Scott Noegel & Alan S. Kaye (eds), 1–17. Bethesda MD: CDL Press, 2004.

Hwang-Cherng, Gong. 2003. Tangut. In Thurgood & LaPolla (eds), 602–620.

Hyman, Larry M. 2004. How to become a Kwa verb. *Journal of West African Languages* 30: 69–88.

Hyman, Larry M. 2011. The Macro-Sudan belt and Niger-Congo reconstruction. *Language Dynamics and Linguistic Change* 1: 3–49. doi:10.1163/221058211X570330

Janhunen, Juha. 1996. *Manchuria: An Ethnic History*. Helsinki: Suomalais-Ugrilainen Seura.

Jahr, Ernst Håkon. 2001. Historical sociolinguistics: The role of Low German language contact in the Scandinavian typological split of the late Middle Ages. *Lingua Posnaniensis* 43: 95–104.

Junge, Friedrich. 2001. *Late Egyptian Grammar*, translated by David Warburton. Oxford: Griffith Institute.

Kandybowicz, Jason. 2008. *The Grammar of Repetition: Nupe Grammar at the Syntax Phonology Interface* [Linguistik Aktuell/Linguistis Today 136]. Amsterdam: John Benjamins. doi:10.1075/la.136

Kari, Ethelbert. 1995. Extensional suffixes in Degema. *Afrikanistische Arbeitspapiere* 44: 149–68.

Keeley, Lawrence H. 1988. Hunter gatherer economic complexity and "population pressure": A cross-cultural analysis. *Journal of Anthropological Archaeology* 7: 373–411. doi:10.1016/0278-4165(88)90003-7

Kennedy, George A. 1951. The monosyllabic myth. *Journal of the American Oriental Society* 71: 161–6. doi:10.2307/595185

Kiessling, Ronald. 2013. On the origin of Niger-Congo nominal classification. In *Historical Linguistics 2011*. [Current Issues in Linguistic Theory 326], Ritsuko Kikusawa & Lawrence A. Reid (eds), 43–65. Amsterdam: John Benjamins. doi:10.1075/cilt.326.05kie

Kihm, Alain & Reintjes, Chris. To appear. Coptic as a contact language.

Klamer, Marian. 2012. Papuan-Austronesian language contact: Alorese from an areal perspective. In *Melanesian Languages on the Edge of Asia: Challenges for the 21st Century*, Nicholas Evans & Marian Klamer (eds), 72–108. Honolulu HI: University of Hawaii Press.

Kusters, Wouter. 2003. *Linguistic Complexity: The Influence of Social Change on Verbal Inflection*. Utrecht: Landelijke Onderzoekschool Taalwetenschap (Netherlands Graduate School of Linguistics).

LaPolla, Randy. 1992. On the dating and nature of verb agreement in Tibeto-Burman. *Bulletin of the School of Oriental and African Studies* 55: 298–315. doi:10.1017/S0041977X00004638

LaPolla, Randy. 2003. Overview of Sino-Tibetan morphosyntax. In Thurgood & LaPolla (eds), 22–42.

Lass, Roger, 1992. Phonology and morphology. In *The Cambridge History of the English Languages*, Vol. II, Norman Blake (ed.), 23–155. Cambridge: CUP. doi:10.1017/CHOL9780521264754.003

Lau, Chun-fat. 1999. "Gender" in the Hakka dialect: Suffixes with gender in more than 40 nouns. *Journal of Chinese Linguistics* 27: 124–31.

Lefebvre, Claire & Brousseau, Anne-Marie. 2002. *Fongbe*. Berlin: Mouton de Gruyter. doi:10.1515/9783110880182

Lepsius, Richard. 1880. *Nubische Grammatik mit einer Einleitung über die Völker und Sprachen Afrika's*. Berlin: Wilhelm Hertz.

Luís, Ana R. 2009. The loss and survival of inflectional morphology: Contextual vs. inherent inflection in creoles. In *Romance Linguistics 2009*. [Current Issues in Linguistic Theory 315], Sonia Colina, Antxon Olarrea & Ana Carvalho (eds), 323–36. Amsterdam: John Benjamins. doi:10.1075/cilt.315.19lui

Lupyan, Gary & Dale, Rick. 2010. Language structure is partly determined by social structure. *PloS One* 5: 1. doi:10.1371/annotation/9b8741e2-0f5f-49f9-9eaa-1b0cb9b8d25f

Marchese, Lynell. 1989. *Kru*. In Bendor-Samuel & Hartell (eds), 119–139.

Matisoff, James A. 1991. Sino-Tibetan linguistics: Present state and future prospects. *Annual Review of Anthropology* 20: 469–504.

Matisoff, James A. 2003. Aslian: Mon-Khmer of the Malay peninsula. *The Mon-Khmer Studies Journal* 33: 1–58. doi:10.1146/annurev.an.20.100191.002345

Matras, Yaron. 2009. *Language Contact*. Cambridge: CUP.. doi:10.1017/CBO9780511809873

McWhorter, John H. 1994. From focus marker to copula in Swahili. In *Proceedings of the Berkeley Linguistics Society (Special Session on Historical Issues in African Linguistics)*, Kevin E. Moore, David Peterson & Comfort Wentum (eds), 57–66. Berkeley CA: Berkeley Linguistics Society.

McWhorter, John H. 2005. *Defining Creole*. Oxford: OUP.

McWhorter, John H. 2007. Language Interrupted: Signs of Non-native Acquisition in Standard Language Grammars. Oxford: OUP. doi:10.1093/acprof:oso/9780195309805.001.0001

McWhorter, John H. 2011. *Linguistic Simplicity and Complexity: Why do Languages Undress?* Berlin: Mouton de Gruyter. doi:10.1515/9781934078402

McWhorter, John H. 2012. Case closed? Testing the Feature Pool hypothesis. *Journal of Pidgin and Creole Languages* 27: 171–82. doi:10.1075/jpcl.27.1.07mcw

McWhorter, John H. 2013. It isn't over: Why it matters whether there is a such thing as a creole. *Journal of Pidgin and Creole Languages* 28: 409–23. doi:10.1075/jpcl.28.2.05mcw

Meinhof, Carl. 1905. Probleme der afrikanischen Linguistik. *Wiener Zeitschrift für die Kunde des Morgenlandes* 19: 77–90.

Meinhof, Carl. 1910. *Die moderne Sprachforschung in Afrika*. Berlin.

Miehe, Gudrun & Winkelmann, Kerstin (eds). 2007. *Noun Class Systems in Gur Languages*, Vol. 1:*Southwestern Gur languages (without Gurunsi)*. Köln: Rüdiger Köppe.

Miestamo, Matti, Sinnemäki, Kaius & Karlsson, Fred (eds). 2008. The simplicity of creoles in a cross-linguistic perspective. In *Language Complexity: Typology, Contact, Change* [Studies in Language Companion Series 94], Matti Miestamo, Kaius Sinnemäki & Fred Karlsson (eds), 265–285. Amsterdam: John Benjamins. doi:10.1075/slcs.94

Mufwene, Salikoko S. 2001. *The Ecology of Language Evolution*. Cambridge: CUP. doi:10.1017/CBO9780511612862

Mühlhäusler, Peter. 1997. *Pidgin and Creole Linguistics*, expanded and revised edition. London: University of Westminster.

Mukarovsky, Hans G. 1977. *A Study of Western Nigritic*, Vol. I. Vienna: Institut für Ägyptologie und Afrikanistik der Universität Wien.

Naden, Tony. 1988. The Gur languages. In Dakubu & Hartell (eds), 12–49.

Naden, Tony. 1989. Gur. In Bendor-Samuel & Hartell (eds), 140–168.

Nichols, Johanna. 1992. *Linguistic Diversity in Space and Time*. Chicago IL: University of Chicago Press. doi:10.7208/chicago/9780226580593.001.0001

Norman, Jerry. 1988. *Chinese*. Cambridge: CUP.

Nurse, Derek. 2007. Did the proto-Bantu verb have a synthetic or an analytic structure? *SOAS Working Papers in Linguistics* 15: 239–56.

Nurse, Derek. 2008. *Tense and Aspect in Bantu*. Oxford: OUP.

Ogie, Ota. 2003. About multi-verb constructions in Edo. In *Proceedings of the Workshop on Multi-Verb Constructions, Trondheim Summer School 2003*, Dorothee Beermann & Lars Hellan (eds). Trondheim: Norwegian University of Science and Technology.

Omoregbe, Esohe Mercy & Aigbedo, William Ighasere. 2012. Agreement patterns within the Edo NP. *European Scientific Journal* 8: 130–47.

Onukawa, Monday C. 1999. The order of extensional suffixes in Igbo. *Afrikanistische Arbeitspapiere* 59: 109–129.

Osam, E. Kweku. 2003. An introduction to the verbal and multi-verbal system of Akan. In *Proceedings of the Workshop on Multi-verb Constructions, Trondheim Summer School 2003*, Dorothee Beermann & Lars Hellan. Trondheim: Norwegian University of Science and Technology.

Ostapirat, Weera. 2005. Kra-Dai and Austronesian: Notes on phonological correspondences and vocabulary distribution. In Sagart, Blench & Sanchez-Mazas (eds), 107–131.

Parkvall, Mikael. 2008. The simplicity of creoles in a cross-linguistic perspective. In Miestamo, Sinnemäki & Karlsson (eds), 265–285.

Paauw, Scott. 2007. A North Papua linguistic area? Paper presented at the Workshop on the Languages of Papua, Manokwari.

Payne, John. 1997. *Describing Morphosyntax*. Cambridge: CUP.

Pienemann, Manfred. 1998. *Language Processing and Second Language Development: Processability Theory* [Studies in Bilingualism 15]. Amsterdam: John Benjamins. doi:10.1075/sibil.15

Plag, Ingo. 2008. Creoles as interlanguages: Inflectional morphology. *Journal of Pidgin and Creole Languages* 23: 114–135. doi:10.1075/jpcl.23.1.06pla

Poppe, Nicholas. 1965. *Introduction to Altaic Linguistics*. Wiesbaden: Otto Harrassowitz.

Pulleyblank, Douglas. 1987. Yoruba. In Comrie (ed.), 971–990.

Pulleyblank, Edwin. 1995. *Outline of Classical Chinese Grammar*. Vancouver: University of British Columbia Press.

Pulleyblank, Edwin. 2002. *Central Asia and Non-Chinese peoples of Ancient China*. Burlington VT: Ashgate.

Ratliff, Martha. 2006. Prefix variation and reconstruction. In *Variation and Reconstruction* [Current Issues in Linguistic Theory 268], Thomas D. Cravens (ed.), 165–78. Amsterdam: John Benjamins. doi:10.1075/cilt.268.09rat

Reh, Mechthild. 1985. *Die Krongo-Sprache*. Berlin: Reimer.

Riddle, Elizabeth M. 2008. Complexity in isolating languages: Lexical elaboration versus grammatical economy. In Miestamo, Sinnemäki & Karlsson (eds), 133–151.

Roberts, Sarah J. & Bresnan, Joan. 2008. Retained inflectional morphology in pidgins: A typological study. *Linguistic Typology* 12: 269–302. doi:10.1515/LITY.2008.039

Ross, Malcolm. 2002. The history and transitivity of western Austronesian voice and voice-marking. In *The History and Typology of Western Austronesian Voice Systems*, Fay Wouk & Malcolm Ross (eds), 17–78. Canberra: Pacific Linguistics.

Sagart, Laurent. 2004. The higher phylogeny of Austronesian and the position of Tai-Kadai. *Oceanic Linguistics* 43: 411–40. doi:10.1353/ol.2005.0012

Sagart, Laurent, Blench, Roger & Sanchez-Mazas, Alicia (eds). 2005. *The Peopling of East Asia: Putting Together Archaeology, Linguistics and Genetics*. London: RoutledgeCurzon. doi:10.4324/9780203343685

Sapir, Edward. 1921. *Language*. New York NY: Harcourt.

Schmitt, Rüdiger. 1989. Altpersisch. In *Compendium linguarum Iranicarum*, Rüdiger Schmitt (ed.), 56–85. Wiesbaden: Ludwig Reichert.

Seifart, Frank. 2012. The principle of morphosyntactic subsystem integrity in language contact: Evidence from morphological borrowing in Resígaro (Arawakan). *Diachronica* 29: 471–504. doi:10.1075/dia.29.4.03sei

Starosta, Stanley. 2005. Proto-East Asian and the origin and dispersal of the languages of East and Southeast Asia and the Pacific. In Sagart, Blench & Sanchez-Mazas (eds), 182–197.

Stahlke, Herbert. 1970. Serial verbs. *Studies in African Linguistics* 1: 60–99.

Sterk, Jan P. 1978. The noun class system of Gade (Nigeria). *African Languages* 4: 24–43.

Stewart, John M. 1989. Kwa. In Bendor-Samuel & Hartell (eds), 217–245.

Thomason, Sarah & Kaufman, Terence. 1988. *Language Contact, Creolization and Genetic Linguistics*. Berkeley, CA: University of California Press.

Thurgood, Graham & LaPolla, Randy (eds). 2003. *The Sino-Tibetan Languages*. London: Routledge.

Thurston, William R. 1987. *Processes of Change in the Languages of Northwestern New Britain*. Canberra: Australian National University.

Trudgill, Peter. 2011. *Sociolinguistic Typology*. Oxford: OUP.

van Driem, George. 1993. The Proto-Tibeto-Burman verbal agreement system. *Bulletin of the School of Oriental and African Studies* 56: 292–334. doi:10.1017/S0041977X00005528

van Driem, George. 2005. Sino-Austronesian vs. Sino-Caucasian, Sino-Bodic vs. Sino-Tibetan, and Tibeto-Burman as default theory. In *Contemporary Issues in Nepalese Linguistics*, Yogendra Prasada Yadava, Govinda Bhattarai, Ram Raj Lohani, Balaram Prasain & Krishna Parajuli (eds), 285–338. Kathmandu: Linguistic Society of Nepal.

Visser, Hessel. 2013. Naro. In Vossen (ed.), 179–206.

Wald, Benji. 1987. Swahili and the Bantu languages. In Comrie (ed.), 991–1014.

Wilkie, M.B. 1930. *Gã Grammar Notes and Exercises*. London: OUP.

Williamson, Kay & Blench, Roger. 2000. Niger-Congo. In *African Languages: An Introduction*, Bernd Heine & Derek Nurse (eds), 11–42. Cambridge: CUP.

Wray, Alison & Grace, George W. 2007. The consequences of talking to strangers: Evolutionary corollaries of socio-cultural influences on linguistics form. *Lingua* 117: 543–78. doi:10.1016/j.lingua.2005.05.005

Yue-Hashimoto, Anne. 2003. Chinese dialects: Grammar. In Thurgood & LaPolla (eds), 84–125.

An analytic-synthetic spiral
in the history of English

Benedikt Szmrecsanyi
KU Leuven

Drawing on techniques familiar from quantitative morphological typology
(Greenberg 1960), this contribution marshals usage- and frequency-based,
aggregate measures of grammatical analyticity and syntheticity to profile the
history of grammatical marking in English between circa AD 1100 and AD
1900, tapping into the Penn Parsed Corpora of Historical English series. Results
indicate that the post-Old English period is clearly not characterized by a linear
drift towards more analyticity and less syntheticity. Instead, analyticity was on the
rise until the end of the Early Modern English period, but declined subsequently;
the reverse is true for syntheticity. In terms of typological analyticity-syntheticity
coordinates, 20th century English texts are actually fairly similar to 12th and
13th century English texts. I suggest that this historical pattern can be interpreted
in terms of a Gabelentz-type spiral.

1. Introduction

We teach beginning students of English Language and Linguistics that the history of
English is characterized by a drift from synthetic to analytic. The textbook story goes
as follows: English has changed

> from a synthetic or inflectional language, which relies on morphological endings
> to mark grammatical function, to an analytic one, which relies on word order
> to convey grammatical elations. From a structural point of view this is the most
> significant change that has occurred in the history of English.   (Fennell 2001:6)

It is clear that this story is true if we compare Old English to Present-Day English. But
as we shall see, when we restrict attention to the post-Old English history of the language, it turns out that there is no longer a linear drift but a cyclical merry-go-round.

This study conceptualizes the analytic-synthetic distinction in a way that makes
possible precise and holistic measurements, drawing on quantitative, frequency- and
usage-based measures inspired by work in quantitative morphological typology (in
particular, Greenberg 1960). I will re-analyze and re-interpret the dataset originally
discussed in Szmrecsanyi (2012), where these measure were applied to the Penn Parsed

DOI 10.1075/la.227.04szm

Corpora of Historical English series. This corpus suite covers the period between circa AD 1100 and AD 1900. The present study thus taps into corpus material to determine the frequency of analytic and synthetic marking, and subsequently calculates an aggregate index of overt grammatical analyticity, which basically measures the text frequency of free grammatical markers, and an aggregate index of overt grammatical syntheticity, which measures the text frequency of bound grammatical markers. So the name of the game in this contribution is calculation of aggregate indices on the basis of naturalistic usage data, inspired by techniques in quantitative morphological typology.

We will see that analyticity peaked towards the end of the Early Modern English period, in the 16th and 17th centuries, and has been on the decline ever since. Conversely, syntheticity had its low point in the Early Modern English period and has been on the increase subsequently. In other words, we seem to be dealing with a cycle (Jespersen 1917) or spiral (Gabelentz 1891) of sorts. One is here, of course, in particular reminded of seminal work by Hodge (1970), who demonstrated that the history of Egyptian is characterized by an analytic > synthetic > analytic cycle.

This article is structured as follows. Section 2 fixes terminology. Section 3 describes the data source. Section 4 discusses the method. Section 5 plots cyclical analyticity-syntheticity fluctuations in a bird's eye perspective. Section 6 explores the linguistic sources of this cyclicity in a jeweler's eye perspective. Section 7 offers some concluding remarks and investigates the extent to which we are dealing with a Gabelentz-Jespersen-Hodge-style cyclical phenomenon.

2.   Terminology

The terms "analytic" and "synthetic" are, of course, staple terms in classical work on the cross-linguistic typology of languages. The labels go back to the 19th century; August Wilhelm von Schlegel is usually credited for coining the opposition. I cannot review the rich history of thought in this area (but see Schwegler 1990 for an excellent literature review). A pertinent problem is that the terms "are used in widely different meanings by different linguists" (Anttila 1989:315). This is why we need to fix terminology right at the outset.

I will be interested, first, in the overt coding of *grammatical* information. Hence, this study will have nothing to say about lexical analyticity and syntheticity. Second, my definition of analytic/analyticity and synthetic/syntheticity is a strictly *formal* one that broadly follows Danchev's definition:

> Formal analyticity evidently implies that the various meanings (grammatical and/ or lexical) of a given language unit are carried by two or more free morphemes, whereas formal syntheticity is normally characterized by the presence of one bound morpheme.
> (Danchev 1992, 26)

I thus operationally define

- *formal grammatical analyticity* as covering all coding strategies that convey gram-matical information via free grammatical markers, which in turn are defined as synsemantic (see Marty 1908) word tokens devoid of independent lexical mean-ing; and
- *formal grammatical syntheticity* as covering all those coding strategies where grammatical information is signaled by bound grammatical markers.

As for analyticity, this study equates synsemantic word tokens with function (also known as structure or empty) words, which are in the present study taken to be mem-bers of closed word classes: conjunctions (e.g. *and, if*), determiners (e.g. *the*), pronouns (e.g. *he*), prepositions (e.g. *in*), infinitive markers (e.g. *to*), modal verbs (e.g. *can, will*), and negators (e.g. *not*). This view of analyticity and of what should count as a function word is fairly customary (see standard reference works such as Bussmann, Trauth & Kazzazi 1996:22 and 471).

With regard to the definition of syntheticity, bound grammatical markers are taken to comprise verbal, nominal, and adjectival inflectional affixes (e.g. past tense -*ed*, plural -*s*, comparative -*er*, and so on), the genitive clitic (as in *Tom's house*), as well as allomorphies including ablaut phenomena (e.g. past tense *sang*), i-mutation (e.g. plural *men*), and other non-regular yet clearly bound grammatical markers. The morphological analysis in this study thus broadly adopts an item-and-process model (Hockett 1954:396) in which grammatically marked forms are seen as deriv-ing from simple forms via some sort of process. What does not feature in this notion of syntheticity is the "zero morpheme'" construct postulated in some morphological approaches to deal with paradigmatic contrasts in finite verb forms – recall that this study is interested in the *overt* coding of grammatical information. Note also that contracted elements ('*s* as in *it's*, *to* as in *gotta*) do not count as bound markers in the present study's approach. Instead, a form such as *gotta* would be analyzed as consist-ing of two free grammatical markers, *got* and *to*, which may happen to be contracted to various degrees in speech.

As for portmanteau morphemes, this study calculates syntheticity indices in the following fashion: what is measured, in a given textual sample, is not the num-ber of inflectional morphemes per sample (which is what Greenberg's original gross inflectional index measured), but the number of words in a sample that bear *at least* one bound grammatical marker. This is not a trivial adjustment, because depending on one's analytical framework e.g. the form *walks* (as in *he walks the dog*) could be analyzed as containing two grammatical morphemes, {non-past} and {3rd person singular}. But in this study's approach, the form *walks* contains exactly one (overt) grammatical marker, -*s*, which may or may not have more than one meaning.

3. Data

This study's data source is the Penn Parsed Corpora of Historical English series (see ⟨http://www.ling.upenn.edu/hist-corpora/⟩). This corpus suite has the following sub-components: The Penn-Helsinki Parsed Corpus of Middle English, second edition (PPCME2) (Kroch & Taylor 2000); the Penn-Helsinki Parsed Corpus of Early Modern English (PPCEME) (Kroch, Santorini & Diertani 2004); and the Penn Parsed Corpus of Modern British English (PPCMBE) (Kroch, Santorini & Diertani 2010). The three corpora yield a total of 605 texts which span slightly less than four million words of running British English text. Each of the texts in this database can be assigned not only to particular periods in the history of English (Middle English, Early Modern English, Late Modern English), but also to specific centuries, starting with the early twelfth century and ending with the early twentieth century. Notice that the texts represent a variety of text types, such as letters, sermons, handbook prose, and history writing. The texts in the Penn Parsed Corpora of Historical English series are all part-of-speech annotated and syntax-parsed using roughly the same tagsets and annotation schemes. As I will explain in the next section, what will take center stage in the present study is the corpus suite's part-of-speech annotation.

4. Method

This study adopts the method described in detail in Szmrecsanyi (2009: 321–325), which I recapitulate below. The method is inspired by a seminal paper (Greenberg 1960) entitled "A Quantitative Approach to the Morphological Typology of Language," in which Joseph Greenberg in turn drew inspiration from work by Edward Sapir. Greenberg demonstrated that seemingly abstract typological notions are in fact amenable to precise quantitative measurements by calculating a number of indices on the basis of *naturalistic texts*. It thus bears highlighting that Greenberg (1960) is an early exercise in quantitative usage-based typology. Of course, the sample size used in Greenberg (1960) were coherent texts of merely 100 words; to mitigate the problem of point estimates deriving from such small sample sizes, Stepanov (1995) suggested basing the calculation of indices on corpora that "will include hundreds of texts from all existing genres, sources, historical periods etc. as one large sample" (Stepanov 1995: 144). This is precisely the kind of analysis that the present study will conduct.

Greenberg specifically defined (i) an index of synthesis, (ii) an index of agglutination, (iii) a compounding index, (iv) a derivational index, (v) a gross inflectional index, (vi) a prefixial index, (vii) a suffixial index, (viii) an isolational index,

(ix) a pure inflectional index, and (x) a concordial index (Greenberg 1960: 187). The *gross inflectional index*, for example, is defined as the number of inflectional morphemes in the analyst's sample divided by the total number of words in the sample (Greenberg 1960: 186–187).

While faithful to the core idea, I take the liberty adapt Greenberg's method. Greenberg did not calculate a plain analyticity index, and so Kasevič and Jachontov (1982: 37) (cited in Kempgen & Lehfeldt 2004: 1237) proposed an "index of analyticity", which would relate the number of synsemantic words in a given text to the total number of words in that text (see also Kelemen 1970: 62 for a similar proposal). Heeding this proposal, this study will calculate two indices:

1. The *analyticity index* (henceforth AI), which is defined as the ratio of the number of free grammatical markers in a sample (F) to the total number of words in the sample (W), normalized to a sample size of 1,000 tokens. Hence: AI = F/W × 1,000.
2. The *syntheticity index* (henceforth SI), which is defined as the ratio of the number of words in a sample that bear a bound grammatical marker (B) to the total number of words in the sample (W), normalized to a sample size of 1,000 tokens. Hence: SI = B/W × 1,000.

The indices have a lower bound of 0, and an upper bound of 1,000 index points.

How does this study determine the number of free grammatical markers in a text, and the number of words in a text that bear a bound grammatical marker? I exploit the part-of-speech (POS) annotation in the Penn Parsed Corpora of Historical English series, which annotates each individual word token in the corpus database for its word class; this includes information on whether nouns, verbs, adjectives, and certain pronouns carry inflections (a detailed description of the Penn Parsed Corpora of Historical English series' POS tagset, including exemplification, is available at ⟨http://www.ling.upenn.edu/hist-corpora/annotation/toc-long.htm#pos⟩). Given the definition of analyticity and syntheticity detailed above, POS tags (or rather the tokens annotated with POS tags) were subsequently placed into four categories: (i) purely lexical tags, such as singular nouns, which are uninteresting for present purposes; (ii) synthetic tags (essentially all tokens that, following Vennemann 1982, 330, show affixation or mutation to indicate grammatical information), (iii) analytic tags (function words), and (iv) a small number of simultaneously synthetic and analytic tags, such as inflected auxiliary verbs and reflexive pronouns in their plural form. Tables 1 and 2 report the exact tag/token-to-category matches, categorizing analytic tags into eleven broad component categories and synthetic tags into four broad component categories.

Table 1. Eleven broad component categories (as defined through POS tags and/or word tokens) loading on the Analyticity Index.[1]

Component category	POS tag(s)
1. conjunctions, complementizers, prepositions, subordinating conjunctions	CONJ (coordinating conjunctions) C (complementizers) P (prepositions, including subordinating conjunctions)
2. determiners	D (determiners) WD (*wh*-determiners)
3. existential *there*	EX (existential THERE)
4. pronouns	PRO (personal pronoun) MAN (indefinite subject pronoun [ME, MAN]) – only in Middle English) WPRO (wh-pronoun)
5. *more/most/less/least*	QR (quantifier, comparative) QS (quantifier, superlative)
6. infinitive markers	TO (infinitival TO, TIL, and AT) FOR (infinitival FOR) FOR+TO (cliticized FOR+TO)
7. modals	MD (modal verb) MD0 (modal verb, untensed)
8. negation	NEG (negation)
9. auxiliary *be*	B* (BE) + verb
10. auxiliary *do*	D* (DO) + verb
11. auxiliary *have*	H* (HAVE) + verb

Table 2. Four broad component categories (as defined through POS tags and/or word tokens) loading on the Syntheticity Index

Component category	POS tag(s)
1. the *s*-genitive	$ (possessive), except for PRO$
2. inflected comparative and superlative adjectives	ADJR (adjective, comparative) ADJS (adjective, superlative)
3. plural nouns	NPRS (proper noun, plural) NS (common noun, plural) OTHERS (OTHER, nominal use, plural)

(Continued)

---

1.   Note that expletive *it* cannot be considered here because it does not have a unique POS tag.

Table 2. (Continued)

Component category	POS tag(s)
4. inflected lexical and primary verbs	VAG (present participle)
	VAN (passive participle, verbal or adjectival)
	VBD (past, including past subjunctive)
	VBN (perfect participle)
	BAG (BE, present participle)
	BED (BE, past, including past subjunctive)
	BEN (BE, perfect participle)
	DAG (DO, present participle)
	DAN (DO, passive participle, verbal or adjectival)
	DOD (DO, past, including past subjunctive)
	DON (DO, perfect participle)
	HAG (HAVE, present participle)
	HAN (HAVE, passive participle, verbal or adjectival)
	HVD (HAVE, past, including past subjunctive)
	HVN (HAVE, perfect participle)
	VBP (present, including present subjunctive) + inflection
	MD (modal verb) + inflection
	BEP (BE, present, including present subjunctive)
	DOP (DO, present, including present subjunctive)
	HVP (HAVE, present, including present subjunctive)
	BE (BE, infinitive) ending in -*en*
	DO (DO, infinitive) ending in -*en*
	HV (HAVE, infinitive) ending in -*en*
	VB (infinitive, verbs other than BE, DO, HV) ending in -*en*

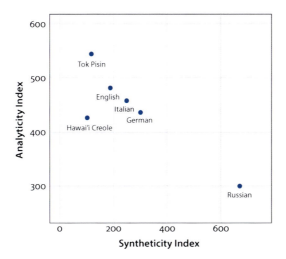

Figure 1. Analyticity Index scores (*y*-axis) against Syntheticity Index scores (*x*-axis) in European languages and two English-based creole languages (adapted from Siegel, Szmrecsanyi & Kortmann 2014)

Exemplification can be found in Section 6 below. On the technical plane, a retrieval script written in the programming language Perl automatically established the text frequencies of the relevant POS-tags (or POS-tag categories) in the data set, and calculated the index scores. Subsequently, the quantitative information was analyzed and visualized using the statistical software package R.

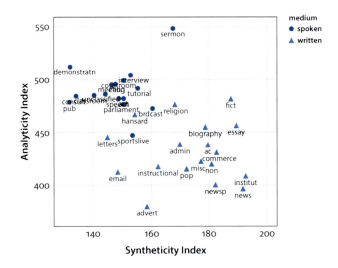

Figure 2. Analyticity Index scores (*y*-axis) against Syntheticity Index scores (*x*-axis) of text types sampled in the British National Corpus (adapted from Szmrecsanyi 2009)

To instill confidence in the method, Figures 1 and 2 show how the method rates different languages and text types in contemporary English. Figure 1 locates a number of different European languages (English, Italian, German, and Russian) as well as two English-based creole languages (Tok Pisin and Hawai'i Creole) in a two-dimensional analyticity-syntheticity plane. It turns out that Russian is the most synthetic and least analytic language in the sample, while Tok Pisin is the most analytic and least synthetic language (Hawai'i Creole is also fairly non-synthetic, but less analytic than Tok Pisin). It is probably the case that Figure 1 is a good representation of many linguists' gut feelings about these languages. Figure 2 applies the method to the various spoken and written text types sampled in the British National Corpus (BNC). Here, we find a very clear split between spoken text types and written text types: spoken text types are more analytic and less synthetic than written text types. Again, this is essentially the pattern that most register analysts would expect to see. For more discussion of these patterns, I refer the reader to the papers mentioned in the Figure captions. The crucial point in terms of the present study is that the method seems to work as advertised. With this in mind, I now go on to explore changes, with regard to analyticity and syntheticity, in the history of English.

5.   The bird's eye perspective: The big merry-go-round

This section investigates the overall development of the two indices in the eight centuries covered in the Penn Parsed Corpora of Historical English series. Table 3 reports mean Analyticity Index scores and mean Syntheticity Index scores by century, averaging over all text types in the corpus. Figure 3 visually depicts the longitudinal trajectories by plotting index scores (y-axis) against real time (x-axis) (level of granularity: individual texts), and approximating the relationship by a fit curve.

Table 3. Mean Analyticity Index and Syntheticity Index by century.

Century	Analyticity Index	Syntheticity Index
12th	449	196
13th	434	151
14th	481	155
15th	470	140
16th	473	141
17th	477	147
18th	464	162
19th	455	166
20th	444	178

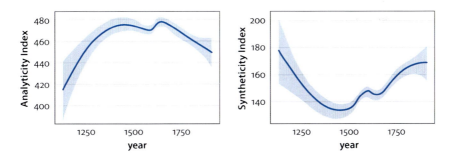

Figure 3. Index level variability by year of creation: LOESS smoothed fit curves with confidence region. Database: all texts in the Penn Parsed Corpora of Historical English series. Left: Analyticity Index. Right: Syntheticity Index

Note, first, that analyticity increased between the twelfth and the fourteenth century, remained fairly constant until the seventeenth century, and decreased subsequently. So in the 20th century, we find on average 444 analytic markers per 1,000 words of running text, which is indeed comparable to the levels in the 12th (449) and 13th (434) centuries. In the 17th century, by contrast, texts in the corpus material exhibit on average no less than 477 analytic markers per 1,000 words of running text.

Syntheticity, in turn, decreased rather robustly between the 12th century, when we find on average 196 inflected words per 1,000 words of running text, and the 15th century, when we find only about 140 inflected words per 1,000 words of running text (see Table 3). However, syntheticity levels rebounded in subsequent centuries. An average 20th century text, for example, in the Penn Parsed Corpus series features no less 178 inflected words per 1,000 words of running text.

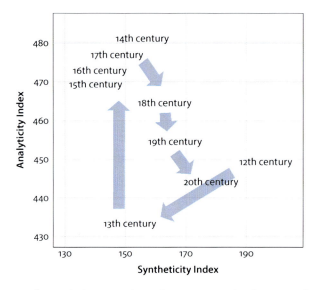

Figure 4. Mean Analyticity Index scores (*y*-axis) against mean Syntheticity Index scores (*x*-axis) by century. Database: all texts in the Penn Parsed Corpora of Historical English series

Figure 4 is a two-dimensional analyticity-syntheticity plane that visually depicts the cyclical nature of the variability. The diagram highlights the fact that analyticity-syntheticity variability after the Old English period can hardly be described in terms of a steady trend, or drift, towards more analyticity and less syntheticity. It is true that the data point for the 12th century is the most synthetic one in Figure 2. Between the 12th and the 13th century, syntheticity decreases robustly, but so does analyticity. Between the 13th to the 14th century, we see a huge surge in analyticity, while syntheticity levels decrease only slightly. Nothing much then happens between the 14th and the 17th centuries; both analyticity and syntheticity levels remain quite stable. Between the 17th and the 20th centuries, however, we observe a steady and incremental drift towards more syntheticity and less analyticity. The data point for the 20th century is both significantly more synthetic and less analytic than the data point for the seventeenth century.

The upshot is that in terms of analyticity-syntheticity coordinates, the 20th century has come almost full circle back to where we started in the 12th century.

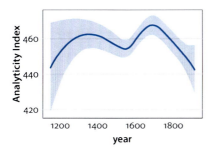
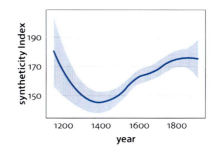

Figure 5. Informative texts ($N = 260$) in the Penn Parsed Corpora of Historical English series – index level variability by year of creation: LOESS smoothed fit curves with confidence region. Left: Analyticity Index. Right: Syntheticity Index

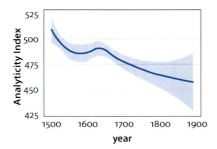
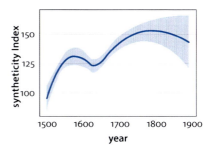

Figure 6. Letters ($N = 219$) in the Penn Parsed Corpora of Historical English series – index level variability by year of creation: LOESS smoothed fit curves with confidence region. Left: Analyticity Index. Right: Syntheticity Index

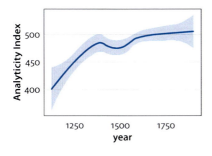
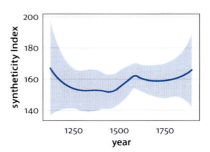

Figure 7. Religious texts ($N = 73$) in the Penn Parsed Corpora of Historical English series – index level variability by year of creation: LOESS smoothed fit curves with confidence region. Left: Analyticity Index. Right: Syntheticity Index

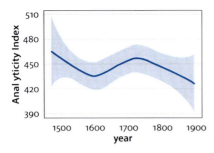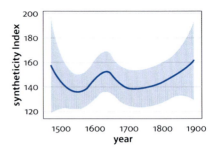

Figure 8. Imaginative texts ($N = 35$) in the Penn Parsed Corpora of Historical English series – index level variability by year of creation: LOESS smoothed fit curves with confidence region. Left: Analyticity Index. Right: Syntheticity Index

Is the merry-go-round in Figure 4 somehow an artefact of the design of Penn Parsed Corpora series, which samples a number of different text types? Are we missing something when we aggregate over these text types? To address these particular questions – rather than to characterize different text types in the Penn Parsed Corpora series, which is not my primary concern – Figures 5–8 canvas the development of the indices in the four major text types represented in the Penn Parsed Corpora series: informative texts, letters, religious texts, and imaginative texts. The developments in informative texts (Figure 5) mirror the overall development (see Figure 3), which is not entirely surprising as informative texts constitute the text category with the best coverage in the Penn Parsed Corpora series. Letters (Figure 6) show a curious pattern: in this text type analyticity is overall on the decline, while syntheticity is on the rise. Moving on, in both religious texts (Figure 7) and in imaginative texts (Figure 8) we see a weak version of the U-shaped syntheticity pattern familiar from Figure 3. But while analyticity is quite steadily increasing in religious texts, it is fairly stable in imaginative texts, with some ups and downs. In conclusion, the overall trajectories to be found in the Penn Parsed Corpora series (see Figure 3) primarily reflect the developments in one particular text type, informative texts. That said, Figure 9 – which replicates the two-dimensional plane in Figure 2 but excludes informative texts from the calculation – shows that even when informative texts are ignored, there is no linear drift, by any stretch of imagination, from syntheticity to analyticity.

6. The jeweler's eye perspective

The previous section has relied on aggregation to study multi-feature, big-picture patterns. In this section, I trade in the bird's eye perspective for the jeweler's eye perspective, and thus engage in an exercise of index deconstruction: what are the linguistic features that are implicated in the patterns discussed in the previous section?

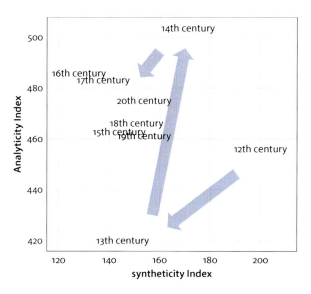

Figure 9. Mean analyticity indices (*y*-axis) against mean syntheticity indices (*x*-axis) by century. Database: all texts except informative prose in the Penn Parsed Corpora of Historical English series

In this spirit, Figure 10 plots the frequency trajectories of the 11 features which are loading on the Analyticity Index. The features whose frequency pattern is broadly in line with the inverted U-shaped Analyticity Index trajectory familiar from Figure 3 are the following:

– Conjunctions, as in (1a), complementizers, as in (1b), prepositions, as in (1c), subordinating conjunctions, as in (1d) (Figure 10a);

(1a) He was just getting into talk with […], **but/CONJ** during the first part of the visit he said very little. (AUSTEN-180X)

(1b) The morning was so wet **that/C** I was afraid […] (AUSTEN-180X)

(1c) but Frank who alone could go to Church called for her **after/P** service (AUSTEN-180X)

(1d) I wished **when/P** I heard them say so, that they could have heard […] (AUSTEN-180X)

– Pronouns, as in (2) (Figure 10d);

(2) They were very civil to **me/PRO**, as they always are (AUSTEN-180X)

– Infinitive markers, as in (3) (Figure 10f);

(3) but this is not thought likely **to/TO** happen (AUSTEN-180X)

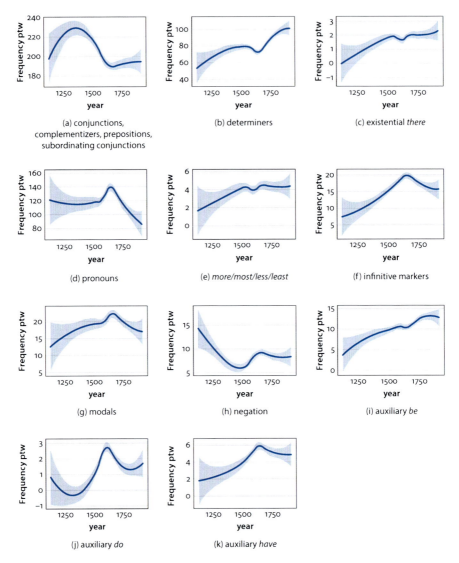

Figure 10. Frequency per thousand words (ptw) of component features/feature groups loading on the Analyticity Index by year of creation: LOESS smoothed fit curves with confidence region. Database: all texts in the Penn Parsed Corpora of Historical English series

–   Modals, as in (4) (Figure 10g);

(4)   He **must/MD** think it very strange that I do not acknowledge the receipt […] (AUSTEN-180X)

–   Auxiliary *do*, as in (5) (Figure 10j);

(5)   My dear Cassandra How **do/DOP** you do ? (AUSTEN-180X)

–   Auxiliary *have*, as in   (6) (Figure 10k);

(6)   he & I **have/HVP** practiced together two mornings (AUSTEN-180X)

Negative markers, as in (7), are on the decline (Figure 10h).

(7)   Mrs. E. Leigh did **not/NEG** make the slightest allusion to my Uncle's Business [...] (AUSTEN-180X)

By contrast, determiners (Figure 10b and (8)), existential *there* (Figure 10c and (9)), the comparative and superlative markers *more/most/less/least* (Figure 10e and (10)), and auxiliary *be* (Figure 10i and (11)) have all become more frequent over the course of time.

(8)   My Mother wrote to her **a/D** week ago (AUSTEN-180X)

(9)   **There/EX** will then be the Window-Curtains [...] (AUSTEN-180X)

(10)   she considers her own going thither as **more/QR** certain [...] (AUSTEN-180X)

(11)   A fortnight afterwards she is to **be/BE** called again [...] (AUSTEN-180X)

A one-way ANOVA which uses a three-partite sub-corpus distinction (PPCME2 versus PPCEME versus PPCMBE) as grouping variable suggests that the following four analytic features (or feature groups) exhibit the most extensive real-time variance: determiners, pronouns, infinitive markers, and auxiliary verbs.

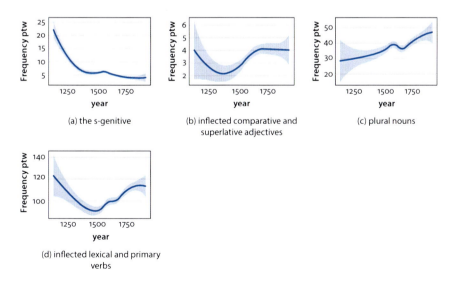

Figure 11. Frequency per thousand words (ptw) of component features/feature groups loading on the Syntheticity Index by year of creation: LOESS smoothed fit curves with confidence region. Database: all texts in the Penn Parsed Corpora of Historical English series

Let us turn to the four features that load on the Syntheticity Index; Figure 11 plots the frequencies of these features against real time. Two of these, inflected comparative and superlative adjectives (Figure 11b and (12)) and inflected lexical and primary verbs (Figure 11d and (13)), have U-shaped frequency trajectories that are similar to the overall trajectory of the Syntheticity Index in Figure 3.

(12)   I can no **longer/ADJR** take his part against you, as I did nine years ago (AUSTEN-180X)

(13)   but as she **found/VBD** it agreable I suppose there was no want of Blankets […] (AUSTEN-180X)

The *s*-genitive (Figure 11a and (14)), on the other hand, is sloping downward, while plural nouns (Figure 9c and (15)) are sloping upward.

(14)   The Duke of Gloucester **'s/$** death sets my heart at ease (AUSTEN-180X)

(15)   I shall be very glad to hear from you, that we may know how you all are, especially the two **Edwards/NPRS** (AUSTEN-180X)

7.   Discussion and Conclusion

Inspired by techniques developed in quantitative morphological typology (Greenberg 1960), this contribution has sketched the development of grammatical analyticity and syntheticity in the Penn Parsed Corpora of Historical English series, which covers the period between the 12th and the 20th century. The key insights can be summarized as follows. First, the period under study is clearly not characterized by a steady drift towards more analyticity and less syntheticity. Instead, analyticity was on the rise until the end of the Early Modern English period, but declined subsequently; the reverse is true for syntheticity. But with regard to the frequency of analytic versus synthetic marking, 20th century English is quantitatively almost back to the analyticity-syntheticity coordinates that characterize 12th century English. Second, we have seen that this pattern primarily reflects the developments in one particular text type that is extremely well represented in the Penn Parsed Corpora series, informative texts (though I hastened to add that the other text types covered in the corpus material – letters, religious texts, imaginative texts – do not exhibit linear drifts either, as we have seen). Third, a jeweler's eye analysis of the linguistic features that are associated with either index revealed that the overall merry-go-round pattern diagnosed in the bird's eye perspective seems to be a function of the frequency trajectories of the following features: conjunctions, complementizers, prepositions, and subordinating conjunctions; pronouns; infinitive markers; modals; auxiliary *do*; auxiliary *have*; inflected comparative and superlative adjectives; and inflected lexical and primary verbs.

So the verdict is that when restricting attention to the post-Old English history of the language, we see a good deal of circularity. This circularity no doubt bears a number of resemblances to Gabelentz-Jespersen-Hodge-style cycles or spirals. That said, there are also a number of important differences and caveats that must be considered:

Time depth. The dataset I have explored in this contribution covers eight centuries. This is a fairly short interval, compared e.g. to the millennia-encompassing analysis presented in Hodge (1970).

Frequency changes. The developments sketched in the present study are primarily about drifts in usage frequency ("fluctuations in analyticity/syntheticity", to borrow a phrase from Schwegler 1990:191). Additions to, or losses from, the inventory of grammatical markers do not take center stage: eight centuries is simply too short a time span to feature substantial inventory changes.

Erosion and replacement not mandatory. It follows that the cyclical developments we are observing in the data are not necessarily about "changes where a phrase or word gradually disappear and is replaced by a new linguistic item" (Gelderen 2009:2). For example, we saw that nouns bearing plural inflections have become more frequent in the course of the past few centuries. But this does not mean, of course, that the English language has acquired new inflectional markers of nominal plurality. It rather means that for some reason (stylistics, content, discourse pragmatics, etc.), language users have come to use existing plural markers more often. Thus Hodge's motto "one man's morphology was an earlier man's syntax" (Hodge 1970:3) is a theme that the present contribution's findings do not necessarily speak to. Sources of renewal in the present contribution's approach are possibly old forms that had never died out.

Aggregation. To explore big-picture cyclical developments, I eschewed the "single-feature study" (parlance of Nerbonne 2008) perspective advocated by e.g. Heine, Claudi & Hünnemeyer (1991:246) and instead studied multi-feature cyclical patterns in an aggregate perspective, adopting a whole-language view in the tradition of e.g. Schlegel (1818) and Sapir (1921).

No discrete steps. Thanks to the usage-based and frequency-oriented method I have been using, it is difficult to distinguish between discrete steps along the lines of e.g. Hoeksema (2009), who distinguishes four stages in the negative cycle.

Quantitative versus qualitative change. Modern analyticity and syntheticity is, of course, qualitatively different from its Early English counterpart. For example, determiners have become increasingly important as an analytic category, but pronouns have been on the decline. Conversely, the possessive marker used to be a more important synthetic marker than it is now, whereas inflected adjectives are on the rise. The point is that contrary developments like these may "gang up", as it were, to create numerically similar Analyticity and Syntheticity Index scores, although the contribution of particular linguistic features may vary quite dramatically. What we are seeing in the data is thus a spiral (Gabelentz 1891), rather than a cycle.

And this takes us to the most important issue to keep in mind: the indices I have been calculating in this study capture but one characteristic – the typological nature and frequency of grammatical marking – that can be used to compare (historical) language varieties and texts. Take texts cmvices1.m1, from the Penn-Helsinki Parsed Corpus of Middle English, and text benson-1908, from the Penn Parsed Corpus of Modern British English. Both texts exhibit very similar index levels (cmvices1.m1: AI – 458, SI -162; benson-1908: AI – 455, SI – 167), but the texts certainly "feel" extremely different, as a cursory glance at the excerpts in (16) and (17) shows.

(16)   Dies ilche modinesse, +deih hie habbe hlot and dale mang alle o+dre sennes, na+del+as hie haue+d ane, +de is hire swi+de neih and swi+de hersum, +de me haue+d swi+de ofte beswiken, +tat is, Vana Gloria, idel wulder o+der idel +gelp. (cmvices1.m1)

(17)   As regards the art of teaching it is difficult to lay down rules, because every man must find out his own method. It is easy to say that the first requisite is patience, but the statement requires considerable modification. (benson-1908)

And so although 20th century English may be similar, in terms of quantitative analyticity and syntheticity, to 12th and 13th century English, there is no way texts from these periods can be confused.

Acknowledgments

Financial support through an Odysseus grant by the Research Foundation Flanders (FWO, grant no. G.0C59.13N) is gratefully acknowledged.

References

Anttila, Raimo. 1989. *Historical and Comparative Linguistics* [Current Issues in Linguistic Theory 6]. Amsterdam: John Benjamins. doi:10.1075/cilt.6
Bussmann, Hadumod, Trauth, Gregory & Kazzazi, Kerstin. 1996. *Routledge Dictionary of Language and Linguistics*. London: Routledge.
Danchev, Andrei. 1992. The evidence for analytic and synthetic developments in English. In *History of Englishes: New Methods and Interpretations in Historical Linguistics*, Matti Rissanen, Ossi Ihalainen, Terttu Nevalainen & Irma Taavitsainen (eds), 25–41. Berlin: Mouton de Gruyter.
Fennell, Barbara A. 2001. *A History of English: A Sociolinguistic Approach*. Oxford: Blackwell.

von der Gabelentz, Georg. 1891. *Die Sprachwissenschaft: Ihre Aufgaben, Methoden und Bisherigen Ergebnisse*. Leipzig: Weigel.

van Gelderen, Elly. 2009. Cyclical change. An introduction. In *Cyclical Change* [Linguistik Aktuell/Linguistics Today 146], Elly van Gelderen (ed.), 1–12. Amsterdam: John Benjamins. doi:10.1075/la.146

Greenberg, Joseph H. 1960. A quantitative approach to the morphological typology of language. *International Journal of American Linguistics* 26(3): 178–94. doi:10.1086/464575

Heine, Bernd, Claudi, Ulrike & Hünnemeyer, Friederike. 1991. *Grammaticalization: A Conceptual Framework*. Chicago IL: University of Chicago Press.

Hockett, Charles F. 1954. Two models of grammatical description. *Word* 10: 210–231.

Hodge, Carleton T. 1970. The linguistic cycle. *Language Sciences* 13: 1–7.

Hoeksema, Jack. 2009. Jespersen recycled. In *Cyclical Change* [Linguistik Aktuell/Linguistics Today 146], Elly van Gelderen (ed.), 15–34. Amsterdam: John Benjamins. doi:10.1075/la.146.04hoe

Jespersen, Otto. 1917. *Negation in English and Other Languages*. Copenhagen: Host.

Kasevič, Vadim & Jachontov, Sergej E. (eds). 1982. *Kvantitativnaja Tipologija Jazykov Azii I Afriki* (A Quantitative Typology of Asian and African Languages). Leningrad.

Kelemen, József. 1970. Sprachtypologie und Sprachstatistik. In *Theoretical Problems of Typology and the Northern Eurasian Languages*, László Dezső & Peter Hajdú (eds), 53–63. Amsterdam: Gruener.

Kempgen, Sebastian & Lehfeldt, Werner. 2004. Quantitative Typologie. In *Morphologie. Ein Internationales Handbuch Zur Flexion Und Wortbildung*, Geert E. Booij, 1235–1246. Berlin: Mouton de Gruyter.

Kroch, Anthony, Santorini, Beatrice & Diertani, Ariel. 2004. *Penn-Helsinki Parsed Corpus of Early Modern English*. ⟨http://www.ling.upenn.edu/hist-corpora/PPCEME-RELEASE-2/index.html⟩

Kroch, Anthony, Santorini, Beatrice & Diertani, Ariel. 2010. *Penn Parsed Corpus of Modern British English*. ⟨http://www.ling.upenn.edu/hist-corpora/PPCMBE-RELEASE-1/index.html⟩

Kroch, Anthony & Taylor, Ann. 2000. *Penn-Helsinki Parsed Corpus of Middle English*, 2nd edn. ⟨http://www.ling.upenn.edu/hist-corpora/PPCME2-RELEASE-3/index.html⟩

Marty, Anton. 1908. *Untersuchungen zur Grundlegung der Allgemeinen Grammatik und Sprachphilosophie*. Halle: Niemeyer.

Nerbonne, John. 2008. Variation in the aggregate: An alternative perspective for variationist linguistics. In *Northern Voices: Essays on Old Germanic and Related Topics Offered to Professor Tette Hofstra*, Kees Dekker, Alasdair MacDonald & Hermann Niebaum (eds), 365–82. Leuven: Peeters.

Sapir, Edward. 1921. *Language: An Introduction to the Study of Speech*. New York NY: Harcourt, Brace and Company.

von Schlegel, August Wilhelm. 1818. *Observations Sur La Langue et La Littérature Provençales*. Paris: Librairie grecque-latine-allemande.

Schwegler, Armin. 1990. *Analyticity and Syntheticity: A Diachronic Perspective with Special Reference to Romance Languages*. Berlin: Mouton de Gruyter. doi:10.1515/9783110872927

Siegel, Jeff, Szmrecsanyi, Benedikt & Kortmann, Bernd. 2014. Measuring analyticity and syntheticity in Creoles. *Journal of Pidgin and Creole Languages* 29(1): 49–85. doi:10.1075/jpcl.29.1.02sie

Stepanov, Arthur V. 1995. Automatic typological analysis of Semitic morphology. *Journal of Quantitative Linguistics* 2(2): 141–150. doi:10.1080/09296179508590043

Szmrecsanyi, Benedikt. 2009. Typological parameters of intralingual variability: Grammatical analyticity versus syntheticity in varieties of English. *Language Variation and Change* 21(3): 319–53. doi:10.1017/S0954394509990123

Szmrecsanyi, Benedikt. 2012. Analyticity and syntheticity in the history of English. In *The Oxford Handbook of the History of English*, Terttu Nevalainen & Elisabeth Closs Traugott (eds), 654–665. Oxford: OUP.

Vennemann, Theo. 1982. Isolation – Agglutination – Flexion? Zur Stimmigkeit Typologischer Parameter. Fakten und Theorien. In *Festschrift für Helmut Sinn Zum 65. Geburtstag*, Sieglinde Heinz & Ulrich Wandruszka (eds), 327–34. Tübingen: Narr.

The interaction between the French subject and object cycles

Mariana Bahtchevanova and Elly van Gelderen*
Arizona State University

In Colloquial French, first and second person preverbal subject pronouns function as agreement markers on the finite verb because they are obligatory and adjacent to the finite verb (e.g. von Wartburg 1943). In other spoken varieties of French, third person pronouns are also agreement markers, having lost gender and number (Fonseca-Greber 2000 for Swiss French). This paper adds new data on third person subjects for Colloquial French, namely third person emphatic pronouns being used on their own, and shows how these data fit the subject cycle. Because, like subject markers, object pronouns are preverbal, they 'interfere' with the preverbal subject agreement markers. Our hypothesis was therefore that preverbal object clitics would be replaced by postverbal pronouns (cf. van Gelderen 2011: 52) or would be deleted, as Lambrecht et al. (1996) had already observed. We investigated postverbal placement of object pronouns and found some evidence of this but, more interestingly, we found that object markers were reinterpreted as agreement markers. The important insights for cyclical change this paper provides are that different person markings can be at different stages, that some stages can be skipped, and that one cycle can influence another.

1. Introduction

It has been observed for a long time that subject pronouns in Modern Colloquial French, especially first and second person ones, are more like agreement markers than like independent pronouns (von Wartburg 1943; Lambrecht 1981). This change has other consequences, such as the appearance of new emphatic subjects. In this paper, we examine instances of third person subject pronouns in various corpora (the *Corpus d'entretiens spontanés*, the *Orléans Corpus*, part of the *ELICOP Corpus*, and the *Corpus*

* Authors are listed in alphabetical order since both have contributed to the data and account. We thank Annette Hornung, Daniela Kostadinovska, William Kruger, JJ LaTourelle, and Sayantan Mukerjee for comments and special thanks are due to Bonnie Fonseca-Greber who made very helpful and specific comments.

DOI 10.1075/la.227.05bah

de français parlé au Québec)[1] and find a lot of variation but definitely a change of the pronoun towards an agreement marker and the loss of that agreement marker. The corpora do not indicate clitic or affix forms but transcribe them mostly as independent words; we follow this. Our glosses do not distinguish among pronoun, clitic, or agreement affix because we think these categories are in transition. For a clear pronoun, we use the English oblique pronoun and, for clear agreement markers, we use person and number markers, such as 1S or 2P.

Secondly, we examine object pronouns because we expect preverbal pronominal objects to be a factor complicating the changes affecting subjects. Subject agreement is not adjacent to the verb if an object (or negative or adverbial) appears in between. Our results show some replacements by postverbal objects and some reanalysis to agreement markers. We investigate how we can see this in terms of a cycle.

The outline is as follows. Section 2 provides an overview of the Subject Cycle in general and in French in particular. Section 3 presents new data on the situation with third person subjects in French. Sections 4 and 5 are concerned with changes in object pronouns in French and how these can be analyzed. Section 6 presents some puzzles and a conclusion.

2. The subject cycle in general and in French

The subject cycle involves the reanalysis of an independent personal pronoun as a subject agreement marker on the verb. Cross-linguistically, there are many examples of the Subject Agreement Cycle, both synchronically and diachronically (cf. van Gelderen 2011). We'll first explain what a subject cycle is and then provide the stages that the French subject has undergone.

The typical stages of the subject cycle are given in (1) where we have used English words for convenience.

(1)   a.   They (often) eat lasagna.
      b.   They'eat lasagna.
      c.   Them th'eat lasagna.
      d.   Them (often) eat lasagna.

In (1a), the pronoun is fully independent and need not be adjacent to the finite verb whereas, in (1b), it is cliticized to the verb. If the pronoun is interpreted as agreement marker, this stage will be one of null subject (or pro-drop). In (1c), the earlier

---

1.   See the reference section for descriptions of these corpora.

independent pronoun is renewed by a new one that is ambiguous between being in topic or in subject position. If *them* is in topic position, the clitic could still count as the subject; if *them* is the subject, the clitic is now a marker on the verb. Stage (1d) is the same as (1a).[2] Languages can thus be seen as being in different stages of the cycle; they can have just pronouns, just agreement, or both.

If languages acquire agreement markers from erstwhile pronouns, one expects them to resemble these and that is indeed the case in many languages (see van Gelderen 2011, Chapter 2). One also expects cross-linguistic surveys of languages to show perhaps a 30% distribution of each stage in (1). There is typological work that provides percentages of agreement and pronouns in the world's languages but, since it is hard to decide in (1b) and (1c) if the agreement occurs, it may be twice 30%, i.e. 60%. This is indeed the case. Bybee (1985) estimates that 56% of languages have verbal agreement with the subject; Siewierska's (2008) data put that at 72% and Dryer's (2013) data at 61%. Subject pronouns appear in 30% of Dryer's (2013) languages (some optionally and some obligatorily). Here too, it is notoriously hard, however, to determine this, especially if we take the pronominal argument languages into account where the verbal affixes count as pronouns (see Jelinek 1984). We conclude the typological data fit the scenario in (1) because the agreement between 56% and 72% illustrates stages (1bc), two-thirds of the cycle.

A language where we have evidence of all the stages in (1) is French. Old French has optional pronouns that need not be adjacent to the verb, as (2) shows for the second person singular *tu* 'you'. Foulet (1961: 330) confirms that all personal pronouns can be separated from the verb in Old French. By the time of Modern (colloquial) French, *je* obligatorily precedes the finite verb, as the ungrammaticality of (3) shows, and this is true for *tu* as well. See Kayne (1975: 82–5) for additional arguments. In addition, a frequent renewal in the form of *moi* (and *toi*) appears, as in (4).[3]

(2) *Si con   tu   **meismes** le preuves*   Old French
     If when you   self   it prove
     'If you prove it yourself.' (⟨http://romandelarose.org⟩, Selden Supra 57, 40v)

(3) **Je probablement ai   lu   ça*   Colloquial French
     1s probably   have read that
     'I've probably read that.'

---

2. See Heine & Song (2011) for sources of pronominal renewal.

3. In the *Corpus d'entretiens spontanés*, this doubling occurs in 8.5% with first person (239 out of 2818 *je/j'*) and, in the *Orléans Corpus*, it occurs in 13% of the first person singulars (187 out of 1424 *je/j'*).

(4) euh **moi je** trouve ce   qui en   souffre   Colloquial French
     Eh   me   1s   find   that who of.it suffers

     le   plus ...
     the most

     'I think that the one that suffers the most is ...' (*Orléans Corpus*).

The forms of all the pronouns with a verb are given in Table 1, both the formal and the colloquial ones. Note that the endings of most of these are only visible in the writing not audible.

Table 1. The present tense of the verb *chanter* 'to sing'

Formal French			Colloquial French		
S	1	je	chante	je	chant	[ʃɑ̃t]
	2	tu	chantes	tu	chant	[ʃɑ̃t]
	3	il/elle	chante	il/elle	chant	[ʃɑ̃t]
P	1	nous	chantons	on	chant	[ʃɑ̃t]
	2	vous	chantez	vous	chantez	[ʃɑ̃te]
	3	ils/elles	chantent	ils/elles	chant	[ʃɑ̃t]

Other phenomena connected to the cliticization/affixation of the subject pronoun to the finite verb are a loss of subject-auxiliary inversion in questions and changes in preverbal negative markers and object clitics. Subject-auxiliary inversion occurs in formal French, as seen in (5a), but as mentioned in e.g. Lambrecht (1981), de Wind (1995), and Auger (1996), it is lost in more colloquial versions shown in (5bc). Inversion, as in (5a), "is extremely rare in spoken French and is expected to disappear ultimately" (de Wind 1995: 24).

(5) a. *Où   es-tu*   Formal French
         where be-2s
         'Where are you?'

     b. *tu es où*   Colloquial French
         2s be where
         'Where are you?'

     c. *où   t'es*   Colloquial French
         where 2s.be
         'Where are you?'

The negative preverbal Formal French *ne*, as in (6a), is left out in Colloquial French, as (6b) shows. Objects in French occur postverbally when they are fully nominal and preverbally when they are clitic pronouns. The preverbal object clitics are undergoing a number of changes that will be discussed more in this paper. The example given in (6) shows the change from preverbal to postverbal object marker and the loss of the negative *ne*. These changes conspire to enable the subject pronoun to cliticize to the verb.

(6)   a.   *je   ne   l'ai   pas   encore   démontré*   Formal French
              1s   NEG   3s.have   NEG   yet   proven

      b.   *j'ai   pas   encore   démontré   ça*   Colloquial French
              1s.have   NEG   yet   proven   that
              'I haven't yet proven that.'

It is usually agreed that the first and second person singulars (*je* and *tu*) have reached the agreement stage. The third person singular is not seen as having reached that stage although Ashby (1977: 18) argues all preverbal pronominal forms form a breath group with the finite verb and there are also many doublings with third person. Third person *il* and *elle* also undergo phonetic reduction before a consonant (Morin 1979: 12). The reason for not considering the pronoun as agreement is that not all DPs allow doubling. For instance, doubling with indefinites, as in (7a), is ungrammatical for most speakers, but we have found instances of generic use in the *Orléans corpus*, namely (7b) and (7c).

(7)   a.   **Un   homme   i(l)   est   venu   me   dire   quelque   chose.*
              a   man   3sM   is   come   me   say   some   thing
              'A man came to tell me something.'

      b.   *si   un   homme   il   a   besoin   d'une   augmentation*
              If   a   man   3sM   has   need   of a   augmentation
              de   quelque   chose.
              of   something
              'If a man needs an augmentation of some kind.'

      c.   *maintenant   si   un gosse   il   apprend   il   apprend*
              now   if   a   kid   3sM   learns   3sM   learns
              'Now if a kid is learning, he is learning'.

The doublings usually occur with definite nominals, as in (8), or with pronouns, as in (9), or with both, as in (10), all from the *Corpus d'entretiens spontanés*. There are generic nominals, as in (10b), and an occasional quantified one, as in (11a). Zribi-Hertz (1994) similarly reports about quantifiers with a third person pronoun in Colloquial French, given as (11b), so speakers of these varieties definitely treat *il* as agreement.

(8)   a.   *Alors   Madame Jagou,   elle   elle   faisait   la   blanchisserie   et*
              so   Madame Jagou,   her   3sG.F   did   the   laundry   and
              le   repassage.
              the   ironing
              'So Madame Jagou used to do the laundry and the ironing'.

      b.   *Et* ***les pièces, elles*** *ont été montées par la*
          and the plays 3PF have been put on by the

          Mère Thérèse
          Mother Therese

          'And the plays were put on by Mother Theresa'.

      c.   ***La maison, elle*** *est 1820.*
          the house 3SF is 1820

          'The house is from 1820'.

(9)   a.   ***Eux, ils*** *sont de gauche.*
          them 3PM are of left

          'They are left-wing'.

      b.   ***Eux, ils*** *vont partir juste un après-midi*
          them 3PM go.FUT.3P leave just an afternoon

          'They are going to leave some afternoon'.

      c.   *donc* ***eux, ils*** *vivent plus mal qu'ils vivaient …*
          therefore them 3PM live more bad than.3PM lived

          'Therefore they live worse than they used to live'.

(10) a.   ***Pompidou, lui, il*** *allait dans un restaurant …*
          Pompidou him 3SM went to a restaurant

          'Pompidou was going to a restaurant'.

      b.   *Parce que* ***le cultivateur français, lui, il*** *est tellement, il*
          because the farmer French him 3SM is so 3SM

          a tellement de matériel
          has so much material

          'Because the French farmer, he is, he has so much material'.

(11) a.   ***Tout chacun*** *il avait son carnet*
          all everyone 3SM had his carnet

          'Everyone had his carnet'.

      b.   ***Personne, il*** *a rien dit*
          nobody 3SM has nothing said

          'Nobody said anything.'   (Zribi-Hertz 1994: 137)

The doubling of third person *lui* and *il* is relatively rare in the *Corpus d'entretiens spontanés*. For instance, there are 12 instances of *lui il* out of 2154 occurrences of *il*, making this doubling 0.6 % of the sentences involving *il*.

    The agreement status of *il* is very clear in other varieties of French. Fonseca-Greber's (2000) study of Spoken Swiss French, illustrates that definite overt subject NPs have additional pronouns around 60% of the time, with human singulars the highest (2000: 329). Surprisingly, doubled pronouns occur more frequently with indefinite subjects, as in (12), on average 77%. Quantifiers, as in (13), are the least likely to be doubled although they still occur about 20% of the time.

(12)   ***une omelette elle*** *est comme ça*   Swiss Spoken French
      an   omelet   3sf   is   like   this
      'An omelet is like this.' (Fonseca-Greber 2000:335).

(13)   *c'est que* ***chacun***   *il*   *a sa manière de …*   Swiss Spoken French
      it.is   that   everyone   3s   has his way of
      'Everyone has his own way of …'   (Fonseca-Greber 2000:338).

The stage in (13) is the last stage in the reanalysis of third person pronouns as agreement markers. Once quantifiers occur with the pronoun, the latter cannot be an argument but has to be an agreement marker. Swiss French is different from other varieties in that number and gender remain marked on the new agreement marker.

Having looked at the status of the first, second, and third person singular, we'll turn to the plurals. The formal and colloquial French pronouns are given in Table 1. First person plural *nous* is replaced by *on* in Colloquial French (cf. Fonseca-Greber & Waugh 2003:108). This *on* also functions as the generic 'one'. In the case of the first person plural, we get doublings, as in (14), from the *Corpus d'entretiens spontanés* with the *nous* as the oblique 'real' pronoun and *on* the agreement marker.

(14)   a.   ***Nous, on*** *a*   *un*   *an*   *de différence. C'est bien, hein?*
           us   1p   has   one   year   of difference.   It is good, right
           'We differ one year in age. Not bad, right?'

      b.   ***nous on*** *appelle ça*   *un k-way.*
           us   1p   call   this   a   windbreaker
           'We call this a windbreaker'.

      c.   *parce que c'est le travail que que, que* ***nous, on*** *ferait*   *pas*
           because it.is   the work   that that   that   us   1p   would.do   neg
           'because it was the work that that we wouldn't do'.

The second person plural is perhaps the 'strongest' pronominal because it is also used for the second person singular polite form, so it has a lot of 'extra baggage', i.e. semantic features. In addition, the ending on the (regular) verb for these subjects is the only one that is distinct in Spoken French (see Table 1). Therefore, doubling, as in (15), is not as common and seems more contrastive. The doublings usually involve singular (polite) subjects; for instance, in the *Corpus d'entretiens spontanés*, they only exist with singular meaning, as in (15).

(15)   *Et*   ***vous vous*** *êtes*   *Parisien*
      and   you   you   are   Parisian
      'And you are Parisian.'

An interesting development is the erosion of *vous* to *z* in (16a), from a song. Although these phonological erosions are not found in the corpora we examined, they occur in Fonseca-Greber and Waugh's data, see (16b), are mentioned in other literature (Morin 1979: 35) and can also be heard.

(16)   a.   ***Z'avez   de   la   chance   qu'on   vous   aime.***
            2p.have PRT the luck   that.1p you   love
            'You are lucky that we love you.'   (Stromae, *Tous les Mêmes*)

       b.   *J-espère   que   **vz-arrivez**   à   réparer ces problems*
            I-hope   that 2p-can   to   repair the problems
            'I-hope y-can get the problems fixed.'
                                                    (Fonseca-Greber & Waugh 2003: 102)

For third person plural, there are signs that the pronoun is an agreement marker. Thus, gender and number are not indicated in (17) when the pronoun becomes the agreement marker. Here *i* is marked for only third person singular although *les tomates* are feminine and plural (see also von Wartburg 1943: 62).

(17)   ***Les   tomates,   i   sont   encore   vertes***   Spoken French
       The tomatoes 3   are   still   green
       'The tomatoes, they are still green.'   (Lambrecht 1981: 40)

So, first and second person singular in Colloquial French have become agreement markers and have undergone changes consistent with a subject cycle. However, it has often been assumed that third person singular and the plurals are (still) not part of this change. In the current section, we have shown that this is not the case and, in the next section, we provide further evidence of this by adding data for the third person.

3.   Changes in the third person subject pronoun

The literature discusses doubling, as in (8) to (17), quite frequently. Doubling is expected if the original subject pronouns have been reanalyzed as agreement markers and the emphatic forms have become the subject pronouns. Thus, technically, there is no doubling but replacement. In this section, we discuss some interesting developments with third person where the agreement marker is left out. We have not seen much discussion of this phenomenon and address it as an acceleration of a stage in the cycle: the new third person agreement marker is left out and the new pronoun might in turn be in a position to be reanalyzed.

All the instances of emphatic pronouns by themselves from the *Corpus d'entretiens spontanés*[4] are given in (18) and (19). In (18), there is only the emphatic *lui* and *i(l)* is missing; the same is true in (19) where the emphatic *eux* appears by itself.

---

4.   Obtained by manually examining all instances of *lui* and *eux*.

(18)   a.   *Et **lui** n'est pas d'ici,   mon beau-fils.*
               and him not.is not from.here my   son-in-law
               'and he's not from here, my son-in-law.'

        b.   *"Oh non, "**lui** dit   "vous savez, ...*
               Oh no   him said you know
               'Oh, no, he said "you know ...".'

        c.   *mais **lui** sait   très bien présenter euh ses thèses et....*
               but   him knows very well present   uh   his theses and ...
               'But he knows how to present his theses very well.'

        d.   *Et **lui** va   sentir les traces et   il   va   les   suivre.*
               and him will smell the track and he will them follow
               'And he will smell the track and will follow them'.

        e.   *le chômeur   qui, **lui**, va se   débrouiller pour faire ...*
               the unemployed who him will REFL find a way to   do   ...
               'The unemployed who will manage to do ...'

        f.   *Et **lui** ne   veut pas quitter sa femme.*
               and him NEG wants NEG leave   his wife
               'And he doesn't want to leave his wife.'

(19)   a.   *Et des   points qui **eux** ne   sont pas jetés au hasard.*[5]
               and some dots   that them NEG   are NEG thrown randomly
               'and some dots that are not randomly marked'.

        b.   *peut-être **eux** se   sont trouvés un peu lésés à un certain*
               Maybe   them REFL are found a   little hurt at a   given

               moment ... de leur vie.
               moment ... of their life
               'Maybe they found themselves a little hurt at a given moment
               of their live'.

        c.   *ils reprochent aux   professeurs sans   voir que **eux** sont*
               3P reproach to-the teachers   without see that them are

               responsables de   ...
               responsible about ...
               'They reproach the teachers without seeing that they are responsible
               for ...'.

        d.   *qui, **eux**, n'ont   pas l'intention   de fonctionner dans*
               who them NEG.have NEG the.intention to function   in

               cet ordre
               this line
               '... (majorities) who have no intention of functioning in the same way'.

---

5. Many of these examples involve relative clauses; we don't know why.

    e.   *il   y a un petit problème ... d'une*
        there is   a   small problem .... with a

        population   maghrébine
        population North African

        *qui, **eux,** ne   voulaient pas   faire de la   musique*
        who them NEG   wanted   NEG   to.do of the music

        'there was a small problem... with a group of North Africans who
        didn't want to play music.'

    f.   **eux** *n'ont   pas besoin nécessitent pas n'ont   pas*
        them NEG.have NEG need   need   NEG NEG.have NEG

        besoin de vacances
        need   of vacation

        'They don't need ... need not ... don't need vacation.'

These occurrences of the oblique pronoun by itself are relatively rare in the *Corpus d'entretiens spontanés* as the total numbers for masculine singular and plural, given in Table 2, show. For the numbers of *il*, we have ignored the *il y'a* construction.

Table 2. Third person masculine and plural subjects
in the *Corpus d'entretiens spontanés*

il	1213	ils	746
lui il	12 (.97%)	eux ils	4 (.5%)
lui	6 (.49%)	eux	6 (.8%)
Total	1231		756

Although the numbers are small, it is striking that many of the pronouns by them-selves precede a negative prefix, as in (18a), (18f), (19a), (19d), and (19f), or an object pronoun, as in (19b). This may mean that the lack of *il(s)* is due to the negative and object that would otherwise intervene.

    In the larger *Orléans Corpus*, *lui* appears as subject by itself more frequently than together with *il* (11 to 5); *il* as subject on its own is of course the most frequent but the exact number is not available.[6] The number of *eux* subjects on its own is smaller, i.e. 5, and that means they take up 0.7% of all third person plural masculine subjects because *ils* occurs 699 times; *eux ils* doesn't appear. The data are given in Table 3. Respective examples are given in (20) and (21).

---

6. The *Orléans Corpus* search engine only gives up to 999 results.

Table 3. Third person subjects in the *Orléans Corpus*

il	999	ils	699
lui il	5	eux ils	0
lui	11	eux	5 (.7%)
Total	751		704

(20) a. *est-ce que **lui**   vous reprend ?*
          is-it that **him** you take back
          'Does he take you back?'

      b. *alors comme **lui**   gagne plus   cher   que moi*
          then as   **him** earn more expensive than me
          'and as he makes more money than me…'

      c. *et **lui** ne   peut pas   prendre de vacances*
          and **him** NEG can NEG take   of vacation
          'and he cannot take any vacation.'

      d. *lui   a   essayé de réparer*
          him has tried to repair
          'He has tried to repair it.'

(21) a. *on a   un appui technique que **eux** n'ont   pas*
          1P have a   support technical that them NEG.have NEG
          'We have technical support that they do not have.'

      b. *…parce que **eux**   voient un seul   ensemble dans*
          …because   them see a single unit   in

          leur départment
          their department
          'because they see a single unit in their department.'

      c. *c'est que **eux**   ont   quelquefois des   avis   à donner qui*
          it.is that them have sometimes some opinions to give   that

          sont intéressants
          are interesting

          'It's that sometimes they have interesting opinions to give.'

      d. *parce que **eux**   sont tranquilles*
          because   them are calm
          'because they are not worried.'

Other interesting renewals of third person pronouns have appeared, e.g. the strengthening of the plural pronouns in some varieties of French (cf. Baissac 1880; Offroy 1975). One such variety is Quebec French, as (22) shows, from the *Corpus de français parlé au Québec*. Like their non-augmented counterparts, the renewed forms can occur without *ils*, as (23) shows. The latter comprise 19% of the total (21 instances of (23) and 91 instances of (22)).

(22)   a.   ***eux-autres***   ***ils***   *ont*   *pris*   *du*   *porto*
            them-others   3P   have   taken   of.the   port
            'They had some port.'

        b.   *l'Armée du Salut*   ***eux-autres***   ***ils***   *sont*   *au* ...
            the.Salvation Army   them-others   3P   are   at
            'The Salvation Army, they are at ...'

(23)   a.   *mais* ***eux-autres***   *sont*   *en*   *ville*   *là*
            but   them-others   are   in   town   there
            'But they are in town.'

        b.   *que* ***eux-autres***   *sont*   *pas*   *conscients*
            that   them-others   are   NEG   aware
            'They are not aware.'

The reinforcement by *autres* 'others' also appears with first and second person plural. It is significant that *ils autres* doesn't appear, another indication that *ils* is no longer the (phrasal) subject in this variety as well.

Having shown that third person pronouns, such as *il* and *ils*, were perhaps late to reanalyze as agreement, we will argue that they are now possibly ahead in terms of the subject cycle because they are left out in favor of the emphatic pronoun. This shows that certain stages in the cycle can be skipped. We'll turn to objects next.

4.   Changes in object pronouns

The preverbal object pronoun interferes with the preverbal subject agreement by separating it from the verb. Because of this interference with the subject cycle, we hypothesized that some changes might occur with the objects as well: (a) some preverbal object pronouns are reanalyzed as postverbal, (b) the object pronoun is itself becoming an agreement marker, and (c) the object pronoun disappears and the verb becomes intransitive. We'll discuss these three possible changes after first examining the frequency of subject markers used on their own as well as their frequency with intervening object and negative clitics. This is important because it constitutes the input for the child learning the language (and changing it).

4.1   Acquisition

In the Corpus d'entretiens spontanés, there are 63 instances of the first person pronoun followed by a clitic, as in (24), and then the inflected form of *avoir* 'have'. There are 16 instances of the negative clitic preceding the verb and 441 instances of *je* immediately followed by this verb, as in (25). That means 84% have *j'* immediately preceding the finite verb and that's the input a child gets for agreement status.[7] There are a few instances with two preverbal clitics, as in (26) but we didn't count those as a separate category.

(24) *Moi, mes quatre enfants, **je les**   **ai**   mis à   l'école...*
      Me, my four   kids,   1s 3P.ACC have put in the.school
      'I've put my four kids in school.'

(25) ***J'ai***   *appris moi-même, avec des livres et   ... parce*
      1s.have learned my-self   with PRT books and ... because

      que j'aimais ça.
      1s.love   that

      'I have taught myself with books because I love it.'

(26) ***Je ne l'ai***   *pas vu*
      1s not 3s.ACC.have not seen
      'I haven't seen it.'

In the *Orléans Corpus*, the percentage of preverbal object pronouns is much lower and therefore the number of cases where *j'* immediately precedes the finite *ai* is high, namely 91%.

Let's say the input of additional material between the subject and verb is between 9% (*Orléans Corpus*) and 16% (*CdES*). This is apparently enough for objects to continue to be able to precede the verb. Children learning French experiment a little, as (27) shows with the non-adult forms in bold. Madeleine is one of the children described in the *Paris Corpus* (cf. Parisse & Morgenstern 2010), available from the Childes database.

(27) a. *là   il   en   boit   **de** **l'eau***
          there 3SM of.it drinks PRT PRT.water
          'He is drinking water.'   (Madeleine, 1.09.03)

      b. ***le***   *ça   mets là*
          3s.ACC that put there
          'Put it there.'   (Madeleine, 1.09.03)

In (27a), *en* doubles the object *de l'eau*, which is not possible in Formal French, although we find it in the corpora, as we'll discuss in Section 4.2. In formal adult French, *en* is used as partitive but, in (27a), it is used as doubling, a sign that the object marker *en* is treated as agreement. In (27b), there are two preverbal objects, *le* and *ça*, which both refer to the

---

7. With the verbs *être* 'to be' and *avoir* 'to have', there is still an audible difference between first person singular and the second/third person. We calculated the numbers for *avoir* because it is a frequent verb and auxiliary.

same object and which are therefore not possible in adult French.[8] Their order is not as expected either because *le* should be closer to the verb and follow it and *ça* should also follow the verb. The child is obviously experimenting with the status of these forms.

If we look at the triggers for these sentences, it is clear the child is not hearing the forms in the input but is making them up. Thus, (27a) is in response to the mother's utterance in (28a) where the mother's sentence lacks the preverbal *en*. The mother repeats it as (28b) after the child's sentence, again without *en*.

(28) a. *et   i(l) boit   **son lait** dans sa … dans sa   tasse*
        and   3sm   drinks his   milk in   his   in   his cup
        'and he drinks his milk from his cup.'   (Madeleine's mother)

    b. *et   oui là   i(l)   peut boire **l'eau***
        and   yes there 3sm   can   drink the.water
        'and, yes, he can drink the water there.'   (Madeleine's mother)

A month or so later, the child has come closer to the adult forms, as (29) shows.

(29) *i(l)   boit   le   lait*
      3sm   drinks the   milk
      'He is drinking the milk.'   (Madeleine, 1.10.07)

In (27a), the child is experimenting with preverbal clitics; in (27b), the use of both *le* and *ça* shows that the status of these forms is not immediately clear to the child. The clitics change to the adult forms quickly but they give us insight into why the language is changing.

4.2 Three changes

As mentioned above, three responses are possible to the problem of a pronoun that is stuck between an agreement marker and the verb, namely (a) its loss, and thereby a loss of transitivity, (b) a change in status, from pronoun to agreement, and (c) a change in position, from preverbal to postverbal object.

Much is known from the literature about the phenomenon in (a) and we therefore won't examine it any further here. Object loss, as between (30a) and (30b), has been documented by Lambrecht & Lemoine (1996), Larjavaara (2000), and Noailly (1997) for adult French and for L1 acquisition by Jakubowicz et al. (1997) and Grüter (2006a) and for L2 acquisition by Grüter (2006b).

(30) a. *Je   l'ai   trouvé hier*
        1s   it.have found   yesterday

---

8. As was pointed out by a reviewer, the first *le* could be an article.

b. ***J'ai***   *trouvé hier.*
1s.have   found yesterday
'I found it yesterday.'

Object loss is of course the least complex way to remove the object pronoun but since it loses a lot of the underlying structure it probably cannot occur full scale.

The second change is related to the status of the pronoun. There are specific changes in the phonology of preverbal markers, as outlined in e.g. Morin (1979). There is variation in how two preverbal syllables with a schwa vowel are pronounced in spoken French: either, as in (31a), the second schwa deletes or, as in (31b), the first schwa deletes. Table 4 provides some of these combinations.

(31)   a.   [ʒəlvwa]

       b.   [ʒləvwa]
          je   le   vois
          1s   him   see
          'I see him.'

Table 4. Portmanteau morphemes with first and second person subjects and other objects

1S subject je			2S subject tu	
and 1S object	je me	[ʒəm] or [ʒmə]	tu me	[tym]
and 2S	je te	[ʃtə]	tu te	[tyt]
and 3SM	je le	[ʒəl] or [ʒlə]	tu le	[tyl]
and 3SF	je la	[ʒəla] or [ʒla]	tu la	[tyla]
and 1P	je nous	[ʒnu]	tu nous	[tynu]
and 2P	je vous	[ʒvu]	tu vous	[tyvu]
and 3P	je les	[ʒəle] or [ʒle]	tu les	[tyle]
and 3SM.DAT	je lui	[ʒəlɥi]], [ʒlɥi], [ʒɥi], or [ʒi]	tu lui	[tylɥi]
and 3P.Dat	je leur	[ʒlœʁ]	tu leur	[tylœʁ]
and en	j'en	[ʒã]	tu en	[tã]
and y	j'y	[ʒi]	tu y	[tɥi] or [ti]

If both subject and object pronouns are reanalyzed as agreement markers, we could analyze [ʒlə] and [ʒəl] in (31) as portmanteau morphemes spelling out the features of the subject and object. The evidence for such a reanalysis would be if *le, y,* and *en* became obligatory with the verbs that select PPs. Instances such as (32), where the clitic and the PP are both present, have indeed become frequent in Colloquial French but haven't reached the stage where they are obligatorily used.

(32)   a.   *J'y   vais à la piscine*
           1s.there go   to the pool
           'I am going to the pool.'

       b.   *J'en   parle de   ce   film*
           1s.about.it speak about that film
           'I am talking about the film.'

There is evidence in the corpora for this change in some speakers, as shown in (33), from the *Orléans corpus*.

(33)   a.   *mais en FRANCE ils en mangent du   pain*
           but in France 3P it eat   PRT bread
           'But in France, they eat bread.'

       b.   *j'en   parle de   ça   en même temps*
           1s.about.it talk about that at same time
           'I talk about it at the same time.'

       c.   *comme des fois on en   discute de   ça*
           like   the times 1P about.it discusses about that
           'Like when we discussed it.'

The third reanalysis that could occur is a change in the position of the pronoun, as from (34a) and (35a) to (34b) and (35b) respectively. This situation is complicated because a myriad of clitics can appear, both locative and argumental *y*, partitive *en*, and various object clitics. We'll restrict ourselves to examining *y* and *le, l',* and *la*.

(34)   a.   *J'y   travaille*
           1s.there work
           'I work there.'

       b.   *Je travaille là*
           1s work   there
           'I work there.'

(35)   a.   *L'agressivité, j'y   travaille*
           Aggression   1s.on.it work
           'Agression, I am working on it.' (from ⟨www.leparisien.fr⟩)

       b.   *Je travaille/pense à   ça*
           1s work/think   on that
           'I'm working on it'

This shift in position is a change we can check for using corpus data. In the *Orléans corpus*, there are 844 instances of *y* – we have excluded the existential *il y a* 'there is/are', idiomatic expressions, and *y* preceding non-finite verbs. This leaves 45 instances of *y* preceding the verb, as in (36).

(36) a. *j' **y**   ai laissé pour ainsi dire ma santé*
              1s.there have left for so say my health
              'I have left my health there so to speak.'

      b. *les cours on **y**   va on y   va pas*
              the classes 1p there go 1p there go NEG
              'We go to classes, we don't go to classes

      c. *ça choque pas on **y** est habitué   maintenant*
              this shocks NEG 1p to.it is accustomed now
              'This doesn't shock (us), we are used to it now.'

      d. *j' **y** suis un peu habituée   du   fait que MICHEL*
              1s.to.it am a   little accustomed to.the fact that MICHEL

              euh il cause anglais très bien
              eh 3s speaks English very well

              'I am somewhat used to the fact that Michel speaks English very well.'

In comparison, the postverbal *là, là-dedans, là-dessus, là-bas,* and *à ça,* as in (37), which can be replaced by *y,* are much more frequent, numbering 70.

(37) a. *qui veulent que leurs enfants aillent jouer **là-dedans***
              who want   that their children go   play   over-there
              'who want for their children to go play over there.'

      b. *il y   a presque personne qui va   **là-dedans***
              3s there is almost nobody who goes there
              'Hardly anybody goes there.'

      c. *ils se   basent **là-dessus***
              they REFL base   there
              'They are based on that.'

We also looked at *le, l',* and *la* objects before finite verbs in the *Orléans Corpus,* as in (38), of which there are 196 occurrences. In comparison, there are 106 cases with a postverbal object *ça,* as in (39), that could be *le,l',* or *la,* i.e. 35% of the combined numbers. The data appear in Table 5.

(38) *la langue de Bretagne je ne   l'a   comprends pas*
        the language of Brittany 1s NEG it.have understood NEG
        'I don't understand the language of Brittany.'

(39) *le gouvernement aura   compris   ça*
        the government   will.have understood that
        'The government will have understood it.'

Table 5. Some pre- and post-verbal objects in the *Orléans corpus*

Preverbal			Postverbal		
locative	y	45	locative	là, etc	70
argument	le, l', la	196	argument	ça	106
Total		241	Total		176

These data indicate that, although preverbal markers are more frequent, the postverbal pronouns are not rare.

In this section, we have seen that preverbal objects occur in the data (possibly between 9 and 16%) but that some of them are lost, reordered, or reanalyzed. These are alternative strategies to avoid preverbal objects. We don't have spoken data from earlier periods so it is hard to see a change in progress. The change in the behavior of pronominal objects triggered by the grammaticalization processes affecting the subject markers can be understood in terms of an object cycle. In the next section, we will examine the processes involved in the object cycle.

5.   The object cycle in general and in French

A typical object cycle is given in (40), again a fictitious case for ease of exposition. Let's say that a language has a fully independent object pronoun, as in stage (40a). Since this pronoun can be coordinated and modified and need not be close to a verb, it is a full phrase. A possible next stage is for speakers to optionally analyze this object pronoun as a head, as in (40b). This head cannot be coordinated or modified and is phonologically dependent on the verb. The next stage might be for the object to be reanalyzed as an agreement marker. Once it has these features, it could be renewed through an emphatic or some other form, as in (40c). The last stage, as in (40d), is similar to the first with the agreement lost and the emphatic counting as the regular argument.

(40)   a.   I saw yesterday her (and him).
       b.   I saw 'r (*and him).
       c.   I saw'r HER.
       d.   I saw her.

As in the case of the subject cycle, if languages reanalyze pronouns as agreement markers, one expects cross-linguistic surveys of languages to reflect this. Siewierska's (2013) data suggest that verbal object marking occurs in 57% of the languages surveyed, i.e. stage (b), but not much is known about the obligatory appearance of object pronouns.

What is the stage of the object cycle that French is in? Kayne (1975: 82) notes that they are clitics and not pronouns in that they cannot be contrastively stressed. They need not appear when nominal objects are present so are not yet agreement markers and seem between stage (40a) and (40b). There are of course frequent doublings, as in (33) above and in (41), but these are not as frequent as subject doublings and have a different prosody from the subject doublings (see Culbertson & Legendre 2008).

(41) ***Celui-là,*** *je l'ai   pas vu.*
      That.there 1s 3s.have NEG seen
      'I haven't seen that one.'

If the changes to the preverbal objects that we have discussed in Section 4.2 continue, however, we expect to see many preverbal object pronouns reanalyze as agreement markers, i.e. from stage (40b) to (40c). So, the reaction of object pronouns to changes in subjects may accelerate the object cycle.

The change where preverbal objects are being replaced by postverbal pronouns is interesting in that this development, when seen in terms of the cycle in (40), seems to be a fast version of the object cycle, skipping the stage where the object clitic is an agreement marker, so from stage (40b) to (40d).

6. Account and puzzles

The Subject Cycle is pretty advanced in spoken French. Pre-theoretically, this means that the object clitic/pronoun doesn't fit the templatic order any more. In this section, we discuss this order and a contemporary generative tree structure where a subject agreement is incompatible with the other clitics.

The preverbal template for French, and for many other Romance languages, is often given as it appears in Table 6 (cf. e.g. Jones 1996: 253) where items from column 4 can appear with those from 1, 2, and 3 and with those from 1 and 5. These combinatorial restrictions are also known as the Person Case Constraint (see e.g. Béjar & Rezac 2003), which basically says that first and second person don't like to be the lowest arguments. This is a complication we won't address.

Structural representations for this template have been given by, among others, Sportiche (1996) and Ciucivara (2009). For Sportiche, each clitic has a voice projection in the head of which the clitic is base generated and to the Spec of which the (empty) argument DP moves at Logical Form; for Ciucivara, there are separate case (KP) and person (PersonP) phrases that clitics move to as they first check their case and then move to a position specific to their person. A derivation of this kind for Standard French in (42) has clitic phrases that house the clitics. These phrases would be above the T to which head the verb moves and the order of object clitics and finite verbs would be derived. The nominative *il* would be in a clitic phrase that is the highest, as in (43).

Table 6. Formal French pronoun/clitic template

Position	1	2	3	4	5	6	7	
	Subject	Negative	1+2+refl se	3	3	LOC	PART/ARG	VERB
			ACC+DAT	ACC	DAT			
	je	ne	me			y	en	
	tu		te					
	il/elle			le/la	lui			
	nous/on		nous					
	vous		vous					
	ils/elles			les	leur			

(42) *Il   me   la   recommandait.*   Formal French
      3SM 1S.DAT 3SF.ACC recommended
      'He recommended her to me.'

(43)

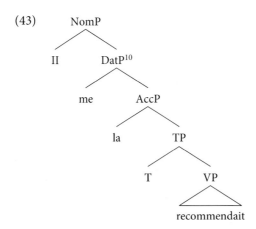

We will now discuss the issue of what is happening to the subject when it becomes agreement in spoken French. We assume with Sportiche and others that a tree with object clitics includes case phrases; we have represented the subject agreement *je* on T (but it could be an Agr(eement)P as well). This configuration, sketched as (44), cannot result in a grammatical output because the object pronouns would not occur between the subject and the verb.

---

9.   Sportiche (1996) actually gives third person direct and indirect object examples and then the order of the AccP and DatP is reversed.

(44)

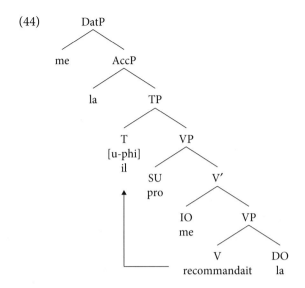

It is therefore either avoided in the spoken colloquial variety, as in (6b), (29b), (33b) and (34b), or reanalyzed as a portmanteau, as in (31) and (32). The structure with portmanteau morpheme for (41) is given in (45).

(45)

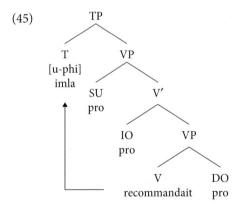

In (45), there is a portmanteau morpheme in T checking the phi-features of the null pronouns in argument positions.

7.   Conclusion

In keeping with the literature on the status of French subject pronouns, we see many changes occurring both with subjects and with preverbal objects. In this paper, after reviewing the situation with the different person markers in Section 2, we add a discussion of some new developments in third person subject pronouns in Section 3. We consider these as an acceleration of the subject cycle in that the agreement prefix is left out and the emphatic form serves as the regular pronoun.

A second point to the paper is to see if there are changes to preverbal object pronouns and, in Section 4, we argue that there are three kinds of changes, namely a loss of the object pronoun, a reanalysis to agreement marker, and a change from pre- to postverbal position. These changes are to be expected because we are mixing object clitics and inflectional subject affixes. The result may be an accelerated object cycle, as pointed out in Section 5. In Section 6, we have provided an account for the changes in object pronouns that result from the changes in subject markers using a generative model with feature checking.

References

Ashby, William. 1977. *Clitic Inflection in French*. Amsterdam: Rodopi.

Auger, Julie. 1996. Subject-clitic inversion in Romance: A morphological analysis. In *Aspects of Romance Linguistics,* Claudia Parodi, Carlos Quicoli, Mario Saltarelli & María Luisa Zubizarreta (eds). Washington DC: Georgetown University Press.

Baissac, Charles. 1880. *Etude sur le patois créole mauricien*. Nancy: Berger-Levrault.

Béjar, Susana & Rezac, Milan. 2003. Person Licensing and the derivation of PCC effects. In *Romance Linguistics. Theory and Acquisition* [Current Issues in Linguistic Theory 244], Ana Teresa Pérez-Leroux & Yves Roberge (eds), 49–62. Amsterdam: John Benjamins. doi:10.1075/cilt.244.07bej

Bybee, Joan. 1985. *Morphology*. Armstrdam: John Benjamins. doi:10.1075/tsl.9

Ciucivara, Oana. 2009. A Syntactic Analysis of Pronominal Clitic Clusters in Romance. Ph.D. dissertation, New York University.

Corpus de français parlé au Québec, CFPQ, is a multi-modal corpus that contains 471,575 words from the current century. ⟨http://recherche.flsh.usherbrooke.ca/cfpq/index.php/site/index⟩

Corpus d'entretiens spontanés, CdES, contains 155,000 words or transcribed spoken French from 1988 to 1990. ⟨https://www.llas.ac.uk/resourcedownloads/80/mb016corpus.pdf⟩

Culbertson, Jenny & Legendre, Géraldine. 2008. Qu'en est-il des clitiques sujet en français oral contemporain? In *Actes du 1er Congrès Mondial de Linguistique Française*, Jacques Durand, Benoît Habert & Bernard Laks (eds), 2651–2662. Paris: EDP Sciences.

Dryer, Matthew. 2013. Expression of pronominal subjects. In *The World Atlas of Language Structures*, Matthew S. Dryer & Martin Haspelmath (eds). Leipzig: Max Planck Institute for Evolutionary Anthropology. ⟨http://wals.info/chapter/101⟩ (8 October 2014).

ELICOP Corpus, includes the Orléans, Tours, and Auvergne corpora. The *Orléans Corpus* (ESLO)contains 902,755 words of transcribed spoken French from 1966 to 1970. ⟨http://bach.arts.kuleuven.be/pmertens/corpus/search/t.html⟩

Fonseca-Greber, Bonnibeth. 2000. The Change from Pronoun to Clitic to prefix and the Rise of Null Subjects in Spoken Swiss French. Ph.D. dissertation, University of Arizona.

Fonseca-Greber, Bonnie & Waugh, Linda. 2003. The subject clitics of European Conversational French: Morphologization, grammatical change, semantic change, and change in progress. In *A Romance Perspective on Language Knowledge and Use* [Current Issues in Linguistic Theory 238], Rafael Núñez-Cedeño, Luis López & Richard Cameron (eds), 99–118. Amsterdam: John Benjamins. doi:10.1075/cilt.238.10fon

Foulet, Lucien. 1919. *Petite Syntaxe de L'ancien Français*. Paris: Honoré Champion. 3rd edn 1961.

van Gelderen, Elly. 2011. *The Linguistic Cycle*. Oxford: OUP.
doi: 10.1093/acprof:oso/9780199756056.001.0001

Grüter, Therese. 2006a. Object clitics and null objects in the acquisition of French. Ph.D. dissertation, McGill University.

Grüter, Therese. 2006b. Object (clitic) omission in L2 French. In *GASLA Proceedings*, Mary Grantham O'Brien, Christine Shea & John Archibald (eds), 63–71. Somerville MA: Cascadilla.

Heine, Bernd & Song, Kyung-an. 2011. On the grammaticalization of personal pronouns. *Journal of Linguistics* 47: 587–630. doi: 10.1017/S0022226711000016

Jakubowicz, Celia, Müller, Natascha, Riemer, Beate & Rigaut, Catherine. 1997. The case of subject and object omissions in French and German. In *Proceedings of the 21st Annual Boston University Conference on Language Development*, Elizabeth Hughes, Mary Hughes & Annabel Greenhill (eds), 331–342. Somerville MA: Cascadilla.

Jelinek, Eloise. 1984. Empty categories, case, and configurationality. *Natural Language and Linguistic Theory* 2: 39–76. doi: 10.1007/BF00233713

Jones, Michael. 1996. *Foundations of French Syntax*. Cambridge: CUP.
doi: 10.1017/CBO9780511620591

Kayne, Richard. 1975. *French Syntax*. Cambridge MA: The MIT Press.

Lambrecht, Knud. 1981. *Topic, Antitopic, and Verb Agreement in Non-Standard French* [Pragmatics & Beyond II:6]. Amsterdam: John Benjamins. doi: 10.1075/pb.ii.6

Lambrecht, Knud & Lemoine, Kevin. 1996. Vers une grammaire des compléments zéro en francais parlé. In *Travaux linguistiques de CERLICO* 9, Jean Chuquet & Marc Fryd (eds), 279–309. Rennes: Presses universitaires de Rennes.

Larjavaara, Meri. 2000. Présence ou absence de l'object. ⟨http://ethesis.helsinki.fi/julkaisut/hum/romaa/vk/larjavaara/presence.pdf⟩

Morin, Yves-Charles. 1979. La morphophonologie des pronoms clitiques en français populaire. *Cahier de Linguistique* 9: 1–36. doi: 10.7202/800076ar

Noailly, Michèle. 1997. Les mystères de la transitivité invisible. *Languages* 127: 96–109.
doi: 10.3406/lgge.1997.2127

Offroy, Geneviève. 1975. Contribution à l'étude de la syntaxe québécoise d'après la langue des journaux. *Travaux de linguistique du Quebec* 1: 257–322.

Parisse, Christophe & Morgenstern, Aliyah. 2010. Transcrire et analyser les corpus d'enfant. In *Acquisition du langage et interaction*, Edy Veneziano, Anne Salazar Orvig & Josie Bernicot (eds), 201–222. Paris: L'Harmattan.

Sportiche, Dominique. 1996. Clitic constructions. In *Phrase Structure and the Lexicon* [Studies in Natural Language and Linguistic Theory 33], Johan Rooryck & Laurie Zaring (eds), 213–276. Dordrecht: Kluwer. doi: 10.1007/978-94-015-8617-7_9

Siewierska, Anna. 2008. Verbal person marking. In *The world Atlas of Language Structures Online*, Martin Haspelmattew Dryer, David Gil & Bernard Comrie (eds). Munich: Max Planck Digital Library, chapter 102. Available online at http://wals.info/feature/102.

Siewierska, Anna. 2013. Verbal person marking. In *The World Atlas of Language Structures*, Matthew S. Dryer & Martin Haspelmath (eds). Leipzig: Max Planck Institute for Evolutionary Anthropology. ⟨http://wals.info/chapter/102⟩ (8 October 2014).

von Wartburg, Walter. 1943. *Einführung in die Problematik und Methodik der Sprachwissenschaft*. Tübingen: Niemeyer.

de Wind, Maarten. 1995. Inversion in French. Ph.D. dissertation, University of Groningen.

Zribi-Hertz, Anne. 1994. La syntaxe des clitiques nominatifs. *Travaux de Linguistique et Litterature* XXXII: 131–147.

PART III

The negative micro-cycles

The negative existential cycle viewed through the lens of comparative data

Ljuba N. Veselinova
Stockholm University

In this paper a family-based sample is used in order to test the model of evolution of standard negation markers from negative existentials suggested by Croft (1991) and known as the Negative Existential Cycle (NEC). The comparative data collected here were analyzed and classified following the definitions of type/stages suggested in the original model. The data collected here were also analyzed from a diachronic perspective and whenever possible also supplied with historical information. It is found that the stages with variation are dominant in the families under study. Consequently they are considered to be far more important for this cycle than the stages without variation. Furthermore, the stages with variation are not only synchronically frequent, they are also diachronically stable as they can be demonstrated to last for very long periods of time. The data collected here also suggest that the NEC is rarely completed within a time span for reasonable reconstruction. This is attributed to the importance of the distinction between negation of actions and negation of existence and its contant renewal in human languages.

1. Introduction

The Negative Existential Cycle (hereafter NEC)[1] was proposed by Croft (1991) as a way of modeling the evolution of standard negation markers (hereafter SN) from existential negators; cf. (1b) and (1d) below for introductory illustrations of these different kinds of negators. As illustrated in (1) below, in Turkish, SN is expressed by a suffix -mA[2] whereas the negation of existential sentences is expressed by the semi-verb *yok* which replaces its positive counterpart *var*. The NEC as laid out by Croft puts forth a

---

1. Kahrel (1996) dubbed this cycle as *The Croft Cycle*; the model is referred to under this name in other works as well, see for instance Mosegaard-Hansen (2011) for a relatively recent reference. Here I am keeping Croft's original denomination *The Negative Existential Cycle*.

2. The quality of the vowel is determined by vowel harmony.

DOI 10.1075/la.227.06ves

hypothesis about the evolution of SN from special existential negators as they gradually expand their use into negating verbs.

(1)   Turkish (Turkic, Common Turkic, Oghuz-Uighur-Kipchak, Oghuz) [tur][3]
    a.   *Gel-ecek*
       come-FUT
       '(S)he will come.'   (van Schaaik 1994: 38)

    b.   *Gel-me-yecek*
       come-NEG-FUT
       '(S)he will not come.'   (van Schaaik 1994: 38)

    c.   *Su   var-dı*
       water exist-PST
       'There was water.'   (van Schaaik 1994: 44)

    d.   *Su   yok-tu*
       water NEG.EX-PST
       'There was no water.'   (van Schaaik 1994: 44)

Before we proceed with the presentation, a few definitions are in order. For the concept of SN, I follow Dahl (2010) and Miestamo (2005). As discussed in these works, SN refers to negation in simple declarative sentences with an overt verb predicate as in (1b) above. In my work, I use the terms SN and *verbal negation* interchangeably. Negation of all other kinds of predications is excluded from SN because in many languages they may be negated by strategies that differ from SN. For the notion of *construction*, I follow Croft (2001: 18), whereby constructions are defined as symbolic units of form and meaning linked by symbolic correspondence. Constructions can be *atomic*, that is consisting of a single lexical item, or they can cover collocational schemas such as *be going to* INF, which expresses future time reference for the verb in the infinitive slot. The term *existential predication/existential sentence* is used here to refer to *grammaticalized existential constructions;* the latter may show one or more of the following characteristics: non-referential subject, usually marked by a non-prototypical subject marking; word order that differs from dominant word orders in the language; special agreement or no agreement between subject and predicate (whenever agreement is relevant); a predicate (item) with a special morphology (see Givón (1979), Hengeveld (1992) Stassen (1997), (Dryer 2007) for further discussion). Finally, the NEC is an example of dynamicization of a typology, that is, a synchronic typology is given a dynamic interpretation. Therefore, I will be using the terms *type* and *stage* interchangeably.

3.   All classifications given here follow Glottolog 2.3, ⟨http://glottolog.org⟩. The ISO-693 code of each language is cited as well.

Despite recent renewed interest in cyclical processes in language change and negative cycles in particular (van Gelderen 2008; 2009), the negative existential cycle has received relatively little attention. The NEC is based on cross-linguistic data. The study presented here is part of a larger project where the ultimate goal is to test the NEC on a family-based sample that covers all major macro-linguistic areas cf. Dryer (Dryer 1992). In this article data from Eurasia predominate; the families compared here include Slavic, Uralic, Turkic and Dravidian; two other areas are represented by one family each, North-West Africa by Berber and Oceania by Polynesiann. Testing the cycle involves (i) checking which of the language types/stages of change suggested in the NEC are actually instantiated in specific families, and (ii) outlining pathways of transition between different types. In other words, by testing this model, my goal is to outline the stages involved in the evolution of a negative existential into a standard negator as well as the processes which lead from one stage to another. These issues have already been discussed for Slavonic, Polynesian and Uralic, see Section 4 below for a more detailed summary of my recent work, (Veselinova 2014; Veselinova 2015).

The comparative data examined here allow for the following generalizations. A time dimension needs to be added to this diachronic model. In the literature on linguistic cycles, see (van Gelderen 2009; Willis et al. 2013: 22), it is typically noted that the rate of change varies considerably from one language to another. Consequently, the duration of a cycle is hard to predict. However, the evolution of negative existentials into markers of standard negation appears to be consistently of a lengthier kind. In fact, the full completion of the NEC appears to occur very rarely within a period that allows for reasonable reconstruction. On the other hand, stages where the negative existential is used for specific sub-domains in the negation of verbs are very frequent and tend to last for very long periods of time. Finally, negative existentials are constantly recreated since they represent a basic functional domain, cf. (Veselinova 2013a). When the NEC turns full circle, the distinction between negation of action and negation of existence is obliterated. This is probably why the NEC is completed so seldom.

This article is organized as follows. In Section 2, I offer an overview of the NEC with pertinent examples. In Section 3, I present the application of the NEC on the language families examined here. In Section 4, I summarize the findings of my recently published work on the NEC. Section 5 is devoted to a diachronic analysis of the comparative data from Berber, Turkic and Dravidian languages. A summarizing discussion concludes the article in Section 6.

2.   Overview of the negative existential cycle

As pointed out above, the NEC is based on cross-linguistic data and consists of six language types. Three of the types suggested in NEC are invariant in their expression of negation in both verbal and existential predications. In the model they are referred to as *stable* types. They alternate with languages that exhibit variation in their negation strategies in either SN or existential negation; the latter are said to be *transitional* types. The terms *stable* and *transitional* are used in both Croft's work and here in a variationist sense. Thus they do not necessarily refer to diachronic stability or instability.

The stable types are labeled A, B, C; the transitional types A~B, B~C, C~A. In type A, there is no distinction between SN and existential negation; one and the same negator, the SN marker, is used for both, cf. (2).

(2) Niue (Austronesian, [...] Polynesian, Tongic) [niu]
Standard negation

a. *Ne nākai fano kehe a ia*
PST NEG go.SG away S 3SG
'He didn't go.'   (Veselinova 2014:1345 citing Polinskaja 1995:71)

Existential negation (=SN)

b. *Nākai hā hinei e tama*
NEG EX here ART boy
'There are no boys here.'
(Veselinova 2014:1345 citing Polinskaja 1995:78)

In type A~B, there is a special existential negator but it is restricted to a specific context. For instance, in Zyryan Komi, cf. (3) below, existential predications in the present tense are negated by the special form *abu*-AGR, as illustrated by (3)a. In non-present tenses, the SN marker has to be used; in Zyryan Komi, as in many other Uralic languages, it is expressed by a negative auxiliary which is used with a special form of the main verb, labeled *connegative* in Uralic linguistics.[4] In the case of negated existential predications with past and future time reference cited in (3)b. the negative auxiliary *o-/e-* agrees with the subject according to number; the main verb is 'be' and it appears in its connegative form *lo*. Both the negative auxiliary and the verb 'be' use suppletive stems for the past versus present/future forms.

(3) Zyryan Komi (Uralic, Permic) [kpv]

a. *taṯin mort-jas abu-ęś*
there human.being-PL NEG.EX-PL
'there are no people there'
(Veselinova 2015: 565 citing Hamari 2007:90)

---

4. See Comrie (1981) and Miestamo (2005) for general overviews of negation in Uralic languages.

b. *Mijan   Mamant kodˀ mort-is̩   vojvil-in̩*
    1PL.GEN Mamant like person-POSS.3SG north-INE

    e–z   na vev̩   i   o–z   lo
    NEG.PST-3 yet be.PST.CNEG.SG and NEG.PRS-3 be.FUT.CNEG.SG

    'So far, there was no person like our Mamant in the north and there
    will not be, [–]'   (Veselinova 2015: 565 citing Arja Hamari p.c.)

In type B, the special existential negator is the only possibility for the negation of existential predications. For instance, in Turkish the SN suffix -*mA* is completely ruled out for their negation, cf. (4b).

(4) Turkish (Turkic, Common Turkic, Oghuz-Uighur-Kipchak, Oghuz) [tur]

    a. *Su   var/var-dı*
        water exist/exist-PST
        'There is/was water.'   (van Schaaik 1994: 44)

    b *Su   yok/yok-tu*
        water NEG.EX/NEG.EX-PST
        'There is/was no water.'   (van Schaaik 1994: 44)

In type B~C, the negative existential is used for the negation of some verbal predications. This is illustrated by data from Zyryan Komi. This language also demonstrates the overlap of two different, non-sequential types of the NEC, an issue to which I will return in 3.2. As demonstrated in (3) above, Zyryan Komi instantiates the transitional stage/type A~B since its negative existential *abu*-AGR is restricted to the present tense. However, the same word *abu* is also used for the negation of verbs in the perfect and pluperfect tenses, cf. (5) below. This in turn calls for classifying the language in type B~C of the cycle as well. When used as a verbal negator, the word *abu* does not take any agreement markers. The use of *abu* in (5) is a good example of a straightforward grammaticalization process: (i) the lexical sense of the item is no longer relevant or even gone, its finite markers are also discarded; (ii) it looks more like an invariable particle and it is used with a fairly abstract function. Within the NEC, type B~C typically represents the diachronic stage where the negative existential is expanding its domain of use; however, as shown by Bulgarian (20) and Old Church Slavonic (21) below, this is not always the case.

(5) Zyryan Komi (Uralic, Permic) [kpv]

    a. *mun-e̩m-a*
        go-PRF-1SG
        'I have gone'   (Hamari 2011)

    b. *Abu   mun-e̩m-a*
        NEG.PRF go-PRF-1SG
        'I have not gone',   (Hamari 2011)

    c.   *me vẹl-i   mun-a*
           1SG be-PST1 go-1SG
           'I was going'   (Hamari 2011, citing Cypanov 2007:255)

    d.   *me vẹl-i   o–g   mun*
           1SG be-PST1 NEG-1 go.CNEG.SG
           'I was not going'   (Hamari 2011, citing Cypanov 2007:255)

In type C, the negative existential is used as SN but the constructions where it is used differ for the negation of verbs and for the negation of existential predications. The negative constructions may differ in terms of morphology or in terms of syntax, or both. The examples below show constructions which differ in terms of morphology from Kannada and in terms of syntactic structure from Māori.

In Spoken Kannada verbal predications are negated by a suffix *-illa* which is attached to a gerundial form of the verb, cf. (6a). The same form, *illa* is used for the negation of existential predications but there it is a free form, cf. (6b).

  (6) Spoken Kannada (Dravidian, South) [kan]

    a.   *anil   ka:le:jige   ho:gu-vud-illa*
           name college.DAT go-NONPST.GER-NEG
           'Anil won't/doesn't go to college'   (Sridhar 1990:111)

    b.   *Khaja:neyalli haNa   illa*
           Treasury.LOC money NEG.EX
           'There is no money in the treasury'   (Sridhar 1990:112)

Māori is used to illustrate a language where the negation constructions for verbal predications and those for existential predications differ in terms of syntax but not in form. Similarly to many other Polynesian languages, negation in Māori is expressed by means of a complex clause, cf. (7b) where the negative verb *kāore* appears in sentence initial position (the position of the main predicate) and the order of the verb complex and the noun complex is reversed in the negated sentence.

  (7) Māori, (Austronesian, […] Nuclear Polynesian, Eastern, Tahitic) [mri]

    a.   *E   tangi ana te   tamaiti*
           GENR weep TA   DET child
           'The child is/was crying',   (Harlow 2007:161)

    b.   *Kāore te   tamaiti e   tangi ana*
           NEG   DET child   TA weep TA
           'The child is/was not crying'   (Harlow 2007:161)

The change of constituent order between (7a) and (7b) indicates subordination; the literal translation of the sentence in (7b) is 'There is no child [who] is crying'. Existential predications are strictly non-verbal in Māori, that is, they do not admit of any tense-aspect marking; the negative verb *kāore* appears sentence-initially but the constituent order remains unchanged in both the affirmative and the negated sentence, cf. (8ab).

(8)   Māori, (Austronesian, […] Nuclear Polynesian, Eastern, Tahitic) [mri]

   a. *He whare wānanga kei   Kirikiriroa*
       DET house learning PREP Hamilton
       'There is a university in Hamilton'   (Harlow 2007: 161)

   b. *Kāore he   whare wānanga i   Taihape*
       NEG   DET house learning PREP Taihape
       'There's no university in Taihape'   (Harlow 2007: 161)

Finally, type C~A of the NEC includes languages where the negative existential is observed not only in verbal predications but it has started to negate the affirmative existential as well. This is illustrated by data from East Futuna. Negation in this language is a very complex phenomenon with several different patterns of variation in both the verbal and the existential domain, cf. (Moyse-Faurie 1997; Moyse-Faurie 1999) and also (Veselinova 2014: 1359–1364). Because of these complex variation patterns, the language is classified in three different types of the cycle (B~C, C, and C~A). For the purposes of this overview, I focus only on the following facts: (i) there is a newly created negator *le'ese*. Cf. (9); it is a univerbation between a negative marker/negative existential *le'e* and the indefinite article *se* cf. also (10)B where they appear orthographically as separate words; (ii) the form *le'ese* can be also used for the negation of the affirmative existential as shown in (10)A; however, it is by no means obligatory in this use as demonstrated by (10)B.

(9)   East Futuna (Austronesian […] Polynesian, Nuclear, Samoic-Outlier, Futunic) [fud]

   Na le'ese māsau a   Kalada i   le   fakatasi
   PST NEG   speak ABS Kalada OBL DEF meeting
   'Kalada did not speak during the meeting.'   (Moyse-Faurie 1999: 122)

(10) East Futuna (Austronesian […] Polynesian, Nuclear, Samoic-Outlier, Futunic) [fud]

   A: *E   le'ese iai   se   lāisi*   B: *E'ai, e   le'e   se   lāisi*
      GENR NEG exist INDF rice   No   GENR NEG INDF rice
      'Isn't there any rice?'   'No, there is no rice.'
                             (Moyse-Faurie 1999: 117)

Languages like East Futuna represent the last stage before the completion of the NEC. When the erstwhile existential negator must be used for the negation of the affirmative existential, we are back at the stage where there is no distinction between verbal and existential negation, cf. (2) above. The cyclical process can then be seen as having turned full circle.

   The cycle is schematically represented in Figure 1 below. Boxes with a solid outline represent stable types; boxes with a dashed outline represent transitional types. In the original graphic representation of the cycle, only the stable types were shown.

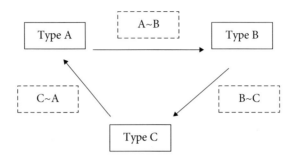

Figure 1. *The Negative Existential Cycle,* adapted from Croft (1991:6)

When the NEC is cited, the general interpretation seems to be that the process evolves from a state where there is no distinction between negation of verbs and negation of existentials to a state where a newly created negative existential establishes a such distinction, and finally to a state where the negative existential ousts the original verbal negator/SN and the state of no distinction between verbal and existential negation is restored again, cf. (Dahl 2010), (Horn 1997), (Hovdaugen & Mosel 1999), (Kahrel & van den Berg 1994), (Mosegaard Hansen 2011), see also (Willis et al. 2013) and (Wilmsen 2014). In other words, in all of the works just mentioned and also in many others, the emphasis lies on the general direction of the cyclical process whereby negative existentials may evolve into more general markers of negation.

The comparative data presented below highlight several aspects of the cycle which have been neglected so far. They include the following: the stages with variation; the sequence of stages in this cycle, and more importantly, the overlap of stages; the time it takes for the NEC to be completed; the nature of negative existentials. In the sections below, I start by presenting the comparative data first by showing how different families are classified in the NEC following the definitions given above. Datasets are presented in pertinent tables in the Appendix.

3.   Application of the cycle on different kinds of samples

A major part of the work conducted here has been devoted to classifying the languages from the world-wide and the family-based samples into the types of the cycle introduced above. Hence I consider it important to present this classification in the graphic form of the cycle in 3.1; a summary and discussion of this classification follows in 3.2.

For the order of the graphs where the families are represented, I follow their geographical location starting from the West and moving to the East. Thus I start with Berber, followed by the families investigated in Eurasia and conclude with Polynesian.

Languages from the family based sample are shown by their ISO-693 codes. For detailed listing of the classification of the world-wide sample, please consult Map 1 in Veselinova (2014: 1383). Languages with complex variation patterns which need to be placed into several types are indicated by a shaded background (such languages are shown by Zyryan Komi in (3) and (5) above, and also by Tamil in (43) below).

3.1 Graphic representation of the collected data

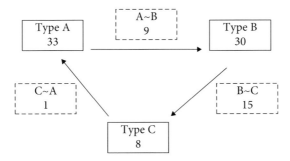

Figure 2. The world-wide sample classified according to the NEC following Veselinova (2014: 1330)

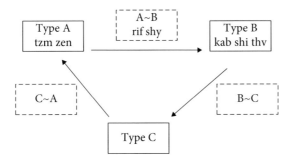

Figure 3. Berber languages classified in the NEC, adapted from (Mettouchi 2009)

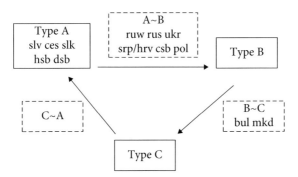

Figure 4. Slavic languages classified in the NEC, adapted from Veselinova (2014: 1336, 1378)

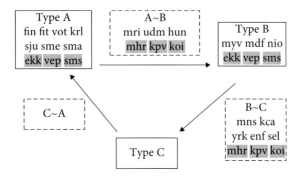

Figure 5. Uralic languages classified in the NEC, adapted from Veselinova (2015: 573–4)

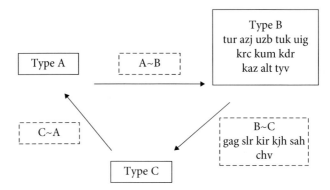

Figure 6. Turkic languages classified in the NEC

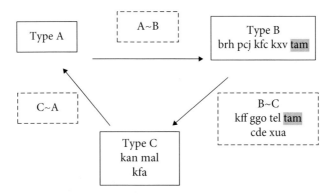

Figure 7. Dravidian languages classified in the Negative existential cycle

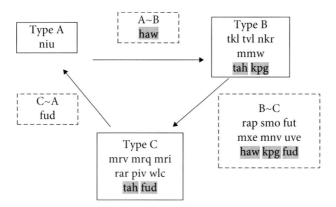

Figure 8. Polynesian languages classified in the NEC, adapted from Veselinova (2014: 1365, 1378–1380)

3.2   Summary and discussion of the types instantiated in the world-wide sample and in the families under study

The classifications presented above allow for the following observations. First, the cycle is instantiated in its entirety in the Polynesian family only and this instantiation is valid when we take into consideration languages with very complex variation patterns, cf. Figure 8. Without invalidating the cycle, this has implications for the length of time required for its completion, especially when the synchronic classifications above are supplied with diachronic information, cf. Section 4 and Section 5 below. Second, the sequence of types as suggested in the original model is not absolute. Croft (1991: 22) does point this out but this is not the way his work is cited so this issue has to be emphasized. The types outlined in the NEC are variationist in nature; thus they tend to co-occur with each other. As shown in 3.2.2 below, there are several cases of overlap between different stages/types in one and the same language. Two of these overlaps appear to be very important as they are observed in several different families and geographical areas and are discussed in more detail in this section. Finally, as will be demonstrated by the counts in Table 1, it is the types with variation that appear to prevail in the families investigated here.

3.2.1   Cross-linguisitic frequency of the NEC types

In Table 1, the raw count (RC) represents the number of languages in a specific type. As shown by the figures above, some languages need to be classified in several types of the NEC due to complex variation patterns. Consequently, the sum (*Sum*) of the raw count shows the number of instantiations of this particular type. The per cent proportion shows the proportion of the RC from the *Sum*.

In the world-wide sample two languages had to be classified into several types (Babole and East Futuna). In the family-based sample, languages with complex variation patterns that had to be classified into several types of the NEC are observed in Uralic, Dravidian and Polynesian. The actual number of languages for these families is 26 Uralic, 12 Dravidian and 22 Polynesian. For Berber, Slavonic and Turkic the sum of the raw count reflects also the number of languages included.

Table 1. Distribution of the different samples across the NEC

	A RC	A %	A~B RC	A~B %	B RC	B %	B~C RC	B~C %	C RC	C %	C~A RC	C~A %	*Sum of RC*
World-wide	33	32.7	9	8.9	30	29.7	15	14.9	8	7.9	1	1.0	97
Berber	2	28.6	2	28.6	3	42.9	–	–	–	–	–	–	7
Slavonic	5	33.3	8	53.3	–	–	2	13.3	–	–	–	–	15
Uralic	11	36. 7	5	16.7	6	20	8	26.7	–	–	–	–	30
Turkic	–	–	–	–	11	64.7	6	35.3	–	–	–	–	17
Dravidian	–	–	–	–	5	35.7	6	42.7	3	21.4	–	–	14
Polynesian	1	3.9	1	3.9	10	38.5	3	11.5	9	34.6	1	3.9	26

As shown in Table 1, in the sample of 95 genealogically and geographically diverse languages, the two most frequent types are types are type A and type B; on the other hand, type C appears to be rather minor. The frequency cline for the world-wide sample is summarized in (11) below.

(11) Frequency cline for world-wide sample
      A (32%) > B (29.7%) > B~C (14.9%)

Generally, this confirms Croft's statement (Croft 1991: 18) that "types A and B are far more common than type C" and that type C~A will be extremely rare. The transitional types are not very well presented in the world-wide sample. Even if type B~C is the third most frequent one cf. (11), it should be also noted that its frequency is substantially lower than those of type A and type B which appear to cover about one third of the sample each.

In the family based sample, type B is by far the most frequent one, followed by the transitional types B~C and A~B, cf. Table 1 above as well as in the graphic representation of the cycle in in the different families in 3.1. The frequency cline for the family based sample is presented in (12) below to facilitate comparison with the most frequent types in the world-wide sample shown in (11).

(12)   Frequency cline for the family-based sample
       B > B~C > A~B

It has to be noted that the only similarity between the world-wide sample and the family-based sample, cf. most frequent types in (11) and (12), is the highly frequent type B, that is, languages with a negative existential which is primarily used for that function. The transitional types B~C and A~B are very frequent in most of the investigated families while these types appear to be rather insignificant in the world-wide sample. Conversely, the stable type A which is observed in one third of the languages in the world-wide sample is present in three families (Berber, Slavic and Uralic) and as good as absent in the other three (Turkic, Dravidian and Polynesian).

3.2.2   *Overlaps of types within the NEC*

As already pointed out, the comparative data from the family-based sample highlight a very important aspect of the NEC namely that the types/stages as outlined in the original model are not sequential but can co-occur within one and the same language. In Section 2 above, the overlap of two transitional types, A~B and B~C was shown using data from Zyryan Komi, cf. Examples (3) and (5) above. Examples of other kinds of overlaps are illustrated below by data from Estonian and Kapingamarangi.

In Estonian we observe an overlap between type A and type B. In this language, SN is expressed by a preverbal particle *ei;* the same particle can be used for the negation of existential predications, as shown in (13a) and (13b). This calls for classifying the language as belonging to type A. However, there is also another particle, *pole*, which can be also used for the negation of existential predications,[5] cf. (13c). Consequently, Estonian can be classified as type B as well.

(13)   Estonian (Uralic, Finnic) [ekk]
       a.   *Maia   ei   laula*
            Maia   NEG   sing.CNG
            'Maia does not sing'   (Miina Norvik, p.c.)
       b.   *külmkapi-s ei   ole   õlu-t*
            fridge-INE   NEG   be.CNG   beer-PART
            'There is no beer in the fridge'   (Diana Krull, p.c.)

---

5.   The special negator *pole* can be used for all kinds of stative predications, cf. Veselinova (2015); however, this is irrelevant for the NEC which is why I am not citing more data from Estonian.

c. *Pole ōlu-t   külmkapi-s*
NEG beer-PART fridge-INE
'There is no beer in the fridge'   (Diana Krull, p.c.)

As shown in (13) above, negation of existential predications in Estonian has two expressions: either the SN marker *ei* or the special negator *pole*. These expressions are in free variation for this function. Consequently, they are considered separate strategies and are classified in appropriate types of the NEC, A and B. Estonian is thus very different from Zyryan Komi, cf. (3) where the use of the special negator *abu*-AGR is restricted to the present tense; the SN strategy has to be used for the negation of existential predications in non-present tenses. The complementary distribution of the special negator and SN in Zyryan Komi motivates the classification of this language in the transitional type A~B.

Another kind of overlap, namely between types B and B~C/C, is shown by Examples (14) and (15) with data from Kapingamarangi, a Polynesian Outlier language from Micronesia. In this language, there are two negative existential *hakarē* and *tēai*, cf. (14b) and (14c). SN is expressed either by the particle *tē* or by the negative existential *hakarē*, cf. (15a–c). In the sources available to me (Elbert 1948) and (Lieber & Dikepa 1974), the SN marker *tē* and the negative existential *hakarē* appear to be in free variation. The same is also valid for *hakarē* and *tēai* when used as negative existentials and related functions.

(14)   Kapingamarangi (Polynesian, Samoic Outlier, Ellicean)[6] [kpg]

a. *Ti   pāhi Ngeiha   i   ai   ti   ēitu*
POSS side northern in/at exist POSS spirit
'There is a spirit at the northern side.'   (Elbert 1948: 17)

b. *Hakarē e   roko*
NEG.EX TA many
'There are not many.'   (Elbert 1948: 30)

c. *koe tēai   tau   mē   e   hai taiā*
2SG NEG.EX 2SG.POSS thing LET's do tomorrow

kitātou   e   hura ki   wērua
1PL.INCL TA go   DIR werua
'If you have nothing to do tomorrow, we'll go to Werua.'
                                                               (Elbert 1948: 30)

---

6.   It should be noted that existence and possession are expressed in one and the same way in Kapingamarangi, either by non-verbal predication with particle *ai* or with the particle *ikoro*. These predications are also negated in one and the same way, either by *tēai* or by *hākare*. Statements to this effect can be read throughout the descriptions available to me.

(15) Kapingamarangi (Polynesian, Samoic Outlier, Ellicean) [kpg]

    a. *Ko   au ku iroa, ko   Iete tē   iroa*
        NOUN.A I   PRS know ACT Iete NEG know
        'I know, Iete does not know.'   (Elbert 1948: 30)

    b. *Au tē   hihai*
        1SG NEG like
        'I do not like it.'   (Elbert 1948: 30)

    c. *Au hakarē   hihai*
        1SG NEG.EX like
        'I don't like it. I don't want any.'   (Elbert 1948: 30)

Given that one of the negative existentials, *tēai,* is dedicated to that function, the presence of type B is postulated in Kapingamarangi. The other negative existential, *hakarē,* is clearly used as an SN marker as well; this in turn requires the postulation of another NEC type for Kapingamarangi, either B~C or C. The uncertainty stems from the fact that it is not clear whether *hakarē* is (i) completely on a par with the particle *tē* the negation of verbal predications or (ii) conditioned by specific grammatical/discourse factors. If (i) is valid, then we would have type C; if (ii) is valid then, this strategy instantiates type B~C. Overall, two stages of the NEC are observed in Kapingamarangi, B and B~C/C. Similar overlaps are also observed in Tahitian and also in Tamil, cf. (41)–(43) below for similar data as well as for a discussion about the diachronic interpretation of these facts.

A comparison of overlapping NEC types brings to light the fact that certain overlaps are cross-linguistically more common than others, and that, in fact, it is possible to offer a typology of overlaps.

As pointed above in Section 3.2.1 and also in this section, the types with variation, B~C and A~B, are not only very frequent in the families examined here but they also co-occur with each other in several different families, cf. Table 2 above. This overlap refers to a situation where a contextually restricted negative existential is extended into the verbal domain; the stable stage of a fully established negative existential is skipped, cf. (3) and (5) from Zyryan Komi. This kind of situation is observed in Uralic, Slavic, Polynesian and Bantu. These families differ substantially in terms of structure and are located in three distinct geographical areas. So it is probably safe to say that it is cross-linguistically valid that a fully established negative existential as the sole negator of existential predication is not a necessary condition for its expansion into other functions.

3.3 Recapitulation of this section

In this section I presented an overview of the application of the NEC to the world-wide sample as well to the family-based sample. The main findings are as follows: (i) the stable types A and B are the most frequent ones in the world-wide sample; (ii) In

Table 2. Languages where overlapping NEC types are observed

Languages classified into several types	Overlapping NEC types
3 Uralic languages (Estonian [ekk], Veps [vep], Skolt Saami [sms])	A and B
3 Uralic (East Mari [mhr], Zyryan Komi [kpv], Permian Komi [koi]), 1 Polynesian (Hawai'ian[haw]), 1 Bantu (Babole [bvx])	A~B and B~C
1 Dravidian (Tamil [tam]), 1 Polynesian (Kapingamarangi [kpg])	B and B~C
1 Polynesian (Tahitian [tah])	B and C
1 Polynesian (East Futuna [fud])	B~C and C and C~A

the family-based sample, type B is by far the most common followed by the transitional types B~C and A~B. In non-technical terms, this means that in the family-based sample, languages with well established negative existential prevail; languages where the negative existential is used within a clearly defined domain of verbal negation (type B~C) are also very common; (iii) finally, it is also very common to observe overlaps of different, non-sequential type/stages of the NEC within one and the same language. Specifically, the most common overlap is that types A~B and B~C co-exist. This means that it is cross-linguistically very common that a contextually restricted special negator expands its domain of use into the verbal domain.

4.   Summary of the findings on Slavonic, Polynesian and Uralic

In my recent work (Veselinova 2014; Veselinova 2015) I offer a critical examination of the NEC based on comparative data from Slavic, Polynesian and Uralic languages. I suggest that the full completion of the NEC appears to take about 2000 years and that it depends on language specific characteristics. In particular, negative existentials are most likely to fully take over the domain of SN in languages where SN is expressed by means of a complex clause, see (16) from Tongan below as well as (7) from Māori above.

(16)   Tongan (Austronesian [...] Polynesian, Tongic) [ton]
       Standard negation

   a.   *Naʻe kei kata ((ʻ)a) e   ongo kiʻi taʻahiné*
        PST still laugh ABS   ART DU   CLF girl.DEF
        'The two little girls were still laughing.'   (Broschart 1999:97)

   b.   *Naʻe ʻikai ke kata ʻa   Pita*
        PST NEG SUB laugh ABS   Pita
        'Pita did not laugh.' ([It] was not that Pita laugh[ed])
                                                       (Broschart 1999: 104)

Based on the comparative and historical data from the families mentioned above, I was also able to outline several different pathways whereby negative existentials come to be used in the domain of verbal negation. They include (i) subordination processes; (ii) the reanalysis of an external negator into a negator external to the proposition; (iii) a direct inheritance of a construction; (iv) the use of negative existentials with nominalized verb forms. Among these pathways, only (iv) shows a great extent of cross-linguistic recurrence; it is illustrated in this section, by Selkup (22) and Hawai'ian (23) as well as in pertinent sections on Berber (5.1), Turkic (5.2) and Dravidian (5.3). The remaining three pathways are briefly presented in this section only as they appear to be cross-linguistically more restricted.

Subordination strategies as in (16) from Tongan above involve the concatenation of predicates in a complex clause structure where a verb with negative content becomes the predicate of the main clause while the negated proposition is in the subordinate clause. These strategies are especially productive in Polynesian languages. Their productivity has led to several renewals of the SN markers and also to at least one round of completion of the NEC. The developments observed in Polynesian lead to the hypothesis that the negative existentials are most likely to fully take over the domain of SN in languages where SN is expressed by a complex clause. This, however, remains to the tested on other languages with such SN strategies.

Negative existentials are commonly used as short answers 'No' and also as negators external to the proposition, cf. (Veselinova 2013a: 118). In fact, there are languages such as Russian where its negative existential *net* is used more often with this latter function as in (17b), than as a sentence predicate as in (17a), see also (ibid. 129–130).

(17)   Russian (Indo-European, East Slavonic) [rus] (Russian National Corpus)

    a.   *Sil   u neë net*
        strength.F.PL.GEN in her NEG.EX
        'She does not have any strength' lit. 'strengths in her there-is-not'
        Russian National Corpus, [Ordinamenti//"Screen and scene",
        2004.05.06]   (Veselinova 2013a: 128)

    b.   *Net, ja tak ne   duma-l   i   tak ne   mečta-l*
        No, I so NEG think-PST.SG.M and so NEG dream-PST.SG.M
        'No, I neither thought nor dreamed that way',
        Russian National Corpus   (Veselinova 2013a: 128)

Following Croft (1991: 21) who cites Schwegler (1988) on this issue, I have assumed that the high frequency of *net* as sentence external negator has led to its reinterpretation as a negator internal to the proposition. The authors just mentioned base their hypothesis on data from Spanish, they do not discuss Russian or related languages. In my study I interpret their idea as applicable on data from Russian and Sino-Russian, a pidgin language spoken around Kyakhta, in the vicinity of the Russian-Mongolian border). In this language, we observe that a form clearly related to Russian *net, netu*, is used as a verbal negator, cf. (18).

(18)   Sino-Russian (Pidgin) Glottocode [kjac1234]
       Naša   ego   ponimaj   netu
       1PL   3SG   understand   NEG
       'We don't understand him.'   (Veselinova 2014: 1337 citing Stern 2002: 23)

An evolutionary path from the function of negative existential to a more general SN marker is suggested in (19) below.

(19)   Negative existential > Negator external to the proposition > SN marker

It has to be emphasized that the pathway outlined in (19) only a hypothesis. The reasons for postulating it are as follows: (i) The form *net* in Russian has effectively become the default word for a short answer 'No!' (ii) In a contact situation, when speakers don't know the language very well, if they hear *net* very often, they are likely to interpret it as the word to use when they negate other words. Thus the negator external to the proposition is interpreted as a negator internal to the proposition. Besides, it may be the case that the evolutionary path presented in (19) is valid for other languages as well. In my current dataset, the facts from Kapingamarangi [kpg], point to a similar development, see (Veselinova 2014: 1352–1356). However, as already stated, while highly probable, this pathway still requires proper documentation.

   In Bulgarian and Macedonian, we observe that the negative existential *njama/nema* is used in an invariant form to negate verbal predications with future time reference, cf. (20).

(20)   Bulgarian (South Slavonic) [bul]
       a.   *Maria   ne   pja   snošti*
            Maria   NEG   sing.3SG.PST   last.night
            'Maria did not sing last night'   (own data)
       b.   *Maria   njama   da   pee   dovečera*
            Maria   NEG.EX   SUB   sing.3SG.PRS   tonight
            'Maria won't sing tonight'   (own data)

Within the context of NEC languages like Bulgarian are interpreted as representing a stage where the negative existential is expanding into the domain of SN but has not taken over verbal negation completely. However, the Slavonic data show that one should be cautious with such conclusions as constructions may be simply inherited from previous stages of the language. This is exactly what took place in Bulgarian and Macedonian. An examination of the constructions that express future in Old Church

Slavonic reveals that in this language there were several possible constructions, cf. (21a) below. One of them involved the use of *imeti* 'have' as an auxiliary followed by the infinitive of the lexical verb.

(21)   Old Church Slavonic (South Slavonic)

    a.   *iměti* 'have' + infinitive
        xotěti 'want' + infinitive
        nachati/vychati 'begin' + infinitive
        bǫde 'be.future' + participle   (Duridanov 1991:418)

    b.   *ne*   *imatъ*   *ostati*   *sьde* *камень* *na* *kamen-i*
        NEG have.3SG.PRS leave.INF here stone   on stone-ACC.SG
        'There will not be left here one stone on another.'
                                                      (Duridanov 1991:418)

Scholars of Old Church Slavonic such as (Xaralampiev 1981:117, 121), Duridanov (1991:418) and likewise Đorđić (1975:200–201) highlight the fact that the construction with *imeti* was much more frequent in negated sentences than in affirmative ones.[7] So the construction with *njama* we see today in Modern Bulgarian in (20c) is directly inherited from Old Church Slavonic; it does not result from the expansion of the negative existential into a new domain of use.

As mentioned above, the use of negative existentials with nominalized verb forms is cross-linguistically the most widespread pathway whereby they can be shown to expand into the domain of verbal negation. This is illustrated briefly in (22) and (23) below. This use of negative existentials is observed in virtually all families studied so far; see further examples from Berber, Turkic and Dravidian languages in Section 5 as well as the summarizing discussion in Section 6.

(22)   Selkup, Taz dialect (Uralic, Samoyedic) [sel]
    man *ilɨ-ptä-mɨ*   *cääŋka*
    1SG live-NMLZ-1SG be.absent.3SG.S
    'I didn't live' lit. 'my living [is] absent'   (Laakso et al. 2011)

(23)   Hawai'ian (Austronesian [...] Polynesian, Nuclear, Eastern, Marquesic) [haw]
    a'ohe *o'u* *'ike/lohe* *aku*   *iā*   *ia*
    NEG.EX 1POSS see/hear DIR.AWAY.FROM.SPEAKER PART 3SG
    'I can't hear him/her' lit. 'not-exist my seeing/hearing away from him/her'
                                           (Kahananui & Anthony 1970:346)

---

7.   See also Birnbaum (1958) as well as Mirčev (1968) on future tense constructions in Old Church Slavonic.

Other results that emerged based on the Slavonic, Polynesian and Uralic data concern notions internal to the NEC such as the sequence of the stages (types) included in it and their cross-linguistic occurrence which were already discussed in 3.2 above. In particular, the stages of the cycle can be shown to be non-sequential; also the stages with variation are dominant in these families and are consequently considered far more important for this cycle than the stages without variation. They are not only synchronically frequent but also diachronically stable as they can be demonstrated to last for very long periods of time. These generalizations are further emphasized below by data from Berber, Turkic and Dravidian.

5.   Diachronic analysis of the comparative data from Berber, Turkic and Dravidian

5.1   Berber

Proto-Berber is dated at about 4500 BCE. Berber cultures were and still are for the most part oral. In the classification used here four groups are distinguished: Kabyle-Atlas, Tuareg, Zenatic and Western Berber. The split of the Western, Tuareg and Zenatic groups is assumed to have occurred around 680-600 BCE. The formation of the modern varieties dated between 300 and 1100 CE, cf. (Kossmann forthcoming: 7).

As demonstrated by the data in Table 3, and also by the discussion in Mettouchi (2009: 293–294), the expressions for SN are cognates so a common standard negator, *wəl/*wər/*wə can be reconstructed for Proto-Berber. Mettouchi (ibid.) states that there is no consensus on the source of the standard negator. The current suggestions include several possible sources which include (i) a particle, (ii) a reduced form of a negative verb, (iii) the result of a univerbation of a negative element with an indefinite meaning 'thing', (iv) a delimiting preposition or a negative adverbial similar to 'never'. In any case, within the limits of the current study, the origin of the standard negator in Berber cannot be traced further than the hypotheses mentioned above.

The negative existentials in Berber languages appear to be either univerbations between the negative particle and a form of the existential verb or a completely unsegmentable item which constitutes a separate lexical-grammatical morpheme, cf. (24).

(24)   Negative existentials in Berber

   a.   Taqbaylit [kab]
        ulaš   < ul + y-əlli +   *ša*
        NEG.EX   NEG 3SG.M-be.N.PFV thing   Mettouchi (2009: 290)

   b.   Tashlhit [shi] *laḥ* no information about origin

   c.   Tuareg [thv] *aba/ba* no information about origin

The following can be said about the NEC in Berber. As shown in Figure 3 above, Berber languages are distributed among three consecutive stages of the cycle: languages where there is no distinction between verbal and existential negation, languages where such a distinction exists but the negative existential is restricted to the present tense, that is, there is variation in the negation of existence which is grammatically conditioned, and finally languages where verbal and existential predications are negated by well delimited strategies. Thus Berber languages follow the general direction of the NEC.

At present there is not enough data that would allow us to assess the diachronic age of the negative existentials or the duration of these stages. Based on what we have, we can suggest that negative existentials have been renewed in the modern history of Berber while the SN marker has remained the same. Such a hypothesis is motivated by the fact that negative existentials are expressed by very different, non-cognate forms in languages which are very closely related; at the same time the SN markers in all Berber languages examined here can be shown to have a common origin, even if the source itself is under debate.

Although there is no evidence that any of the negative existentials is currently expanding into the verbal domain, it is worth noting that they appear to follow the general cross-linguistic tendency to be used with nominalized verb forms, cf. (25).

(25)   Taqbaylit [kab] (Afro-Asiatic, Berber, Northern)
        ulaš   lbyi
        'NEG.EX willingness'
        'There is/was/has (had) been no will (to help)'   (Mettouchi 2009: 293, 289)

As pointed out above, the use of negative existentials with nominalized verb forms is verb forms is very common in Uralic languages and is likewise observed in Polynesian. It will be further illustrated below by Turkic and Dravidian data. In Veselinova (2013a), I argue that negative existentials state the absence of an entity rather than negating its presence. This semantic feature is prototypical of negative existentials cross-linguistically. Thus it appears that when the marker of absence is interpreted as a negator of an action, the action itself is perceived as an entity and appears with an appropriate encoding, cf. further discussion on this in 6.5.

5.2   Turkic

According to Golden (1998: 16) Proto-Turkic was formed between 3000–500 BCE. The main branches of this family are Bolgar and Common Turkic. Their split is dated around 400 CE, (Golden 1998: 18). Old Turkic is the earliest documented variety[8] of

---

8.   Erdal (2004: 10) states that Old Turkic is not to be confused with Proto-Turkic; nor is it to be considered the ancestor of Common Turkic in the sense (Vulgar) Latin is thought of for Romance languages.

Turkic languages, the runic inscriptions where it is reflected date from 720 CE (Erdal 2004:4).

The comparative data in Table 7 of the Appendix indicate that the verbal negator can be safely reconstructed as the suffix *-mA- cf. also Grønbech (1955) and Erdal (1979). Similarly, reflexes of the negative existential *yok* are found in all modern languages. Hence a lexeme *yo:k* can be reconstructed for Proto-Turkic as well. Marcel Erdal (p.c.) argues that in the proto-language, the word must have been a verbal noun related to the verb stem *yod-* 'wipe out, obliterate', cf. also cognates in (26) from Qarakhanid, a literary variety developed during the 10th–11th centuries during the Qarakhanid dynasty in Central Asia.

(26)   Qarakhanid, LINGUIST List code [xqa]

    a. *yod-ug*   'disaster'
    b. *yok yodun* 'destruction'   Marcel Erdal (p.c.)

Again, Marcel Erdal (p.c.) maintains that at some prehistoric stage *yo:k* was not so much part of the grammar but rather a lexical item which must have had competitors for expressing non-existence and absolute absence. The reanalysis whereby it acquired the function of negative existential must have taken place at some prehistoric stage since all Turkic languages have make a distinction between verbal and existential negation and the expressions for both have apparent cognates in most Turkic languages.

The following can be said with regard to *yok* breaking into the domain of verbal negation. It is used with nominalized verb forms in virtually all modern Turkic languages. Such constructions show different degrees of conventionalization and pragmatic markedness. For instance in Modern Turkish, the neutral way to negate a verbal predication is with *-mA* as shown in (27). However, emphatic[9] negation is expressed by *yok* in combination with participial/nominalized form of the verb and the subject marked by the genitive case, cf. (27b).

(27)   Turkish (Turkic, Common Turkic, Oghuz-Kipchak-Uyghur) [tur]

    a. *Kadın   Ali-ye   bak-ma-di*
        Woman   Ali-DAT   look-NEG-PST
        'The woman didn't look at Ali.'   (van Schaaik 1994:46)

---

9. Marcel Erdal (p.c.) objects to the term *emphatic*. His motivation for this is that all meaning is entrenched in a particular situation and the utterances listed below are used in very specific situations. Consequently, they are not exactly in free variation but rather in complementary distribution. The reason I have chosen to keep the term *emphatic* here is that in terms of frequency, negation with the suffix *-mA-*is the most common way for negating verbs in Turkish; in this sense it is less marked than the construction where *yok* is used.

b. *Kadın-ın   Aliy-e   bak-tığ-ı   yok-tu*
woman-GEN Ali-DAT look-PTCP.PST-AGR NEG.EX-Past
'The woman didn't look at Ali at all.'/lit. 'There was
no woman's-to-Ali-looking'   (van Schaaik 1994: 46)

Van Schaaik compares the sentence in (27b) with the Dutch sentence *Het bestaat niet dat de vrouw naar Ali keek* which is equally emphatic and involves an existential construction as well. The literal translation of the Dutch expression is 'It doesn't exist that the woman looked at Ali'.

A very similar situation is observed in Modern Uyghur. As shown by the data in (28), the most emphatic negation in this language is expressed by a participial/nominalized verb in combination with *yok*.

(28)   Modern Uyghur (Turkic, Common Turkic, Oghuz-Kipchak-Uyghur) [uig]

   a. *Emine Ali-ni   kör-mi-gen*
Emine Ali-ACC see-NEG-PST.PTCP
'Emine didn't see Ali'   Arienne Dwyer (p.c.)

   b. *Emine Ali-ni   peqet kör-mi-gen*
Emine Ali-ACC only   see-NEG-PST.PTCP
'Emine didn't see Ali at all'   Arienne Dwyer (p.c.)

   c. *Emine Ali-ni   kör-gen   yoq*
Emine Ali-ACC see-PST.PTCP NEGEX
'Emine didn't see Ali AT ALL, (not at all, not even a glimpse)!!'
                                                Arienne Dwyer (p.c.)

In other Turkic languages such as Gagauz the existential construction in both the affirmative and the negative domain has been extended to verbs for the expression of the habitual past. It should be noted though that the negator *-mA* is not in any way ousted; it is used for negating most finite verbal constructions in the language.

(29)   Gagauz (Turkic, Common Turkic, Oghuz-Kipchak-Uyghur) [gag]

   a. *var-dır   gör-düüm*
exist-PST see-NMLZ.POSS
'I saw [everything]' (in a general way) lit. 'There is my vision'
                                                (Pokrovskaja 1964: 154)

   b. *yok-tur   al-dı*
not.exist-PST take-NMLZ.POSS
'He didn't take [anything whatsoever]' (in a general way) lit.
'There is not his taking'   (Pokrovskaja 1964: 154)

   c. *yaz-mæ-ær-ım*
write-NEG-PROG-1SG
'I am not writing'   (Pokrovskaja 1964: 160)

The use of *yok* with nominalized verb forms follows one and the same construction in all Turkic languages cited above. It is presented schematically in (30).

(30)   Construction where *yok* is used as a verbal negator

    a.   Verb-PTCP.POSS-PERSON   +   *yok*
    b.   Verb-NMLZ.POSS-PERSON   +   *yok*

In both (30)a and (30)b above, we can see that *yok* is used with a non-finite form of the verb that receives possessive and person marking.

In addition to the constructions in (30), *yok* is also involved in a number of other univerbations, the most notable of which is probably the suffix *-QALAQ*; its vowels are subject to vowel harmony and the quality of its consonants assimilates to surrounding context, hence the indeterminate form. Its origin is described by Erdal (p.c.) as involving a participial suffix, a particle *ele* borrowed from Mongolic plus *yok* and pronominal marking.

(31)   Origin of *-QALAQ*
    -gAn-ele-yok-PERSONAL_PRONOUNS > *-QALAQ*
    PTCP-PART-NEG.EX-PERSONAL_PRONOUNS   Marcel Erdal (p.c.)

The resulting morpheme *-QALAQ* is probably best described as a separate gram which indicates that an expected action or state have not yet occurred but are expected to do so soon, cf. (32) and (33).

(32)   Khakas (Turkic, Siberian, South) [kjh]
    al-ɣalax-pın
    take-NOT.YET-1SG
    'I haven't taken yet but I am about to take'   Marcel Erdal (p.c.)

(33)   Altai (Turkic, Siberian, South) [alt]
    kör-gölög-im
    see-NOT.YET-1SG
    'I haven't seen yet but I will'   Marcel Erdal (p.c.)

Marcel Erdal (p.c.) considers the constructions in (30) to have existed in Turkic languages for a long time. However, as demonstrated by the data above, they have reached different degrees of grammaticalization and conventionalization in different Turkic varieties. In some, they are still marked variants of the verbal negator; in others they have taken over the negation of a particular category but not the entire domain of SN. The negative existential *yok* used in other constructions related to verb negation as well, see (32) and (33) where it has become fused with the morphological marking of the verb to form a separate verbal category. Yet, although *yok* does interact with verbal negation to a great degree, it is in no way close to ousting the verbal negator in any modern Turkic language. The state of variation with *-mA* for some verbal categories and the Verbal Noun + *yok* has evidently been maintained for a long time. This aspect of the cycle has to be brought to the fore since it has not been discussed at all. When citing the negative existential cycle, authors tend to emphasize the general possibility for a negative existential to take over the domain of standard negation. As the comparative data here suggest what is highly significant is that (i) the cycle is rarely fulfilled within the limits for reasonable reconstruction; (ii) stages of variation like the ones demonstrated with data from Turkic languages above can be maintained for very long periods of time.

5.3 Dravidian

Proto Dravidian is dated at 4000 BCE (Steever 1998:11ff). Krishnamurti (2003) identifies three groups: Northern, Southern (I & II)[10] and Central. The Northern group consists of two languages, Brahui and Malto. It is assumed to have split very soon after 4000 BCE. The split of the Southern group is set by Steever (ibid.) around 1500 BCE; Old Tamil, one of the major Southern languages, is considered to have been formed as a separate variety between 300 BCE and 700 CE. Four Dravidian languages, Tamil, Kannada, Malayalam and Telugu, have a long written tradition; the earliest Tamil inscription dates from 254 BCE (Steever 1998:4). The rest of Dravidian languages represent oral cultures.

Negation in Dravidian languages is a complex phenomenon which deserves a separate article.[11] For the purposes of this overview, the most important facts to cite follow below. In the pertinent literature, cf. (Payne 1985), Dahl (2010), Miestamo (2005) (the list here is, of course, not exhaustive), Dravidian languages are commonly used as an example of neutralization of tense-aspect and likewise of finiteness distinctions under negation. These neutralizations are illustrated briefly by data from Tamil in (34). As demonstrated in (34a), in the affirmative, Tamil verbs inflect for tense; the person and number of the subject are also indexed on the verb form; for 3rd person subjects, even the gender of the subject is indexed, cf. (34b). When negated, verbs lose their tense distinctions and the finiteness distinctions of person, number and gender, cf. (34c); the person-number-gender marker *ai* in that example belongs to the suffixed auxiliary *ill-ai*; it does not reflect the person-number-gender of the subject, see (36) and ensuing discussion.

---

10. The group identified by Krishnamurti as Southern II appears as South-Central in other classifications.

11. Some general comparative works on Dravidian languages include Andronov (2003), Krishnamurti (1990), Krishnamurti (2003), Steever (1998).

(34) Modern Tamil (Dravidian, Southern) [tam]

    a. *naaḷai-kku*   *matraasu-kku·p poo-kiṟ-eeṉ*
        tomorrow-DAT Madras-DAT   go-PRS/FUT-1SG
        'I am going to Madras tomorrow'   (Lehmann 1993:67)

    b. *raja kumaar-ukku-k katav-ai·t tiṟa-ntu   koṭu-tt-aan*
        Raja Kumar-DAT   door-ACC open-PPL give-PST-3SG.M
        'Raja opened the door for Kumar'   (Lehmann 1993:227)

    c. *ravi neeṟṟul/   ippootu/ naaḷai   var-a·v-ill-ai*
        Ravi yesterday/ now/   tomorrow come-INF-be.not-3PL.N
        'Ravi didn't come yesterday'/'Ravi doesn't come now'/
        'Ravi won't come tomorrow'   (Lehmann 1993:231)

As indicated by Figure 7 and Table 8, in Dravidian languages there is a distinction between SN and negation of existence. Most Dravidian languages have one negative existential; Tamil has two. In this section only the one which is cognate with the negative existentials in the rest of the family is shown in (35b).

(35) Modern Tamil (Dravidian, South) [tam]

    a. *peey uṇ-ṭu*
        ghost exist-3SG.N
        'Ghosts exist'   (Lehmann 1993:230)

    b. *peey ill-ai*
        ghost not.exist-3PL.N
        'Ghosts do not exist'   (Lehmann 1993:230)

The comparative data in Table 8 demonstrate that SN in Dravidian languages is expressed by several strategies which have different effects on the negated verbs. One is a suffix *-ā-/-(v)u-* (Southern & Northern/Central group); when this suffix is used, verbs keep their finite marking and all tense distincitons are lost, cf. (38) below with pertinent discussion. The other SN strategy is the suffix *–(i)llai/-illai* or the auxiliary *illa*; its exact shape or the degree of its morphological bondedness will vary from one language to another. The forms *–(i)lle/illa* are used only with non-finite forms of the negated verb, that is, with infinitives or with other nominalized forms; they are obviously related to the negative existential *illai* cited in (35)b above. When used with different nominalized forms of the negated verbs, the resulting constructions have different temporal reference, cf. (41b), (42), (44), (46).

    Krishnamurti (2003:353) suggests the reconstruction of the negative suffix **-ā-* for Proto-Dravidian. Two negative verbs **alla* 'to be not so and so' and **cila,* 'not be', are also reconstructed for the proto-language. One reflex of **alla* is found as a negative existential in modern Brahui, cf. Table 8. Since this particular verb is not transferred to the domain of SN, it will not concern us further here.[12] Just like the Turkic *yo:k*, *cila* is said to have had another, more specific lexical meaning in some, non-specified, proto-stage. Burrow and Emeneau (1984:222–223) cite the sense 'death, want, non-existence'. Some reflexes are of *cila* in the modern languages are shown in (36) below.

(36)   Cognates of *cila* in the modern Dravidian lgs

    a.   Parji (Central) [pci]   *cila*
    b.   Gondi (Southern II) [ggo]   *sil*
    c.   Kuvi (Southern II) [kxv]   *hil*-PERSON.NUMBER.GENDER
    d.   Kannada (Southern I) [kan] *illa*
    e.   Tamil (Southern I) [tam]   *illai/ille*

The cognates of *cilla* cited in (36) are most often invariable forms in their respective languages, with the obvious exception of *hil-* in Kuvi where a full paradigm is said to exist for this verb. In Tamil *illai* appears with several orthographic variants when transliterated into English; there are also authors such as Lehmann (1993) who choose to indicate its root morpheme *ill-* and the suffix *-ai* '3PL.N'. However, despite its morphological transparency, the form *illai* is the only form of the erstwhile verb *cila* in Tamil and just as invariable as the negative existentials in the other Dravidian languages. Krishnamurti (2003:356) states that a full paradigm can be reconstructed for the verb *cila* in Proto-Dravidian. According to this author, this verb was used as a main verb but also as a negative auxiliary early on in Dravidian languages, cf. data from Old Tamil in (39) below.

Essentially, the data on the verb *cila* illustrate a typical grammaticalization cline which can be summarized in (37).

(37)   Grammaticalization of *cila*
(i)   lexical item *cila* 'death, want, non-existence' with a full paradigm >
   (ii)   verb with a more abstract sense 'not be, not exist' >
      (iii) fossilized forms with transparent morphology, 'not exist, SN' >
         (iv)   invariant forms, no transparent morphology 'not exist, SN' >
            (v)   semi-bound or bound SN suffix

However, what is important for this study, is the fact that even when the reflexes of *cila* have become expressions of SN, the distinction between negation of action and negation of existence is still maintained. It has apparently existed in the Dravidian family for several millennia. Moreover, reflexes of *cila* appear to have been used for

---

12.   The reflexes of *alla* are used for negation of attributive predications in several modern Dravidian languages, cf. for instance Tamil *Kumaar vakkiil alla* 'Kumar is not a lawyer', (Lehmann 1993:230).

the negation of verbs for a very long time as well, cf. data from Old Tamil in (39) below.

Dravidian languages allow for several important generalizations with regard to the NEC. First, we observe that stages of variation in the expressions of negation of SN last for extended periods of time. Second, negative existentials represent a very basic functional domain and expressions for it are recreated all the time. Third, when a word expands its function into a new domain, this does not necessarily imply loss of function in its previous domain;[13] I will come back to this issue when I compare Jespersen Cycle with NEC and generally the idea of a completed cycle, cf. 6.5. Data from Tamil and Kannada will be used to highlight these generalizations.

5.3.1   Tamil

In Old Tamil, negative suffix -ā- assimilates to the markers of person, number and gender thus yielding portmanteau morphs, cf. (38) for the paradigm of the verb viṭu 'leave'.

(38)   Old Tamil (Dravidian, South) [oty]

viṭ-een	leave-NEG.1SG
viṭ-aay	leave-NEG.2SG
viṭ-aaṉ	leave-NEG.3SG.M
viṭ-aaḷ	leave-NEG.3SG.F
viṭ-aa-tu	leave-NEG-3SG.N
viṭ-oom	leave-NEG.1PL
viṭ-iir	leave-NEG.2PL
viṭ-aar	leave-NEG.3PL.M/F
viṭ-aa	leave-NEG.3PL.N

(Lehmann 1993:69)

The negative forms in (38) are not marked for tense. They can be interpreted as referring to past, present or future, depending on context. Evidence from Old Tamil shows that negative statements with past time reference were formed using a reflex of *cila, cf. (39) below. It is unclear whether the two negation strategies were in free variation or in complementary distribution.

(39)   Old Tamil (Dravidian, Southern) [oty]

   a. *kuṭux-t-il-e:n*   >   *kuṭuttile:n*
      give-PST-NEG-I
      'I didn't give'   (Agesthialingom & Shanmugam 1970:66)

   b. *kuṭux-t-il-an*   >   *kuṭuttilan*
      give-PST-NEG-he
      'he didn't give'   (Agesthialingom & Shanmugam 1970:66)

---

13.   Cf. Veselinova (2014:1357–1358) for very similar data and observations based on Tahitian [tah] and Kapingamarangi [kpg] and likewise data from Turkic in the preceding section.

In Modern Tamil only one of the finite forms shown in (38) is used. It is the form inflected for third person, singular number and neuter gender, e.g. *viṭ-aa-tu* and corresponding forms for other verbs.[14] According to Lehmann (1993:69), these forms are interpreted with future time reference or as expressing habituality, cf. (40); despite the morphological indication of 3SG.N, they can be used with both singular and plural subjects, regardless of their gender.

(40) Tamil (Dravidian, South) [tam]

     pas iṅkee var-aa-tu
     bus here come-NEG-3SG.N
     'The bus won't come here'   (Lehmann 1993:228)

In addition to negation expressed by the suffix *-ā-*, there are two auxiliaries *maaṭṭu* 'will not' and *illai* 'be not'. Both of these appear with the main verb in the infinitive.

(41) Tamil (Dravidian, South) [tam]

    a. *viṭ-a   maaṭṭ-eeṇ*
       leave-INF will.not-1SG
       'I won't leave'   (Lehmann 1993:69)

    b. *naaṇ viṭ-a·v-ill-ai*
       I   leave-INF-be not-3PL.N
       'I did not leave'/'I do not leave'   (Lehmann 1993:69)

Apart from appearing on verbs by bound or semi-bound forms, the verb *illai* is also used with nominalized clauses to negate the existence of the event denoted by such clauses, (Lehmann 1993:230), cf. (42). Such constructions are routinely interpreted as expressing habitual negativity.

(42) Tamil (Dravidian, South) [tam]

    a. *Kumaar koovil-ukku·p poo-kiṛ-atu   ill-ai*
       Kumaar temple-DAT   go-PRS-NMLZ not.exist-3PL.N
       'Kumaar never goes to the temple'

As pointed on numerous occasions throughout this paper, cross-linguistically, it is very common for negative existentials to be used with nominalized forms of verbs. Such uses receive different tense-aspect interpretations in different languages, cf. also Koptjevskaja-Tamm (1993, in passim) on this issue.

    In Tamil, negation of existence has two alternative expressions. One is the fossilized form *illai* which is sometimes further analyzed into a stem and an affix although

---

14. From a typological point of view, it is, of course, no surprise that exactly the third person singular neuter form survives in the modern language, cf. Greenberg (1966:65–69) and also the psychological model offered in Bybee (1985).

the affix no longer has the subject indexing function. The other is the form *kiṭai·y-aa-tu*, cf. (43c). Both *illai* and *kiṭai·y-aa-tu* replace the positive existential *untu*.

(43)   Tamil (Dravidian, South) [tam]

    a.   *peey   un-ṭu*
        ghost   exist-3SG.N
        'Ghosts exist'   (Lehmann 1993:230)

    b.   *peey   ill-ai*
        ghost   not.exist-3PL.N
        'Ghosts do not exist'   (Lehmann 1993:230)

    c.   *peey   kiṭai·y-aa-tu*
        ghost   exist-NEG-3SG.N
        'There are no ghosts'   (Lehmann 1993:81)

In diachronic terms, the form *kiṭai·y-aa-tu* is obviously younger than the form *illai* since it (*kiṭai·y-aa-tu*) is formally transparent and its meaning appears to be compositional. However, verb *kiṭai·y* occurs only under negation, and only with this combination of affixes, cf. (Lehmann 1993:81). So it is, in fact, an invariant form, despite its transparent morphology. What seems to be happening in Tamil is that while the older negative existential *illai* has expanded into the verbal domain, a new negative existential dedicated to non-existence only is being developed. A very similar situation is observed in Kapingamarangi, cf. (14) and (15) above. Of course, there does not have to exist any causal connection between one negative existential that expanded its function and the creation of a new one. However, it is important to point out that a new expression for negated existence has effectively emerged. Consequently, the distinction between SN and existential negation is "re-affirmed"; the cycle having reached stage B~C or C on *illai* is back at stage B with *kiṭai·y-aa-tu*.

5.3.2   *Kannada*

The durability of the distinction between SN and existential negation is likewise illustrated by data from Kannada. The facts from this language also bring further confirmation to the generalization that when a form expands its functions into one domain, it does not necessarily lose its older functions.

Kannada is a good example of diglossia as there are substantive differences between the literary and the spoken language on many levels. With regard to negation, it has to be said that one and the same strategy seems to be used to negate verbs with past time reference in both Literary and Spoken Kannada. Clear differences for the expressions of SN are observed for verbs/simple verbal sentences with present/future time reference.

The construction used to negate verbs with past time reference involves the *-(a)l* infinitive of the negated verb and an invariant form of the negative existential *illa*, cf. (44).

(44)   Literary & Spoken Kannada (Dravidian, South) [kan]
Avn   ninne   nan   maneeg   bar-l-illa
He   yesterday   my   house   come-INF-NEG
'He didn't come to my house yesterday'   (Schiffman 1983: 114)

Negation of verbs with present/future time reference is done by means of two different strategies in Literary Kannada. One is by means of finite verb forms whereby the verb stem is directly followed by portmanteau suffixes that combine senses such as 'NEG' as well as information on tense, person, number and gender, cf. (45). The other negation strategy for verbs with present/future time reference is a construction where the negated verb appears as a nominalized form followed by the negative existential *illa* as an auxiliary cf. (46a). In Spoken Kannada we observe both this latter strategy or negation by a portmanteau suffix, cf. (46b–c).

(45)   Negation by suffixation in Literary and Spoken Kannada

Literary Kannada   Spoken Kannada

a. *naanu maaD-enu*   d. *naanu maaD-e*
   I   do-NEG.PRS.FUT.1SG   I   do-NEG.PRS.FUT.1SG
   'I do not do it'/'I will not do it'   'I do not do it'/'I will not do it'
          (Schiffman 1983: 113)   (Schiffman 1983: 113)

b. *avanu maaD-anu*
   he   do-NEG.PRS.FUT.3SG.M
   'he does not do it'/'he will not do it'
          (Schiffman 1983: 113)

c. *avaLu maaD-aLu*
   she   do-NEG.PRS.FUT.3SG.F
   'She will not do it'
          (Schiffman 1983: 113)

(46)   Negation by *illa* (or related forms)

Literary Kannada   Spoken Kannada

a. *maaDu-vu-du*   *illa*   b. *maaD-ood*   *illa*
   do-PRS.ADJ.PART-NMLZ   NEG.EX   do-PRS/FUT.NMLZ   NEG.EX
   doesn't do/won't do   'doesn't go/won't go'
          (Schiffman 1983: 114)   (Schiffman 1983: 114)

                                              c. *maaD-olla*
                                                 do-NEG.PRS/FUT
                                                 'doesn't go/won't go'
                                                        (Schiffman 1983: 114)

Among the three possible forms cited for Literary Kannada in (45a–b), only one is used in spoken Kannada. This is the first person singular, and that in a highly reduced form, see (45d). The construction with *illa* used with a nominalized verb form shown in (46a) in Literary Kannada is observed in two variants in Spoken Kannada, cf. (46b–c) where we observe different degrees of fusion and obliteration of morphological transparency. In (46b) the participial and the nominalizing suffix are fused while *illa* is still a free form. In (46c), the suffix *-ood* 'PRS/FUT.NMLZ' is fused with *illa* to yield a new portmanteau morph *-olla* 'NEG.PRS/FUT'.

The data cited above show that the negative existential *illa* in Kannada is used for verbal negation in a variety of constructions, which presumably also have different diachronic age. Yet, the function of *illa* as a negative existential is completely retained, cf. (47).

(47) Kannada (Dravidian, South), [kan]

    a. *Khaja:ney-alli haNa   ide*
        treasury-LOC money is
        'There is money in the treasury'   Madhuri Doss (p.c.)

    b. *Khaja:ney-alli haNa   illa*
        treasury-LOC money NEG
        'There is no money in the treasury'   (Sridhar 1990: 111)

So with Kannada we have yet another example of a form expanding from one domain into another but also keeping its older functions. Whether we should view the forms of *-illa* cited as SN markers and *illa* as a negative existential as instantiations of one and the same word or an example of a lexical split is of course a matter of definition and further discussion.

6. Summary and concluding discussion

In this paper I used comparative data from six unrelated language families in order to test the model of evolution of SN markers from negative existentials, cf. Croft (1991). The comparative data collected here show that the model needs to be elaborated in several respects.

First, the stages with variation in either the expression of SN or in the expression of negative existence are cross-linguistically more common that the stages without variation. This synchronic dominance is also matched by diachronic stability in that such stages of variation can be maintained for extended periods of time. Furthermore, the stages are non-sequential; co-occurrence of stages is observed in several unrelated languages. It is also possible to outline a typology of overlaps so they do show cross-linguistic validity.

Second, the data collected here also enable us to outline several pathways whereby negative existentials break into the domain of SN. They include subordination strategies, reanalysis of external negators into negator internal to the proposition, direct inheritance of constructions and finally, the use of negative existentials with nominalized forms of lexical verbs. The latter is by far the most common one cross-linguistically.

Third, that lexical items with a negative content appear to participate into processes very similar to those for negative existentials entering the NEC. Consequently, the model should be probably extended to cover those as well.

Fourth, the family-based sample shows that the NEC is instantiated completely in the Polynesian family only; the remaining five families show only partial instantiations of the cycle. While it does not invalidate it per se, it does have implications for its duration. The diachronic analysis and historical data suggest that the cycle is rarely completed within the time span of observable reconstruction. This is attributed to the constant renewal of expressions for negative existentials.

Each of these issues is allotted its own subsection. Finally, a brief comparison between the Jespersen Cycle and the NEC concludes this section and also the article.

6.1   The dominance and also frequent overlap of types with variation

As shown in 3.2, two types with variation in either the expression of SN (B~C) or in the expression of negated existence (A~B) are most frequent in virtually all of the families investigated here. As we recall, see Section 2, these two types cover languages where there is grammatically conditioned variation in the expression of standard/verbal negation (type B~C) or in the negation of existence (type A~B). To put it in non-technical terms: we can observe that is very frequent that a language has a negative existential which is used for some clearly delimited part of the SN domain; it is also common for a language to have a negative existential that is restricted to a specific context, typically the present tense. Moreover, it is also very common that a contextually restricted negative existential to extend to the verbal domain. The synchronic frequency of stages of variation and their overlap is also matched by diachronic durability as such stages can be shown to last for very long periods of time, cf. data on Turkic in 5.2 and from Dravidian in 5.3.

6.2   The use of negative existentials in nominalized constructions

As already pointed out, there are several ways whereby negative existentials can be extended into the domain of verbal negation but only one is attested in a nearly all investigated families and can consequently be described as cross-linguistically frequent. This is the use of negative with nominalized forms of the verbs which are negated. Such use is present in all families except Slavonic, cf. (22) from Selkup (Uralic), (23) Hawaiian (Polynesian), (25) from Kabyl (Berber), (27) through (29) for various Turkic languages and (41), (42), (44) and (46) for data from Dravidian languages. Nominalizations are common in Central and Eastern Asia, cf. (Yap et al. 2011) so there may be some areality effect here. However, since the use of negative existentials stretches beyond Asian languages, the motivation for this use is most probably grounded in more general factors. In Veselinova (2013a), I argue that negative existentials represent a separate function domain. One of their striking cross-linguistic characteristics is that they tend to require special constructions where their pivot appears in generic form. The negative existential construction enjoys different degrees of productivity in different languages, just like the affirmative existential construction, cf. (Koptjevskaja-Tamm & Wälchli 2001) for Circum-Baltic languages. In some languages these constructions are very productive, in others they are restricted to the negative existential domain. In languages where negative existentials are carried over to the domain of SN via their use with nominalized verbs, such constructions are obviously productive. Nominalized verb constructions are have been treated at length in the literature, cf. (Alexiadou & Rathert 2010; Chung 1973; Comrie & Thompson 1985; Gerner 2012; Koptjevskaja-Tamm 1993; Nikolaeva 2007). It is not possible to present here a full treatment of the various tense-aspect-modal interpretations a nominalized construction may receive. In fact, quite opposite interpretations are possible in different areas and regions cf. Koptjevskaja-Tamm (1993). The important point here is that when negative existentials are used to negate an action, it is encoded as an entity. The interpretation of the construction as a whole in terms of tense-aspect values depends on the specific language.

6.3   Other lexicalizations of negation into the NEC

As indicated by data from Tamil in (41a), lexicalizations of other negative senses may take over specific parts of the domain of SN. Croft (1991: 14–15) comments on the issue of the role of negative lexicalizations and their use to negate imperatives. In this study, I focused on negative existentials and only briefly mentioned other lexicalizations of negation such as 'will.not'. However, in many languages we observe other special negative expressions such as 'not.be of identity', 'not-yet', not-know' to name a few, see Veselinova (2013b) for a preliminary list. These expressions are also observed to take over some sub-domains of SN, cf. data from Kanuri, a Nilo-Saharan language where the negative existential *bâ* is used to negate verbs in the imperfective cf. (48c) while the attributive negator *gɔ̀nyi* has been grammaticalized as the SN negator for verbs with future and near-past time reference, cf. (48d–e).

(48)   Kanuri (Nilo-Saharan, Saharan, Western, Kanuri)

   a.   *cídà   bâ*
        work   not exist
        'there is no work'   (Hutchison 1981: 170)

b. *kə́remá kúlolan   cidajîn-bâ*
Now   farm.LOC work.3SG.IPFV.NEG
'now she is not working on the farm'
(Miestamo 2005: 296–7 citing Cyffer 1998: 39)

c. *Álì bàrèmà gə̀nyi*
Ali farmer not.be
'Ali is not a farmer'   (Hutchison 1981: 178)

d. *wanée músa kû   silemân cúru-nnyí*
maybe Musa today film   see.3SG-FUT.NEG
'Maybe Musa will not see a film today'
(Miestamo 2005: 296–7 citing Cyffer 1998: 40)

e. *bíska   músa kánoro lezə́-nyi*
yesterday Musa Kano.DIR go.NEAR_PST.3SG-NEG
'Yesterday Musa did not travel to Kano',
(Miestamo 2005: 296–7 citing Cyffer 1998: 287)

The whole issue of incorporating other lexicalizations of negation into the NEC should receive more attention. Negative existentials will always be dominant in this cycle since they are by far the most common lexicalizations of negation. But in the long run, it would probably be appropriate to find a more general name for the cycle, like for instance, the Negative Lexical Cycle.

6.4 The constant renewal of the negative existentials

Several of the languages investigated here have two negative existentials, one of which is diachronically younger than the other, cf. (14) from Kapingamarangi and (43) from Tamil. The comparative data from the Uralic family also shows that negative existentials have been created and re-created throughout the history of the family, cf. Table 6 as well as Veselinova (2015). If we see negative existentials as a basic functional domain, then we can say that there is a functional pressure for their creation. As Zeshan (2004: 51) points out "events and states such as not liking, not knowing, not having are all identifiable human experiences". This is why these concepts are often expressed by lexicalized expressions cross-linguistically in both spoken and signed languages. However, the constant renewal of expressions for negative existentials has also implications for the cyclical processes where they participate. Specifically, when a new negative existential is created alongside an older one, we can say that the negative existential cycle starts anew. However, it is typically also the case that the older negative existential acquires newer functions as a verbal negator while keeping its special one for the negation of existence, cf. data from Tamil (5.3.1) and Kannada (5.3.2) above. Thus for the older negative existential, cycle has never really been completed. Another way to interpret this is to say that the distinction between negation of actions and negation of availability is so important in human languages that it is constantly maintained. This brings us to the last point of this discussion and that is the comparison between Jespersen Cycle and the NEC.

6.5   Jespersen Cycle vs. the NEC

The cyclical process dubbed Jespersen Cycle, cf. (Dahl 1979 and also Devos & van der Auwera 2010; van der Auwera 2010) for relatively recent references, refers to processes whereby a lexical item, say French *pas* 'step', which has little or nothing to do with negation, is gradually incorporated into the SN construction and eventually comes to oust the older SN negator. This is the case of *pas* 'step' which has come to replace *ne* 'NEG' in Spoken French. However, the word *pas* still exists with its older sense 'step' in French; so yet again, we see that expansion in one domain does not necessarily mean loss of function in the older domain. In fact, that particular development in French should rightfully be described as a lexical split. In Spoken French there are effectively two homonymous forms, the negator *pas* and the lexical item *pas*. One important aspect of Jespersen cycle is that when it is "completed", a new form ousts an older form for the function of a general negator but in essence, a very basic category such as SN receives a new expression. Whether the source, in the French case *pas* 'step', keeps its older sense is in a way immaterial since it does not really belong to the negative domain.

With the NEC, an item that does belong to the negative domain, although not to SN, is gradually incorporated into verbal negation. However, the distinction between negation of actions and negation of availability/existence appears to be a very basic one in human languages. When the NEC is "completed", this important distinction is obliterated. In the data examined here we have seen evidence that stages of NEC where negation of actions and negation of existence are kept apart can be maintained for a long time even when the existential negator is partially used in the domain of SN. We have also seen that expressions for negative existentials are also constantly renewed. At the end, whether we say that the NEC is rarely completed or constantly re-started becomes a matter of perspective. But unlike the Jespersen Cycle where typically categories from different semantic domains meet and the cycle renews expressions for the more abstract one, with the NEC, the meeting is between categories that belong to one and the same general domain. As such the distinction between them is important which is why is it also maintained and the NEC rarely comes to full completion.

Abbreviations

A	agent	DEF	definite
ABS	absolutive	DET	determiner
ACC	accusative	DIR	directional
ACT	active	DU	dual
AGR	agreement	EX	existential
ART	article	F	feminine
CLF	classifier	FUT	future
CNEG	connegative	G	gender
DAT	dative	GEN	genitive

GENR	generic TA		PERS	person
GER	gerund		PFV	perfective
INCL	inclusive		PL	plural
INDF	indefinite		POSS	possessive
INE	inessive		PREP	preposition
INF	infinitive		PRF	perfect
IPFV	imperfective		PROG	progressive
LOC	locative		PRS	present
M	masculine		PST	past
N	neuter		PTCP	participle
NEC	Negative Existential Cycle		S	subject
NEG	negation/negative		SG	singular
NMLZ	nominalization		SN	Standard negation
NONPST	non-past		SUB	subordinator
NUM	number		TA	tense-aspect
OBL	oblique		TNS	tense

Appendix

Table 3. Data from Berber languages, adapted from (Mettouchi 2009: 288–289)

GROUP	LANGUAGE NAME [ISO CODE]	SN	NEGATIVE EXISTENTIAL	TYPE IN NEC
Kabyle-Atlas	Taqbaylit (West) [kab][15]	*u(r)*	*ulaš*	B
	Taqbaylit (East) [kab]	*u(r)*	*ulaš*	B
	Tashelhit [shi]	*ur*	*laḥ*	B
	Tamazight [tzm]	*ur*	*ur- əlla* *ur -EXIST*	A
Tuareg	Tuareg [thv]	*ur*	*aba/ba*	B
Zenatic	Tarifit [rif]	*ur*	*u(r) … (ša)/ ulaš*	A~B
	Tashawit[16] [shy]	*u(r/d)*	*ud-illi/ ulliš*	A~B
Western Berber	Ghadamsi [zen]	*wəl*	*wəl d*	A

---

15. There are no separate codes for West and East Taqbaylit (Kabyle) in either the Ethnologue or the Glottolog. However, since Mettouchi makes a distinction between these two varieties, I am listing them separately as well. They do not show any differences as regards their expressions of standard negation and their expression of negative existentials.

16. The language name is spelled *Tachawit* in most online language catalogue systems. However, since I am citing Mettouchi's work here, I chose to follow the spelling used by this author.

Table 4. Overview of the standard and existential negators in the Slavonic dataset adapted from Veselinova (2014: 1378). Unless otherwise indicated, the forms of the ascriptive and existential negators are 3SG.PRS *Type* type from the Negative Existential Cycle assigned to a particular language

Group	Language Name	SN	Existential negator	Type
East	Byelorussian [ruw]	*ne*	*njama* 'not.have'	A~B
	Russian [rus]	*ne*	*net* 'not.exist, not.have'	A~B
	Ukrainian [ukr]	*ne*	*nema/nemae,* 'not.have'	A~B
South	Bulgarian [bul]	*ne*	*njama,* 'not.have'	B~C
	Macedonian [mkd]	*ne*	*nema,* 'not.have'	B~C
	Serbian/Croatian [srp/hrv]	*ne*	*nema,* 'not.have'	A~B
	Slovene [slv]	*ne*	*ne obstaja* 'NEG exist'	A~B
West	Czech [ces]	*ne-*	*ne-existujou* 'NEG-exist.PL.PRES'	A
	Slovak [slk]	*ne-*	*ne-jestvujú/existujú* 'NEG-exist.PL.PRS' (nieto)	?A~B →A
	Kashubian [csb]	*nie*	*ni ma,* 'not.have'	A~B
	Polish [pol]	*nie*	*nie ma,* 'NEG have'	A~B
	Upper Sorbian [hsb]	*nie-*	*nie-dawa* 'NEG-give' *nie-eksistuja* 'NEG-exist.PL.PRES'	A
	Lower Sorbian [dsb]	*nie-*	*nje-dajo* 'NEG-give' *nje-eksistěruju* 'NEG-exist.PL.PRES'	A

Table 5. Overview of the standard and existential negators in the Polynesian dataset adapted from Veselinova (2014: 1378–80)

Group	Sub-group I	Sub-group II	Language Name [ISO-693]	SN		Negative existential	Type
				Form	*Part of speech*		
Tongic			Tongan [ton]	*'ikai*	higher verb	*'ikai*	C
			Niue [niu]	*nakai ai fakaai tē*	higher verb > particle	*nakai hā* 'EX' *ai fai* 'be/do/have'	A
Nuclear Polynesian	East	Rapa Nui	Rapa Nui [rap]	*kai* (R) *eko* (R) *'ina*	particle particle particle	*'ina*	B~C
	East Central	Marquesic	Hawai'ian [haw]	*'aòle* *aòhe*	higher verb > particle	*'aòle* *aòhe*	A~B & B~C
			Mangareva [mrv]	*e kore* *kakkore*	higher verb higher verb	*kore*	C

(*Continued*)

Table 5. (Continued)

Group	Sub-group I	Sub-group II	Language Name [ISO-693]	SN		Negative existential	Type
				Form	*Part of speech*		
			Marquesan, North [mrq]	*'aòe* *'ae* *tē*	Particle particle particle	*'aòe* *'ae*	C
		Tahitic	Maori [mri]	*kaōre*	higher verb	*kaōre*	C
			Tahitian [tah]	*a'ita/aòre, ê'ita/eòre*	higher verb > particle	*'a'ita, 'aòre*	B & C
			Rarotongan [rar]	*kāre*	unclear	*kāre*	C
	Samoic Outliers	Samoan	Samoan [smo]	*lē*	Particle	*leai*	B~C
		Tokelauan	Tokelauan [tkl]	*hē*	Particle	*heai*	B
		Ellicean	Tuvaluan [tvl]	*hē*	Particle	*heai*	B
			Kapingamarangi [kpg]	*tē* *hakarē*	Particle Particle	*tēai* *hakarē*	B & B~C
			Nukuoro [nkr]	*de*	Particle	*deai*	B
		Futunic	Emae [mmw]	*sē*	Particle	*ikai*	B
			Futuna, East [fud]	*lee'se* *se* *le'aise*	higher verb particle higher verb	*le'e le'ai* *se* POSS PREDICATION	B~C & C & C~A
			Futuna, West [fut]	*se...ma*	Particle	*fikai* *jikai*	B
			Mele-Fila [mxe]	*(se-)...kē*	(prefix-)... Particle	*saai*	B
			Rennell-Bellona [mnv]	*he'e*	Particle	*si'ai*	B
			Vaeakau-Taumako [piv]	*sikiai* *hiai*	Higher verb > particle	*siai* *hiekhiloa* *khiloa*	C
			Uvean, West [uve]	*hē*	Particle	siai	B
	East Uvean Niuafoòu		Wallician [wls]	*mole*	Higher verb	*mole*	C

Table 6. Overview of the standard and existential negators in the Uralic dataset adapted from Veselinova (2015: 385–6)

GROUP	LANGUAGE NAME [ISO-CODE]	SN	Neg Ex	TYPE
Finnic	Estonian [ekk]	*ei* + VERB.FINITE.FORM	*ei/pole*	A, B
	Finnish [fin]	*e*-TNS.PERS.NUM + VERB.CNEG	*e*-TNS.PERS.NUM + VERB.CNEG	A

(*Continued*)

Table 6. (Continued)

GROUP	LANGUAGE NAME [ISO-CODE]	SN	NEG EX	TYPE
	Meänkieli [fit]	*e*-TNS.PERS.NUM + VERB. CNEG	*e*-TNS.PERS.NUM + VERB. CNEG	A
	Votic [vot]	*e*-TNS.PERS.NUM + VERB. CNEG	*e*-TNS.PERS.NUM + VERB. CNEG	A
	Karelian [krl]	*e*-TNS.PERS.NUM + VERB. CNEG	*e*-TNS.PERS.NUM + VERB. CNEG	A
	Ingrian [izh]	*e*-TNS.PERS.NUM + VERB. CNEG	*e*-TNS.PERS.NUM + VERB. CNEG	A
	Veps [vep]	*ei* + VERB.FINITE.FORM	*ei/pole*	A, B
Saami	Ume Saami [sju]	*i*-TNS.PERS.NUM + VERB. CNEG	*i*- TNS.PERS.NUM + VERB. CNEG	A
	North Saami [sme]	*i*-TNS.PERS.NUM + VERB. CNEG	*i*- TNS.PERS.NUM + VERB. CNEG	A
	South Saami [sma]	*i*- TNS.PERS.NUM + VERB. CNEG	*i*- TNS.PERS.NUM + VERB. CNEG	A
	Skolt Saami [sms]	*ij* 'be.CNEG'/*i'lla* etc.	*ij* 'be.CNEG'/*i'lla* etc.	A, B
Mari	Western Mari [mrj]	*a*- TNS.PERS.NUM + VERB. CNEG	*uke*	A>B
	Eastern Mari [mhr]	*o*-TNS.PERS.NUM + VERB. CNEG *uke* in PROG constructions	*uke*	A>B, B>C
Mordvin	Erzya [myv]	*a, eź-/eś-* + *ul'ems* 'be' (PST)	*aras, (a) eź-/eś-* + *ul'ems* 'be' (PST)	B
	Moksha [mdf]	*af, apak- əź-/iź uləms* (PST)	*aš, ajaš əź-/iź uləms* (PST)	B
Permic	Udmurt [udm]	*ö*-TNS.PERS.NUM + VERB. CNEG	*övöl*	A>B
	Komi-Zyryan [kpv]	*o-/e-*.PERS.NUM + VERB. CNEG *abu* + VERB.2nd PST (PRF)	*abu*-AGR	A>B, B>C
	Komi-Permyak [koi]	*o-/e-*.PERS.NUM + VERB. CNEG	*abu*-AGR	unclear
Ugric	Hungarian [hun]	*nem* + VERB.FINITE.FORM	*nincs*	A>B
	Mansi [mns]	*at, āt'im* [PST]	*āt'i, āt'im*	B>C
	Northern Khanty [kca]	*at, ? ăntom*	*ăntom*	B>C
Samoyedic	Nganasan [nio]	*ńi*	*d'aŋku*	B
	Tundra Nenets [yrk]	*ńi-, ńi-* V-CNEG; V-IPFV.PTCP *jaŋku-*	*jaŋku*-TNS-AGR, *juŋku*-TNS-AGR	B>C
	Forest Enets [enf]	*ńi-*	**d'ago**	B>C
	Selkup [sel]	*ašša // čääŋka* [PST, PRF]	*čääŋka*	B>C
	Kamas [xas]	*ej/e-*[FUT]	*naga*	unclear

Table 7. Data from Turkic languages

GROUP I	GROUP II	LANGUAGE [ISO-693 CODE][17]	SN	EXISTENCE	TYPE IN NEC	SOURCE[18]
Common Turkic	Oghuz-Kipchak-Uyghur, Oghuz	Turkish [tur]	*VERB-mA-TNS-PERS.NUM*	*yok*	B	Eyüp Bacanlı (p.c.)
		Azerbaijani [az]	*-mA/-mAr*	*yox-TENSE*	B	(Öztopçu 2000:, in passim)
		Gagauz [gag]	*-mA* *yok+VERB-NMLZ-POSS*	*yok*	B>C	(Pokrovskaja 1964:, in passim)
		Uzbek [uzb]	*-maz-*	*yo'k* *namevcut* *namavjud*	B	Eyüp Bacanlı (p.c.)
		Salar [slr]	*verb-NMLZ-yohtur/yoxtar* *-mA*	*yokh/youkhtur*	B>C	(Qualin et al. 1993; Tenishev 1976)
		Turkmen [tuk]	*-mA*	*yok*	B	ASKED FOR A NAME
	Oghuz-Kipchak-Uyghur, Uyghur	Modern Uyghur [uig]	*-mA*	*yoq*	B	(Engesaeth et al. 2009)

(Continued)

17. Current language code systems such as ISO-693, *World Atlas of Language Structures* (WALS), LINGUIST List and Glottolog differ in their coverage. For instance, unique codes for dead language are found in the LINGUIST List only; consequently, the codes used for the Turkic languages investigated here may come from several systems; this is indicated in table attributes or pertinent footnotes.

18. The Source cited here is a source for the data on negation. The classification according to types in the NEC is my own.

Table 7. (Continued)

GROUP I	GROUP II	LANGUAGE [ISO-693 CODE[17]]	SN	EXISTENCE	TYPE IN NEC	SOURCE[18]
Oghuz-Kipchak-Uyghur, Kipchak		Karachaj-Balkar [krc]	-mA VERB-PTCP + tül/tüyül	jok	B[19]	(Abaev 1993)
		Kumyk [kum]	-mA	yok	B	Eyüp Bacanlı (p.c.)
		Karaim [kdr]	-mA	yoktur[20]/yokt/yok/yo	B	(Csató 2001; Musaev 1964; Musaev 2003)
		Kazakh [kaz]	-mA	zhok	B	ASKED FOR A NAME
		Kirghiz [kir]	-bA -PERF.PRCP-PERSON.POSS + žok	žok	B>C	ASKED FOR A NAME
	Siberian Turkic, South	Altai [alt]	-MA[21]	d'ok	B	Eyüp Bacanlı (p.c.)
		Tuva [tyv]	-BA	čok	B	(Cypanov 2007)
		Khakas [kjh]	-MAn čoyil in PERFECT, HAB.PRS, with some converbs	čoyil	B>C	(Baskakov & Inkizhekova-Grekul 1953: 366. In passim), (Anderson 1998: 46–47, in passim)
	Siberian Turkic, North	Sakha/Yakut [sah]	-BA -bAt 'neg.aor' prs.prog: prs.part.3poss + suokh 'non-existing'	suokh-NUM 'NEG. EX'-NUMBER	B>C	(Petrova 2011), Eyüp Bacanlı (p.c.)
Bolgar		Chuvash [chv]	-mA(s) s'uk? VERB.FUT (mostly in the spoken register)	s'uk	B>C	(Andreev 1992), (Krueger 1961)

19.   The data are just bare bones for Kumyk.

20.   Unlike *bart* 'exist, be', *yokt(ur)* does not take person-number suffixes. It is frequently used as a sentence tag and as the general word 'No'.

21.   Even the consonant of the negation suffix is subject to numerous assimilations, cf. Baskalov (1972:62).

Table 8. Data from Dravidian languages, see also (Lindblom 2014) for additional data

Subgroup	Language name	SN		Negative existential	Type in NEC	Source
		pst	NEG by suffix has no temporal value, except where indicated			
North	Brahui [brh]	VERB-$t(a)$- PERS.NUM.G	VERB-$f(a)$-/-$p(a)$-PERS. NUM.G	$alla$-v-PERS.NUM aff-PER.NUM.G[22]	B	(Andronov 1980: 70–79)
Central	Parji [pci]	VERB-e/-o PERS.NUM.G	VERB-a- PERS.NUM.G	$cila/cila$-	B	(Burrow & Bhattacharya 1953: 64, 67)
Southern II	Chenchu [cde]	VERB-INF + $lēdu/lē$	verb-a-/-$\bar{o}$- PERS.NUM.G / VERB-NMLZ + $lēdu$ 'negative progressive'	$lē$- PER.NUM.G	B~C	(Trivedi 1978: 58, 74, 80)
	Gondi [ggo]	VERB-PRET+sil	VERB-$\bar{o}$-/ -v- PERS.NUM.G	sil	B~C	(Lincoln 1969: 162, 111, 134)
	Konda [kfc]	VERB-t- PERS.NUM.G	VERB-$ʔ$- PERS.NUM.G	sil- PERS.NUM.G	B	(Krishnamurti 1969: 283, 289)
	Koya [kff]	VERB-INF-ill-PERS.NUM	VERB-o-/-$\bar{o}$-/-$\bar{u}$-/-v-/-$v\bar{o}$-/-$v\bar{u}$-/-$\bar{e}$-PERS.NUM.G	ill- PERS.NUM.G	B~C	(Tyler 1969: 99, 83, 96–97)
	Kuvi [kxv]	VERB-$ʔa$-PERS.NUM.G / VERB-NEG.PST.PTCP + hil-$ʔasi$	VERB-$ʔo$-/-$ʔ$-/-$ʔ\bar{o}$-PERS. NUM.G	hil-$ʔa$-PERS.NUM / hil-$ʔo$-PERS.NUM.G	**B~C**	(Israel 1979: 62–63, 135–136, 166)
	Telugu [tel]	VERB-INF + $lēdu$ 'not. exist.3SG'	VERB-a- PERS.NUM.G	$lē$- PERS.NUM	B~C	(Krishnamurti & Gwynn 1985: 218, 159, 142)
Southern I	Literary Kannada [kan]	VERB-INF-$illa$	VERB-a- PERS.NUM.G / VERB-NMLZ + $illa$	$illa$	B~C	(Schiffman 1983: 113–114)

(Continued)

22. Andronov (1980:79) states that the stem a- takes the negative suffix f and subsequent person-number marking. This is certainly the historical situation but synchronically the negative forms of the verb 'be' are unanalyzable units so any further morphological analysis is superfluous.

Table 8. (Continued)

Subgroup	Language name	SN	pst — NEG by suffix has no temporal value, except where indicated	Negative existential	Type in NEC	Source
	Spoken Kannada [kan]	VERB-INF-*illa*	VERB-*e* / VERB-NMLZ.INFORMAL + *illa* / VERB-NMLZ-*Vlla*	*illa*	C	(Schiffman 1983: 113–114)
	Kodava=Kodagu [kfa]	VERB.NMLZ-*le*/-*ille*	VERB.NMLZ-*le*	*ille*	C	(Ebert 1996: 22)
	Alu Kurumba [xua]	VERB-NMLZ-*le*	VERB-*ar*/*yi*-PERS.NUM.G	*ille*	B~C	(Kapp 1982: 141, 151, 52)
	Malayalam [mal]	VERB.PST-*illa*	VERB.PRS-*illa* / VERB.FUT1-*illa* / VERB.NEG.FUT2-*illa*	*illa*	C	(George 1971: 53, 30)
	Tamil [tam]	-*ill*-	VERB-*á*-PER.NUM.G	*illa*	B~C	(Lehmann 1993: 209)

References

Abaev, Vasily I. 1993. *Obshie elementy v jazyke osentin, balkarcev i karachaevcev*. Leningrad: Izdatel'stvo Akademii Nauk SSSR.

Agesthialingom, Sakthievel & Shanmugam, S.V. 1970. *The Language of Tamil Inscriptions 1250–1350 A.D*. Annamalainagar: Annamalai University.

Alexiadou, Artemis & Rathert, Monika (eds) 2010. *The Syntax of Nominalizations across Languages and Frameworks*. Berlin: De Gruyter. doi:10.1515/9783110245875

Anderson, Gregory D.S. 1998. *Khakas*. Munich: Lincom.

Andreev, I.A. 1992. *Uchebnik po chuvashkogo jazyk dlja russkix* Cheboksary: Chuvashkoe knizhnoe izdatel'svo.

Andronov, Mihail Sergeevič. 1980. *The Brahui Language*. Moscow: Nauka Publishing House, Central Department of Oriental Literature.

Andronov, Mihail S. 2003. *A Compararive Grammar of the Dravidian Language*. Wiesbaden: Otto Harrasowitz.

Baskakov, Nikolaj A. 1972. *Dialekt kumandincev (Kumandy-kizi): grammatičeskij očerk, teksty, perevody i slovar' (Severnye dialekty altajskogo ojrotskogo jazyka)*. Moskva: Izdatel'stvo "Nauka".

Baskakov, Nikolaj A. & Inkizhekova-Grekul, A.I. 1953. *Khakassko-pusskij slovar'/Okolo 14000 slov. S prilozheniem ocherka Khakasskij jazyk*. Moskva: Gosudarstveno izdatel'stvo inostrannykh i natsionalnykh slovarej.

Birnbaum, Henrik. 1958. *Untersuchungen zu den Zukunftsumschreibungen mit dem Infinitiv im Altkirchenslavischen*. Stockholm: Almqvist & Wiksell.

Broschart, Jürgen. 1999. Negation in Tongan. *Negation in Oceanic Languages*, Even Hovdaugen & Ulrike Mosel, 96–114. Munich: Lincom.

Burrow, Thomas & Emeneau, Murray Barnson. 1984. *A Dravidian Etymological Dictionary*. Oxford: Clarendon Press.

Burrow, Thomas & Bhattacharya, Sudhibhushan. 1953. *The Parji Language: A Dravidian Language of Bastar*. Herford: Steven Austin and Sons.

Bybee, Joan. 1985. *Morphology* [Typological Studies in Language 9]. Amsterdam: John Benjamins. doi:10.1075/tsl.9

Chung, Sandra. 1973. The syntax of nominalizations in Polynesian. *Oceanic Linguistics* 12: 641–86. doi:10.2307/3622869

Comrie, Bernard. 1981. Negation and other verb categories in the Uralic languages. In *Congressus Quintus Internationalis Fenno-Ugristarum, Pars VI: Dissertationes sectionum: Phonologica et morphologica, syntactica et semantica*, O. lkola (ed.), 350–355. Turku: Suomen Kielen Seura.

Comrie, Bernard & Thompson, Sandra A. 1985. Lexical nominalization. In *Language Typology and Syntactic Description*, Timothy Shopen (ed.), 348–98. Cambridge: CUP.

Croft, William. 1991. The evolution of negation. *Journal of Linguistics* 27: 1–39. doi:10.1017/S0022226700012391

Croft, William. 2001. *Radical Construction Grammar: Syntactic Theory in a Typological Perspective*. Oxford: OUP. doi:10.1093/acprof:oso/9780198299554.001.0001

Csató, Éva Ágnes. 2001. Karaim. *Minor Languages of Europe*, Thomas Stolz (ed.), 1–24. Bochum: Universitätsverlag Dr. N. Brockmeyer.

Cyffer, Norbert. 1998. *A Sketch of Kanuri* [Grammatische Analysen, Afrikanischer Sprachen 9]. Cologne: Rüdiger Köppe.

Cypanov, Evgenij Aleksandrovič. 2007. *Vidza olan! Samouchitel' komi jazyka* Syktyvkar: Izdatel'stov Anbur.

Dahl, Östen. 1979. Typology of sentence negation. *Linguistics* 17: 79–106.

Dahl, Östen. 2010. Typology of negation. *The Expression of Negation*, Lawrence R. Horn (ed.), 9–38. Berlin: Mouton de Gruyter.

Devos, Maud & van der Auwera, Johan. 2010. Jespersen cycles in Bantu: Double and triple negation. *Africana Linguistica* 16: 155–181.

Đorđić, Petar. 1975. *Staroslovenski jezik*. Beograd: Matica Srpska.

Dryer, Matthew S. 1992. The Greenbergian word order correlations. *Language* 68: 81–138. doi:10.1353/lan.1992.0028

Dryer, Matthew S. 2007. Clause types. In *Language Typology and Syntactic Description*, Timothy Shopen (ed.), 224–75. Cambridge: CUP.

Duridanov, Ivan. (ed.) 1991. *Gramatika na starobulgarskija ezik*. Sofia: Izdatelstvo na Bulgarskata Akademiia na Naukite.

Ebert, Karen. 1996. *Koḍava*. Munich: Lincom.

Elbert, Samuel H. 1948. *Grammar and Comparative Study of the Language of Kapingamarangi. Texts and Word Lists* [Coordinated Investigation of Micronesian Anthropology (1947–1949), CIMA report 3]. Seattle WA: Pacific Science Board, National Research Council.

Engesaeth, Tarjei, Yakup, Mahire & Dwyer, Arienne M. 2009. *Greetings from Teklimakan: A Handbook of Modern Uyghur*. Lawrence KS: University of Kansas Scholar Works.

Erdal, Marcel. 1979. The chronological classification of Old Turkish texts. *Central Asiatic Journal* 23: 151–175.

Erdal, Marcel. 2004. *A Grammar of Old Turkic*. Leiden: Brill.

van Gelderen, Elly (ed.) 2009. *Cyclical Change* [Linguistik Aktuell/Linguistics Today 146]. Amsterdam: John Benjamins. doi:10.1075/la.146

van Gelderen, Elly. 2008. Negative cycles. *Linguistic Typology* 12: 195–243. doi:10.1515/LITY.2008.037

George, Karimpumannil Mathai. 1971. *Malayalam Grammar and Reader*. Trivandrum: St. Joseph's Press Trivandrum-14.

Gerner, Mattias. 2012. The typology of nominalization: Review article on Foong Ha Yap, Karen Grunow-Hårsta & Janick Wrona, *Nominalization in Asian Languages: Diachronic and Typological Perspectives*, Amsterdam: John Benjamins, 2011. *Language and Linguistics* 13: 503–544.

Givón, Talmy. 1979. *On Understanding Grammar* New York NY: Academic Press.

Golden, Peter B. 1998. The Turkic peoples: A historical sketch. In *The Turkic Languages*, Lars Johanson & Éva Á. Csató (eds), 18–29. London: Routledge.

Greenberg, Joseph. 1966. *Language Universals, With Special Reference to Feature Hierarchies* [Janua Linguarum, Series Minor 59]. The Hague: Mouton.

Grønbech, Kaare. 1955. Bemerkungen über das alttürkische Verbum. *Zeitschrift der Deutschen Morgenländischen Gesellschaft* 105: 69–70.

Hamari, Arja. 2007. The Negation of Stative Relation Clauses in the Mordvin Languages. Ph.D. dissertation, University of Turku.

Hamari, Arja. 2011. Negation in Komi. Presented *Negation in Uralic Languages* workshop, Stockholm University, 24 November. Published in *Negation in Uralic Languages* [Typological Studies in Language 108], Matti Miestamo, Anne Tamm & Beáta Wagner-Nagy (eds), 239–264. Amsterdam: John Benjamins. doi:10.1075/tsl.108.09ham

Harlow, Ray. 2007. *Māori: A Linguistic Introduction*. Cambridge: CUP. doi:10.1017/CBO9780511618697

Hengeveld, Kees. 1992. Non-verbal predicability. In *Meaning and Grammar: Cross-linguistic Perspectives* [Empirical Approaches to Language Typology 10], Michel Kefer & Johan van der Auwera (eds), 135–160. Berlin: Mouton de Gruyter.

Horn, Laurence R. 1997. All John's children are as bald as the king of France: Existential import and the geometry of opposition. *Papers from the Regional Meetings, Chicago Linguistic Society, 1997*, 33(1): 155–179.

Hovdaugen, Even & Mosel, Ulrike. 1999. *Negation in Oceanic Languages*. Munich: Lincom.

Hutchison, John P. 1981. *The Kanuri Language: A Reference Grammar*. Madison WI: African Studies Program, University of Wisconsin.

Israel, Motchakon. 1979. *A Grammar of the Kuvi Language, with Texts and Vocabulary*. Trivandrum: Dravidian Linguistics Association.

Jespersen, Otto. 1917. *Negation in English and Other Languages*. København: Hovedkommissionær: Andr, Fred, Høst & Søn, KGL. Hof-boghandel, Bianco Lunos Bogtrykkeri.

Kahananui, Dorothy M. & Anthony, Alberta P. 1970. *E Kama'ilio Hawai'i Kakou (Let's Speak Hawaiian)*. Honolulu HI: The University Press of Hawaii. Reprinted in 1975.

Kahrel, Peter & van den Berg, René (eds). 1994. *Typological Studies in Negation* [Typological Studies in Language 29]. Amsterdam: John Benjamins. doi:10.1075/tsl.29

Kahrel, Peter. 1996. Aspects of Negation. Ph.D. dissertation, University of Amsterdam.

Kapp, Dieter B. 1982. *Ālu-Kuṟumbaru Nāyan: Die Sprache der Ālu-Kuṟumbas: Grammatik, Texte, Wörterbuch* Wiesbaden: Otto Harrasowitz.

Koptjevskaja-Tamm, Maria & Wälchli, Bernhard. 2001. The Circum-Baltic languages: An areal typological approach. In *The Circum-Baltic Languages: Typology and Contact* [Studies in Language Companion Series 54–55], Östen Dahl & Maria Koptjevskaja-Tamm (eds), 615–751. Amsterdam: John Benjamins.

Koptjevskaja-Tamm, Maria. 1993. *Nominalizations*. London: Routledge.

Kossmann, Maarten G. Forthcoming. Berber subclassification. In *The Oxford Handbook of African Languages*, Rainer Vossen (ed.). Oxford: OUP.

Krishnamurti, Bhadriraju & Gwynn, J.P.L. 1985. *A Grammar of Modern Telugu*. Oxford: OUP.

Krishnamurti, Bhadriraju. 1969. *Koṇḍa or Kūbi: A Dravidian Language (Texts, Grammar, and Vocabulary)*. Hyderabad: Tribal Cultural Research and Training Institute, Government of Andhra Pradesh.

Krishnamurti, Bhadriraju. 1990. Stative Expressions in Indian Languages (Some Semantic and Syntactic Aspects). *Osmania Papers in Linguistics*, 16–17: 39–71.

Krishnamurti, Bhadriraju. 2003. *The Dravidian Languages*. Cambridge: CUP. doi:10.1017/CBO9780511486876

Krueger, John R. 1961. *Chuvash Manual: Introduction, Grammar, Reader and Vocabulary*. Bloomington IN & The Hague: Indiana University Publications & Mouton.

Laakso, Johanna, Wagner-Nagy, Beáta, Sarolta Viola, Márta, Sutter, Regula, Bradley, Jeremy, Mus, Nikolett & Köstbauer, Maria. 2011. Typology of Negation in Ob-Ugric and Samoyedic Languages. Vienna.

Lehmann, Thomas. 1993. *A Grammar of Modern Tamil*. Pondicherry: Pondicherry Institute of Linguistics and Culture.

Lieber, Michael D. & Dikepa, Kalio H. 1974. *Kapingamarangi Lexicon*. Honolulu HI: University Press of Hawaii.

Lincoln, Neville John. 1969. *A Descriptive Analysis of the Adilabad Dialect of Gondi*. Ithaca NY: Cornell University.

Lindblom, Camilla. 2014. Negation in Dravidian Languages. A Descriptive Typological Study of Verbal and Non-verbal Negation in Simple Declarative Sentences. MA thesis, Stockholm University.

Mettouchi, Amina. 2009. The system of negation in Berber. In *Negation Patterns in West African Languages and Beyond* [Typological Studies in Language 87], Norbert Cyffer, Erwin Ebermann & Georg Ziegelmeyer (eds), 287–306. Amsterdam: John Benjamins. doi:10.1075/tsl.87.14met

Miestamo, Matti. 2005. *Standard Negation: The Negation of Declarative Verbal Main Clauses in a Typological Perspective.* Berlin: Mouton de Gruyter.

Mirčev, Kiril. 1968. Kăm istorijata na bădešte predvaritelno (futurum exactum) vreme v bălgarskija ezik. *Izvestija na Instituta za Bălgarski Ezik* 16: 357–62.

Mosegaard Hansen, Maj-Britt. 2011. Negative cycles and grammaticalization. In *The Oxford Handbook of Grammaticalization*, Heiko Narrog & Bernd Heine (eds), 570–579. Oxford: OUP.

Moyse-Faurie, Claire. 1997. *Grammaire du futunien.* Nouméa: Centre de Documentation Pédagogique.

Moyse-Faurie, Claire. 1999. Negation in East Futunan. In *Negation in Oceanic Languages*, Even Hovdaugen & Ulrike Mosel (eds), 115–31. Munich: Lincom.

Musaev, Kenesbaj Musaevic. 1964. *Grammatika karaimskogo jaqyka. Fonetik i morfologija.* Moskva: Izdatel'svo Nauka.

Musaev, Kenesbaj Musaevic. 2003. *Sintaksis karaimskogo jazyka.* Moskva: Rossijskaja Akademija Nauk. Institut jazykoznanija.

Nikolaeva, Irina. 2007. *Finiteness: Theoretical and Empirical Foundations.* Oxford: OUP.

Öztopçu, Kurtuluş. 2000. *Elementary Azerbaijani.* Santa Monica CA & Istanbul: Tütk Dilleri Araştırmaları Dizisi.

Payne, John R. 1985. Negation. In *Language Typology and Syntactic Description,* Vol I: *Clause Structure*, Timothy Shopen (ed.), 197–242. Cambridge: CUP.

Petrova, Nyuguyana. 2011. Lexical and Clause-linkage Properties of the Converbal Constructions in Sakha (Yakut). Ph.D. dissertation, State University of New York at Buffalo.

Pokrovskaja, Ljudmila A. 1964. *Grammatika gagauzskogo jazyka. Fonetika i morfologija.* Moskva: Akademija Nauk SSSR: Institut Jazykoznanija.

Polinskaja, Maria. 1995. *Jazyk Niue.* Moskva: Izdatel'skaja firma "Vostochnaja literatura" RAN.

Qualin, Ma,Wanxiang, Ma & Zhicheng, Ma. 1993. *Salar Language Materials.* Philadelphia PA: Department of Asian and Middle Eastern Studies, University of Pennsylvania. doi:10.1075/tsl.29.03sch

van Schaaik, Gerjan. 1994. Turkish. In *Typological Studies in Negation*, [Typological Studies in Language 29], Peter Kahrel & René van den Berg (eds), 35–50. Amsterdam: John Benjamins.

Schiffman, Harold F. 1983. *A Reference Grammar of Spoken Kannada.* Seattle WA: University of Washington Press.

Schwegler, Armin. 1988. Word-order changes in predicate negation in Romance languages. *Diachronica* 5: 21–58. doi:10.1075/dia.5.1-2.03sch

Sridhar, S.N. 1990. *Kannada.* London: Routledge.

Stassen, Leon. 1997. *Typology of Intransitive Predication.* Oxford: Clarendon Press.

Steever, Sanford. 1998. Introduction to the Dravidian languages. In *The Dravidian Languages*, Sanford Steever (ed.), 1–39. London: Routledge.

Stern, Dieter. 2002. Russische pidgins. *Die Welt der Slaven* 47: 1–30.

Tenishev, Èdgem R. 1976. *Stroj salarskogo jazyka.* Moskva: Nauka.

Trivedi, Govind Mohan. 1978. *Linguistic Study of the Chenchus of Andhra Pradesh.* Calcutta: Anthropological Survery of India, Government of India.

Tyler, Stephen B. 1969. *Koya: An Outline Grammar.* Berkeley CA: University of California Press.

van der Auwera, Johan. 2010. On the diachrony of negation. In *Expression of Negation*, Lawrence R. Horn (ed.), 73–101. Berlin: Mouton de Gruyter.

Veselinova, Ljuba. 2013a. Negative existentials: A cross linguistic study. *Italian Journal of Linguistics: Special Issue on Existential Constructions* 25: 107–146.

Veselinova, Ljuba. 2013b. Lexicalized negative senses: A cross-linguistic study. Paper presented at the 10th Biennal Conference of the Association for Linguistic Typology, Leipzig, Germany.

Veselinova, Ljuba. 2014. The negative existential cycle revisited. Linguistics 52: 1327–1369.

Veselinova, Ljuba (with Hedvig Skirgård). 2015. Special negators in the Uralic languages: Synchrony, diachrony and interaction with standard negation. In *Negation in Uralic Languages* [Typological Studies in Language 108], Matti Miestamo, Anne Tamm & Beáta Wagner-Nagy (eds). Amsterdam: John Benjamins. doi:10.1075/slcs.108

Willis, David, Lucas, Christopher & Breitbarth, Anne. 2013. Comparing diachronies of negation. In *The History of Negation in the Languages of Europe and the Mediterranean*, David Willis, Christopher Lucas & Anne Breitbarth (ed.), 1–50. Oxford: OUP. doi:10.1093/acprof:oso/9780199602537.003.0001

Wilmsen, David. 2014. *Arabic Indefinites, Interrogatives and Negators. A Linguistic History of Western Dialects.* Oxford: OUP. doi:10.1093/acprof:oso/9780198718123.001.0001

Xaralampiev, Ivan. 1981. Starobălgarskite sredstva za izrazjavane na bădešti dejstvija i săvremennite formi za bădešte vreme. *Bălgarski Ezik* 31: 116–22.

Yap, Foong Ha, Grunow-Hårsta, Karen & Wrona, Janick (eds). 2011. *Nominalization in Asian Languages: Diachronic and Typological Perspectives* [Typological Studies in Language 96]. Amsterdam: John Benjamins. doi:10.1075/tsl.96

Zeshan, Ulrike. 2004. Hand, head, and face: Negative constructions in sign languages. *Linguistic Typology* 8: 1–58. doi:10.1515/lity.2004.003

Jespersen cycles in the Mayan, Quechuan and Maipurean languages*

Johan van der Auwera & Frens Vossen
University of Antwerp

This study looks for evidence for the Jespersen Cycle, which is typically the development from one single negator to another one via a strengthening stage in which both are present, in the Mayan, Quechuan and Maipurean languages. For Mayan and Quechuan languages the evidence is solid, and what is particularly interesting is that the strengthening would seem to have happened twice and that in both families an irrealis marker served to make the negation emphatic. In Maipurean languages the most important development is the extension of a prenominal privative marker ('without') to clausal negation, which if it shows up preverbally to a verb that already has postverbal negation, would show us a Jespersen Cycle which, untypically, operates from right to left.

1. Introduction

'Jespersen Cycle' is the name given by Dahl (1979:88) to a process in which a single clausal negator is joined by another negator (which often developed from a non-negative construction), thus expressing a semantically simple negation twice, and then disappears, leaving only the 'new' negator. The classical illustration is French: the original negator *ne* was joined by *pas*, thus giving *ne … pas,* and now, in colloquial registers, just *pas*. The label honors the Danish linguist Otto Jespersen, whose 1917 book on negation starts off with an early and clear description of this process.

The last 20 years has seen a lot of work on this process, and from various frameworks (typology, as in van der Auwera 2009, generative grammar, as in van Gelderen 2008, and optimality theory, as in de Swart 2010). The main results are the following:

i. Though it is not to be denied that Jespersen (1917) was early and clear, we now realize that the account was not the earliest and that it was not fully correct either.

---

* Thanks are due to Elly van Gelderen, Edith Pineda-Bernuy and Clifton Pye for their comments and to the Research Foundation Flanders for the financing.

DOI 10.1075/la.227.07auw

An important earlier account was that of Meillet's (1912) and Meillet is also more correct: whereas Jespersen claimed that the reason for the appearance of a second negator was that the first negator was too weak, Meillet claimed that the first negator was not too weak for negation as such, but too weak for emphatic negation (i.e. for expressing *not at all* rather than just *not*). Meillet explicitly took the cycle (which he called a 'spiral') to constitute a case of grammaticalization – the 1912 paper is in fact the very paper in which Meillet introduced the term 'grammaticalization'.

ii.   The Jespersen cycle was originally noticed for Germanic and Romance and languages of North Africa (with Gardiner 1904 on Egyptian, antedating even Meillet). For these languages, we now have more detailed studies (e.g. Willis et al. 2013). We are also beginning to have studies for languages other than those of Western Europe and the Mediterranean, see Devos & van der Auwera (2013) on Bantu, Vossen & van der Auwera (2014) on Austronesian, and van der Auwera & Vossen (in print) on Austronesian and Austro-Asiatic.

iii.   We are beginning to realize that the Jespersen Cycle, at least in its second, doubling stage, does not seem to be a rare phenomenon. Thus, Van Alsenoy (2014: 187–188) finds it in 1 out of 6 languages in a variety sample of 179 languages, a figure that is very similar to what Dryer (2013) reports for his WALS data set of 1189 languages.

iv.   We have come to realize that the process allows a lot more variation than the original work on Germanic, Romance and North African prepared us for. Thus the new negative in the doubling stage need not come from a minimizer (such as French *pas* 'step') or a negative pronoun (such as English *not*). It may, for instance, result from the answer particle *no* (as in some Bantu languages, see Devos and van der Auwera 2013). Also, the doubling stage need not be followed by a new single negator stage. There could be a tripling and even a quadrupling stage (van der Auwera, Vossen & Devos 2013).

v.   We are beginning to understand the relation between the Jespersen Cycle and word order. From the body of existing research it would appear that the cycle typically operates from the left of the verb to the right of the verb. This means that the old negator tends to be preverbal and the new one postverbal. But this is only a tendency and it is to be noted also that the term 'verb' is vague: it can refer to a lexical verb or to an auxiliary verb (Dahl 2010: 24, van der Auwera 2011: 853), and both can be the pivot for the circle (e.g. in Brabantic Belgian Dutch, van der Auwera 2012).

vi.   We are also beginning to understand the relation between the Jespersen Cycle and what Miestamo (2005) has called 'constructional asymmetry'. This asymmetry is found when a positive and a negative sentence do not only differ with respect to the absence vs. the presence of the negator but also in the presence vs. absence of finiteness. Consider Example (1), taken from the Dravidian language Kannada.

(1)   Kannada (Miestamo 2005: 78, based on Sridhar 1990: 112, 220)

    a.   raSmi   na:Le   haLe:bi:Dige   ho:g-utt-a:Le
        Rashmi   tomorrow   Haledib.DAT   go-NPST-3SG.F
        'Rashmi goes to Haledib tomorrow.'

    b.   anil   ka:le:jige   ho:gu-vud-illa
        Anil   college.DAT   go-NPST.GER-NEG
        'Anil won't/doesn't go to college.'

The negator is only *illa*, but when added to a positive sentence, the lexical verb loses its finiteness and, in the non-past construction illustrated in (1), it has to take a gerundial form. There is nothing inherently negative about the non-past gerundial suffix *-vud*, but since it is an obligatory feature of negation, it could be reanalyzed as constitutive of negation, not unlike *pas*, which in its original 'step' meaning did not express negation either.

vii.   Finally, we are gaining a clearer picture of how the Jespersen Cycle relates to other processes of negation renewal, such as the 'Croft Cycle' (Croft 1991; Veselinova 2014, this volume) or other cyclical processes (van Gelderen 2011).

In this paper we turn to the languages of the Americas. We are not the first to do so. The first one might well be Kroskrity (1984) on Arizona Tewa, though there was no reference to the concept of the Jespersen Cycle – for interpreting the Arizona Tewa facts from a Jespersen perspective we have to wait until van der Auwera (2009: 54). Then there is Mithun (1995) on Iroquoian, van Gelderen (2008: 220–227; 2011: 325–329) on Athabascan languages (and other languages of that area), Romero (2012) on K'iche' Maya and Pineda-Bernuy (2014) on the Quechuan languages. For reasons of space, we restrict this study to three families, viz. the Mayan, Quechuan and Maipurean languages – for a study of the totality of the American languages see Vossen (in preparation). The three families all have *ma* as a preverbal negator, but not necessarily as the only one (see Pye this volume for Mayan). This fact is interesting and poses the question to what extent this similarity is due to inheritance, contact, coincidence or a combination of these factors (Matteson 1972: 71; Greenberg 1987: 315; Payne 1990: 76–77). We will not touch upon this controversial issue here. This issue furthermore relates to the classification of the languages of the Americas. In this respect we follow the *Ethnologue* classification (www.ethonologue.com), also with respect to the names and the spellings of languages and languages families. When we discuss a language that is not in the *Ethnologue* or when there is no clear correspondence – this is especially true when we come to Quechuan – we use the name and the spelling of the source.

Another restriction is that we will only discuss standard negation much in the sense of Miestamo (2005), i.e. verbal declarative main clause negation. So we discuss the equivalents of (2), but not the equivalents of the constructions in (3).

(2)   I have not climbed Mount Everest.

(3)   a.   He said that he had not climbed Mount Everest.
      b.   Don't climb Mount Everest.
      c.   Nobody had climbed Mount Everest before Tenzing Norgay and
           Edmund Hillary.
      d.   I am not a mountaineer.

In one respect we depart from Miestamo (2005), as we will discuss both emphatic
negation and constructional asymmetry, to the extent at least that we see evidence in
the three families that the markers that are responsible for the emphasis or the asymmetry are reinterpreted as exponents of negation.

2.   Negation in the Americas

We have surveyed negation strategies in 530 languages of the Americas.[1] In Table 1
we classified the findings as to whether the negators are obligatorily single preverbal
('NEG V'), obligatorily single postverbal, at least optionally double (but not triple)
with a preverbal and a postverbal part, at least optionally triple, or use yet some other
strategy. The verb relative to which we classify languages and constructions can be an
auxiliary. If the negation is itself an auxiliary we take the lexical verb as the point of
reference. We also compare our numbers with those of earlier studies.

Table 1. A survey of surveys[2]

Source	NEG V	V NEG	NEG V NEG	Triple	Other	Σ
Miestamo 2005	53	37	14	0	8	112
Dryer 2013	190	149	50	0	5	394
This study	256	148	104	5	17	530

The comparison of the three studies is approximative only, because Dryer (2013), different from us and Miestamo (2005), takes the verb with respect to which the position of

---

1.   Our sources are grammars and articles. For most of them we rely on specialists explicitly
making a claim on negation in their language(s) or, often, in the dialect(s) of these languages.
When we only rely on example sentences, whether in the grammars and articles or in texts,
we show this – in the tables of Sections 3 to 5 – with a question mark in front of the name of
the language.

2.   We cannot include Van Alsenoy (2014), for there is no information on single postverbal
or triple negation.

the negation is classified to be the lexical verb. Of these datasets only Miestamo's is a true sample, but it is also the smallest data set. He found double negation in 12.5% of his languages, a bit less than Van Alsenoy's (2014: 187–188) worldwide average of 1 out of 6, i.e. 17%. What is remarkable is the high percentage of V NEG languages (33%), which goes counter to the assumed world-wide preference for preverbal negation (Dahl 1979; Dryer 1988, 2013). The data sets in Dryer (2013) and in our own study are not representative but they are much larger. Both data sets show that double negation occurs in percentages not too far from the Van Alsenoy and Miestamo figures: 12.7% in Dryer 2013 and 19.6% in our study – only counting the NEG V NEG types. In agreement with Miestamo's sample, the two datasets also show V NEG to be surprisingly frequent (from 27.9% in this study to 37.8% in Dryer 2013). In a classical Jespersen Cycle a single postverbal negator will be a third stage, following a doubling stage. For at least two families, such a scenario is very plausible. The first such family is the Mayan family.

3.   Negation in the Mayan languages

Romero (2012) is first and foremost a diachronic study of negation in one Mayan language, viz. K'iche', based on texts from the 16th, late 19th and 20th centuries. We present his data and his interpretation but also our own partially different interpretation.

In the earliest K'iche' documents negation was marked by a preverbal negator *ma,* which is an ancient negator reconstructed for Proto-Maya (Pye this volume), or a negator-enclitic compound. (4) illustrates the negator-enclitic compound *mak'u* consisting of the negator *ma-* and the adversative enclitic *-ku.*

(4)   16th century K'iche' Quechua (Romero 2012: 82)
ma-k'u   ʃ-Ø-ucin-ik   ʃ-e-tʃaw-ik
NEG-CL   COMP-3SG.A-succeed-PF   COMP-3PL.A-speak-PF
'But they didn't succeed in speaking.'

Romero (2012: 83) documents 11 such compounds, each conveying a different nuance. Though the enclitics are optional and the bare negator *ma-* is perfectly possible, in roughly 90% of the attestations Romero (2012: 82, 84) finds a negator-enclitic compound. In roughly 15% of the attestations (both of the bare negator and of the compound) there is also a marker *ta* or *tax* (Romero 2012: 84), which is independently used as an irrealis (optative, subjunctive) marker. (5a) illustrates the non-negative irrealis use, and (5b) the negative use. This marker occurs in what Romero (2012: 82) calls a post-head position, which in the cases we are interested in boils down to a postverbal position.

(5)   16th century K'iche' (Romero 2012: 88, 87)
a.   r-umal   nima-k'aʃk'ol
     3SG.E-cause   great-pain

mi-ʃ-Ø-ki-ɓan   tʃi-q-e
RPST-COMP-3SG.A-3PL.E-do   LOC-1PL.E-for

ʃ-ox-kam   tax   ʃ-ox-satʃ   tax   putʃ
COMP-1PL.A-die   IRR   COMP-1PL.A-lose   IRR   also

'Because of the great suffering they did onto us, we would have died, we would have been lost too.'

b. man(a)   k-Ø-a:wil   tax
    NEG   INC-3SG.A-2SG.E-see   IRR
    'You didn't see it at all.'

Romero (2012: 82–88) assumes, without any argumentation, that for *ta(x)* the irrealis meaning is the oldest one, which may get lost in the negative context, in which case it becomes a negative polarity item. Our own view is different: let the irrealis meaning indeed be the oldest meaning, but since negation is an excellent irrealis context, there is no reason to assume that the irrealis meaning is no longer present in the negative context. It is, of course, semantically redundant. But not necessarily pragmatically. The use of *ta(x)* indeed appears to be strongly associated with one particular emphatic negator-enclitic compound, viz. *man(a)* 'not at all', already illustrated in (5b). This is an example of a grammar of 1560, and the grammarian claimed that *ta(x)* is obligatory for *man(a)* (Romero 2012: 87). This is an overstatement, for Romero finds uses of *man(a)* without *ta(x)*, but even in his own material half of the time *ta(x)* is found together with *man(a)* and in the other half the negative-enclitic is an adversative 'but not' compound (Romero 2012: 84), which we take as a kind of emphasis, too. So we propose that what *ta(x)* did was to add emphasis. Whether or not *ta(x)* was always emphatic, i.e. also in non-negative contexts, is not clear. Romero (2012: 85) does not discuss any negative polarity context other than negation.

By the end of 19th century, two things had happened. First, the 16th century variation between bare *ma* and the 11 *ma-* compounds was strongly reduced: 85% of Romero's examples now have *man(a)* (Romero 2012: 90). Romero does not make clear to what extent the uses are still emphatic, but given the very high percentage, it must have been bleached considerably – and we know that by 1923 the bleaching had been completed (Romero 2012: 92). Second, in half of the cases, *ta(x)* was present (Romero 2012: 90–91). Again, Romero does not make clear to what extent the subset of *man(a)* uses with *ta(x)* were emphatic. We know that *ta(x)* will lose emphatic nuance (assuming as we do, but not Romero, that it had one) and that it will become an obligatory part of negation. The fact that *ta(x)* was present in only half of the cases makes sense on the assumption that it could still mark emphasis.

By 1923, only *mana* survived as the preverbal negative and it was obligatorily accompanied by *ta(x)* (Romero 2012: 91). And right now *ta(x)* is beginning to occur

as the sole exponent of negation.[3] (6) is a contemporary example of the *(man(a)) ....*
ta(x) strategy.

    (6)   Modern K'iche' (Romero 2012:85)
           (man) w-etaman   ta   u-watʃ
           NEG   1SG.E-know NEG 3SG.E-face
           'I do not know him/her.'

We thus see that K'iche' shows a clear progression from a single preverbal strategy to
a double, embracing one and then to a simple postverbal one. This is very much like a
classical Jespersen Cycle, but it is a little special for two reasons. First, in our analysis
the bleaching of an emphatic strategy to a non-emphatic one happened twice: it happened to the *na* part of *man(a)* as well as to the *tax* part, and the two processes did
not happen in sync. Second, the *tax* emphasizer has its origin in an irrealis marker. Of
note, though not so special, is that if one characterizes the Jespersen Cycle in terms of
five stages, as in (7), the K'iche' Cycle has not been completed yet. K'iche' is in stage 4,
because the preverbal negative remains optional.

    (7)   Stage 1   Stage 2   Stage 3   Stage 4   Stage 5

           NEG V   NEG V (NEG)   NEG V NEG   (NEG) V NEG   V NEG

So much for the diachronic aspects of the work by Romero. He also makes the
comparative remark (Romero 2012:79, 92) that there are other K'ichean languages with double negation, more particularly, Kaqchikel, Tz'utujil, and Q'eqchi',
which did not reach the fourth stage, except for varieties that were in close contact with K'iche'. We have checked a few more Mayan languages (compare again
Pye this volume). All of the languages listed in Table 1 have a preverbal (cognate
of) *ma* and in some there is also a postverbal (cognate of) *ta(x)*. With a five stage
model our sources suggest the classification in Table 2. Stage 1, 2 and 3 languages
are illustrated in (8) to (10). It is important to stress that putting a language in
Stage 1 is a little misleading: there is no guarantee at all that it will ever move to
Stage 2.

---

3. Romero (2015) shows that in one variant of K'iche' the cycle is going another round, with
a clause-final copy of *ta* being added to *ta* or even to *man ... ta*. The first case results in a new
doubling pattern and the second in tripling. Such processes are known from Jespersen Cycles
in other languages (van der Auwera 2009; van der Auwera, Vossen & Devos 2013). Romero
(2015) invokes a notion of 'negative concord', but this is uncalled for.

Table 2. A Jespersen Cycle hypothesis for the Mayan languages

Stages	Languages		Sources
1	Chol	Cholan-Tzeltalan	Vázquez Alvarez 2002: 26–28; Coon 2006
	Itza'	Yucatecan	Hofling 2000: 185–186, 432–444
	Jakalteko	Q'anjob-'alan-Chujean	Grinevald Craig 1977: 26–30; Day 1973: 80–81
	Mopan	Yucatecan	Verbeeck 1998: 90–91
	Aguacatenango Tzeltal	Cholan-Tzeltalan	Kaufman 1971: 108
	Bachajón Tzeltal[4]	Cholan-Tzeltalan	Slocum 1980: 82
2	Pokomchi'	K'ichean	Mayers 1958: 129, 143
	Q'eqchi'	K'ichean	Romero 2012: 79, 93[3]
	Tzutujil	K'ichean	Romero 2012: 79, 92[5]
3	?Achí	K'ichean	Neuenswander & Shaw 1971: 272
	Kaqchikel	K'ichean	Romero 2012: 79, 92; Stenson 1998: 224
	Chuj	Q'anjob-'alan-Chujean	Williams & Williams 1966: 324–325, 329–330; Buenrostros 1991: 35, 68; Hopkins 1967: 120–122, 128–129, 138, 144
	Poqomam	K'ichean	Santos Nicolás & Pérez Waykan 1998: 231–233, 264–267, 387–399, 338–339
4	K'iche'	K'ichean	Romero 2012: 86
5	Ø		

(8) Bachajón Tzeltal (Slocum 1980: 82)
    ma? oc-em-uk-on
    NEG enter-PRF-MODAL-1SG
    'I haven't entered.'

(9) Pokomchi' (Mayers 1958: 19, 12)

    a. mi ma' ix-kacuy l'elejeb k'ij …
        if NEG endure the.nine days
        'If we do not endure the nine days …'

    b. xpon i rek pero ma' xuc'a ta rib'
        3SG.go to search but NEG did NEG uncover.it
        'He went to search but he did not uncover it.'

---

4. Bachajón Tzeltal could be a stage 2 language, for, as Example (8) shows, the verb form contains a so-called 'modal suffix'. This could be an irrealis marker not unlike what we see in K'iche' and, later also, in Quechuan. However, the nature of this suffix is unclear. It shows up with perfective verbs (and with the copula), as well as in intransitive hortatives (*let's*) constructions (Slocum 1980: 82).

5. Romero (2012) does not make clear whether doubling is necessary or just possible.

(10)   Pocomam (Santos Nicolás & Pérez Wyakan 1998: 369, no glosses)
        man ki'k'oona   ta pan paat kotaq ak'un
        NEG   NEG
        'The children didn't play in the house.'

It is clear that the Jespersen Cycles basically only plays in the K'ichean family. The
one exception of the non-K'ichean language is Chuj. Map 1 shows how the stages are
distributed in space.[6] The isoglosses show the Mayan Jespersen Cycle to have a clear
centre (Stage 4) and a clear periphery (the potential Stage 1). The isoglosses for Stage 2
and 3 are close to each other and thus less clear, but they do not cross each other.

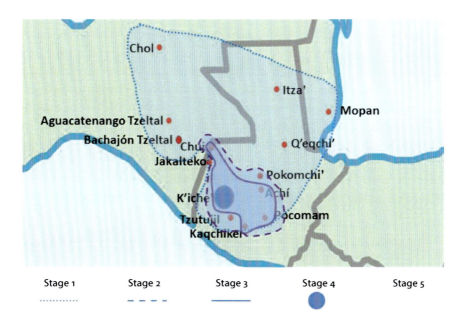

Map 1. A Jespersen Cycle hypothesis for the Mayan languages

4.   Negation in the Quechuan languages

For Quechuan we have our own synchronic survey and of that of Pineda-Bernuy
(2014), done independently. The latter also treats the 16th century variety called

---

6.   We used the 'Interactive Reference Tool' of the *World Atlas of Language Structures* (http://
wals.info) to make the maps of this paper. The maps only indicate the current location of the
languages. This is problematic for linguistic similarity may relate to the geographical proximity of the earlier and possibly very different location of languages.

lengua general. In this variety there are, according to Pineda-Bernuy (2014: 118–119), two strategies. One uses a preverbal *mana* and the second uses *mana* together with a postverbal suffix *-chu*.

(11)   16th century Quechua (Pineda-Bernuy 2014: 119, 118)

    a.   kiki-lla-n-ta-paŝ   mana qishpi-chi-ku-n
         self-LIM-3-AC-AD   NEG   save-CAUS-REFL-3
         'They didn't even save themselves.'

    b.   yacha-ŝpa-taq-mi   mana waqaycha-n-chu
         know-SUB-CONTR-AS   NEG   obey-3-NEG
         'But, although they know, they didn't obey.'

The form *mana* is similar to what we found in Mayan, esp. the *ma* component. For Quechua *-na* Pineda-Bernuy (2014: 116, 122) hypothesizes an irrealis origin. This is different for Mayan *-na,* of which the earliest use was taken to be an emphasis maker.

Of the two Quechuan strategies, i.e. *mana* alone and *mana* with the postverbal suffix *-chu,* the one with just *mana* is argued by Pineda-Bernuy (2014) to be the oldest one. The main argument concerns the analysis of *-chu*.[7] Like Quechuan *-na* this *-chu* suffix is an irrealis marker, at least to the extent one can infer this from the modern varieties (Pineda-Bernuy 2014: 88, 114, 122). In most modern Quechuan languages *-chu* marks interrogation, which is arguably an irrealis use. This is illustrated in (12). (13) is an example of a non-negative non-interrogative irrealis use.

(12)   Cusco Quechua (Pineda-Bernuy 2014: 86)
     ¿Juan llank'a-rqa-n-chu?
     Juan work-PST-3-Q
     'Did John work?'

(13)   Quechua (Pineda-Bernuy 2014: 123)
     chay-qa huk martes   p'unchay-chu hina, puri-ri-mu-yku ...
     that-TOP one Tuesday day-IRR   like walk-INCH-DIR-1EXCL
     'We may have left on Tuesday ...'

The association of a negator with irrealis again invites a comparison with Mayan. For Mayan we argued that there was a postverbal irrealis marker that was added to

---

7.   Another argument is that in varieties that normally use *mana* plus *-chu* there are constructions with just *mana* in what could be considered to be frozen constructions (Pineda-Bernuy 2014: 107). Also, Pineda-Bernuy (2014: 92) points out that in all modern Quechua languages subordinate clauses only use *mana*. Since subordinate clauses are often conservative (cp. van der Auwera 2009: 62 on an older negator surviving in the subordinate clauses of Dutch dialects), this too, we propose, could be seen as an argument.

a negator to make the negation emphatic. This is also what Pineda-Bernuy (2014:94, 119) proposes, though not on the basis of an analysis of old texts, but on what she analyzes as what is happening in the contemporary conservative Quechuan languages of the extreme North and South. In these varieties, Ecuadorian Northern Quechua and Argentinian Southern Quechua, called 'Peripheral' (Pineda-Bernuy 2014:86), the neutral negation uses only *mana*, but for emphasis -*chu* is added (Pineda-Bernuy 2014:93–95).

(14) Ecuadorian Northern Quechua (Pineda-Bernuy 2014:93)
      Pedro kayna   mana shamu-rka
      Pedro yesterday NEG   come-PST
      'Pedro didn't come yesterday.'

(15) Argentinian Southern Quechua (Pineda-Bernuy 2014:95)
      mana llamka-n-chu Pedro
      NEG work-3-NEG   Pedro
      'Pedro DOES NOT work.'

What is happening in these peripheral varieties now, she argues, must have happened in the non-peripheral varieties earlier.

It is also interesting that in both Mayan and Quechuan languages the strengthening with a postverbal element, *ta(x)* in Mayan and -*chu* in Quechuan, happened to a *ma*- marker that was itself strengthened with a -*na* element.

For the modern Quechuan languages, our survey includes the languages shown in Table 3. Chinchay and Yungay languages are both 'Peripheral' in the sense used in *Ethnologue*, which is wider than the use used in Pineda-Bernuy (2014). As there are many question marks, indicating that our categorization is based on examples rather than explicit claims (see Note 2), the hypothesis must remain very tentative. Note also that we have included a doubling strategy in which either the preverbal or the postverbal negator can be absent (2 or 4). This could be seen as an alternative to stage 3. Like in an ordinary stage 3, both negators are available, but both are separately optional. Stage 2 languages have already been illustrated in (14) and (15), but they concerned varieties covered only by Pineda-Bernuy (2014). (16) to (18) illustrate stage 3, 4 and 2-or-4 languages.

(16) Cajamarca Quechua (Coombs 2008:51)
      čay runa biyudu-qa-s   wambritu-n-guna-ta-qa mana
      this man little.son-3-PL-O widower-3-PL-O-TOP   NEG

      ati-rqa-n-ču   qara-y-ta
      can-PST-3-NEG   feed-INF-O

      'This widower couldn't feed his sons.'

Table 3. A Jespersen Cycle hypothesis for the Quechuan languages

Stages	Languages	Families	Sources
1	Ø		
2	Chimborazo	Northern Chinchay	Beukema 1975: 120–122
	Inga de San Andrés	Northern Chinchay	Levinsohn 1974: part 1: 39–40; part 2: *passim*; Levinsohn 2008: *passim*
	?San Martin	Northern Chinchay	Phelps 2008a: *passim*
	?Huallaga	Central	Weber 1987: *passim*
	?North Junín Tarma	Central	Black 1987: *passim*
	?de la Unión	Southern Chinchay	Kindberg 1987: *passim*; Phelps 2008b: *passim*
3	Imbabura	Northern Chinchay	Miestamo 2005: 100–101
	?Pastaza	Northern Chinchay	Zahn & Toedter 1987: 38
	?Saraguro	Northern Chinchay	Weber & Orr 1987: *passim*
	?Cajamarca	Yungay	Carlson de Coombs 1975b: 12; Coombs & Carlson de Coombs 2008: *passim*
	?Lambayeque	Yungay	Shaver & Shaver 2008: *passim*; Shaver 1987: *passim*
	?Ambo	Central	Tolliver 1987: *passim*
	Ayacucho	Southern Chinchay	Carlson de Coombs 1975a: 19; Weber & Phelps 1987a: *passim*
	Bolivian	Southern Chinchay	Loriot 1975: 12; Sherman et al. 1967: 93–94
	Cochabamba	Southern Chinchay	Lastra 1968: 35, 45, 55–56
	Cusco	Southern Chinchay	Loriot 1975: *passim*; Weber & Phelps 1987b: *passim* ;
	?de la Unión	Southern Chinchay	Phelps 2008b: *passim*
4	?Corongo Ancash	Central	Hintz 2008: *passim*
	?Huamalies	Central	Smith 1987: *passim*; Benson 1987: *passim*
	?Pachitea	Central	Smith 2008: *passim*
5	Ø		
+			
2 or 4	?Huaylas	Central	Miller 2008: *passim*
	?Margos-Yarowilca-Laurochoca	Central	Bean 2008: *passim*

(17)   Corongo Ancash Quechua (Hintz 2008: 7)
  ke:-man   mana pwe:de-:xa-n-tsu ni   ba:je-y-ta
  this-GOAL   NEG   can-PST-3-NEG   neither descend-INF-O

  ni   su:bi-y-ta
  neither ascend-INF-O

  'There they couldn't go down or go up.'

(18)   Corongo Ancash Quechua (Hintz 2008:72)
        bwe:nu, i   ka-:xo-n-tsu   nina-n-kuna-xa
        good   but have-PST-3-NEG fire-3-PL-TOP
        'OK, but I don't have fire.'

The generalization that appears is fairly clear: the central languages are the most progressive ones, which does not mean that all of them are, possibly followed by Yungay languages, and the more conservative ones are the Chinchay languages, both in the North and in the South. That the center is most progressive may well accord with the little we know about the earlier stages. The 17th century variety that survives in some documents was spoken in a reasonably central area. So at least in that area the languages had already started the cycle. Map 2 is the cartographical representation of Table 3.

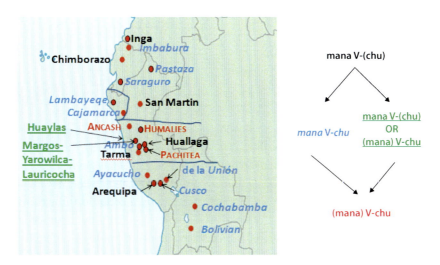

Map 2.   A Jespersen Cycle hypothesis for the Quechuan languages

The survey in Pineda-Bernuy (2014)[8] differs in coverage and, for the languages covered in both, also in the details, but the general picture is the same: the center, though not every language spoken there, is most progressive.

---

8.   The survey that will succeed both studies is Pineda-Bernuy's forthcoming doctoral dissertation (Pineda-Bernuy, in preparation).

5. Negation in the Maipurean languages

In the *Ethnologue* the Maipurean family (also known as 'Maipuran' and 'Arawak') splits up into Northern and Southern Maipurean. We have synchronic data on 36 languages, 18 Northern and 18 Southern ones, but virtually no data on diachrony.[9] We again find a negative preverbal *ma* marker, and we could, superficially, sketch a five stage scenario like the ones offered for Mayan and Quechuan. However, the situation is more complicated and less clear, but in a way also more interesting, also methodologically.

A first point to note is that although negative *ma* is 'one of the most stable features of the Arawak family' (Aikhenvald 2012:186) and it 'is one of the small number of morphemes that most historical works on Arawak languages agree in attributing to Proto-Arawak' (Payne 1991:377–378; Michael 2014b: 276, 285), its diachronically primary and synchronically main use is that of a nominal privative marker ('without N', 'N-less') and not a marker of standard negation (Michael 2014b: 276–282; Aikhenvald 2014:109, 116–118).

(19)   Arawak (Patte 2014:64)
        ma-mana   da-yadoalan
        PRIV-cutting.edge my-knife
        'My knife is without cutting edge.'

That the privative use is synchronically dominant is beyond doubt. That it is also the historically primary one is a hypothesis, which is based on two things. First, it is based on the synchronic dominance: many if not most Maipurean languages have a productive privative use or at least show some relic constructions, and few of the languages have a standard negative use. Second, one can draw up a scenario through which the privative use develops into the standard negation use: from the noun-oriented stative, derivational privative use to the verb oriented non-derivational a-stative standard negation use via a verb-oriented derivational stative use (giving e.g. a 'not know' verb)[10] (Michael 2014b: 280–287).

Secondly, there is much more variation in the preverbal negative slot. Whereas for Mayan and Quechuan languages described in the previous sections, the preverbal marker was *ma* or a construction containing *ma*, in Maipurean *ma* is a minority option: we only found it in at best 9 of the 36 languages. Nevertheless, *ma* is special in the sense that it is the only marker that occurs in both Northern and Southern Maipurean, which again testifies to its age. And as in Mayan and Quechuan there are

---

9.   We have data on Maipure, which became extinct at the end of the 18th century (Zamponi 2003) and on older Tariana (see below).

10.   The intermediate status of verb oriented stative use is itself also reflected in the synchronic distribution (see Michael 2014b: 276–277).

also complex forms. In Table 4 we thus include Parecis *maisa* and *maiha*, assuming with Brandão (2014: 172) and Michael (2014b: 278), that *maisa* and *maiha* contain the very same privative or negative ancestral *ma-*. The nature of these complex forms is unclear: Michael (2014b: 289) speculates that they could originally be negative existentials, which would then illustrate a 'Croft cycle' (Croft 1991; Veselinova 2014). We also include Yanesha' *ama*, though we note that the language appears to have been influenced strongly by Quechuan (Michael 2014b: 279, referring to Wise 1976, and Wise 1986: 616, who explicitly states that Yanesha' borrowed *ama* from Quechuan).[11]

Thirdly, there is also much more variation in the postverbal slot. In Mayan the second marker was always *ta* and in Quechuan it was always *-chu*. In the 10 Maipurean languages for which we have found a postverbal negative, there are few that clearly betray cognacy – see Tables 4, 5 and 6. The fact that most postverbal negators are different is not in support of a Jespersen Cycle, but it does not constitute counterevidence either. For French, for example, the doubling initially involved more than just *pas* (original meaning 'step'), but also *point* (originally meaning 'point') and *miette* (original meaning 'crumb').

In Table 4 we tabulate the 9 Maipurean languages that allow a *ma* form in the preverbal slot in a Jespersen Cycle format.

Table 4. A Jespersen Cycle hypothesis for the Maipurean languages that have a preverbal *ma-* negator

Stages	NEG1	NEG2	Languages	Families	Sources
1	*ma*		Baniwa	Northern	Aikhenvald 2002: 132
	ma		Baré	Northern	Cunha de Oliveira 1998: 160
	m-		Garifuna	Northern	Munro & Gallagher 2014: 20
	mainda		Bahwana	Northern	Aikhenvald 2014: 117
	maisa, maiha		Parecis	Southern	Brandão 2014: 172
	ma/m(a-)/ma m-(a-)		Piro	Southern	Facundes 2014: 144
2	Ø				
3	*ama*	*-o/e*	Yanesha'	Southern	Duff-Tripp 1997: 179; Michael 2014b: 257
4	*(ma)*	*-kade*	Tariana	Northern	Aikhenvald 2014
	(ne)	*kásu*			
5	Ø				
+					
2 or 4	*ma*	*kho(ro)*	Arawak	Northern	Patte 2014: 56, 67–68

---

11. We do not include Nanti *matsi*, for its use is restricted to what Michael (2014a: 194–196) calls 'metalinguistic negation', the denial of a proposition explicit or implicit in the previous discourse.

We see that the synchrony is compatible with a Jespersen Cycle. Even though, as stated above, *ma* was originally a privative, there is no reason why it could not have entered a Jespersen Cycle after it had turned into a marker of standard negation.

Map 3 translates most of Table 4 into cartography.[12] Different from the maps for Mayan and Quechuan there is no clear transition from a centre to a periphery. The reason that Tariana and Yanesha' have arguably progressed further is not that they are the centre of a zone reflecting progress in the cycle. This makes one suspicious. It is perhaps interesting that the languages of potentially stages 2 to 4 are spoken in the Center and the South West. That *ma* is well established in Yanesha', however, is probably due to interference from Quechua (and this may be the case for Piro too, which allows preverbal doubling). We will now discuss and illustrate the languages of the various hypothesized stages.

Map 3. A Jespersen Cycle hypothesis for the Maipurean languages that have a preverbal *ma*- negator

---

12.   We do not give a special symbol for Arawak.

Stage 1 is, of course, simple and as such fully neutral with respect to the Jespersen Cycle hypothesis. Baniwa illustrates the type, but very little seems to be known about the language.

(20) Baniwa (Aikhenvald 2002: 132)
      ma-kapa-kana
      NEG-see-PASS
      'wasn't seen'

In Baré the *ma* construction is marginal – the grammarian glosses it as 'privative' – and the dominant construction is a doubling pattern with preverbal *hena* and a postverbal enclitic *wa(ka)* (Cunha de Oliveira 1998).

(21) Baré (Cunha de Oliveira 1998: 162, 152)

   a. na-ma-kudasa-n   nu-kameni-e
       1SG-NEG-light.up-IMPRF   1SF-fire-POSS
       'I put out my fire.'

   b. txabati hena a-hukada waka
       bird   NEG   S-sing   NEG
       'The bird is not singing.'

Apart from illustrating a stage 1 of the Jespersen Cycle Baré illustrates how *ma* enters the domain of standard negation. Garifuna is categorized as a stage 1 language, but this is a little doubtful, as the verb often ends in *-n* (see Munro & Gallagher 2014: 23–24 for discussion). This makes it a candidate for a stage 2 language. The categorization of Parecis is problematic too, as it shows structural asymmetry, requiring the negated verb to have a progressive or nominalizing affix (Brandão 2014: 172). As mentioned already, Piro is strange too, for it allows preverbal *ma* doubling.

We have no stage 2 language and very little evidence for the possible stage 3 language, Yanesha'.

(22) Yanesha' (Duff-Tripp 1997: 197, unglossed)
      ama name'ñen=o
      'I don't obey.'

The most interesting case is Tariana, which has been described on various occasions by Aikhenvald (2002: 132–136, 2003, 2014), with details on dialectal and diachronic variation.[13] Let us first discuss the major dialect, that of the Wamiarikune clan (Aikhenvald 2014: 105). A non-future clause is negated with a preverbal prefix *ma-* and a postverbal suffix *-kade*.

---

13. We will use the most recent, 2014 description, unless a difference or a better example makes it worthwhile to bring in an earlier account.

(23) Tariana (Aikhenvald 2003: 400)
yanaki   ma-ira-kade-mha   nuha
whisky NEG-drink-NEG-PRES.NONVIS I
'I didn't drink whisky.'

When the verb does not support a prefix, then only -*kade* is found.[14]

(24) Tariana (Aikhenvald 2003: 401)
nuha   keɾu-kade-mha
I   angry-NEG-PRES.NONVIS
'I am not angry.'

When the verb is future and it allows a prefix, then we get *ma-* again as well as a suffix, but the suffix is a different one, i.e. not the 'normal' *kade*, but *kasu*, which is an 'intentional' suffix, taking care of a 'quasi future', an alternative to the real futures, viz. the certain future with -*de* and the uncertain future with -*mhade*.

(25) Tariana (Aikhenvald 2014: 92)
nuha ma-nu-kásu
I   NEG-come.INT
'(I) won't come.'

(26) Tariana (Aikhenvald 2014: 93)
nu-nu-kasú/-de/-mhade.
I-come-INT/FUT.CERT/FUT.UNCERT
'I intend to come/I will come (definitely)/Maybe I will come.'

In (25) Aikhenvald (2014: 93) glosses *kásu* as FUT.NEG, but there is no need to. All we see – and Aikhenvald (2014: 92) sees that too – is that a distinction in the positive domain is neutralized in the negative domain – a case of paradigmatic asymmetry (Miestamo 2005). When the future verb does not allow a prefix, then *ma-* is absent, *kásu* appears again – but with obligatory stress on the first syllable.

(27) Tariana (Aikhenvald: 2014: 93)
wha iya   putʃa-kásu
we   rain be.wet/make.wet-FUT.NEG
'Rain won't make us wet.'

However, in 90% of the corpus examples with *kásu* without *ma*, there is a preverbal particle *ne* (Aikhenvald 2014: 94) The exact function of *ne* is unclear. On the one hand,

---

14. (24) is not an example of standard negation, for neither Aikhenvald (2014) nor the earlier accounts supply one. Prefixless verbs are typically stative, but not necessarily so (Aikhenvald 2014: 88).

Aikhenvald characterizes it as emphatic and glosses it as 'not at all'. On the other hand, its presence 'may be motivated by phonological reasons' (Aikhenvald 2014: 94), for

> [s]stress is the only means of distinguishing a positive *hamíya-kasù* [secondary stress on the last vowel, JvdA & FV] 'is going to be heavy' and a negative *hamiya-kásu* 'won't be heavy'. 'The emphatic negative serves to ensure the negative meaning is expressed with clarity'. (Aikhenvald 2014: 94)

Furthermore, the very fact that 90% of the examples have *ne* strongly suggests that it is not emphatic, at least, not in this context, though not, one supposes, when it occurs together with both *ma* and *kade* and constitutes tripling.

(28) Tariana (Aikhenvald (2014: 102))
di-na   du-wana-tha-pidana
3SG.NF   O.3SGF-call-FRU-REMPST.REP

ne-ma-dia-kade-pidana
NEG.EMP-NEG-return-NEG-REMPST.REP
'She called him in vain, he DID NOT come.'

Nearby East Tucanoan, Aikhenvald (2014: 102–104) further points out, has a similar particle, with arguably similar uses,[15] but Aikhenvald (2014: 103) does not go so far as to claim that the Tariana particle is borrowed from East Tucanoan – maybe only some aspects of the pattern are, which is typical for the contact interference between Tariana and east Tucanoan (Aikhenvald 2014: 111–115). Intererestingly, East Tucanoan standard negation is normally only postverbal and this, Aikhenvald (2014: 111) thinks, could have influenced Tariana too.

Let us now turn to the information about other dialects and about earlier stages of the language. According to Aikhenvald (2014: 105–106) some dialects only have the *-kade* (or *-de*) suffix.[16] From a Jespersen Cycle perspective these would be progressive stage 5 dialects. However, Aikhenvald (2014: 105) further mentions that the suffix also occurs – as the only exponent of negation – in the speech of a lady who speaks an archaic version of a dialect that would otherwise have double negation. Of course, this statement only concerns one speaker, who is furthermore described as 'ethnically' Piratapuya (father Piratapya, mother Tariana). Piratapuya is an East Tucanoan

---

15. The argumentation that the uses are similar in Tariana and Tucanoan is not very strong. The Tucanoan examples all involve the expression of negative indefiniteness, i.e. the counterparts to *nobody* and *nothing*.

16. There is also one dialect that is like the Wamiarikune dialect described so far, but that also has a *-maka* suffix, which occurs without the *ma* prefix and which is emphatic (Aikhenvald 2014: 105). Aikhenvald does not integrate this observation in any argumentation and we can't either.

language, so perhaps her speech was not only archaic but also influenced by East Tucanoan. Then there is also a little direct historical evidence. Aikhenvald (2014:106) claims that in an older text, dating back to 1831, there is one negative verb and it has both *ma-* and *-kade*. The second oldest text, Aikhenvald (2014:106) continues, dates from 1886, and here we again have one negative verb, this time a verb with just *-kade*. All in all, the cross-dialectal and historical evidence is scanty, of course, yet scanty as it is, it is compatible with a Jespersen scenario: at least the doubling goes back to at least 1831 and the postverbal negator construction goes back to at least 1886. Furthermore, if single negation was already around in 1886 it is perfectly possible for Aikhenvald's Piratapuya Tariana speaker to speak archaic Tariana with just one negator.

But there is another hypothesis. What we have seen with Baré is that *ma* enters the domain of standard negation. In the case of Baré *ma* enters this domain as an alternative to the 'normal' negation. There is no reason why *ma* couldn't enter the domain as an enrichment of the normal negation rather than as an alternative. From this perspective, single postverbal *-kade* and *-kasú* are older than the constructions in which these combine with *ma-*. One could consider the enrichment as a stage 2 in a 'Jespersen Cycle in reverse'. A point of support for doubling happening on the left is also the use of the preverbal *ne*. Aikhenvald calls it 'emphatic', which accords well with a classical Jespersen Cycle, as does the fact that the emphasis seems to have bleached – in any case, *ne* is added preverbally to a verb with a postverbal negator. The fact that *ma-* is only possible for verbs allowing prefixes is interesting too: prefixless verbs are normally stative and for this very reason they should be more hospitable to *ma*, given the hypothesis offered by Michael (2014b) sketched above, but they are not. One would assume that the morphological division between prefixed and prefixless verbs is an old one and then it makes sense to interpret the impossibility of *ma* with prefixless verbs as old verbal morphology preventing the less old entry of *ma* into verbal inflection. All in all, given this pan-Maipurean perspective the hypothesis that *ma* is an innovation makes most sense to us.[17]

Then we come to Arawak and its hypothesized 2-or-4 stage. The language can negate with a preverbal *ma-* or a postverbal *kho(ro)*, but they cannot occur together.

(29)   Arawak (Patte 2014:67, 69)

    a.   m-aithi-n   d–a   no
         NEG-know-INF 1SG-AG-DV 3F.O
         'I don't know it.'

---

17.   Aikhenvald ends her most recent account (2014:113) with the sober conclusion that it is an open question whether or not the standard negation use of *ma-* is archaism or an innovation or – in Jespersenian terms – a stage 4 in a classical cycle or a stage 2 in a reversed cycle. Earlier she was more in favor of the classical scenario (Aikhenvald 2002:133).

b. d-aitha   kho no
    1SG.AG-know NEG 3F.0
    'I don't know it.'

This is superficially like the *mana V chu* construction of Quechuan, which in two varieties would allow either the preverbal part of the postverbal part. However, there is a big difference too. In Quechua, the two parts, though both optional, could occur together. This is not the case in Arawak. Like for Baré and, we think, Tariana, it is the pan-Maipurean perspective that explains Arawak and Patte (2014) argues this too: the *ma* negative is a fairly limited extension of the older privative use, as in (19). Like in Baré it can replace an older construction, though whereas in Baré the older construction was a doubling construction, here it is a postverbal single negator construction. From this perspective, there is no Jespersenian connection between *ma* and *kho(ro)*. Interestingly, however, a Jespersen Cycle could still be useful. Even if *kho(ro)* is not plausibly an enrichment of an original *ma* negator, it could have been an enrichment of something else. We don't know anything about this earlier element, but that *kho(ro)* would indeed have resulted from enrichment makes sense if Patte (2014: 56) is right that *kho(ro)* is 'probably' related to a word meaning 'little', *kho(ro)* could then be a minimizer just like *pas, point* and *miette*. Michael (2014b: 288) furthermore lists *khoro* with a whole set of negative markers with a voiceless velar stop, he wonders whether they might be cognates and explicitly asks whether these elements could be involved in a Jespersen Cycle. However, he shelves both questions for future research.[18] One problem is that some of these voiceless velar stop negators are preverbal.

All in all, the evidence for a Jespersen Cycle involving the *ma-* negator in the Maipurean languages is meagre. Different from the *ma* form in Mayan and Quechuan, in which we indeed see a *ma* form that allows enrichment by a form with an originally non-negative form and eventually replacement, what seems to be going on with Maipurean *ma* is that it enters the domain of negation and either enriches or replaces another negative construction. If it enriches the earlier negative construction – in Tariana – we do have a Jespersen Cycle, but it has the non-classical directionality from the right to left – a hypothesis that makes sense to explain Tariana preverbal *ne* too. Also, as the hypothesized etymology of Arawak *kho(ro)* suggests all of this does not mean that there is no classical Jespersen cycle for the elements other than *ma*.

Let us briefly turn to the Maipurean languages in which *ma* does not have a standard negation function (see also Derbyshire 1986: 520–524; Aikhenvald 2014: 116–118;

---

18. Aikhenvald (2014: 109–110) also lists languages with a voiceless velar negator, but does not dare to speculate and, at least with respect to Tariana -*kade* and -*kásu*, she claims that they have no 'straightforward cognates'.

Michael 2014b: 254). Table 5 presents a Jespersen Cycle hypothesis for the Northern languages.

Table 5. A Jespersen Cycle hypothesis for the Northern Maipurean languages that lack negative *ma*

Stages	NEG1	NEG2	Languages	Sources
1	*noho-*		Goajiro	Mansen & Mansen: 1984: 212; Adelaar 2004: 119; Granadillo 2014: 82–83
	auna		Wapishina	Michael 2014b: 245
	nii		Resígaro	Allin 1976: 299, 302–303, 309–310, *passim*
	játa		Yavitero	Granadillo 2014: 84
	uká		Kawiyari	Michael 2014b: 238
	khen(im)		Ehe-Khenim Kurripako	Granadillo 2014: 75–76
	hó-ka[19]		Achagua	Wilson 1992: 8, 131
	càmi(ta[20]*)*		Piapoco	de Klumpp 1985: 132–133; Michael 2014b: 247, 250, 251
2	*ka*	*=ma/me*[21]	Palikur	Dooley & Green 1977: 3, 9; Michael 2014b: 245–293
3	*ya-*	*-pia*	Baniva	Granadillo 2014: 83–84
	uncá	*-ke/-lá*	Yucuna	Aikhenvald 2014: 118
4	*ya-*	*-pia-*	Warekena	Aikhenvald 1998: 264–269
5		*-pe*	Añun	Patte 1986: 183–185; Michael 2014b: 255

As the appearance of lookalikes suggests, Jespersen Cycles may have played a role. If *uncá* in Yucuna is a cognate to *uká* in Kawiyari (and to *nuca* of the extinct language Maipure, not in the table but documented in Zamponi 2003: 50), then we have progression from stage 1 to stage 3, perhaps even via Palikur's stage 2 construction with *ka* and *=ma/me*. Also, if *játa* in Yavitero is a cognate to *ya-* in Baniva and Warekena, we have a progression from stage 1 to stages 3 and 4 and even to stage 5, if at least *pe* in Añun is a cognate to *pia* (cp. Michael 2014b: 289).

Table 6 is the set-up for the Southern languages.

---

19. *-ka* is analyzed as an affirmative particle.

20. *-ta* is analyzed as a focal particle.

21. In standard negation the second part, which is possibly a reflex of the privative, only shows up in limited contexts, including at least progressives (Michael 2014b: 282–283). It may serve emphasis (Derbyshire 1986: 521).

Table 6. A Jespersen Cycle hypothesis for the Southern Maipurean languages that lack negative *ma*

Stages	NEG1	NEG2	Languages	Sources
1	*aitsa*		Wauja	Ball 2014: 150
	ónka/nka		Baure	Baptista & Wallin 1967: 36, 79
	vai/vi		Ignaciano	Ott & Ott 1967: 88–89, 127–128, 134–135
	kuna/n(a)=		Apurinã	Facundes 2014: 125–127
	aa-		Iñapari	Facundes 2014: 144
	ako		Kinikinau	De Souza 2007: 96–99
	wo/wi/wo'i		Trinitario	Rose 2014: 217–218
	te(ra)/ga(ra)		Machiguenga	Carlson 1985: 57, 82, 85, 88, 90; Michael 2014a: 211
	te(ra)/ha(ra)		Nanti	Michael 2014a: 186
	te/teni/quero kero		Nomatsiguenga	Shaver 2008: 6–7; Michael 2014a: 211
	te/eero		Asháninca	Michael 2014a: 211
	te/eiro		Ashéninca	Michael 2014a: 211
	tee/aato		Caquinte	Swift 1988: 34, 37, 46; Michael 2014a: 211
	ako/hyoko		Terêna	Michael 2014a: 211
2	Ø			
3	Ø			
4	Ø			
5		*-tu*	Canamarí	dos Anjos Gonçalves da Silva 2011: 193

As Table 6 makes clear, there is little evidence for a Jespersen Cycle. All languages but one have a preverbal negator only.[22] Only Canamarí has a postverbal *-tu* suffix, but there is no direct evidence explaining it as the outcome of a Jespersen Cycle, though the very fact that all the other languages have preverbal negators only does suggest that Canamari too once only had a preverbal negator. Interestingly, half of the stage 1 languages exhibit a constructional asymmetry of a type that is reminiscent of Mayan and Quechuan. Nanti, Asháninca, Ashéninca, Machiguenga, Nomatsiguenga, and Caquinte, all of the members of the Campa subfamily, as well Terêna and Trinitario, have systems of realis and irrealis marking of the verb that is sensitive to negation. In Trinitario the system is simple: standard negation requires the verb to be marked for irrealis (with the marker *-a*).

---

22.   Note that Baure *ónka* looks like Northern Kawiyari *uká* and Yucuna *uncá* and that Wauja *aitsa* resembles Parecis *maisa*, listed in Table 4 (cp. Michael 2014b: 289).

(30)   Trinitario (Patte 2014: 217)
        wo-po   ta-ni-ko-a   to   waka
        NEG-PRF 3NH-eat-ACTC-IRR ART.NH COW
        'The cows do not eat any more.'

In the other languages the system is complex. In Nanti, for example, there are two preverbal negators, one considered realis and the other irrealis, each combining with a realis or irrealis suffix on the verb, but not in a straightforward way. The details of this system need not concern us here (see Michael 2014a, 2014b: 269–269). What is relevant is that we know from Mayan and Quechuan that irrealis marking that accompanies a negator can be used for emphasis and can bleach into an exponent of negation. This has not happened here though, but there is a potential, perhaps, if Swift (1988: 46) is right, already realized in Caquinte.

6.   Conclusion

Compared to the state of the art in the general study of the Jespersen Cycle, sketched in the introduction, the paper aimed at progress in the following way. First, we continued expanding the search for Jespersen Cycles in the world at large with a closer look at three big families of Central and South America, viz. Mayan, Quechuan and Maipurean. Second, we have increased our understanding of the relation between asymmetric negation and the Jespersen Cycle. In each of the three families, there was or is constructional asymmetry with negation optionally or obligatorily involving irrealis marking (or, to take care of languages like Nanti, realis marking), and in two of the families it is relatively clear that the irrealis marking has been reinterpreted as an exponent of negation, via a stage in which the irrealis marking made the negation emphatic. Third, we have also aimed at increasing our understanding of the relation between the Jespersen Cycle and word order. In particular, in Tariana the more plausible analysis introduced a new negator to the left of the verb, thus allowing us to speak of a 'Jespersen Cycle in reverse'. Fourth, we have tried to throw light on the interaction of the Jespersen Cycle and the process by which nominal privatives turn into negators.

At a more specific level of analysis, we hope to have contributed to a better understanding of the dynamics of negation in Mayan, Quechuan and Maipurean and we have put our finger on an intriguing similarity between Mayan, in particular K'ichean, and Quechuan: it is not just a fact that in both families the Jespersenian renewal is linked up with irrealis marking, but in both families strengthening has occurred twice, the first time even with the same -na morpheme.

Abbreviations

A	absolutive		LIM	limitative
ACC	accusative		LOC	locative
ACTV	active		NEG	negation
AD	additive		NF	non-feminine
AG	agent		NH	non-human
ART	article		NONVIS	non-visual
ASI	adverbalizer, equal subject		NPST	non-past
ASS	assertive		O	object
CAUS	causative		PASS	passive
CERT	certain		PF	phrase-final marking
CL	clitic		PL	plural
COMP	completive		POSS	possessed
CONTR	contrastive		PRES	present
DAT	dative		PRF	perfective
DIR	direction		PRIV	privative
DV	dummy verb		PST	past
E	ergative		Q	question
EMP	emphatic		REMPST	remote past
EXCL	exclusive		REP	reported
F	feminine		RFL	reflexive
FRU	frustrative		RPST	recent past
FUT	future		S	subject
GER	gerund		SG	singular
IMPRF	imperfective		SUB	subordinator
INC	incompletive		TOP	topic
INCH	inchoative		UNCERT	uncertain
INF	infinitive		1	first person
INT	intentional		3	third person
IRR	irrealis			

References

Adelaar, Willem F.H., with the collaboration of Muysken, Pieter C. 2004. *The Languages of the Andes*. Cambridge: CUP. doi:10.1017/CBO9780511486852

Aikhenvald, Alexandra Y. 1998. Warekena. In Derbyshire & Pullum (eds), 225–439.

Aikhenvald, Alexandra Y. 2002. *Language Contact in Amazonia*. Oxford: OUP.

Aikhenvald, Alexandra Y. 2003. *A Grammar of Tariana*. Cambridge: CUP. doi:10.1017/CBO9781107050952

Aikhenvald, Alexandra Y. 2012. *The Languages of the Amazon*. Oxford: OUP. doi:10.1093/acprof:oso/9780199593569.001.0001

Aikhenvald, Alexandra Y. 2014. Negation in Tariana: A North Arawak perspective in the light of areal diffusion. In Michael & Granadillo (eds.), 86–120. doi:10.1163/9789004257023_006

Allin, Trevor R. 1976. *A Grammar of Resígaro*. Dallas TX: Summer Institute of Linguistics & the University of Texas.

Ball, Christopher. 2014. Negation in Wauja discourse. In Michael & Granadillo (eds), 147–269. doi:10.1163/9789004257023_008

Baptista, Priscilla M. & Wallin, Ruth. 1967. Baure. In Matteson (ed.) 27–84.

Bean, Mark. 2008. Achkaypa willapan. In Weber & Meier (eds), 117–140.

Benson, Bruce. 1987. Huamalíes. In Weber (ed.), 26: 87- 101.

Beukema, Ronald William. 1975. A Grammatical Sketch of Chimborazo Quichua. Ph.D. dissertation, Yale University.

Black, Nancy. 1987. Junín. In Weber (ed.), 141–159.

Brandão, Ana Paula. 2014. Standard and non-standard negation in Paresi. In Michael & Grandadillo (eds), 169–183.

Buenrostros, Christina. 1991. Gramática chuj. Honors thesis. Escuela Nacional de Antropología e Historia, Mexico City.

Carlson, Sylvia Elizabeth. 1985. A Discourse Analysis of a Machiguenga Text. MA thesis, The University of Texas at Arlington.

Carlson de Coombs, Heidi. 1975a. Sufijos de persona en Quechua de Ayacucho. In *Datos Etno-Linguïsticos no 5*, 1–23. Lima: Instituto Lingüístico de Verano con el Ministerio de Educacion.

Carlson de Coombs, Heidi. 1975b. La clausula relative en quechua de Cajamarca. In *Datos Etno-Linguïsticos no 5*, 24–42. Lima: Instituto Lingüístico de Verano con el Ministerio de Educacion.

Coombs, David & Carlson de Coombs, Heidi. 2008. Suq runash byudu kidaran. In Weber & Meier (eds), 51–60.

Coon, Jessica. 2006. Existentials and negation in Chol (Mayan). In *CamLing: Proceedings of the fourth University of Cambridge Conference in Language Research*, Charles Chang et al. (eds), 51–58. Cambridge: Cambridge Institute of Language Research.

Croft, William. 1991. The evolution of negation. *Journal of Linguistics* 27: 1–39. doi:10.1017/S0022226700012391

Cunha de Oliveira, Christiane. 1998. Negation in Baré: A diachronic explanation. In *IV Encuentro Internacional de Lingüística en el Noroeste*, Tomo I: *lenguas indígenas*, 151–165. Hermosillo, Sonora: Unison.

Dahl, Östen. 1979. Typology of sentence negation. *Linguistics* 17: 79–106. doi:10.1515/ling.1979.17.1-2.79

Dahl, Östen. 2010. Typology of negation. In *The Expression of Negation*, Laurence R. Horn (ed.), 9–38. Berlin: De Gruyter Mouton.

Day, Christopher. 1973. *The Jacaltec Language*. Bloomington IN: Indiana University Press.

de Klumpp, Deloris. 1985. La oracion simple en piapoco. *Artícolos en Lingüística y Campos Afines* 13: 116–168.

Derbyshire, Desmond C. 1986. Comparative survey or morphology and syntax in Brazilian Arawakan. In Derbyshire & Pullum (eds), 469–566.

Derbyshire Desmond C. & Pullum, Geoffrey K. (eds). 1986-1991. *Handbook of Amazonian Languages*, Vol. 1: (1986)/Vol. 3 (1991)/Vol. 4 (1989). Berlin: Mouton de Gruyter.

De Souza, Ilda. 2007. Koenukunoe emo'u. A língua dos índios Kinikinau. Ph.D. dissertation Universidade Estadual de Campinas.

Devos, Maud & van der Auwera, Johan. 2013. Jespersen cycles in Bantu: Double and triple negation. *Journal of African Languages and Linguistics* 34: 205–274. doi:10.1515/jall-2013-0008

Dooley, Robert A. & Green, Harold G. 1977. Aspectos verbais e categorias discursivas da língua Palikur. *Série Lingüística* 7: 7–28.

dos Anjos Gonçalves da Silva, Zoraide. 2011. Fonologia e Gramática Katukina-Kanamarí. Ph.D. dissertation, Free University of Amsterdam.

Dryer, Matthew S. 1988. Universals of negative position, In *Studies in Syntactic Typology* [Typological Studies in Language 17], Michael Hammond, Edith Moravcsik & Jessica Wirth (eds), 93–124. Amsterdam: John Benjamins. doi:10.1075/tsl.17.10dry

Dryer, Matthew S. 2013. Order of negative morpheme and verb. In *The World Atlas of Language Structures Online*, Matthew S. Dryer & Martin Haspelmath (eds). Leipzig: Max Planck Institute for Evolutionary Anthropology. ⟨http://wals.info/chapter/143⟩ (11 December 2014).

Duff-Tripp, Martha. 1997. *Gramatica del idioma Yanesha' (Amuesha)*. Lima: Instituto Lingüístico de Verano.

Facundes, Sidi. 2014. Negation in Apurinã (Arawak). In Michael & Granadillo (eds), 121–146. doi:10.1163/9789004257023_007

Gardiner, Alan H. 1904. The word. *Zeitschrift für Ägyptische Sprache und Altertumskunde* 41: 130–135.

van Gelderen, Elly. 2008. Negative cycles. *Linguistic Typology* 12: 195–243. doi:10.1515/LITY.2008.037

van Gelderen, Elly. 2011. *The Linguistic Cycle. Language Change and the Language Faculty*. Oxford: OUP. doi:10.1093/acprof:oso/9780199756056.001.0001

Granadillo, Tania. 2014. On negation in Kurripako Ehe-Khenim. In Michael & Grandadillo (eds), 74–85.

Greenberg, Joseph. 1987. *Language in the Americas*. Stanford CA: Stanford University Press.

Grinevald Craig, Colette. 1977. *The Structure of Jacaltec*. Austin TX: The University of Texas.

Hintz, Daniel J. 2008. Achkë. In Weber & Meier (eds), 71–78.

Hofling, Charles Andrew. 2000. *Itzaj Maya Grammar*. Salt Lake City UT: University of Utah Press.

Hopkins, Nicholas Arthur. 1967. The Chuj Language. Ph.D. dissertation, University of Chicago.

Jespersen, Otto. 1917. *Negation in English and Other Languages*. København: A. F. Høst & Søn.

Kaufman, Terrence. 1971. *Tzeltal Phonology and Morphology*. Berkeley CA: University of California.

Kindberg, Eric. 1987. Arequipa. In Weber (ed.), 181–209.

Kroskrity, Paul V. 1984. Negation and subordination in Arizona Tewa: Discourse pragmatics influencing syntax. *International Journal of American Linguistics* 50: 94–104. doi:10.1086/465817

Lastra, Yolanda. 1968. *Cochabamba Quechua Syntax*. The Hague: Mouton. doi:10.1515/9783111357409

Levinsohn, Stephen. 1974. *Una gramatica pedagogica del Inga*. Place: Lingüístico de Verano & Ministerio de Gobierno, Colombia.

Levinsohn, Stephen H. 2008. Inga de San Andrés, Alto Putumayo, Colombia. In Weber & Meier (eds), 21–36.

Loriot, James. 1975. *Notas sobre referencia en un texto Quechua de Cuzco*. Lima: Instituto Lingüístico de Verano & Ministerio de Educacion.

Mansen, Karis B. & Mansen, Richard A. 1984. *Aprendamosn Guajiro. Gramática pedagógica de Guajiro*. Bogotá: Editorial Townsend.

Matteson, Esther (ed.). 1967. *Bolivian Indian Grammars,* 1. Norman OK: Summer Institute of Linguistics of the University of Oklahoma.

Matteson, Esther. 1972. Toward Proto Amerindian. In *Comparative Studies in Amerindian Languages*, Esther Matteson, Alva Wheeler, Frances L. Jackson, Nathan E. Waltz & Diana R. Christian (eds), 21–89. The Hague: Mouton. doi:10.1515/9783110815009

Mayers, Marvin K. 1958. *Pocomchi Texts, with Grammatical Notes*. Norman OK: Summer Institute of Linguistics of the University of Oklahoma.

Meillet, Antoine. 1912. L'évolution des formes grammaticales. *Scientia* 12: 384–400. Reprinted in Antoine Meillet, 1926, *Linguistique historique et linguistique générale*, 130–148. Paris: H. Champion.

Michael, Lev. 2014a. Negation in Nanti. In Michael & Granadillo (eds), 184–215. doi:10.1163/9789004257023_010

Michael, Lev. 2014b. A typological and comparative perspective on negation in Arawak languages. In Michael & Granadillo (eds), 241–300. doi:10.1163/9789004257023_012

Michael, Lev & Granadillo, Tania (eds). 2014. *Negation in Arawak Languages*. Leiden: Brill. doi:10.1163/9789004257023

Miestamo, Matti. 2005. *Standard Negation. The Negation of Declarative Verbal Main Clauses in a Typological Perspective*. Berlin: Mouton de Gruyter.

Miller, Mike. 2008. Achikë. In Weber & Meier (eds), 79–90.

Mithun, Marianne. 1995. Affixation and morphological longevity. In Yearbook of Morphology 1994, Geert Booij & Jaap van Marle (eds), 73–97. Dordrecht: Kluwer. doi:10.1007/978-94-017-3714-2_3

Mosegaard Hansen, Maj-Britt & Visconti, Jacqueline (eds). 2014. *The Diachrony of Negation* [Studies in Language Companion Series 160]. Amsterdam: John Benjamins. doi:10.1075/slcs.160

Munro, Pamela & Gallagher, Caitlin E. 2014. Garifuna negatives. In Michael & Granadillo (eds), 13–53. doi:10.1163/9789004257023_003

Neuenswander, Helen L. & Shaw Mary. 1971. Achí. In Mary Shaw (ed.). *According to our Ancestors: Folk Texts from Guatemala and Honduras*, 39–58, 251–273. Norman OK: Summer Institute of Linguistics of the University of Oklahoma., 39–58, 251–273.

Ott, Willis G. & Ott, Rebecca H. 1967. Ignaciano. In Matteson (ed.), 85–137.

Patte, Marie France. 1986. La langue añun (arawak). Etude descriptive. Ph.D. dissertation, Université de Paris IV.

Patte, Marie-France. 2014. Negation in Guianese Lokono/Arawak. In Michael & Granadillo (eds), 54–73. doi:10.1163/9789004257023_004

Payne, David L. 1990. Some widespread grammatical forms in South American languages. In *Amazonian Linguistics. Studies in Lowland South American Languages*, Doris L. Payne (ed.), 75–87. Austin TX: University of Texas Press.

Payne, David L. 1991. A classification of Maipuran (Arawakan) languages based on shared lexical retentions. In Derbyshire & Pullum (eds), 355–499.

Phelps, Conrad M. 2008a. Suk kwentu ishkay wamrakunapa. In Weber & Meier (eds), 61–70.

Phelps, Conrad M. 2008b. Warmakunata mikyu yachaq awlamanta. In Weber & Meier (eds), 161–168.

Pineda-Bernuy, Edith. 2014. The development of standard negation in Quechua: A reconstruction. In Mosegaard Hansen & Visconti (eds), 83–127.

Pineda-Bernuy, Edith. In preparation. *The Development of Negation in Quechua*. Ph.D. dissertation, Australian National University.

Romero, Sergio G. 2012. A Maya version of the Jespersen's cycle: The diachronic evolution of negative markers in K'iche' Maya. *International Journal of American Linguistics* 78: 77–96. doi:10.1086/662638

Romero, Sergio. 2015. The emergence of negative concord in Santa María Chiquimula K'ichee' (Mayan): A variationist perspective. *Language Variation and Change* 27: 187–201. doi:10.1017/S0954394515000058

Rose, Françoise. 2014. Negation and irrealis in Mojeño Trinitario. In Michael & Granadillo (eds), 216–240. doi:10.1163/9789004257023_011

Santos Nicolás, Francisco, José & Gonzalo Benito Pérez Waykan, José. 1998. *Rukorb'aa; poqom q'orb'al. Gramática Poqiom (Poqomam)*. Cholsamaj: Centro Educativo y Cultural Maya.

Shaver, Dwight & Shaver, Gwynne. 2008. Aĉakay: Wasikaqmanta. In Weber & Meier (eds), 37–50.

Shaver, Dwight. 1987. Lambayeque. In Weber (ed.), 29–35.

Sherman, Grace, Spenst, Henry, Spenst, Ila & Wrisley, Betsy. 1967. Quechua. In *Bolivian Indian Grammars, 2*, Esther Matteson (ed.), 27–97. Norman OK: Summer Institute of Linguistics of the University of Oklahoma & Yarinacocha: Ministerio de Educación & Instituto Lingüístico de Verano.

Shaver, Harold Swanson. 2008. Campa Nomatsinguenga: Tiemps del verbo, *Datos Etno-Lingüísticos = Colección de los archiveso del ILV*. Lima: Instituto Lingüístico de Verano.

Slocum, Marianna C. 1980. A sketch of Bachajon Tzeltal clause and sentence structure. SIL *Mexico Workpapers* 3: 79–92.

Smith, Terrence. 1987. Pachitea. In Weber (ed.), 113–129.

Smith, Terry P. 2008. Janĉhäna. In Weber & Meier (eds), 149–160.

Sridhar, S.N. 1990. *Kannada*. London: Routledge.

Stenson, Nanay. 1998. Spanish loans in Cakchiquel. In *Studies in American Indian Languages. Description and Theory*, Leanne Hinton & Pamela Munro (eds). Berkeley CA: University of California Press.

Swift, Kenneth E. 1988. *Morfolofía del caquinte (Arawak preandino)*. Lima: Instituto Lingüístico de Verano.

de Swart, Henriëtte. 2010. *Expression and Interpretation of Negation. An OT Typology*. Dordrecht: Springer. doi:10.1007/978-90-481-3162-4

Tolliver, Ralph. 1987. Ambo. In Weber (ed.), 131–139.

Van Alsenoy, Lauren. 2014. *A New Typology of Indefinite Pronouns, With a Focus on Negative Indefinites*. Ph.D. dissertation, University of Antwerp.

van der Auwera, Johan. 2009. The Jespersen cycles. In *Cyclical Change* [Linguistik Aktuell/ Linguistics Today 146], Elly van Gelderen (ed.), 35–71. Amsterdam: John Benjamins. doi:10.1075/la.146.05auw

van der Auwera, Johan. 2011. Review article of *Expression and Interpretation of Negation,* by Henriëtte de Swart. *Language* 87: 845–865. doi:10.1353/lan.2011.0086

van der Auwera, Johan. 2012. Wat het Nederlands ons kan leren over de Jespersencyclus. *Nederlandse Taalkunde* 17: 403–413. doi:10.5117/NEDTAA2012.3.DISC543

van der Auwera, Johan & Vossen, Frens. In print. Negatives between Chamic and Bahnaric. *Journal of the Southeast Asian Linguistics Society*.

van der Auwera, Johan, Vossen, Frens & Devos, Maud. 2013. Le cycle de Jespersen à trois ou quatre négations. In *La linguistique de la contradiction,* Jacques François, Pierre Larrivée, Dominique Legallois & Franck Neveu (eds), 19–30. Bern: Peter Lang.

Vázquez Alvarez, Juan Jésus (2002). *Morfología del verbo de la lengua chol de Tila, Chiapas*. México: Centro de Investigaciones y Estudios Superiores en Antropología Social.

Verbeeck, Lieve. 1998. *Linguistic Acculturation in Mopan Maya: A Study of Language Change in Belizan Mopan due to Spanish and English Culture and Language Contact*. Munich: Lincom.

Veselinova, Ljuba. 2014. The Negative Existential Cycle revisited. *Linguistics* 52: 1327–1369.

Vossen, Frens. In preparation. Towards a Typology of the Jespersen Cycles. Ph.D. dissertation, University of Antwerp.

Vossen, Frens & van der Auwera, Johan. 2014. The Jespersen cycles seen from Austronesian. In Mosegaard Hansen & Visconti (eds), 47–82.

Weber, David. 1987. Huallaga. In Weber (ed.), 103–111.

Weber, David (ed.) 1987. *Juan del Oso*. Yarinacocha: Ministerio de Educación & Instituto Lingüístico de Verano. [Serie Lingüística Peruana 26]

Weber, David & Orr, Carolyn. 1987. Saraguro. In Weber (ed.), 25–27.

Weber, David & Phelps, Conrad. 1987a. Ayacucho. In Weber (ed.), 169–179.

Weber, David & Phelps, Conrad. 1987b. Cusco. In Weber (ed.), 211–237.

Weber, David J. & Meier, Elke (eds). 2008. *Achkay, mito vigente en el mundo quechua*. Lima: Instituto Lingüístico de Verano.

Williams, Barbara & Williams, Kenneth L. 1966. Chuj. In *Lenguas de Guatemala*, Marvin K. Mayers (ed.), 311–330. Guatemala: Ministerio de Educación.

Willis, David, Lucas, Christopher & Breitbarth, Anne (eds). 2013. *The History of Negation in the Languages of Europe and the Mediterranean*, Vol. 1: *Case Studies*. Oxford: OUP.

Wilson, Peter J. 1992. *Una descripción preliminar de la gramatica del Achagua (Arawak)*. Bogotá: Instituto Lingüístico de Verano.

Wise, Mary Ruth. 1976. Apuntes sobre la influencia inca entre los amuesha, factor que oscurese la classificación de su idioma. *Revista del Museo Nacional* 42: 355–366.

Wise, Mary Ruth. 1986. Grammatical characteristics of PreAndine Arawakan languages of Peru. In Derbyshire & Pullum (eds), 567–642.

Zahn, Charlotte & Toedter, Christa. 1987. Pastaza. In Weber (ed.), 37–53.

Zamponi, Raoul. 2003. *Maipure*. Munich: Lincom Euroup.

Mayan negation cycles*

Clifton Pye
University of Kansas

The Jespersen Cycle (1917) remains the definitive example of the linguistic cycle. A reconstruction of the history of negation marking in the Mayan languages shows that while some Mayan languages exhibit the beginning of a typical Jespersen Cycle, the majority of Mayan languages evidence different types of negation cycles. Differences in the domain of negation strengthening and the absence of postverbal negation strengthening provide evidence of the unique structure of Mayan languages. This evidence suggests that constraints on negation cycles are just as important as the cycles themselves in examining cross-linguistic variation in the structure of negation.

1. Introduction

To this day the Jespersen Cycle remains the most widely cited example of a linguistic cycle (Jespersen 1917, van der Auwera 2009). Predicate negation invites strengthening by adding negative sensitive elements which gradually usurp the role of the original negation marker and eventually replace it. French, for example, recruited the noun *pas* 'step' to strengthen its preverbal negation marker *ne*. Negation cycles are attested in a wide range of language families including Indo-European, Chinese and Athabaskan (Hoeksema 2009, van Gelderen 2011). Indeed, negation cycles are so common that their absence is almost more in need of explanation than their presence.

   In this chapter I reconstruct the history of negation marking in the Mayan languages and show that while one Mayan language exhibits the beginning of a classic

* I thank Terrence Kaufman, David Mora Marin, Brent Metz, Robert Rankin, Johan van der Auwera and Elly van Gelderen for their suggestions on earlier versions of this reconstruction. Barbara Pfeiler helped with negation in Yukatek, Gilles Polian helped with Tzeltal negation, Pedro Mateo Pedro helped with negation in Q'anjob'al, Ana Elizabeth López Ramirez helped with Mam negation, and Alejandro Curiel helped with Tojolab'al negation. I also thank the participants at SSILA in Portland (January 4, 2013) and at the Cycles II Workshop held at Arizona State University (25–26 April 2014) for their comments on an earlier version of the reconstruction. I take responsibility for all errors or misinterpretations. This research is funded in part by grants from the National Science Foundation (BCS-0613120 and BCS-0515120) as well as a grant from the General Research Fund of the University of Kansas.

DOI 10.1075/la.227.08pye

Jespersen-type negation cycle, the majority of Mayan languages provide no evidence for a clause-internal negation cycle that uses indefinite nouns or verbs. Instead, Mayan languages employ a host of adverbial clitics to strengthen negation in a clause-external position. The difference in the domain of the negation cycle reflects the unique syntactic organization of the Mayan languages. This evidence suggests that the identification of different types of negation cycles illuminates fundamental differences in the domain of negation.

2. The Mayan languages

The Mayan language family contains thirty languages spoken by people living in Mexico, Guatemala, Belize and Honduras (Kaufman 1974). The language family is divided into six main branches with a linguistic history of four thousand years (England 1994; Kaufman 1990). I assume the historical relations proposed in Kaufman's (1976) genetic classification of the Mayan languages as shown in Figure 1. Robertson (1992, 1999) and Campbell (1984) suggest alternative models of Mayan diversification.

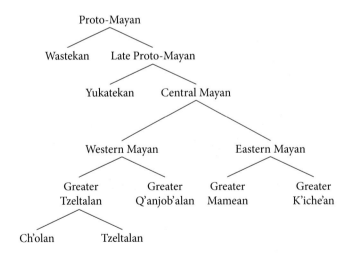

Figure 1. Kaufman's (1976) genetic classification of Mayan languages

Mayan languages have a predominantly verb-initial word order and are morphologically ergative, head-marking languages. The Mayan verb complex marks tense/aspect, subject and object agreement, direction of motion, derivation status, transitivity, verb class, and mood in addition to the main verb. Subject and object drop is frequent, while focused and topicalized constituents move to the left periphery before the predicate. I provide examples of Mayan predicates/sentences in (1).

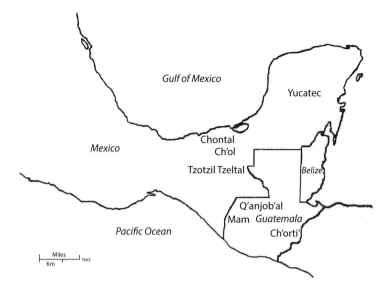

Figure 2. Geographic Distribution of Mayan Languages

(1)   Mayan predicates[1]

a.   K'iche'
x-at-ul-inw-il-oh
CMP-ABS2-come-ERG1-see-IND.TV
'I came to see you.'

b.   Mam (England 1983: 170)
ma tz'-ok-tzaj   w-ii'n–a
REC ABS3-enter-come   ERG1-by-ENC
'I brought it inside' (lit. 'It came inside by me')

c.   Teenek (Edmonson 1988: 143)
'u   'ots-e-l-ak

---

1.   All K'iche' words are shown in the practical orthography developed by the Proyecto Lingüístico Francisco Marroquín (Kaufman 1974) with a single exception: I use <'> rather than <7> for the glottal stop. The other orthographic symbols have their standard IPA values except: <ä> = /ɨ/, <b'> = /ɓ/, <ch> = /tʃ/, <ch'> = /tʃ/, <j> = /x/, <ñ> = /ɲ/, <ty> = /c/, <tz> = /ts/, <tz'> = /ts'/, and <x> = /ʃ/ in all languages but Mam, Popti' and Q'anjob'al and /ʂ/ in those languages. Abbreviations: 1 = first person singular, 2 = second person singular, 3 = third person singular, 4 = first person plural; ABS – absolutive; AP – antipassive; CL – classifier; CMP – completive aspect marker; DER – derviation; E – existential; EMPH – emphatic; ENC – enclitic; ERG – ergative; EXH – exhortative; INC – incomplete aspect marker; INAN – inanimate; IND – indicative; IRR – irrealis; IV – intransitive verb; N – noun phrase; NEC – necessitative particle; NEG – negation; PASS – passive; PL – plural; POT – potential aspect marker; QY/N – yes/no question; REC – recent tenst; SUBJ – subjunctive; TERM – termination; TOP – topic; TS – thematic suffix; TV – transitive verb; V – verb complex; VP – verb phrase.

ABS3 enter-TS-INC-IRR
'If he should enter'

The Mayan verb complex differs in fundamental ways from the structure of verbs in European languages. The sentence-initial position of the verb complex, the ergative morphological and syntactic structure, the obligatory head-marking morphology, and the aspect based event marking provide a distinctly Mayan perspective on events. I have shown elsewhere that the verb complex has a stative character that undergoes cyclical replacement of the aspect markers (Pye 2009, 2011). Negation marking further highlights the structural differences with European languages and offers unique insights into the structure of Mayan languages. Negation is much more than a simple contrary proposition. Negation creates a blank slate for languages to carve out original distinctions between negative propositions. In this paper I reconstruct negation marking in the six main branches of the Mayan languages. This exercise shows how the original Proto-Mayan system of negation marking changed over the past 4,000 years as well as how negation marking changed in response to contingent features in the individual languages.

Negation marking is not a monolithic feature in the Mayan languages anymore than it is in European languages (Biberauer 2009, van der Auwera 2009). The variety

Table 1. Negation marking in Tzeltal, Q'anjob'al and Mam[a]

Context	Tzeltal[b]	Q'anjob'al[c]	Mam[d]
Incompletive	**ma** (x-)k-il neg (cmp-)erg1-see 'I do not see it'	**maj** in way-i neg abs1 sleep-ind **k'am** ch=in way-i neg inc=abs1 sleep-ind 'I do not sleep'	**nti'** xch'upchin b'ixh? neg_exist hair_wash she 'she does not hair_wash?'
Potential		**maj**=ach way-oq neg=abs2 sleep-pot 'you will not sleep'	**mii'n** ø-tzaaj jb'aal ja'la neg abs3-fall rain today 'it will not rain today'
Imperative	**ma** x-aw-uts'in-on neg cmp-erg2-bother-abs1 'don't bother me'	**manchaq**	**mii'n** tz'ok t–q'o'n jal neg down erg2-put it 'don't put it'
Existential	**ma ay-uk** > **may-uk** neg exist-irrealis 'it is not'	**k'am** nab' neg_exist rain 'there is no rain'	**nti'** chib'aj neg_exist meat 'there is no meat'
Stative	**ma** mut-**uk** neg bird-irrealis 'it is not a bird'	**man** hin mexhtol **oq** neg abs1 teacher pot 'I am not a teacher'	**miyaa'** matiij-ø neg_inan big 'it is not big'
Discourse	**no** (< Spanish)	**k'am**=aq no=pot	**mii'n** no

[a]Blank cells indicate that no information is available for the language.
[b]Polian (2013).
[c]Mateo Pedro, pc (2010).
[d]field notes (2010).

and quirkiness of negation contexts provides linguistic reservoirs where languages develop new negation contrasts or conserve older forms. Table 1 illustrates the information on negation that is available for three Mayan languages.

Grammars seldom provide an exhaustive analysis of negation in all contexts as evidenced by the blank cells in Table 1. I chose a subset of negation contexts for my reconstruction that maximizes the number of contexts that are described in the Mayan grammars that I consulted. I compared the negation markers in six contexts: the incompletive and potential aspects, the imperative mood, the existential verb, stative predicates, and anaphoric or discourse contexts. Linguists who work on Mayan languages broadly distinguish between these contexts, although the contexts differ in subtle ways between the languages. I base my description on the formal properties of the words used in these contexts rather than their precise functional descriptions. The incompletive aspect corresponds to habitual, progressive or current descriptions of events. The potential aspect is used for future events. Stative negation includes both nominal and adjectival predicates, e.g. 'The house is not big.' Most Mayan languages have a distinct existential verb that lacks inflection for aspect. The anaphoric or discourse forms of negation occur as responses to commands or *yes/no* questions.

This list of negation contexts is far from exhaustive. I do not include the forms of negation used in the admonitive, prohibitive, subjunctive, completive and perfect moods and aspects in my investigation either because the same forms are used in these contexts or more frequently because the information is lacking on negation in these contexts. A host of negative words, e.g. K'iche' *ma juun* 'not one, nothing' exist outside of these negation contexts. These negative words also inform the reconstruction of predicate negation marking by preserving negative forms that changed in predicate negation. The diversity of negation forms indicates that negation in natural languages is more complex than a simple logical operation.

3. Historical reconstruction

Kaufman (2001:384) reconstructs three Mayan negation markers for proto-Mayan or Late proto-Mayan. He claims that the marker with the shape *yAb' is proto-Mayan based on its reflexes in Wastek and Ixil. He reconstructs two other negation markers *maa' and *mii for Late proto-Mayan, i.e. after Wastek's separation from the rest of Mayan family. Kaufman claims that these two markers cannot be derived from one another by any recurrent (morpho)phonological process.

I begin by reconstructing negation forms for each subbranch of the family before moving to a reconstruction based on the initial subbranch recontructions. This process ends with a reconstruction of Proto-Mayan negation that differs from Kaufman's reconstruction in its attention to the contexts of use and interaction with adverbial clitics. I note the problems that occur at each stage of the reconstruction. I use a uniform terminology that reconciles different descriptions of the tense/aspect markers in all of the languages. I assume the reconstruction of Mayan phonological changes presented in Kaufman (1969) and Campbell (1984).

3.1   Greater K'iche'an

The Greater K'iche'an branch includes the languages K'iche', Sakapultek, Sipakapense, Tz'utujil, Kaqchikel, Poqomam, Poqomchi', Q'eqchi' and Uspantek. Table 2 displays the forms of negation used in the selected aspectual and modal contexts for a subset of Greater K'iche'an languages. All tables include the sources of my information on negation for each language. The final column in each table contains the reconstruction for the languages in the table.

Table 2. Negation marking in the Greater K'ichean languages

Context	K'iche'[a]	Kaqchikel[b]	Tzutujil[c]	Poqom[d]	Q'eqchi'[e]	Uspantek[f]	Proto-K'ichean
incompletive	(man) V ta(j)	man V ta	ma V ta	ma V ta	moko V ta	ta' V	*ma ta V
potential	(man) V ta(j)	man V ta	ma V ta	ma pot ta V	ink'a' V	(ki) ta' V	*mi na V
imperative	(man) V ta(j)	mani V	ma V ta	ma V	ma V	ma V	*ma V
existential	maj/man E taj	manäq	ma E ta	ma'xtaj	maak'a'	(ki) ta'	*ma ki ta E
stative	(man) N ta(j)	man N ta	ma N ta	ma N ta	moko N ta maawa' N	ta' N	*ma ki N
discourse		manäq	mani'	ma'xtaj	ink'a'	ta'n	*mi na oq

[a]Larsen (1988); Mondloch (1978).
[b]Brown et al. (2006).
[c]Dayley (1985).
[d]Malchic et al. (2000).
[e]Caz Cho (2007).
[f]Can Pixabaj (2007).

Uniform negation marking in Mayan languages is the result of paradigm leveling which results from the extension of a single negation marker to different contexts. K'iche', Kaqchikel and Tzutujil extended an initial *ma* or a *man* negation marker. The variety of negation markers seen in Q'eqchi' is a reflex of the variation that I reconstruct for Proto-Greater K'iche'an. In particular, Q'eqchi' preserves a contrast between Proto-Mayan *maa/*mii that is missing in the other Greater K'iche'an languages. The Q'eqchi' data support the hypothesis that the Late proto-Mayan language restricted the use of *maa and *mii by aspect and modality. Much of the similarity between K'iche', Kaqchikel and Tzutujil can be explained by their recent separation and close geographic proximity.

Negation marking in Mayan languages is complicated by its interaction with adverbial clitics. For K'iche' Romero (2012) notes that "Enclitics had a diverse though not always well-understood series of roles in Classical texts. Colonial grammarians were baffled by their syntax and semantics, so unlike anything they knew from the grammars of Romance, Latin, Greek, Arabic, and Hebrew …" (82). This situation remains the case in modern grammars of the Mayan languages. The interaction between negation and adverbial clitics raises two problems: 1. accounting for the morphophonological realization of the negator clitic compounds; and 2. explaining the placement of negation marking.

Mayan languages have extensive processes of vowel harmony and vowel elision. Caz Cho (2007:65) describes the variable realization of vowels in twelve Q'eqchi' communities. Significantly, the incompletive aspect marker is realized as [nak, nek, nok, nik, na, and n] depending upon the vowel in the subsequent subject marker. The negation marker *moko* is sometimes realized as [muku] (102). The variable realization of negation marking is also present in other Greater K'iche'an languages. Modern K'iche' speakers produce the initial negation marker as [mana, man, ma, na, in, n or ø]. Larsen (1988:433) observed that "All of the examples of the form *man* which I have observed in the Momostenango dialect seem to occur in rather formal discourse; however, even in those contexts, the form *ma* seems to be more common." Can Pixabaj (2007:403) notes that the initial negation marker *ma* in Uspantek can be omitted when focused constituents are negated in preverbal position.

Romero (2012) found that the negation marker *ma* was followed directly by the enclitics (*wi, na, pu, ki, k'u, b'a, b'i*) in sixteenth century K'iche' documents, whereas it appears almost exclusively with the clitic *na* in a nineteenth century text. Table 3 provides Romero's list of the negator clitic compounds and their discourse role in the colonial K'iche' text the *Popol Wuj*. Table 3 includes negator clitic compounds from Romero's Table 2 that he did not include in his glossed list of compounds. The clitic sequences *ma+k'u+xa+b'i* and *ma+pu+xa+b'i* show that the clitics could be combined in ways that the clitic glosses do not predict.

The negator *ma* also combines directly with the irrealis clitic *ta(j)*. Romero (2012) provides examples of *ma+ta* compounds in both Colonial and Modern K'iche'. One of his examples from Colonial K'iche' is shown in (2).

(2)   Colonial K'iche' (Popol Wuj, folio 18v from Romero 2012:88)
Ma **ta** keje xib'an chike iwats', ix wi
Ma **ta** keje x-ø-i-b'an   chi-k-e   iw-ats',
NEG **irr** thus com-ABS3-ERG2.PL-do to-ERG3.PL-for ERG2.PL-brother

ix   w–i
ABS2.PL   ERG1-grandchildren

'Would that you hadn't done that to your elder brothers,
you my grandchildren!'

Table 3. K'iche' negator-clitic compounds and their discourse role in the *Popol Wuj* (Romero 2012:83)

ma+wi	causal or temporary sequence
ma+xa+b'i	causal or temporary sequence, discontinuity
ma+k'u	adversative relation to preceding clause
ma+na	strong negative force
ma+pu	adversative relation to preceding clause
ma+b'a	counterfactual possibility
ma+ki	strong negative force
ma+k'u+xa+b'i	not glossed
ma+pu+xa+b'i	not glossed
ma+xa	not glossed
ma+ni	not glossed

These observations support reconstructing the origin of the K'iche' and Kaqchikel negation marker *man* from a contraction of the negator clitic compound *ma+na*. Tzutujil and Poqom retain the negator *ma* without adding a clitic. Uspantek uses the compound *(ki)+ta'* for verbal and existential negation. Can Pixabej (2007:405) mentions that the compound *kita'* is the negative form of the existential *wi'*. Adding the initial negator *ma* for focused constituents to the compound *kita'* would produce the compound *ma+ki+ta'* that is similar to negator clitic compound *ma+ki* in K'iche'. This account of the origin of the Uspantek negation compound *kita'* is mirrored in other Mayan languages and shows how the Proto-Mayan negator *maa* is sometimes replaced by the following clitics. Uspantek now has the general negator *ta'*.

A similar process of clitic compounding and contraction is seen in Q'eqchi'. I derive the Q'eqchi' negator *moko* from the same compound seen in K'iche' and Uspantek *ma+ki*. The vowels in *moko* are problematic, but then the incompletive aspect marker *nak-* in Q'eqchi' also has variable vowel realizations. The origin of the Q'eqchi' negator *ink'a'* is more problematic, but essentially explicable in terms of the process of negator clitic compounding and erosion. I propose a derivation from a Greater K'iche'an compound *mi+na+k'a'*. This origin coincides with the use of the clitic *na* in K'iche'. Caz Cho provides a complete list of the negation markers in his Table 4.4 for twelve Q'eqchi' communites (223). All twelve communites use the marker *ink'a'* for discourse negation and all but one use *ma* for imperative negation. Five communities use the form *ink'a'* in potential contexts and seven use *moko … ta*. My reconstruction for Greater K'iche'an treats the Q'eqchi' negator *ink'a'* as a reflex of the Proto-Mayan negator *mii* and the other Q'eqchi' negators as reflexes of the Proto-Mayan negator *maa*.

The Q'eqchi' negation forms provide the basis for reconstructing contrasting negation markers *maa and *mii for Greater K'iche'an.

The second problem raised by negation marking in the Greater K'iche'an languages is the use of the *ta* clitic in post-predicate position. The clitic *ta* occurs in post-predicate position in K'iche', Kaqchikel and Tzutujil, whereas the clitic *ta'* occurs in pre-predicate position in Uspantek. The clitic *ta* occurs in preverbal position in Poqom in the potential aspect and in the post-predicate position in other contexts.

Romero (2012) proposes assimilating negation in K'iche' to Jespersen's Cycle of negation marking in that the omission of the initial negator *ma* frequently leaves the post-predicate clitic *ta(j)* as the sole negation marker in K'iche'. For example, the negative existential in K'iche' is frequently produced as *k'oo taj* instead of *ma k'oo taj*. (NEG EXIST IRR 'It is not there'). Modern K'iche' speakers have not eliminated the initial negation marker entirely, as shown in (3), and preserve *ma* as the sole negation marker in the nominal phrase *ma juun* 'not one'.

(3)   Modern K'iche' negation marking
       ay, ma katchab'etaj **ta** b'a xa ne
       ay, ma k-at-chab'e-taj   **ta**   b'a   xa   ne
       ay, NEG INC-ABS2-understand-PASS **IRR** indeed only maybe
       'Ay, maybe you are not indeed (only) understood.'

Modern K'iche' is unique in this respect. The other Greater K'iche'an languages do not reduce the initial negation marker, and Mayan languages outside of the K'iche'an branch still rely upon an initial negation marker. The Colonial K'iche' examples show that K'iche' speakers added the clitics *na* and *ki* directly after the negation marker. Q'eqchi' added the clitics *k'a'* and *wa'* to the negation marker, and Uspantek eliminated the negator *maa, but retained the negation marker *ta'* in pre-predicate position. Caz Cho notes that several Q'eqchi' communities use the topic marker *a'an* with the negation marker *moko ... ta* for emphasis (217). He states that in the context of negation the topic marker is reduced to [a]. In his example (shown in 4), the topic marker *a* appears immediately after the clitic *moko* and attracts the irrealis clitic *ta*, which ordinarily follows the subject *li qana'chin* 'the woman'.

(4)   Q'eqchi' topic negation (Caz Cho 2007:217)
       moko a ta li qana'chin xk'ayink re li mis
       moko a   ta li qana'chin x-ø-k'ay-i-n-k   r-e   li mis
       NEG   top irr the woman   com-ABS3-sell-der-ap-iv ERG3-of the cat
       'It was not the woman who sold the cat.'

The post-predicate position of the clitic *ta* in K'iche', Kaqchikel and Tzutujil requires explanation. For *ta(j)* to be reinterpreted as a marker of negation, it had to appear after the predicate phrase. Both Colonial and Modern K'iche' speakers place clitics in the post-predicate position when the predicate is in clause-initial position. Norman (1976) provides an example of irrealis marking in a post-predicate position (5).

(5)   Modern K'iche' (Norman 1976: 48)
      … kaqab'an jun mo:d cheech kaqawor **ta** nee rii iwee ix …

(1)   … k-ø-qa-b'an   jun mo:d   chi-ee-ch
      … INC-ABS3-ERG1.PL-do one method to-for-term

      k-ø-qa-wor   **ta** nee   rii iw-ee   ix …
      INC-ABS3-ERG1.PL-perforate   **irr** maybe the ERG2.PL-for ABS2.PL

      '… we will find a way that maybe we could perforate yours …'

The example in (5) shows that clitics marking irrealis (*ta*) and modal force (*nee*) for the entire clause appear after the verb *kaqawor*, which occurs in the clause-initial position. The irrealis marker *ta(j)*, like the other enclitics, only appears in the second position in a clause. The movement of the adverbial clitics, including *ta(j)*, to the postverbal position is evidence of a structural reanalysis of negation in K'iche', Kaqchikel and Tzutujil. In effect, the initial negation marker *ma* had to became integrated into the verb complex enough for the second position to be redefined as the post-predicate position. The integration of the initial negation marker *ma* into the K'iche' verb complex created the condition in which the clitic *ta(j)* came into the scope of the predicate and could replace the clause-initial negator *ma*. K'iche', Kaqchikel and Tzutujil are the only Mayan languages that display this level of reanalysis of negation marking.

On the basis of these data, I postulate the proto-Greater K'iche'an forms listed in Table 2, and assume that the negation markers in the individual languages were derived by the following processes:

1.   Proto-K'iche'an originally restricted the negation particle *mii to discourse and potential contexts. Most of the Greater K'iche'an languages extended the negation marker *ma* to all contexts of negation. Uspantek reduced the clitic compound ma+ki+ta' to (ki)ta'. Q'eqchi' reduced the clitic compound mi+na+k'a' to *ink'a'* and preserved the Proto-Greater K'iche'an distinction between *maa and *mii.

2.   K'iche', Kaqchikel and Tzutujil reanalyzed the initial negation marker as part of the verb complex and moved the second position enclitics to the post-predicate position. These languages innovated the use of the irrealis marker *ta(j)* to reinforce negation marking in the post-predicate position. Q'eqchi' is conservative in its restricted use of the irrealis marker. The other K'iche'an languages extended the irrealis marker to other contexts. Kaqchikel preserves a proto-K'iche'an irrealis suffix *+oq in the discourse negation marker *manäq* (< ma+na+oq, NEG+NEC+IRR).

3.   Q'eqchi' may have preserved a combination of *maa plus *ki realized as the marker *moko* in incompletive and stative contexts. The vowel harmony between verb prefixes and subject markers in Q'eqchi' explains why the vowels in *moko* are

/o/ rather than /i/. The Q'eqchi' marker is an older form because it is possible to reconstruct a similar form for proto-Greater Tzeltalan.

4. Proto-Greater K'iche'an had a restricted use of a *na clitic with negation. Modern K'iche' adds *na to the negative conjunction *wemna* 'if not' (< we-ma-na IF-NEG-NEC), the negative question *laamna* 'is not?' (<laa-ma-na QY/N-NEG-NEC), *pineemna* 'even though ... not' (<pine ma-na even_though-NEG-NEC) and *jas chemna* 'why not (<jas_chee ma-na why-NEG-NEC) (Mondloch 1978: 121–122). Kaqchikel extended a fused *na with the negation particle *ma* to all contexts. Tzutujil preserves a reflex of *na in the discourse negation marker *mani'* which is close to the Kaqchikel imperative negation marker *mani.* These changes are shown in Table 2.

The Greater K'iche'an languages demonstrate three main historical changes to negation. First, they eliminated two Proto-Mayan markers *yAb and *mii by extending the *maa form throughout the paradigm. Second, they added adverbial clitics to the original negation marker. Finally, K'iche', Kaqchikel and Tzutujil reanalyzed the initial negator *ma* as part of the predicate, and moved the clitics, including the irrealis particle *ta(j)* to a new second position after the predicate. The irrealis clitic *ta* was reanalyzed as the primary marker of negation in Uspantek and Modern K'iche', but in pre- and post-predicate positions respectively.

3.2   Greater Mamean

The Greater Mamean branch consists of the languages Ixil, Awakatek, Teko (Tektitek), and Mam. Table 4 provides the negation forms for Ixil, Awakatek and Mam as well as my reconstruction for proto-Mamean.

Table 4. Negation marking in the Greater Mamean languages

	Ixil[a]	Awakatek[b]	Tektitek[c]	Mam[d]	Proto-Mamean
incompletive	ye' V/jit – aspect	kyi'	k'onti' V	miti' V	*k'o ya'/*mii E V
potential	ye' V/jit	kyil	nla'	mii'n V	*k'o ya'/*mii na V
imperative	ye' V		k'on V	mii'n V	*ya'/*mii na V
existential	ye' E	kyi' E	k'onti'	miti' [nonhuman] mi'aal [human]	*k'o ya' E/*mii E
stative	ye'l N		nya'tx N	miyaa' N	*mii ya' N
discourse	ye'le	kye'		mii, mii'n	*mii na

[a]Ayers (1991).
[b]Tuyuc (2001).
[c]Pérez Vail (2007).
[d]England (1983).

I reconstruct a Proto-Mamean negation system with reflexes of both *yAb' and *mii on the basis that Ixil and other Mayan languages employ multiple negation markers in many contexts. Ayres (1991:190) states that both negation markers ye' and jit are used with verbs, but that speakers prefer the use of ye'. It is possible that jit derives from the morphemes mii+oj+at, NEG+IRR+exist. If so, Ixil, like Mam, extended an existential negation marker to verbal predicates. Ixil retains the negative marker mi in the form mita'n 'not one'. This word provides support for reconstructing both *ye' and *mii negation markers for proto-Mamean.

Mam has two main forms of negation: miti' (nti') and mii'n. The form nti' shows incipient weakening of the initial negation marker. England (1983) states that the form miti' is derived from a contraction of the negation marker and the existential, i.e., mi at (NEG exist). England lists an alternate form mixti', which includes a clitic ix. This reconstruction assumes that Proto-Mamean extended existential negation to verbal predicates on the basis of the Ixil, Tektitek and Mam data.

Croft (1991) classified Mam as a language that extended existential negation to negate verbal predicates, and suggested that this process constitutes a new type of negation cycle (see also Veselinova's chapter in this volume). The existential cycle of negation begins when a language has different forms for existential and predicate negation. The next step in the cycle takes place when the language extends the existential form to mark predicate negation. The cycle is then renewed when the language forms a new contrast between existential and predicate negation. My reconstruction for Proto-Eastern Mayan, the ancestor of Greater Mamean and Greater K'iche'an, illustrates the first step in the existential cycle, while modern Mam and Tektitek take the cycle to the next step (6).

(6)   The existential cycle in Mam

		Predicate Negation	Existential Negation
a.	Proto-Eastern Mayan	*maa ta V	*k'o ya'/*mii na E
b.	Mam	miti' V	miti' (< mi+at, NEG+exist)
c.	Tektitek	k'onti' V	k'onti' (< k'on+at, NEG+exist)

Croft does not explain the motivation for this extension nor the specific contexts in which the extension occurred. The extension of existential negation to verbal predicates provides evidence that negation occurs outside of the verbal predicate in Mayan languages. Rather than negating the verbal predicate directly, negation in Mayan languages occurs in a separate clause with the verbal predicate in a complement clause. The extension of existential negation in Tektitek and Mam may be literally translated as 'It is not the case that …'. This analysis explains why the extension occurs in indicative verbal predicates before an extension to non-indicative predicates. I count negative existential extension and the process of negative strengthening by clitic addition as evidence that negation has a separate structural position that is outside of the verbal predicate in Mayan languages.

The second Mam negation form derives from the combination of the negative marker *mii* and the necessitative clitic *na*. England's Mam grammar lists a host of other negation markers, including the negative verb *-ky'i'* 'not want', *miky'* 'not like this', *ky'eenan* 'no one', *ii, iichaq* 'it doesn't matter', *eeq'a* 'not a chance! (between men)' and *kye'* 'not a chance! (between women)', *ooy* 'not a chance!', *na'x* 'still not' and *yiin* 'a little'. Some of these forms are similar to the Awakatek and Tektitek forms. Pérez Vail (2007: 230) analyzes the Tektitek form *k'onti'* as a compound of the negation marker *k'on* and the existential. The Tektitek form preserves a reflex of the negation compound *k'o+na*, and Awakatek and Mam preserve reflexes of the negation compound *k'o+ya'*.

Mam has a third negation form *miyaa'* for stative predicates. Stative negation takes the form of *ye'l* in Ixil and *nya'tx* in Tektitek. The Mam and Tektitek forms preserve a combination of the Proto-Mayan negators *yaa* and *mii*. These forms provide the basis for my reconstruction of the Proto-Mamean stative negation as the compound *mii ya'*. This reconstruction also shows that the change from *yaa* to *ye'l* occurred after Ixil separated from the other Mamean languages.

In sum, negation exhibits different changes in the Mamean and K'iche'an languages. Ixil and Awakatek preserved a reflex of the Proto-Mayan negation form *yAb' and extended it throughout the contexts of negation. Mam extended a reflex of the Proto-Mayan *mii form across the contexts of negation. Tektitek and Mam augmented the form of verbal negation by extending existential negation to indicative contexts. Mam added a clitic like the necessitative clitic *na* in some contexts of negation, while Awakatek and Tektitek added a clitic like *k'o*. On the basis of the Mamean and K'iche'an languages I conclude that the Eastern Mayan languages tended to level the negation paradigm by extending one or another form across the negation contexts. They also augment negation by adding various clitics and the existential verb in a separate negation clause. The Mamean languages did not introduce the irrealis clitic *ta(j)* after the verb like the K'iche'an languages.

3.3   Eastern Mayan

Based on the reconstructions of negation for the Greater K'iche'an and Greater Mamean languages, I reconstruct the negation markers for Eastern Mayan as shown in Table 5. The reconstruction assumes that Eastern Mayan maintained distinct negation forms along the lines of Ixil. It also assumes the use of *ma and *mii in different contexts that roughly corresponds to a division between indicative and imperative modality. The forms for imperative and discourse negation require minimal changes. The K'iche'an languages abandoned the *ya' forms, while the Mamean languages lost the *ta clitic.

The incompletive reconstruction preserves the clitic *ta of Greater K'iche'an, but not the extension of existential negation in Greater Mamean. The extension of existential negation to verbal predicates is a Mamean affair.

Table 5. Reconstruction of negation marking for Eastern Mayan

	Greater K'iche'an	Greater Mamean	Eastern Mayan
incompletive	*ma ta V	*k'o ya'/*mii E V	*maa ta V
potential	*mi na V	*k'o ya'/*mii na V	*ya'/*mii na V
imperative	*ma V	*ya'/*mii na V	*ya'/*maa V
existential	*ma ki ta E	*k'o ya' E/*mii E	*k'o ya'/*mii na E
stative	*ma ki N	*mii ya' N	*mii ya' N
discourse	*mi na oq	*mii na	*mii na oq

These assumptions make the reconstruction of existential negation a critical piece. My reconstruction extends the Greater K'iche'an necessitative particle to the existential and stative contexts, while Greater Mamean did not. Greater Mamean extended existential negation, including the existential, to verbal predicates. The reconstruction for proto-Eastern Mayan requires a choice between *maa and *mii as alternatives to *ya'. I reconstruct both forms for Proto-Eastern Mayan in the Greater K'iche'an contexts. Greater Mamean extended *mii to all contexts while the Greater K'iche'an languages extended *maa.

4.   Ch'olan

The Ch'olan languages display a diversity of negation forms which demand an explanation. Above all else, these languages provide further evidence of the ways in which Mayan negation interacts with a variety of adverbial clitics. Table 6 provides the forms of negation for the Ch'olan languages Chontal, Ch'ol, Ch'orti' and Ch'olti' as well my reconstruction for Proto-Ch'olan. The Ch'olan languages form a subbranch of the Greater Tzeltalan family.

The Ch'olti' data come from the seventeenth-century Morán manuscript and, thus, represent an earlier stage of development (Robertson et al. 2010). This manuscript uses the negation marker *el* in both future and imperative contexts (7).

(7)   Ch'olti' future and imperative negation (Robertson et al. 2010: 183)
      el   a-muk-u
      NEG   ERG2-bury-IND$_{TV}$
      'Do not hide them.' or 'You will not bury them.'

Table 6. Negation marking in the Ch'olan languages

	Chontal[a]	Ch'ol[b]	Ch'orti'[c]	Ch'olti'[d]	Proto-Ch'olan
incompletive	mach V	ma' E V	ma V	ma V	*ma V
potential	mach V	mach ik V ame V ik ame mach ik V	ma'chi V	el V	*ye' V/ *ma V
imperative	mach V	mach V	ma'chi V	el V	*ye' V/ *ma V
existential	mach E	ma' E(+ik)		may E matak	*ma E
stative	mach N	mach(+ik) N	ma N	ma N	*ma N
discourse		ma' E	ma ix		*ma

[a]Keller & Plácido Luciano (1997).
[b]Vázquez Álvarez (2002).
[c]Baquiax (2004).
[d]Robertson et al. (2010).

Ch'ol exhibits a different development in its negation system. Ch'ol extended existential negation (*ma 'añ*, NEG EXIST; ma' E in Table 6) to verbal predicates in a wide range of contexts as well as to contexts of discourse negation. The extension of existential negation to indicative verbal predicates echoes the extension seen in Tektitek and Mam, but existential negation extends to more contexts in Ch'ol.

Vázquez Álvarez (2002) provides a fascinating description of the interaction between the negation particles and other particles in Ch'ol, including the subjunctive clitic *ik* and the dubitative clitic *ka*. These clitics follow the main verb in affirmative predicates, but follow the negation particle in negative predicates. The examples in (8) appear in Vázquez Álvarez's thesis. He does not gloss the particle *ba'añ* in (8b).

(8) Ch'ol (Vázquez Álvarez 2002: 165)
  a. wäy-äl-ety+ik
     sleep-CMP-ABS2+SUBJ
     'If you would sleep.'
  b. mach+ik ba'añ wäy-äl-ety
     NEG+SUBJ ? sleep-CMP-ABS2
     'If you would not sleep.'

Ch'ol provides an important insight into the way in which the adverbial clitics attach to negation markers in the Mayan languages. Whereas the entire verb complex, including the initial negative marker, serves as a clitic host in K'iche', the initial negative marker hosts second position clitics in other Mayan languages.

Ch'ol reinterpreted existential negation *ma'*+ *añ* as a single negation marker that hosts the second position clitics. Vázquez Álvarez (2002) provides examples of clitics attached to the existential negation *ma'añ* (9). The Ch'ol negation marker *ma* no longer acts as a clitic host by itself (i.e. resulting in the unacceptable form *ma+ik añ*).

(9)   Ch'ol existential negation with clitic (Vázquez Álvarez 2002:174)

　　a.   ma'añ+ik　　　wiñik
　　　　NEG_exist+SUBJ　man
　　　　'If there was not a man.'

　　b.   ma'añ+ik　　　wäy-äl-ety
　　　　NEG_exist+SUBJ　sleep-CMP-ABS2
　　　　'If you were not sleeping.'

Vázquez Álvarez describes one other negation marker in Ch'ol, the clitic *ame*. This clitic is only used in subjunctive contexts and does not host clitic raising (10a). This negation marker also combines with the negation marker *mach* to produce an interrogative reading (10b). In this combination, *mach* hosts the subjunctive clitic in the usual manner.

(10)   The Ch'ol subjunctive negation particle *ame* (Vázquez Álvarez 2002:178)

　　a.   ame wäy-ety+ik
　　　　NEG sleep-ABS2-SUBJ
　　　　'You are not going to sleep.'

　　b.   ame mach+ik　　wäy-ø+ix
　　　　NEG NEG+SUBJ　sleep-ABS3+now
　　　　'Is he not going to sleep now?'

This evidence suggests that *ame* was introduced after clitic raising was generalized to the negation markers *mach* and *ma'añ*. The example in (10a) shows that the negative marker *ame* by itself does not host the second position clitic +ik. The clitic +ik does attach to the compound negation marker *ame mach* in (10b). The example in (10b) also provides evidence of a process that Mayan languages use to strengthen negation marking through the use of multiple clitics.

Wisdom's Ch'orti' dictionary (1950) contains negation entries with the forms *ma ix* 'no, not yet' and *ma achi* 'no, not yet' that suggest a *ma* form for discourse negation that was followed by the clitics *ix* 'a going' and *achi* (no entry). It lists the form *maachiix* 'already not, no longer' (< ma-achi-ix), which shows that both particles could be used in combination with the negation marker. The Ch'orti' forms suggest that the *mach* negation marker in Chontal and Ch'ol was derived from the contraction of **maa* with the particle *achi*.

In sum, the Ch'olan changes resemble the Eastern Mayan changes. Once again, we find examples of paradigm leveling, clitic augmentation and the extension of existential negation to new contexts.

4.1 Greater Tzeltalan

Table 7 provides the negation markers for Tzotzil, Tzeltal and Tojolab'al, as well as the reconstructions for Proto-Ch'olan and Greater Tzeltalan. Kaufman (1976) places Tojolab'al in the Greater Q'anjob'alan branch, whereas Robertson (1992) groups Tojolab'al with Tzotzil and Tzeltal. The negation forms in Tojolab'al are more similar to the forms in Tzotzil than the forms in Q'anjob'al, and better inform the reconstruction for Greater Tzeltalan. Tojolab'al is close to Tzotzil and Tzeltal geographically and there is a possibility that the similarity between the negation forms in Tojolab'al and Tzotzil is the result of borrowing rather than a shared history. Borrowing does account for the differences between Tojolab'al and Tzotzil that support a historical relation rather than borrowing.

Table 7. Negation marking in the Greater Tzeltalan languages

	Tzotzil[a]	Tzeltal[b]	Tojoab'al[c]	Proto-Ch'olan	Greater Tzeltalan
incompletive	mu(k') V	ma'(ba) V	mi	*ma V	*ma V
potential	mu V	ma' V	mi	*ye' V/ *ma V	*ye' V/*ma V
imperative	mu (me) V	ma' V	mok	*ye' V/ *ma V	*ye' V/*ma V
existential	mu'yuk, muk'	ma'yuk	mi E uk mey uk	*ma E	*mii E uk
stative	mu N uk, ma'uk N	ma' N uk	mi N uk	*ma N	*mii N uk
discourse	ch'abal	ma'uk	miyuk	*ma	*ma uk/*mii uk

[a]Haviland et al. (nd).
[b]Slocum et al. (1999).
[c]Curiel pc (2014).

Tzotzil contrasts the use of two negation markers *mu* and *muk'*. Laughlin (1975:241) states that:

> *mu* generally contrasts with *muk'*, implying speaker's unwillingness to carry out action; *mu xibat* 'I will not go' *muk' xibat* 'I am not going'. When occurring with interrogative particle, *mu* implies speaker's desire that person addressed carry out action; *mi mu xabat* 'Won't you go?' *mi muk' xabat*? 'Aren't you going?'

Clitic raising to negation markers also occurs in the Tzeltalan languages. Aissen (1987:13) notes that *muk'* occurs in combination with *bu* to form the complex *muk' bu* 'never'. Tzeltal uses the form *ma'ba* in the perfect aspect of verbal predicates (Slocum et al. 1999: 292). Tojolab'al has the negation form *mixa* 'not anymore' that contrasts with the discourse form *miyuk* (mi+uk). These forms provide evidence that Greater Tzeltalan permitted its negation markers to host raised clitics.

Tzotzil, Tzeltal and Tojolab'al extended different forms across the contexts of negation. The differences provide further evidence that Greater Tzeltalan had a contrast between *maa and *mii negation markers. The different forms in the Tzeltalan languages parallel those of the Eastern Mayan branch, and show that the contrast existed at the time the two branches separated. The Tzotzil grammar of Haviland et al. notes that the stative negation form *ma'uk* N is used for contrastive focus, while *mu* N *uk* is neutral. A focus contrast would explain why Greater Tzeltalan allowed both *ma and *mii forms in the same contexts. My reconstruction only shows contrasting forms for discourse negation, but the contrast probably existed throughout the paradigm.

This reconstruction includes the following changes from Greater Tzeltalan to the present-day languages:

1. The proto-language used the irrealis clitic *+uk in existential, stative and discourse contexts. Ch'ol uses the clitic +ik in these contexts, while Chontal and Ch'orti' do not. Tzeltal and Tzotzil may have borrowed the clitic from Ch'ol, but they did not borrow Ch'ol's negation markers. It is more likely that the clitic was inherited from the proto-language and lost in Chontal and Ch'orti'. I have changed the reconstructed Proto-Ch'olan forms accordingly. The Tzeltal word *manchuk* 'if not' provides evidence that Greater Tzeltalan retained a combination of *ma+na.

2. The Tzeltalan languages extended the *maa and *mii forms across different contexts of negation. The same process occurred in the Ch'olan languages, and probably occurred in all of the Greater Tzeltalan languages simultaneously around the seventeenth century. The languages may have used the *maa and *mii forms contrastively in the same contexts.

5.   Greater Q'anjob'alan

Reconstructing negation for proto-Q'anjob'alan is challenging due to the diversity of forms that are present in Greater Q'anjob'al. The Greater Q'anjob'alan branch includes the languages Tojolabal, Chuj, Q'anjob'al, Akatek, Popti' (Jakaltek) and Mocho'. Q'anjob'al provides a living example of a Mayan language that supports multiple negation markers in the same contexts. Table 8 shows the negation markers for Q'anjob'al, Akatek and Popti'.

Table 8. Negation marking in the Q'anjob'alan languages

	Q'anjob'al[a]	Akatek[b]	Popti'[c]	Proto-Q'anjob'alan
incompletive	k'am/toq + aspect V	k'am + aspect	mach V	*k'am/*toq V
potential	maj – aspect V	manoj	ma+oj+ab	*ma na oj V
imperative	manchaq V	manchaj	mach V	*ma na cha oq V
existential	k'am – E/toq + E	k'am – E	mach – E	*k'am/*toq
stative	man N oq	man N+oj	mat N+oj	*ma na N oq
discourse	k'am aq/manchaq/maj		mach+oj	*ma na cha oq

[a]Mateo Pedro pc (2010).
[b]Stz'ib'eneb'al Ti'e Jak'atan – Gramática normativa Akateka (2007).
[c]Grinevald Craig (1977).

There are few points of similarity between Q'anjob'al and Popti'. The two languages share a common potential form (Q'anjob'al *maj*; Popti' *majab*). Grinevald Craig (1977: 29) states that the negation marker *majab* is used in negative exhortatives (11). She analyzes *majab* as *mat-oj-ab* (NEG-IRREALIS-EXH), but states in a footnote that this contraction is not accounted for phonologically. At the very least, this form provides evidence that this negation marker hosts the exhortative clitic +*ab*, which attaches to the verb in affirmative exhortatives.

(11) Popti' negative exhortative   (Grinevald Craig 1977: 29)
      ta chaltu' maj-ab   ch-ø-ul   xo' catin
      if that_so NEG-EXH INC-ABS3-come CL Catherine
      'If that is so, would that Catherine not come!'

Grinevald's proposal that this form includes the irrealis clitic +*oj* is interesting. If Popti' originally had a negation marker *ma* that contracted with +*oj*, the derivation of Q'anjob'al *maj* would be easier to account for. Q'anjob'al uses the negation marker *maj* to negate verbs in completive and potential aspects. The aspect markers (*ma*)*x* (completive) and *hoq* (potential) do not appear with *maj* in these contexts (12). It is likely that the negation marker *maj* in both Q'anjob'al and Popti' derives from the combination of *ma* with the irrealis clitic +*oj*.

(12) Q'anjob'al negation with *maj* (Mateo Pedro, pc 2010)
      a. completive aspect
          maj+ach   way   ewi
          NEG+ABS2 sleep yesterday
          'You did not sleep yesterday.'

b.   potential aspect
maj+ach   way-oq
NEG+ABS2   sleep-POT
'You will not sleep.'

The Popti' negation marker *mach* is identical to the Chontal marker, but occurs in different contexts. Grinevald Craig (1977:26) derives the Popti' form *mach* from the contraction of the negation form *mat* with the existential *ay* on the basis that the existential does not occur with *mach* in negative existential constructions (13). Kaufman (2001) proposes a derivation of *mach* from the combination of *ma* and *+ti* 'unfocused'. Popti' uses the negation marker *mat* in stative contexts. Kaufman would need to explain why *ma+ti* became *mach* in some contexts, but not in the stative context. This contraction may have originated in other contexts and been extended to existential negation.

(13)   Popti' existential negation (Grinevald Craig 1977:27)
mach   hin melyu
NEG_exist   my money
'I do not have money.'

Q'anjob'al uses the form *k'am* to mark negation with verbs in the incompletive aspect as well as the existential. The form *k'am* appears with the incompletive aspect marker *chi* on verbs (14a), but without the existential *ay* (14b). As Table 8 shows, Q'anjob'al also uses the negation marker *toq* on verbs in the incompletive aspect (14c) as well as with the existential (14d). In these contexts *toq* occurs with both the aspect marker and the existential.

(14)   Q'anjob'al negation with *k'am* and *toq* (Mateo Pedro, pc 2010)

a.   k'am chi-ø   uj   ha-way-i
NEG   INC-ABS3   can   ERG2-sleep-IND$_{IV}$
'You cannot sleep.'

b.   k'am nab'
NEG   rain
'There is no rain.'

c.   toq   ch-ø-je'
NEG   INC-ABS3-can
'S/he cannot.'

d.   toq   ay   nab'
NEG   exist rain
'There is no rain.'

The incompletive negation forms are interesting in that they show that Q'anjob'al, like Ch'ol and Ixil, tolerates multiple forms of negation. This fact makes plausible the idea that Late Proto-Mayan also had multiple negation markers with the forms *yAb' and *maa. The Q'anjob'alan languages show how the negation markers interact with markers for aspect and modality. This evidence makes plausible the idea that Late Proto-Mayan would have different forms of negation markers in different aspects and modalities.

Q'anjob'al uses the form *manchaq* in imperative and discourse contexts of negation. My reconstruction assumes that *manchaq* derives from a combination of *ma+na.

6. Central Mayan

Table 9 shows the reconstructions for Greater Tzeltalan, Q'anjob'alan and Eastern Mayan along with a reconstruction for Central Mayan. There are many points of similarity between the reconstructions for Greater Tzeltalan and Eastern Mayan. The Q'anjob'alan reconstructions help to fill in some gaps. The Eastern Mayan reconstruction features the clitic +oq in the discourse contexts, while the Greater Tzeltalan reconstruction features the clitic +uk in existential, stative and discourse contexts. The Q'anjob'alan forms support the use of this clitic in incompletive, imperative, existential, stative and discourse contexts. The Q'anjob'alan forms also support the reconstruction of a *ma na combination in imperative and discourse contexts.

Table 9. Reconstruction of negation marking for Central Mayan

	Greater Tzeltalan	Q'anjob'alan	Eastern Mayan	Central Mayan
incompletive	*ma V	*k'am/*toq V	*maa ta V	*maa ta V
potential	*ye'/*ma V	*ma na oj V	*ya'/*mii na V	*ya'/*maa na V
imperative	*ye'/*ma V	*ma na cha oq V	*ya'/*maa V	*ya'/*maa na V
existential	*mii E uk	*k'am/*toq	*k'o ya'/*mii na E	*mii na E oq
stative	*mii N uk	*ma na N oq	*mii ya' N	*mii na N oq
discourse	*ma uk/*mii uk	*ma na cha oq	*mii na oq	*mii na oq

The incompletive and existential forms rely on the reconstructions for Greater Tzeltalan and Eastern Mayan. The reconstruction of the potential and imperative forms are problematic since the three branches have different reconstructed forms of negation in these contexts. I have used a combination of the Q'anjob'alan and Eastern Mayan forms for the Central Mayan reconstructions since it is possible that Central Mayan had two forms of negation marking. Ch'olti' preserved the original distribution of the *ya' form, which Ixil later extended to other contexts. The reconstruction for Central Mayan shows the following changes took place in Greater Tzeltalan, Q'anjob'alan and Eastern Mayan:

1. Proto-Mayan *q changed to /k/ in Greater Tzeltalan resulting in the clitic +uk. Greater Tzeltalan extended the use of the particle *ka to most contexts. The Greater Tzeltalan languages apart from Ch'olti' lost the negation marker *ya'.
2. The Q'anjob'alan languages shifted the clitic +oq to a pre-verbal position in incompletive, imperative and existential contexts. The Q'anjob'al negation marker *toq* may derive from a contraction with +oq. The Q'anjob'alan languages retained the particle *na in imperative and stative contexts. These languages lost the negation marker *ya', and the languages Q'anjob'al and Akatek innovated the negation markers *k'am* and *toq*.

7.   Proto-Mayan

Table 10 compares the reconstruction of negation for Central Mayan with the negation markers of Teenek (Wastek), Yukatek and Itzaj. Teenek and the now extinct language Chikomuseltek form the Wastekan branch of Mayan languages. Yukatek, Itzaj, Mopan and Lakantun form the Yukatekan branch of languages (Hofling 2006). Teenek extended the form *yab* to most contexts of negation, while Itzaj extended the form *ma'*.

Yukatec retains a contrast between the *maa and *mii forms of negation, which supports the reconstruction of these forms for Proto-Mayan. The Yukatek form *min* supports a *mii na reconstruction for existential negation in Late Proto-Mayan. Yukatek also supports the reconstruction of a *mii form for stative negation.

Yukatek, like most other Mayan languages lost the Proto-Mayan *yab' negation marker. It also lost the *+oq clitic in contexts of negation. Yukatek innovated the use of the trapping particle *i'* in contexts of verbal negation (Durbin & Ojeda 1978). This particle appears at the end of the verb phrase rather than immediately after the verb complex. Durbin and Ojeda (1978) analyze this particle as a marker of the scope of focus in contexts of negation. The trapping particle is unrelated to the irrealis and subjunctive particles that appear with negation in other Mayan languages.

Teenek extended the marker *yab* to most contexts of negation, but also uses the form *ibaaj* in many contexts. Teenek provides evidence for reconstructing a Proto-Mayan negation marker *ya'. I reconstruct the vowel /a/ rather than /e/ based on my Eastern Mayan reconstruction.

Table 10. Negation marking in Teenek, Yucatec and Proto-Mayan

	Teenek[a]	Yukatek[b]	Itzaj[c]	Central Mayan	Proto-Mayan
incompletive	yab ats V	ma' V (i')	ma' V	*maa ta V	*maa ta V
potential	yab V	ma' V	ma' V	*ya'/*maa na V	*ya' ba/*maa na V
imperative	yab/ibaaj V	ma' V	ma' V	*ya'/*maa V	*ya' ba/*maa V
existential	yab/ib its E	min E	ma'(y)an	*k'a ya'/ *mii na E oq	*ya'/*mii na E oq
stative	ibaaj N	mix N	ma' N	*mii na N oq	*mii ba N oq
discourse	ii/iib/ibaaj	ma' (i')	ma(la)	*mii na oq	*mii na oq

[a]Edmonson (1988).
[b]Pfeiler pc (2010).
[c]Hofling (2000).

The final vowel of the *ba* particle still surfaces when *yab* is followed by the emphatic particle *its* (15). Without the vowel /a/, the contraction *yab+its* would surface as *yabits*. This reconstruction accounts for the reflexes *el* and *ye'* that occur in Ch'olti' and Ixil respectively.

(15) Teenek negation with emphatic particle   (Edmonson 1988: 494)
      ma   ti xowee' yabaa-its 'in   k'al-e-ø
      until at today not-EMPH ABS1 go-TS-CMP
      'Even now I haven't gone.'

Note that this example includes a particle *ma* that looks suspiciously like the negation marker in the K'iche'an and Greater Tzeltalan languages.

Edmonson notes that the negative marker *ibaaj* can sometimes surface as simply [ii]. Mam has a similar form. One possibility is that at some point Teenek added the particle *ba to the Proto-Mayan negation marker *mii to create *mii+ba > *iiba > iib. I assume that Teenek extended *ibaaj* to the discourse context after separating from the other Mayan languages. This reconstruction assumes that Proto-Mayan used the combination *ya' ba or *ya' le to mark negation.

The reconstructed forms for Proto-Mayan include the particle *na reconstructed for Central Mayan. Yukatek supports the reconstruction of *na for existential negation. Teenek adds the emphatic clitic +*its* in this context.

8.   Conclusion

I summarize the historical changes to negation in the Mayan languages in (16).

(16)   Reconstruction of Proto-Mayan negation

Proto-Mayan
inc *maa ta V
pot *ya' ba/*maa na V
imp *ya' ba/*maa na V
exis *ya'/*mii na E oq
stat *mii ba N oq
dis *mii na oq

Wastek
inc yab+ats V
pot yab V
imp yab/ibaaj V
exis yab/ib+its E
stat ibaaj N
dis ii/iib/ibaaj

Late Proto-Mayan
inc *maa ta V
pot *ya'/*maa na V
imp *ya'/*maa na V
exis *ya'/*mii na E oq
stat *mii na N oq
dis *mii na oq

Yukatekan
inc *ma V
pot *ma V
imp *ma V
exis *min E
stat *mix N
dis *ma

Central Mayan
inc *maa ta V
pot *ya'/*maa na V
imp *ya'/*maa V
exis *k'a ya'/*mii na E oq
stat *mii na N oq
dis *mii na oq

Western Mayan
inc *ma ta V
pot *ye'/*ma na V
imp *ye'/*ma V
exis *k'am/*mii na E oq
stat *mii na N oq
dis *ma na oq/*mii na oq

Eastern Mayan
inc *maa ta V
pot *ya'/*mii na V
imp *ya'/*ma V
exis *k'o ya'/ *mii na E
stat *mii ya N
dis *mii na oq

Proto-Greater Tzeltalan
inc *ma V
pot *ye'/*ma V
imp *ye'/*ma V
exis *mii E+uk
stat *mii N+uk
dis *ma+uk/*mii+uk

Proto-Q'anjob'alan
inc *k'am/*toq V
pot *ma na oj V
imp *ma na cha+oq V
exis *k'am/*toq
stat *ma na N+oq
dis *ma na cha+oq

Proto-Mamean
inc *k'o ya'/*mii E V
pot *k'o ya'/*mii na V
imp *ya'/*mii na V
exis *k'o ya' E/*mii E
stat *mii ya N
dis *mii na

Proto-K'iche'an
inc *ma ta V
pot *mi na V
imp *ma V
exis *ma ki ta E
stat *ma ki N
dis *mi na oq

Proto-Cholan
inc *ma V
pot *ye'/*ma V
imp *ye'/*ma V
exis *ma E
stat *ma N
dis *ma

Proto-Tzeltalan
inc *ma V
pot *ma V
imp *ma V
exis *mii E+uk
stat *mii N+uk
dis *ma+uk/*mii+uk

The history of Mayan negation exhibits three broad types of change:

1. Extension

This reconstruction assumes that Proto-Mayan had a Q'anjob'alan-like structure that employed multiple negation forms in several contexts. As Kaufman claimed, Proto-Mayan had the three negation markers *ya', *maa and *mii. While Proto-Mamean may have retained these options, the other branches eliminated the options by excluding one or more of the negation markers in various contexts. Teenek and Ixil extended *ya', K'iche', Chontal and Popti' extended *maa, while Mam and Tojolab'al extended *mii. Yukatek, Ch'olti' and Q'eqchi' retained a contrast between separate negation markers, but restricted their use to specific contexts rather than allowing different forms to be used in the same contexts.

Extension (Anttila 1972; Harris & Campbell 1995) is a well recognized historical process that occurs outside the domain of cyclic change, assuming that extension crosses different contexts of use while cyclic change occurs within the same context of use. Croft (1991) proposed treating the extension of existential negation to the verbal domain as a type of cyclic change. His proposal does not recognize the various types of extension that are possible in the domain of negation as shown by the history of Mayan extension. The Mayan languages do not support a more general type of cyclic change namely cyclic extension. It is best to treat the extension of existential negation in the Mayan languages as instances of paradigm leveling rather than as instances of cyclic extension.

2. Division

Extension would not be possible without the presence of different negation morphemes in the first place. A Jespersen Cycle cannot start without a competition between different forms. Negation presents a rich cognitive domain for division because it seems reasonable to distinguish the negation of an existential predicate from the negation of a stative predicate, and both of these from responses to questions or commands. The present-day Mayan languages Ch'ol, Ixil and Q'anjob'al provide evidence of a widespread tendency in the languages to multiply the negation markers used in the same contexts. Division is different from the strengthening of negation marking that characterizes the typical Jespersen Cycle.

3. Clitic addition

Historical change to negation in the Mayan languages is best characterized as one of clitic addition. Mayan languages employ clitics to mark irrealis, subjunctive, dubitive, necessative and emphatic contexts. The clitics appear after the predicate in affirmative clauses, but cliticize onto negation markers in negative clauses. Mayan clitics constitute a source of negative coloring that is distinct from the use of indefinite noun phrases to strengthen negation in European languages. Clitic addition hints at a fundamental structural difference between the European and Mayan languages.

I previously proposed a complementation cycle for the Mayan languages in which the languages recruit auxiliary verbs to mark aspect, grammaticalize the auxiliaries onto the verb complex, and then lose the aspectual prefixes setting the stage for the addition of new auxiliary verbs (Pye 2009). I suggest that Mayan negation be integrated into the complementation cycle as a negative state predicate that takes a complement clause of some type. This analysis treats Mayan negation as a form of logical negation with an interpretation like 'It is not the case that …'. Such an analysis explains why Mayan languages extend existential negation to other contexts.

An analysis of Mayan negation as a negative state predicate accounts for the movement of adverbial clitics to the negation marker. The clitics modify the negation predicate, and can be read as modifying the negative assertion rather than the verb predicate. The addition of the clitics to the negative marker prevents the negation markers from cliticizing onto the verb complement and therefore prevents negation in most Mayan languages from undergoing a classic form of the Jespersen Cycle. Instead, adverbial clitics attach onto the negation marker which results in the changes that I and other Mayanists postulate for the negative markers, e.g. Teenek *ya' + *ba > *yab* and K'iche' *ma + *na > *man/na/n*.

I suggested several cases where clitic addition may be responsible for a short-circuited form of a Jespersen Cycle, namely the Teenek derivation *mii + *ba > i(ba) and the Ch'olti' derivation *ya' + *le > el. The derivation for Ixil (*mi+*oj+*at > jit) is more tentative, but of the same type. I label these short-circuited forms of a Jespersen Cycle because they take place within the domain of the negative state predicate that has the negation marker as its head. This domain does not take indefinite noun complements, and so European-style negative strengthening is ruled out.

It is striking that the Mayan languages that do not add clitics to the negation marker, e.g. K'iche', set the stage for a more prototypical Jespersen Cycle. The K'iche'an languages reinterpreted the negation marker as a clitic and thereby set the stage for the loss of the initial negation marker in some contexts. The original negation marker can be preserved in some contexts long after it has disappeared from the verbal domain.

Mayan negation also behaves differently from negation in the Iroquoian languages. Mithun (2014) outlines processes of negation renewal in the Iroquoian language family. The Iroquoian languages descend from a proto-language with a polysynthetic morphology. Wyandot verbs, for example, have partative, translocative, (factual), duplicative, irrealis, cislocative and agreement prefixes. The Wyandot negation marker *t-~te'-* may appear before either the duplicative, irrealis or cislocative prefixes. This reshuffling increases the saliency of the negation marker by moving it from an inner prefix position to an outer prefix position. This fluctuation shows that negation in the Iroquoian languages has a domain within the verb complex rather than outside the verb complex as in the case of Mayan negation.

In this chapter I showed that negation marking is especially sensitive to the underlying linguistic structure of a language, and that languages exhibit a variety of historical changes to negation. The typical form of the Jespersen Cycle is expected in analytic languages with post-verbal modifiers that can be recruited to modify the negative intent. Polysynthetic languages such as the Iroquoian languages strengthen negation by shifting the position of the negative morphemes to an outer position within the verb complex. Mayan negation occurs in a position outside of the verb complex and recruits adverbial clitics to modify the negation markers directly rather than the predicate phrase. We will not know what historical paths that negation takes until we have investigated negation in all languages.

References

Anttila, Raimo. 1972. *An Introduction to Historical and Comparative Linguistics*. New York NY: MacMillan.

Aissen, Judith L. 1987. *Tzotzil Clause Structure*. Dordrecht: Reidel.
    doi: 10.1007/978-94-009-3741-3

Ayers, Glenn. 1991. *La grammatica Ixil*. La Antigua Guatemala: Centro de Investigaciones regionales de Mesoamérica.

Baquiax Barreno, Modesto (coordinador). 2004. *U'tirach e Ojroner Maya Ch'orti': Gramática descriptiva ch'orti'*. Ciudad de Guatemala: Academia de Lenguas Mayas de Guatemala.

Biberauer, Theresa. 2009. Jespersen off course? The case of contemporary Afrikaans negation. In van Gelderen (ed.), 91–130.

Brown, R. McKenna, Maxwell, Judith M. & Little, Walter E. 2006. *La Ütz Awäch? Introduction to Kaqchikel Maya language*. Austin TX: University of Texas Press.

Campbell, Lyle. 1984. The implications of Mayan historical linguistics for glyphic research. In *Phoneticism in Mayan Hieroglyphic Writing*, John S. Justeson & Lyle Campbell (eds), 1–16. New York NY: Institute for Mesoamerican Studies, State University of New York at Albany.

Can Pixabaj, Telma Angelina. 2007. *Jkemiik Yoloj li Uspanteko: Gramática Uspanteka*. Guatemala: Cholsamaj.

Caz Cho, Sergio. 2007. *Xtz'ilb'al rix li aatinak sa' Q'eqchi': Informe de variación dialectal en Q'eqchi'*. Guatemala: Cholsamaj.

Croft, William. 1991. The evolution of negation. *Journal of Linguistics* 27: 1–27.
    doi: 10.1017/S0022226700012391

Dayley, Jon P. 1985. *Tzutujil Grammar*. Berkeley CA: University of California Press.

Durbin, Marshall & Ojeda, Fernando. 1978. Negation in Yucatec Maya. *Journal of Mayan Linguistics* 1: 53–60.

Edmonson, Barbara Wedemerer. 1988. A Descriptive Grammar of Huastec (Potosino Dialect). Ph.D. dissertation. Tulane University, New Orleans LA.

England, Nora C. 1983. *A Grammar of Mam, a Mayan Language*. Austin TX: The University of Texas Press.

England, Nora C. 1994. *Autonomia de los idiomas Mayas: Historia e identidad*. Guatemala City: Editorial Cholsamaj.

van Gelderen, Elly (ed.). 2009. *Cyclical Change* [Linuistik Aktuell/Linguistics Today 146]. Amsterdam: John Benjamins. doi:10.1075/la.146

van Gelderen, Elly. 2011. *The Linguistic Cycle: Language Change and the Language Faculty*. Oxford: OUP. doi:10.1093/acprof:oso/9780199756056.001.0001

Grinevald Craig, Colette. 1977. *Jacaltec: The Structure of Jacaltec*. Austin: TX: University of Texas Press.

Harris, Alice C. & Campbell, Lyle. 1995. *Historical Syntax in Cross-Linguistic Perspective*. Cambridge: CUP. doi:10.1017/CBO9780511620553

Haviland, John, Robinson, Stuart & Gutierrez, Esteban *Sk'op Sotz'leb: The Tzotzil of Zinacantán*. ⟨http://www.zapata.org/Tzotzil⟩

Hoeksema, Jack. 2009. Jespersen recycled. In van Gelderen (ed.), 15–34.

Hofling, Charles Andrew. 2000. *Itzaj Maya Grammar*. Salt Lake City UH: University of Utah Press.

Hofling, Charles Andrew. 2006. A sketch of the history of the verbal complex in Yukatekan Mayan languages. *International Journal of American Linguistics* 72: 367–396. doi:10.1086/509490

Jespersen, Otto. 1917[1966]. *Negation in English and other Languages*. Copenhagen: A.F. Høst.

Kaufman, Terrence. 1969. Teco: A new Mayan language. *International Journal of American Linguistics* 35: 154–174. doi:10.1086/465050

Kaufman, Terrence S. 1974. Idiomas de Mesoamérica [Seminario de Integración Social 33]. Guatemala: Editorial José de Pineda Ibarra.

Kaufman, Terrence S. 1976. Archaeological and linguistic correlations in Mayaland and associated areas of Mesoamerica. *World Archaeology* 8: 101–118. doi:10.1080/00438243.1976.9979655

Kaufman, Terrence S. 1990. Algunos rasgos estructurales de los idiomas Mayances. In *Lecturas Sobre la Lingüística Maya*, Nora C. England & Stephen R. Elliott (eds), 59–114. Antigua, Guatemala: CIRMA.

Kaufman, Terrence S. 2001. Outline of Comparative Mayan Grammar, I: Morphology and Particles. Ms.

Keller, Kathryn C. & Luciano G, Plácido. 1997. *Diccionario Chontal de Tabasco*. Tucson AZ: Summer Institute of Linguistics.

Larsen, Thomas W. 1988. Manifestations of Ergativity in Quiché Grammar. Ph.D. dissertation, University of California, Berkeley.

Laughlin, Robert. 1975. *The Great Tzotzil Dictionary of San Lorenzo Zinacantan*. Washington DC: Smithsonian Institution Press.

Malchic Nicolás, Bernardo, Manuel, Mó Isém, Romelia & Tul Ras, Augusto. 2000. *Rub'iral ruk'ihaal wach Poqom q'orb'al: Variación Dialectal en Poqom*. Guatemala: Cholsamaj.

Mithun, Marianne. 2014. What cycles when and why? Paper presented at the Linguistic Cycle Workshop II, Arizona State University, Tempe AZ.

Mondloch, James L. 1978. *Basic Quiché Grammar* [Institute for Mesoamerican Studies. Publ. 2]. Albany NY: State University, New York.

Norman, William. 1976. Quiché text. In *Mayan Texts*, I, Louanna Furbee-Losee (ed.), 40–60. *International Journal of American Linguistics, Native American Texts Series*. Chicago IL: University of Chicago Press.

Pérez Vail, José Reginaldo.2007. *Xtxolili Yool B'a'aj: Gramática Tektiteka*. Guatemala: Cholsamaj.

Polian, Gilles. 2013. *Gramática del Tseltal de Oxchuc*. México DF: CIESAS.

Pye, Clifton. 2009. Cycles of complementation in the Mayan languages. In van Gelderen (ed.), 265–284.

Pye, Clifton. 2011. Mayan stative predication. In *Proceedings of Formal Approaches to Mayan Linguistics* [MIT Working Papers in Linguistics 63], Kirill Shklovsky, Pedro Mateo Pedro & Jessica Coon (eds), 191–207. Cambridge MA: MITWPL.

Robertson, John S. 1992. *The History of Tense/Aspect/Mood/Voice in the Mayan Verbal Complex*. Austin TX: University of Texas Press.

Robertson, John S. 1999. A Ch'oti'an explanation for Ch'orti'an grammar: A postlude to the language of Classic Maya. *Mayab* 11: 5–11.

Robertson, John S., Law, Danny & Haertel, Robbie A. 2010. *Colonial Ch'olti': The Seventeenth-century Morán Manuscript*. Norman OK: University of Oklahoma Press.

Romero, Sergio F. 2012. A Maya version of Jespersen's Cycle: The diachronic evolution of negative markers in K'iche' Maya. *International Journal of American Linguistics* 78: 77–96. doi:10.1086/662638

Slocum, Marianna C., Gerdel, Florencia L. & Cruz Aguilar, Manuel. 1999. *Diccionario Tzeltal de Bachajón, Chiapas*. Mexico: Instituto Lingüístico de Verano.

Tuyuc Sucuc, Cecilio (coordinador). 2001. *Xtxoolb'iliil Qayool: Gramática descriptiva awakateka*. Guatemala: Academia de Lenguas Mayas de Guatemala.

van der Auwera, Johan. 2009. The Jespersen cycles. In van Gelderen (ed.), 35–71.

Vázquez Álvarez, Juan. J. 2002. Morfología del verbo de la lengua chol de Tila.. MA thesis, Centro de Investigaciones y Estudios Superiores en Antropología Social, Instituto Nacional Indigenista, Chiapas.

Wisdom, Charles. 1950. *Ch'orti Dictionary*. Microfilm notes deposited at the University of Chicago. Transcribed and transliterated by Brian Stross. ⟨http://www.utexas.edu/courses/stross/chorti/⟩

PART IV

Pronominal, quantifier, and modal micro-cycles

The diachrony of pronominal agreement

In Ute and maybe elsewhere

T. Givón

University of Oregon and White Cloud Ranch, Ignacio, Colorado

This paper examines Ute clitic pronouns and contrasts them with other reference-coding devices, such as demonstratives, independent pronouns, zero anaphora, and flexible word-order. It concludes that most independent pronouns are used in contexts of referential discontinuity and most zero and clitic pronouns show extreme referential continuity–a one-clause anaphoric gap. This shows evidence of a typical cycle having taken place: as pronouns weaken into clitics and affixes, they lose referential independence which then needs to be expressed by demonstratives. In addition, the fronting of pronouns and nominal groups is strongly associated with referential or thematic discontinuity whereas the post-posing of pronouns and nominals goes with referential continuity. The chapter also contributes to structural questions: why do pronouns cliticize to verbs and why do they do so in certain positions.

1. Introduction[1]

In an important typological paper, Edith Moravcsik (1974) observed that the cross-linguistic distribution of pronominal agreement on the verb seemed to obey the following hierarchic generalizations:

(1) **Synchronic typological distribution**:
   a.   subject > object
   b.   definite > indefinite
   c.   animate/human > inanimate/non-human
   d.   agent > dative > patient

---

1. This paper is based in part on ch. 7 of my *Ute Reference Grammar* (Givón 2011). I am indebted to Zarina Estrada, Jane Hill, Francisco Queixalos, Spike Gildea and Marianne Mithun for helpful discussion of the Ute data and how they relate to pronominal clitics elsewhere.

Although these generalization were couched in synchronic-typological terms, it is easy to see that these hierarchic claims pertain to the diachronic extension along functional continua.

In a subsequent attempt to explain Moravcsik's typological observations (Givón 1976), I then suggested that:

(2)   a.   The hierarchies in (1) were the then-fashionable **topicality hierarchies** (Hawkinson & Hyman 1974; Silverstein 1976);

     b.   Pronominal agreement on the verb was the diachronic product of stressed independent pronouns becoming de-stressed in anaphoric contexts, and consequently cliticizing on the verb.

     c.   Topicalized-pronoun constructions, such as L-dislocation or R-dislocation, were implicated in the diachronic development of clitic pronouns (2b).

This paper focuses more closely on the diachronic rise of pronominal agreement ((2b,c) above). That is, on the sequence of changes also referred to as "the pronoun cycle" (van Gelderen 2011; van Gelderen in this volume), as in:

(3)   **Diachrony of pronominal agreement**:

     a.   stressed/independent PRO > unstressed/clitic PRO
     b.   unstressed/clitic PRO > verbal pronominal agreement
     c.   verbal pronominal agreement > zero

In the intervening years, the diachronic observations (3) has held up with relatively few exceptions.[2] However, the synchronic distributional prediction (1a), at the time based on data skewed heavily toward Indo-European, Semitic and Bantu or typologically-similar languages, turns out to have fared less well. In particular, one language, Ute, presents a glaring counter-example to prediction (1a), suggesting an alternative hierarchic control:

(4)   absolutive > ergative

This is particularly striking since Ute is in all other respects a quintessential nomina-tive/accusative language.[3]

In this paper I describe the synchronic behavior of clitic pronouns in Ute, in the context of the use of other anaphoric devices–demonstratives, independent pronouns, zero anaphora as well as flexible word-order. While the data is synchronic,

---

2.   The whole notion of 'topicality' used in the 1970s turns out to have been hazy and prob-lematic, and eventually required re-analysis (Givón ed. 1983, 1988, 1992).

3.   A much older, non-pronominal verbal agreement system in Ute, the plural-subject agree-ment, is controlled by the nominative (Givón 2011, ch. 2).

the goals remain profoundly diachronic–understanding the evolution of pronominal agreement.

The rise and fall of pronominal agreement paradigms has often been considered a prime example of a diachronic "cycle" (van Gelderen 2009; 2011; this volume). I have no serious objection to such designation, provided the notion of "cycle" is clearly understood. First, what makes a multi-step development such as (3) above a "cycle" is the last step (3c), the inexorable phonological erosion of all bound morphology back to *zero*, whereby the whole process can, and often does, start all over again (Givón 1971).

Second, and more vexing: Each step in a so-called "cycle" or, by another terminology, "grammaticalization chain" (Heine 1992), is independently motivated. It is the universality of the individual steps and of their functional motivation that makes particular "chains" or "cycles" seem universal.

And third, since a grammatical morpheme or syntactic construction can arise from **multiple sources**, and often gives rise to **multiple products**, the universality of an entire "chain" or "cycle" is, to some extent, an illusory epiphenomenon (Givón 2013). Put another way, as in biological evolution, local diachronic changes, constrained locally, tend to have global consequences without necessarily being globally constrained.

2.   Referential coherence in discourse

The use of independent pronouns, clitic pronouns, pronominal agreement and zero anaphora is part and parcel of the grammar of referential coherence in connected, multi-clausal discourse. In this paper I will take most of the details of this core area of grammar for granted, but a few basic notions need to be mentioned.[4]

The most visible sub-elements of coherence in discourse are:

(5)   **Sub-elements of thematic coherence:**
    a.   referents (participants)
    b.   spatiality
    c.   temporality
    d.   aspectuality
    e.   modality and speech-acts
    f.   actions/events
    g.   perspective (narrative voice)

---

4.   For the gory details see Givón (ed. 1983, 1988, 1992) as well as the relevant chapters in Givón (2001).

These sub-elements of thematic coherence tend to persist across multiple adjacent clauses; that is, across whole **clause chains**, but tend to change at chain boundaries.

The clause chain is the minimal unit of thematic coherence in discourse. At chain boundaries–chain-initial or chain-final position–the continuity of the sub-elements of coherence (5) tends to be lowest. In contrast, at chain-medial positions thematic continuity tends to be highest. The structure of clause-chains may be given schematically, as:

(6)   **Chain structure (schematic):**
… #RD, CI, CM, CM, CM, CM,(…), CF#…

RD = re-orientation device
CI = chain-initial clause
CM = chain-medial clause(s)
CF = chain-final clause
# = chain boundary

Thematic continuity may now be described from two distinct perspectives:

–   **anaphoric**, pointing to the preceding discourse; and
–   **cataphoric**, pointing to the succeeding discourse.

The RD element at the beginning of chains is typically an anaphorically-pointing device, or **coherence bridge**. The CI clause has, typically, weak anaphoric links but strong cataphoric ones, introducing new participants, location, time, etc. into the discourse. Once introduced, these new coherence elements tend to persist across the new chain. CM clauses tend to display maximal continuity both anaphorically and cataphorically. While CF clauses tend to have just as high anaphoric continuity but minimal cataphoric continuity, being thus a mirror image of CI clauses.

3.   Demonstratives and definite articles

The deictic system in most languages is closely connected, diachronically, to the third-person pronoun system, as well as to definite articles. It is thus useful to describe Ute demonstrative first.

3.1   Demonstrative modifiers

The demonstrative (deictic) system of Ute is based on a three-way distinction of **spatial position** vis-à-vis the speaker, a distinction that is coded by three prefixes:

(7)   a.   near the speaker: 'i-
       b.   away-visible: ma-
       c.   away-invisible: 'u-

Demonstrative words, in addition to the three-way deixis, are also marked for the case-role contrast of subject vs. non-subject, and then for the three-way distinction between inanimate, animate-singular and animate-plural. The full inventory of Ute demonstratives is then given in (8) below.

(8) Demonstratives forms:

	near-speaker		away-visible		away-invisible	
	subject	object	subject	object	subject	object
inanimate:	'í-cha	'i-cha-y	má-rʉ	ma-rʉ	'ú-rʉ	'u-ru
animate-SG:	'í-na	'i-na-y	máa	máa-y	'ú-wa	'u-wa-y
animate-PL:	'í-mʉ	'i–mʉ	má-mʉ	ma-mʉ	'ʉ-mʉ	'u–mʉ

The use of these demonstratives as pre-nominal modifiers, pointing to referents in the shared speech situation, may be seen in:

(9) a. **Subject:** 'ícha tʉpʉychi tavasi-kya-tʉ 'this rock is dry'
               this/s rock/s dry-ANT-NOM

   b. **Object:** 'icha-y tʉpʉychi pʉnikya '(s/he) sees this rock'
              this/o rock/o see/IMM

   c. **Subject:** máa na'achichi wʉʉka-y 'that (vis.) girl is working'
               that/s girl/s work-IMM

   d. **Object:** máa-y na'achichi pʉnikya '(s/he) sees that (vis.) girl'
              that/o girl/o see/IMM

   e. **Subject:** 'úmʉ máamachi-u wʉʉka-qha-pʉga 'those (invis.)
               those/s women-PL work-PL-REM women worked'

   f. **Object:** 'umʉ máamachi-u pʉnikya-pʉga '(s/he) saw those
               those/o women/o-PL see-REM (invis.) women'

In natural discourse, the distal pre-nominal demonstratives are often used almost like **definite articles**. This usage is only subtly different from the use of the unstressed post-nominal distal demonstratives as definite articles (see below). To illustrate this, consider the opening passage of a traditional narrative:[5]

(10) a. kh-'ura 'uwas yʉʉpʉchi 'ura-pʉga.
       then-be 3s/s porcupine/s be-REM
      'there was once a porcupine.

---

5. "Porcupine, Sinawav and buffalo cow", told by Mollie B. Cloud. All Ute texts examples cited in this paper are taken from Givón (ed. 1985).

    b.   kh-'ura   tuachi-u-gwa-pʉga,   wáay-kunani.
        then-be child-PL-have-REM   two-O
        Well, he had children, two of them.

    c.   kh-'ura   tuachi-u-av   supay-kwa-pʉga.
        then-be child-PL-OWN leave-go-REM
        But then he deserted his children.

    d.   "i-vaa-sap-'uru   mʉni pagha'ni-nʉ" máy-pʉga,
        here-at-MOD-it/O   you/s wander-IMP say-REM
        "You-two just wander around here" he told them,

    e.   nʉ'   'ay-ku   tʉna-khwa-vaa-chi" máy-pʉga-'uru.
        1s/s say-SUB hunt-go-IRR-NOM   say-REM-it/O
        while I go hunting" he told them.

    f.   'ú-'uni-chi-'ura   'ura-vaachi 'ú   yʉʉpʉchi..
        RED-do-NOM-be   be-BKGR   **that/s** **porcupine/s**
        he always does it, **that porcupine…**'

This use of stressed pre-nominal demonstratives is limited to the distal ones, and is most likely the diachronic precursor of the unstressed post-nominal definite articles.[6]

3.2   Demonstratives as definite articles

Distal demonstratives can be de-stressed and placed after the head noun, and used as **definite articles** that can modify both subject and non-subject nouns. As noted earlier, this use is not obligatory. In terms of word-level phonology, these unstressed morphemes are probably clitics/suffixes on the preceding word, though here we will continue to write them as separate words. The set of distal demonstratives used as articles is:

(11)

category	subject	object
inanimate	'úru	'uru
animate-SG	'ú	'uway
animate-PL	'úmʉ	'umʉ

As a somewhat simplified examples of their use, consider:

(12) a. kh-'ura 'áapachi **'u**   tʉkuavi **'uru**   tʉka-pʉga
         then-be boy/s   **the/sʉ** meat/o **the/o** eat-REM
         'then the boy ate the meat'

---

6.   The most common universal source of definite articles are the distal demonstratives. As stressed deictic pointers, they appear in Ute before the noun. The use in (10f) may be the intermediate stage before they become post-nominal definite articles.

b. xh-'ura kani-naagh<u>a</u>-tukh<u>wa</u> **'uru** y<del>u</del>ga-p<del>u</del>ga
   then-be house-in-to **the/o** enter-REM
   'then (s/he) entered into the house'

c. tuachi **'uway** t<del>u</del>kuavi **'uru** magha-p<del>u</del>ga
   child/o **the/o** meat/o **the/o** feed-REM
   '(s/he) fed the meat to the child'

d. t<del>u</del>ka'nap<u>u</u> **'ur<u>u</u>** yaqh-kya
   table/s **the/s** break-ANT
   'the table broke'

e. máam<u>a</u>chi-u **'um<u>u</u>** táata'wachi-u **'um<del>u</del>** p<del>u</del>nikya-qha-p<del>u</del>ga
   women/-PL **the/s** men/o-PL **the/o** see-PL-REM
   'the women saw the men'

In connected discourse, post-nominal definite articles are used as one of several
devises to mark referents that have been introduced previously into the discourse and
are now being **re-introduced**. But they can also be used upon first introduction, as in
the following two examples:[7]

(13) a. 'uwas-kway 'in<u>i</u>-kway 'ura-p<del>u</del>ga, **Sinawavi 'u,**
        he/s-MOD WH/s-MOD be-REM **Sinawav/s the/s**

   Sinawav<u>i</u> 'ura-p<del>u</del>ga...
   Sinawav/s be-REM

   'There was once this one what's-his-name, **the Sinawav,** it w<del>u</del>as
   Sinawav...'

b. kh-'ura **wáa-mamachi-u 'um<u>u</u>** 'ura-p<del>u</del>ga,
   then-be **two-woman-PL the/s** be-REM

   'inii-u-sap<u>a</u>   'ura-p<del>u</del>ga-vaach<u>i</u>.
   WH-PL-MOD   BE-REM-BKGR

   '...so then there were **the two women,** whoever they were.'

   'úm<u>u</u>-'ura 'úu-pa-am<del>u</del>   paghay'w<u>a</u>-p<del>u</del>ga-vaach<u>i</u>...
   3p/s-be   there-DIR-they walk-REM-BKGR
   they were walking that-a-way...'

3.3 Demonstratives as pronouns

Stressed demonstratives can also be used pronouns, that is, standing by themselves for
a referent that is assumed to be familiar to the hearer. In the case of demonstrative pronouns, this presumption of familiarity is initially based on the shared current speech
situation. What is more, the independent third-person pronouns in tables (15)/(16)

---

7. "How Sinawav got his yellow eyes", told by Mollie B. Cloud.

below are diachronically derived from the non-proximate demonstrative set in table (8) above. Thus, the pronominal use of the demonstratives, as in (14) below, may be the diachronic precursors of their use as independent pronoun.

(14)   a.   'ícha̱-'ara tʉpʉychi̱   'ura-'ay   'this one (prox., inan.) is a rock'
             this/s-be rock/PRED be-IMM

       b.   **marʉ**   ka-'ásti-wa   'I don't want that one (vis. inan.)'
             that/o   NEG-want-NEG

       c.   'úmʉ-'ura   ka-'ay-wa-tʉ-mʉ   'those ones (invis., an.) are no good'
             those/s-be   NEG-good-NOM-PL

4.   Pronouns

4.1   Independent personal pronouns: Discontinuity and contrast

As noted above, the personal pronouns in Ute are historically derived from the set of non-proximate demonstrative pronouns in (8) above, with addition of the first- and second-person forms. In third-person pronouns, the **positional** distinction of far-visible vs. far-invisible is still observed. The first person forms are partially marked for a three-way **number** distinction: singular, dual, plural. In the non-singular first persons, an **inclusive-exclusive** distinction is also observed. Finally, all pronouns display the **case-role** distinction of subject vs. non-subject.

(15)   **Independent subject pronouns**

person	singular	dual	plural
1st	nʉ́' 'I'	támi̱ 'we (incl. you)'	táwi̱ 'we (incl. you)'
		nʉ́mʉ 'we (excl. you)'	
2nd	'ʉ́mʉ 'you'	mʉ́ni 'you-pl.'	
3rd-vis.	máa-s 's/he'	má-mʉ 'they'	
3rd-invis.	'uwa-s 's/he'	'u-mʉ-s 'they'	

(16)   **Independent non-subject pronouns**

person	singular	dual	plural
1st	nʉ́na-y 'me/'my'	tami 'us/our (incl. you)'	tawi 'us/our (incl. you)'
		nʉ́mʉ-y 'us/our (excl. you)'	
2nd	'ʉmʉ–y 'you'/'your'	mʉni 'you/your-pl.'	
3rd-vis. obj:	máa-y 'him/her/his'	ma-mʉ 'them'	
poss:	máa-y-a-s 'his/her'	mamʉ-a-s 'their'	
3rd–invis. obj:	'uwa-y 'him/her'	'u-mʉ 'them'	
poss:	'uwa-y-a-s 'his/her'	'u-mʉ-a-s 'their'	

Stressed independent pronouns are used universally in contexts of **referential discontinuity** or **contrast**. As a brief illustration of this, consider the following English examples. In English, the writing system obscures the difference between stressed-independent and unstressed-anaphoric-clitic pronouns, a difference that is crystal clear in the spoken language.[8] Thus compare:

(17) a. **Continuity: zero anaphora:**
          John talked to Bill and then [0] left. (> John left)

      b. **Continuity: unstressed/anaphoric pronoun:**
          John talked to Bill. Then **he** left. (> John left)

      c. **Discontinuity: stressed/independent pronoun:**
          John talked to Bill. The **HE** left. (> Bill left)

      d. **Non-contrast: unstressed/anaphoric pronoun:**
          John talked to Bill and Mary. **He** wasn't happy. (> John wasn't happy)

      e. **Contrast: stressed/independent pronoun:**
          John talked to Bill and Mary. **HE** was unhappy, but **SHE** didn't care.
          (> Bill was unhappy; Mary didn't care)

The first context of referential discontinuity where independent pronouns are used in Ute is that of introduction of new participants into the discourse, be it at a story-initial or story-medial position. In either position, the pronoun is most commonly augmented with the suffix -'*ura* 'be' or -'*uru* 'that/it', both marking the referent as **important** or **topical**. Consider first the various story-initial referent introductions in:

(18) a. wíitʉs   'ura-na-pʉga-vaachi-'uru…[9]
          long.ago   be-HAB-REM-BKGR-that
          'It was long ago…

              'úmʉ-'uru pa'avi-u núuchi-u 'ura-qa-paachi-'uru…
              3p/s-be   insect-PL person-PL be-PL-BKGR-that
              the insects were humans…'

      b. 'uwas 'íni-kway… Sinawavi   'ura-pʉga…[10]
          3s/s WH-MOD   Sinawav/s be-REM
          'There was once what's-his-name… **Sinawav**…'

---

8.   For a detailed study of this issue, see Givón (2002, ch. 3).

9.   "Sinawav racing the birds and betting", told by Julius Cloud.

10. "Sinawav the copycat", told by Harry Richards.

    c.   'uwas-'ura 'ura-puga-vaachi̱, núu-maroghoma-puga-tu̱...[11]
        3s/s-be   be-rem-BKGR   person-create-REM-NOM
        'There was Him long ago, The Creator...'

    d.   'uwas 'ura-puga sinawavi̱... 'umu̱ chaquura-y-u 'umu̱-kway...[12]
        3s/s   be-REM Sinawav/s 3p/o crane-o-PL 3p/o-MOD
        'There was once Sinawav... and the cranes, whatever they...'

Independent pronouns, often with the suffixes *-'ura,* or *-'uru,* are also used to introduce new participants in the middle of the discourse, as in:[13]

  (19) a. ...'ú-vway-aqh-'uru tu-tugaa-puga-vaachi̱ 'uwas,
           there-at-it-that RED-bet-REM-BKGR 3s/s
           '...So then at one time he kept betting,

      b. kava-nana-chigya-pu̱ tu-tugaa-puga.
           horse-RECIP-race-NOM RED-bet-REM
           he kept betting on horse races.

      c. **mámu̱...** 'umu̱ wu̱-wu̱siaa-gha-tu-mu̱,   'umu̱-vwaa-n
           3p/s   3p/o RED-feather-have-NOM-PL/o 3p/o-at-LOC

           'ay-puga 'uwas...
           say-REM 3s/s
           So he told the feathered ones (birds)...'

Referent-marking devices are not only sensitive to referential continuity, but also
to **thematic continuity.** Thus, consider the English usage in (20) below, where zero
anaphora cannot be used across a chain boundary, and anaphoric pronouns must
be used:

  (20) a. Bill ate his breakfast, then **[0]** took off.

      b. *Bill ate his breakfast. Then **[0]** took off.

      c. Bill ate his breakfast. Then he took off.

The next common use of stressed independent pronouns is reminiscent of their English usage in (17) above. In Ute, the contrast is between zero anaphora and the independent pronoun. When two topical referents have already been introduced into the
discourse, for as long as the same referent continues–typically across a clause-chain–
zero-anaphora is the most common referential device used. When reference shifts to

---

11. "Ute creation story", told by Julius Cloud.

12. "Sinawav and the seven stars", told by Mollie B. Cloud.

13. "Sinawav racing the birds and betting", told by Julius Cloud.

the other topical participant, most commonly the independent pronoun is used, all by itself. Thus consider:[14]

(21) a. ...'ú-vway-aqh-'ura-'uru   nana-chigya-qha-pᵾga,
          there-at-it-be-that   REC-race-PL-REM
          '...So then they raced,

      b. nanᴓs puku-vwa-n-av...   'uwas   ságharᵾ-mᵾ
          each/s horse/o-at-on-OWN   3s/s   white-AN/O

          puku-gwa-tᵾ   'ura-pᵾga...
          horse/o-have-NOM   be-REM

          each (riding) his own horse... **he** had a white horse...'

Sinawav had already been introduced in the preceding paragraph, as have the group of birds he challenged to a horse-race. The first topic of the new paragraph in (21a) is that group. The **switch-reference** back to Sinawav is marked by the independent pronoun 'uwas 's/he'.

The next set of examples involves episodes with two previously-introduced topical participants. The description is now switching back and forth from one to the other, either in mid-chain or when opening a new chain. The independent pronoun is used here as a **switch-reference** device.[15]

(22) a. ...'áa-gha   máy-kya-pᵾgay-kᵾ, 'ú-vwaa
          gentle-PART   say-PL-REM-SUB   there-at

          pagha'ni-pᵾga **'uwas**...
          walk.about-REM **3s/s**

          '..as they were whispering (among themselves), **he** paced around there...'

      b. ...puku-'u.. nᵾ-nukwᵢ-na-pᵾga,, na-rukwᴀ   qha-qharᵾ-na-pᵾga,
          horse-his   RED-run-HAB-REM   REFL-under RED-run-HAB-REM
          '...his horse... it kept running, running with his head bent down,

          "máy-kya-'u!"   máy-pᵾga **'uwas**...
          say-ANT-3s   say-REM   **3s/s**
          "I've told you about him!" **he** said...'

      c. ...pa'a-ka-'átᵾ-tᵾsu'a-pᵾ-a.
          complete-NEG-well-feel-REM-NEG
          '... and **he** (the other guy) felt real bad (about it).'

---

14. Ibid.

15. Ibid.

'ú-vway-aqh-unuv-'ura-'uru   'uwas chaghacivi tᵾga-gha-tᵾ
there-at-it-TOP-be-that/o   3s/s   near   come-PAR-NOM
And sure enough, **he** (Sinawav) was a short-distances racer

'ura-pᵾga-vaachi̱...
be-REM-BKGR
he was...'

d.   ...túu-vᵾni-vɵrɵ-pᵾga-ni   'uwasᵾ-ga.
     ...dark-look-go.about-REM-like 3s/s-EM

'umᵾs máy-kya-pᵾgay-'u..[16]
3p/s   say-PL-REM-3s

'...he kept looking about him with wild eyes. So **they** told him...'

e.   ...'u-vwaa-tukh<u>wa</u>   pɵrɵ-pᵾga 'umᵾsu-ga.[17]
     there-at-go   go/PL-REM 3p/s-EM
     '...and they were coming that way.

'úu-pa-s<u>ᵾ</u>   'uwasᵾ-ga   ka-sari-vaani-kwa-pᵾ-a
there-DIR-C   3s/s-EM   NEG-delay-IRR-go-REM-NEG
So right there **he**(,) without delay(,)

kukwapi   'uru
firewood/o   the/o

ma-mágu'na-ta-qha-na-av   na'a-ti-pᵾga...
RED-gather-PASS-ANT-REL-OWN   fire-CAUS-REM

lighted up the firewood that had been gathered (by him)...'

f.   ..."kani-m<u>a</u>   naguch'a–y, 'iyᵾpᵾy-aa-n!"
     house-LOC   burn-IMM   kinswoman-POSS-1s

'áy-kya-pᵾga 'umᵾsu-ga.
say-PL-REM   3p/s-EM

'..."your house is burning, my kinswoman!" **they** told him.[18]

"ma-mani-ta-sap<u>a</u>-'ara   márᵾ" máy-puga 'uwas...
RED-do.like-PASS-MOD-be   that/s say-REM   3s/s
"That one always does it this way" **he** said...'

---

16.   "Sinawav burning his own house", told by Bertha B. Groves.
17.   Ibid.
18.   Ibid.

g.   ...tuguy-whqa-vѳrѳ-na-puga-'ura. [19]
     hungry-search-walk-HAB-REM-be
     '... he (Sinawav) was walking about hungry searching (for food).

'ú-vwa-aqh-'ura   'u-vwaa-tu-'ura   'íni̱-kway   'ura-puga...
there-at-it-be   there-at-DIR-be   WH/S-MOD   be-REM

mu̱kwapi   maay-puga,
spider/O   find-REM

so then right there there was **what's-his-name**... he found a spider,

pacha'ay-kyay-ku̱.   'ú-vway-aqh-'ura   **'uwas**
stick-ANT-SUB   there-at-it-be   **3s/s**

magu̱ni̱-puga, tu̱ka-vaa-chi̱-'u.
pounce-REM   eat-IRR-NOM-3s

who had been stuck there. So the he pounced, aiming to eat it.

'ú-vway-aqh-'ura   **'uwas-'uru**   'áy-puga...
there-at-it-be   **3s/s-that**   say-REM

so then he (the spider) told him...'

What emerges from these examples is a strong interaction between the use of independent pronouns for switch-reference, pragmatically-controlled word-order (Section 5 below), and the use of large chain-initial conjunctions.[20] When switch-reference is affected in a chain-medial (or chain-final) clause, the pronoun marking the returning subject/topic is **post-verbal**. When switch-reference is at a chain-initial position, especially when a higher thematic-boundary is marked by a large conjunction or adverbial, the returning subject/topic is **pre-verbal**. This conforms to the generalization (see Section 5 below) that the pre-verbal position of the referent in Ute marks **referential discontinuity**, provided the referent is an **important** topic.[21]

4.2   Clitic anaphoric pronouns vs. zero anaphora

4.2.1   *Preliminaries*

The use of unstressed/clitic anaphoric pronouns in Ute is optional. Such pronouns, short and unstressed, can refer to either the subject, the object, or the possessors. What

---

19.   "Hungry coyote races skunk for the prairie dogs", told by Mollie B. Cloud.

20.   For clausal conjunctions and their interaction with other elements of thematic coherence, see Givón (2011, ch. 18).

21.   In this, Ute follows general tendencies in the pragmatics of word-order flexibility, where important discontinuous topics tend to be pre-posed (Givón 1988, 2001, vol. I, ch. 5).

is more, they can be suffixed not only to the verb, but to any word in the clause, especially the first word. They are, thus so-called 'second position clitics'. The set of suffix pronouns, transparently reduced versions of the set of independent pronouns, are given in table (23) below.

(23)   **Clitic pronouns:**

person	singular	dual	plural
1st	-nʉ 'I/me/my'	-rámi̱ 'we/us/our' (incl. you)	-ráwi̱ 'we/us/our' (incl. you)
			-nʉmʉ 'we/us/our (excl. you)'
2nd	-mʉ 'you/your'		-amʉ 'you/your'
3rd-vis.AN	-'a 's/he/her/him/his'		-amʉ 'they/them/their'[22]
3rd-invis.AN	-'u 's/he/her/him/his'		-amʉ 'they/them/their'
3rd-INAN	-aqh 'it/its'		-aqh 'they/them/their'
	-ukh 'it/its'		-ukh 'they/them/their' [23]

As noted earlier above, the "most common chain-medial continuing-reference device, cross-linguistically as well as in Ute, is **zero anaphora**. Three vexing questions now arise concerning the use of clitic anaphoric pronouns in Ute:

– What controls the choice between suffix-clitic pronouns and zero anaphora, given that both mark highly continuous referents?
– What controls the choice between marking the subject, the object, or both, when the verb is transitive and thus has both a subject and an object?
– Under what condition, if at all, can clitic pronouns appear when the subject or object noun also appear in the clause–as **pronominal agreement**?

It is not clear that we will be able to answer these questions in full, given that discourse-pragmatics choices by speakers are often subtle. Studying the frequency distribution of the relevant forms in text may help resolve some of these issues. But the optional use of grammatical devices often depends on the speaker's subconscious cognitive and thematic choices that are not fully amenable to statistical manipulation.

4.2.2   Zero anaphora as default choice for referential continuity

When the referential environment is uncluttered, with no referential conflict or competition, zero anaphora over long stretches of narrative is the common norm in Ute

---

22.   The clitic pronoun -'a ('s/he') is rarely used, and is probably on its way out.

23.   The clitic pronoun -ukh is much less common than -aqh, but is still used. The factor(s) that control the choice between -aqh and -ukh are not clear.

discourse. One may find it, typically, in story-initial context, where for a while the first-introduced participant dominates the discourse. As an example, consider:[24]

(24) a. yoghovʉchi̱ 'u,   [0] pagha'ni-na-pʉga-'ura,
         Coyote/s   the/s   walk.about-HAB-REM-be
         'Coyote, **he** kept wandering about,

     b. kach [0] 'ini-a-sapa̱ paqha-na-pʉ-a,   [0] ⊖⊖-'ay-kwa̱-pʉga,
         NEG   WH-O-MOD   kill-HAB-REM-NEG   bone-be-go-REM
         he hadn't killed anything (for a long time), **he** became bone-skinny,

     c. ka-'ini-aa-sapa̱   [0]
         NEG-WH-O-MOD

         paqha-na-pʉ-a,   [0] tʉgʉy-whqa-vɵrɵ-na-pʉga-'ura.
         kill-HAB-REM-NEG   hungry-search-walk-HAB-REM-be
         he hadn't killed anything (for a while), **he** was walking about searching hungry.

     d. 'ú-vway-aqh-'ura 'ú-vwaa-tʉ-'ura 'i̱ni-kway   'ura-pʉga…
         there-at-it-be   there-at-DIR-be WH-MOD   be-REM
         Then, right there, there was what's-his-name…

     e. mu̱kwapi [0] maay-pʉga, [0] pacha'ay-kyay-ku̱.
         spider/o   find-REM   stick-ANT-SUB
         he found a spider, as **it** was stuck (there).

     f. 'ú-vway-aqh-'ura 'uwas magʉni̱-pʉga, [0] tʉka-vaa-chi̱-'u.
         there-at-it-be   3s/s   pounce-REM   eat-IRR-NOM-3s
         so right away HE (Coyote) pounced, intending to eat **it** (spider).

     g. 'u-vyay-aqh-'ura 'uwas-'uru 'áy-pʉga:
         there-at-it-be   3s/s-that   say-REM
         so then HE (Spider) said:

     h. "ʉ́mʉy-'ura nʉ́' 'anʉ-pa'a-tugwa-n pɵni-kya-vaani?"
         2s/o -be   1s/s WH-long-go-LOC   full-ANT-FUT
         "How long would I keep you full?"

     i. [0] 'ay-pʉgay-'u, "nʉ́-nugway tʉvʉchi̱
         say-REM-3s   I/SU-TOP   very

         míi-pʉ-vʉ-chi̱   'ura-'ay"
         small-DIM-DIM-NOM be-IMM
         he told **him**, "and I am such a tiny little thing"

     j. [0] 'áy-pʉgay-'u…
         say-REM-3s
         he told **him**…'

---

24. "Hungry coyote races skunk for the prairie dogs", told by Mollie C. Cloud.

From (24a) to (24e), even with the introduction of the second participant, zero anaphora marks the continuing referent. And the ambiguity of that device in (24e) is easily resolved by **situation knowledge**. Once the two participants start interacting, beginning with (24f), clitic pronouns begin to appear. Since both participants are animate-singular, the clitic pronoun -'*u* is in principle ambiguous. In (24f) it is perhaps resolved by the following general principle:

(25)   "If the subject is zero-marked in the preceding clause and then persists as subject, it will continue to be zero-marked; so that the ambiguous clitic on the transitive verb must refer to the object".

Note, however, that principle (25) may be on occasion superfluous. Thus, the clause where a clitic pronoun appears first (24f) is a **purpose clause**, whose equi-subject is obligatorily marked as zero. The only referential reading of the clitic pronoun in that clause must therefore be the object–spider, especially given who was intending to eat whom.

The next ambiguous clitic pronouns in (24i) and (24j), both with the verb 'say'/'tell', do not afford us an easy choice of case-role interpretation. If the verb was unambiguously the intransitive 'say', only a subject interpretation of the pronoun ('he' = spider) would have been possible. However, the same verb in Ute also means the transitive 'tell'. My interpretation of the pronouns here as referring to the object ('him' = Coyote) is based on a reasoning akin to principle (25): Spider has been re-instated as the subject/topic in (24g), with an independent pronoun, and then continues to be the active participant in (24h,i,j). Continued marking with the default zero anaphora seems called for, thus assigning the clitic pronoun to the object–Coyote. But is this reasoning sound? And can it be supported by cases where the pronoun is *not* ambiguous; that is, when the subject and object differ in number, or animacy, or person? Or when the verb is intransitive? We will explore such cases in the next section.

4.3   Subject vs. object clitics: In search of a general principle

In this section we will examine only examples of the use of clitic pronouns where the case-role is clear and unambiguous. This can be done when either singular-plural, animate-inanimate, or transitivity information disambiguate the reference of the pronoun. A few instances of 1st and 2nd person pronouns–all from quoted speech–are also examined. The examples below are all taken from one long, complex story.[25]

(26)   a.   ...tavi-navichi-pʉga, 'úmʉ chaqura-u, 'uwa-vaa-chʉ...
            step-MASS-REM   3p/s crane-PL   him-at-DIR
            '...they landed, those cranes, just next to him...

---

25. "Sinawav and the Seven Stars", told by Mollie B. Cloud.

'uwas-'ura: "'agha-ni-uchaa?" 'áy-puga-**amu**…
3s/s-be   WH-do-INC   tell-REM-**3p**
so he asked **them**: "What are you fixing to do?"…'

b.   …kh-'ura-'uru 'uni-'a-puga,
      then-be-that do-ASP-REM
      '…so he went along (with them),

      whsiaavi ma-magha-puay-agay-'u, nani súu-kus…
      feather/O RED-give-REM-ASP-**3s**   each/s one/O
      and they each gave **him** one feather…'

c.   …kh-'ura "togho-y-nug<u>wa</u> maru whsiaavi
      then-be good-IMM-TOP   that/O feather/O

      t<u>u</u>-tuvu-cha'a–n<u>u</u>"   máy-puga.
      RED-pluck-catch-IMP   say-REM

      '…then: "It would be better if we pluck his feathers off" said
      (one of them).

      kh-'ura kw<u>a</u>-kwávi-gha-**amu** tu-tuvu-ch<u>a</u>'a-pugay-**ku** 'umus…
      then-be RED-lie/PL-PAR-**3p**   RED-pluck-catch-REM-**it** 3p/s
      So then while **they** were all asleep (someone) plucked it (feathers)…'

d.   … "n<u>ú</u>-aa   muni ka-ta'wa-puari-nu-wa-t<u>u</u>?"
      1s/s–Q 3p/G NEG-man-help-IMP-NEG-NOM

      máy-puga núgway,
      say-REM   TOP

      '…"can't I be your helper please?" he pleaded,

      ch<u>a</u>qura-y-u 'umu yagha-khwa-miya-kw-**amu**…
      crane-G-PL   3p/G cry-go-go/PL-SUB-**3p**
      as **the cranes** kept going about crying…'

e.   …resti-kya-khay-k<u>u</u>-'ura,
      rest-PL-ANT-SUB-be
      '…whenever they stopped to rest,

      su'i-mi   qova-m<u>i</u>-amu tugwa-amu,
      pee-HAB face-LOC-3p   go-3p

      yua-vaa-t<u>u</u>-**amu** tavi-navich<u>i</u>-k<u>u</u>-'uru…
      plain-at-DIR-**3p** step-MASS-SUB-that

      he would pee in front of them toward-them, whenever **they** landed
      in open country…'

f.   …kh-'ura-'uru 'uwas p<u>u</u>-p<u>ú</u>i-gyay-ky<u>a</u>-'uru,   tapu'ni-puga.
      then-be-that 3s/s RED-sleep-PAR-ANT-that wake.up-REM
      '…so then finally after having slept on and on, he woke up.

      'umu-aa-t<u>u</u>   ya-yagha-puga 'ava-**amu** yáasi-u-k<u>u</u>…
      3p/G-POS-NOM   RED-cry-REM   far-**3p**   fly-INC-SUB
      One of them kept honking as **they** were flying away…'

g.   …'ú-vway-aqh   pa'a-'uwa-vɵrɵ-puga,
     there-at-it   complete-jump-go-REM
     '…so he started/kept jumping up and down,

    su̱-súpay-kya-puay-aghay-'u…
    RED-leave-PL/ANT-REM-CONC-3s
    they had left **him** behind…'

h.   …'umus-'ura   'i-vaa-chu   nɵ̱ɵghwa-tu   pa̱-páqha-khwa̱-puga,
     3p/s-be   here-at-DIR   pregnant-NOM/O   RED-kill-go-REM
     '…and indeed they killed a pregnant one right there,

    'uwa-nukwa̱-'uru   'ura-puga-miya-'u,
    3s-TOP-that   be-REM-go-3s
    and indeed it was **that one**,

        ku-nɵɵ-pɵrɵ-pu-amu̱,   'ú   núu-ruachi̱…
        mouth-carry-go-NOM-3p   that/s   human-child/s
        they mouth-carried (her), that child (from the woman)…'

i.   …máy-puay-aghay-'u,   nana-qhay-ku-'u.
     say-REM-CONC-3s   grow-ANT-SUB-3s
     '…("Go back to your kin") he told her, when **she'd** grown up.

    'uwas-'ura   payu-kwa-puga,   'ú   mamachi̱   'u…
    3s/s-be   return-go-REM   3s/s   woman/s   the/s
    so then she went back, that (young) woman…'

j.   …kh-'ura   'uwas-'uru   'umu   kwá-navichi̱-tu-mu-'uru
     then-be 3s/s-that   those/o   run-MASS-NOM-PL-that/o
     '…so then he (raced) those fast runners

    'umu   nana-chigya-puga-amu̱…
    those/o   REC-race-REM-3p
    he raced **them**…'

k.   …"…'uru   tuka-miya-ku̱"   máy-pagha-puga-amu̱.
     that/o   eat-go/PL-SUB   say-go-REM-3p
     '…"…when you keep eating that" he kept telling **them**.

    'umus   kh-'ura   wucha-rupu'na-qha-mi,
    they   then-be   calf.muscle-cramp-PL-HAB
    They kept having calf-muscle cramps,

        'áagha-kwá-khwa̱-pga-amu̱-'ura   'uwas…
        WH-win-go-REM-3p-be   he
        that's how he beat **them**…'

l.   …'uni-kya-puga   'umus   'uru,   ya'ay-kwa-qhay-ku-'u…
     do-PL-REM   3p/s   that/o   die-ASP-ANT-SUB-he
     '… so they did that, after he died…'

m.   …ꞌuwas súwiini púa-ꞌu máy-vaachi̲:
      3s/s   one/s   kin-3s   say-BKGR
    ‛…So one of his kinsmen said:

      "kachʉ-**ꞌa** pini-vʉni-kya-paa-ꞌwaa-ni   máy-kya-na̲-**ukh**
      NEG-**3s**   back-look-PL-IRR-NEG-FUT   say-ANT-REL-**it**

      ꞌuwas" máy-pʉga…
      3s/s   say-REM

      "don't look back! (that's) what he told us" he said…'

n.   …kh-ꞌura ꞌumʉs-ꞌuru ꞌuni-kya-pʉga, púupa   máy-pʉ-na-ꞌu…
      then-be 3p/s-that   do-PL-REM   manner say-NOM-REL-**3s**
    ‛…so then they did it, just the way **he** said…'

There are **10** cases of unambiguous **subject** pronouns in the sample. Fully **9** of them appear with **intransitive** verbs, where object interpretation of the clitic pronoun is not an option. The lone exception is the transitive verb 'carry-by-the-mouth' in (26h). This clause is in a way a natural exception, being nominalized, so that its subject pronoun is, technically, a **genitive** pronoun. In nominalized clauses in a nominative language, there is a strong tendency for the subject to out-compete the object for the genitive slot–if there is only one.[26] This lone exception aside, the data so far, however meager, conforms to principle (25). That is, the **continuous subject** tends to claim zero anaphora. And the continuous **absolutive** argument–be it object of transitive or subject of intransitive–tends to have a stronger claim to the optional clitic pronoun.

To further investigate this seeming absolutive tendency, 8 consecutive stories in our collection were counted for unambiguous agent-referring pronouns in transitive clauses. The four examples in (27) below are the only ones found in this large sample:

(27)   a.   …bag-i yáaꞌwa-rʉ-**ꞌu**…[27]
        bag-O carry-HAB-**3s**
        ‛…**he** (always) carries a bag…'

    b.   …ꞌumʉ-ꞌura   wáa-mamachi-u   ꞌáy-pʉay-aghay-**ꞌu**…[28]
        them/O-be two-women/O-PL say-REM-CONC-**3s**
        ‛…**he** told the two women…'

---

26.   See discussion in Givón (2001, vol. II, ch. 11).

27.   "How Sinawav got his yellow eyes"; told by Mollie B. Cloud.

28.   Ibid.

c. …ma-machugwa-pᵾga-s-**'u**-'ura…[29]
 RED-squeeze-REM-C-**3s**-be
 '…**he** squeezed it tight together…'

d. …kani-gyay-ku̱-**amu̱**-'ura… [30]
 house-have-SUB-**3p**-be
 '…when/where **they** had a house…'

So far, then, the absolute distribution of clitic pronouns is a near-categorial tendency in Ute.

Another question raised by Example (26) concerns the distribution of **pronominal agreement** in the data. That is, cases where the pronoun co-exists with its co-referent noun (or stressed independent pronoun) in the same clause. There are only four such cases in our larger sample. Of these 4 cases, 3 represent subject agreement, 1 object agreement. We will return to this issue in Section 7.4., below.

Let us now examine the examples where the unambiguous reference of clitic pronoun is due to the fact that they refer to 1st or 2nd persons (speaker/hearer) inside quoted-speech. Consider:[31]

(28) a. …"i-vaa-**numu̱** 'ani-ki̱
  here-at-**1p**   do-IMM walk-go-IMM

  pᴓrᴓ-khwa-y, nagukwi̱-kya-ta-miya-agha" máy-kya-pᵾga…
  fight-PL-PASS-go-have   say-PL-REM

  '…here **we** are flocking about, there's going to be a war" they said…'

 b. …"súwiini 'áy-pᵾga" "kach-**in** 'ásti-wa máay 'uni-'a-vaa-ku̱…"…
  one/s   say-REM   NEG-**1s**   want-NEG 3s/G   do-ASP-IRR-SUB
  '…so one of them said: "**I** don't want that he do (this)…"…'

 c. …" 'uru-'ura nᵾnay ya'ay-kwa-qhay-ku-**n**,
   that-be   1s/G   die-ASP-ANT-SUB-**1s**
  '…"so after **I** die,

  'uru kukwapi-paa-tugwa-n   wᵾnay-kya-**n**" máy-pᵾga-'ura…
  that/o   firewood./O-DIR-go-on   throw-PL/IMP-**1s**
  please throw **me** on that pile of firewood"…'

 d. "…máy-kya-**nu̱**-s 'ura-sap. ᵾvᵾs…"
  say-ANT-**1s**-C   be-MOD   end
  '…**I**'ve spoken, this is it. Finished…'

---

29. Ibid.

30. "Sinawav burning his own house", told by Bertha B. Groves.

31. "Sinawav and the seven stars", told by Mollie B. Cloud.

Of the **4** examples where the pronoun refers to the subject, **3** involve intransitive verbs. Only **1** (28b) involves a transitive verb. However, that verb, 'want', takes a non-finite, nominalized complement clause whose subject is, technically, a **genitive**. While the form of the demonstrative subject *máay* 'that one' is ambiguous, and could also be the object form, it is not clear that the verb 'want' in that clause has a nominal object. To all intent and purpose, then, it behaves syntactically like an intransitive verb. The absolutive distribution of clitic pronouns seems to hold here as well.

Lastly, the only object pronoun ('me') in these examples, in (28c), is a continuing referent preceded by its co-referent ('I') as subject of the preceding clause. Such referential continuity is consonant with our principle (25).

One must note that while most clitic pronouns appear alone, a few cases suggest the co-presence of the subject and object pronouns in a transitive clause, cliticized to the same word. The six such examples in (29) below are all double-pronoun forms found in our 8-story sample.[32]

(29) a.   ...sa'a-khwa̱-pʉay-agha-amʉ̱,[33]
             boil-go-REM-CONC-3p
             '...he boiled them,

             kh-'ura 'uway   Sinawavi-**aqh-amʉ̱** magha-pʉga-amʉ̱
             then-be that/o Sinawav/o-**it-3p**   feed-REM-them
             then he fed **it/them** to Sinawav...'

      b.   doctor   'ura-pʉga-vaachi̱-'u-'uru...[34]
             doctor/s be-REM-BKGR-he-that
             '...he was a doctor...

             maay-pʉgay-**'u̱-amʉ̱**, doctor-i   'uway...
             find-REM-**3s-3p**   doctor-o   him
             they finally found **him**, the doctor...'

      c.   ...'umʉ̱-gaa-ni pʉ-pʉni-vaa-tʉ̱-'u-amʉ̱   'ura-pʉga-s...[35]
             3p-TOP-like RED-look-IRR-NOM-3s-3p be-REM-C
             '...and they themselves were going to come and check on him regularly...'

---

32.   The 8-story sample comprises of "Sinawav and the seven stars" (Mollie B. Cloud); "Sinawav names the trees and bushes" (Bertha B. Groves); "Sinawav the copycat" (Harry Richards); "Sinawav the copycat" (Mollie B. Cloud); "How Sinawav got his yellow eyes" (Mollie B. Cloud); "Porcupine, buffalo-cow and Sinawav" (Mollie B. Cloud); "Sinawav racing the birds and betting" (Julius Cloud); "Sinawav burning his own house" (Bertha B. Groves).

33.   "Sinawav the copycat", told be Mollie B. Cloud.

34.   "How Sinawav got his yellow eyes", told by Mollie B. Cloud.

35.   Ibid.

d. …"'agha-ni-**aqh-amu**-kwa 'uni-kya-y 'umusu-ga?"… [36]
WH-do-**it-3p**-MOD   do-PL-IMM 3p/s-TOP
'…how could **they** possibly do **it**?…'

e. 'agha-ni-**aqh-amu** kh-'ura muni   maru-s   'uni-kya-ku?..[37]
WH-do-**it-2p**   then-be you/GEN that/o-CONJ do-PL-SUB
'…how is it possible when **you** do **it**?…'

f. …"…naruvu-**n-ukh-'uru**" máy-puga…[38]
       habit-**1s-it**-that   say-REM
'…"…it is a habit of mine" he said…'

Of these examples, (29a) is clearly aberrant, since the two pronouns both refer to the object, once as 'it', then as 'them'. Examples (29b,c,d,e) are genuine. In all four, the object pronoun precedes the subject pronoun. Finally, Example (29f) is dubious, since it involves the possessive pronoun 'my' followed by the implied subject 'it'. One may conclude that double clitic pronouns are indeed an option in Ute, but an exceedingly rare one.

4.4   Pronominal agreement

As we have seen from the admittedly restricted sample in (28) above, clitic pronouns can on occasion co-occur in the same clause with their co-referent noun or independent pronoun. How frequent is this optional pronominal agreement in Ute, and is its text distribution predictable? In the single story that contributed the data in (28), only three examples of pronominal agreement were identified. They are re-produced in (30) below:

(30) a. …kh-'ura 'uwas-'uru 'umu kwá-navichi-tu-mu-'uru,
       then-be 3s/s-that 3s/o run-MASS-NOM-PL/o
'…so then he (raced) those fast runners,

   'umu nana-chigya-puga-amu…
   3p/o REC-race-REM-3p
   he raced **them**…'

b. …'umus-'ura 'i-vaa-chu néeghwa-tu pa-páqha-khwa-puga,
      they-be   here-at-DIR pregnant/o RED-kill-go-REM
'…and indeed they killed a pregnant one right there,

   'uwa-nukwa-'uru 'ura-puga-miya-'u…
   3s-TOP-that   be-REM-go-3s
   and indeed it was **that one**…'

36. "Sinawav burning his own house", told by Bertha B. Groves.

37. Ibid.

38. "Sinawav the copycat", told by Harry Richards.

c.   … "nʉ́-aa   mʉni   ka-taˈwa-pʉariʼi-nʉ-wa-tʉ̱?"   máy-pʉga   núgway,
     1s/s–Q   2p/G   NEG-man-help-IMP-NEG-NOM   say-REM   TOP
'…"can't I be your helper please?" he pleaded,

chạqura-y-u   'umʉ   yagha-qha-miya-ku-amʉ̱…
crane-G-PL   3p/G   cry-PL-go/PL-SUB-3p
as **the cranes** kept going about crying…'

Two facts stand out in this minuscule sample:

– The pronouns on the verb in two out of the three cases agree with highly topicalizing **independent pronouns**.
– Pronominal agreement has the same **absolute** distribution–subject of intransitive or object of transitive–as seen with clitic pronouns in general.

To probe the validity of these two suggestive distributions, the count was extended to
the same 8-story sample from our collection.[39] Only clitic pronouns whose case-role
was unambiguous were counted. The results are given in table (31) below.

(31)   **Text distribution of pronominal agreement (only 3rd person)**

controller	Preceding NP	Following NP	Preceding PRO	Following PRO	total
S (intr.)	1	9	9	2	21
O (tr.)	2	10	1	5	18
A (tr)	/	/	/	1	1
total:	3	19	10	8	40

There are several striking facts about this distribution. First, it recapitulates the over-
whelming **absolute** distribution of clitic pronouns in Ute. Only **1** instance of pronominal agreement with the agent-of-transitive was found.

Second, the interaction of pronominal agreement with word-order is of some
interest. Object-controlled pronominal agreement tends, at the level of 15/18, to
involve **post-posed** NPs or independent pronouns. For intransitive subject pronouns,
however, the situation is more complex. If the controller is an NP, **9/10** times it is **post-
posed**. But if it is an independent pronoun, **9/11** times is **pre-posed**.

And third, the frequency of optional pronominal agreement in the total use of
clitic pronouns in our 8-story sample is also of some interest. There were **168** cases
of clitic pronouns without agreement in our sample. The frequency distribution of
optional pronominal agreement in our 8-story sample was thus **40/208 = 19.2%**.

---

39.   See fn. 31, above.

4.5   Cliticization locus: 'Second-position clitics'?

Another option in the use of clitic pronouns in Ute involves the type of word they affix themselves to. To illustrate the great variety of host words available to the clitic pronouns, consider the following examples, the first eight (32a-h) from one story:[40]

(32)   a.   **Verb:** …'uwas-'ura: "'agha-ni-uchaa?" '**ay-puga**-amu…
            3s/s-be   WH-do-INCEP   **say**-REM-them
            '…"what are you fixing to do?" he **asked** them…'

       b.   **LOC-adverb:** …'i-vaa-numu 'ani-ki
            here-at-1p   do-IMM

            pөrө-kwa-y   nagukwi-kya-ta-miya-gha…
            go/PL-go-IMM   fight-PL-PASS-go-PAR

            '…**here** we are flocking (because) there'll be fighting…'

       c.   **LOC-nominal:** …yua-vaa-tu-amu   tavi-navichi-ku-'uru…
            plain-at-DIR-3p   step-MASS-SUB-that
            '…when they would land **in the open country**…'

       d.   **Negative word:** …kach-in 'ásti-wa   máay   'uni-'a-vaa-ku…
            '…NEG-1s   want-NEG   that.one/o do/be-ASP-IRR-SUB
            '…I **don't** want him to be (here with us)…'

       e.   **Time-ADV:** …'umu-aa-tu   ya-yagha-puga 'ara-amu yáasi-ku…
            them-PAR-NOM/S RED-cry-REM   **far**-3p   fly/PL-SUB
            '…one of them kept honking when they flew **frther away**…'

       f.   **Interjection:** …"uvus-1s chika-ghwa"…
            end-3s   fetch-go/IMP
            '…**alright**, go fetch him…'

       g.   **Pronoun:** …'umus-'u…pi-vía-amu   máy-vaachi…
            3p/s-3s   RED-mother-their say-BKGR
            '…**they**… their mother said…'

       h.   **Conjunction:** …"…." 'áy-puga 'uwas **ú-vway-aqh-'u**…
            say-REM 3s/s   **there**-at-it-3s
            '…"…." he said **then**…'

       i.   **Object noun:** kh-'ura **sinawavi**-khu 'uru   magha-puay-aghay-'u…[41]
            then-be **Sinawav**/o-it   that/o feed-REM-CONCL-3s
            '…then he fed it **to Sinawav**…'

---

40.   "Sinawav and the seven sisters", told by Mollie C. Cloud.

41.   "Sinawav the copycat", told by Mollie B. Cloud.

j. **Subject pronoun:** …'uwas-ukh 'úu-pa   'uni-pᵾga…[42]
               3s/su-it   there-DIR do-REM
               '…so **he** did just that…'

k. **Manner ADV:** …má-ra-tᵾ-aa-ni-amᵾ   'uni-pᵾga-sᵾ… [43]
               that-be/like-NOM-O-do-3p do-REM-C
               '…so they did **exactly that way**…'

l. **WH-word:** …'ipᵾ-m-sᵾ-aa-khᵾ 'inay tᵾaani-vaa-tᵾ-sᵾ 'inay?…
               WH-INS-C-Q-it   this/o skin-IRR-NOM-C this/o
               '…**what** shall I skin this one with?…'[44]

Two questions are of interest about the distribution host-words of clitic pronouns:

– What is the ratio of verb-attached pronouns?
– What is the ratio of first-word-attached ('second position') clitics?

The answer to both questions is important for our understanding of the diachrony of cliticization and the rise of pronominal agreement. In search of an answer, the frequency distribution of all clitic pronouns in our 8-story sample was again counted. The results are given in table (33) below.

(33) **Host-word distribution of clitic pronouns (incl. 1st & 2nd person)**

      host position in the clause

host word	first	other	total
verb	90 (45.4%)	108	198 (73%)
non-verb	59 (81.9%)	13	72
total:	149	123	270

The text distributions given in table (33) may be summarized as follows:

– Verbs constitute **73%** of clitic pronoun-hosting words.
– Non-verbal host words appear **81.9%** of the time at the clause-initial position ('2nd position clitics').
– Verbal host words appear only **45.4%** of the time at the clause-initial position ('2nd position clitics').

---

42. Ibid.

43. "How Sinawav got his yellow eyes", told by Mollie C. Cloud.

44. "Porcupine, buffalo cow and Sinawav", told by Mollie B. Cloud.

The implications of these distributions to the diachronic rise of pronominal agreement will be discussed further below.

The last question that needs to be answered concerns the ratio of zero-anaphora vs. anaphoric clitic pronouns in a Ute text. Zero anaphora was counted only in clauses where the referent is marked by neither a noun nor an independent pronoun. Clitic pronouns were counted regardless of whether they stand alone or constitute pronominal agreement. We counted here only the first of our 8-story sample.[45] The results are given in table (34) below.

(34)   **Zero anaphora vs. anaphoric clitic pronouns**

zero anaphora	clitic pronouns	total
114 (70.7%)	48 (29.3%)	162

The implications of this distribution will be discussed in sec. 6., below.

5.   Flexible word-order and referential coherence

In spite of the obvious OV-related features of Ute morpho-syntax, Ute currently displays a flexible word-order, sensitive primarily to discourse-pragmatic factors. Much like the use of clitic pronouns, the pragmatics of word-order flexibility in Ute is complex, subtle, and defies easy generative statements. What is more, the use of word-order options in Ute interacts with the use of both independent and clitic pronouns, as well as with the choice of chain-initial re-orientation devices (RDs).

As an illustration of word-order flexibility in spoken Ute narrative, consider the following examples, all clauses that fall under a single intonation contour; that is, clauses that do not involve left- or right-dislocation.[46]

(35)   a.   'iya-na   muni-'ura agha-paa pɵrɵ-qwa-gha   'ani-kị?
              here-LOC 2p/s-be   WH-DIR   walk/PL-go-PAR do-IMM
              LOC   S   LOC   PART-ADV   V
              '...Where are y'all going flocking through here?...'

         b.   muni-'ura núnay kach 'u-vwaa-tʉ   nóoghwa-y-'ura
              2p/s-be   1s/o   NEG   there-at-DIR carry-IMM-be
              S   O   LOC   V
              '..."Won't you please carry me there?"...'

---

45.   "Sinawav and the seven stars", told by Mollie B. Cloud.

46.   Ibid.

c. 'umu-aa-tu̠   ya-yagha-puga 'a-vaa-amu̠
   one-PAR-NOM/s RED-cry-REM   there-at-they
   S   V   LOC
   '...one of them kept crying there...'

d. 'uru   máy-puga 'umus
   that/o say-REM   3p/s
   O   V   S
   '...they said that...'

e. 'uwas-'ura payu-kwa-puga 'ú   mamachi̠ 'u
   3s/s-be   return-go-REM 3s/s woman/s the/s
   S   V   S
   '...so she returned home, that woman...'

f. ma-vaa-tugwa-su-ni mawisi-vaani mama-'áyh-pu-chi̠
   there-at-go-c-like appear-FUT   woman-teenager-DIM-NOM
   LOC   V   S
   '...a young woman will appear right there...'

g. 'umus-nukwa̠-'ura-'uru   suwa-kwáa-khwa̠-puay-aghay-'u
   3p/s-TOP-be-that   almost-win-go-REM-CONC-him
   S   V

   'uwayas   sinawavi
   3s/o   Sinawav/o
   O
   '...they almost beat Sinawav (in the race)...'

h. 'uni-kya-puga 'umus 'uru
   do-PL-REM   3p/s   that/o
   V   S   O
   '...so they did that...'

The first general pragmatic principle of word-order flexibility in Ute is in fact a universal principle that is attested in all languages regardless of word-order flexibility or rigid word-order type:[47]

(36) **Pre-posing a discontinuous topical referent:**

   a. If an important referent/topic is continuous, i.e. was active in the preceding clause (1-clause anaphoric gap), it will be marked by **zero anaphora** or **clitic pronoun**.

   b. If the topical referent is introduced into the discourse for the first time, or is re-instated after a large gap of absence (3-clauses or more anaphoric gap), it will be marked as a full noun and **pre-posed** to the beginning of the clause.

---

47. For an extensive discussion and documentation, see Givón (ed. 1983, 1988; 2001, ch. 5).

c. But if the gap of absence is relatively small (ca. 2–3 clauses anaphoric gap), so that **chain-medial switch-reference** is involved, the re-instated referent is also **pre-posed**, but as an **independent pronoun**.

Principles (36) single out three universal types of grammatical devices that are used to code topical referents in three distinct discourse contexts:

–   **Maximal referential continuity**: zero-anaphora or anaphoric pronouns
–   **Chain-medial switch reference**: pre-posed independent pronouns or small NPs
–   **Chain initial first introduction or re-introduction**: Pre-posed large NPs

Let us illustrate how Ute word-order conforms to principles (36). Consider first the introductory paragraph of a story, in (37) below, which illustrates the initial introduction of the two main participants.[48]

(37)   a.   wíitʉs 'ura-pʉga, **sinawavi̱** 'ura-pʉga, **sinawavi̱** 'u 'ura-qa,
             past   be-REM   **Sinawav/s** be-REM   **Sinawav/su** **the/su** be-ANT
             'It was long time ago, there was Sinawav, there was that Sinawav,

       b.   pөө-pa   paghay-kwa-pʉga.
             road-DIR walk-go-REM
             he was going down the road.

       c.   kh-'ura   **púuch'achi̱** 'ura-pʉga-sʉ̱,
             then-be   **mouse/s**   be-REM-C
             and then there was also Mouse,

       d.   sicha'wa-miya-kway,
             trick-HAB-MOD
             he used to plays tricks,

       e.   **kwasi-a-'u**   pe̱vi'wi-kwa-mi,
             tail-G-his/3s pull-go-HAB
             he used to pull his tail,

       f.   manu-khʉ̱-tʉ   mani-miya-sʉ̱,
             all-O-NOM/O   do.like-HAB-C
             he would do that all the time,

       g.   qa̱-qháarʉ-mi   kh-'ura 'uni-gya.
             RED-run-HAB   then-be do-PAR
             then he would run away doing that.

---

48.   "Sinawav names the trees and bushes", told by Bertha B. Groves.

h. **'uwas-'ura** ka-puka-manay-pɵrɵ-'a–tu̱   'ura-puga-vaachi̱,
   3s/s-be NEG-very-move-go-have/NEG-NOM be-REM-BKGR
   Now *he* (Sinawav) was never very fast-moving,

i. ka-túsapa mani-'wa-na-pu̱a-vaachi̱…
   NEG-hurry do.like-NEG-HAB-REM/NEG-BKGR
   he could never move like that in a hurry [gesture]…

j. ka-qomɵ'na-pu̱a-vaachi̱.
   NEG-turn-REM/NEG-BKGR
   he could never turn (very fast).'

In (37a) the first major participant (Sinawav) is introduced as a **pre-posed** subject NP (SV order), twice. It continues in the next clause (37b) as **zero** subject. In (37c) the second main participant (Mouse) in introduced, again as a **pre-posed** subject NP (SV order), who then continues as **zero** subject over the next four clauses (37d,e,f,g). In the midst of that run (37e), a minor participant, Sinawav's tail, is introduced as a **pre-verbal** object (OV order). In clause (37h), a mid-paragraph switch-reference back to Sinawav is affected by the pre-posed **independent pronoun** (SV order) with the topicalizing suffix -'*ura* 'be'; after which Sinawav continues as **zero** subject for two more clauses (37i,j).

Once the two main participants have been introduced and given some background description, the next macro-paragraph launches into the body of the story. Most of the back-and-forth switch-reference cases in this long paragraph, given in (38) below, are coded by **pre-posed independent pronouns** (same as in (37h) above).

(38)   a. pina-khwa̱-'ura **'uwas** tu̱vu̱chi na'ay'a̱-puga,
          follow-go-be **3s/s** very angry-REM
          '…then finally he (Sinawav) got real angry,

       b. na'ay'a̱-ku̱-'u 'uni-pu̱ga-vaachi̱.
          angry-BEN-3s do-REM-BKGR
          he got angry at him (Mouse) for what he was doing.

       c. 'ú-vway-aqh na'ay'a̱-qhay-ku̱…
          there-at-it angry-ANT-SUB
          So when he got angry…

       d. sicha'wa̱-pu̱ga-vaachi̱-'u kh-'ura qha̱-qháaru̱-puga,
          trick-REM-BKGR-him then-be RED-run-REM
          (because) (Mouse) had tricked him and then ran away,

       e. páaqhachi-naagha̱ yu̱ga-khwa̱-puga.
          hole/o-in enter-go-REM
          and (he) entered into a hole.

    f.   páaqhachi-naagha̱   yu̱ga-khwa-pu̱gay-ku̱   'uwas,
        hole/o-in   enter-go-REM-SUB   **3s/s**
        So when he entered into a hole,

    g.   **'u̱u̱u̱u̱**... 'iya-kwa-pu̱ga   tíi   páaqhachi-naagha̱.
        "eeee"... here-go-REM   high hole/o-in
        "eeee"... he went high up there into the hole...'

There is no topic/subject switch in the first clause of this paragraph (38a). Nonetheless, Sinawav is recapitulated with a **pre-posed independent pronoun**. The reason is that the use of pre-posed pronouns is not sensitive only to referential discontinuity, but also more generally to **thematic discontinuity**. While the two tend to coincide, when thematic discontinuity–in this case a paragraph break–occurs without referential discontinuity, the continuing topical referent is recapitulated anyway.

Another departure from the strict rule occurs in (38b), where switch reference back to Mouse occurs without any marked device. But it occurs in a subordinate 'because' clause, and the speaker relies on knowledge of the story's contents to disambiguate the reference. Finally, in (38f), in spite of the continuing referent (Mouse), a **post-posed** independent subject pronoun (OVS order) is used. While this is not strictly necessary, it conforms with another general tendency found in our oral texts, to be discussed further below.

In the third paragraph of our story, several switch-reference turns occur in rapid succession, most of them well marked by the pre-posed independent pronoun:

(39) a.   **'uwas-'ura**   'áy-pu̱gaa-[ni]:
          3s/s-be   say-REM-like
          So then he (Sinawav) thought:

       b.   "'ipu̱-sapa̱-'uru 'ura-gupu̱ pa'a-toghwa-tu̱
           WH-MOD-that be-SUBJUN   complete-right-NOM/s
           "What would possibly be so long

       c.   kh-'ura **nu̱'** 'u-ma   'uni-ku̱ chu̱kur'a-gupu̱...
           then-be **1s/s** there-LOC do-SUB poke-SUBJUN
           so that I may poke it in there...

       d.   piyoghwa-khwa̱ **'uway** pana-khwa̱?"
           pull-go   **3s/o**   return-go
           and pull him back out of there?"

       e.   manu-khu̱-tu̱-aa-su̱ 'uni-pu̱ga,
           all-o-NOM-o-c   do-REM
           So he tried all kinds of things,

       f.   'ivichi ku̱u̱-pu̱ga, cu̱kur'a-pu̱ga, 'u̱u̱-pa-tu̱   tíi
           stick/o-take-REM poke-REM   there-DIR-DIR high
           he took a stick an poked it, high up there,

g. kachu-'u   sapigya-puha.
   NEG-3s   can-REM/NEG
   But he couldn't (get him).

h. **púuch'achi** 'u   kiya-ku-kwa-pugay-'u   'i-na-khwa-paa   tíi,
   mouse/s   3s/s   laugh-BEN-go-REM-3s   here-LOC-go-at   high
   That mouse just laughed at him high up there,

i. 'ini-'a-pugay-'u-kway:
   do-ASP-REM-3s-MOD
   he just did it (teased him) like that:

k. " 'avatu-mu"   sicha'wa-qha-'u.
    big-AN   tease-ANT-3s
   "You are big" he teased him

l. **'uwas**-'uru 'ay-na-puga   náaaaa…
   3s/s-that   say-HAB-REM   náaaa
   he used to call him that náaaa….

m. "'avatu wa'a-qa-tu"   máy-na-pugay-'u.
    big   penis-have-NOM   say-HAB-REM-him
   "The one with the big penis" he used to call him.

n. **'uwas**-'ura 'ú-ra-ku,
   3s/s-be   that-be-EM
   He (Sinawav) was indeed like that,

o. 'áy-na-puga-vaachi,   'íi-pa-kwa-su-'ura…
   say-HAB-REM-BKGR   here-DIR-go-c-be
   he (Mouse) used to call him that, it was (long) like this [gesture]…

p. **'uru**   'ura-qa…   **'uru**   'uni-aa-gha-y   wíitus-'uru,
   that/o be-ANT   **that/o** POSS-o-have-IMM past-that
   it was that… that thing he had long ago.

q. pa'a-togho-puga-vaachi   **'urusu-ga**.
   complete-straight-REM-BKGR **that/s-TOP**
   it was so long, that thing.

r. 'íi-pa   kh-'ura   **'uwas**
   here-LOC then-be   3s/s

   wachu-vɘrɘ-na-puga-vaachi 'avatu-kwa-na-va'agha.
   put-go-HAB-REM-BKGR   shoulder/o-go-LOC-over

   so that he used to carry it over his shoulder.

s. 'ú-ra-ku-'u   sicha'a-na-puga-vaachi-'u.
   that-be-EM-him   tease-HAB-REM-BKGR-3s
   they used to tease him for being like that'.

The first switch-reference occurs in (39a), from Mouse back to Sinawavi. The next
one, in (39c), is to 'I' within the direct-quoted speech. The next one in (39h) is back

to Mouse. All are marked with **pre-posed** independent pronouns. In (39-l) the use of an independent pronoun seems to be superfluous, given that Mouse continues topical referent. But such usage may be due to a thematic break. But in (39n), (39p) and (39r) the **pre-posed** independent pronoun is again used to mark switch-reference. Finally, the **post-posed** independent pronoun (VS order) in (39q) is used in the context of referential continuity (see again directly below).

We turn now to trying to understand the communicative context of **post-posed** independent pronouns or larger NPs. What stands out in the use of this word-order, VS or VO, are two features:

(40) **Post-posed independent pronouns or larger NPs:**

   a.   The referent tends to be highly continuous, most commonly with an anaphoric gap of **one clause** (co-reference in the preceding clause).

   b.   The discourse context is most commonly the **chain-final**, paragraph-final, or episode-final clause.

All the examples of the VO order found in paragraphs (37), (38) and (39) above conform to both principles (40a,b). What is more, the conditions under which the VS word-order is used in Ute are reminiscent of the use of R-dislocation in spoken English.[49]

6.   Discussion

If one looks at the text distribution of independent pronouns, clitic pronouns and pronominal agreement in Ute oral texts, the first question that leaps to mind is synchronic:

(41) **Synchronic coherence:**
      Are all these usage options rule-governed? Can one come up with a tight generative statement for the use of Ute pronouns?

The answer is both yes and no, depending on what one means by 'rule-governed'. If by 'rule governed' one means the traditional generative statement, with purely syntactic conditioning of the choice of options, the answer is surely no. If, on the other hand, one means that the choices are non-random, and motivated by communicative or cognitive factors, the answer is probably yes. The text distributions we have seen above are not communicatively random even when the choices seem wide-open and subtle. The vast majority of independent pronouns are indeed used in contexts for topic switching. The vast majority of the clitic pronouns display an absolute distribution. The vast

---

49.   See Givón (1983a,b).

majority of zero anaphora distributes in the context of extreme referential continuity–one-clause anaphoric gap. The pre-posing of independent pronouns and larger NPs is strongly associated with referential or thematic discontinuity. And the post-posing of independent pronouns and larger NPs is strongly associated with both high referential continuity and termination of the thematic unit. Most clitic pronouns are suffixed to the verb. Still, none of these statistical associations are absolute. Exceptions abound, and the choices the speakers make are often too subtle to pin down. And lastly, in the case of three usage options–choice of anaphoric pronouns vs. zero anaphora, of optional pronominal agreement, and of the host-word for clitic pronouns–variation may outstrip clean rule-governedness.

The level of variation one sees in these three areas begs for a diachronic interpretation of the data, so that one may wish to ask the second, obvious question:

(42)   Is the distribution of the optional variations noted above diachronically coherent?

The tentative answer is yes indeed, in the context of the diachronic rise of anaphoric pronouns and pronominal agreement. Earlier work on the subject suggested the following generalizations:[50]

(43)   **Anaphoric pronouns and pronominal agreement**:
   a.   Clitic anaphoric pronouns arise from independent pronouns by de-stressing, phonological attrition and functional 'de-marking'.
   b.   The anaphoric distance of zero anaphora and clitic anaphoric pronoun is, most typically, the same–one clause back.
   c.   Obligatory grammatical agreement arises from optional clitic-anaphoric pronouns, via generalization and de-marking, and in interaction with an 'optional' word-order device–left- or right-dislocation.

Our Ute data are fully compatible with generalizations (43a,b) above. What is more, the Ute data can help resolve two questions that previous work had left open:

–   Why do anaphoric pronouns cliticize where they do?
–   What is the detailed mechanism of their cliticization to the verb?

As it happens, the Ute synchronic situation catches the language in the midst of the change from **first-position clitics** to **verb suffixes**, with the majority of pronouns–73%–already cliticized to the verb. The key to answering the first question is to remember our diachronic generalization (43a) above:

---

50.   See Givón (1976, ed.1983).

– Clitic pronouns arise from independent pronouns, and independent pronouns in Ute most typically a pre-posed; that is, they appear early in the clause. When they become de-stressed and cliticize, the host to their cliticization would be the preceding full-size word in the clause.

The answer to the second question requires keeping in mind generalization (43b) and what we know about zero anaphora:

– Zero anaphora is the most common referent-marking device in natural discourse. Which means that the most common clause-type in language is the one-word clause–the verb by itself, with an anaphoric subject and, to a lesser degree, anaphoric object.[51] The verb is thus likely to be the most frequent first word in the clause, thus the most frequent candidate to host second-position clitics.

Lastly, one has to account for the possible interaction between second position clitics and flexible word-order. Here again, the synchronic situation of Ute is illuminating. The pre-posed position of Ute independent pronouns is not governed by a pronoun-specific rule, but rather by the general word-order pragmatic principle (sec. 5, above):

– A discontinuous topical referent is most likely be pre-posed.

One may thus be tempted to go on a limb and make the following typological generalization:

(49)   **Diachronic-typological generalization:**
Languages that currently display obligatory pronominal agreement are either now, or have been in the past, languages with flexible word-order *and* second-position pronominal clitics.

As for the **absolute**–rather than nominative–control of clitic pronouns and pronominal agreement in Ute, I suspect the Numic sub-family, and indeed Uto-Aztecan in general, might be a fertile ground for investigating this phenomenon. The pronominal clitic situation in Pima Bajo (Estrada 2011) apparently to involve absolutive control, as in Ute. Pronominal agreement in Nahuatl (Peralta 2010), for 3rd persons, is a close variant of the Ute situation: clitic pronouns on the verb are controlled by the object in transitive clauses, with zero-anaphora for the subject of *both* transitive intransitive clauses. Lastly, Hill's (2011) work on Cupan (Takic), while describing several diachronically more mature agreement systems that are not identical to Ute, contains many hints that may help explain the typological diversity–thus diversity of diachronic pathways that give rise to – pronominal agreement.

---

51.   See DuBois (1987).

Abbreviations of Grammatical Terms

AN	animate	OWN	possessive reflexive
ANT	anterior	PAR	participle
BG	background	PASS	passive
CAUS	causative	PL	plural
CL	closure	POSS	possessed
DIM	diminutive	PR	predicate
DIR	directional	Q	yes/no question
FUT	future	REC	reciprocal
G	genitive	RED	reduplication
HAB	habitual	REFL	reflexive
IMM	immediate	REM	remote
IMPER	imperative	S	subject
INC	inchoative	SUB	subordinator
INCP	inceptive	TOP	topic
IRR	irrealis	WH	WH question word
LOC	locative	1s	1st person singular
MASS	mass	1P	1st person plural
MOD	modal particle	2s	2" person singular
NEG	negative	2P	2" person plural
NOM	nominalizer	3s	3rd person singular
O	object	3P	3rd person plural

References

DuBois, John. 1987. The discourse basis of ergativity. *Language* 63(4): 805–855. doi: 10.2307/415719

Estrada-Fernández, Zarina. 2011. Systemas pronominales en pima bajo: Formas, fonciones y sus patrones de gramatización. *Seminario de complexidad sintáctica 2011*, Universidad de Sonora, Hermosillo.

van Gelderen, Elly. 2009. *Cyclical Change* [Linguistik Aktuell/Linguistics Today 146]. Amsterdam: John Benjamins. doi: 10.1075/la.146

van Gelderen, Elly. 2011. *The Linguistic Cycle: Language Change and the Language Faculty*. New York: Oxford University Press.

Givón, T. 1971. Historical syntax and synchronic morphology: An archaeologist's field trip. In *Proceedings of the Chicago Linguistic Society 7*. Chicago IL: CLS.

Givón, T. 1976. Topic, pronoun and grammatical agreement. In Li (ed.), 149–188.

Givón, T. (ed.). 1983. *Topic Continuity in Discourse: Cross-Language Quantified Studies* [Typological Studies in Language 3]. Amsterdam: John Benjamins. doi: 10.1075/tsl.3

Givón, T. 1983a. Topic continuity and word-order pragmatics in Ute. In Givón (ed.), 141–214. doi: 10.1075/tsl.3.04giv

Givón, T. 1983b. Topic continuity in spoken English. In Givón (ed.), 343–364. doi: 10.1075/tsl.3.08giv

Givón, T. (ed.). 1985. *Ute Traditional Narratives*. Ignacio CO: Ute Press.

Givón, T. 1988. The pragmatics of word order: Predictability, importance and attention. In Hammond et al. (eds), 243–284. doi:10.1075/tsl.17.18giv

Givón, T. 1992. The grammar of referential coherence as mental processing instructions. *Linguistics* 30: 5–55. doi:10.1515/ling.1992.30.1.5

Givón, T. 2001. *Syntax: An Introduction*, 2 Vols. Amsterdam: John Benjamins. doi:10.1075/z.syn1

Givón, T. 2002. *Bio-Linguistics: The Santa Barbara Lectures*. Amsterdam: John Benjamins. doi:10.1075/z.113

Givón, T. 2011. *Ute Reference Grammar*. Amsterdam: John Benjamins. doi:10.1075/clu.3

Givón, T. 2013. On the diachronic 'ethical dative'. In *Functional-Historical Approaches to Explanation: In Honor of Scott DeLancey* [Typological Studies in Language 103], Tim Thornes, Erik Andvik, Gwendolyn Hyslop & Joana Hansen (eds), 43–66. Amsterdam: John Benjamins. doi:10.1075/tsl.103.03giv

Hammond, Michael, Moravcsik, Edith & Jessica Wirth (eds). 1988. *Studies in Syntactic Typology* [Typological Studies in Language 17]. Amsterdam: John Benjamins. doi:10.1075/tsl.17

Hawkinson, Annie & Hyman, Larry. 1974. Topic hierarchies in Shona. *Studies in African Linguistics* 5(2): 147–170.

Heine, Bernd. 1992. Grammaticalization chains. *Studies in Language* 16(2): 335–368. doi:10.1075/sl.16.2.05hei

Hill, Jane H. 2011. Pronouns in the Cupan languages. *Seminario de Complexidad Sintáctica 2011*, Universidad de Sonora, Hermosillo.

Li, Charles N. (ed.). 1976. *Subject and Topic*. New York NY: Academic Press.

Moravcsik, Edith. 1974. Object-verb agreement. In *Working Papers in Language Universals* 15. Stanford CA: Stanford University.

Peralta-Ramírez, V. 2010. Procesos de seguimiento de referente dentro de clausulas encadenadas en el discurso náhuatl. *Seminario de Complexicad Sintácticc 2010*, Universidad de Sonora, Hermosillo.

Silverstein, Michael. 1976. Hierarchy of features and ergativity. In *Grammatical Categories in Australian Languages*, Robert M.W. Dixon (ed.). Canberra: Australian Institute of Aboriginal Studies.

The degree cycle*

Johanna L. Wood
Aarhus University

The grammaticalization of the demonstratives *this*, *that* and *thus* is investigated with respect to their functions as degree adverbs using empirical data from dictionaries and historical and modern corpora. It is first argued that *thus* participates in the CP cycle. With respect to *this* and *that,* data relevant to the development of the degree adverb function is presented and possible relevant constructions identified. It is argued that the degree adverb function of *that* possibly occurs later than the historical dictionaries indicate. The degree adverb function of *this* is challenging to trace due to the apparent overlap with *thus*.

1. Introduction

Since the recent renewed interest in cycles of language change, a number of different macro and micro cycles have been proposed, but so far little attention has been given to degree words or a possible degree cycle within the Cycles framework. Degree adverbs are constantly being renewed. Stoffel (1901:2) discusses how adverbs that originally express absolute qualities, such as *pure* and *full,* weaken to become intensifiers (degree adverbs), and that "the process is always going on, so that new words are in constant requisition, because the old ones are felt to be inadequate to the expression of the idea of completeness of a quality, or of a quality to the very highest degree of which it is capable under the circumstances". Likewise, Tagliamonte (2008:362) remarks that "competition, change, and recycling among intensifiers have been going on in English since the Old English period", pointing out that Old English *swiþe* was replaced by *full,* then *right,* all with the meaning 'very'. The class of degree words is fairly open in some respects, but still fairly closed in other respects. On the one hand, degree words like *dead* and *wicked* are easily recruited into expressions like *it is dead useful* and *it is wicked cold out*, and just as easily discarded; on the other hand degree

* I am grateful to participants at the Linguistic Cycle Workshop II, held at Arizona State University, 25–26 April 2014, and to Elly van Gelderen, Sten Vikner and Jane Trayer for comments and suggestions. Also thanks to Joseph Sterrett for his enthusiasm in discussing the examples from Shakespeare.

DOI 10.1075/la.227.10woo

words like the adverb *so* (Old English *swa*) show no signs of retreating. According to a recent study, Tagliamonte (2008: 368) finds that *so* is almost on par with *very* as the second most frequent degree adverb in Toronto English, following the most frequent, *really*. One possible significant factor when considering the difference between those that disappear (or abandon their degree function) and those that do not is that some degree words (*full, right, wicked* etc.) are derived from lexical words whereas others, notably *so, such* and those that will be investigated here (*this, that, thus*) are functional and have long been so. Although they are recruited to express degree they have a number of other grammatical functions and belong to more than one non-lexical word class.

In this chapter, the focus will be on three degree words that belong to this second, more functional, group: *thus, this* and *that*. Such a focus will take the discussion into both the CP and the DP and possible connections between them. A number of recent and not so recent studies have focused on language external factors associated with degree words. For example, Stoffel (1901: 101) and Jespersen (1922: 249–50) associate them with hyperbolic language and women's speech, Paradis (1997) and Macaulay (2006) associate them with young people, and recent sociolinguistic work e.g. Ito and Tagliamonte (2003). Tagliamonte (2008) has investigated external variables of age and gender, as well as internal ones. However, the focus in this chapter is on language internal change of degree words and whether and how this relates to a possible cycle. I start by investigating the clausal adverb, *thus*, both historically and with respect to its retreat in present-day English and go on to discuss the DP in the analysis of the degree adverbs *this* and *that*. The early history of the demonstrative manner adverb *thus* is so bound up with the degree adverb *this* that one adverb cannot be discussed without the other. The remaining focus is on two other demonstratives, specifically the degree adverbs, *this* and *that*. The word *that* is a relevant starting point for investigating possible degree cycles since it has already been shown to be involved in two cycles: as a determiner in the DP and a complementiser in the CP. This third change, to a degree adverb, is arguably related in some way, particularly as far as feature loss is concerned.

The change from the demonstrative *that* to definite article *the* in early Middle English is well described. In this micro cycle, the demonstrative changes syntactic position (from specifier to head), changes its feature content (loses deictic features) and becomes a definite article. Subsequently, demonstratives tend to be reinforced with locative adverbs in many languages, including English, where *this here* and *that there* are frequently heard, although not considered part of the standard (van Gelderen 2011: 210–17). The focus in this investigation is a more recent, less well described, change in which the demonstrative becomes a degree adverb, modifying an adjective in both predicates, as in *I didn't think the winter would be that/this bad*; and in DPs, as in *I didn't expect that/this bad a winter*. In the dictionaries, degree use of *this* and *that* is first attested in late Middle English, although my preliminary investigation in this chapter will find little evidence before the 19th century. Unlike the development of the definite article and the complementiser, this change involves the proximal *this* as well as the distal *that*. A third related demonstrative, the adverb *thus,* clearly has a different function in present-day English, as e.g. a manner adverb (*We turned up the heat; thus we stayed warm*). However, historically *thus* is part of the same paradigm as *this,* being derived from the instrumental case, *þȳs,* of Old English *þes þis þeos,* 'this' (Wright 1902:228). In this chapter, after some theoretical background in Section 2, I first situate *thus* in the CP cycle and show, in Section 3, how it has changed since Old English and is being replaced in present-day English. The second and third parts of the paper, Sections 4 and 5, focus on method. In a preliminary investigation of degree *that* (in Section 4) and degree *this* (in Section 5), I start with the historical dictionaries and corpora and try to find the time period and the type of data relevant to the reanalysis of *that* and *this*. There are some challenges to be met here, particularly in Section 5 with regard to the degree adverb *this*. Although there is a clear functional split between *this* and *thus* in present-day English, this has not always been the case. It will be seen that the separate functions of *thus* and *this* are not so clearly defined in earlier English.

Demonstrative expressions are a widely researched topic cross linguistically, particularly interesting in grammaticalization as they demonstrate that not only lexical items, but also grammatical items, may be the source in grammaticalization processes. Diessel (1999:160) suggests that all languages have, in their basic vocabulary, a class of deictics which do not derive from a lexical source but are, in a sense, primitives. This observation has been built on in analyses that decompose the various demonstratives. See, for example, Klinge (2005:185–186) who suggests a relationship between English *the, this, that, there, then, thence, thither, therefore* and *thus,* all with demonstrative semantics related to *th* plus vowel. Koenig's (2015) investigation into the role of demonstratives of manner, degree, and quality in the development of grammatical markers mentions a possible cycle involving demonstratives. One of the characteristics of the cycle is loss and renewal, and he claims that *so, such,* and *thus,* in their manner adverb function, are currently being replaced by expressions such as *like this* and *this way.* Additionally, it has been noted both by Koenig (2015:75) and Wood (2002:113; 2014:7) that in present-day English *such* is being renewed with *like* to *suchlike.* Since *such* in Germanic is already a grammaticalised form of 'so' formed from *swa,* 'so' + **liko,* 'body', 'form', the same process has happened twice in one word. In Section 3 another example of a cycle within a word will be seen, in *thus,* where the manner features are renewed with the suffix *-ly,* the modern equivalent of Old English *-lice,* to give *thusly.*

Returning to cycles and the recycling referred to by Stoffel (1901) and Tagliamonte (2008), there are obvious differences between changes involving words like *full, right* and *pure* etc. and those mentioned by Koenig (2015), which involve functional words like *so, such* etc. Although they all become degree words, lexical items such as *full* show typical patterns, developing fairly rapidly into degree adverbs, subsequently widening their collocation behaviour and (eventually) become archaic and obsolete (Partington 1993; Ito & Tagliamonte 2003; Tagliamonte 2008; Peters 1994). However, the already grammaticalised items, *this, that, so, such, as,* also change, but do not fit straightforwardly into the established framework of grammaticalization in which degree adverbs are formed by delexicalisation (Partington 1993: 183). Although interesting, investigation of the delexicalisation of lexical words like *full* etc., and the subsequent loss of their degree function, is beyond the scope of this chapter and the focus will be on *this, that* and *thus*.

I start in Section 2 by outlining the theoretical framework. In terms of structure, the cycle involves the determiner phrase (DP), where the demonstrative originates, the adjective phrase (AdjP) and its functional structure and the clause (CP). The characteristics of the items under discussion are often described in terms of the semantic categories' manner', 'kind/quality' and 'degree' and I also introduce these properties (Bolinger 1972; Ghesquière & van de Velde 2011; Anderson & Morzycki 2015; Koenig 2015). In Section 3, I examine *thus* and evaluate the claim that it is being replaced in present day English, arguing that it is part of the already described CP cycle (van Gelderen 2011: 247–259). In Sections 4 and 5, I follow various 'leads' in the investigation of *that* and *this,* starting with information in the historical dictionaries in order to discover when the change took place and which data might be relevant in the reanalysis. Although I find characteristics indicative of a cycle with *thus,* no indications of a cycle are found with *that* and *this.*

The development of *that* into a complementiser is older than the written record, and so it is possible for the degree adverb *that* to have developed through a stage involving the complementiser *that* as in (1)c, or, through a stage involving a clausal adverb as in (1)a, or as in (1)b directly, without any clausal interaction.

(1)   a.   Demonstrative> clausal adverb> degree modifying adverb
      b.   Demonstrative> degree modifying adverb
      c.   Demonstrative> complementiser > degree modifying adverb

The path in (1)c is less likely, otherwise different explanations would be needed for *this* and *that,* as only *that* is a complementiser. In Section 4 the evidence points to *that* following the path in (1)b. However, in Section 5 the data show that for *this* the choice between(1)a and (1)b is complicated by the close connection between the demonstrative determiner *this,* degree adverb *this,* and the adverb *thus.*

The historical data is taken from the Oxford English Dictionary on Historical Principles (henceforth OED), the Middle English Dictionary (henceforth MED) the Helsinki Corpus (henceforth HC) and the Corpus of Historical American English (henceforth COHA) plus specific individual texts. It should be noted regarding the OED dates that the earliest entry is not always the earliest example and could be predated. Also, in Middle English, the composition date and manuscript dates are often a

considerable number of years apart, and therefore the dates cannot be taken as definitive.[1] For contemporary data I use the British National Corpus (henceforth BNC) and
the Corpus of Contemporary American English (henceforth COCA). It should also be
mentioned that there is some confusion in the current literature regarding the terminology used for degree adverbs. Quirk et al. (1985) refer to the entire set as 'intensifiers' (as does Bolinger 1972), split into amplifiers (*terribly, very, so*), compromisers
(*rather, fairly*) and diminishers (*slightly, partly*). Others omit downtoners and take the
term 'intensifier' to mean only items on the upper part of the scale, excluding compromisers and diminishers (e.g. Tagliamonte 2008). See Paradis (1997) for other terms. In
order to circumvent this problem, I use 'degree adverb' as a neutral term.

2. Theoretical background

Cycles, simply put, are changes where a phrase or word gradually disappears and is
replaced by a new linguistic item. Generally the changes leading up to the disappearance are those which are associated with what is known as grammaticalization. Within
formal theory (Roberts & Roussou 2003; van Gelderen 2004), grammaticalization is
seen as reanalysis in which a lexical item becomes functional or a functional item
becomes more functional, essentially becoming more closely associated with the left
periphery. Van Gelderen (2004: 11–12) puts this in terms of two economy principles:
the Head Preference Principle, (Be a head, rather than a phrase) and the Late Merge
Principle (Merge as late as possible). Research into grammaticalization from a functional perspective has, for the most part, focused on clines, stepwise changes from one
stage to another, which are generally argued to be unidirectional. Little attention has
been paid to renewal. The Cycles approach takes into account the replacement/renewal
aspect of grammaticalization, arguing that certain language changes are cyclic, or
rather, since the replacement is with a different item, the result is not cycles, but spirals.

2.1 Syntactic structure

Below, I first briefly outline my assumptions regarding the structure of clauses and
nominals. Since the introduction of the DP, a number of clausal/nominal parallels have
been proposed including parallel structures of the general form in (2):

(2)   a.   Clausal structure: [CP [AgrP [VP]]]
       b.   Nominal structure: [DP [AgrP [NP]]]

---

1. The OED often gives both an original manuscript date and the (later) date of the quoted
source and I leave both dates for clarity of reference. When the individual text might be significant I have left it for reverence otherwise I quote the general source and the date.

The clause consists of the VP layer, where thematic roles are assigned. The area designated AgrP in (2)a is for agreement, traditionally called T(ense)P(hrase), though other types of agreement may be involved (see van Gelderen 2013: 10–11 for an overview). With respect to the clause, generally mood can be expressed by adverbs and adverbials in the CP layer (e.g. *frankly, probably*) and in the TP layer (e.g. *possibly*). Aspect can be expressed in the TP layer (e.g. *often*) and the VP layer (e.g. *completely*). A fine grained analysis of adjective ordering is given by Cinque (1999:106). Partington (1993:180–82) discusses the "modal to intensifier shift" e.g. for *really,* and a modal stage is expected for lexical content words. With respect to *thus,* and changes involving grammatical words, it is not clear whether or not similar stages occur. However, evidence of participation in the CP cycle, will come from position, in the lower part of the clause in earlier English and the higher part of the clause in later English before possibly disappearing from contemporary use. A shift from the VP manner adverb to a CP discourse orientated function is also expected.

I assume that the basic structure of the nominal has a similar agreement area e.g. Num(ber)P(hrase), (Ritter 1988, 1991) although other agreement projections are not excluded. As a starting point for nominal structure I take the surface order of nominal elements argued for in Epstein (1999:18) and the structure she proposes is shown in (3). This structure, she argues, provides the minimum number of nodes required for an English DP. All the lexical items shown in (3) may be thought of as "determiner-like" (See also Denison 2006: 284).

(3)

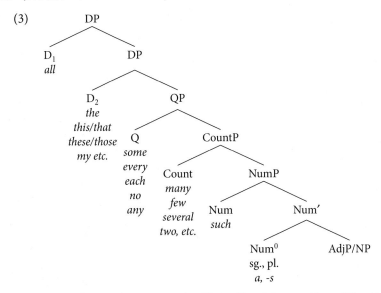

Two positions of particular note are the DP itself and the specifier of NumP. The specifier of NumP is the surface position of fronted degree modifiers, e.g. the moved constituent *that bad* in *I didn't expect that bad a winter* (Wood & Vikner 2011, 2013).

Although the position of numerals is sometimes thought to be the specifier of NumP, Epstein (1999:17) argues that the possible positions of *such* shown in (4), preceding the indefinite article but following numerals, means that a separate node is needed for numerals, placing *such* in Spec-NumP.

(4) a. I read such a book yesterday.
  b. I read two such books yesterday.
  c. I read one such book yesterday.
  d. *I read a such book yesterday.

As for *this* and *that,* I follow the widely accepted view that the definite article *the* is merged as the head of DP and demonstrative determiners are in Spec-DP, having moved from a lower position (Alexiadou et al. 2007; Bernstein 1997; Brugè 2002; Giusti 1997, 2002). Finally, it should be noted that, generally, adjective phrases in English immediately precede the noun. Different proposals put adjectives either directly into the tree stem or in the specifiers of functional categories. Since this is unimportant for the present discussion, I will remain neutral on this detail.

As well as the position of the demonstratives *this* and *that* within the DP structure, it is also relevant to consider the position of degree *this* and *that* in relationship to the adjective phrase. The syntax of degree phrases is less clear than that of the nominal. In Jackendoff's (1977) proposal, the degree phrase occupies the specifier of the adjective phrase, whereas other proposals (e.g. Abney 1987:298–321; Bresnan 1973; Corver 1997) suggest functional structure for the adjective phrase as well as for clauses and nominals. The functional structure is particularly relevant in explaining the difference between the degree adverbs *less* and *too* as shown in (5) and (6). As seen with *less* in (5), 'fond of Mary' can be replaced by the pro-form *so,* but in (6) *too* has to be replaced by *much so.*

(5) a. John is less fond of Mary.
  b. In fact he is <u>less so</u> than Bill.
  c. *In fact he is <u>less much so</u> than Bill.

(6) a. John is too fond of Mary.
  b. *In fact he is too so.
  c. In fact he is <u>too much so.</u>

In Corver's (1997) explanation of this, the extended projection of the adjective phrase has two heads, Deg° and Q° and *too* is merged as the head of DegP, whereas *less* is merged lower, as the head of QP.

(7) $[_{DegP}Deg [_{QP}Q AP]]$

Hence, in (6)c, when *fond of Mary* is replaced by the proform *so*, the head of QP is lexically realized by *much*. The examples in (8) show *that* and *this* pattern with *too* and not with *less*.

(8) a. John is that/this fond of Mary.
     b. *In fact he is that/this so.
     c. In fact he is that/this much so.

If the structure in (7) is correct, then *this* and *that* are functional heads in the extended projection of the adjective phrase and the change from demonstrative *this* and *that* to degree adverb *this* and *that* involves two changes from one XP (DP) to another XP (AdjP) and from specifier to head in accordance with the Head Preference Principle. See Bernstein (1997) for arguments that demonstratives are specifiers.

Building further on the two different approaches (Jackendoff vs, Bresnan/Corver), Neeleman et al. (2004) propose abandoning a uniform analysis of degree expressions. They argue that degree expressions that pattern with *too* are functional heads which c-select an adjective phrase complement (these they call class-1 expressions). Those that pattern with *less* are modifiers that may select any XP (class-2 expressions). From this falls out the difference between degree adverbs that select only adjectives, class-1 (e.g. *very*) and those that select adjective phrases and additionally select other phrasal categories, class-2 (e.g. *fairly* and *sorely*). As can be seen in (8), *this* and *that* pattern with *too*, and therefore, are class-1 degree adverbs in present day English and are functional heads under this approach as well.

2.2   Semantic categories

As well as structural position, three semantic properties are relevant: 'kinds', 'manners', and 'degrees'. Discussion of the interaction between 'kind' and 'degree' in English degree words goes back at least as far as Bolinger (1972). Most recently, Anderson & Morzycki (2015) have highlighted the close semantic connection between, 'kinds', 'manners', and 'degrees' and Koenig (2015) has described the grammaticalization of demonstratives with particular reference to the three categories, 'quality' 'manner' and 'degree'. So far, the research that links 'kind' and 'degree' has focused on *such* and its cognates. For example, Wood (2002) attempts a synchronic syntactic analysis to distinguish 'kind' *such*, and 'degree' *such* and the diachronic question has been addressed comparatively for English and Dutch (Ghesquière & van de Velde 2011). It is well known that while *such* may express 'kind' and 'degree', it does not express manner, which is taken up by the etymologically related *so*. Similarly, with *this* and *that*, the manner function is taken up by an etymologically related item, *thus*.

Of course, these semantic properties are not limited to DP modifiers and many adverbs can function both as adverbial modifier in the DP and as clausal adjunct, e.g. *fairly* which in (9) is a manner adjunct in the clause and in (10) is a degree modifier in the DP:

(9)   I think that can be fairly said   (COCA: spoken)

(10)   Well, it's a fairly significant downsizing   (COCA: spoken)

However, not all adverbs have this dual clausal/nominal syntax in present-day English and some adverbs are found exclusively as adjectival modifiers in the DP. In present-day English the modifiers *this* and *that* select only adjective phrases and one of the crucial questions is whether the change of *this* and *that* to modifiers took place exclusively in the DP or whether there was an intermediate clausal stage. The possible paths are set out in (1) a, b, c above. These relationships point to potentially interesting aspects of the cycle: interaction between the DP cycle and the CP Cycle, and the path taken when lexical items move between the two.

3.   The CP Cycle and *thus*

As was mentioned above, the adverb *thus* is part of the same Old English proximal demonstrative paradigm as *this*. In present-day English, *thus* is an adjunct adverbial in the clause and, unlike adverbial *this* and *that*, selects other phrases in addition to adjective phrases. In this section, I argue that *thus* participates in the cyclic change known as the CP cycle.

In the analysis of the changes undergone by clausal degree adverbs, van Gelderen (2011:252) shows that lower adverbs (VP adverbs) develop additional functions as higher adverbs (CP adverbs) in the cycle. The high adverbials are subsequently lost. For example, two Old English adverbs, *siker, sikerly* meaning 'sure' and *soþlice*, meaning 'truly' are now obsolete and have been replaced. The method is to look at the position of adverbs in Old English in relationship to the verb and to consider the adverb's meaning and function. A cartographic approach to the order of adverbs is taken, with speech act adverbs as the highest, as was outlined in Section 2. Other indicators include the amount of preposing, and also adverbs with the ending *-lice* compared with adverbs without the short adverbial *-e* ending. Incorporation of *-lice* tends to happen later. It should be noted, however, that *thus* is not expected to go through the same adverbial stages as e.g. *sikerly* and *soþlice,* because, as was previously mentioned, the process is not stagewise delexicalisation, but rather an already functional element (a demonstrative) becoming more functional.

In 3.1, I show that in earlier English *thus* tended to be a VP manner adverb in a low (VP) position and in later English moves to a higher position on the left periphery, as adverbs are shown to do in the CP cycle. In a more leftward position *thus* still sometimes has a manner meaning although often it can be ambiguous between manner and a discourse connector meaning 'therefore'. Additionally, in Section 3.2, I present data to show that *thus* is declining in present-day English. The conclusion is that the clausal adverb *thus* participates in the CP cycle, and appears to be regressing in present-day English.

3.1   Position of clausal *thus*

In Old English, in the OE 1–2 section of the Helsinki Corpus (covering the years 850–950) a leftward position of *thus* is evident as in (11) from *Leechdoms, Wortcunning, and Starcraft of Early England*. Here, although *thus* is preposed, it still has a manner meaning; the verb *make* lends itself easily to this.

(11)   *þus   mon   sceal   eagsealfe   wyrcean,   genim   streawberian...*
       Thus   man   shall   eye-salve   make,   take   strawberries...
       'In this way eye-salve is made, take strawberries....'   (HC: OE1-2. 850–950)

However, in (12), from the 891 entry of the *Anglo-Saxon Chronicle*, although I have translated *thus* with a manner reading, another interpretation could be 'therefore', in which case it is possible to leave *thus* out without significantly changing the meaning. Ambiguous examples like (12) are required for reanalysis and language change.

(12)   *þus   hie   wæron   genemnde, Dubslane & Maccbethu & Maelinmun.*
       Thus   they   were   named   Dubslane & Maccbethu & Maelinmun
       'They were named in this way: Dubslane & Maccbethu. & Maelinmun.'
                                                        (HC: OE1-2. 850–950)

Although I suggested that (12) could be read as 'therefore', according to the OED, *thus* is not found meaning, "in accordance with this; accordingly, and so; consequently; therefore" until the 12th century. In (13), although *thus* is adjacent to the verb, it still appears to be ambiguous, whereas in (14) and (15), *thus* is preposed and no longer has a manner meaning.

(13)   *And   þus   a   departet   mit   mukel   reunes:*
       And   thus   are   departed   with   much   sorrow

       þe   souel   into   helle..   þe   bodi   into   herþe.
       the   soul   into   hell...   the   body   into   earth.
       'And thus, with much sorrow, the soul goes to hell, the body into the earth.'
                                                        (1250 *Body & Soul*)

(14)   *Ðuss   hire   is   Marthen   geswyncfulle   lif...*
       Thus   here   is   Marth-GEN   full-of labour   life...
       'And here is Martha's hardworking life...'
                                (a1150 (c1125) *Homily for the Feast of the Virgin Mary*)

(15) *Þus, wummon, ȝif þu hauest were   after þi   wil ...*
      Thus woman,   if you have   husband after your will ...
      'Therefore, woman, if you have the husband you want ...'
                              (c1225 (?c1200) *Hali Meiðhad*.Bod 34)

In the Middle English text *The Poems of William of Shoreham*, dated approximately 1320 and written in the Kentish dialect, there are several examples in which *thus* (spelled *þos*) precedes the subject.

(16) *Þos   we beþ al   awey-ward*
      Thus   we are all away-turn
      'Thus we are all astray (line 29)

(17) *And þos   þat chyld to nyȝt   y-bore*
      And thus that child to night brought-forth
      'And thus that child born tonight' (line 859)

Hence by early Middle English, *thus* starts to occur in the leftward position in the clause and may be considered a discourse connector in the CP as well as a manner adverb in the VP. In present day English, a manner reading is possible, as in (18), although it sounds rather stilted and *thus* is more usual as a clause linker as in (19).

(18) Molly Bloom's final soliloquy is above all a celebration of that freedom, and the freedom <u>thus</u> won. (BNC: spoken)

(19) legislation was specifically geared at Local Education Authorities that do not look after their schools, and <u>thus</u> schools are able to opt out ...
                                                          (BNC: spoken)

Finally, one of the criteria that van Gelderen uses, the difference between the adverb with -*e* and the adverb with -*lice,* is not a useful indicator of change in Old and Middle English, but, I claim, it is indicative of 20th century renewal. According to the OED (s.v. *thusly*), *thusly* was first used at the end of the 19th century and is colloquial. There are only two examples in the BNC from the same fictional text. Surprisingly, in American English at least, *thusly* appears to be becoming more frequent and less colloquial. In COHA, between 1810 and 1950, there is only a total of 8 examples of *thusly*, whereas there are 13 examples in 1990 and 11 in 2000. The early examples bear out the OED's comment that *thus* is colloquial, as shown in (20) below, which is from a fictional text depicting a non-standard speaker.

(20) If Tallmage, in his sermin, sez he b'lieves there's a hell, you want to be sure to rite it up <u>thusly</u>:   (1885, COHA: fiction)

However, the more recent examples, such as (21) from the *Wall Street Journal* are not colloquial.

(21)   Bob Reade, who coaches football at Augustana College here, sums up the physical attributes of his players <u>thusly</u>:   (1986, COHA: news)

This new, initially non-standard, use of inflected *thus* could be interpreted as a renewal of the manner function within one word. In COCA, of the 80 examples of *thusly* in non-fiction texts (spoken and written, excluding fiction), only 8 are discourse connectors (CP adverbs) and the remainder are VP adverbs. Renewal will be discussed further in the following section.

3.2   Reinforcement loss and renewal

One of the indications that an item participates in a cycle is its loss, renewal and replacement (which, as mentioned, is actually a spiral, as the exact same starting point is never regained.) Cycles often involve renewal with new lexical items, which add interpretable semantic features to replace those that are being lost. As was mentioned above, the recent development of *thusly* is one indication of renewal where manner features are reintroduced with the suffix *-ly*. Historically, there are sporadic examples of renewal. The Old English suffix *-wise* means 'in such a way' or 'manner' or 'fashion'. For example, *likewise* means 'in the same manner' and *otherwise* means 'in a different manner'. When *thus* starts to be reinforced with *-wise* it could be an indication that the manner features are weakening, although the locative features remain. Example (22), of two manuscript versions of the 14th century *Cursor Mundi*, not only shows *thus* reinforced with *wise*, but also *this*. In Section 5 *thus* and *this* will be shown to be used interchangeably.

(22)   a.   'Sun', scho said, 'wirk noght <u>þus</u> <u>wise</u>.'
                                     [*Göttingen* MS.] (line 11971)

       b.   Sun', scho said, 'wirk noght' <u>þis</u> <u>wise</u>.'
                                     [*Vespasian* MS.]
            Son, she said, work not thus wise/this wise
            "Son', she said, 'do not behave in this way."

Another reinforcer found in northern texts is *-gate*, meaning 'way':

(23)   Þus-gat was sant Iohan slan
       Thus   was   St.   John   slain
       'St John was killed in this way'   (a1325) *Cursor Mundi* (*Vesp.*) line.13192)

There are no modern examples of *thus wise* (or *thuswise*) in the BNC and only two in COCA, both from fiction, possibly to give an archaic tone to the text. Something similar is found in COHA, only one non-fiction example, from the 1918 *Chicago Tribune* newspaper.

(24)   One sarcastic commentator remarked <u>thuswise</u>: "It's pretty tough for poor old Goethe".

There are, however, other ways in which *thus* may be replaced. Koenig (2015:106), who points out that "reinforcements of the basic demonstratives by additional morphological material is particularly visible in Romance languages" goes on to remark that in English "the exophoric uses of the relevant demonstratives are generally expressed by combination of manner-denoting prepositions or nouns (*like, way*) and basic demonstratives like *this* and *that*". In other words, a more modern version of (24): *Do not work thuswise* could be: *Do not work like this/that,* or *Do not work in this/that way.*

As already mentioned, it is also notable that *thus* in present-day English can in many instances be easily replaced by *therefore* or *consequently,* as in (25):

(25)   Because there are millions of Hispanic voters in Texas, the Governor doesn't want to alienate them. <u>Thus</u> he opposed a border fence which is absolutely necessary.   (COCA: spoken)

Replacement, as discussed above, is one indication that *thus* is participating in the CP cycle. Three other indications that *thus* is possibly is being lost, are that it is considered archaic, is declining in frequency according to corpus evidence, and is fossilizing in the phrase *thus far*.

Although *thus* is still used in present-day English, it is certainly considered archaic, a possible indication that it is being lost. The OED says *thus* is "Now chiefly literary or formal" in all its meanings. Corpus searches reveal that *thus* appears to be declining in present-day English, as the frequency is falling, and it is found only in the more formal genres. In modern spoken British English, the BNC has 84 examples of *thus*, only 11 of which are from conversation; the others are from more formal registers: speeches, broadcast discussions, courtrooms etc. In COCA, the spoken genre has the lowest frequency of *thus*, with a frequency of 14 words per million words of text, compared with the academic genre with 489 words per million words of text. The use of *thus* is overwhelmingly most frequent in academic speech, which tends to be more formal. In COHA, which of course is entirely written, and from which it is possible to extract data from individual years, the frequency per million words has been dropping rapidly in the last century and a half:

Table 1. Decline of *thus* in COHA

Year	1840	1900	1950	2000
Words per million words of text	620	327	188	77

Table 1 shows that from a peak of 620 words per million words in 1840, *thus* has been declining rapidly.

A final indication that *thus* is declining is that, in present day English, it appears to be fossilizing in the fixed phrase *thus far*, meaning the end point of a scale. In the spoken part of COCA, which is broadcast data, taken from public radio current affairs and discussion programmmes, 47% of the examples are of *thus far*.

(26)   The debates thus far have not answered those questions   (COCA: spoken)

(27)   And we've had improvements in three of the four months thus far.
(COCA: spoken)

The fixed phrase *thus far* is found proportionally more frequently in the spoken part of COCA, while there are only two examples in the BNC, although this is perhaps more of a reflection of the differences between the two corpora. The BNC data is more colloquial conversation, whereas the spoken part of COCA is mainly taken from radio discussion programmmes. A more colloquial way of expressing *thus far* would be *so far*.

Although further investigation is needed to confirm this, the preliminary conclusion is that in early Middle English *thus* started to be used less as a VP manner adverb and more as a discourse organizer on the clausal left periphery. This could be seen as tendency towards 'Late Merge' of *thus* (and possible subsequent loss) as part of the CP cycle. Evidence of loss of *thus* comes from: replacement with e.g. *like this, thusly* and *therefore*; designation as archaic in dictionaries and use in more formal genres; frequency decline in the corpora; fossilization in *thus far*.

Before leaving this section, it should be mentioned that a third function of *thus*, as a degree modifier, is found very early on as in (28) and (29):

(28)   *Ne   seah ic elþeodige þus   manige men   modiglicran.*
NEG saw I foreign   thus many   men brave-looking
'I've never seen this many brave-looking men abroad.' (OE: *Beowulf.* 336–7)

(29)   *Sege me, beceapode ge   ðus   micel landes?*
Say   me, sold   you thus much land.GEN
'Tell me, did you sell this much land?'   (1000 *Ælfric Homilies*)

Examples (28) and (29) show Old English examples of *thus* that are distinctly odd in present-day English, where *this* (or *so*) would be more natural instead of *thus*. Degree *thus* will be further discussed in Section 5.

4. Degree *that* and *this*

As was mentioned in the introduction, the demonstrative *that* has been shown to be involved in two cycles: one nominal, the DP cycle (Lyons 1999; van Gelderen 2007; van Gelderen 2011: 197–244) and one clausal, the CP cycle (van Gelderen 2011: 259–264).

(30) Demonstrative >article   (loses interpretable locative features)
(e.g. *se* > *þe* > *the*, (reanalysis of the masculine distal in late Old English)

(31) Demonstrative > complementiser   (loses interpretable *phi* features)
(e.g. *þæs* and *þæt* >*that*, (reanalysis before the written record)

A third, possibly related reanalysis involving the demonstrative is the development of the present-day English degree adverbs, specifically the change that resulted in present-day English degree modifiers *this* and *that*. In Section 4.1 below, I outline the theoretical and historical background, and in 4.2 I discuss the type of data that are relevant for investigating the change. As with *thus,* the type of data relevant for triggering a change is ambiguous. Unlike *thus,* there are no indications of a cyclic change with degree *this* and *that.*

4.1 Background to *this* and *that*

The focus in Sections 4 and 5 is on the degree modifiers *that* and *this*, as in the examples from British and American English shown in (32)–(35).

(32) I don't want to be <u>this thin</u>, I want to put it on again.   (BNC: spoken)

(33) I never thought I'd be <u>this old</u> when the fantasy came true. (COCA: spoken)

(34) They've taken somebody else on so things can't be <u>that bad</u>.   (BNC: spoken)

(35) You were never really <u>that good</u> at sports.   (COCA: spoken)

Also relevant is a newer expression in which *this/that* + adjective modifies a count noun and precedes the definite article as in (36)–(37).

(36) It wasn't <u>that great a speech</u>, but for Dole it was wonderful.

(COCA: spoken)

(37) Well, I'm not sure he would have gone there with <u>this large a deployment</u>.

(COCA: spoken)

Although the historical dictionaries give (scattered) examples of adverbial *that* as early as the 15th century, my preliminary searches (discussed below) found very few pre-19th century examples; a tentative conclusion is that *that* as a nominal degree modifier did not occur with any significant frequency before the 19th century. Examples such as

(36) and (37) are not reported in the OED (possibly because the entry has not been fully updated since 1912), and my searches found pre-indefinite article *that* and *this* first attested in COHA in the 19th century.

Expressions of the type [degree modifier + adjective + *a*] first occur in the 13th century (Fischer 1992: 211) although a quotation search in the OED shows that each modifier is first attested at a different time: *how* from the 14th century, *so* from the 16th century, *too* from the early 17th century (Wood 2003: 315–16). There are no OED examples of pre-indefinite article *this* and *that*. The earliest examples found in COHA are (38) and (39).

(37)   "Is it <u>that bad a place</u> for the schoolmasters, then? I often hard the schoolmaster was abroad;' an' maybe it's too manny o' them's abroad. "

(1858, COHA: fiction)

(38)   "These horses mighty lucky to have <u>this good a place</u> to stay. Yankees come yesterday and made off with three of Colonel Miles' four-year-olds."

(1937, COHA: fiction)

These two fictional examples are notable in that they are of dialogue spoken by non-standard speakers. Language change usually starts in speech and in the early stages is often judged to be colloquial, and so examples of this type are an indication that the change may be in its early stages.

With these 19th century changes, it is evident that *this* and *that* have joined the special set of English functional degree adverbs which includes *so, how, as,* and *too,* and which may precede the indefinite article along with the adjective. When these adverbs precede the article, they must be accompanied by the adjective. Note the ungrammaticality of **that a great speech* and **this a large deployment*. Additionally, as was already discussed in Section 2, *that* and *this* pattern in the same way as *too* in requiring '*much*-insertion' as was seen in (6) and (8) above. The significance of (32)–(35) is that they show *this* and *that* selecting an adjective phrase as part of the functional structure of the adjective phrase. The fact that the degree adverb plus adjective moves as a constituent in (36)–(37) is evidence that *that* and *this* are functional degree heads in the extended projection of the adjective phrase. The structure of the adjective phrase was discussed in Section 2 (see (7) above) and is shown in tree structure below with *this/that* as head of DegP.

When the degree adverb moves, it must do so as a constituent with the adjective. Its landing site is the specifier of NumP within the DP (see Wood & Vikner 2011, 2013).

The main questions, then, are when and how this change took place and when and how the modern examples in (32)–(37), in which *this* and *that* select an adjective phrase, develop. There are three possible development paths of the degree modifiers, which were set out in (1) above and are repeated here in (41).

(40)

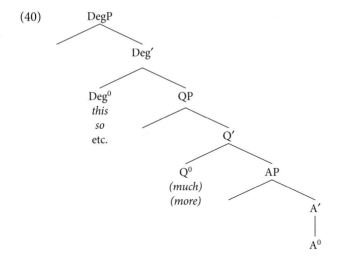

(41) a.   Demonstrative> clausal adverb> degree modifying adverb
      b.   Demonstrative> degree modifying adverb
      c.   Demonstrative> complementiser > degree modifying adverb

First, consider how the change relates to the tree structures discussed in the introduction. In (42) the essential parts of the DP structure are shown. The demonstrative determiners, which are merged low in the structure, need to check number in NumP, whereas the definite article does not, and is merged as the head of DP. Regarding the degree adverbs, demonstrative *that* has to 'escape' from the main stem of the DP to the functional part of the adjective phrase shown in (40). This could be directly, completely within the DP, or via an intermediate clausal stage in which it first became a VP adverb at the clausal level and subsequently moved into the AdjP. Once the change has taken place, the degree adverbs *that* and *this* presumably are directly merged as functional heads in the adjective phrase.

(42)

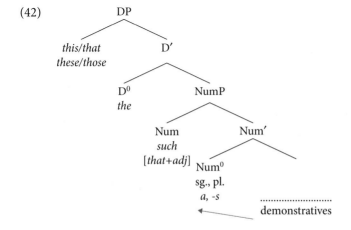

Demonstratives are well known to be a common (but not the only) source for degree adverbs, there being a small step from pointing i.e. drawing attention to the 'kind' or 'quality' of an entity, which demonstratives do, to pointing up (Bolinger 1972:61; Klein 1998:60). A crucial stage in the reanalysis is for *that* to be able to select an adjective phrase.

In 4.2 below, I report on searches for the data that would provide evidence for the paths (41)a, (41)b, or (41)c. As was mentioned, (41)c, a change from complementiser to a degree adverb is the least likely, and so this possible path will be addressed only briefly. The suggestion that the path (41)b could be a significant part of the change comes from the historical dictionaries. According to the Oxford English Dictionary, both *this* and *that* at one time were clausal adjuncts (adverbs) with the meaning "To that extent or degree; so much" (OED s.v. *that* adv.) and "To this extent or degree; as much as this; thus", (OED s.v. *this* adv.), although the clausal function is said to be now obsolete. The possible use of *that* and *this* as clausal adverbs is relevant to the cycle because it points to the likelihood of (41)a being the path, one in which *this* and *that* became first clausal adverbs, adjoined to the VP in the clause and then nominal degree modifiers, part of the functional structure of the adjective phrase. A grammaticalization path via the clause is taken by e.g. *fairly*, see (9) and (10) above, originally a clausal adverb, and subsequently a modifier in the DP (Nevalainen & Rissanen 2002). In Section 4.2 below, I sketch out the route that I followed in a preliminary investigation of *that*. I first identify constructions that are possible sources of the reanalysis of *that* via the path in (41)a but conclude that these constructions were not frequent in English at the relevant time, and therefore not likely to have influenced the change. I then go on to suggest possible nominal sources, evidence for the path in (41)b. In order for reanalysis to occur, ambiguous examples, having two interpretations, are a prerequisite and have to occur somewhat frequently. A crucial stage in the reanalysis is for *that* to be able to select an adjective phrase. Although the historical dictionaries give early examples of degree *that*, my search did not find constructions where degree *that* selects an adjective occurring with any frequency until the 19th century.

4.2   Reanalysis of *that*: Possible paths

As was explained in Section 2, some degree adverbs can be both sentential and nominal (selecting several different categories), whereas others such as *very* select only adjectives or other adverbs. Although the degree adverb *that* and the related *this* select only adjectives in present-day English, this need not have always been the case. First, I explore whether *that* has, in the past, functioned as a verb phrase adverb, in other words, if the path in (41)a is the likely one. The OED claims that *that* once functioned as a verb modifier, but that the function was rare and is now obsolete. I consider these data from historical dictionaries and argue that *that* is likely to always have been a nominal modifier. I also consider examples of *that* preceding a past participle, relevant for the adjective selection stage, as past participles can be used adjectivally. The conclusion is that such examples are not frequent in the data considered here. Finally, I discuss both examples in which *that* selects an NP and examples in which *that* selects an AdjP, all with a possible degree reading.

Both the Middle English Dictionary (MED) and the Oxford English Dictionary (OED) quote examples of *that* used as a clausal degree adverb in Middle English, but the examples in the MED are earlier, from 1225, whereas those in the OED start in 1450. The two (pre-1450) MED examples, (43) and (44) do not clearly show *that* functioning as a clausal degree adverb.

(43) *Þe deofel þet to soþe..rixat   in-nan him*
 the devil that to truth reigns within him

  þet he nulle   nefre forleten   his sunne.
  that he NEG.want never abandon his sin
  'the devil has such a strong hold on him that he will never abandon his sin.'
  (1225 (?OE) *Lambeth Homilies*)

(44) *Ic ham ȝeue reste...from non   on saterdei a þa   cume*
  I him give rest...from noon on Saturday of then comes

  monedeis lihting, þet efre forð to domes   dei.
  Monday's dawn   that ever forth to judgment day.

  'I give him peace from noon on Saturday until dawn on Monday
  that continuously until judgement day.'   (1225 (?OE) *Lambeth Homilies*)

First, in (43) the meaning of *that* adv. is given as "To such an extent, so; in such a way, thus" (MED s.v. *that* adv.), in which case *that* would modify the verb *rixat* with the meaning 'the devil reigns within him to such an extent'. I suggest that a more likely analysis is for *that* to be a complementiser introducing a result clause. Also, in (44), *that* need not be an adverb; it could be a cataphoric pronoun or a relative marker, with the meaning 'the aforementioned peace (will be continued) until judgement day'. These two early examples are not likely to be significant in the change.

As mentioned, if the path in (41)a (via a clausal adverb to a nominal modifier), is the correct one, then constructions with a past participle are significant, as they can be ambiguous between being verbal and adjectival. In (45), also from the MED, 'hated' could be understood either as a past tense or a past participle used adjectivally, modifying Sir Gareth.

(45) *Where he hated, he wolde be avenged with murther,*
  Where he hated he would be avenged with murder

  and that hated sir Gareth.
  and that hated sir Gareth

  '*Where he hated he* [Sir Gawain] *wanted to be avenged with murder and Sir Gareth hated that.*'   (a1470 *Malory Wks*)

Consultation of the original text shows that *that* certainly is not degree *that* but a preposed pronoun. The meaning is that Sir Gareth hated the aforementioned trait of vengefulness in his brother. In other words, *that* does not modify *hated* but is a pronoun, the object of hated, referring to the vengeful character of Sir Gawain. The ambiguity come from the pronoun reference, as the 'he' who would be avenged is not Sir Gareth, but someone else, Sir Gawain. Although ambiguous, and could possibly be a site for reanalysis, it is not likely that this type of construction would occur frequently, particularly as the preposed pronoun is a result of object verb word order, which was lost in English by the Early Modern period (Pintzuk & Taylor, 2006).

Two other early MED examples from the mid-15th century, (46) and (47) are the earliest clear attested instances of nominal modification. Clearly, here degree *that* modifies a past participle understood adjectivally.

(46)   *Seke she is, and <u>that</u> ouer-doon. But if that she amend soon*
      sick she is and so   over-done But if that she amend soon

      Of hir liue sore I   me drede.
      Of her life I   sor me dread.

      'She is sick and so done-in, unless she recovers soon I very much fear for her life.'
      (1450 *Gener.*)

(47)   *His sekenes <u>þat</u> encrest,   he gert   beere him*
      His sicknes that increased he readied bear him

      ferr and nere Aboute þe   contre   on a bere.
      far and near. About the country on a bier
      'His sickness got so bad that he had himself carried back and forth around the country on a litter.'
      (1450 *St.Cuthbert*)

In both examples, the degree reading comes from the correlative clause which reports the (possible) result arising from the degree of exhaustion in (46) and from the increase in sickness in (47). However, searches in the Helsinki Corpus (between 1420 and 1640) failed to uncover any more participle examples with *that*, from which my preliminary conclusion is that ambiguous participles were not frequent. The conclusion regarding the path in (41)a is that I found no convincing evidence that *that* was once a VP modifier. Although examples in which *that* occurs adjacent to a past participle are likely sites for reanalysis, this preliminary investigation has not found such examples to be frequent.

Although the OED shows three pre 19th century examples of degree adverb *that*, in fact, overall, the degree modifier expression does not appear to have been very frequent before the 19th century. The first OED example of *that* as an adverb is (47) above, and then there is a chronological gap until the second, (48), which is from 1616, about 150 years later and the third, (49), which is even later into the 17th century.

(48) If I had been <u>that unhappy</u> as to have such a foolish thing, I would have
      given him no copy of it if I had suspected his ill intention
                                    (1616 in J. Russell *Haigs of Bemersyde*)

(49) This was carried with <u>that little noise</u> that..the..Bishop was not awaked
                                                                        (OED: 1670)

Considering first (49), a DP (*that little noise*) occurs as a complement of the preposition, *with*, and *that* selects a NP in which there is a head noun *noise*, and a gradable
adjective, *little*. Although *that* is the demonstrative determiner in a determiner plus
noun combination, the following comparative clause, and the fact that the adjective is
gradable, open up the possibility of a degree reading for *that*. The implicature is that
there must have been a very small amount of noise in order to achieve the result: *little
noise*. The phrase could equally well be rendered as *such little noise*. There do appear to
be other examples similar to (49).

(50) in all our agonies and troubles, deuoutly to resort prostrate vnto the
      remembraunce of <u>that bitter agony</u>, which our Sauiour suffred before his
      passion at the Mount.   (HC: EModE 1. 1500–1570)

Significantly, what (48) and (49) have in common with each other and with (46) and
(47) is the resultant clause that leads to a degree reading. The extra clause creates the
implicature that high degree is involved. However, apart from (48) none of the early
examples from the historical dictionaries show *that* selecting a bare adjective.

Returning, then, to (48), in this example, which looks very modern, there is a
predicate adjective followed by a comparative clause with *as*. Since this is a promising
example, I searched the entire text of (48) *The Haigs of Bemersyde* for more context
(already shown above in (48)), which confirms the degree reading. The 'foolish thing'
refers to a few lines of incriminating writing. I also searched the entire text for other
examples of adverbial *that*, but the search did not reveal anything remarkable. It is
perplexing that examples of degree *that* seem to be sparse before the 19th century,
with the OED giving only the three examples above and none from the 18th century.
Examples in which *that* directly selects an adjective, as in (48), are even sparser. This
lack of data may or may not be significant. It could be that there is little 18th century
data, or it could simply be that dictionaries are not meant to be exhaustive.

Since two of the 19th century OED examples are from Charles Dickens' novels,
I searched the novel *David Copperfield*, and looked for examples in COHA. Remarkable is that many of the early examples I found appear to be fictional depictions of
non-standard speakers. In (51), the speaker is the character Ham Peggoty, generally
thought of as a lower class character. All three of the fictional examples are of reported
speech and nonstandard spelling and grammar is used to show non-standard speakers.

(51)   "Odd times, I think that if I hadn't had her promise fur to marry me, sir, she
was <u>that trustful</u> of me, in a friendly way, that she'd have told me what was
struggling in her mind, and would have counselled with me, and I might
have saved her".   (1850 *David Copperfield*, Charles Dickens)

Although the data in COHA range from1810–2000, there do not appear to be COHA
examples earlier than (52) and (53), from the mid 19th century.

(52)   "Why, now, yer' d better b'leve her sperits isn't the best! Why, she' s <u>that bad</u>,
Miss Fannie, she actually been a cryin' when I put the baby in her arms".
(COHA 1856 *Dred: A Tale of the Great Dismal Swamp*;
Harriet Beecher Stowe)

(53)   "But – sich things as these" – the mountaineer wiped off a tear with his
coat-sleeve – "burns me an' weakens me an' hurts my eyes <u>that bad</u> that I
kin scarcely look a man straight forrard in the face".
(COHA: 1867 *Tiger-Lilies: A Novel*)

Usually language change starts in spoken language and its early stages is often considered "mistakes" or colloquial. Recall that examples of the type [*that* + adjective + *a*].
such as that shown in (38). are first found around the same time as this in American
English (1858). It is also notable that examples like (51)–(53) do not start to occur
with any frequency until the 20th century and then most frequently with adjectives
such as *bad, good, easy, simple*. This co-occurrence may be coincidental, or it may be
evidence that the degree modifier construction, in which *that* selects an adjective, did
not start to occur with any significant frequency until the 19th century. It may be that
the 15th–18th century examples are sporadic and too infrequent to be significant in
the change.

Before leaving the nominal, there is one other significant construction to consider, ambiguous pronouns. Recall, (47) above, partially repeated here as (54) in which
I analysed *that* as degree adverb.

(54)   *His sekenes þat encrust   …*
His sickness that increased …
His sickness increased to the extent that …

In an alternative reading of (54), *that* could be pronoun, referring to the sentence
topic, 'his sickness'. A similar example with an ambiguous pronoun is shown in (55).
Here, *that* could either be a degree adverb or the object of *do*.

(55)   The rules I have already given will I suppose doe <u>that</u> better than all the
Apothecarys shops and medicines in the County.
(HC: EModE 3. 1640–1710)

I will leave for future work the question of the frequency and significance of these examples.

Finally, I have not mentioned (41)c, a change from complementiser to degree adverb. There are two reasons: first such a change seems the least likely internal syntactic change and secondly, the simplest initial assumption is that *this* and *that* follow similar paths, and a path via the complementiser would not include *this*. This is a line of enquiry to follow once the other two have been ruled out.

In this section, I considered the possible paths followed by demonstrative *that* in changing to a degree adverb. I have shown the type of data required if the path is clausal but found no convincing evidence for degree *that* to have been clausal. I then went on to discuss the types of nominal expression that may be significant. I also found, in a preliminary investigation that degree *that* may have developed later than the OED examples indicate. In Section 5, I show that whereas there is likely no interaction with the clause in the case of *that*, the situation is not nearly so clear with *this* due to the presence of the manner adverb *thus*, part of the same paradigm as *this* in Old English.

5.   Degree adverb *this* (and *thus*)

As was mentioned at the end of Section 3, from the very earliest records *thus* is found as a degree modifier, as was shown in (28) and (29), repeated here as (56) and (57).

(56) *Ne   seah ic elþeodige þus   manige men modiglicran.*
     NEG saw I foreign   thus many   men brave-looking
     I've never seen this many brave-looking men abroad.

                                                   (OE: *Beowulf.* 336–7)

(57) *Sege me, beceapode ge   ðus   micel landes?*
     Say   me, sold   you thus much land.GEN
     'Tell me, did you sell this much land?'   (1000 *Ælfric Homilies*)

These examples are ambiguous in that *thus* could be translated as present-day English degree adverb *this* (as I did above) or as *thus* as a clausal adverb modifying *saw* and *sell*. Even later into Early Modern English, a similar ambiguity arises as in (58).

(58)   Therefore let me be <u>thus bold</u> with you.

                                      (1616 Shakespeare *Taming of Shrew*)

It seems that there are two present-day survivors from the Old English paradigm for the proximal demonstrative, *this* (*þis*.NOM.NEUTER) and *thus* (*þ̄ys*.INSTR). The puzzle is that their functions appear to overlap into Middle and Early Modern English, and there is a brief period (1420–1593) where *this* is reported in contexts where *thus* would be expected. The OED (s.v. *this* adv.) has five examples dating between 1400 and 1593 which show *this* as a sentence adverb, but with the comment "in some instances, perhaps an alteration of *thus* adverb". Therefore difficulty arises when deciding whether *this* or *thus* is meant and consequently whether *this* ever was clausal. Do the examples actually show *this* as a clausal degree adverb or is *this* really just *thus*?

According to the OED, *thus* has a number of spelling variants: *ðus, þus, þuss, þusse, þos, þous, thws, thuss, thus. tuss, tus, tas; dus, sus, yus*. Although there are many variant spellings, and some variation in the vowel, all the variants are back vowels and there no spellings with a front vowel ⟨i⟩. So ⟨thus⟩ is, apparently, always *thus*, whereas ⟨this⟩ could be either *this* or "an alternation" of *thus*.

Consider first the straightforward examples; the earliest examples of *this* as an adjectival degree modifier, quoted in the MED and the OED are from the mid 15th century.

(59) *Do yowr dylygens To clense þe Soull wyche ys þis fowl*
Do   your   diligence to   cleanse the   soul   which is   this foul
Take care to cleanse the soul which is this foul   (1475 *Wisd.*)

(60) *I wepe for sorow, Lorde! I begyn awake,*
I   weep   for   sorow,   Lord!   I begin   awake

I that þis longe hath slumberyde in syne.
I that this long   have slumbered   in sin.
'I weep with sadness Lord! I begin to awaken, I that this long have
slumbered in sin.'   (1475 *Wisd.*)

(61) *Nowe yt seemes well that hee would attayne royaltee;*
Now   it   seems   well   that   he   would   attain   royalty

elles <u>*this bould*</u> *durst hee not bee*
else   this bold   dare   he   not be
'Now it appears likely that he will attain status otherwise he would not dare
to be this bold.'   (1591(?a1425) *Chester Pl*)

The OED suggests that Middle English *this* is frequently found with adjectives of quantity, and that in these expressions *this* is possibly "felt" as a pronoun in the expression 'as much as this', which then went on to modify other adjectives and adverbs, "grading into an intensive". For example, in (62) *this much* is an argument of *received* with an elided noun (e.g. *money* or *recognition* or *favour*).

(59) This myche have I received from her majestye.   (OED: 1586)

One difficulty with the OED suggestion is that in order to be significant in the 15th century reanalysis of *this* to a degree adverb, *this much* expressions would have to be frequent earlier than the 16th century, which is when the earliest OED examples of *this much* are found. My search of the Middle English sections of the Helsinki Corpus (1150–1500) for *much* (spelling: *moch; moche: much; muche, mych; myche*) found 2 examples of *thus much* with elided nouns and three of *this much* with an overt noun. A search of the Early Modern sections of the Helsinki Corpus (1500–1710) for all spellings of *much* found 17 examples of *thus much* and none of *this much*. Often *thus much* expressions are ambiguous[2] and *thus* could either be a degree adverb with the meaning 'I will tell you as much as this' or *thus* could be a CP adverb and the meaning 'Hereby, I will tell you a great deal of information'. Such ambiguity is seen in (63) and (64).

(63) *Thus muche of hir beautee telle   I   may*
      'This much I   may tell   about her beauty.'
                                          (1395 Chaucer *CT.Mch.*)

(64) *Thus muche   I wol yow seye*
      'This much will I say to   you.'   (1395 Chaucer *CT.Cl.*)

In fact, expressions with *thus much* + noun are found very early on as was seen in (29) repeated here as (65).

(65) *Sege me, beceapode ge   ðus   micel landes?*
      Say   me, sold   you thus much land.GEN
      'Tell me, did you sell this much land?'   (1000 *Ælfric Homilies*)

In conclusion, the OED data showing degree *this* occurring first in late Middle English appear clear. Although I followed the lead suggested by the OED, that *this much* expressions are significant in the reanalysis, I did not find them occurring with any frequency.

Next, the OED examples from between 1400 and 1593 which show *this* as a sentential adverb with a manner reading will be examined. The confusion is over whether speakers are really using *this* as a clausal manner adverb or are using *thus* as a variant of *this*. The suggestion that *this* as a clausal manner adverb has its source in the instrumental case of Old English *this* fits for *thus* but not for *this*. Instrumental case

---

2.   As Sten Vikner points out, in one of the readings, (*thus, much* …) there is an intonation break, whereas there is no break in the degree adverb reading (*thus, much*). One way to tease these apart might be by looking at the metre.

was found only in early texts in Old English, and if instrumental case is the source of manner adverb *this*, examples of manner *this* would be expected before the 15th century, a time when case marking had all but disappeared in English. Therefore, below, I look more closely at the examples of *this* as a manner adverb to investigate the possibility that they could be either "typos" (writers sometimes write *this* in mistake for *thus*) or have an alternative analysis (as was shown above for *that* which could, in some cases, be analysed as a complementiser and in others as a pronoun).

The earliest OED example of *this* as a manner adverb is (66), where the author appears to use *þis* first as a determiner (*this lamb*) and then as a manner adverb (*had this* [thus] *run*).

(66)   *When* þis *lomb had* þis *y ron* þrye þe *tomb* abouȝt
        When this lamb had this run thrice the tomb about
        'When this lamb had this [thus] run three times around the tomb.'
                                                            (1420 *Chron. Vilod.*)

However, examination of a subsequent part of the same text shows that later the author distinguishes between determiner *this*, determiner *that* and manner *thus* and therefore is not consistent in using *this* as an adverb. As can be seen from (67), þat and þis are clearly both determiners (*that same place* and *this Easter lamb*) and *thus* is a discourse level adverb (CP adverb).

(67)   *Hit went aȝeyn in to* þat *same place*
        It   went again in to that same place

        From þe *whyche hit come first ouȝt*
        From the which it   came first out

        & þus þis *astere-lomb apered* þere
        and thus this easter lamb appeared there

        'It went again into that same place from which it first came out and thus this Easter lamb appeared there.'

The conclusion for the example of þis in (67) is that þis could be read as a 'typo' for þus, although the entire text would need to be examined to confirm this.

Considering the remaining four examples, a possible alternate analysis for (68) is an appositive construction, two DPs.

(68)   And this the King of Scottland depairtit out of France (OED 1578).

However, three other examples of *this* are not so easily explained, as in these it does seem that the writers are using *this* as a manner adverb. In particular (69), from Shakespeare, is difficult to explain in any other way.

(69)   *What am I that thou shouldst contemne me* this?
        'What am I that you   should   scorn   me so?'
                                                            (1593 *Venus & Adonis*)

In isolation, *this* in (69) could be a simple typo, i.e. *this* written when *thus* is intended, but the early versions of the manuscript show no typos or print anomalies (Joseph Sterret p.c.) and the poem continues as in (70), where the word has to be *this* if it is to rhyme with *kiss*.

(70)   Or what great danger, dwells upon my sute
       VVhat were thy lips the worse for one poore kis?

The meaning appears to be 'in this way', i.e. a manner adverb. Since some editors gloss *contemne* as 'deny' an attractive analysis is for *this* to be a pronoun, giving the line the meaning 'deny (to) me this (kiss)'; the problem here is that *contemne* is a transitive verb meaning, 'scorn, disdain, slight' which selects a direct object, either a DP or an infinitive with *to*, and there is no support for *contemne* taking an indirect object (*me*). Equally problematic appear to be (71) and (72) where the reading again is a manner adverb.

(71)   *And þis   he ȝalde   þe spyrit.*
       And this he yielded the spirit
       'And thus he died.'   (OED 1400)

(69)   *I wyll not haue it, so I wyll haue it this.*
       I will not have it so I will have it this.
       'I will not have it, unless I can have it like this.'   (OED 1529)

In conclusion, three of the examples above, (69), (71) and (72) open up the possibility that that there is period in late Middle English/Early Modern English where *this* is used as a manner adverb.

There is clearly a close relationship between *this* and *thus,* as they are part of the same paradigm. However, the differences between *this* and *thus* in the historical data are difficult to tease apart. Although I argued above that *that* is likely to have always been a nominal adverb (and not clausal), the situation is not clear when it comes to *this*. In conclusion, early 15th century examples of degree *this* selecting an adjective are quite clear, unlike *that,* for which I found very few early examples of adjective selection. However, it proved difficult to tease apart examples of *this* and *thus*. Further investigation is beyond the scope of this chapter.

6.   Conclusion

In this chapter I have discussed diachronic changes involving demonstratives, a universal category the members of which are intrinsically deictic. Although *that* and *this* have changed fairly recently, so that in present-day English they express degree, they differ from the degree expressions most commonly addressed in the literature on language change. The type of grammaticalization most often examined is from lexical categories to functional (grammatical) categories and in this case functional elements become more functional.

First, it was argued that *thus* participates in a cyclic change known as the CP cycle. The evidence presented relates to changes in its position, meaning, and loss and replacement in present-day English. Although in earlier English *thus* is a manner adverb in the VP, its position in present-day English tends to be on the clausal left periphery and its function tends to be discourse orientated. The older meanings, however, are not completely lost, as is common in grammaticalisation. In present-day English *thus* may be replaced in its manner (VP) use by *this way*, *like this*, *like so* or even *thusly*, and in its discourse (CP) use by e.g. *therefore*. Evidence that *thus* is archaic and possibly being lost comes from: the fall in frequency as evidenced by corpora, its presence in academic speech rather than in conversation, and the fossilized expression *thus far*. In terms of the cycle, this change follows one of the two economy principles, "late merge". Nothing was said about the "head preference principle" with respect to *thus* and I assume it does not apply to *thus*.

The second and third parts of the chapter went on to discuss the development of degree adverbs from the demonstratives *this* and *that*, both of which are determiners and pronouns. From what has been reported here, it is clear that although some aspects of grammaticalization are apparent (specifier to head, and association with the left periphery of the adjective phrase) there are no indications that specific changes affecting the functional structure of the adjective phrase can be said to be cyclic, as no loss is apparent.

The question of degree *this* and *that* was approached from a methodological perspective, based on information from the historical dictionaries and building on corpus evidence. The degree adverbs *this* and *that* originate low in the DP as demonstratives but in degree expressions move into a new XP to become heads in the functional structure of the adjective phrase. Three possible grammaticalization paths were suggested and two were investigated: whether the nominal degree adverb developed via an intermediate clausal adverb, or whether the changes took place completely within the DP. Little evidence was found for the clausal route for *that*, but with *this* it was difficult to decide whether speakers and writers were using *this* or *thus*.

In terms of structural position, two structures were introduced. In the structure (42) demonstratives are assumed to be merged low in the DP and move to the specifier of DP as determiners, whereas the indefinite article is directly merged as the head, D°. In the structure (40), the position within the adjective phrase is relevant with respect to *this* and *that*, which are argued to be functional elements in the degree phrase. The structural change involves demonstratives changing from a specifier position in one XP to a head position in another XP, i.e. two changes.

In terms of features, the adverb uses of *that* and *this*, as in (32)–(35), have retained deictic (locative) features, as has the demonstrative determiner. On the other hand, the complementiser has grammaticalised from the demonstrative through loss of deictic features. As for number agreement, the degree adverbs only occur in the singular. Regarding the interaction of 'kind', 'manner' and 'degree', Bolinger (1972:61) points out the usual diachronic path is from 'identification' to 'degree', so we might expect the degree reading of *this* and *that* to develop later, which is what is observed.

In terms of future work there are a number of interesting avenues to explore. First, the initial investigation of *that*, in Section 4, found colloquial examples from the 19th century where *that* selects an adjective, and it was claimed that these examples indicate that degree expressions were fairly novel at that time. However, the historical dictionaries put a much earlier date than the 19th century on degree *that*. Although I was not able to find much relevant data, particularly for *that* selecting an adjective, it may be because I was not looking in the right places. The Helsinki Corpus is a mixture of various representative genres, and it may be that there simply was not enough text of the relevant genre in the relevant time period. A closer look these same data, possibly in targeted texts, such as plays and court transcripts, is needed to establish more accurate dates for the changes, as well as to examine the types of construction in use at the time the reanalysis took place. Likewise, the initial investigation of *this* in Section 5 uncovered the need for more data. Here some information on historical phonology and some early data might help to show how *thus* and *this* are differentiated in early Old English.

Another possibly interesting avenue is a cross-linguistic approach. Klein (1998: 40–45) remarks that it would be unexpected for Dutch *dat* to become an adverb of degree as it cannot be used to point to degree, and therefore a grammatical shift would be required first.

(73) Du. a. *Deze stock is ook <u>dat lang</u>.
      En.. b. This stick also is <u>that long.</u>

(74) I shan't need more than ten minutes, if you can hold the fort <u>that long.</u>
                                                                (OED1962)

This grammatical shift must have taken place in English but not in Dutch, as such constructions are perfectly fine in English. Also, as far as I am aware, no cognates of *thus* have survived into the modern Germanic languages and the early history of other Germanic languages may help to uncover why.

A third interesting avenue is the interaction of *this* and *that* with negation. The expression *all that* + adjective is a negative polarity item, and *He is all that old* sounds distinctly odd; compare with *He is not all that old*. Kayne (2010) points out that the contrast in (75) shows that *this* and *that* are not completely parallel.

(75) He is not all that /*this smart.

A final observation, then, is the question: to what extent are *this* and *that* similar and to what extent are they different? They display some similar syntax, both are determiners and pronouns and both have the syntax of fronted degree modifiers preceding the indefinite article (*this/that bad a day*). I started my investigation assuming that they both became degree modifiers by the same route at approximately the same time. That assumption was not supported by the data I reported; significant differences in timing (*this* was found to select an adjective much earlier than *that*) were found. Also, it proved difficult to disentangle *this* from *thus*. Nevertheless, I hope to have at least made some initial suggestions as to how an investigation into degree cycles could proceed in the future.

Sources

British National Corpus (BNC) ⟨http://corpus.byu.edu/bnc⟩
Corpus of Contemporary American English (COCA) ⟨http://corpus.byu.edu/coca/⟩
Corpus of Historical American English (COHA) ⟨http://corpus.byu.edu/coha⟩
Middle English Dictionary (MED) ⟨http://quod.lib.umich.edu/m/med/⟩
Oxford English Dictionary (OED) on-line ⟨www.oed.com⟩
Bosworth, Joseph. *An Anglo-Saxon Dictionary Online.* ⟨http://bosworth.ff.cuni.cz/031500⟩ (1 June 2015).
Konrath, Matthias. 1902. *The poems of William of Shoreham, re-edited from the unique manuscript in the British Museum* London: Early English Text Society, Kegan Paul, Trench, Trübner & Co. ⟨https://archive.org/details/poemswilliamsho00konrgoog⟩ (28 June 2015).
Russell, John. 1881. *The Haigs of Bemersyde. A Family History.* Edinburgh: William Blackwood and Sons. ⟨https://archive.org/stream/haigsofbemersyde00russuoft/haigsofbemersyde-00russuoft_djvu.txt⟩ (28 June 2015).

References

Abney, Steven P. 1987. The English Noun Phrase in its Sentential Aspect. Ph.D. dissertation, MIT.
Alexiadou, Artemis, Haegeman, Lilianne & Stavrou, Melita. 2007. *Noun Phrase in the Generative Perspective.* Berlin: Mouton de Gruyter. doi:10.1515/9783110207491
Anderson, Curt & Morzycki, Marcin. 2015. *Degrees as kinds. Natural Language and Linguistic Theory* 33 (3): 791–828.
Bolinger, Dwight. 1972. *Degree Words.* The Hague: Mouton. doi:10.1515/9783110877786
Bresnan, Joan. 1973. Syntax of the comparative clause construction. *Linguistic Inquiry* 4(3): 275–343.
Bernstein, Judy B. 1997. Demonstratives and reinforcers in Romance and Germanic languages. *Lingua* 102: 87–113. doi:10.1016/S0024-3841(96)00046-0
Brugè, Laura 2002. The positions of demonstratives in the extended nominal projection. In Cinque, G. (Ed.) *Functional Structure in DP and IP,* Guglielmo Cinque (ed.), 15–53. Oxford: OUPress.
Cinque, Guglielmo. 1999. *Adverbs and Functional Heads: A Crosslinguistic Perspective.* Oxford: OUP.

Corver, Norbert. 1997. *Much*-support as last resort. *Linguistic Inquiry* 28(1): 119–64.

Davies, Mark. (2004-). *BYU-BNC*. (Based on the British National Corpus from Oxford University Press). Available online at http://corpus.byu.edu/bnc/.

Davies, Mark. (2008-). *The Corpus of Contemporary American English: 450 million words, 1990-present*. Available online at http://corpus.byu.edu/coca/.

Davies, Mark. (2010-). *The Corpus of Historical American English: 400 million words, 1810-2009*. Available online at http://corpus.byu.edu/coha/.

Denison, David. 2006. Category change and gradience in the determiner system. In *The Handbook of the History of English,* Ans van Kemenade & Bettelou Los (eds). Oxford: Blackwell.

Diessel, Holger. 1999. *Demonstratives: Form, Function and Grammaticalization* [Typological Studies in Language 42]. Amsterdam: John Benjamins. doi:10.1075/tsl.42

Epstein, Melissa. 1999. On the singular indefinite article in English. In *Syntax at Sunset* [UCLA Working Papers in Linguistics], Gianluca Storto (ed.), 3: 14–58.

Fischer, Olga. 1992. Syntax. In *Cambridge History of the English Language*, Vol 2, Norman Blake (ed.), 168–289. Cambridge: CUP.

van Gelderen, Elly. 2004. *Grammaticalization as Economy* [Linguistik Aktuell/Linguistics Today 71]. Amsterdam: John Benjamins. doi:10.1075/la.71

van Gelderen, Elly. 2007. The definiteness cycle in Germanic. *Journal of Germanic Linguistics* 19(4): 275–305. doi:10.1017/S147054270700013X

van Gelderen, Elly. 2011. *The Linguistic Cycle: Language Change and the Language Faculty*. Oxford: OUP. doi:10.1093/acprof:oso/9780199756056.001.0001

van Gelderen, Elly. 2013. *Clause Structure*. Cambridge: CUP. doi:10.1017/CBO9781139084628

Ghesquière, Lobke & Van de Velde, Freek. 2011. A corpus-based account of the development of English *such* and Dutch *zulk*: Identification, intensification and (inter)subjectification. *Cognitive Linguistics* 22(4): 765–797. doi:10.1515/cogl.2011.028

Giusti, Giuliana. 1997. The categorial status of determiners. In *The New Comparative Syntax*, Liliane Haegeman (ed.), 95–124. London: Longman.

Giusti, Giuliana. 2002. The functional structure of noun phrases. A bare phrase structure approach. In *Functional structure in DP and IP: The Cartography of Syntactic Structures*, Vol. 1, Guglielmo Cinque (ed.), 54–90. Oxford: OUP.

Ito, Rika & Tagliamonte, Sali A. 2003. Well weird, right dodgy, very strange, really cool: Layering and recycling in English intensifiers. *Language in Society* 32: 257–279. doi:10.1017/S0047404503322055

Jackendoff, Ray S. 1977. *X'-Syntax. A Study of Phrase Structure*. Cambridge MA: The MIT Press.

Jespersen, Otto H. 1922. *Language: Its Nature, Development and Origin*. London: George Allen & Unwin.

Kayne, Richard. 2010. Why isn't this a complementizer? In *Comparisons and Contrasts,* Richard Kayne. Oxford: OUP.

Klein, Henny. 1998. *Adverbs of Degree in Dutch and Related Languages* [Linguistik Aktuell/ Linguistics Today 21]. Amsterdam: John Benjamins. doi:10.1075/la.21

Klinge, Alex. 2005. The Structure of English Nominals: A Study of Correlations between Form, Distribution and Function. Ph.D. dissertation, Copenhagen Business School.

Koenig, Ekkehard. 2015. Manner deixis as source of grammatical markers in Indo-European languages. In *Perspectives on Historical Syntax* [Studies in Language Companion Series 169], Carlotta Viti (ed.), Amsterdam: John Benjamins. doi:10.1075/slcs.169

Lyons, Christopher. 1999. *Definiteness*. Cambridge: CUP. doi:10.1017/CBO9780511605789

Macaulay, Ronald. 2006. Pure grammaticalization: The development of a teenage intensifier. *Language Variation and Change* 18: 267–283. doi:10.1017/S0954394506060133

Neeleman, Ad, van de Koot, Hans & Doetjes, Jenny. 2004. Degree expressions. *The Linguistic Review* 21(1): 1–66. doi:10.1515/tlir.2004.001

Nevalainen, Terttu & Rissanen, Matti. 2002. Fairly pretty or pretty fair? On the development and grammaticalization of English downtoners. *Language Sciences* 24: 359–380. doi:10.1016/S0388-0001(01)00038-9

Paradis, Carita. 1997. *Degree Modifiers of Adjectives in Spoken British English*. Lund: Lund University Press.

Partington, Alan. 1993. Corpus evidence of language change: The case of intensifiers. In *Text and Technology: In Honour of John Sinclair*, Mona Baker, Gill Francis & Elena Tognini-Bonelli (eds), 177–92. Amsterdam: John Benjamins. doi:10.1075/z.64.12par

Peters, Hans. 1994. Degree adverbs in Early Modern English. In *Studies in Early Modern English*, Dieter Kastovsky (ed.), 269–88. Berlin: Mouton de Gruyter.

Pintzuk, Susan & Taylor, Ann. 2006. The loss of OV order in the history of English. In *The Handbook of the History of English*. Ans van Kemenade, & Bettelou Los, (eds.). Oxford: Blackwell.

Quirk, Randolph, Greenbaum, Sidney, Leech, Geoffrey & Svartvik, Jan. 1985. *A Comprehensive Grammar of the English Language*. London: Longman.

Ritter, Elizabeth. 1988. A head movement approach to construct-state nominal. *Linguistics* 26: 909–929. doi:10.1515/ling.1988.26.6.909

Ritter, Elizabeth. 1991. Two functional categories in noun phrases: Evidence from modern Hebrew. In *Syntax and Semantics* 25, Susan Rothstein (ed.), 37–62. San Diego CA: Academic Press.

Roberts, Ian & Roussou, Anna. 2003. *Syntactic Change: A Minimalist Approach to Grammaticalization*. Cambridge: CUP. doi:10.1017/CBO9780511486326

Stoffel, Cornelis. 1901. *Intensives and Down-toners: A Study in English Adverbs*. Heidelberg: Carl Winter.

Tagliamonte, Sali. 2008. *So different* and *pretty cool*! Recycling intensifiers in Toronto, Canada. *English Language and Linguistics* 12(2): 361–394. doi:10.1017/S1360674308002669

Wood, Johanna L. 2002. Much about *such*. *Studia Linguistica* 56: 91–115. doi:10.1111/1467-9582.00088

Wood, Johanna L. 2003. Number phrase and fronted pre-modifiers in Middle English. In *Proceedings of the 2003. Western Conference on Linguistics*.

Wood, Johanna L. & Vikner, Sten. 2011. Noun phrase structure and movement: A cross-linguistic comparison of *such/sådan/solch* and *so/så/so*. In *The Noun Phrase in Romance and Germanic - Structure, Variation and Change* [Linguistik Aktuell/Linguistics Today 171], Petra Sleeman & Harry Perridon (eds), 89–109. Amsterdam: John Benjamins. doi:10.1075/la.171.07woo

Wood, Johanna L. & Vikner, Sten. 2013. What's to the left of the indefinite article? – Et sådan et spørgsmål er svært at svare på (What's to the left of the indefinite article? – A such a question is difficult to answer). In *Gode ord er bedre end guld - Festskrift til Henrik Jørgensen*, Simon Borchmann, Inger Schoonderbeek Hansen, Tina Thode Hougaard, Ole Togeby & Peter Widell (eds), 515–540. Aarhus: Section for Scandinavian Studies, Aarhus University.

Wood, Johanna L. Reinforcement and renewal: Germanic *'so a'*: The Linguistic Cycle Workshop II, Arizona State University, Tempe, AZ, 25–26 April 2014.

Wright, Joseph. 1902. *Old English Grammar*. London: OUP.

Modality and gradation

Comparing the sequel of developments in 'rather' and 'eher'

Remus Gergel

University of Graz / Saarland University

This paper focuses on some effects and possible causes in the concatenation of two micro-developments undergone by words like *rather*. While the first one maps its semantics from an original temporal-based comparison to modal meanings, the second takes it from modal ordering to the modification of gradable predicates. A comparison is drawn with the parallel sequel of developments observed in the case of German *eher* ('sooner, rather') especially with respect to the apparently distinct flavors of modal ordering available in the two items.

1. Introduction and background

The goal of this paper is to analyze key aspects in the meaning, structure, and history of the representation of words like *rather*. I take them to remain in need of both diachronic and synchronic explanation despite the interest and work that has been conducted from several perspectives (e.g. Thompson 1972; Dieterich & Napoli 1982; König & Traugott 1988; Rissanen 2008; Gergel 2009; van der Auwera & De Wit 2011; Kratzer & von Fintel 2014). Given the comparative nature of such words and the modal flavors involved, the issues addressed will be tied directly to semantic change in the areas of intensionality and degrees (cf. e.g. Kratzer 2012 for theoretical discussion). In a nutshell, the paper investigates the hypothesis that two major spirals are involved, where I use the term to mean essentially "language change taking place in a systematic manner and direction" (van Gelderen, this volume). I will present telling contrasting data from German *eher* ('sooner, earlier, rather'), a word which seems to be undergoing a partially similar change with regard to some of the major semantic building blocks, but which also presents an interesting counterfoil due to distinct morphosyntactic patterns and readings.

DOI 10.1075/la.227.11ger

The essentials of the first change undergone by *rather* are – at least at first glance – quickly told: an earlier temporal-based comparative adverb ('sooner, earlier, more quickly') has developed modal as well as metalinguistic meanings. The new meanings of *rather* can be paraphrased roughly as "more preferably" in the modal cases and perhaps as "more appropriately" in the case of the metalinguistic ones. According to Giannakidou and Yoon (2011), the meaning of metalinguistic comparatives can ultimately be subsumed under preference as well.[1] Metalinguistic comparatives are not the specific concern of this paper, but I will point them out when there are potential confounds. I will show that a range of meanings is possible on trajectories like those of *rather* and that they have a common core in the original <u>ordering relation</u>. The contrast with German *eher* will be argued to be useful in illustrating the variety of meanings with a change that is still 'in progress' (in the sense of being transparent synchronically). I will follow, but also sharpen in some respects, an earlier account of such developments (Gergel 2009) with respect to timing issues, possible triggering factors, and the range of possible and available meanings.

In a second diachronic step to be investigated (let's call this spiral number two), a modificational use comes into existence (cf. (1)). In this connection, I will also compare English *rather* to German *eher* in discussing the development. An interesting fact is that despite differences in the shifts towards modal meanings (i.e. inherited from the initial spiral with its origins in temporality), the end results of the two follow-up spirals are exactly parallel data as in (1), which I will refer to – for descriptive purposes – as modificational *eher/rather*:

(1)   a.   *Leo ist eher groß.*
      b.   *Leo is rather tall.*

The overall development of German *eher,* 'earlier' is quite close in terms of the basic trajectory undergone. Although there are quite drastic distributional restrictions, as I will point out, *eher* can still be recognized as a temporal comparative in appropriate contexts, alongside modal and modificational uses. At the same time, I will show that rolling up the case of *eher* does considerably more than serving decorative purposes. It helps uncover key points in each of the two spirals. Regarding the first spiral (temporal to modal), the contrast with *eher* will show interesting differences. Modality can be involved in more ways than this is visible in English today (and it is not always straightforward to reconstruct modal flavors from earlier stages). This will raise the question why English *rather* is so narrowly connected to preferential (i.e. ultimately bouletic) modality in current usage. With respect to the second spiral (modal to modifier, as in

---

1. But see Morzycki (2011) for a different view of metalinguistic comparatives, which is based on the semantic notion of imprecision.

rather tall), the comparison with German will reveal interesting similarities despite a different chronology and qualitative differences in the first spirals. The organization of the paper follows the developments and the cross-linguistic comparisons take place within the respective sections. Thus, section two concentrates on the first spiral. That is, after a consideration of the temporal input morphemes, it will consider the modal flavors obtained. In the third section, the focus will be on the development leading up to the modificational use. The fourth section will specifically discuss issues related to the domain of cycles or spirals with respect to the two developments under investigation.

2. Comparative temporality shifting to modality

2.1 Essentials of the trajectory: The temporal-based scale and facets of its erosion

2.1.1 *English* rather

In this section, I present – and seek to sharpen the analysis of – some of the key facts related to *rather's* early history. The Old English cognates of *rather* could function as adjectives (viz. *(h)ræþ* and variants) and adverbs (cf. *(h)ræþe,* also with many variants; overall, adverbs of the stem are more broadly attested than adjectives, e.g. in the YCOE; Taylor et al. 2003). The meanings of the adverb are temporal-based in the sense that they range along the lines of 'soon', 'early', 'quick(ly)', 'swift(ly)'. The adverb and the adjective are almost indistinguishable morphologically, as in most cases of adverbs and adjectives in Old English. A version *hrædlice* existed in Old English, i.e. with the cognate of the modern adverbial ending *-ly*, but it interestingly did not take off towards the regularized use of *-ly* in Middle English.[2] Illustrations for Old English temporal-based *rath(er)* are given in (2) (from the Penn-Helsinki-York corpora of historical English, in this case the YCOE corpus, Taylor et al. 2003; cf. Gergel 2009).

(2) a. *On Sunnandæge mon sceal **hraðor** arisan to uhtsange.*
      'On Sunday   one shall earlier rise   to morning song.'
                                    (cobenrul, BenR:11.35.4.476)

---

2. Later on, Lowth's notorious prescriptive grammar of 1762 complains explicitly about the lack of adverbial endings in adverbial contexts in the writings of several English authors (including Shakespeare), but it does not go as far as to invoke a form for *rather* that is morphologically (overtly) marked as adverbial, i.e. no *rathly is proposed, even though historically the ingredients for such a form would have been available. We will see below that an impediment towards such a development might have been a striking dispreference for the positive form altogether already in the Middle English period.

b. *Quirinus þa   eode to ðam cwarterne **hraðe**,*
   'Quirinus then went to the   prison   quickly.'

(coaelhom, ÆHom 24:78.3806)

c. *Forþon   hi   ne   besceawiaþ no   **hu   late** hi   on þysne*
   therefore they not   consider   not how late they on this

   *middangeard acennede wurdon, &   **hu   raþe** hi   him*
   world   born   were   and how soon they him

   eft   of gewitan sceolan,...
   afterwards of depart shall

   'Therefore they didn't consider how late they were born on this world
   and how soon they would depart from it.'

(coblick, HomS_17_[BlHom_5]:59.88.735)

While the sentence in (a) illustrates a comparative form (*hraðor*), the adverb we are
interested in (just as the adjective) could naturally also feature the positive, as shown
in (2c). Example (2c) features an implicit question in which *raþe*, 'early', contrasts with
the antonym *late*, 'late': *hu late/hu-raþe*, 'how late/how early'.[3] *Hu* in (2c) is an interrogative degree word in conjunction with the positive form *raþe*. More degree words
could co-occur with the positive forms of *rather*, for instance *swiðe*, 'very'; i.e. we can
assume a largely well-behaved distribution of a gradable adverb.

   Positive and comparative forms of *rather* can still express temporal meanings in
the Middle English period, as illustrated in (3) (originally from PPCME2, Kroch &
Taylor 2000):

(3) a. *and al **so raþe** he was iwarisd of his maladie.*
        'and all so soon he was cured of his sickness.'

(CMKENTSE, 218.108)

   b. *for þat Sonday was of þe **raþer** ʒere, and nouʒt of þe*
      for that Sunday was of the earlier year and not   of the

      newe ʒere þat...
      new year that...

      'because Sunday was of the earlier year and not of the new year that...'

(CMPOLYCH, VI, 101.709)

---

3. Differences between senses of e.g. immediacy, rapidity and earliness will not be discussed
here (cf. e.g. Stern 1931 and references cited there). What such senses have in common is the lin-
earity of a temporal scale (or of closely related scales). My focus is on the transition towards scales
which are distinct from temporality, such as modality. Stern (1931: 185ff) entertains the possibility that temporal-based changes pertaining to swiftness – more generally, not in the context
of expressions like *rather* – could take place in either direction. A crucial feature of the meaning
change on which the focus is placed here is that it is unidirectional and predicted to be so.

If *rathe* was a well-behaved adverb originally (i.e. with a positive in the first place) and *rather*, the original comparative, is the only form existing today, we need to raise at least the following question: what was the relationship between the positive, the comparative (and the superlative)? Let us consider the superlative briefly, an example of which is given in (4)– drawn from the YCOE corpus (Taylor et al. 2003).

(4) *&   for oft   hit wyrð **raðost**   forloren þonne hit wære*
     and for often it   is   fastest/earliest lost   when   it   is

     leofost gehealden.
     dearest held   (cowulf,WHom_13:12.1225)

It turns out that we may set the superlative *per se* aside in terms of the key quantitative developments that may have influenced the perception and the grammatical properties of the form. Such a form was attested (as illustrated above), but it never played a large quantitative role. For example, the 1.5 million-words YCOE corpus only has 25 examples of the superlative and the PPCME2 (Kroch & Taylor 2000) happens to contain no examples that are annotated as superlative.[4] This clearly does not mean that the superlative did not exist in Middle English, but simply that it was infrequent enough in a balanced corpus in which comparatives and positives were attested (s. below). A full productive paradigm of the original adverb and adjective could then ultimately not be upheld, given that the superlative seems to have been the first of its members to be prone to disuse on a broad basis.

But there is a development that I take to be more important towards singling *rather* out as a special item: a rise in the ratio of comparative forms (to the clear detriment of any other adverbial forms, i.e. not only the negligible superlative, but especially the positive) in the transition from Old to Middle English. While the temporal readings are still available in Middle English (and hence the development may go unnoticed), they are increasingly only expressed in the contexts of comparative morphemes. Moreover, the *-er* form and its variants are increasingly the only ones available at all in Middle English. For comparison: in the YCOE corpus there are (only) 51 comparative forms in a total of 535 adverbial *rath-* forms. This yields a proportion of 9.53% of comparatives in the total of forms used adverbially. But in Middle English (based on the PPCME2 corpus once more), the proportion is of 73/105, i.e. at a total 69.52% of comparative forms in the overall number of adverbial forms. This indicates a ratio of the comparative that increased more than seven times between the averaged Old and Middle English periods.

---

4. I searched the following forms in the corpus notation of the two corpora: *rath*, ra+t*, ra+d*, reth*, rad*, hrath*, hra+t*, hra+d*, hreth*, hrad** coupled with the condition that they be superlatives. Notation: +t substitutes thorn, +d eth, and *is a wild card (given that there are various endings attested).

The overall incidence of the adverb decreases, but the comparative forms (i.e. *rather* and its spelling variants) become the clear absolute majority in this pool of data over time.

Establishing the exact disappearance date of *rath* forms can naturally only be given as a general tendency (archaic or other singular late uses cannot be excluded), but it appears that in the Early Modern English period it was hardly available in the general vocabulary of the then-emerging standard. There are three indications which lead me to this affirmation. One early piece of indication is that while Chaucer could still use *rath(er)* temporally, Caxton appears to be clearly more hesitant about it; the ambitious distributor of the new printing medium uses *rather*, but prefers to do so only with non-temporal meanings. Furthermore, dictionaries are known to take time to fully adapt to both new and disappearing forms. Taking such considerations into account, contemporary or later dictionaries can offer auxiliary evidence. The anonymous dictionary of 1598 entitled *The Works of our Ancient and Learned English Poet, Geoffrey Chaucer* (cf. Lancashire 2015) considers it necessary to translate *rath*. A later dictionary edited by John Ray (*A Collection of English Words not Generally Used*; 1674; see Lancashire 2015) considers *rath* to be a word that is explicitly not in general use and paraphrases it in the context of two expressions, listed one after the other as follows: "Rathe in the morning. i.e. early in the morning. Rath-ripe fruit, i.e. early fruit, fructus præcoces". Last but not least, the PPCEME, Kroch et al. 2004, records no entries for positive *rath*. The PPCEME extends the original Helsinki basis for Early Modern English, i.e. it is a relatively large corpus within the family of syntactically annotated historical corpora. Even if the question of negative data remains (as always in historical linguistics), I take the findings presented to be indicative (by and large, i.e. at least in the grammars of most speakers) of the disappearance of the form *rath* and of temporal readings during Early Modern English. Having delimited the rough timeline of the temporal-based adverb, I turn to its analysis.

Borrowing the technology from von Stechow's (2009) synchronic proposal for the semantics of comparisons of time, a simplified representation of *rather* on its basic temporal reading can be rendered as in (5) below with the corresponding semantic types indicated in brackets. I assume that the same representation applies to *eher*, 'earlier' on the temporal reading and to any similar comparative temporal adverb (e.g. *sooner*).

(5)   Logical Form for temporal *rather* ('earlier')

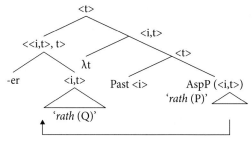

As the arrow indicates, movement at the level of interpretation is crucially involved in this representation. (A more detailed background of the relatively standard semantic assumptions made is given in Gergel (2009)). The ontology involved includes saturated constituents such as ⟨t⟩ (truth values), which can be 'opened up' via movement of the type known from Quantifier Raising. In fact, what we have in (5) is nothing but QR over times (entities of type ⟨i⟩). The type ⟨i,t⟩ stands for a set of times (or equivalently: the characteristic function of such a set). Following a common analysis in the semantics of comparison (cf. Heim 2001; Beck 2011 and references therein), the comparative morpheme is bracketed with the Q constituent above (i.e. the explicit 'than' clause/phrase, or the implicit term of comparison, as is frequently the case). More can be said about the representation, but suffice it for now to keep track of the fact that it involves movement as long as *rather* is interpreted as temporal.

To summarize, *rather* and *rath* had temporal meanings in Old and Middle English, but the positive gradually falls into disuse during the Early Modern period, after its frequency had already been considerably lowered in Middle English compared to Old English. The temporal comparative originally denoted by *rather* can be analyzed as a moved dependency at the level of Logical Form, i.e. a type of Quantifier Raising.

2.1.2 *German* eher

The ongoing development in the case of Modern German *eher,* 'early, soon' shows differences (it is not a cognate of *rather*), but a distributional similarity with the situation we have noticed for *rather* after the Middle English period is as follows: despite its availability as a temporal comparative adverb, *eher* does not show a well-attested and truly temporal positive adverbial form. [5] The stem with a temporal meaning is

---

5.   This does not mean that forms such as *eh(e)* cannot be found, but they show uses that have developed into different things; some instances are idiomatic as in the expression *wie eh und je,* 'as ever', or they have developed quite specialized meanings such as 'anyways, certainly' in Southern varieties of German; I give a version of the latter with ellipsis in a dialogue, specifically the fragment answer in (iB), a use observed, for instance, in Austrian varieties:

(i) A: *Das bekomme ich auch hin.* B: *Ja,   eh!*
        this get   I   too   PRT   yes, EH
        'I can get this done too.'   'Yes, certainly!'

Eh had originally been a comparative itself in Old High German, translating Latin *prius,* 'earlier', (cf. Grimm & Grimm 1854–1961). (Modern) dictionaries such as *Duden* do not indicate temporal meanings of the positive adverb *eh(e)* at all (correctly, I believe). Finally, there is still a use of *ehe* in the sense of 'before' and in conjunction with full clauses. I assume that this is a preposition that takes full clauses due to the semantic equivalence of 'earlier than' and 'before'. The reason I do not call this a complementizer is that it co-occurs with *dass,* 'that', itself in sentential contexts immediately preceding it: *ehe dass,* 'before (that)'. Old English forms of

strikingly restricted in its distribution beyond the comparative. For example, the following sentences are marked at best:

(6) a. *Wie eh(e) stehst du   auf? (ok: früh, 'early' instead of eh(e))
         how early get   you   up
         'How early do you get up?'

     b. *Er   war so eh(e) dran.   (ok: früh, 'early' instead of eh(e))
         he   was so early on-it
         'He was so early.'

This kind of behavior contrasts with both Old and Middle English, where the positive form not only existed freely with temporal meanings, but it could also be used with degree words, such as so or the interrogative hu, 'how', as we have seen. Neither an overt positive such as sehr 'very' nor e.g. an equative construction so...wie, 'as... as', appear to be quite right with eh, although they are just fine with the near-synonyms such as früh or bald, both meaning 'early'.[6]

A superlative form ehest- is still available on temporal readings, cf. e.g. (7):

(7) Der eheste   Termin   ist in zwei Wochen.
     the earliest appointment is   in two   weeks
     'The earliest possible appointment is in two weeks.'

But the impression of temporal normality is slightly perturbed in this corner of the paradigm as well. The example in (7) involved an adjective. First, a salient reading of (7) has a modal side message, as indicated in the translation. Second, the adverb am ehesten often induces a salient modal reading in current use.[7] I will not go through an entire list of degree constructions here, but in a few respects, the appearance of eher may seem to be more advanced in the relevant sense than e.g. Middle English rather,

---

rath(er) did not appear to select complementizers this way (thank you to a reviewer for raising the question). I take this to indicate that selecting for a complementizer cannot be a necessary condition for the development of modal meanings as those coupled with rather.

6.   I leave aside a discussion of measure phrases (e.g. 2m tall) in the domain of temporality because their availability is even more restricted cross-linguistically, perhaps even to the point of being idiosyncratic. Even though German is often thought to be a language with a broad use of measure phrases (Schwarzschild 2009), the temporal domain is more restricted in this area. This also holds for früh/spät, 'early/late', unlike with their English counterparts, which are freely available (cf. five minutes early/late); the combination of too and a measure phrase is felicitous with früh, but not with eh. More generally, an acceptability study could offer a wider picture of the contrastive restrictions and their magnitudes.

7.   Cf. e.g. the following example brought up by a reviewer with a salient modal reading:

    (i)   Er wird am ehesten   am Mittwoch   kommen.
          he will on EH.SUP.   on Wednesday come
          'He will most likely come on Wednesday.'

which for instance still allowed the degree word *so* with the positive (e.g. in Chaucer; cf. e.g. Gergel 2009).

A restriction with regard to the interface of meaning and intonation also becomes apparent in examples such as (8).

(8) *Die kleinere Insel   wird éher   verschwinden.*
      the smaller island will sooner disappear
      'The smaller island will disappear sooner.'

For the sentence in (8) to receive a temporal reading, a pitch accent on the adverb is required (as indicated) and the predicate *verschwinden*, 'disappear' is deaccented. Its meaning can then be understood temporally as in the translation. More specifically, the comparison is with some contextually given entity via a phrasal comparative; e.g. by comparing the time interval when the smaller island will disappear with an interval given one way or another in the context (say the year 2050, due to expectations related to climate change). The comparison will then be based on asserting that the actual disappearance will be even earlier than at such an interval. A second possibility is that we compare, still on the time scale, but with another entity; e.g. the smaller island will disappear sooner than a contextually salient larger island. An additional pitch accent on the adjective appears to enhance this reading. In both cases, the comparison stays on the temporal scale. I will return to modal readings of the same type of configuration and the corresponding intonation in Section 2.2.2.

Summarizing: at first sight, *eher* seems to be a well-behaved modal comparison that wears its temporal-modal ambiguity on its sleeves synchronically, just like *rather* might have done at earlier stages. However, we have seen that restrictions are imposed on the form-interpretation mappings of temporal *eher*. Among other restrictions, we noted that the form *eh* still exists, but while the comparative can be used with temporal meanings, the form *eh*, when used as an adverb (and not in the complementizer domain) only has non-temporal meanings in Present-day German. The additional restrictions observed enhance the point that we are not seeing semantic change in progress quite the way we might have expected to see it. On a currently popular view (e.g. Eckardt 2012 in a compositional framework), we might expect an overload of implicatures to cause a random and relatively regular item to change its core meaning. But there is an additional point. The item which has changed its core semantics is not a random synonym (e.g. *frü(er)*), but *eh(er)*, an item with a restricted distributional picture on its temporal meanings. Although the distributional restrictions are not identical, the same more general point appears to have held for *rather* in Late Middle and Early Modern English given that its appearance was increasingly restrictive.

2.2 Modal elements

2.2.1 Rather *as a modal relator marking preferences in Present-day English*
While there is no trace of a temporal meaning left in Present-day English (PDE) *rather*, there is a quite prominent modal meaning, namely one of preference in it. This

becomes apparent together with *would*, but also in isolation in appropriate contexts, as illustrated in (9) and (10), respectively. The *would*-less construction in PDE requires *rather* to be adjacent to the *than* clause. The constituent consisting of *rather* and the *than* clause can be fronted as a whole, or stay postposed, as long as the requirement for them to be adjacent (on the preference reading) is met. The usual prosodic preferences for longer constituents to go last may interact of course too (this is an orthogonal issue).

(9) *Ben would rather eat the berries.*

(10) *Ben ate the berries rather than take the meat from the fridge.*

(11) *Rather than take the meat from the fridge, Ben ate the berries and stayed hungry.*

In such sentences there is no temporal meaning conveyed as an assertion and we encounter *rather* on its re-analyzed modal meaning. A first Logical Form representation that integrates the new meaning can be given as in (12) (cf. also Gergel 2009).

(12) Logical Form for the reanalyzed modal structure

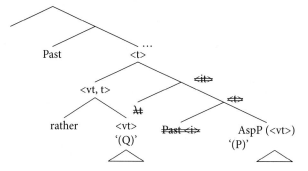

In (12), the elements that were referring to times prior to the reanalysis (i.e. the ones containing ⟨i⟩ in their semantic types), cannot do so any longer and are eliminated from the interpretable structure. This corresponds to structural reduction in the relevant part at the level of interpretation. A higher Past node is added at the top of the tree. But this is attached to the LF that is already organized, i.e. to locate ranked preferences in time. What I assume, then, for preferential *rather* itself is that it ranks propositions P and Q with respect to desirability, requiring P to be more desirable than Q on such a scale. The pertinent propositions are viewed as sets of possible situations (or events) and P is considered more desirable than Q with respect to an individual's – say, a's – preferences. (This is usually the subject, i.e. Ben above.) The simple entry in (13) captures this fact:

(13) $[[rather]] = [\lambda q: q \in D_{\langle v,t \rangle}.[\lambda p: p \in D_{\langle v,t \rangle}.\ q <_{Des,a} p]]$

Assuming such an entry and a structure along the lines of (12) (see Gergel 2011 for further discussion regarding some of the effects involved in *rather* including actuality in the past) helps us make a case for structural reduction and for the elimination of a movement dependency. The latter has been widely discussed in diachronic syntax (Roberts & Roussou 2003; van Gelderen 2004). I suggest such mechanisms may also have an effect, and explanatory power, at the level of interpretation, as indicated in (12) above.

In what follows, I will argue that while preferences and bouletic modality are indeed a key component in the representation of *rather*, this is not part of a universal requirement for such spirals out of temporal readings. In general, it is one type of modality that can arise. I will proceed by beginning with an illustration of the modal flavors of German *eher*. I will then return to *rather* to show that historically it had some other modal flavors as well. Although we will inspect different modal flavors, I will claim that the key semantic notion will still be an ordering as in (13).

2.2.2 *The modal flavors of* eher

This section discusses *eher*'s modal readings. The focus will be on the readings that can be conveyed by *eher* alone, but I will also note a variety of modal readings that are available when *eher* supports other (visible) modals.

A preliminary is in order: I will not discuss the potential temporal-precedence reading of *eher* in all cases in which it is available. A related point is that even though sentences containing *eher* can be ambiguous, in speech they are often disambiguated, not only via context, but also via intonation, albeit the relationship is not one-to-one. Consider (14), repeated from above, and its basic paraphrases in (15).

(14) *Die kleinere Insel   wird eher   verschwinden.*
     the smaller island will EHER disappear

(15) a. 'The small island will disappear sooner.'
     b. 'The small island is more likely to disappear.' [8]

We have seen that the temporal reading in (14) requires a deaccented predicate *verschwinden* and a pitch accent on the adverb. But this is a one-way implication. Consider things from the other perspective. When the focus is on the adverb in a sentence such as (14), the temporal reading becomes highly prominent, but – and this is where a good biconditional fails – it is not necessarily the only one. We turn to the modal reading next.

---

8. An additional reading that a reviewer points out is that the smaller island is likely to disappear (notice: without 'more'). I assume that one possibility is for this reading to be analyzed with an underspecified term of comparison. Another interesting possibility, I assume, is that *eher* decomposes on such readings at the level of interpretation into something like a (phonologically null) positive and 'likely'.

The distribution of the modal paraphrase given in b. is straightforward to get with a focus on the predicate, i.e. *verschwinden*, 'disappear' in (14). A speculation which comes to mind is that, since we are dealing with an epistemic reading, epistemic modality is less likely to bear focus. But this possible tendency (Drubig 2001) has exceptions even with epistemic modals and it turns out to be just a tendency in this case as well. Although the pertinent reading is less salient, focus on the adverb can be compatible with a modal reading as well. As is to be expected when focus interferes, the alternatives will vary. A focal accent on the predicate would typically be compatible with a context in which a straightforward possible alternative to 'disappear' is e.g. 'not disappear' (other alternatives can be invoked too, if they are made relevant). The focus on the adverb, on the other hand (on a modal reading), can bring out the higher likelihood of the small island to disappear (as opposed to, say, the likelihood of a contextually salient larger island to disappear, which may not disappear at all).[9]

Consider the modal readings possible for *eher* more closely. Recall that the primary reading of *rather* was related to preferences. But the modally flavored examples we have considered so far that featured *eher* had epistemic readings. Let us consider some more.

(16) *Es wird eher   regnen.*
      it   will rather rain
      'It is more likely to rain.'

(17) *Heute Abend   legt eher   Uwe auf.*
      today evening sets rather Uwe up
      'It's quite likely that Uwe will be the DJ tonight.'

---

9. An interesting issue in the case of modal readings of *eher* arises also in interaction with the particle *noch*, 'still', which is itself also ambiguous between a temporal and other scalar meanings (in part similarly to English *still*). König (1991) and Hofstetter (2013) discuss some tendencies of *noch*, though not in connection with *eher*:

(i) *Die kleinere Insel   wird eher   noch   verschwinden.*
     the smaller island will EHER still disappear

In a context such as (i) *noch* cannot receive a focus (though it can easily do so in other degree contexts, e.g. *nóch größer*, 'even taller'). But the sentence is ambiguous at least between the two paraphrases in (ii):

(ii) a. 'The small island is more likely to still disappear' (e.g. *still* within the next decade).
     b. 'The small island is more likely to disappear.' (than say the large island, and there is a presupposition that none of them is very likely to disappear).

While these are two distinct readings, I attribute them to the interaction with *noch* and leave a larger discussion of the corresponding effects to further research.

Examples such as (16) and (17) show a similar pattern. A descriptive generalization we can draw so far is: uncertainty readings in connection with predictions are particularly prominent for instances of *eher* which are not accompanied by modals. Whether the relevant sentences contain an explicit future tense (*werden*) or not, is not a key factor. The present tense can convey future meanings in German. The sentences do not indicate the source of evidence directly (as bona-fide evidentials would do; contrast *sollen*, an established hear-say modal in German), but they have clear epistemic readings nonetheless, which are compatible with evidential backgrounds. Context setters such as 'according to {the evidence/everything we know/the weather forecast/the latest rumors/etc.}' are compatible with such sentences. Furthermore, there are also genuine present-tense and past-tense contexts that can be found in which epistemic readings of *eher* are prominent:

(18)   *Lisa kennt   eher   die Antwort.*
     Lisa knows rather the answer
     'Lisa is more likely to know the answer.'

(19)   *(Ich glaube,) gestern   hat eher   Uwe aufgelegt. Oder?*
     I   think   yesterday has rather Uwe up-set   or
     'I think it's more likely that Uwe DJ-ed yesterday. Didn't he?'

On an epistemic reading, the context would naturally be such that the speaker does not possess the information regarding the individual who knows the answer in (18), or who was the relevant DJ the day before utterance time in (19), respectively. But they take the alternatives asserted in each case to be more likely than others. What I assume, then, is that we are dealing with a particular type of epistemic modal item in such cases. It induces an ordering of propositions and requires one to be more likely than the other. The likelihood ordering can be based on different types of evidence and inferences and it is usually the speaker's assessment on the basis of the evidence and facts given. Thus, I assume that *eher* is a very similar building block as *rather* (recall (13))– in that on its prominent modal reading, it induces an ordering of propositions. A difference lies in the fact that while *rather* appears to have grammaticalized to order propositions primarily with respect to desires, *eher* orders them primarily with respect to likelihood based on knowledge and evidence. We will see momentarily more ways of ordering propositions via *eher* as well, but we need to get a potential confound out of the way first. Consider, therefore, (20).

(20)   *Sie   haben eher   Heuschrecken gegessen.*
     they have rather locusts   eaten
     'Rather, they ate locusts.'

A prominent reading of (20) is metalinguistic. A preference reading for it seems to be hardly available with *eher*. What is more: substituting *eher* by a different comparative, *lieber*, 'more preferably' would give an impeccable preference reading and this fact might lead us to suspect that *eher* is just not available for marking desires.[10] Trying to replicate the exact morphosyntax of the English preference construction from (21) yields a structure which is standardly marked in (22) at best.

(21)   *They ate locusts rather than give up their pride.*

(22)   ?*Sie   haben   Heuschrecken   gegessen   eher   als   ihren   Stolz   aufgeben.*
        they   have   locusts   eaten   rather than   their pride give.up

But there are ways out of the apparent impasse. An interesting means to facilitate the construction is via full-fledged finite clauses including the complementizer *dass,* 'that':

(23)   *Sie   haben   eher   Heuschrecken   gegessen   als   dass   sie   ihren   Stolz*
        they   have   rather locusts   eaten   than that   they their pride

       aufgegeben   haben.
        given.up   have

       'They ate locusts rather than give up their pride.'[11]

The adjacency requirement between *rather* and that *than* clause in (21) does not hold for preference *eher,* but that does not change the basic semantics. If anything, the clause containing the complementizer makes it even clearer that we are dealing with propositions. The newly introduced clausal pattern does not require us to revise what we noticed previously about likelihood readings. Epistemic likelihood is just as available with *als dass* clauses as they were with the reduced (or implicit) comparatives introduced earlier:

(24)   *Man   hat   eher   ein   6er   im   Lotto,   als   dass   man   einen   Mitarbeiter*
        one   has   rather a   6   in   lotto   than that   one   a   worker

       des   Supermarktes   findet.
        of.the supermarket   finds

       'It's more likely to get all 6 numbers at lotto right than to find a supermarket worker.'[12]

---

10.   Recall that we are considering *eher* without the addition of overt modals here. Together with a bouletic modal such as *wollen,* 'want', such doubts should not arise. Crucially for now, we contrast the preference effect which both *rather* and German *lieber* can induce on their own and which *eher* appears to be lacking.

11.   Adapted and simplified from ⟨http://www.stryjak.de/land_ohne_grenzen.html⟩. As a reviewer points out, another way to improve the acceptability of (22) is by placing *eher* in front of *Heuschrecken* (in this point as in (23)) and then participle morphology on the second main verb of (22) (*aufgegeben,* 'given up').

12.   Adapted and simplified from ⟨http://www.spiegel.de/forum/wirtschaft/servicegedanke-deutschland-wir-haben-geoeffnet-bitte-bleiben-sie-fern-thread-131045-11.html⟩. (Guessing six numbers right in a German lotto game is the best possible result.)

To summarize what we have seen so far: *eher* alone can convey both preferences and epistemic modality. This may seem a larger domain of modality than the preferences conveyed by modern *rather*, but there are restrictions, too. Notably, *eher* does not seem to naturally convey deontic modality on its own. I will refrain from speculating why this is the case (it is well-known that certain modals develop uses that are predominantly found with certain modal bases only). I will next show, however, that *eher* can appear in an even wider range of contexts when it supports additional modals.

The following example is ambiguous in multiple ways (I consider a subset of the possible readings below):

(25)   *Das Restaurant muss eher   schließen.*
       the   restaurant   must sooner/rather close

Importantly, the readings of *eher* and of the modal can cross-classify. With a temporal reading of *eher*, there are a range of modal meanings involved: (i) on a deontic one, for example, the restaurant needs to close earlier these days because the law has changed and restaurants in the relevant part of the world must close at an earlier time than they used to; (ii) on an epistemic reading, the restaurant must be closing earlier these days based on the evidence – Jami comes home at 10 PM and she has noticed, when driving past the restaurant, that the lights at the place have recently always been off, unlike at earlier times, when it used to close at midnight; (iii) on a circumstantial/teleological reading (these could be distinguished easily further – but notice that it is not unusual for modal readings to be conflated either), the necessary closing of the restaurant at an earlier time than previously is taking place in order to save costs (since there were no customers at late hours), etc. This covers some key modal readings in conjunction with temporal *eher*.

Let's now turn to modal readings of *eher* in the example in (25). The same modal readings just observed can still obtain (and more refined contexts can bring out more flavors as mentioned), but the meaning of *eher* will typically co-vary with the modal itself, as in a modal harmony context. There is a difference however from modal-harmony contexts. There is a clear ordering induced here by the non-temporal use of *eher*. What's at stake, then, is the restaurant's closing (not closing earlier). For instance, on a deontic reading, the necessity for the salient restaurant to close is higher than the necessity for something else to happen (e.g. for some other entity to close – say, the same owner has another property and s/he'll be more forced to close the restaurant, because the other property is faring better). On an epistemic reading, e.g. when the interlocutors are wondering what's going to happen and assess probabilities on the basis of the available evidence in a context that includes the restaurant in question, one of them can assert that it's more likely that the restaurant will close (compared to the likelihood that something else will happen). We are then comparing the strengths of requirements, likelihood predictions etc.

With the additional contribution of an overt ability modal, *eher* can also have an epistemic reading which is independent of the modal. On such a reading *eher* takes scope over the ability modal. But it can also have a reading on which a gradation is undertaken on abilities to answer a question under discussion.

(26)   *Katarina kann das eher   beantworten.*
       Katarina can   this rather answer
       'Katarina is more likely to be able to answer this (e.g. than somebody else).'
       'Katarina's ability to answer this is higher (e.g. than another salient person's ability).'

Finally, there are also contexts in which *eher* may appear neither to perform gradations on modality, nor (only) to harmonize in the usual way, but in which it (arguably) neutralizes the factor of modal force entirely. An interesting issue which von Fintel & Kratzer (20014: 178) point out is that in certain configurations, *eher* seems to neutralize the semantic contribution of modals. The following three sentences are thus claimed to be truth-conditionally equivalent:

(27)   *Das ist **eher** eine japanische als   eine chinesische Maschine.*
       this is more a   Japanese than a   Chinese   machine
       'This is more likely a Japanese than a Chinese machine.'

(28)   *Das **kann** eher eine japanische als   eine chinesische Maschine sein.*
       this might more a   Japanese than a   Chinese   machine   be
       'This is more likely a Japanese than a Chinese machine.'

(29)   *Das **muss** eher eine japanische als   eine chinesische Maschine sein.*
       this must more a   Japanese than a   Chinese   machine   be
       'This is more likely a Japanese than a Chinese machine.'

I am not sure whether scalar effects can be ruled out entirely (e.g. between the *kann* and *must* variety), but the sentences are very close to one another in their meanings. We may add a fourth variant including an epistemic use of the future and the optional addition of the particle *wohl* ('probably'):

(30)   *Das wird (wohl) **eher** eine japanische als   eine chinesische*
       this will PRT   more a   Japanese than a   Chinese
       Maschine sein.
       machine   be
       'This is more likely a Japanese than a Chinese machine.'

But let's also note that to the extent that truth-conditional equivalence exists, it must be restricted. Consider, for instance, (31) (from Gergel 2009, modeled after an attested economic forecast). We do not get equivalent statements by inserting different modals in (32)–(35):

(31)   *Der Industriesektor wird **eher**   nicht wachsen.*
       the industry sector will rather not   grow

(32) *Der Industriesektor **kann eher** nicht wachsen.*
      the industry sector can   rather not   grow

(33) *Der Industriesektor **muss eher** nicht wachsen.*
      the industry sector must rather not   grow

(34) *Der Industriesektor **darf eher** nicht wachsen.*
      the industry sector may   rather not   grow

(35) *Der Industriesektor **braucht eher** nicht zu wachsen.*
      the industry sector needs   rather not   to grow

The key difference lies in the modal base. The salient reading of (32) is clearly circumstantial. For instance, the economic set-up is such that the industrial sector cannot grow. However, (33)–(35) (with (35) featuring an NPI modal) have most readily deontic readings (other readings are possible as well), which – even if the may be related to one another – are clearly distinguishable. For instance (34) is a much stricter kind of prohibition on growth than the others. Unlike (35), (33) displays wide scope of the modal over negation; etc.

Evidential/hear-say *sollen* can also be inserted in such contexts, as can epistemic *dürfte* and a colloquial version of *wollen* (cf. Gergel & Hartmann 2009 on some such flavors of *wollen*):

(36) *Der Industriesektor **soll eher** nicht wachsen.*
      the industry sector shall rather not   grow
      'The industry sector is supposed rather not to grow.'

(37) *Der Industriesektor **dürfte eher** nicht wachsen.*
      the industry sector might   rather not   grow
      'The industry sector might rather not to grow.'

(38) *Der Industriesektor **will eher** nicht wachsen.*
      the industry sector wants rather not   grow
      'The industry sector rather doesn't want to grow.'

The effects are similar, but the sentences are not quite equivalent; both differences of salient modal bases and scalar effects obtain.

This does not exhaust the modal readings of *eher*,[13] but it should offer an idea how the word can function in conjunction with modals in a multitude of ways and order the possibilities that are available further. I return to this point in Section 3.

---

13. There are also metalinguistic readings, which I leave aside (they are not very different from English *rather* on metalinguistic readings). There are also further readings, on which *eher* orders possibilities, but on a different modal base than the overt modal. *Eher* can be epistemic (as we have seen) and, at the same time, interestingly order different types of necessities.

2.2.3   *Further modal flavors in* rather

The usual flavor from the domain of modality that is associated with Modern English *rather* is one of preference (Huddleston & Pullum 2002). While *eher* and *rather* do not convey an identical range of modal flavors, I investigate in this section whether more modal flavors can be associated with *rather* diachronically (where the usual diachronic provisos hold). I first point out that epistemic readings might have been available, then consider co-occurrence with other modals, and finally point out an additional co-occurrence pattern which I take to have been another crucial factor in *rather's* ultimate anchoring to the domain of preferences.

Consider the following examples from the Middle English and Early Modern period, respectively (retrieved via the PPCME2, Kroch & Taylor 2000, and the Innsbruck Corpus of Middle English, Markus 2010):

(39)   *Trowist thow that Marye grucched of Martha?*
Believe you that Mary grouched of Martha

Nay, but rather Martha of Marye.
nay, but rather Marthy of Mary
'Do you think that Mary was angry at Martha? No, but rather Martha at Mary.'
(CMAELR4,16.471–2)

(40)   *Wherby I knowe certeynli, as I fere me/   that she ys rather*
whereby I know certainly as I fear myself that she is rather

ded   than a lyue'
dead than alive   (W. Caxton's_Blanchardyn_and_Eglantine)

E.g. consider a scenario for (25) in which we are talking about several (deontic or circumstantial) necessities and don't know which one is more likely to hold in the actual situation. In such a context, *eher* can state that the necessity of the restaurant to close is more likely (according to the evidence available to one of the interlocutors) than for something else to (be forced to) happen. Also, I did not discuss weak deontic modality in an overt modal, but similar effects can obtain. For instance, (i) can mean that the addressee is allowed to go out tonight (more so than some other relevant possibility). *Rather* can harmonize quite similarly.

(i)   *Du darfst heute Abend   eher   ausgehen.*
you may   today evening rather go.out
'You may rather go out tonight.'

There are also additional syntactic possibilities; e.g. in (i) *eher* can immediately precede *heute Abend* (in which case a salient contrast would include 'tonight'), as – with some acceptability – *rather* could also immediately precede *tonight* in the English translation.

The narrator of (37) raises a rhetorical question regarding the biblical context of the two sisters Mary and Martha and offers the answer that one possibility is more likely than the other. It is questionable whether there is a preference on the side of the narrative voice with regard to the two past possibilities (pace possible didactic purposes of such texts). And there is certainly no preference of the subject as in the PDE preference pattern displayed by *rather,* e.g. previously in (10). On the other hand, there is a source of evidence (e.g. the biblical passages in the New Testament cited) that make the outcome given as the more likely one, namely that Martha was angrier at (and in other versions: envious of) Mary. We cannot know whether the sentence was ultimately *intended* to have an epistemic reading. Some sort of metalinguistic reading may almost always be invoked and other readings may be possible too. However, if metalinguistic readings are understood as preferences, then there is no obvious preference-holder involved in the example (again, neither with respect to the narrator nor to the two individuals mentioned). Quite plausibly, then, a particular type of epistemic reading, which comes down to deciding between the likelihood of two possibilities, could be sanctioned by the context.[14] In the same vein, the sentence in (40) appears to rest on an ignorance/uncertainty background, even though no explicit question is formulated here. The king uttering the words in the narrative passage does not know whether the queen referred to is dead or alive (pace the perhaps misleading use of *certainly*). He fears the worst. This again makes an epistemic reading likely.

The width of potential modal readings can also be grasped via modals co-occurring with *rather*. This is presumably the case at any point in time, but particularly so at the transition from Middle to Modern English. Consider, for instance, the 15th century text *Le Morte Darthur* by Thomas Malory and printed by Caxton. A search for *rather* on the Corpus of Middle English Prose and Verse within this text reveals 26 entries. Out of these tokens, only one lacks a modal altogether. While *will/would* appears frequently (in the corresponding forms, *wylle, wolde* etc.), this is not the only modal to co-occur with *rather*. *Shall* is one candidate that does not necessarily convey volition. *Ought* is another one, as shown below:

(41) *Affermyng that I ouȝt   rather tenprynte his   actes and noble*
      affirming   that I ought rather to print   his   acts   and noble

---

14. The difficulties of establishing particular readings as epistemic notably holds for the modals themselves too (cf. e.g. Denison 1993; Gergel 2014 for some discussion). A possible marginal argument for the current sentence to be understood in a context in which alternatives that are not known are weighed against each other is also that an early Middle English version of the same text contained a <u>matrix</u> *whether* in the question, a marker typically used when one of two alternatives was expected to be true in earlier English.

> *feates /* than of godefroye of boloyne
> feats   than of Godfrey   of Boullion
>
> 'Affirming that I rather ought to print his acts and noble feats than those
> of Godfrey of Boullion.'   (*Le Morte Darthur*, Caxton's Preface, p. 1)

(41) is from Caxton's own preface; he reports having been under more pressure to print King Arthur's story than other individuals' (Godfrey being one of them). *Ought* is deontic and *rather* grades it further.

Besides co-occurrence with modals, which could be quite high at times, as we have seen, there are additional factors that may well have shaped the transmitted meaning of *rather* further. I mention one related construction here that I take to be particularly relevant, which was still available – if on the decline – during Caxton's time of writing and *inter alia* in the text introduce above:

(42)   *and* **rather** *than my lady shold*   *lese her heed/yet had I*
and rather than my lady should lose her head/yet had I

leuer   *lese my hede*
more.preferably lose my head
                                (*Le Morte Darthur*, Book 8, Ch. XXV, p. 311)

(42) conveys that the reported speaker (viz. Tristan, upon complaining about an odd and as he calls it 'foul' custom at the castle at which he arrives) prefers to lose his own head over the possibility of his wife's losing hers. Note that while the embedded clause contains *rather*, the main clause features *leuer*, 'more preferably'. This pattern appears four times in the total of 26 examples of *rather* in *Le Morte Darthur*. Constructions such as *I had rather* (hardly transparent for many speakers in PDE) are also a follow-up of the same lexical fall into disuse of the original preferential marker *leuer*.

3.   More ordering and scalar structures operated on by eher and rather

In this section, I will investigate how the ordering semantics has given rise to the modificational use of *rather/eher* in conjunction with adjectives.

3.1   Ordering

I suggest that the crucial part that was transmitted in the meaning of *rather* and *eher* from the original temporal-based semantics is the ordering relationship. While we have already seen specific illustrations of how the ordering could be implemented in the case of *rather* and *eher* (cf. Section 2.2), I slightly extend the empirical scope of the observations in what follows. I begin by illustrating – inspired by claims to the contrary in recent literature – that the word is also able to operate between modalized finite clauses.

Von Fintel and Kratzer (2014) point out the apparent impossibility of modal comparisons with *eher*. What is claimed is that only a temporal meaning arises in (43). On an intended non-temporal reading, a puzzling ungrammatical status is claimed to arise:

(43) **Jockl **wollte** diesen Mord eher begehen als er **konnte.***
      Jockl wanted this murder rather commit than he could

A qualification is, however, in order. There is no semantic puzzle involved in cases such as (43). With a change of syntactic configuration, the construction becomes fully acceptable:

(44) *Jockl **wollte** diesen Mord begehen **eher** **als** **dass** er es*
      Jockl wanted this murder commit rather than that he it

      ***konnte**/gekonnt hätte.*
      could/ could has(Konj.II)

      'The degree to which Jockl wanted to commit the murder is higher than the degree to which he was/would have been able to do it.'

The pattern is, moreover, extendable to other modals in the respective clauses joined by *eher*; cf. (45)–(46), the latter being modeled after a naturally occuring example.

(45) *Jacky **musste** den Gast aufnehmen **eher** **als** **dass** sie es **wollte**/*
      Jacky had.to the guest take.up rather than that she it wanted/

      gewollt hätte.
      wanted has(Konj.II)

      'The degree to which Jacky was obliged to take upt the guest was higher than the degree to which she was/would have been willing to do it.'

(46) *Gerade die Wanderung war wirklich anstrengend,*
      precisely the hike was really strenuous

      laut Karte sollte die mittelschwer sein, aber zwischendurch
      according.to map should it middle-heavy be but in-between

      ***musste** man eher klettern **als** **dass** man laufen **konnte**.*
      had.to one rather climb than that one walk could

      'It's precisely the hike that was really strenuous; according to the map, it should have been medium difficulty, but at times you had to climb, more than you could walk.' (adapted from usahochdrei.wordpress.com/)

The ordering between clauses seems to be the crucial common core that *eher/rather* constructions have. Notice that *rather* operating between two modalized clauses is quite common in late Middle and early Modern English too. The relevant common use is illustrated in (47) below:

(47) *...rather than I **sholde** be dishonoured, there **wolde** som good*
      rather than I should be dishonored there would some good

> *man   take   my quarell.*
> man   take.up my fight   (CMMALORY,36.1143)

Rather/eher operates between two modalized clauses in such configuration and the German examples shown, respectively. But there is a subtle difference. In German, such constructions stay with a relatively unspecified nature, i.e. without imposing an additional kind of modality which is superordinate to the two clauses. That means, we are really comparing degrees e.g. of wanting and being able to etc. – the very phenomenon von Fintel and Kratzer seem to allude to (even if they happened not to consider the right constructions in this case).

The latter point brings out the general type of ordering mechanism which the earlier temporal comparative can give rise to. I cannot rule out that some early English examples had (the potential of having) such meanings; on the contrary this is a possible scenario. The flavor I get from the contexts of examples like those in (47), which are common e.g. in Caxtonian prose, is a preference after all, but one that is added on top of the two internally modalized clauses. The lady reported to utter (47) has in fact a preference for the matrix proposition over the subordinate one.

3.2   Modifying adjectives

We have so far seen that a range of meanings available with *rather* and *eher* still contain a common element of ordering two entities (in the broadest sense, i.e. including propositions). There is, however, an interesting further use which both words have developed – cf. (48) (repeated from (1)) – and which is less obviously related to the temporal reading.

(48)   a.   *Leo ist eher groß.*
        b.   *Leo is rather tall.*

Consider features shared by *eher* and *rather*. While sentences such as (48a) and (48b) can also have metalinguistic readings, they have clear meanings that make use of the structure of scales, as I will illustrate. The metalinguistic use of *eher/rather* is most naturally accompanied by a *than* clause, while the scalar modificational use of interest here does typically not allow one. Adding *than* phrases/clauses makes the scalar meaning disappear in (49):

(49)   a.   *Leo ist eher groß als schlank.*
        b.   *Leo is rather tall than thin.*

Whether the structure is phrasal or underlyingly fully expanded into a clause (*rather than he is thin* – and similarly in German with the optional use of a 'Konjunktiv II', i.e. the irrealis form of the copula as an alternative to the indicative) in general has little bearing on the unique reading which remains; see Lechner (2001) on comparative ellipsis. Only a metalinguistic meaning remains in (49), a straightforward rendering of which is that it is more appropriate to describe Leo as tall than as thin.[15]

If we factor out the meatalinguistic reading, modificational *eher* and *rather* show further distributional restrictions with respect to degree constructions. *Than* phrases are odd also when possible comparisons would be sensible. If the term of comparison remains implicit, then *rather* (and *eher*) can function as a non-met-alinguistic marker (of showing a small difference interval) with a comparative of the adjective itself, but such a non-metalinguistic reading appears considerably harder to construe with other degree constructions including the superlative of the adjective:

(50) a. *Leonie is rather taller.*
    b. *#Leonie is rather the tallest.*

Let me return to the basic configurations such as (48), however, which have a clearly distinct and scalar reading induced by *rather/eher*. The basic insight that we may use is that the interval which is denoted as the positive (i.e. *Leo is _ tall*) is typically higher than the average (cf. e.g. Kennedy & McNally 2005 and von Stechow 2009 on the positive).

(51)   ----------xxxxxxxxx--
        pos tall

Keeping context-sensitivity in mind, one thing that <u>*rather* tall</u> and <u>*eher* groß</u> can be thought to convey is that Leo's height is within a certain interval of the relevant dimension, but that this interval is just below the interval denoted by the positive. On my initial view, its core meaning does nothing more than that. There are several types of side-messages (for simplicity, I assume that they are implicatures here, without much hinging on it for the present course; cf. Eckardt 2006 for their relevance in change). For instance, ignorance could be one – e.g. the speaker doesn't know the exact height or, alternatively, the latter is not particularly relevant to be told. Another possibility is some form of politeness, i.e. that the speaker does not wish to appear as e.g. too evaluative or offending; this will come out best in the use of *eher/rather* with adjectives such as e.g. *intelligent, old, cheap, expensive* or *dumb*.[16] But note that such adjectives as well as the previously used dimensional class (*tall*; but cf. also *wide, broad, deep*) are

---

15. Naturally, not only properties, but also e.g. individuals can be compared metalinguistically. Cf. von Fintel & Kratzer (2014) for observations on such comparisons.

16. This may be more prominent in certain types of speech/writings or perhaps even more predominantly at certain periods than at others (based on the data available). For instance, out of 62 modificational uses of *rather* in the currently expanding PPCMBE corpus (Kroch et al. 2010 has been used), 45 have a clear negative expressive evaluation (cf. (i)) in their respective

open-scale adjectives (Kennedy & McNally 2005). Consider the use of *eher/rather* with some closed-scale adjectives:

(52)   a.   *eher {fertig/voll/leer/unsichtbar}*
       b.   *rather {done/full/empty/invisible}*

In such cases, the meaning of *rather* (factoring out metalinguistic readings) is that the endpoint of the scale is not reached and that the degree reached is relatively close to it. Without denying the role of imprecision and approximation in natural language, notice that the meaning on this use of *rather* does not necessarily entail imprecision. A pragmatic halo of imprecision would be involved e.g. if we said a glass is full even if a few more drops could fit into it (Lasersohn 1999). We can invoke the contrast with *more or less*, which is close, but not identical in its effect. The use of *rather* under unmarked scalar circumstances means that the endpoint is not reached. An interesting further scalar effect obtains in comparison with *almost*. *Almost* would require the degree reached on the scale (e.g. in *almost full*) to be even closer to the endpoint. *Almost* and *rather* do not normally co-occur (except on metalinguistic readings with *rather* then preferably preceding *almost* as in a.):

(53)   a.   **rather almost full*
       b.   **almost rather full*

Just like the use of *rather* in the modal domain was in fact quite broad, on closer inspection, there is an interesting breadth of use in the scalar domain. The distinction discussed above, namely between open and closed scales, can in general be characterized by the use of different modifiers, one of the key observations in Kennedy and McNally (2005). Accordingly, there should be classes of modifiers that are more felicitously used with one respective class of predicates. For instance, the modifier *well* is fully felicitous and often attested with a predicate such as *acquainted* (involving a closed scale) and not felicitous with *surprised* (which operates on an open scale). Conversely, *very* is felicitous with the latter predicate and odd with the former.

But Kennedy and McNally focus on deverbal predicates and their interesting paper does not discuss *rather*, which can felicitously be used in both types of scalar domains with adjectives as well as deverbal forms. In view of the descriptive suggestions made above, modificational *rather* has, however, slightly distinct meanings in each of the two scalar domains. To summarize so far, then: in the case of open scales, it

---

contexts, 11 a positive one, and 6 are neutral or unclear. More such pragmatic questions of use can certainly be addressed (cf. Rissanen 2008 for some), but they go beyond present scope.

(i)   *In Germany things look rather critical and threatening.*
       (VICTORIA-186X,1,271.697)

denotes membership in an interval that is located, via context, typically just below the interval denoted by the positive (i.e. 'very' or a zero form) on the relevant scale. In the other case, it denotes non-adjacent closeness to the endpoint and it is situated – within the linear order of a scale – after the extension of *almost*, which comes in-between in the closed-scale environments.[17]

But how do we get from the relator ordering entities in the modal senses to the modifier use? I divide the answer into two parts. I illustrate some key data immediately below and return to the conceptual part that I suggest has been involved in Section 4.2 in the context of the second spiral involved. First note that before modifying uses become visible in the data (recall their scarcity as late as in the Early Middle English period), there was a frequent use of *rather* that seemed to operate between scalar opposites of some sort, or antonyms. Borrowing Rissanen's terminology for descriptive purposes, I call this a contrastive use:[18]

(54) *Also Marie oweth **rather** to sytte with the **poor** þan with*
     also Mary owes rather to sit with the poor than with

     *þe **rich**; **rather** to **obey** than to be **abeyde**; rather to kepe **silence***
     the rich rather to obey than to be waited rather to keep silence

     *than to **speke**; **rather** to be **alon** solytarie þen be conn_staunte*
     than to speak rather to be alone solitary than be constantly

---

17.   That is, I see *eher* as behaving distinctly in the two environments for the purposes of the current descriptive account. It remains unclear (to me) whether the two types of behavior are to be unified, e. g if *almost* itself can be reduced to some version related to the positive (as suggested for example by Gergel & Stateva 2014 for quantificational contexts independent of *rather*). On an independent note that may bring *almost* closer to the current concerns, König and Traugott (1988: 119) briefly note a use of *bald*, 'soon', which comes down to meaning *almost*:

    (i) *Ich warte jetzt schon bald eine halbe Stunde.*
       'I have been waiting for nearly half an hour.'

18.   Rissanen (2008) is one of the few contributions within the numerous ones on *rather* to also consider the modifier use (many others, including e.g. König & Traugott 1988 or Gergel 2009 do not treat it; but cf. Hall 1881 for interesting notes alluding to the modificational reading as well). I take such contributions to be of the highest merit philologically, even if e.g. Rissanen (2008: 357) seems to seriously doubt that there is much common ground between the temporality the first development started out with and the modificational end result of the development, even though he sees metonymy as plausible. The fact that the development takes place quite similarly with etymologically unrelated items like *rather* and *eher* (but also in other languages e.g. French *plutôt*, or Romanian with a non-related expression again; Gergel 2011) is an indication that there must be mechanisms which *can* produce such a sequence of two spirals in the change of natural language meaning.

> *amonge* the grete of the world or amonge his wordily frindes.
> among   the great of the world or among his worldy friends
> (*The Revelations of Saint Birgitta*, a1475, 33:3)

Interestingly, some of the earliest examples of modifiers that can be culled from the parsed corpora of English (PPCEME) have a contrastive reading, as do some of the earliest apparent examples from German (via the Cosmas II corpus):

(55) *And dygnyties geuen vnto wycked folke, do not make them* **worthy**,
      but shewethe and declareth them rather **vnworthy**.
      (BOETHCO-E1-P1,46.506–7)

(56) *Ueberhaupt muß ich bekennen, daß die Kunstrichter in*
      generally   must I   admit   that the art_judges in

      Ansehung meiner eher   nachsichtsvoll, als   strenge gewesen sind.
      regard   mine   rather lenient   than strict   bin are
      'I must admit, quite generally, that the jurors have been rather lenient than strict in my case.' (1767, Moses Mendelssohn, Cosmas II)

The pattern persists into the Late Modern periods. For instance, out of 40 examples of *rather* modifying adjectives in 31.721 tokens in the 1800s within the syntactically annotated corpora, 8 example can be interpreted as contrastive within the token, as illustrated in (57):

(57) *some in the progress of formation, instead of being* **soft and crumbling** *like lumps of brown sugar, as some stalactites are, were flexible, something like a* **rather tough** *paste.* (RUSKIN-1835,1,21.558)

4. More on how *rather* and *eher* spiraled twice

4.1 From temporal to modal: Why does 'rather' spiral to preference readings?

The exploration of linguistic cycles or spirals has seen a broad range of research in recent years. Cases like *rather* and *eher* are certainly distinct from the more proto-typical cycles such as the famous negative one. Part of this may have to do with the much clearer distribution of labor in the case of negation. What comes in, every time a negation system gets such a boost, is an item that gains the ability to reverse the truth value of a sentence (or which yields the complement set if one thinks in terms of propositions as sets of possible worlds). Negation is intricate enough historically and synchronically, but we could still say: comparatively simple. In the case of modality, we have a many-to-many mapping. There are typically several modal markers for many modal flavors both before and after an earlier comparative may become a marker of modality. What happens with *rather* is thus certainly only one part of the fuller range of modal meanings. It is also not the case that anything comes back to its original position (e.g. of a temporal comparative). Hence – to the extent that such labels have theoretical significance – we may be dealing with a spiral in which new items seem to undergo trajectories also seen with earlier items (comparing e.g. modal contexts of *sooner*) and furthermore seen in other languages.

The only additional issue that I would like to raise in this subsection, is what kind of modality may constitute the more general pattern and – if such a pattern exists – why is the other pattern attested nonetheless? In a nutshell, we have seen that while several flavors are available, bouletic modality is the prevalent pattern for Modern English *rather* and a particular type of ordering epistemic modality the one prevalent for German *eher*. Somewhat similar changes are attested in several languages (cf. e.g. König & Traugott 1988; Gergel 2011), and a statistical analysis which should extend to more languages than the Indo-European ones focused on so far should be able to tell which flavors are most frequent. (Notice, again, that more markers for the respective types of modality are available even at one stage of the same language.) From the simple comparison conducted within the limits of this paper, however, it appears that a development as in the case of German, towards epistemic modality and a more general type of comparison, may be a fundamental pattern. Examples with a similar potential have also been attested in English, as I have sought to illustrate with historical data. But why is, then, *rather* in Modern English ultimately tied so closely to preferences? I suggest that one major reason may lie in the disappearance of earlier preference constructions in English, and in particular one which is still preserved in German and other Germanic languages, namely *lieber*, 'more preferably'. *Leofer, lever* (and again, many alternative forms) were productive patterns in Old English and still available up until Middle English. That is, one particular type of meaning, which the more general type of scaffolding based on ordering in *rather* came to eventually replace, was the one pertaining to the relative preference of two propositions.

4.2 On the spiral to the modificational use; and most specially, why it is one

I propose (i) that the type of configuration-meaning pairing which I call modificational is a follow-up of the spiral development we have investigated in some detail from temporal to modal ordering elements [19] and (ii) that it is an independent sequel, insofar as

---

19. I focus on how *eher* behaves with gradable adjectives (and by extension with properties that can be re-interpreted as gradable in some sense or another), but it should be clear that the configuration is not restricted categorically; cf. (i) and (ii).

(i) *Her mobile was rather on the cheap side.*
(ii) *He was rather average.*

it uses the input of the first development (as one means of introducing carriers of such modificational meanings), but it is not automatically triggered by it.

First notice that the modificational use seems to show up systematically in the late Modern English period in English and at around the same time, on first estimates, in German. This may appear as out of sync if we put into the picture that the change from temporal to modal has been fully completed in English for a long time, but it is still at least transparent in current German. That is, the first development seems not to condition (much less automatically trigger) the timing of the second one. Furthermore, there are words in several languages that undergo some part of the development from temporal to modal (e.g. English *sooner* in the context of *would*, or European Portuguese, also without the addition of additional modals), but which do not show the second development:

(58) *sooner tall* (intended as: 'rather tall')

(59) *mais depressa alto* (E. Portuguese, intended as 'rather tall, Conceição Cunha, p.c.)

There is some indication why the modificational use and the modal uses seem to be quite distinct, as we have seen. But I claim that there is a diachronic semantic link that offers itself to consideration directly from the observations we have put together above. Recall that we had ordering involved, as schematically represented in (60):

(60) *rather/eher* as ordering: A before/more preferably than/ more than B

```
        A              B
_____x_____x_____
```

In some cases, as we have seen, the scale may not be so obvious at all and it only becomes detectable by virtue of the use of *eher/rather*. If A and B are properties and we have A holding of an individual more than B does, then we are close by at the meaning associated with the metalinguistic reading.

The contrastive readings we have seen may be relevant in two ways. One lies in the expressive power of contrasting properties that may have enhanced this in the process of change (as expressive use of language may well linger on etc.). But there is also a more specific way. The contrastive use may also have had the effect of placing the meanings involved very clearly onto one and the same scale. Whether the 'opposing' ends were on a scale or not, using them as such defines the scale. The scale is more clearly defined since its positive extensions are often mentioned: e.g. *poor/rich, worthy/unworthy* etc.

(61) xxxxxxxxxx ———————x——xxxxxxxxx
      pos *unworthy*   pos *worthy*

If an entity x is closer to the extension of *pos worthy* than to that of *pos* unworthy, then x is somewhere above the average perhaps, but typically – for originally pragmatic reasons: slightly – below the extension of *pos worthy*.

Notice that stating that x has the latter property (i.e. of being slightly below the pos interval) is then truth-conditionally equivalent to the earlier meaning that happened to have been set up by the opposing poles. This may be a case in which so-called constant entailments (Beck 2012) operate in language change (Beck & Gergel to appear; Gergel & Beck 2015). Truth-conditional equivalence in a subset of contexts may lead to the adoption of a different analysis. Crucially, this offers a window onto explaining the modificational use of *rather* and *eher* from of the way ordering relationships and scales have been used.

4.3 Summary and outlook

This paper has suggested that two inter-related developments are involved in *rather* and *eher,* the first one leading to modality and a general type of ordering relation (prominently used for preferences in English and epistemic possibilities in German), and one leading to modificational uses in both languages. While parts of the changes have been previously observed, the paper has sought to sharpen the reconstruction of the possible causal effects and the analysis of the semantic essentials towards a more predictable account of such changes. In terms of observations relating to the cycle, we have seen that *rather* – with its salient modern preference use – came to be used in such a way in part because a substitute turned out to be useful for the eventual demise of other such preference markers (while German still has the counterpart *lieber*). The question what exactly the specific epistemic markers and modifiers came in for is, however, less straightforward and desires further research.[20]

Acknowledgments

I am very grateful to the audiences of the second ASU workshop on linguistic cycles and of a talk at the Institute for Linguistics in Budapest, respectively, for inspiring comments to the related material presented. A sincere thank you also to the partici-

---

20. The question of the possibly late rise of epistemic markers is an old one in the domain of the modals (cf. e.g. Denison 1993). A somewhat similar possibility – under which new means enter a language without necessarily substituting for something specific, but rather by expanding it – has been interestingly raised by Johan van der Auwera at the second workshop on cycles with respect to the modificational use. It may thus be the case that the nominal and adjectival projections into which *rather* intruded simply expanded over time. We could phrase this in terms of syntactic articulation of the nominal domain and presumably richness in terms of semantic flavors expressed. Recent work such as Wood (this volume) or van de Velde (2011) may be interesting starting points for pursuing this more general question pertaining to the expansion of means further.

pants of my research seminar in December 2014 and a thoughtful reviewer for their valuable feedback on this work.

References

van der Auwera, Johan & De Wit, Astrid. 2011. The English comparative modals – A pilot study. In *Distinctions in English Grammar, Offered to Renaat Declerck*, Cappelle, Bert & Naoaki Wada (eds), 127–147.Tokyo: Kaitakusha.

Beck, Sigrid. 2011. Comparatives and superlatives. In *Semantics: An International Handbook of Natural Language Meaning*, Klaus von Heusinger, Claudia Maienborn & Paul Portner (eds), 1341–1390. Berlin/New York: Mouton de Gruyter.

Beck, Sigrid. 2012. Pluractional comparisons. *Linguistics and Philosophy* 35: 57–110. doi:10.1007/s10988-012-9111-3

Beck, Sigrid & Gergel, Remus. To appear. The diachronic semantics of English *again*. Ms. University of Tübingen and University of Graz.

Corpus of Middle English Prose and Verse. University of Michigan. ⟨http://quod.lib.umich.edu/c/cme/⟩

Denison, David. 1993. *English Historical Syntax*. London: Longman.

Dieterich, Thomas G. & Napoli, Donna J. 1982. Comparative *rather*. *Journal of Linguistics* 18: 137–165. doi:10.1017/S0022226700007283

Drubig, Hans-Bernhard. 2001. On the syntactic form of epistemic modality. Ms, Tübingen.

Eckardt, Regine. 2012. Grammaticalization and semantic reanalysis. In *Semantics: An International Handbook of Natural Language Meaning*, Vol. 3, Klaus von Heusinger, Claudia Maienborn & Paul Portner (eds), 2675–2702. Berlin: Mouton de Gruyter.

von Fintel, Kai & Angelika Kratzer. Modal Comparisons: Two dilletantes in search of an expert. In *The Art and Craft of Semantics: A Festschrift for Irene Heim,* Vol. 1 [MIT Working Papers in Linguistics 70], Luka Crnic & Uli Sauerland (eds), 175–179. Cambridge MA: MITWPL.

van Gelderen, Elly. 2004. *Grammaticalization as Economy* [Linguistik Aktuell/Linguistics Today 71]. Amsterdam: John Benjamins. doi:10.1075/la.71

van Gelderen, Elly. 2011. *The Linguistic Cycle: Language Change and the Language Faculty*. Oxford: OUP. doi:10.1093/acprof:oso/9780199756056.001.0001

Gergel, Remus. 2009. *Rather* – on a modal cycle. In *Cyclical Change* [Linguistik Aktuell/Linguistics Today 146], Elly van Gelderen (ed.), 243–264. Amsterdam: John Benjamins. doi:10.1075/la.146.14ger

Gergel, Remus. 2011. Structure-sensitivity in actuality: Notes from a class of preference expressions. *University of Pennsylvania Working Papers in Linguistics* 17: 115–124.

Gergel, Remus. 2014. Dimensions of variation in Old English modals. Ms. University of Graz.

Gergel, Remus & Beck, Sigrid. 2015. Early Modern English *again*: A corpus study and semantic analysis. *English Language and Linguistics* 19: 27–47. doi:10.1017/S1360674314000355

Gergel, Remus & Cunha, Conceição. 2009. Modalidade e inferências do mundo real em Português Europeu. *Rasal Lingüística* 111–128.

Gergel, Remus & Hartmann, Jutta. 2009. Experiencers with (un)willingness: A raising analysis of German 'wollen'. In *Advances in Comparative Germanic Syntax* [Linguistik Aktuell/Linguistics Today 141], Artemis Alexiadou, Jorge Hankamer, Thomas McFadden, Justin Nuger & Florian Schäfer (eds), 327–356. Amsterdam: John Benjamins.

doi:10.1075/la.141.14exp

Giannakidou, Anastasi & Yoon, Suwon. 2011. The subjunctive mode of comparison: Metalinguistic comparatives in Greek and Korean. *Natural Language and Linguistic Theory* 29: 621–655. doi:10.1007/s11049-011-9133-5

Grimm, Jacob & Grimm, Wilhelm. 1854–1961. *Deutsches Wörterbuch von Jacob Grimm und Wilhelm Grimm*; [DWB]. ⟨http://dwb.uni-trier.de/de/⟩

Hall, Fitzedward. 1881. On the Origin of "Had Rather Go" and Analogous or Apparently Analogous Locutions. *The American Journal of Philology* 7: 281–322.

Heim, Irene. 2011. Degree operators and scope. In *Audiatur Vox Sapientiae. A Festschrift for Arnim von Stechow* (= Studia Grammatica 52), Caroline Féry & Wolfgang Sternefeld (eds.), 214–239. Berlin: Akademie-Verlag.

Hofstetter, Stefan. 2013. Selected Issues in the Theory of Comparison: Phrasal Comparison in Turkish and a Cross-Linguistic Perspective on Intensifiers, Negative Island Effects and the Distribution of Measure Phrases. Ph.D. dissertation, University of Tübingen.

Huddleston, Rodney & Pullum, Geoffrey. 2002. *The Cambridge Grammar of the English Language*. Cambridge: CUP.

Kennedy, Christopher & McNally, Louise. 2005. Scale structure, degree modification, and the semantics of gradable predicates. *Language* 81: 345–381.

König, Ekkehard. 1991. *The Meaning of Focus Particles*. London: Routledge.

König, Ekkehard & Traugott, Elizabeth C. 1988. Pragmatic strengthening and semantic change: The conventionalizing of conversational implicature. In *Understanding the Lexicon*, Werner Hüllen & Rainer Schulze (eds), 110–124. Tübingen: Niemeyer.

Kratzer, Angelika. 2012. *Modals and Conditionals: New and Revised Perspectives*. Oxford University Press.

Kratzer, Angelika & von Fintel, Kai. 2014. In *The Art and Craft of Semantics: A Festschrift for Irene Heim*, vol. 1, Luka Crnic & Uli Sauerland (eds), 175–179. MITWPL 70.

Kroch, Anthony, Santorini, Beatrice & Delfs, Lauren. 2004. *Penn-Helsinki Parsed Corpus of Early Modern English*. University of Pennsylvania.

Kroch, Anthony, Santorini, Beatrice & Diertani, Ariel. 2010. *Penn Parsed Corpus of Modern British English*. University of Pennsylvania.

Kroch, Anthony & Taylor, Ann. 2000. *Penn-Helsinki Parsed Corpus of Middle English*, 2nd edn. University of Pennsylvania.

Lancashire, Ian. 2015. *Lexicons of Early Modern English*. University of Toronto. ⟨leme.library.utoronto.ca⟩

Lasersohn, Peter. 1999. Pragmatic halos. *Language* 75: 522–551. doi:10.2307/417059

Lechner, Winfried. 2001. *Ellipsis in Comparatives*. Berlin: Mouton de Gruyter.

Markus, Manfred. 2010. *Innsbruck Computer Archive of Machine-Readable English Texts* [ICAMRET]. Innsbruck: English Department, University of Innsbruck Austria.

Morzycki, Marcin. 2011. Metalinguistic comparison in an alternative semantics for imprecision. *Natural Language Semantics* 19: 39–86. doi:10.1007/s11050-010-9063-5

Rissanen, Matti. 1999. On the adverbialization of 'rather': Surfing for historical data. *Language and Computers* 26: 49–59.

Rissanen, Matti. 2008. From 'quickly' to 'fairly': On the history of *rather. English Language and Linguistics* 12: 345–359. doi:10.1017/S1360674308002657

Roberts, Ian & Roussou, Anna. 2003. *Syntactic Change: A Minimalist Approach to Grammaticalization*. Cambridge: CUP. doi:10.1017/CBO9780511486326

Schwarzschild, Roger. 2009. Measure phrases as modifiers of adjectives. *Recherches Linguistiques de Vincennes* 34: 207–228.

von Stechow, Arnim. 2009. Times as degrees. In *Quantification, Definiteness and Nominalization,* Anastasia Giannakidou & Monika Rathert (eds), 214–233. Oxford: OUP.

Stern, Gustaf. 1931. *Meaning and Change of Meaning with Special Reference to the English Language.* Göteborg: Elander.

Taylor, Anthony, Warner, Ann, Pintzuk, Susan & Beths, Frank. 2003. *The York-Toronto-Helsinki Parsed Corpus of Old English Prose.*

Thompson, Sandra A. 1972. Instead of and rather than clauses in English. *Journal of Linguistics* 8: 201–357. doi:10.1017/S0022226700003285

Wood, Johanna. 200 Germanic *so* and *such*. Paper presented at the Linguistic Cycle Worshop II, Arizona State University.

van de Velde, Frank. 2011. Left-peripheral expansion of the English NP. *English Language and Linguistics* 15: 387–415. doi:10.1017/S1360674311000086

All you need is another 'Need'

On the verbal NPI cycle in the history of German*

Łukasz Jędrzejowski
Universität Potsdam

In this chapter, I will examine the verbal NPI cycle in the history of German including three NPIs: *dürfen*, *bedürfen* and *brauchen*. In doing so, I will illustrate that *dürfen* used to function as an NPI in older stages and that it lost its NPI status due to a semantic change. The received wisdom has it that *dürfen* was then replaced by *brauchen* (cf. Bech 1951; Kolb 1964; Lenz 1996; Paul 1897). I will challenge this view and provide evidence illustrating that *dürfen* was first replaced by *bedürfen*, while *bedürfen* has being replaced by *brauchen* in the last three centuries. In my view, *bedürfen* builds a bridge between *dürfen* and *brauchen*. Remarkably, as there is no need to preserve both predicates in Modern German, *bedürfen* as NPI is about to disappear giving way to *brauchen*. In what follows, I argue that *dürfen*, *bedürfen* and *brauchen* constitute a linguistic cycle in the sense claimed by van Gelderen (2009, 2011, this volume) and illustrate, both synchronically and diachronically, that although these three predicates have a lot in common, they differ in several respects. Their differences, however, do not weaken the cycle analysis. Quite the opposite, they provide direct evidence for typical hallmarks of a linguistic cycle, whereby "toward the end of the cycle, similar events start again, but they are (slightly) different and happen at a difference pace" (van Gelderen 2011: 3). As it will turn out, these properties hold for the NPI cycle in German as well.

* I am grateful to two anonymous reviewers and Elly van Gelderen for helpful comments and suggestions which considerably improved the readability of this paper. Earlier versions of this work were presented at the workshop *Linguistic Cycles II* at the Arizona State University (April 2014) and at the workshop *Cartographier les Mondes Possibles* at the Université Paris-Sorbonne (October 2014). I thank both audiences as well as Simon Blum, Melitta Gillmann, Katrin Goldschmidt, André Meinunger, Malika Reetz and Luisa Steinhäuser for helpful discussions. Of course, all remaining errors and shortcomings are my own responsibility.

1.   Introduction

Following the seminal work by Bech (1955/57) German infinitival clauses embedded under a matrix verb can be divided into two main groups: (i) complements with the infinitival marker *zu* 'to' (= 2nd status complements) and (ii) complements without *zu* (= 1st status complements). Modern German possesses approximately 1400 infinitive-embedding predicates[1] and the majority of them selects for the 2nd status complements. However, a small group of predicates breaks rank and allows complements with and without the infinitival marker. To this group belong *lernen* 'learn', *lehren* 'teach', *helfen* 'help' and *brauchen* 'need'. The following corpus examples demonstrate this situation for *brauchen*:[2]

(1)   Du   brauchst   nicht   [$_{INF}$ zu   warten]³   [2nd status]
      you   need   NEG   to   wait.INF
      'You need not wait.'

                                    (DeReKo, *St. Galler Tagblatt*, 28/12/2011)

(2)   Die Fahrer   brauchen   nicht   [$_{INF}$ warten]   [1st status]
      the drivers need   NEG   wait.INF
      'The drivers need not wait.'

                                    (DeReKo, *Braunschweiger Zeitung*, 7/9/2012)

(2) is in contrast to what Haider (2009: 276) says about *brauchen*: "Modals select a bare infinitive, except for *brauchen* (need), which selects a *zu*-infinitive." (2) appears also to be unexpected, in particular in a written language, given what König and Gast (2012: 112) state: "*zu* is required by prescriptive grammarians but often omitted in casual speech". However, what (1) and (2) connects are two features building the core of the present paper. In both cases *brauchen* is a negative polarity item (henceforth: NPI) and expresses a modal attitude of the speaker towards the embedded proposition (but see also Section 4 for *brauchen* occurring in positive contexts). In this connection, I label *brauchen* as a modal NPI. In addition to *brauchen*, German also possesses the

---

1.   This information comes from a clause-embedding database set up at the Centre for General Linguistics (ZAS) in Berlin.

2.   The following abbreviations are used in this paper: 1/2/3 – 1st/2nd/3rd person, ACC – accusative, COND – conditional mood, COR – correlate, DAT – dative, GEN – genitive, INF – infinitive, INTP – intensifier particle, IPP – infinitivus pro participio, MP – modal particle, NEG – negation, PASS.AUX – passive auxiliary, PL – plural, PST – past tense, PTCP – participle perfect, REFL – reflexive pronoun, SG – singular.

3.   Using the label INF I do not refer to any functional projection here (but see Evers 1990). I use it for purely expository purposes indicating that one of the matrix verb arguments is realized as an infinitive clause.

archaic predicate *bedürfen*, which to my knowledge has not been dealt with in the literature so far. *Bedürfen* expresses a similar modal attitude towards what is embedded and seems to be an NPI as well when an infinitival clause is embedded (cf. 3 below). At first appearance, *bedürfen* does not really differ from *brauchen*. However, the former seems to admit only 2nd status complements:

(3)   Die Vertreter des   Bundes   haben wiederholt erklärt,
      the   delegates of.the association have   repeatedly explained

      dass die Veranstaltungsverordnung (…) dessen   nicht bedarf,
      that   the meeting.regulation   COR.GEN NEG   need

      von der Kirche   anerkannt   zu werden
      by   the Church acknowledged to PASS.AUX.INF

      'The association representatives have repeatedly declared that there is no need for the meeting regulation to be acknowledged by the Church.'
                                         (ZAS data base, DWDS, 1972)

One might argue that *zu* has to be present in (3) because the correlate *dessen* triggers its presence. However, even if the correlate *dessen* seems to be optional to some native speakers of German, meaning it can be dropped, *zu* still appears to be obligatory. One of the anonymous reviewers, a native speaker of German, judges (3') as ungrammatical:

(3')   ?Die Vertreter des Bundes haben wiederholt erklärt, dass die
      Veranstaltungsverordnung (…) nicht bedarf, von der Kirche
      anerkannt zu werden

The main objective of this chapter is to show, in particular from a diachronic perspective, that *brauchen* and *bedürfen* constitute an NPI cycle, whereby the former has been replacing the latter. In addition, I will extend the diachronic analysis to a third predicate, i.e. to *dürfen* and argue for the following NPI cycle in the history of German

(4)   *dürfen > bedürfen > brauchen*

where > indicates the replacement mechanism of one predicate by another. What is in particular interesting about these predicates is that all of them exist in Modern German, but only *brauchen* is used productively as an NPI. *Bedürfen* is about to disappear from the use as a clause-embedding predicate, whereas *dürfen* is defined as a modal verb and no longer as an NPI. I will show, though, that *dürfen* used to occur in negative environments in older stages of German and that it underwent a semantic change leading to the need of recruiting a new NPI, namely *bedürfen*.

    This chapter is organized as follows. Section 2 is concerned with *brauchen* and its modal verb properties, where I provide empirical evidence underpinning the view that *brauchen* is not only an NPI, but also a modal verb, both from a semantic and from a morphosyntactic point of view. In Section 3, I compare *brauchen* to *bedürfen* and illustrate that the latter cannot be classified as a modal verb. Instead, I define it as a modal predicate. Having pointed out the most striking similarities and differences between *dürfen*, *brauchen* and *bedürfen*, I outline the NPI cycle , describe its individual micro-cycles and show that as a whole it can be defined in terms of what van Gelderen (2009, 2011, this volume) labels as a linguistic cycle (Section 4). In this regard, I argue that there is an initial stage with a single verb expressing a modal meaning under negation. At some point another verb with a very similar meaning or even with the same meaning and NPI status is added. Their coexistence creates a period of variation, which is ultimately resolved when the original verb in its NPI use is lost. The availability of two variants in a single period leads to a functional competition, whereby one NPI drives the other out of the language (cf. Kroch 1994, 2000). Finally, Section 5 summarizes the results.

2.   *Dürfen* and *brauchen* as modal verbs

In this section I examine the predicate *brauchen* and compare its behavior with the modal verb *dürfen* 'may'. The main aim is to demonstrate that *brauchen* can be classified as a modal verb, both semantically and morphosyntactically. As argued by Reis (2001), there is a closed group of verbs in German, which can be defined as modal verbs. To this group belong the following six verbs: *dürfen* 'may', *können* 'can', *mögen* 'may', *müssen* 'must', *sollen* 'should', and *wollen* 'want'. I decided on purpose to compare *brauchen* with *dürfen*, as the latter used to function as an NPI in older stages of German as well and behaved as *brauchen* in Modern German does. In her other paper, Reis (2005) also argues for a modal verb status of *brauchen*. In what follows, I will elaborate on Reis' (2001, 2005) arguments, discuss new corpus examples corroborating her claims and, finally, provide new evidence underpinning the view that *brauchen* is to be considered a modal verb.

2.1   Semantics

In order to delineate the class of modal verbs and distinguish them properly from modal predicates (e.g. *in der Lage sein* 'to be able'), I propose the following definition of modal verbs:

(5)   A verb is a modal verb iff it is evaluated against a non-epistemic and against an epistemic modal base.[4]

---

4.   For the sake of convenience, I distinguish between epistemic and non-epistemic modalities. Whereas to the first group belong epistemic, evidential and metaphysical (in the sense claimed by Condoravdi 2001) interpretations of modal verbs, the latter group encompasses deontic, bouletic, circumstantial and teleological modalities (for more details see Kratzer 1981, 1991).

Semantically, we expect every modal verb to take two different modal bases. I refer to this property as modal polyfunctionality and consider it to be one of the main hallmarks of being a modal verb (cf. Reis 2001 and Maché 2013). *Dürfen* is not exceptional in this respect:

(6) dass sie als jüdisches Kind nicht mehr
     that she as Jewish   child NEG more

     in die Schule gehen durfte   [non-epistemic]
     in the school go.INF may.3SG.PST
     'that she as Jewish child was not allowed to go to the school any longer'
                 (DeReKo, *Niederösterreichische Nachrichten*, 24/5/2012)

(7) Es ist   aber klar, dass etwas   schief
     it be.3SG but clear that something awry

     gegangen sein   dürfte[5]   [epistemic]
     go.PTCP   be.INF may.3SG.COND
     'But it is clear that something might have gone wrong.'
                 (DeReKo, *Burgenländische Volkszeitung*, 24/1/2013)

Whereas in (6) *durfte* is evaluated against a non-epistemic modal base and it takes a deontic conversational background in the sense claimed by Kratzer (1981, 1991), *dürfte* in (7) can only be interpreted epistemically. *Brauchen* patterns with *dürfen* allowing two different modal bases. As the following corpus examples demonstrate, *brauchen*, used non-epistemically, can be narrowed down by different conversational backgrounds:

(8) Zu zahlen braucht   der Azubi   nichts   [deontic]
     to pay.INF need.3SG the apprentice NEG
     'The apprentice need not pay.'
                 (DeReKo, *Mannheimer Morgen*, 8/7/2003)

(9) Klar ist,   dass der FCW diese Saison
     clear be.3SG that the FCW this   season

     keinen Gegner   zu fürchten braucht   [circumstantial]
     NEG   opponent to fear.INF need.3SG

     'It is clear that this season the FCW need not stand in awe of an opponent.'
                 (DeReKo, *St. Galler Tagblatt*, 19/4/2013)

---

5. If *dürfen* is evaluated against an epistemic modal base, it must bear the subjunctive morphology. This peculiarity does not have to hold for the other five modals. Maché (2013: 93–105) discusses interesting differences between *dürfte* and the other modal verbs used epistemically. Notice, however, that these differences have no impact on the approach taken here, and I ignore them in this paper.

(10)   der   den Ball nur   noch ins   leere   Tor
       who   the ball only   yet   into.the empty   gate

       zu schieben brauchte   [teleological]
       to push.INF need.3SG.PST

       'who only needed push the ball into the empty net'
                                 (DeReKo, *St. Galler Tagblatt*, 2/11/1999)

What we have seen so far is that *brauchen* can express different kinds of modality associated with a non-epistemic modal base (see also Section 2.2. below and independent
data on the IPP effect, which disambiguates the reading of the embedded modal giving rise solely to a non-epistemic reading). In order to be classified as a modal verb,
brauchen should also be able to take an epistemic modal base. Such cases have been
already reported in the literature (for more examples see Ulvestad 1997):

(11)   Das braucht   nicht der Fall zu sein
       that need.3SG NEG the case to be.INF
       'That need not be the case.'   (Takahaši 1984: 21)

(12)   Das braucht   nicht zu stimmen
       that need.3SG NEG   to be.right.INF
       'That need not be correct.'   (Vater 2010: 108)

(13)   Wir haben   die Telekom längst   gebeten,
       we have.3PL the Telekom long.age ask.PTCP

       vor Ort   nachzusehen.   Das braucht   Herr   Kunz
       at place after.to.look.INF this need.3SG Mister Kunz

       gar   nicht gemerkt   zu haben,   weil   der Techniker
       INTP NEG notice.PTCP to have.INF because the technician

       dafür   nicht unbedingt   ins   Haus   muss.
       therefore NEG   necessarily   into.the house must

       'We already asked the Telekom company to check his connection long ago.
       Mister Kunz does not have necessarily noticed it because the technician
       does not need to enter the house to do so.'
                         (DeReKo, *Nürnberger Nachrichten*, 23/11/2006; cited in
                                                       Maché 2013: 294; ex. 87)

Based on (8)–(13), we can thus classify *brauchen* as a modal verb. In this connection Maché (2013: 171) states: "*brauchen* is attested with an epistemic interpretation.
However, the number is much smaller than is expected. Accordingly, *brauchen* can be
considered as a verb with a marginally developed epistemic interpretation."

    Although *dürfen* and *brauchen* both are consistent with non-epistemic as well as
with epistemic modal bases, there is one important difference between them. *Dürfen*,

as opposed to *brauchen*, has no NPI status, meaning that it can occur in positive environments, while *brauchen* cannot (but see Section 4 below).[6] If we drop the negation operators in (8) and in (10), only (6) remains felicitous (see also Vater 2010: 108):

(6′)   ^{OK}dass sie als jüdisches Kind in die Schule gehen durfte

(8′)   *Zu zahlen braucht der Azubi

As I will show in Section 4, *dürfen* used to act as an NPI in older stages of German and it was replaced by *bedürfen*.

2.2   Morphosyntax

1st status complements. One of the major hallmarks of being a modal verb refers to 1st status complements in the sense claimed by Bech (1955/57), i.e. infinitives without the infinitive marker *zu* 'to':

(14)   Wir dürfen nicht warten
       we   may   NEG   wait.INF
       'We may not wait.'   (DeReKo, *Rhein-Zeitung*, 05/01/2008)

The classical modal verbs never take 2nd status complements (but see Section 4 below on *dürfen* in older stages of German). *Brauchen* started selecting bare infinitives already in the 19th/20th century and in spoken colloquial German they are even the preferred complement type. Van der Wouden (2001: 198) states that "the use of *zu* with *brauchen* is disappearing, especially from the spoken language." According to Maché (2013), Sanders (1908) was the first to attest one of the first examples, which is traced back to 1862 and in which *brauchen* selects for a bare infinitive:

---

6.   One of the reviewers draws my attention to Hoeksema (2008) who observed that the Dutch NPI *hoeven* 'need' can occur in one positive environment, namely in restricted relatives with the quantifier *alles* 'all':

(i)   Alles   wat   we   hoeven te weten staat   in   dit   kleine boekje
      all   what   we   need   to know   stand.3SG in   this little booklet
      'All we need know is in this little booklet.'   (Hoeksema 2008: 111, ex. 3a)

(ii) is a German paraphrase of (i):

(ii)   [?]Alles, was wir (zu) wissen brauchen, steht in dem kleinen Büchlein

Judgements vary as to the acceptability of (ii). Some of my informants accept (ii), whereas others judge it as ungrammatical claiming that the sentence is only acceptable if the infinitive marker *zu* 'to' is dropped and *brauchen* replaced by *müssen* 'must'. I leave this issue open for further research.

(15) ich hätt'   mich bloß nicht einmischen brauchen
      I   have.1SG.COND REFL MP   NEG   barge.in.INF need.INF
      'It was not necessary that I barged in.'
                    (Sanders 1908:101, cited in: Maché 2013:157; ex 371)

Remarkably, from the 20th century onwards the pattern *brauchen* + bare infinitive
started occurring in formal language as well. Compare the following example from a
linguistics book:

(16) Für HV und Aux des   Konstituentensatzes brauchen
      for HV and Aux of.the   constituent.clause   need.3PL

      keinerlei Einschränkungen angegeben   werden
      NEG   restrictions   specify.PTCP PASS.AUX.INF
      'For HV and Aux of the constituent clause there is no need to   specify any
      restrictions.'   (Bierwisch 1963:134)

Although *brauchen* can still embed 2nd status complements (cf. example 1 above) and
although a quantitative analysis would reveal a more clear picture of what kind of the
infinitive is favored in individual text types, we observe a general diachronic increase
of 1st status complements. Therefore, I conclude that *brauchen* patterns with the classical modal verbs embedding bare infinitives (see also van der Wouden 2001 for differences between Dutch *hoeven*, English *need*, German *brauchen* and their infinitive
complements with regard to the opposition 1st versus 2nd status).

Principle of compactness. Another property often discussed in connection with
modals is what Haider (2009:314), in his representational analysis, calls the principle
of compactness. According to him, German (and Dutch) modal verbs form verb clusters consisting of at least two verbal elements between which no non-verbal material
may occur. Verbal clusters are monosentential, constitute one verbal domain and its
verbal members must be adjacent to each other, indicating that neither two negation
operators nor independent adverbial modifications are allowed to occur:[7]

---

7. This sharply contrasts with control CP-infinitives embedded under, for example, factive
predicates (e.g. *bereuen* 'regret'):

       (i)   während der Lehrer bereut,   [_CP nach Bonn umgezogen zu sein]
             while   the teacher regret.3SG   to   Bonn move.PTCP to be.INF
             'while the teacher regrets to have moved to Bonn.'

       (ii) während der Lehrer nicht bereut, [_CP nach Bonn nicht umgezogen zu sein]

       (iii) während der Lehrer heute bereut, [_CP gestern nach Bonn umgezogen zu sein]

See Haider (2009:272–353) and Sternefeld (2008:567–9, 625–33) for more details on control
CP-infinitives in Modern German and possible analyses.

(17) *[während er nicht darf] [sie   nach Hause begleiten]
while he NEG may   her.ACC to   home accompany.INF
Intended: 'while he may not walk her home'

(17′) ^{OK}während er sie nach Hause nicht [$_{cluster}$ [$_V$^{0}begleiten [$_V$^{0}darf]]]

(18) *[während er nicht darf] [sie nach Hause nicht begleiten]

(19) *[während er gestern durfte] [sie morgen nach Hause begleiten]

Haider (2009) analyzes verbal clusters as head-to-head adjunction structures, which are supposed to be absent in VO-languages. Reis (2001), in turn, based on Bech (1955/57) amalgamates this property (*obligatorische Kohärenz* 'obligatory coherence') with 1st status complements and uses the term strong coherence (*starke Kohärenz*) of modal verbs.[8] Regardless of how we analyze and label this property, we expect *brauchen* to adhere to these rules too. And as it turns out, *brauchen* in fact obeys the principle of compactness:[9]

(20) *[während er nicht brauchte] [sie nach Hause begleiten]

(20') ^{OK}während er sie nach Hause nicht
[$_{cluster}$ [$_V$^{0} begleiten [$_V$^{0} brauchte]]]

(21) *[während er nicht brauchte] [sie nach Hause nicht begleiten]

---

8. The strong coherence hypothesis is too strong, though. As Hinterhölzl (2006:131) shows, *wollen* 'want' breaks rank and projects biclausal structures under certain conditions. However, as Schallert (2014:249) points out, only *wollen* can behave this way. According to him, the other modal verbs appear to be degraded in biclausal contexts.

9. It is worth noticing that even if one would find examples in which *brauchen* took 2nd status complements, i.e. *zu*-infinitives, and a non-verbal intervening material occurred, they would not speak against the principle of compactness and against the analysis advocated in this paper. First, the principle of compactness holds only for predicates embedding 1st and 3rd status complements as well as for selected predicates combining with 2nd status complements (e.g. *wissen* 'know'). Second, examples with an intervening material would not be instances of sentential complements (= CPs), instantiating extraposition of the embedded clause. Instead, they would rather represent the Third Construction, i.e. an amalgamation of arguments of the matrix and the embedded clause (see den Besten & Rutten 1989 and Wöllstein-Leisten 2001). This is mainly due to the subject-to-subject raising status of modal verbs. As all modal verbs, except for the desiderative uses of *wollen* 'want' and *möchte* 'would like to', are to be treated as subject-to-subject raising verbs, both synchronically (cf. Reis 2001; Wurmbrand 1999) and diachronically (cf. Axel 2001 for Old High German, 750–1050), I analyze *brauchen* as a subject-to-subject raising verb as well, meaning that the matrix subject is base-generated in the embedded structure and then A-moved up to the higher clause (see below for more details). This approach is not novel here. Reis (2007) develops a similar analysis for the aspectual use of *versprechen* 'promise' and *drohen* 'threaten'.

(22)   *[während er gestern (nicht) brauchte]
        [sie morgen nach Hause (nicht) begleiten]

As the examples given in (20)–(22) indicate, *brauchen* must be adjacent to the verbal head it embeds and allows neither distinct verbal/negation domains nor independent temporal modifications. Malika Reetz (pers. comm.) points out to me that the situation in (20)–(22) does not change if *brauchen* selects for 2nd status complements.

IPP effect. The next property characterizing the German modal verb system is related to the IPP effect. When a modal verb is embedded under the perfect auxiliary *haben* 'have' and when it, simultaneously, takes an infinitive in the 1st status, the modal itself has to be spelled out as an infinitive (cf. Schmid 2005 and Schallert 2014 for a general overview of the IPP effect in Germanic standard languages and dialects):[10]

(23)   Es ist   ein Wunder, dass er dies so lange
        it be.3SG a   miracle that he this so long

        hat   tun   OKdürfen/*gedurft
        have.3SG   do.INF/PTCP may.INF/PTCP

        'It is a miracle that he was allowed to act this way so long.'
                              (DeReKo, *Mannheimer Morgen*, 21/9/2009)

Now, if *brauchen* is expected to behave like the classical modal verbs, it should exhibit the IPP effect. This is borne out:

(24)   Das Bundesverfassungsgericht   fällt   heute und
        the Federal.Constitutional.Court hand.down.3SG   today and

        morgen   zwei Urteile, über die   es sich die deutsche
        tomorrow   two verdicts over which   it REFL the German

---

10.   One of the anonymous reviewers points out that *dürfen* can occur as participle perfect. This is true if *dürfen* embeds no infinitive:

(i)   Und er hätte   kraft   Amtes   sogar gedurft
       and he have.3SG.COND by.virtue.of agency   even may.PTCP
       'And ex officio, he had even been allowed (to do this).'
                              (DeReKo, *Braunschweiger Zeitung*, 24/10/2011)

For the reviewer *gedurft* is possible, though not necessary, in solitary predicative use, i.e. as a full verb. Obviously this issue does not deserve further study but it is sufficient in the present to establish the distinction that I want to make here between functional and lexical verbal heads.

Einheit nie　den　Kopf hätte　　　　zerbrechen brauchen
unity　NEG　the　head　have.3SG.COND break.INF　need.INF
'Today and tomorrow, the Federal Constitutional Court will hand down two
verdicts about which they would not have had to break their heads without
the German Unity.'　　　　　(DeReKo, *Nürnberger Nachrichten*, 23/4/1991)

(24) underpins one of the observations made by Reis and Sternefeld (2004):

> Thus, limiting the domain of application to complements, the IPP phenom-
> enon is clearly tied to infinitival status in that (i) no predicate shows the IPP
> effect when taking *zu*-infinitival complements, (ii) all predicates productively
> allowing IPP take 1st status complements.　　　(Reis & Sternefeld 2004: 498)

(ii) is undoubtedly true for *dürfen*, as the example (23) demonstrates. (i), however,
is too strong,[11] as *brauchen* can take *zu*-infinitives (= 2nd status complements) and,
simultaneously, exhibit the IPP effect, both with the indicative as well as with the conditional morphology on the perfect auxiliary *haben* 'have' (see the Appendix for more
corpus examples):

(25)　In Duisburg hat　　　man an　　so etwas
　　　In Duisburg have.3SG　one about so something

　　　gar　nicht erst zu denken　　brauchen
　　　INTP NEG　first to think.INF　need.INF

　　　'In Duisburg, nobody had to think about such a thing.'
　　　　　　　　　　　　　(DeReKo, *Nürnberger Nachrichten*, 19/10/2006)

(26)　Die Fehler　　hätten　　　　niemanden zu grämen　　brauchen
　　　the mistakes have.3PL.COND NEG　　　to trouble.INF　need.INF
　　　'The mistakes would have had to trouble nobody.'
　　　　　　　　　　　　　(DeReKo, *Nürnberger Nachrichten*, 27/11/2006)

---

11. Note that (i) sharply contrasts with what we observe in Modern Dutch. Ter Beek
(2008: 39) points out that the IPP effect is optional with selected predicates taking 2nd status
complements, e.g. with *proberen* 'try':

(i)　omdat　Jan het meisje heeft geprobeerd/proberen te bellen
　　　because Jan the girl　has　try.PTCP/INF　　　to call.INF
　　　'because Jan has tried to call the girl'

However, if the verbal cluster is broken up by an argument, no IPP effect occurs, cf. Rutten
(1991: 68) for appropriate examples (but see also Haegeman & Riemsdijk 1986 for a different
situation in Flemish Dutch). Dutch possesses approx. 50 infinitive-embedding predicates
taking 2nd status complements and allowing the IPP effect, for an overview see in particular
Ponten (1973: 75) and ter Beek (2008: 37). It still remains to be investigated, especially from a
diachronic point of view, what led to these differences between Dutch and German.

The data from (24) to (26) strongly support the view that *brauchen* ought to be classified as a modal verb. First, if it takes bare infinitives and is embedded under the analytic perfect tense form, it consequently exhibits the IPP effect. Second, even if *brauchen* licenses 2nd status complements, it is not barred from being licensed in IPP contexts in line with all other modal verbs. Many speakers analyze *brauchen* as a modal verb and analogously use the IPP pattern. Of course, one can also find corpus examples as in (27), in which *brauchen* selects a *zu*-infinitive and in which it is spelled out as participle perfect:

(27)   Dafür   allerdings   hätte   er   nicht
       that.for   however   have.3SG.COND   he   NEG

       in   die   Politik   zu   gehen   gebraucht
       in   the   politics   to   go.INF   need.PTCP

       'However, he would not have had to go into politics.'
                  (DeReKo, *Süddeutsche Zeitung*, 15/12/1995)

As *brauchen* can embed 2nd status complements, (27) is expected to occur. What would appear to be more surprising, though, were cases in which *brauchen* took bare infinitives and occurred as participle perfect. I could not find any corpus examples illustrating this pattern.

Omission of the third person singular suffix. The classical modal verbs have been addressed in the literature in terms of their morphological make-up. They represent the class of preterite-present verbs, indicating that they lack the 1st and 3rd person singular suffixes in the present tense and that they display a vowel alternation in the stem when spelled out in the present and the past tense (for a critical overview see Maché 2013: 12–14). Even if there is no agreement in the literature on whether *brauchen* belongs to the strong or to the weak verb class (cf. Scaffidi-Abbate 1973), morphologically *brauchen* patterns with *dürfen* allowing the omission of the present tense suffix *-t* in the 3rd person singular:

Table 1. Present Tense paradigms of *dürfen* and *brauchen*

		dürfen	*brauchen*
Singular	1st person	*darf* – ø	*brauch* – (e)
	2nd person	*darf* – st	*brauch* – st
	3rd person	*darf* – ø	*brauch* – t/ø
Plural	1st person	*dürf* – en	*brauch* – en
	2nd person	*dürf* – t	*brauch* – t
	3rd person	*dürf* – en	*brauch* – en

The following corpus examples undergird this similarity:

(28) Doch   vor   Gott brauch   man sich   nicht
     however ahead God need.3SG one   REFL NEG

     zu verbergen oder zu verstellen
     to hide.INF   or   to dissimulate.INF

     'However, there is no need to hide away or to dissimulate in the eyes of God.'
                                        (DeReKo, *Mannheimer Morgen*, 13/2/2013)

(29) Sie brauch   nicht zu arbeiten
     she need.3SG NEG to work.INF
     'She need not work.'   (DeReKo, *Rhein-Zeitung*, 20/7/2002)

Van der Wouden (2001: 198–9) makes a similar observation: "German *brauchen* appears to be following the English example, so to speak, in assimilating to the other modal verbs by optionally dropping the third person singular *t*" (for a different view see Maitz & Tronka 2009).

Absence of the covert subject PRO. According to Haider (2009: 316) monoclausal infinitival constructions lack a covert subject, PRO (property h in his account). This is in accordance with Wurmbrand (1999) and Axel (2001), who claim the same for Modern German and Old High German, respectively, and who show that modal verbs are subject-to-subject raising verbs (see also Footnote 9). Subject-to-subject raising verbs do not assign a theta-role to their subjects and can be identified, among others, by embedding weather predicates, e.g. *regnen* 'rain' (see Colomo 2011: 27 for a recent overview of diagnostic tests in German). Both *dürfen* and *brauchen* allow embedding of *regnen*:

(30) Es$_i$ hätte   weniger t$_i$ regnen   dürfen
     it   have.3SG.COND less   rain.INF may.INF
     'It could have rained less.'
                                   (DeReKo, *Braunschweiger Zeitung*, 5/9/2008)

(31) Es$_i$ braucht nicht t$_i$ zu regnen
     it   need.3SG NEG   to rain.INF
     'It need not rain.'   (Ulvestad 1997: 228)

What it means is that *es*, both in (30) and in (31), is base-generated as an argument of *regnen*, not of *dürfen* or *brauchen*; and then it A-moves up to the higher clause leaving a trace in the embedded structure. In other words, *brauchen* is to be classified as a subject-to-subject raising verb.[12]

---

12. Maché & Abraham (2011: 260) observe that in selected dialects of German *brauchen* occurs as a subject-to-object raising predicate imposing restrictions on the embedded verbal

Extraction of the main verb. Haider (2009: 320–1) also highlights another property typical of verbal clusters and absent in CP control infinitives (property o in his analysis). Compare the following examples (taken from Haider 2009):

(32) *Mitzuteilen$_i$ hat   er versucht [ihr   etwas   t$_i$]$_{CP}$
       to.tell.INF   have.3SG he try.PTCP her.DAT something
       'To tell her something, he has tried.'

(33) Ihr$_i$ hat er versucht [PRO t$_i$ etwas mitzuteilen]$_{CP}$

(34) Mitzuteilen$_i$ hat$_j$ er ihr etwas [t$_i$ versucht t$_j$]$_{VC}$

(35) Mitteilen$_i$ wird$_j$ er ihr   etwas   [t$_i$ müssen   t$_j$]$_{VC}$
       to.tell.INF will.3SG he her.DAT something   must.INF
       'Tell her something, he will have to.'

Versuchen 'try' can embed two kinds of complements: sentential complements (= CPs) and verbal clusters (= VPs). Structurally, they differ in one important respect. Whereas the main verb of a CP cannot be extracted out of the clause, e.g. by topicalization, as shown in (32), this operation is possible in verbal clusters building no potential syntactic barriers blocking the movement. (34) and (35) are a case in point. As (33) demonstrates, topicalization is possible for non-verbal constituents, but not for the main verb itself. Haider (2009) provides evidence for this argument using the subject control predicate *versuchen* and the modal verb *müssen*. If German modal verbs are taken to build a homogenous group, *dürfen* and *brauchen* ought to pattern with *müssen*. The following corpus examples confirm this:

(36) Wünschen$_i$ wird$_j$ man sich noch etwas   [t$_i$ dürfen   t$_j$]$_{VC}$
       wish.INF   will.3SG one REFL yet something   may.INF
       'One will be allowed to wish himself something else.'
                                              (DeReKo, *Die Presse*, 12/12/2000)

(37) Nach oben gehen$_i$ hätte$_j$ er auch nicht [t$_i$ brauchen t$_j$]$_{VC}$
       to   up   go.INF   have.3SG.COND he also NEG   need.INF
       'He wouldn't have had to go upstairs.'
                                              (DeReKo, *Die Südostschweiz*, 21/1/2010)

---

head. According to them, the raised subject must stem from a stative locative verb such as *liegen* 'lie', *sitzen* 'sit' or *stehen* 'stand'. (i) illustrate this usage from Viennese:

(i) I brauch di   da   jetzt net deppat umanand sitz
     I need   you.ACC there now NEG stupid around sit.INF
     'It doesn't help me if you sit around here now.'

It seems to me that *brauchen* in (i) is also used as an NPI. However, space considerations prevent me from being able to provide a detailed analysis of *brauchen* employed in (i) and I ignore it here.

Epistemic modality under temporality. The last property to be discussed in this section concerns the issue of how different kinds of modalities interact with temporality. Cross-linguistically, modal verbs are assumed to occupy two distinct syntactic positions. If they receive a non-epistemic interpretation, they are interpreted as Mod-heads merging below TP. If, on the other hand, modal verbs are used as epistemic or evidential operators, they outscope TP:

(38) $Mod_{evidential}P > Mod_{epistemic}P > TP > Mod_{non\text{-}epistemic}P > VP$

(38) is in accordance with the rigid hierarchy of functional projections proposed in Cinque (1999, 2006) and advocated in Butler (2004: 138–175, 2006). I illustrate the syntactic relationships between TP and two distinct modal flavors of modal verbs taking, again, *dürfen* as an example:

(39)   Er   hat   abwaschen   dürfen   T(Past) > Mod
        he   have.3SG   do.the.dishes.INF may.INF
        'He was allowed to do the dishes.'

(40)   Er   wird   abwaschen   dürfen   T(Future) > Mod
        he   will.3SG   do.the.dishes.INF may.INF
        'He will be allowed to do the dishes.'

(41)   Er   dürfte   abgewaschen   haben   Mod > T(Past)
        he   might.3SG   do.the.dishes.PTCP have.INF
        'He might have done the dishes.'

From (39)–(41) we can infer that syntactically neither the past perfect auxiliary *haben* 'have' nor the future auxiliary *werden* 'will' can outscope epistemic modality. If they co-occur with modal verbs, they disambiguate their interpretation and only a non-epistemic interpretation is available. If a modal verb takes an epistemic modal base, as in (41), the speech act time and the epistemic evaluation time collapse, even if the event time itself is rooted in the past. Accordingly, the embedded proposition falls under scope of epistemic modality (see also Hacquard 2006, 2010, who provides semantic arguments for the hierarchy given in 38). Given this line of reasoning, if *brauchen* is supposed to be considered a modal verb, it is expected to take an epistemic modal base and to behave as *dürfte* in (41) does. And, again, this prediction is borne out, compare (42):

(42)   Der Täter   braucht   nicht am   Tatort   gewesen zu sein
        the culprit need.3SG   NEG at.the crime.scene be.PTCP to be.INF
        'It wasn't necessarily the case that the culprit was present at the crime scene.'
                                                    (André Meinunger, pers. comm.)

The epistemic evaluation time outscopes the event time. This can be deduced from the fact that in (42) *brauchen* bears the present tense morphology, although the embedded proposition is rooted in the past.

2.3   Interim summary

So far we have seen that *brauchen* patterns with the six classical modal verbs in many respects. Table 2 gives an overview of the selected modal verbs properties examined in the preceding section:

Table 2. *Brauchen* and its modal verb properties

		Modal verbs	*Brauchen*
1.	Modal polyfunctionality	✓	✓
2.	1st status complements (= bare infinitives)	✓	✓
3.	Principle of compactness	✓	✓
4.	Single verbal domain	✓	✓
5.	Single negation domain	✓	✓
6.	IPP effect	✓	✓
7.	Omission of the 3rd person singular suffix *-t*	✓	✓
8.	Absence of the covert subject PRO	✓	✓
9.	Extraction of the main verb	✓	✓
10.	Epistemic modality > temporality	✓	✓

As a lexical V-head *brauchen* also selects for DP complements marked for the Accusative case. In this case *brauchen* is a transitive V-head:

(43)   Wir brauchen [$_{DP}$ deine Hilfe]$_{ACC}$
       we   need.1PL   your help
       'We need you help.'   (DeReKo, *Braunschweiger Zeitung*, 6/6/2006)

Lenz (1996) points out that in impersonal constructions *brauchen* can still embed DP complements marked for the Genitive case, as (44) illustrates:

(44)   Es braucht [$_{DP}$ keiner weiterer Erklärungen]$_{GEN}$ mehr
       it need.3SG   NEG   further   explanations   more
       'No further explanations are required.'   (Lenz 1996: 396; ex. 9)

One of the anonymous reviewers notes that *brauchen* allows DPs only with a dummy subject that is not theta-marked. Notice, however, that *brauchen* is not an NPI when DP complements are embedded. In these cases, it can also occur in positive contexts (cf. 43 above). I therefore assume three different lexical entries for *brauchen*

$$brauchen1 + DP \rightarrow [[brauchen]] = \lambda x \lambda y[\text{brauchen'}(x,y)]$$
$$brauchen2 + INF \rightarrow [[brauchen]]^{w,f} = \lambda q_{\langle st \rangle}.w' \in \cap f_{\text{NON-EPIST}}(w): q(w') = 1$$
$$brauchen3 + INF \rightarrow [[brauchen]]^{w,f} = \lambda q_{\langle st \rangle}.w' \in \cap f_{\text{EPIST}}(w): q(w') = 1$$

occupying three different structural positions:

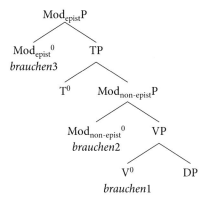

Figure 1. Merge positions of *brauchen* in Modern German

When used as a transitive lexical head, *brauchen* merges within the VP phrase. If it combines with an infinitive, both in the 1st and 2nd status, it behaves like a modal verb and can merge below as well above the classical T-node.[13] The lower position always results in a non-epistemic interpretation. *Dürfen*, in turn, deviates from *brauchen* in one important respect. It cannot select for DP complements:[14]

---

13.   There exist different empirical reasons to abandon the TP/IP layer in the clause structure of Modern German. Most of them come from representational analyses collected in Haider (2009: 45–85) and in Sternefeld (2008: 507–558).

14.   Of course, in older stages of German *dürfen* could select DP complements, as today's *bedürfen* and *brauchen* can, for a considerable amount of Old High German examples see Graff & Massmann 1840: 205 (see also Fritz 1997: 10 and Maché 2013: 93–5). One of the reviewers asks w.r.t. (45) and (46) how one can analyze the example given in (i):

    (i)   Ich   darf   das/es   nicht
          I   may.3sg   that/it   NEG
          'I'm not allowed to do that'

Note that neither *das* nor *es* can be analyzed as canonical DP complements. First, they cannot be replaced by a full lexical DP. Second, they refer to an elided infinitival phrase, meaning that *dürfen* still quantifies over a set of events and not over a set of objects.

(45)   *Wir dürfen [$_{DP}$ deine Hilfe]$_{ACC}$

(46)   *Es darf [$_{DP}$ keiner weiteren Erklärungen]$_{GEN}$ mehr

Hence, for *dürfen* two lemmas can be postulated:

$$dürfen1 + INF \rightarrow [[dürfen]]^{w,f} = \lambda q_{\langle st \rangle}.w' \in \cap f_{NON\text{-}EPIST}(w): q(w') = 1$$
$$dürfte2 + INF \rightarrow [[dürfte]]^{w,f} = \lambda q_{\langle st \rangle}.w' \in \cap f_{EPIST}(w): q(w') = 1$$

Their syntactic positions do not differ from those of *brauchen2* and *brauchen3*. This being said, we can conclude that *dürfen* and *brauchen* belong to the same verb group representing the class of modal verbs. Johan van der Auwera (pers. comm.) raises the question if the arguments favoring the modal verb status of *brauchen* are strong enough in order to be allowed to use the term modal verb. In other words, we can analyze the above facts the other way round. For instance, embedding of 2nd status complements can be deemed to be one of the violations against the modal verb status. In my view, there are several arguments to reject such an approach though. First, among approximately 1400 infinitve-embedding predicates in Modern German only *brauchen* patterns with the other modal verbs in so many respects. I am not aware of any matrix predicate – without having undergone a semantic change – taking first 1st status complements and switching then to 2nd status complements over time. Of course, the cases in which *zu* 'to' as an infinitival marker has not been grammaticalized yet have to be excluded. None of the modal verbs is losing the possibility to express epistemic modality or starts attaching the third person singular suffix *-t* to the stem. What we basically observe is an accommodation of *brauchen*, not of the modal verbs. Second, the classical modal verbs, as opposed to *brauchen*, are analyzed as preterite-present verbs. Note that *wissen* 'know', another preterite-present verb, never became a modal verb although it can express a non-epistemic modality:

(47)   Die Feuerwehr   weiß   zu feiern
       the fire.department know.3sg to celebrate
       'The fire department can celebrate (properly).'
                          (DeReKo, *Niederösterreichische Nachrichten*, 12/5/2010)

As reported by Speyer (2015:14, Footnote 10), already in Middle High German (1050–1350) we can find cases "in which *wissen* is construed as a control verb like French *savoir*: *Il sais faire quelque chose* – 'he is able to do something'". Note, however, that although *wissen* as infinitive-embedding predicate is older than *brauchen* and although it does not merge with the third person singular suffix *-t*, it did not develop into a modal verb, as *brauchen* did. *Wissen* can neither embed 1st status complements, nor can it express epistemic modality (for more arguments see Jędrzejowski 2015a: Chap. 5):

(48) *Er weiß   krank (zu) sein
      he know.3sg ill   (to) be.inf
      Intended: 'He might be ill.'

Now the question arises if *bedürfen* expressing a similar modality and behaving like *brauchen* (cf. 3 above) can be analyzed as a modal verb and as an NPI, too. As the following section will show, there is no affirmative answer to this question.

3. *Bedürfen* as a modal predicate

In this section, I shall focus on *bedürfen* and examine its main semantic as well as morphosyntactic properties. As it will turn out, *bedürfen* can encode a non-epistemic modality, but its behavior deviates in many respects from that of *brauchen*, leading to the conclusion that it cannot be considered a modal verb.

3.1 Semantics

If *bedürfen* is assumed to act as a modal verb, it necessarily has to be evaluated against a non-epistemic and against an epistemic modal base. As for the former, we have already seen in (3) that *bedürfen* can take a non-epistemic modal base. The context in which (3) occurs narrows down *bedürfen*'s reading giving rise to a teleological modality interpretation, i.e. referring to what is possible or necessary for achieving a particular goal. Since *bedürfen* as infinitive-embedding predicate is supposed to be old-fashioned in Modern German and since this pattern is about to disappear, it is a hard task to find appropriate examples. It is reasonable to recall that *bedürfen* constitutes a bridge between *dürfen* and *brauchen* in the NPI cycle. Accordingly, *bedürfen* is expected to be perceived as an old-fashioned predicate. Since *brauchen* is used as a dominant NPI in Modern German, *bedürfen* fades into the background. Therefore, it is necessary to scrutinize examples from older stages of German. (49) and (50) are from the 19th century:

(49) doch zu trinken   bedurfte   ich nicht   [bouletic]
      though to drink.inf need.1sg.pst I   neg
      'Though, I did not have do drink.'
                                            (GOE, *Aus meinem Leben. Dichtung und Werke*, 1809–13)

(50) Wiederum den Kaufmann (…) zu beobachten,
      again   the trader   to observe.inf

      bedarf   die Regierung   nicht   [circumstantial]
      need.3sg the government neg
      'It is not necessary for the government to observe the trader again.'
                                            (HK5, J. G. Fichte, 1800, *Der geschlossene Handelsstaat*)

Contrary to *brauchen*, *bedürfen* occurs already in Middle High German (1050–1350) as a modal NPI. (51) illustrates its use with a circumstantial conversational background:

(51)   In   bedorft   da   nicht belangen   [circumstantial]
        him.ACC need.3SG.PST there NEG care.INF
        'He did not have to care (about it).'
                                              (MBD, *Garel von dem bluenden Tal*, line 20902)

Now, the question immediately arises if *bedürfen* can also take an epistemic modal base. As it turns out, it cannot. First, I have examined over 800 examples from older stages of German containing *bedürfen* used as an NPI and embedding an infinitive, be it in the 1st or in the 2nd status. None of these examples can be interpreted epistemically. Second, if epistemic modality encoded by modal verbs is supposed to be a young development in the history of German and if some speakers can still use *bedürfen* with non-finite complements (cf. 3), we expect epistemic modality readings to occur. Note, however, that this is not the case, as *bedürfen* cannot replace *brauchen* when the latter quantifies epistemically over the embedded proposition:

(52)   *Der Täter bedarf nicht am Tatort gewesen zu sein

(53)   *Das bedarf nicht zu stimmen

(54)   *Das bedarf Herr Kunz gar nicht gemerkt zu haben, weil der Techniker
        dafür nicht unbedingt ins Haus muss

This is mainly due to the fact that *bedürfen* never grammaticalized into an epistemic quantifier, which, in turn, would correspond to the meaning of *brauchen3*. Instead, it started being replaced by *brauchen*. When *brauchen* began behaving as a modal NPI, there was no need to preserve both predicates as NPIs and the older one, *bedürfen*, lost its NPI status. Following this line of reasoning, *bedürfen* never got a chance to develop further into an epistemic quantifier. This also accounts for why native speakers of German no longer use *bedürfen* as an NPI when an infinitive is embedded:

(55)   Um   ein Gesamtresümee (…) zu ziehen,
        in.order a   total.summary   to draw.INF
        bedarf   es den groben Blick auf die zwei (…)
        need.3SG it the rough look on the two
        Schwerpunkte dieser Arbeit zu werfen
        areas   of.this work   to throw.INF
        'In order to conclude, one needs to take a look at the two focus areas of this
        work.'   (AK, p. 28)

Let us now contrast (3) with (55). In both cases *bedürfen* selects for a 2nd status complement. However, they differ in one important respect: Whereas in (3) it occurs in a negative context, no such environment is to be observed in (55). If *brauchen* is an NPI in Modern German, one should be allowed to use it in (3), but not in (55). Remarkably, our assumptions are borne out:

(3″) Die Vertreter des Bundes haben wiederholt erklärt, dass die Veranstaltungs-verordnung von der Kirche nicht anerkannt zu werden braucht

(55′) *Um ein Gesamtresümee zu ziehen, braucht es den groben Blick auf die zwei Schwerpunkte dieser Arbeit zu werfen

However, one diachronic problem arises in this context. Maché (2013: 180) observes that "*brauchen* had already developed the full range of functions by the end of the 18th century." If we assume this to be true, we expect *bedürfen* to begin occurring in positive environments much earlier than in the 21st century (cf. 55). Again, we find empirical evidence supporting this view. (56) stems from the 19th century:

(56) Sie, Pauline, bedürfen es, an ein starkes, muthiges
      you Pauline need.3PL it at a strong brave

      Herz   sich   zu   schließen
      heart REFL   to   form.a.friendship.INF

      'You, Pauline, need to form a friendship with a strong and brave heart.'
      (HK4, Louise Otto, 1846, *Schloß und Fabrik*)

In conclusion, from the semantic point of view *bedürfen* cannot be classified as a modal verb.[15] It does not meet the polyfunctionality criterion. Additionally, it does not have to occur in negative environments in Modern German when an infinitive clause is embedded.

3.2 Morphosyntax

1st status complements. Due to the fact that *bedürfen* as an infinitive-embedding predi-cate is not often employed in Modern German as *brauchen* is, it is difficult to figure out whether the infinitival marker *zu* must be present or not (Melitta Gillmann, pers. comm.). But in older examples from the 19th century its presence seems to be indis-pensable. (3) is a case for an embedded passive infinitive, while (49) illustrates that the dependent main verb *trinken* 'drink' can be topicalized. In both cases *zu* occurs. *Zu* is also licensed in active as well as in *bekommen* passive infinitives, as (57) and (58) demonstrate, respectively:

---

15. This contrasts with what Brandner (2006: 247) says about *bedürfen*: "On the other hand, Ebert (1976) cites examples from eNHG where *zu*–marking can be found even in the comple-ments of modal verbs".

(57)   ich bedarf   jetzt nichts zu wissen
       I   need.1SG now   NEG   to know.INF
       'I need not know anything.'
           (HK4, Therese Huber, 1829, *Drei Abschnitte im Leben eines guten Weibes*)

(58)   Ich bedarf   nur   eine beantwortet   zu erhalten
       I   need.1SG only one   answer.PTCP   to get.INF
       'You need to answer only one (question).'
                                      (HK4, Therese Huber, 1822, *Ellen Percy*)

Interestingly enough, I could find no examples younger than from 1650, in which *bedürfen* is used as an NPI taking 1st status complements. We observe a similar situation even in Early New High German (1350–1700). Ebert (1976) provides the following example:

(59)   Maria bedorfft   nit in Tempel zegon
       Maria need.3SG.PST   NEG in temple to.go.INF
       'Maria did not have to go to the temple.'   (Ebert 1976: 100)

His examples clearly demonstrate that 2nd status complements outnumber their 1st status counterparts. This appears to be unexpected to some extent. As Jędrzejowski (2015b) shows, verbal functional heads encoding aspectuality, modality or temporality could embed 1st status complements even in the 19th century. (60), for example, is a case in point:

(60)   Die Leitung   solcher Arbeiten haben   französische
       the leadership of.such works   have.3PL French

       Genieoffiziere, wodurch   dieselben weit rascher gefördert
       genius.officers by.what   the.same   far   quicker sponsor.PTCP

       werden,   als   sonst (…) hier geschehen   pflegt
       PASS.AUX.INF   than usually   here happen.INF   use.3SG

       'French genius officers are leading such works, whereby they are sponsored quicker than it usually happens.'
                        (KHZ, *Mainzer Journal*, 13/10/1849; cited in Jędrzejowski 2015b)

Pflegen is an aspectual head requiring a habitual operator in the sense claimed by Boneh and Doron (2012) binding the event variable. In Modern German it is consistent only with 2nd status complements. *Bedürfen*'s 1st status complements occur very early. Most of them are to be traced back to Middle High German, compare (51) above and (61):

(61)   dú   bedarf   nit verre gan
       you need.2SG NEG far   go.INF
       'You need not go far.'
                        (M. von Magdeburg, 1210–1282, *Das Fließende Licht der Gottheit*)

It is worth mentioning, however, that the absence of *zu* as infinitive marker in (51) and (61) might be due to its late grammaticalization (cf. Abraham 2004 or Speyer 2015 for more details). What all this boils down to is that there is no empirical evidence showing that *bedürfen* can embed 1st as well as 2nd status complements in the way, as *brauchen* in Modern German can.

Principle of compactness. (3) already illustrates that the principle of compactness does not hold for *bedürfen*. The non-verbal material intervenes between verbal heads splitting the clause into, potentially, two verbal domains. To be more precise, the PP *von der Kirche* 'by the Church' intervenes between the matrix predicate *bedürfen* and the embedded passive infinitive *anerkannt zu werden* 'to be acknowledged.' If we assume *bedürfen*, contrary to *brauchen*, to allow two independent verbal domains, we should also be able to modify the matrix clause and the embedded clause by two separate negation operators or by distinct temporal adverbials. Notice, however, that this is not possible:

(62)   *Die Vertreter des Bundes haben wiederholt erklärt, dass die
        Veranstaltungsverordnung (…) dessen nicht bedarf, von der Kirche
        nicht anerkannt zu werden

(63)   *Die Vertreter des Bundes haben wiederholt erklärt, dass die
        Veranstaltungsverordnung (…) gestern dessen nicht bedurfte,
        (heute) von der Kirche (heute) anerkannt zu werden

We can deduce from (62) and (63) that *bedürfen* admits only one verbal domain. As argued by Haider (2009: 278), "if we destroy compactness, we ascertain that a given variant is the non-clustering variant." What we have seen in Section 2.2 is that *brauchen* has to cluster; otherwise we end up with ungrammatical sentences. Hence, *bedürfen* and *brauchen* behave differently. Having said that, however, we have to provide an appropriate analysis for (3). Theoretically, we can assume that the finite matrix verb *bedarf* has been inverted, meaning it does not belong to the verbal cluster. This scenario would explain the occurrence of the PP *von der Kirche* between the matrix verbal head *bedarf* and the left edge of the cluster *anerkannt zu werden*. Another possibility would be to analyze the whole infinitive complement as a control CP-complement. There are two strong arguments, though, that speak against such an analysis. First, *bedürfen* is a subject-to-subject raising verb (see below), which do not extrapose their infinitival complements by definition. Second, the infinitive clause cannot be of the CP-size, as it appears to be resistant to the CP-hood tests: It admits neither two separate negation domains nor two independent adverbial modifications. Hence, this scenario must be ruled out. There are two other options of how we can analyze (3), one of which seems to me to be the most promising solution. In principle, we can assume the entire embedded infinitive to be an extraposed VP complement.

But this view cannot be upheld. Similar to the CP analysis, we have to reject this possibility due to the fact that CPs can be extraposed while VPs cannot (cf. Sternefeld 2008:418). What remains is a Third Construction analysis. Two arguments support this view. First, if *bedürfen* is believed to have a subject-to-subject raising verb status, then it assigns no thematic role to its subject, indicating that subjects are base generated in the embedded structure and A-move to the higher clause. What emerges is an amalgamation of arguments of the matrix and the embedded clause (= Third Construction). Though this is not surprising, as the most modal verbs are subject-to-subject raising verbs. What appears to be more supportive for the Third Construction analysis is another property. (3) contains the correlate *dessen* marked for the Genitive case and cataphorically referring to the follow-up clause. I repeat it here for the sake of convenience:

(3) Die Vertreter des Bundes haben wiederholt erklärt,
     the delegates of.the association have repeatedly explained

dass die Veranstaltungsverordnung (…) [dessen]$_i$ nicht
that the meeting.regulation COR.GEN NEG

bedarf, [von der Kirche anerkannt zu werden]$_i$
need.3SG by the Church acknowledged to PASS.AUX.INF

'The association representatives have repeatedly declared that there is no need for the meeting regulation to be acknowledged by the Church.'

The correlate is licensed by the matrix predicate *bedürfen*. Being related to the infinitival clause, i.e. to one of the matrix predicate arguments, leads again to an amalgamation of arguments. Thus, the Third Construction analysis seems to describe the structure given in (3) at best. But as appealing as it might be, it is crucial to keep in mind that *bedürfen* does not have to obey the principle of compactness, as *brauchen* does.

IPP effect. I was not able to find any cases in the history of German, in which *bedürfen* would exhibit the IPP effect being typical of the classical modal verbs. But it does not automatically mean that *bedürfen* was barred in such environments. As Maché and Abraham (2011:258; ex. 39) show, some matrix predicates could exhibit the IPP effect in the history of German only occasionally. Old-fashioned *dünken* 'seem' is one of them, compare (64) from Early New High German (see Demske 2008 for *dünken*'s distribution in Old High German):

(64) den sie hetten jn
      because they have.3PL.COND them.DAT

rechtschaffene Leut duencken seyn
righteous people seem.INF be.INF

'because they had seemed to them to be righteous people'
                                    (Ulrich Schmid, 1567, *Neuwe Welt*, page 20)

Hinterhölzl (2009) finds a similar example with the habitual predicate *pflegen* embedding an infinitive in the 2nd status:

(65) unbesonnen Urteil   hab   ich jederzeit zu verachten pflegen
      imprudent   judgement have.1sg I   always   to despise.inf use.inf
      'I always used to despise imprudent judgements.'
                            (Martin Opitz, *Poemata* 8; cited in Hinterhölzl 2009: 203)

In other words, it would not be surprising if one came across an appropriate example. But on the other hand, it is unlikely to find many examples resembling the structure given in (64) or in (65). First, in contrast to Dutch German does not really tolerate the IPP effect with 2nd status complements (see Footnote 11). Only *brauchen* is allowed to occur. Other infinitive-embedding predicates are barred from IPP environments. Second, as we have seen above *bedürfen* embeds 1st status complements neither in New High German (1700–1900) nor in Modern German (1900 –). What remains are Middle High German (1050–1350) and Early New High German (1350–1700). However, I have analyzed all occurrences of *bedürfen* in BFK, an Early New High German corpus, and found no proper IPP examples. More diachronic corpus studies would probably reveal a clearer picture of whether or not *bedürfen* used to occur as *Ersatzinfinitiv*.

Omission of the third person singular suffix. Since *bedürfen* inherited the morphological make-up from its ancestor *dürfen*, it does not merge with the third person singular suffix *-t*, meaning it cannot be observed whether the suffix can be omitted or not.

Absence of the covert subject PRO. Based on the fact that *brauchen* can embed weather predicates, we have argued for a subject-to-subject raising verb analysis. I could not find similar examples with *bedürfen*. But we do have evidence for its subject-to-subject raising status. As pointed out above, *bedürfen* can license all kinds of infinitives: active infinitive (57), passive infinitive (3) and *bekommen* passive infinitive (58). In other words, it does not seem to impose any selectional restrictions on its subject. In addition, the example given in (51) supports our analysis:

(51) [In]$_i$ bedorft da nicht t$_i$ belangen

Bedürfen merges with the embedded structure *jemanden belangen* 'to care'. *Belangen*, in turn, assigns an [ACC]value to its internal argument, *in* 'him' in (51). However, *in* does not merge within the middle field. It is base generated in the embedded structure and A-moves to the matrix [Spec, CP]. It ends up occupying the classical prefield position. In this context, *bedürfen* patterns with *brauchen*. This argument has no persuasive power, though, when analyzed on its own. Other predicates like *scheinen* 'seem' and *versprechen* 'promise' are subject-to-subject raising verbs as well, but they are far away from being treated as modal verbs.

Extraction of the main verb. In order to exclude the CP-status of infinitives embedded under *bedürfen*, we should be able to build a verbal cluster. I take (49) – repeated here as (66) for convenience – to be our point of departure

(66)   doch zu trinken bedurfte ich nicht

and modify it slightly to acquire a verbal cluster:

(66′)   zumal ich nicht [zu trinken bedurft habe]$_{VC}$

We can now extract the main verb out of the embedded infinitive:

(66″)   doch   zu trinken$_i$ habe$_j$ ich nicht   [t$_i$ bedurft   t$_j$]$_{VC}$
         though   to drink.INF   have.1SG   I   NEG   need.PTCP
         'Though, I did not have do drink.'

At first sight, *bedürfen* behaves as the classical modal verbs do. However, it ought to be kept in mind that this property is not decisive here. It is tightly linked with the other properties characterizing the class of modal verbs. This is mainly due to the fact that other modal predicates like *wissen* 'know' allows extraction of the main infinitive as well (since not all native speakers of German accept (67'), I put a question mark in front of it):

(67)   der   mich   und meine   Arbeit   [zu schätzen
        who   me.ACC   and   my   job   to   appreciate.INF

        gewusst   hat]$_{VC}$
        know.PTCP   have.3SG   (DeReKo, *Burgenländische Volkszeitung*, 17/9/2008)

(67')   ?zu schätzen$_i$ hat$_j$ er mich und meine Arbeit [t$_i$ gewusst t$_j$]

Hence, it is not surprising that *bedürfen* as modal predicate permits topicalization of the dependent infinitive.

Epistemic modality under temporality. Since *bedürfen*, as opposed to *brauchen*, cannot take an epistemic modal base, this criterion is not suited to check its modal verb status.

3.3   Interim summary

Based on what we have observed in this section, we can conclude that *bedürfen* is not a modal verb. Table 3 gives an overview of to what extent *bedürfen* is different from modal verbs:

Table 3. Modal verbs, *bedürfen* and their properties

		Modal verbs	*Bedürfen*
1.	Modal polyfunctionality	✓	–
2.	1st status complements	✓	–

(Continued)

Table 3. (Continued)

		Modal verbs	*Bedürfen*
3.	Principle of compactness	✓	–
4.	Single verbal domain	✓	–/✓
5.	Single negation domain	✓	✓
6.	IPP effect	✓	not attested
7.	Omission of the 3rd person singular suffix -*t*	✓	inherited from *dürfen*
8.	Absence of the covert subject PRO	✓	✓
9.	Extraction of the main verb	✓	✓
10.	Epistemic modality > temporality	✓	does not apply

In my view *bedürfen* is a modal predicate. Similar to modal verbs it can take a non-epistemic modal base, but contrary to them it is not capable of expressing epistemic modality. This difference makes *bedürfen* belong to the class of modal predicates, i.e. predicates barred from epistemic contexts. To this group also belong *wissen* 'know', *in der Lage sein* 'be able', *vermögen* 'be able', *im Stande sein* 'be capable of', etc. What *brauchen* and *bedürfen* connects, though, are DP complements marked for the Genitive and the Accusative case:

(68) Allerdings bedarf es dazu [$_{DP}$ einer Wetterbesserung]$_{GEN}$
      however need.3SG it to.this a weather.improvement
      'However, a weather improvement is needed for this.'
                                    (DeReKo, *Mannheimer Morgen*, 6/4/2013)

(69) [$_{DP}$ Viele Vorbereitungen]$_{ACC}$ bedarf eine solche Produktion
      many preparations need.3SG a such production
      'Many arrangements are required for such a fabrication.'
                                    (DeReKo, *RheinZeitung*, 4/8/1998)

In this regard, they do not quantify over a set of events, as modal verbs do, but over a set of objects, meaning they are not modals. As (68) and (69) also show, *bedürfen* is not an NPI when a DP complement occurs. Keeping all these facts in mind, we are forced to postulate two lexical entries for *bedürfen*:

$$\textit{bedürfen}1 + \text{DP} \rightarrow [[\textit{bedürfen}]] = \lambda x \lambda y [\text{bedürfen'}(x,y)]$$
$$\textit{bedürfen}2 + \text{INF} \rightarrow [[\textit{bedürfen}]]^{w,f} = \lambda q_{\langle st \rangle}.w' \in \cap f_{\text{NON-EPIST}}(w): q(w') = 1$$

Both of them merge below the T-node:

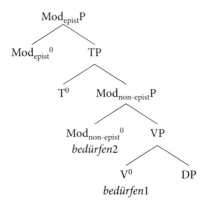

Figure 2. Merge positions of *bedürfen* in German

*Bedürfen*1 is a lexical V-head favoring Genitive DP complements. *Bedürfen*2, in turn, is a modal predicate. Its interpretation can be narrowed down by different conversational backgrounds associated with a non-epistemic modal base. In the next section, I will outline the modal NPI cycle including *dürfen*, *bedürfen* and *brauchen* and show how they are related diachronically.

4. The verbal NPI cycle

Having described the most important semantic as well as morphosyntactic properties of *dürfen*, *brauchen* and *bedürfen* in (Modern) German, one more general question remains to be addressed: To what extent are these three predicates related to each other from a diachronic point of view? In order to elaborate on this issue, I divide the German language into the following historical periods and adopt the notion of linguistic cycles, recently advocated in the generative tradition by van Gelderen (2009, 2011, this volume). In this connection, I follow van Gelderen (2009:2) and define a linguistic cycle as a complex diachronic process including "changes where a phrase or word gradually disappears and is replaced by a new linguistic item." In addition, van Gelderen (2011:3) points out that "[t]oward the end of the cycle, similar events start again, but they are (slightly) different and happen at a different pace." I argue that *dürfen*, *bedürfen* and *brauchen* constitute a linguistic cycle as given in (4):

(4)   *dürfen* > *bedürfen* > *brauchen*

I dub this cycle modal NPI cycle and argue that all three predicates exemplify a competition among functional heads leading to one form ousting the other (see also

Table 4. Historical stages of German

Language period	Abbreviation	Dates
Old High German	OHG	750–1050
Middle High German	MHG	1050–1350
Early New High German	ENHG	1350–1700
New High German	NHG	1700–1900
Modern German	MG	1900–present

Kroch 1994, 2000 on a constraint against the coexistence of functionally equivalent items). This neatly accounts for why *brauchen* and *bedürfen* coexist and are still used side by side if they quantify over a set of objects. When they embed DP complements, they merge as lexical V-heads. As convincingly illustrated by Kroch (1994, 2000), open class lexical items do not compete. Thus, only the NPI uses of *bedürfen* and *brauchen* are participating in the competition. The question we also need to ask is what is responsible for the cyclical changes. In other words: what triggers the cycle? To answer this question I follow Martins (2000), Jäger (2010) and Willis (2012) who examine possible change pathways in indefinite systems across different languages. Mainly, they show that an indefinite item can develop either into an NPI being restricted exclusively to negative contexts or into an item developing more affirmative distributions over time. In the former case a plus-valued NEG-feature is introduced. In the latter case, in turn, a minus-valued NEG-feature needs to be postulated. As Jäger (2010:817) states, both scenarios instantiate two independent processes and no change from the plus-valued feature to the minus-valued feature is to be observed. Now, based on what we have seen so far, we can safely argue that *dürfen*, *bedürfen* and *brauchen* as NPIs occur in so called strong NPI contexts, i.e. in the scope of a c-commanding negative operator, and that they all exemplify a loss of the [+NEG]-feature. Following Jäger's (2010) classification of main polarity types of contexts, *dürfen*, *bedürfen* and *brauchen* as NPIs are [+affective] and [+negative]:

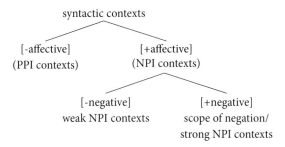

Figure 3. Main polarity types of contexts according to Jäger (2010)

Note that the approach taken here deviates from those by Bech (1951), Kolb (1964), Lenz (1996), Maché (2013) and Paul (1897) in one important respect. I do not claim that *brauchen* replaced *dürfen*. In my view, *bedürfen* forms a bridge between both predicates and links them. This mainly follows from the fact that *brauchen* began selecting infinitive complements first in the 18th/19th century (cf. Kolb 1964:75; Maché 2013:180; Scaffidi-Abbate 1973:24; among many others), whereas *dürfen* ceased being used as an NPI already in the 16th/17th century. I extracted and analyzed 153 examples from GMC, a diachronic corpus from the period 1650–1800, in which *dürfen* embeds an infinitive clause. In 88 examples (= 58%) *dürfen* occurs in negative contexts. The remainder (= 65 examples) of the attested examples contains neither a negation operator nor an expression triggering a negative quantification over the embedded proposition. In all examples *dürfen* selects for 1st status complements. Several points deserve our attention here. From a MG perspective we expect *dürfen* not to embed 2nd status complements. However, as in older stages *dürfen* was employed as an NPI, 2nd status complements could occur:

(70) du   darfst   kein Kundschaft (…) z'bstellen
      you need.2SG NEG custom   to.order.INF
      'You need not to order any customers.'
                                  (Niklaus Manuel 1485–1530, cited in: Korhonen 2006:1467)

(71) nun sprichstu waz darf   ich das   zu biten
      now talk.you   what need.1SG I   that to beg.INF
      'Now you talk, what necessitates me beg for that?'
                                  (Geiler Keiserberg, 1518, cited in: Scaffidi-Abbate 1973:26)

Ebert (1976:100) investigating infinitive clauses in ENHG states that "there are also a dozen examples of *zu* + inf. with *dürfen, mügen, söllen* and *wöllen*." (70) and (71) confirm his findings. If *dürfen* had replaced *brauchen* directly, we should be able to find some examples in GMC with 2nd status complements. A plausible explanation for their absence might be that *dürfen* is no longer used as an NPI, but as a modal verb. This also accounts for why it can occur in positive environments, meaning that its occurrence in negative contexts does not necessarily imply its NPI status. (72) illustrates that *dürfen* cannot be analyzed as an NPI anymore:

(72) Nun darf   ich weinen
      now may.1SG I   cry.INF
      'Now I may cry'   (GMC, 1771)

In fact, neither does (72) contain a negation operator, nor can *darf* be rendered as today's *brauchen*. Furthermore, if *brauchen* had replaced *dürfen*, the former is supposed to occur as an NPI already in GMC. In total, I was able to find 109 *brauchen* examples. Table 5 gives an overview of the embedded complements:

Table 5. *Brauchen* and its complements in GMC

DP	infinitive	*dass*-clause
105	3	1

Only in 3 cases *brauchen* is in fact used as an NPI embedding an active infinitive. However, what is more interesting in the light of our discussion here is the dependent *dass*-clause licensed in an impersonal negative context:

(73) Es brauchts nicht, dass ich es (…) seh
      it   need.it NEG   that I   it   see.1SG
      'I do not have to see it.'   (GMC, 1737)

As pointed out by Kluempers (1997:87), cases like those under (73) are supposed to be regarded as an intermediate step between *brauchen*1 and *brauchen*2. *Brauchen* in (73) realizes its internal argument as a clause headed by the complementizer *dass* 'that'. The clause itself is anaphorically referring to the correlate *es* 'it' cliticized on the matrix verb. In addition to that *brauchen* occurs in a negative context. However, as illustrated by Maché (2013:153–4, 179) impersonal structures are to be attested in positive contexts as well. At this point, we can postulate the following development of *brauchen*:

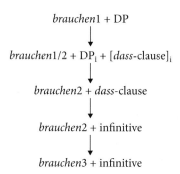

Figure 4. The development of *brauchen* as an NPI

If the pattern *brauchen*2 + *dass*-clause is a precondition for the canonical use of *brauchen* as an NPI, i.e. with an infinitive, then the GMC data show that it is still developing in the period from 1650–1800. In other words, if *brauchen* would have replaced *dürfen* immediately, we would expect more *brauchen*2 occurrences with an infinitive and no *dass*-clauses, especially as the latter appear to be absent in MG[16] and

---

16. Maché (2013:154) finds some interesting examples in DeReKo with *brauchen* used impersonally. However, he claims that "the impersonal variant of *brauchen* found in DeReKo

dürfen no longer occurs in its NPI function. Accordingly, a gap emerges between *dür-fen* and *brauchen*, which, in my opinion, is filled by *bedürfen*. The following example from GMC confirms this assumption indirectly:

(74)   daß   weder   Ständer, Riegel,   noch   Balcken
       that neither posts   transoms   nor   timbers

       zerschnitten   zu   werden   bedarf
       cut.PTCP   to   pass.aux.INF need.3SG
       'that it is not necessary to cut posts, transoms or timbers'   (GMC, 1751)

In (74) *bedürfen* occurs as an NPI. The negative interpretation comes about the complex negation *weder noch* 'neither nor' presupposing a plural NP. But what appears to be more intriguing about (74) is the fact that *bedürfen* embeds a passive infinitive, implying that the NP *Stränder, Riegel, Balcken* underwent a case conversion from [+ACC] to [+NOM] and became the clause subject. We therefore expect *bedürfen* to occur in plural. However, this is not the case. Instead it occurs in singular and there is no syntactic agree relation between the matrix predicate and its subject. It indicates that *bedürfen* as NPI was developed much further than *brauchen*. Additionally, as I pointed out in Section 3.1, *bedürfen* occurs already in MHG as an NPI, whereas *brauchen* does not. Hence, *bedürfen* must be an older predicate. Elly van Gelderen (pers. comm.) raises the question if the NPI cycle given in (4) could encompass more predicates related to the meaning of *brauchen* used as an NPI. One of the candidates would then be *gebrauchen* 'use'. Several facts indicate that it cannot be the case. In the first place, *gebrauchen*, contrary to *brauchen*, cannot embed infinitives in MG:

(75)   *Die Fahrer   gebrauchen   (es/dessen)   (nicht)   (zu)   warten
        the drivers use.3PL   it.ACC/GEN   NEG   to   wait.INF
       Intended: 'The drivers need not wait.'

Thus, it is reasonable to examine *gebrauchen* in older stages. As for OHG, Graff & Massmann (1837: 280–1) do not provide any examples in which *gabrûhan* would embed an infinitive. What we find instead are DP complements, the majority of them is marked for the Genitive case. In addition, OHG *gabrûhan*'s meaning corresponds in most cases to the meaning of MG *gebrauchen*. There are some instances in which *gabrûhan* is used in the meaning of *brauchen* and in which the prefix *ga-* fulfills a perfectivizing function, but then, again, it selects a DP complement, not an infinitive. Grimm & Grimm (1878: 1826–36) highlight two interesting examples from the 16th/17th century. One of them is given in (76):

---

occurs above all in Swiss newspapers. This high frequency of this pattern in Swiss German could be due to language contact: there is a similar pattern in French that corresponds almost one by one to its German counterpart: *il faut* 'it necessitates.'"

(76) der mensch gebraucht des feuers   sich zu wermen
      the man   need.3SG   the fire.GEN REFL to warm.INF
      'The man needs the fire in order to warm himself.'

    a.   der mensch [$_{VP}$ gebraucht [$_{DP}$ des feuers]] sich zu wermen
    b.   *der mensch [$_{VP}$ gebraucht [$_{INF}$ des feuers sich zu wermen]]

In (76), *gebrauchen* embeds the Genitive-DP *des feuers* and not, as the brackets in the
(b) paraphrase indicate, an infinitive clause containing the DP *des feuers*. The infinitive
clause is not a part of *gebrauchen*'s internal argument. Instead, it should be analyzed
as an adjunct clause having a purpose reading. Now, if *gebrauchen* cannot realize its
internal argument as an infinitive clause, it cannot be considered a modal predicate/
modal verb. Nor can it be classified as an NPI.

In what follows I outline the NPI cycle and its major steps. However, it ought to
be stressed at this point that a linguistic cycle proceeds gradually, i.e. one should not
be surprised if we find two members of a diachronic cycle appearing within a language
period. Such situations are expected. Our departure point is *dürfen* in OHG. Diewald
(1999: 350) investigating Otfrid's *Evangelienbuch* identifies 16 examples with *thurfan*.
All of them occur in negative contexts. However, as Lühr (1997: 169–171) points out
already in OHG *thurfan* could be rendered as today's *dürfen*, meaning that it does not
necessarily have to be analyzed as an NPI and that it starts losing its NPI status as early
as in OHG:

> Was nun das Verb *dürfen* angeht – die gotische Entsprechung þaurban bedeutet
> 'nötig haben, bedürfen, Mangel leiden' und 'müssen' […] -, so wird dieses im
> Tatian noch nicht mit dem Infinitiv verbunden, mit dem Infinitiv kommt es bei
> Otfrid nur verneint vor und bei Notker verneint und bejaht (Lühr 1997: 169) (As
> far as the verb *dürfen* is concerned – the Gothic counterpart þaurban means 'be
> in need of, require, be in want' and 'must' […] -, it does not select for infinitives
> in Tatian, in Otfrid's *Evangelienbuch* infinitives occur only in negative contexts,
> while in Notker's texts also positive environments are to be attested with *thurfan*,
> Lühr 1997: 169; my translation, ŁJ)

Lühr's claim is confirmed by the data collected by Graff & Massmann (1840: 205), who
provide OHG examples illustrating the use of *thurfan* in positive environments. The
following two examples are a case in point:

(77) uuaz tarf   ih choson
      what may.1SG I speak.INF
      'What may I say?'

(78) daz sia durfe   riuuuen
      that she may.3SG regret.3SG
      'that she may regret'

If *thurfan* ceases being used as NPI already in OHG, a gap is emerging, which, according to a linguistic cycle, is supposed to be filled by another predicate. There are two suitable predicates that potentially could replace *dürfen*: *bedürfen* and *gedürfen*. As both of them consist of *dürfen* and of a prefix, they seem to be appropriate candidates from a morphological point of view. As a matter of fact, *bedürfen* prevails and *gedürfen* disappears from the use altogether. Grimm & Grimm (1878: 2054) define *gedürfen* as *verstärktes dürfen* 'intensified dürfen' and point out no differences in comparison to *dürfen*. As the prefix *ge-* is usually analyzed as a perfectivizing strategy, there is probably no need to distinguish between *dürfen* and *gedürfen* as two different predicates. Accordingly, they express the same attitude towards the embedded proposition and represent one predicate with different aspect values. Over time the morphological marking of the perfective aspect is no longer available in German (cf. Leiss 1992) leading to the loss of *gedürfen*. Lenz (1996: 394) has observed that *brauchen* exists already in OHG and that it takes DP complements marked for the Genitive, Dative and Accusative case. Thus, one might ask why *brauchen* does not start filling the gap already in OHG. This is mainly due to the fact that *brauchen* undergoes a semantic change first in the 16th/17th century and in older stages of German it is associated with other meanings paraphrased in Table 6:

Table 6. The semantic change of *brauchen* according to Lenz (1996)

Gothic	*brûkjan*	genießen 'enjoy', Anteil haben 'have a share', sich erfreuen 'rejoice'
OHG	*brûhhan*	genießen 'enjoy', nutzen 'utilize', ausüben 'exert'
MHG	*brûchen*	verwenden 'use', benutzen 'utilize'
ENHG	*brauchen*	verwenden 'use', benötigen 'need'
NHG	*brauchen*	benötigen 'need'

According to Table 6, OHG *brûhhan* does not even equal today's *brauchen*1, although both of them act as lexical heads embedding DP complements. Semantically, *brûhhan* is a far cry away from *thurfan*, indicating that *bithurfan* appears to be a better candidate. If this is true, we need to provide empirical evidence for this claim. I was not able to find any OHG examples in which *bithurfan* would select for infinitives. Graff & Massmann (1840: 207–8) register a considerable number of DP complements, no infinitive complements though. Diewald's (1999: 350) analysis does not yield a different outcome: "Alle *bithurfan*-Belege […] sind mit nominalem Objekt konstruiert" (in all attested examples *bithurfan* merges with a nominal object; my translation, ŁJ). Grimm & Grimm (1854: 1239–41) note first infinitive complements in MHG. However, in the light of the definition of a linguistic cycle given above, we expect such a state of affairs. First, the replacement does not happen abruptly, but gradually. In addition, as I mentioned at the beginning of this chapter, MG possesses approximately 1400 infinitive-embedding predicates. The OHG situation looks differently. If one counts OHG infinitive-embedding predicates based on the studies by Demske (2001), Denecke (1880) and Johnk (1979), one ends up with approximately 200 predicates selecting either for 1st or for 2nd status complements. The number of infinitive-embedding predicates increased sevenfold. Hence, it is not surprising that *bedürfen* selects no infinitives in OHG. Second, although *thurfan* paves the way for *bithurfan*, we expect both predicates to coexist as NPIs for a time. A search query in MBD confirms this assumption. In almost all infinitive contexts, *dürfen* is used as an NPI. I could not find any examples with *bedürfen* occurring in a positive context:

(79)   darftû   niht mê   vrâgen
        need.you NEG more ask.INF
        'You need not ask anymore.'
        (MBD, *Iwein*, line 552)

(80)   Das bedarfftu   nit sorgen
        that need.3SG.you NEG care.INF
        'You need not care about that.'
        (MBD, *Die Crone*, line 13844)

Based on that, I assume for OHG *thurfan* two lexical entries:

*thurfan*1 + DP -> [[thurfan]] = $\lambda x \lambda y$[thurfan'(x,y)]
*thurfan*2 + INF -> [[thurfan]]^{w,f} = $\lambda q_{\langle st \rangle}.w' \in \cap f_{\text{NON-EPIST}}(w): q(w') = 1$

Whereas *thurfan*1 merges, similar to *brauchen*1 and *bedürfen*1, as a lexical V-head embedding DP complements mostly marked for the Genitive case (see Footnote 14), I consider *thurfan*2 a modal predicate taking a non-epistemic modal base. Its meaning corresponds to those of *bedürfen*2 and *brauchen*2. As time passed, it undergoes a semantic change (= modal shift), loses the [+NEG]-feature, develops into a modal verb losing the possibility to embed DPs and acquiring the ability to quantify epistemically. OHG *bithurfan*, in turn, is neither a modal predicate nor a modal verb. It can solely quantify over a set of objects and not over a set of events, meaning it is a lexical V-head. It grammaticalizes in the transition from OHG to MHG acquiring the [+NEG]-feature and the modal predicate properties delineated in Section 3. Hence, in MHG both *dürfen* and *bedürfen* merge as Mod-heads below the T-node. Both predicates compete for a while in the history of German due to several factors. First, morphologically they do not differ to a large extent, as both of them consist of the same stem. Second, already in OHG they express a similar modal attitude towards what is embedded. Hence, in some contexts they could replace each other. Third, although *dürfen* starts losing its NPI status already in OHG, this process spans over several centuries. Diewald (1999) and Lenz (1996) illustrate that its old meaning *be in need of* can still be identified in selected idiomatic phrases in MG. This also explains why *dürfen* could select for 2nd status complements (cf. 70 and 71 above). If *dürfen* and *bedürfen* compete until the 16th/17th century and if the grammaticalization of *zu* as infinitival marker spreads to other predicates over time, as Jędrzejowski and Goldschmidt (2015) show, (70) and (71) do not surprise. In ENHG the competition between *dürfen* and *bedürfen* abates. In BFK I could find 131 examples with *dürfen* embedding an infinitive. In 49 (= 37%) cases *dürfen* no longer occurs as an NPI. *Bedürfen*, in turn, occurring 12 times in the corpus appears as NPI throughout, thus gaining traction over *dürfen*. *Brauchen* is still attested as a lexical V-head (= *brauchen*1) merging with nominal complements or infinitive purpose adjuncts headed by the silent complementizer *um* 'in order to'. Having acquired the semantics of *brauchen*1 at the end of the ENHG period or at the beginning of NHG, *brauchen* starts competing with *bedürfen*. Its development has been already depicted in Figure 4 above. At some point *bedürfen* begins losing its NPI status and *brauchen* starts to substitute for it. The only difference between *dürfen* and *bedürfen* on the one hand and *brauchen* on the other is that the former never grammaticalized into epistemic quantifiers as NPIs. Only *brauchen* acquired this possibility. Finally, if *dürfen*, *bedürfen* and *brauchen* in fact constitute a cycle and if the first two of them lost their NPI status over time, we might want to expect *brauchen* to loss its NPI status, too, when an infinitive is embedded. This would even be in accordance with the definition of a linguistic cycle. Interestingly enough, independent studies provide evidence pointing to this direction. Maché (2013: 169) observes that German L1 learners overgeneralize and can use *brauchen* in positive environments. (81) is an utterance heard in a bookstore:

(81) doch Papa   das brauchst du   kaufen
      MP   daddy that need.2SG you buy.INF
      'Oh yes, daddy, you need to buy this.'   (Maché 2013: 169; ex 375)

Vainikka & Young-Scholten (1994) make similar observations with respect to adults German L2 learners having acquired either Korean or Turkish as their L1. Similar to German both languages are OV languages, but unlike German they do not exhibit V-to-C movement in declarative root clauses. As the authors point out, some speakers produce a good number of sentences with a finite verb raised to C. The following example illustrates this and, simultaneously, shows that also German L2 acquirers overgeneralize being able to use *brauchen* in positive contexts:

(82) Jetzt brau Wohnungsamt   fragen
      now   need housing.authority ask.INF
      'Now (I) need to ask (the) housing authority.'
      (Vainikka & Young-Scholten 1994: 289; ex 25a)

Apart from the language acquisition data, there are also German dialects in which *brauchen* can be licensed in positive contexts. Maché (2013) notices two examples from the North Rhine-Westphalia region:

(83) Jeder Kinositzer   braucht   ein eigenes Bild
      each   cinema.sitter   need.3SG   a   proper   picture

      berechnet   zu bekommen, da die Abstände vom
      calculate.PTCP   to get.INF   as the distances from.the

      Bild   der   einzelnen Besucher viel   zu gravierend sind
      picture of.the single   visitors   much too serious   be.3PL

      'It is necessary that each cinema goer gets an individually calculated picture
      as the distances from the picture of each visitor are too varied.'

                                  (Maché 2013: 170; ex. 378)

(84) Jetzt brauch   ich meine Pillen nehmen,
      now   need.1SG   I   my   pills   take.INF

      und dann geh   ich ins   Büro
      and then go.1SG   I   in.the office

      'Now, I just need to take my pills and then I'll go to the office.'

                                  (Maché 2013: 170; ex. 379)

However, as appealing as (83) and (84) might appear to be, it still remains to be investigated if *brauchen* loses its NPI status in this region or if it never acquired it. It is well known that dialects can often remain resistant to the changes that took place in a standard language. Brandner (2006), for example, demonstrates that in Alemannic control CP-infinitives the infinitive marker *zu* 'to' does not occur, resembling the situation known from older stages of German. In Modern German, however, the presence of *zu* is a must-have in almost all control cases. A similar scenario may have happened to *brauchen* in North Rhine-Westphalia. If *brauchen* could always be employed in positive contexts, (83) and (84) do not support the approach taken here. On the other hand, if *brauchen* lost its NPI status, (83) and (84) do yield more evidence for continuation of the modal NPI cycle in the history of German. This being said, one intriguing question arises. If *brauchen* ceases being used as an NPI, another verbal candidate fitting in the cycle must be recruited. What verb would suit best remains open here.

5. Conclusion

The main objective of this chapter has been to outline the modal NPI cycle in the history of German involving three verbal NPIs: *dürfen*, *bedürfen* and *brauchen*. It has been shown that the three predicates behave differently in Modern German, although all of them express a modal attitude of the speaker towards the embedded proposition and although all of them used to function as NPIs in older stages of German. As for Modern German, I have argued that *bedürfen* in contrast to *dürfen* and *brauchen* cannot be classified as a modal verb and labeled it as a modal predicate. Diachronically, it has been illustrated that *dürfen*, *bedürfen* and *brauchen* competed with and replaced each other in a cyclical manner.

Primary sources

AK – Alexander Klaaßen. 2014. Entstehungsbedingungen europäischer Konstitutionen zwischen 1830 und 1848. Eine Untersuchung anhand der Verfassung der Paulskirche. BA thesis, Universität Potsdam.
BFK – *Das Bonner Frühneuhochdeutschkorpus* ⟨http://www.korpora.org/Fnhd/⟩
DeReKo – *Cosmas II* ⟨http://www.ids-mannheim.de/cosmas2/⟩
GMC – *GerManC Korpus, Historische Texte aus der Zeit von 1650 bis 1800.*
GOE – *Goethe-Korpus, 1772–1828.*
HK4 – *Deutsche Literatur von Frauen, 1650–1923.*
HK5 – *Philosophie von Platon bis Nietsche, 1713–1924.*
KHZ – *Mannheimer Korpus Historischer Zeitungen, 1737–1877.*
MBD – *Mittelhochdeutsche Begriffsdatenbank* ⟨http://mhdbdb.sbg.ac.at⟩

References

Abraham, Werner. 2004. The grammaticalization of the infinitival preposition – Toward a theory of 'grammaticalizing reanalysis'. *Journal of Comparative Germanic Linguistics* 7(2): 111–170. doi:10.1023/B:JCOM.0000007343.96479.7f
Axel, Katrin. 2001. Althochdeutsche Modalverben als Anhebungsverben. In *Modalität und Modalverben im Deutschen* [Linguistische Berichte Sonderheft 9], Reimar Müller & Marga Reis (eds), 37–60. Hamburg: Helmut Buske.
Bech, Gunnar. 1951. *Grundzüge der semantischen Entwicklungsgeschichte der hochdeutschen Modalverba*. Kopenhagen: Munksgaard.
Bech, Gunnar. 1955/57. *Studien über das deutsche verbum infinitum*. Kopenhagen: Munksgaard.
ter Beek, Janneke. 2008. Restructuring and Infinitival Complements. Ph.D. dissertation, Rijksuniversiteit Groningen.
den Besten, Hans & Rutten, Jean. 1989. On verb raising, extraposition, and free word order in Dutch. In *Sentential Complementation and the Lexicon* [Linguistic Models 13], Dany Jaspers, Wim G. Klooster, Yvan Putseys & Pieter A.M. Seuren (eds), 41–56. Dordrecht: Foris.
Bierwisch, Manfred. 1963. *Grammatik des deutschen Verbs* [Studia Grammatica 2]. Berlin: Akademie-Verlag.
Boneh, Nora & Doron, Edit. 2012. Hab and Gen in the expressions of habituality. In *Genericity*, Alda Mari, Claire Beyssade & Fabio Del Prete (eds), 176–191. Oxford: OUP. doi:10.1093/acprof:oso/9780199691807.003.0006
Brandner, Ellen. 2006. Bare infinitives in Alemannic and the categorial status of infinitival complements. *Linguistic Variation Yearbook* 6: 203–268.
Butler, Jonny. 2004. Phase Structure, Phrase Structure, and Quantification. Ph.D. dissertation, The University of York.

Butler, Jonny. 2006. The structure of modality and temporality (or, towards deriving something like a Cinque Hierarchy). *Linguistic Variation Yearbook* 6: 161–201.

Cinque, Guglielmo. 1999. *Adverbs and Functional Heads. A Cross-Linguistic Perspective.* Oxford: OUP.

Cinque, Guglielmo. 2006. *Restructuring and Functional Heads.* Oxford: OUP.

Colomo, Katarina. 2011. Modalität im Verbalkomplex. Halbmodalverben und Modalitätsverben im System statusregierender Verbklassen. Ph.D. dissertation, Universität Bochum.

Condoravdi, Cleo. 2001. Temporal interpretation of modals: Modals for the present and for the past. In *Stanford Papers on Semantics*, David Beaver, Stefan Kaufmann, Brady Clark & Luis Casillas (eds), 1–30. Stanford CA: CSLI.

Demske, Ulrike. 2001. Zur Distribution von Infinitivkomplementen im Althochdeutschen. In *Modalität und Modalverben im Deutschen* [Linguistische Berichte Sonderheft 9], Reimar Müller & Marga Reis (eds), 61–86. Hamburg: Helmut Buske.

Demske, Ulrike. 2008. Raising patterns in Old High German. In *Grammatical Change and Linguistic Theory. The Rosendal papers* [Linguistik Aktuell/Linguistics Today 113], Thórhallur Eythórsson (ed.), 143–172. Amsterdam: John Benjamins. doi:10.1075/la.113.06dem

Denecke, Arthur. 1880. *Der Gebrauch des Infinitives bei den althochdeutschen Übersetzern des 8. und 9. Jahrhunderts.* Leipzig: Druck von Pöschel & Trepte.

Diewald, Gabriele. 1999. *Die Modalverben im Deutschen. Grammatikalisierung und Polyfunktionalität* [Germanistische Linguistik 208]. Tübingen: Max Niemeyer. doi:10.1515/9783110945942

Ebert, Robert Peter. 1976. *Infinitival Complement Constructions in Early New High German* [Linguistische Arbeiten 30]. Tübingen: Max Niemeyer. doi:10.1515/9783111355832

Evers, Arnold. 1990. The infinitival prefix *zu* as INFL. In *Scrambling and Barriers* [Linguistik Aktuell/Linguistics Today 5], Günther Grewendorf & Wolfgang Sternefeld (eds), 217–238. Amsterdam: John Benjamins. doi:10.1075/la.5.11eve

Fritz, Gerd. 1997. Historische Semantik der Modalverben. In *Untersuchungen zur semantischen Entwicklungsgeschichte der Modalverben im Deutschen* [Germanistische Linguistik 187], Gerd Fritz & Thomas Gloning (eds), 1–157. Tübingen: Max Niemeyer. doi:10.1515/9783110940848.1

van Gelderen, Elly. 2009. Cyclical change, an introduction. In *Cyclical Change* [Linguistik Aktuell/Linguistics Today 146], Elly van Gelderen (ed.), 1–12. Amsterdam: John Benjamins. doi:10.1075/la.146

van Gelderen, Elly. 2011. *The Linguistic Cycle. Language Change and the Language Faculty.* Oxford: OUP. doi:10.1093/acprof:oso/9780199756056.001.0001

Graff, Eberhard Gottlieb & Massmann, Hans F. *Althochdeutscher Sprachschatz oder Wörterbuch der althochdeutschen Sprache,* Vol. 1: 1834; Vol. 2: 1836; Vol. 3: 1837; Vol. 4: 1838: Vol. 5: 1840; Vol. 6: 1842. Berlin: Nikolai.

Grimm, Jacob & Grimm, Wilhelm. *Deutsches Wörterbuch,* Vol. 1: 1854; Vol. 4: 1878. Leipzig: Verlag von S. Hirzel.

Hacquard, Valentine. 2006. Aspects of Modality. Ph.D. dissertation, MIT.

Hacquard, Valentine. 2010. On the event relativity of modal auxiliaries. *Natural Language Semantics* 18: 79–114. doi:10.1007/s11050-010-9056-4

Haegeman, Liliane & van Riemsdijk, Henk. 1986. Verb projection raising, scope, and the typology of rules affecting verbs. *Linguistic Inquiry* 17(3): 417–466.

Haider, Hubert. 2009. *The Syntax of German.* Cambridge: CUP.

Hinterhölzl, Roland. 2006. *Scrambling, Remnant Movement, and Restructuring in West Germanic.* Oxford: OUP. doi:10.1093/acprof:oso/9780195308211.001.0001

Hinterhölzl, Roland. 2009. The IPP-effect, phrasal affixes and repair strategies in the syntax-morphology interface. *Linguistische Berichte* 218: 191–215.

Hoeksema, Jack. 2008. Distributieprofielen van negatief-polaire uitdrukkingen: Een vergelijking van het Nederlands, Engels en Duits. *Tabu* 37(34): 111–195.

Jäger, Agnes. 2010. *Anything* is *nothing* is *something*: On the diachrony of polarity types of indefinites. *Natural Language and Linguistic Theory* 28(4): 787–822. doi:10.1007/s11049-010-9113-1

Jędrzejowski, Łukasz. 2015a. Subjektanhebungsverben im Deutschen. Ihre Entstehung, Entwicklung und Komplemente. Ph.D. dissertation, Universität Potsdam.

Jędrzejowski, Łukasz. 2015b. *Somebody that I used to know*, or: How do habitual verbal heads emerge? The case of German *pflegen* 'use(d) to'. Ms, Universität Potsdam.

Jędrzejowski, Łukasz & Goldschmidt, Katrin. 2015. On the status of the infinitival marker *zu* 'to' in the history of German. A corpus-based analysis. Ms, Universität Potsdam.

Johnk, Linn Dale. 1979. Complementation in Old High German. Ph.D. dissertation, The University of Texas at Austin.

Kluempers, John David. 1997. *The Grammaticalization of a Verb: The Role of 'Nicht Brauchen' in the German Modal Verb System.* Ann Arbor MI: UMI.

König, Ekkehard & Gast, Volker. 2012. *Understanding English-German Contrasts,* [Grundlagen der Anglistik und Amerikanistik 29], 3rd enhanced edn. Berlin: Erich Schmidt.

Kolb, Hermann. 1964. Über *brauchen* als Modalverb. *Zeitschrift für Deutsche Sprache* 20: 64–78.

Korhonen, Jarmo. 2006. Valenzwandel am Beispiel des Deutschen. In *Dependenz und Valenz. Ein internationales Handbuch der zeitgenössischen Forschung*, Vol. 2, Vilmos Ágel, Guta Rau, Herbert Ernst Wiegand, Hugo Steger & Gerold Ungeheuer (eds), 1462–1473. Berlin: de Gruyter.

Kratzer, Angelika. 1981. The notional category of modality. In *Words, Worlds, and Contexts. New Approaches in Word Semantics* [Research in Text Theory 6], Hans-Jürgen Eikmeyer & Hannes Rieser (eds), 3874. Berlin: De Gruyter.

Kratzer, Angelika. 1991. Modality. In: *Semantik: Ein internationales Handbuch zeitgenössischer Forschung*, Arnim von Stechow & Dieter Wunderlich (eds), 639–650. Berlin: De Gruyter.

Kroch, Anthony. 1994. Morphosyntactic variation. In *Proceedings of the Thirtieth Annual Meeting of the Chicago Linguistics Society,* Vol. II: Katharine Beals (ed.), 180–201. Chicago Il: Chicago Linguistic Society.

Kroch, Anthony. 2000. Syntactic change. In *The Handbook of Contemporary Syntactic Theory*, Mark Baltin & Chris Collins (eds), 629–739. Oxford: Blackwell.

Leiss, Elisabeth. 1992. *Die Verbalkategorien des Deutschen. Ein Beitrag zur Theorie der sprachlichen Kategorisierung* [Studia Linguistica Germanica 31]. Berlin: De Gruyter.

Lenz, Barbara. 1996. Wie *brauchen* ins deutsche Modalverbsystem geriet und welche Rolle es darin spielt. *Beiträge zur Geschichte der deutschen Sprache und Literatur* 118(3): 393–422.

Lühr, Rosemarie. 1997. Zur Semantik der althochdeutschen Modalverben. In *Untersuchungen zur semantischen Entwicklungsgeschichte der Modalverben im Deutschen* [Germanistische Linguistik 187], Gerd Fritz & Thomas Gloning (eds), 159–175. Tübingen: Max Niemeyer.

Maché, Jakob. 2013. On Black Magic – How Epistemic Modifiers Emerge. Ph.D. dissertation, Freie Universität zu Berlin.

Maché, Jakob & Abraham, Werner. 2011. Infinitivkomplemente im Frühneuhochdeutschen – satzwertig oder nicht? In *Frühneuhochdeutsch – Aufgaben und Probleme seiner linguistischen*

Beschreibung [Germanistische Linguistik 213–215], Oskar Reichmann & Anja Lobenstein-Reichmann (eds), 235–274. Olms: Hildesheim.

Maitz, Péter & Krisztián Tronka, Henk. 2009. *Brauchen* – Phonologische Aspekte der Auxiliarisierung. *Zeitschrift für Dialektologie und Linguistik* 76(2): 189–202.

Martins, Ana Maria. 2000. Polarity items in Romance: Underspecification and lexical change. In *Diachronic Syntax: Models and Mechanisms*, Susan Pintzuk, George Tsoulas & Anthony Warner (eds), 191–219. Oxford: OUP.

Paul, Hermann. 1897. *Deutsches Wörterbuch*. Halle: Max Niemeyer.

Ponten, Jan Peter. 1973. Der Ersatz- oder Scheininfinitiv. Ein Problem aus der deutschen und niederländischen Syntax. *Wirkendes Wort* 23(2): 73–85.

Reis, Marga. 2001. Bilden Modalverben im Deutschen eine syntaktische Klasse? In *Modalität und Modalverben im Deutschen* [Linguistische Berichte Sonderheft 9], Reimar Müller & Marga Reis (eds), 287–318. Hamburg: Helmut Buske.

Reis, Marga. 2005. Wer *brauchen* ohne zu gebraucht … Zu systemgerechten 'Verstößen' im Gegenwartsdeutschen. *Cahiers d'Études Germaniques* 48: 101–114.

Reis, Marga. 2007. Modals, so-called semi-modals, and grammaticalization in German. *Interdisciplinary Journal for Germanic Linguistics and Semiotic Analysis* 12: 1–57.

Reis, Marga & Sternefeld, Wolfgang. 2004. Review article of Wurmbrand 2001. *Linguistics* 42(2): 469–508.

Rutten, Jean. 1991. Infinitival Complements and Auxiliaries. Ph.D. dissertation, Universiteit van Amsterdam.

Takahaši, Terukazu. 1984. Über den subjektiven Gebrauch des Modalverbs *brauchen*. *Sprachwissenschaft* 9: 21–22.

Sanders, Daniel. 1908. *Wörterbuch der Hauptschwierigkeiten in der deutschen Sprache*, 38th edn, Julius Dumcke (ed). Berlin: Langenscheidt.

Scaffidi-Abbate, August. 1973. *Brauchen* mit folgendem Infinitiv. *Muttersprache* 83: 1–45.

Schallert, Oliver. 2014. *Zur Syntax der Ersatzinfinitivkonstruktion. Typologie und Variation* [Studien zur deutschen Grammatik 87]. Tübingen: Stauffenburg. doi:10.1075/la.79

Schmid, Tanja. 2005. *Infinitival Syntax. Infinitivus Pro Participio as a Repair Strategy* [Linguistik Aktuell/Linguistics Today 79]. Amsterdam: John Benjamins.

Speyer, Augustin. 2015. AcI and control infinitives: How different are they? A diachronic approach. In *Journal of Historical Linguistics* 5(1): 41–71. Special issue *The Diachrony of Infinitival Patterns: Their Origin, Development and Loss,* guest-edited by Ulrike Demske & Łukasz Jędrzejowski. doi:10.1075/jhl.5.1.02spe

Sternefeld, Wolfgang. 2008. *Syntax. Eine morphologisch motivierte generative Beschreibung des Deutschen*, 3rd edn. Tübingen: Stauffenburg.

Ulvestad, Bjarne. 1997. On the use of *brauchen* versus *müssen*. In *Modality in Germanic Languages. Historical and Comparative Perspectives* [Trends in Linguistics. Studies and Monographs 99], Toril Swan & Olaf Jansen Westvik (eds), 211–231. Berlin: De Gruyter.

Vainikka, Anne & Young-Scholten, Martha. 1994. Direct access to X′-theory. Evidence from Korean and Turkish adults learning German. In *Language Acquisition Studies in Generative Grammar* [Language Acquisition and Language Disorders 8], Teun Hoekstra & Bonnie D. Schwartz (eds), 265–316. Amsterdam: John Benjamins. doi:10.1075/lald.8.13vai

Vater, Heinz. 2010. *Möchten* als Modalverb. In *Modalität/Temporalität aus kontrastiver und typologischer Sicht* [Danziger Beiträge zur Germanistik 30], Andrzej Kątny & Anna Socka (eds), 99–112. Frankfurt: Peter Lang.

Willis, David. 2012. Negative polarity and the quantifier cycle: Comparative diachronic perspectives from European languages. In *The Evolution of Negation: Beyond the Jespersen Cycle* [Trends in Linguistics. Studies and Monographs 235], Pierre Larrivée & Richard Ingham (eds), 285–323. Berlin: De Gruyter.

Wöllstein-Leisten, Angelika. 2001. *Die Syntax der dritten Konstruktion. Eine repräsentationelle Analyse zur Monosentialität von 'zu'-Infinitiven im Deutschen* [Studien zur deutschen Grammatik 63]. Tübingen: Stauffenburg.

van der Wouden, Ton. 2001. Three modal verbs. In *Zur Verbmorphologie germanischer Sprachen* [Linguistische Arbeiten 446], Sheila Watts, Jonathan West & Hans-Joachim Solms (eds), 189–210. Tübingen: Max Niemeyer.

Wurmbrand, Susanne. 1999. Modal verbs must be raising verbs. In *Proceedings of the* 18th *West Coast Conference on Formal Linguistics (WCCFL 18)*, Sonya Bird, Andrew Carnie, Jason D. Haugen & Peter Norquest (eds), 599–612. Somerville MA: Cascadilla Press.

Appendix

Here, I provide 15 corpus examples extracted from DeReKo and illustrating that *brauchen* selecting a 2nd status complement can exhibit the IPP effect.

(1)　Und fürs　Foyer hätten　　　　wir auch
and for.the foyer have.1PL.COND we also

gar keinen Eintritt　zu bezahlen brauchen.
INT no　　admission to pay.INF　need.INF

'And for the foyer we would have had to pay no admission at all.'
(DeReKo, *Nürnberger Nachrichten*, 18/9/2006)

(2)　Aber Flavio Cotti hätte　　　　nicht zu kommen brauchen.
but　Flavio Cotti have.3SG.COND NEG　to come.INF need.INF

'But Flavio Cotti wouldn't have had to come.'
(DeReKo, *Zürcher Tagesanzeiger*, 19/6/1998)

(3)　Wie sich am　Samstag zeigen　sollte,
how REFL at.the Saturday show.INF should.3SG

hätten　　　die Suchenden nur wenige Meter
have.3PL.COND the searchers　only few　meters

zu gehen brauchen.
to go.INF need.INF

'As it turned out on the Saturday, the searchers would have had to go only a few meters.'
(DeReKo, *Rhein-Zeitung*, 24/6/1996)

(4)　Natürlich hätte　　　　der General damals　　nicht
of.course have.3SG.COND the general at.that.time NEG

Innenminister　zu sein　brauchen.
Interior.Secretary to be.INF need.INF

'Of course, the general would not have had to be Interior　Secretary at that time.'
(DeReKo, *St. Galler Tagblatt*, 18/9/2008)

(5)   Er   hätte   nur Ja   zu sagen   brauchen.
      he   have.3SG.COND only yes to say.INF need.INF
      'He would only have had to say "Yes".'
                                      (DeReKo, *Hannoversche Allgemeine*, 19/4/2008)

(6)   Durch   reifliche Überlegung hätte   sich das Trio
      through careful   consideration have.3SG.COND REFL the trio

      gar   nicht in diese Bredouille zu bringen   brauchen.
      INTP NEG   in this stew   to bring.INF   need.INF

      'After a careful consideration, the trio would not have had to get into a scrape.'
                                      (DeReKo, *Rhein-Zeitung*, 28/3/2007)

(7)   (…) ein Programm (…), dessen   sich   auch eine größere
           a   schedule   of.which REFL   also a   bigger

      Gemeinde nicht hätte   zu schämen   brauchen.
      township NEG   have.3SG.COND to be.ashamed.INF need.INF

      ' (…) a program, which a bigger township would not have   had to be ashamed of.'
                                      (DeReKo, *Nordkurier*, 7/7/2008)

(8)   Elmar Willebrand machte   deutlich, dass Asklepios
      Elmar Willebrand make.3SG.PST   clear   that Asklepios

      das Geld   nicht hätte   zu zahlen   brauchen.
      the money   NEG   have.3SG.COND to pay.INF   need.INF
      'Elmar Willebrand made clear that Asklepios would not have had to pay the money.'
                                      (DeReKo, *Nordkurier*, 18/9/2002)

(9)   daß ich nicht hätte   zu fahren brauchen
      that I   NEG   have.3SG.COND to go.INF need.INF
      'that I would not have had to go'   (DeReKo, *Süddeutsche Zeitung*, 10/7/1993)

(10) obwohl er   sie   nicht hätte   zu stellen   brauchen
      although he her.ACC   NEG   have.3SG.COND to put.INF   need.INF
      'although he would not have had to ask it (= this question)'
                                      (DeReKo, *Nürnberger Nachrichten*, 10/10/2005)

(11) Sie kümmert sich geräuschlos um   Dinge, um   die
      she care.3SG REFL silently   about things about which

      sie sich nicht hätte   zu kümmern brauchen
      she REFL NEG   have.3SG.COND to care.INF need.INF

      'She cares about things without a lot of fuss, which she would not have had to care
      about.'   (DeReKo, *Rhein-Zeitung*, 29/6/2001)

(12) Es gibt   jedoch eine O2 World, hinter der   sich
      it give.3SG though an   O2 World behind which REFL

      der Architekt nicht hätte   zu verstecken brauchen.
      the architect NEG   have.3SG.COND to hide.INF   need.INF

      'There is an O2 World, though, behind which the architect would not
      have had to hide.'   (DeReKo, *die tageszeitung*, 10/9/2008)

(13) dass ich (…) nur   ein   Stück Brot   hätte   zu kaufen brauchen
      that I   only one   piece bread have.3SG.COND to buy.INF need.INF
      'that I (…) would have had to buy only one piece bread.'

(DeReKo, Weltwoche, 14/11/2013)

(14) den   er   nicht hätte   zu fürchten brauchen
      which he   NEG   have.3SG.COND to fear.INF need.INF
      'which he would not have had to fear'

(DeReKo, Nürnberger Nachrichten, 27/4/1996)

(15) Sie ist   die einzige der   Bewerberinnen,
      she be.3SG   the only   of.the enrollees

      die   nichts hätte   zu tun   brauchen.
      who   NEG   have.3SG.COND to do.INF need.INF

      'She is the only enrollee, who would have had to do nothing.'

(DeReKo, Süddeutsche Zeitung, 9/3/2005)

The grammaticalization of 要 *Yao* and the future cycle from Archaic Chinese to Modern Mandarin*

Robert Santana LaBarge
Arizona State University

In this paper, I argue that the grammaticalization of the Chinese word 要 *yāo/yào* shows an instance of the future cycle. Similar to English *will*, 要 *yāo/yào* has developed new functional meanings apart from its earlier semantic meanings of Compulsion and Volition, including deontic and future time uses. I adopt the theory of Late Merge (van Gelderen 2004) as a descriptive account to argue that while full verb 要 *yāo/yào* is in the VP, the deontic and future time uses are in the Aspect Phrase and Mood Phrase respectively. I present evidence of scope differences in Modern Mandarin to support this thesis, and also briefly suggest that a "Problems of Projection" approach (Chomsky 2013, 2014) to grammaticalization may motivate the Late Merge phenomenon. Lastly, I show that although the older uses of 要 *yāo/yào* still exist in Modern Mandarin, they are increasingly likely to be replaced by renewed forms, as predicted in the cycle framework.

* I would like to thank the following people for their help and support: my native-speaker informants Echo Can Gao, Jianing Liu, Jill Yuching Yang, and Xia Zhang; Timothy C. Wong for his expertise and productive conversation; and Elly van Gelderen and William Kruger for presenting with me as part of a panel on linguistic cycles at the 11th Conference of the High Desert Linguistics Society at University of New Mexico in Albuquerque. An early version of this paper was presented there, and so many thanks go to Joan Bybee and all the UNM graduate students and conference participants who attended our panel and provided many helpful comments. Also thanks to three reviewers who have made extremely helpful comments during the writing of this paper. Any remaining mistakes are my own.

DOI 10.1075/la.227.13lab

1. Introduction

Over the course of more than two thousand years, new uses of the Chinese word 要 *yāo/yào*[1] (pronounced [jâʊ] in Modern Mandarin) have emerged as the result of grammaticalization. Early uses of the word were as a full verb with multiple meanings involving semantic notions of Compulsion and Volition, while more recent uses include that of an auxiliary modal indicating future time.[2] (1) and (2) show examples along this cline, while (3) shows that the full verb usage is being 'renewed' or 'reinforced' by a new lexical item. This is evidence for the presence of *cyclical change* (as in van Gelderen 2009, 2011):

Archaic Chinese (ca. 350 B.C.E)

(1)   非 …   要   譽…
      fēi   yāo   yù
      not   want fame
      '[A man may] not want/seek fame…'
                                        (孟子 *Mèngzǐ*, 公孫丑上 Gōngsūn Chǒu Part 1, Ch. 6).

Modern Mandarin

(2)   明天,   我   要   去   中國[3]
      míngtiān   wǒ   yào   qù   Zhōngguó
      tomorrow   I   will go   China
      'Tomorrow, I will go to China'.

(3)   我   想要   去   中國
      wǒ   xiǎngyào   qù   Zhōngguó
      I   would like go   China
      'I would like/want to go to China'.

Although this is only a survey study, the grammaticalization of 要 *yào* appears to be similar to the historical path of the English word *will*, which has itself been studied in considerable depth (Visser 1969; Aijmer 1985; among many others). The English examples below show a similar cline of grammaticalization and cyclical change:

Old English (ca. 700–1000 C.E)

(4)   *Will-e   ic   asecg-an…*
      Want-1s   I   say-INF
      'I want to say…'   (*Beowulf*, line 344).

---

1.   Full verb uses of 要 in Archaic Chinese take the first tone (*yāo*) instead of the fourth (*yào*). For simplicity's sake, I use Mandarin to gloss Archaic and Ancient Chinese throughout, but these eras of Chinese had quite different pronunciation. See Ulving (1997).

2.   Nominal and adjectival forms exist as well, but will not be covered here.

3.   All examples are from my own fieldwork unless otherwise specified.

Modern English

(5)   a.   *I will say...*
       b.   **I will to say...*

(6)   a.   *I want to say...*
       b.   *I wanna say...*

In (4), *will* shows agreement with its Subject *ic* (first-person singular) and takes the non-finite complement clause *āsecgān*, evidence that it is a true full matrix verb[4] (Aijmer 1985: 12). In (5a), *will* has no agreement with its Subject, and also does not force a non-finite subordinate reading of the verb *say*, as in the ungrammatical (5b). Hence, it is a modal auxiliary instead of a verb. A new verb (*want*) has come to take the place of the old *will* (6a), but it too is beginning to grammaticalize (6b).[5] Given this evidence, both English and Chinese are displaying instances of the *future cycle* (van Gelderen 2011).

But unlike *will* in Modern English, 要 *yào* in Modern Mandarin can be used either as a full verb *or* as a modal auxiliary (Li & Thompson 1981: 174).[6] Although a widely-observed phenomenon in other languages (Traugott 1989: 33), this has led to controversy among grammarians and linguists regarding the actual syntactic status of 要 *yào*, some of whom consider it to be an adverb (Li & Thompson 1981: 174–176). It is the goal of this chapter to show that the modern variable uses of 要 *yào* and their connection with the ancient uses are not at all idiosyncratic – like *will* and other verbs turned modals (Haegeman 1983; Kratzer 1977; Sarkar 1998), there is an underlying account unifying each usage. And these usages do, in fact, have a principled account as predicted by the cycle framework of formal grammaticalization theory. The syntactic upshot, then, means that for Modern Mandarin 要 *yào*, the current future time modal reading places it in the head of the Mood Phrase, having grammaticalized to

---

4.   In Old English, verbs that eventually become modals are sometimes known as "pre-modals" (Lightfoot 1979). Traugott (1989: 37) notes that many of them behave differently from true full verbs, including *sculan* ('shall') and *motan* ('must'), which "never appear in nonfinite forms". Although she does not include *will* with these latter two, for the reason shown in (4), we still may include *will* as a pre-modal based on Lightfoot's criteria (p. 114).

5.   Incorporation of the infinitive marker *to* into the full verb *want* seems to have created an new auxiliary, *wanna*. *Say* is then 'promoted' to the position of matrix verb. For example, a search engine query reveals several hundred instances of third-person subject-verb agreement with an intervening *wanna*, as is "he wanna goes…".

6.   There are exceptions for English – full verb uses of *will* exist in purposely archaic, literary, or religious contexts.

this position from the VP (in Archaic Chinese) via the Aspect Phrase (as a deontic in Ancient Chinese):[7]

(7)

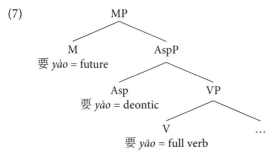

The forms of (7) still exist in Modern Mandarin, but in many cases new multisyllabic variants have appeared with a disambiguating role:

(8)

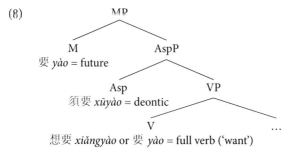

The paper proceeds following the diachrony of 要 *yāo/yào*: Section 2 briefly covers its verbal history throughout the Archaic period (texts range from ca. 475 B.C.E. – 350 B.C.E), noting that the different meanings of the word during this time can be reduced to a common semantics, either Volition or Compulsion. This, I argue, invites subsequent meaning change and modal usage as in Traugott (1989).

Section 3 analyzes the period of 要 *yào*'s transition into deontic and future modal auxiliaries (in the sense of Palmer, 2001, p. 8–9), presenting evidence from texts in Ancient Chinese (ranging from ca. 100 C.E. – 200 C.E). I discuss the grammaticalizing concept of Late Merge (van Gelderen 2004:28), and propose a way by which it may have led to the reanalysis of 要 *yào* into an auxiliary.

In Section 4, I assign the deontic use of 要 *yào* to the head of a Asp(ect) Phrase and the future use of 要 *yào* to the head of a M(ood) Phrase, as in (7) above, bringing in data from Modern Mandarin for support. Specifically, I use recent research on Mandarin sentence final particles (Erlewine, to appear) to show that the sentence final particle 了 *le* takes narrow scope under the modern future use of 要 *yào* while taking scope

---

7.   For an explanation as to the connection between deontics and the AspP, see Section 4.

over the newly-renewed deontic 須要 *xūyào* 'must'. This supports the cartographic ordering of the Mood Phrase and Aspect Phrase in van Gelderen (2004: 155–178) and the grammaticalizing tendency of modals to pass through deontic interpretations into epistemic (Bybee & Pagliuca 1987; Shepherd 1982; Traugott 1989).[8]

Section 5 discusses other recent renewals of 要 *yào*, noting that Modern Mandarin speakers are beginning to strongly prefer alternatives to 要 *yào*'s full verb usage and the future cycle is in the process of its completion (yet still incomplete), hence contributing to both the renewal and current syntactic ambiguity of 要 *yào*.

2.   要 *Yāo* as a full verb in Archaic Chinese

In this section, I analyze the syntactic and semantic status of 要 *yāo* (cf. fn. 3) in the Archaic period of Chinese. Texts from this time show that 要 *yāo* functions as a verb with a fully-developed argument structure, and has multiple but related meanings, including: 'meet', 'desire/seek', 'compel/force', 'subdue/agree', and 'submit'.[9] I present examples of each below, noting that what unites them are underlying notions of Compulsion and Volition,[10] and that these meanings set the stage for the grammaticalization of the verbal usage into the modal auxiliary usage (Lightfoot 1979; Bybee & Pagliuca 1987: 109–111; cf. fn. 4).

Perhaps the earliest instance of 要 *yāo* comes from a line in the 詩經 *Shī Jīng* (sometimes called *The Book of Songs*, or *The Classic of Poetry* in English), which is

---

8.   The cartographic ordering requires two Aspect Phrases, a phenomenon which I also discuss in Section 4. One big-picture question remains problematic: How do we allow certain words to grammaticalize into higher positions while still retaining their lower usages (as is the case here for 要 *yào*)? One solution might be a sort of "self-renewal", whereby multiple lexical entries exist for words that have been grammaticalized, including a full-verb option that fills the lower position needing renewal. But I assume, generally, as in evolutionary biology, that the creation of new categories (or species) does not entail the disappearance of the older category (or species). Perhaps a more enlightening question is how the lower category falls out of use.

9.   The meanings as presented here are simplified, naturally. The most important point is that 要 *yāo*, as a full verb, has argument structure as a matter of course.

10.   This polysemy may be the result of the interactions between the underlying semantics of 要 *yāo* (a semantics of Compulsion or Volition) with varying 'flavors' of v and resulting argument structure formation (Folli & Harley, 2004). In other words, there may not be multiple lexical entries for 要 *yāo*, but one basic meaning which changes depending on syntactic context.

among the oldest of Chinese texts. Here, 要 *yāo* requires an Object (我 *wǒ*, 'I/me'), but allows pro-drop in the Subject position:

Archaic Chinese (1046 B.C.E.–771 B.C.E)

(9) 要   我   乎   上 宮,   送   我   乎   淇   之   上   矣
     yāo *wǒ* *yú* *shàng gōng* *sòng* *wǒ* *yú* *qí* *zhī* *shàng* *yǐ*
     meet   me   PREP Shanggong   deliver me   PREP Qi   POSS   top   PART
     '[She will] meet me in Shanggong and accompany me to the mouth of the
     river Qi'   (詩經 *Shī Jīng*, 桑中 "Sāng Zhōng", stanza 1, line 3).

The meaning of 要 *yāo* in (9) is that of 'meet' with the intention of performing some subsequent action, in this case, two lovers meeting and eloping or running away together.[11] This is expected, given that Bybee & Pagliuca (1987: 109) list verbs of movement along with verbs of desire and obligation (what I have called Compulsion and Volition) as the most common potential source for future time markers. Perhaps by extension, 要 *yāo* in this case may be thought of as belonging to all three categories. But any notion of 'meeting' and subsequent movement (which may be bundled with Volition),[12] or any physical action at all for that matter, is subsumed by Compulsion in later uses several centuries later. (10) appears in the 論語 *Lúnyǔ*, or Confucian *Analects*, a series of aphorisms attributed to China's great teacher and collected by his disciples:

Archaic Chinese (ca. 475 B.C.–221 B.C)

(10) 雖   曰   [pro] 不   要   君[13]   吾   不   信   也
     suī   *yuē* [pro] *bù* *yāo*   *jūn*   *wú* *bù* *xìn*   *yě*
     though said   [pro] not   force   lord   I   not   believe PART
     'Although [it may be] said that [Zang Wu Zhong] did not force his lord,
     I don't believe this'   (論語 *Lúnyǔ*, 憲問 "Xiàn Wèn" chapter, paragraph 14).

The Compulsion semantics here can be seen in larger context in which (10) was written. Here, Confucius is chastising the actions of a certain minister Zang Wu Zhong for asking his lord to do something on that minister's behalf. Zang Wu Zhong is not

---

11. As far as I can tell, there are no instances of 要 *yāo* meaning 'to meet' unintentionally, as in 'to run into', or 'to come across'.

12. I take the 'meet' reading of 要 *yāo* here to be at least a combination of Compulsion and Volition – one is compelled to meet with a lover out of desire or lust, but the physical act of meeting is done out of one's own will.

13. Some translators, such as James Legge, appear to consider 君 *jūn* as an adjunct and 要 *yāo* as a noun, probably due to parallel passages in which 要 *yāo* does not take an object. This results in a translation of "using force with his lord". If this is true, it is not evidence against the thesis that 要 *yāo* can act as a full verb with argument structure, but rather points to the notion that there exists a separate (nominal) lexical entry for 要 *yāo*.

physically forcing his lord to complete an action, but is rather 'putting him in an awkward position', where the lord feels some pressure or compulsion to satisfy Zang Wu Zhong's request, but under ordinary circumstances shouldn't have been asked at all.

The Compulsion semantics continues with what might be considered 要 *yāo*'s most recognizable meaning, 'to desire', 'to seek', or 'to want', which is probably directly derivable from (10). Example (11) is an expanded version of (4), and is from the 孟子 *Mèngzǐ*, or *Mencius*, the eponymous text of another important philosopher in China's Confucian tradition. In the larger context, Mencius notes that human behavior is inherently good, as a man who sees a child about to fall into a well will, without thought for himself or toward his possible fame for doing so, grab the child before it's too late:

Archaic Chinese (ca. 350 B.C.E)

(11)	非	所	以	[pro]	要	譽	於	鄉	黨
	fēi	*suǒ*	*yǐ*	[pro]	*yāo*	*yù*	*yú*	*xiāng*	*dǎng*
	not	PART	PART	[pro]	want	fame	PREP	country	fellows

朋	友	也
péng	*yǒu*	*yě*
friend	friend	PART

'This [action to save a child from imminent danger] is not a means by which a man [would do to] seek fame from his fellow countrymen and friends'
(孟子 *Mèngzǐ*, 公孫丑上 Gōngsūn Chǒu Part 1, Ch. 6).

The difference between (10) and (11) then, is that in (10), the Subject is *causing* the Object to experience compulsion (putting his lord in a position where he feels forced), whereas in (11), the Subject himself is *experiencing* compulsion (i.e., the type of desire that comes from the thought of receiving fame or praise for one's actions) (cf. fn. 8).

(12) below appears to be derived from the 'meet' or 'seek' meanings above, and seems again to have an underlying semantics of Compulsion. That is, 要 *yāo* here does not mean 'agreement' in the common English sense of two people having the same opinion on a particular matter in an equal relationship, but rather is closer to a plea agreement or plea bargain between two parties:

Archaic Chinese (ca. 389 B.C.E)

(12)	使	季 路	要	我	吾	無	盟	矣
	shǐ	*Jì Lù*	*yāo*	*wǒ*	*wú*	*wú*	*méng*	*yǐ*
	send	Ji Lu	accord	me	I	no	covenant	PART

"Send Ji Lu to accord [with] me, I have no covenant"
(左傳 *Zuǒ Zhuàn*, Book 12, 哀公 Āi Gōng Year 14).

In this section, I've provided evidence that the Archaic Chinese verb 要 *yāo* has multiple meanings. Though mostly used contemporaneously, the oldest meaning is likely to be that of 'meet', which appears to have both Compulsion and Volitional semantics. As the underlying semantics changes from Volition to Compulsion, other versions of 要 *yāo* appear, including 'force', 'desire', 'subdue', and 'submit'. Important is the fact that the early verbal uses of 要 *yāo* contain argument structure, and are all related despite their polysemy. Volition and Compulsion semantics end up setting the stage for 要 *yāo*'s appearance as a modal auxiliary during the Ancient period.

3.   要 Yào as a modal auxiliary in Ancient Chinese

3.1   Deontics and futures

Section 2 argued that the early meanings of 要 *yāo* included semantic notions such as Volition and Compulsion. In this section, I appeal to the notion of Late Merge (van Gelderen 2004) to explain why 要 *yāo* in turn grammaticalizes into an auxiliary position (first as a deontic and then as a future), becoming 要 *yào* and taking a VP as its complement. I begin by discussing the qualities of the various early modal instantiations of 要 *yào* before I give possible accounts for the motivation behind its structural change.

The first auxiliary uses of 要 *yào* appear in the Ancient period, around the second century C.E. As expected (cf. Bybee & Pagliuca 1985; Shepherd 1982; Traugott 1989), they begin as deontic modals, indicating "the necessity or possibility of acts performed by morally responsible agents" (Lyons 1977:823) and (crucially) lacking argumenthood. More specifically, the earliest classes of modal auxiliaries have a meaning akin to 'you are required to X', as explicated by Traugott (1989:36) and Lyons (1982:109). Haegeman (1983:105) defines similar modals as being rooted in "external initiation", where "the decision [to act] is prompted by the situation and is a response to a request, offer, invitation, etc. from the interlocutor". Following Palmer (2001:81), we may call the structure in (13) *hortative* or *jussive* (as special types of imperatives), or possibly even *optative* (Bybee 1985:171):

Ancient Chinese (111 C. E)

(13)   要   以   俱   死   立   信
      yào   *yǐ*   *jù*   *sǐ*   *lì*   *xìn*
      must PART accompany death stand faith
      'It is imperative that you [risk] death with us for the sake of good faith'
                    (漢書 *Hàn Shū*, 張耳陳 餘傳 "Zhāng Ěr Chén Yú Zhuàn" Chapter,
                            Section 36; translation by Dobson, 1974, p. 804).

Shortly after, around the third century C.E., another deontic modal usage appears, with a meaning of 'I require you to X', or in this case, 'I require myself to X' (Traugott 1989:36;

Lyons 1982: 109). Examples (14) and (15), then, may be labeled *injunctive* (cf. Beekes 1995: 245) in that they represent a speaker imploring himself towards a particular action (cf. the 'internal initiation' of Haegeman 1983: 105), and also correspond to Bybee's (1985: 171) category of *volitional* mood markers. These examples are still spurred by external pressure, but the ultimate decision to act comes from the speaker:

Ancient Chinese (ca. 200 – 300 C. E)

(14) 我　要　自　當　以　　信　義　　　　待　人
wǒ yào zì dāng yǐ　xìn yì　　　 dāi rén
I　must self act　PART faith righteousness treat man
'I must deal with this myself and treat others with good faith'
(三國志 *Sān Guó Zhì*, 魏書 "Wèi Shū" Chapter, Section 28;
translation by Dobson 1974: 804).

(15) 吾　要　當　立　效　以　　報　　曹　公　乃　去
wú yào dāng lì　xiào yǐ　　bào　Cáo gōng nǎi qù
I　must do　stand effect PART requite Cao lord so left
'I had to do something of merit in order to requite the Lord of [Cao] and so
I left'　　　　　　　　　　　　　(三國志 *Sān Guó Zhì*, 蜀書 "Shǔ Shū"
Chapter, Section 36; translation by Dobson 1974: 804).

(16) below appears in the same text as (13) above, a century before (14) and (15), and may in fact be interpreted in a number of ways:[14]

Ancient Chinese (111 C. E)

(16) 人　生　　要　死　何　為　　苦　心
rén shēng yào sǐ hé　wéi　kǔ xīn
man born　will die why PART pain heart
'All men, being born, must/will die. Why should this pain my heart?'
(漢書 *Hàn Shū*, 武五子傳 "Wǔ Wǔ Zǐ Zhuàn" Chapter, Section 31).

(16) is ambiguous, particularly given the context in which it appears. Here, a protagonist is facing execution, which spurs him to write a poem lamenting his fate. Since his execution is obligatory (i.e. deemed by law), 要 *yào* could be seen as deontic, in which case the translation might be rendered as 'A man [in such a situation, facing imminent execution], being born, must die. Why should this pain my heart?' Being honor- or duty-bound, he may be seeking solace in the fact that he can accept his fate

---

14. If (16) is interpreted as future, this may appear to be a counterexample of the unidirectionality of grammaticalization that I have been arguing in support of. However, what is of concern in this regard is the fact that the deontics dominated *as a group* at this time and have since been almost entirely replaced by the future usage in Modern Chinese. One particular (and curious) usage does not change the general tendency.

as determined by the law. Likewise, 要 *yào* may be epistemic, referring to a "piece of knowledge or information" (Kratzer 1977: 338). In this sense, the protagonist knows, from experience or rational conclusion, that "all men, being born, must die…".

The data presented so far are summarized in Table 1 below. 要 *Yāo/yào* has changed from a semantics of Volition to a semantics of Compulsion (meaning that the deontic quality of 要 *yāo/yào* started early, even in the fully verbal uses). The Compulsion semantics is fully entrenched by the time the modal usage arises, which also establishes 要 *yào* as an auxiliary (lacking argument structure). This change from verb to modal auxiliary, which is the only real instance of grammaticalization presented so far, is delineated via shading. The final column displays the approximate date of emergence for each particular form:

Table 1

Form	Meaning	Class	Semantics	Arguments?	Emergence
要 *yāo*	'meet'	full verb	Volition	Yes	ca. 1046 B.C.E
要 *yāo*	'desire', etc.	full verb	Compulsion	Yes	ca. 475 B.C.E
要 *yào*	'[you] must'	deontic (hortative)	Compulsion	No	ca. 111 C.E.
要 *yào*	'[I] must'	deontic (injunctive)	Compulsion	No	ca. 200 C.E.

3.2 Forming auxiliary modals from full verbs

I have argued so far that the Archaic Chinese full verb 要 *yāo* grammaticalized into a modal auxiliary during the Ancient period several centuries later. I have also argued that in this sense, 要 *yāo* has followed a path similar to that of certain full verbs in (Old) English, such as *will* in Example (1). This phenomenon, of full verbs becoming modal auxiliaries, has been investigated in depth by a number of previous researchers (Aijmer 1985; Bybee & Pagliuca 1987; van Gelderen 1993; Haegeman 1983; Lightfoot 1979; Traugott 1989; Visser 1969; among many others). One question, of course, is how the leap from full verb to auxiliary modal is made. Below, I investigate the cartography of the auxiliary layer and propose a method by which 要 *yāo/yào* enters this layer.

3.2.1 *AspP and MP*

I argue that the auxiliary layer should be split into three phrases TP, MP, and AspP. Evidence "comes from [the possibility of] adverbials in the Specifiers of [those] positions" (van Gelderen 2004: 159), and is argued in-depth by Cinque (1999). Other authors such as Boye (2012: 221) propose a universal ordering of CP – MP – TP and he notes (p. 226) that Bybee has proposed a similar ordering: MP – TP – AspP. Compelling evidence is provided by van Gelderen (2004), however, that the ordering of these elements is in fact TP – MP – AspP (pp. 155–178), and with respect to modals, argues that "deontics are lower in the tree, i.e. connected to Asp, and epistemics are higher, i.e. in a category between T and Asp [namely M]", which "suggests that elements 'climb' higher up in the tree as they grammaticalize" (p. 157). A tree structure showing this general ordering is given in (17) below:

(17)

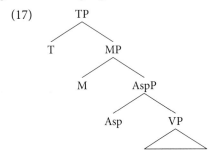

Since AspP is projected immediately above VP, we might assume that this is where the deontics of (14)–(16) are housed. That Aspect might be connected to (deontic) modals might at first seem curious, but van Gelderen makes two points. The first is that.

> "deontics [in English] originate historically as perfect, i.e. stative, verbs (*can* means 'to know', *motan* [i.e. *must*] 'to have measured', and the non-preterite-present *will* is originally 'to want') and express that original unboundedness through being in Asp. So when modals occur in Asp, the main verb cannot be stative. With a stative verb, the unboundedness must be expressed by checking Asp or by *have/be* in Asp" (p. 163).

Her examples ((12) and (13), p. 162) appear below as (18) – in the first example, *must/may* appears in Asp and *read* in V, in the second example, *be* attempts to check features by moving to Asp, but is blocked by *must/may* in that position:

Modern English

(18) a. *He must/may read that letter.*

  i.e. Someone forces/allows him to read that letter (deontic reading/ eventive verb).

  b. *#An orange must/may be healthy.*

  i.e. Someone forces/allows an orange to be healthy (deontic reading/ stative verb).[15]

---

15. Speakers' judgments vary here, a fact possibly related to interpretation of deontic modality along a strong/weak cline. Under the "strong" reading, as in (19b), an agent is forcing the state of healthiness unto an orange, and the result is ungrammatical. Under the "weak" reading, the statement is much less agentive and the sense of obligation is far less. Grammaticality is clearer with non-stative verbs (cf. "Milk must be kept in the fridge [if you don't want it to spoil]", but can be extended under the right circumstances ("An orange must be healthy

Aside from the historical connection between Aspect and deontic modals, as well as the inability for deontics to take stative verbs as complements, van Gelderen points out that deontic modals in English cannot take perfect or progressive auxiliaries as their complements (because they are base-generate in the same position, Asp), while epistemic modals can, being base-generated in M (her examples, p. 161):

Modern English

(19) a. *I can have read that book. (deontic and perfective)

b. *I can be swimming. (deontic and progressive)

(20) a. He must have read that letter. (epistemic and perfective)

b. He must be looking for that letter. (epistemic and progressive)

Like van Gelderen, I will assume the 要 *yào* of (13)–(15) is deontic and thus occupies the head of the AspP. Later instances of 要 *yào* (i.e. in Modern Chinese, see Section 4 below) are more clearly future, similar in some ways to epistemics, and so fit in M. This works nicely because, to recap, we have a diachronic model for 要 *yāo/yào* moving 'up the tree' one step at a time, from V to Asp to M.

3.2.2 *Late Merge and labeling*

Now that we have a model to describe the cartography of auxiliary positions above V, and thus can provide stopping points for the upwards grammaticalization of certain auxiliaries, we must ask how such movement could be motivated to begin with. To help solve this problem, I utilize the concept of Late Merge developed in van Gelderen (2004, p. 18).

Consider (21) below. This example repeats (10), but uses a third-person personal pronoun instead of *pro* for clarity.[16] The meaning is 'he forces [his] lord':

(21)

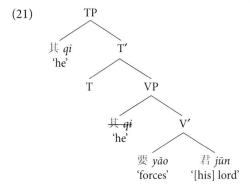

---

in order to get picked for our homemade orange juice"). See Coates (1983: 34–36) for a discussion of the strong/weak cline for deontics.

16. I add a TP on top of the VP to represent the T/M/A layer, but it could just as well be MP or AspP (generally speaking).

Since in the Spell-Out form of (21) the Subject has moved the Spec of TP, 要 *yāo* could theoretically occupy either V or T (or M or Asp) and yield identical surface structures. This fact must pose some parsing difficulties for the acquirer of a language, who receives only the surface structure as evidence, and doesn't know if (a) 要 *yāo* is generated in V and stays there, (b) 要 *yāo* is generated in V and moves to a higher head, or (c) 要 *yāo* is base-generated in a higher position. If the acquirer assumes the final hypothesis, then we have an instance of Late Merge, and 要 *yāo* successfully grammaticalizes.

But what might be the origin of the change that leads to this confusion? There are a number of possibilities. The first is with regards to c(omplement)-selection (à la Grimshaw 1979). If the c-selection abilities of a given verb are expanded beyond (human or non-human) nouns to propositions as a whole, then the structure Subject-Verb$_1$-Verb$_2$ may arise, as in (1)'s 'Wille ic asecgan'. In order for 要 *yāo* to begin to take propositional/verbal arguments, its c-selection would not have necessarily needed to change (from taking N to V), but simply become underspecified (taking either N or V), and 要 *yāo* would begin to appear in V$_1$-V$_2$ concatenated structures. Further, if 要 *yāo* lost its ability to mark Subjects as well, then the language acquirer has evidence that 要 *yāo* should in fact be in the first auxiliary position (Asp) and V$_2$ in the matrix verb position V$_1$. Hence, S-V$_1$-V$_2$ becomes S-Asp-V$_1$.

The 'promotion' of a full verb to an auxiliary could be the consequence of labeling difficulties, as outlined in Chomsky (2013, 2014). For him, the operation Merge creates binary sets out of lexical items which receive labels to be interpreted at the sensory-motor and conceptual-intentional interfaces. The labeling of sets proceeds naturally from the members of those sets. In cases where a head H merges with a phrase XP, the labeling algorithm labels the resulting set {H, XP} with the label of H. An example would be labeling a verb with its complement – the set {V, COMP} would be labeled V (as a full phrase).

Difficult cases include sets of the type {XP, YP} and {H, H}, which are not intuitive for the labeling algorithm. For the former, labeling proceeds by identifying agreeing features. For the later, labeling proceeds by internally merging (moving) one of the heads to a higher position. For example, (22) below shows movement of one head (H$_1$) from a lower position to a higher position. The lower copy is invisible to the labeling algorithm, and so the first structure gets labeled naturally as H$_2$, becoming a phrase. The resulting structure can merge with the moved head.

(22)   H$_1$ (= YP)

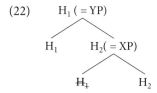

Late Merge follows naturally from the labeling difficulties of the type {H, H}. If structures of the type S-V$_1$-V$_2$ emerge naturally from the underspecification of the c-selection features of 要 *yāo*, the higher verb (要 *yāo*) must move in order to allow labeling to proceed. Since the next highest phrase is AspP, 要 *yāo* begins to occupy this position, and the auxiliary is formed.

Is it possible that something like this actually happened with 要 *yāo*? In many instances, it is difficult to tell given the (lack of) morphology in Chinese, which does not directly distinguish between auxiliaries and full verbs, or between finite verbs and non-finite verbs. For example, one might analyze (15) (repeated as (23) below) as containing a full verb 要 *yāo*, hence making 當 *dāng* ('do', 'make') the verb of a subordinate clause with 自 *zì* ('self') as its Subject:

(23)

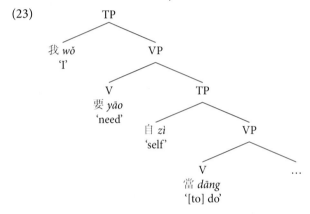

Conversely, (24) gives an auxiliary-verb analysis, in which case 自 *zì* 'self' would be an adverbial adjunct (i.e., 'by myself'), as a subordinate Subject would not be able to intervene between a modal auxiliary and a verb (hence, I've excluded it from the structure in (24)):

(24)

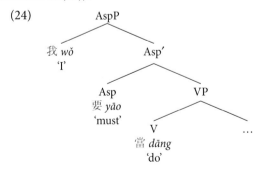

Despite this ambiguity, (24) is likely the correct analysis. Syntactically, (14) and (15) are quintessential – there are no examples of ECM Subjects appearing after 要 *yāo* and before a subordinate verb. This leads me to believe that 自 *zì* in (14) is in fact an adverbial, which along with evidence already discussed, means that 要 *yào* is indeed an auxiliary. The question as to whether (23) could have existed at one time, or that (24) is grammaticalized out of something like (23), remains. The evidence for Subject-要 *yāo*-Verb$_2$ structures, where the second verb is unambiguously a full (subordinate or non-finite) verb is unfortunately lacking. There is evidence, namely in Modern Chinese, of concatenated V$_1$-V$_2$ structures with 要 *yào* as a full verb, and I am not inclined to believe that such a structure arose anew. I turn next to an analysis of some of these contemporary structures.

4. The syntactic structure of deontic and future 要 *Yào* in Modern Chinese

In this section, I show that the future use of 要 *yào* is the prevailing one in Modern Chinese. Deontic uses exist as well, but are often represented by renewed forms (You 1998). As suggested above, I argue that the future 要 *yào* occupies the head of a Mood Phrase. To support this, I turn to examples in Modern Chinese which show that certain usages of 要 *yào* must occupy a position higher than certain modern Aspect markers and deontics. I identify that position as M, and (by analogy) identify the previous Ancient deontic use of 要 *yào* as Asp.

4.1 The ambiguous status of 要 *Yào* in Modern Chinese

There are multiple meanings of 要 *yào* in Modern Mandarin (for an overview, see You (1998)). These meanings can be divided into two major classes, verbal and auxiliary. Regarding the verbal class, two options are possible: 要 *yào* can take an NP or VP complement and in either case means 'desire', 'seek', 'wish', 'want' (You 1998: 162). This is shown below, with word classes appearing as subscripts:

Modern Mandarin

(25) a. 我 $_{VP}$要 $_{NP}$蘋果
    wǒ   yào   píngguǒ
    I   want   an apple
    'I want an apple'

 b. 我 $_{VP1}$要 $_{VP2}$洗澡
    wǒ   yào   xǐzǎo
    I   want   bathe
    'I want to take a bath'

The usage in (25b) tends to present a problem. As I've mentioned above, juxtaposing two VPs leads to some ambiguity as to whether or not the first VP is in fact that category or is instead an auxiliary. For example, there is no morphology on VP$_2$ in (25b) that would indicate that 洗澡 *xǐzǎo* is a subordinate verb, just as there is no indication that VP$_1$ (in either example) is a matrix verb. Furthermore, there is no overt CP complementizer intervening between the two verbs to indicate subordination. And since 要 *yào* is also a modal auxiliary in Modern Mandarin (cf. (28) below), it is difficult to tell whether (25b) means 'I want to take a bath' or 'I will take a bath'.

You (1998:163) shows that there is a real syntactic and semantic difference between (25a) and (25b), which disambiguates between full verb and auxiliary uses. I interpret his evidence as indicating that 要 *yào* in (25a) is a full verb 要 *yào* in (25b) is an auxiliary, as auxiliaries cannot be suffixed with aspect markers such as 了 *-le*. This supports the Late Merge analysis I gave above, where a V$_1$-V$_2$ structure is more likely to be interpreted as Aux-V$_1$.

Modern Mandarin

(26) a. 我 $_{VP}$要了 $_{NP}$蘋果
          wǒ yào-le pǐngguo
          I   want-Asp an apple
          'I wanted/asked for an apple'

      b. *我 $_{VP1}$要了 $_{VP2}$洗澡
          wǒ yào-le xǐzǎo
          I   want-Asp bathe
          *'I (have) wanted to take a bath'

In fact, (26b) shows that 要 *yào* is in fact an auxiliary in that case. For example, if 要 *yào* were a full verb in (26b), it should be able to raise and adjoin to the head above it (i.e., 了 *-le* in Asp), which is what I assume is happening in (26a). (27) shows this:

(27)

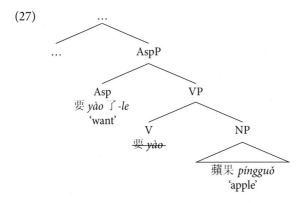

Given the ungrammaticality of (26b), the move-and-attach account of (27) can only apply to (26a). For (26b), two possibilities arise: either 要 *yào* is deontic, and hence is competing to occupy the same position with 了 *-le* (both being base-generated in Asp), or 要 *yào* is future (occupying M) and 了-*le* has no verb to attach to.[17] Either result is ungrammaticality.

Let us turn now to the future time use of 要 *yào*. (28) below uses 要 *yào* in such a way that the predicate is fully expected, pending some unforeseen circumstance (and this is solidified through the use of the adverbial 明天 *míngtiān*). It is incompatible with a full-verb reading of 要 *yào*:

Modern Mandarin

(28)   明天,   我們   要   去   中國
         míngtiān   *wǒmen*   *yào*   *qù*   *Zhōngguó*
         tomorrow   we   will   go   China
         'Tomorrow, we will [need to, ought to][18] go to China' *not*
         #'Tomorrow, we want to go to China'

(28), in other words, is asserting that it is in fact *tomorrow* that we will be going to China (not today). This is the future time/auxiliary reading. Conversely, a full verb reading meaning something like 'it is tomorrow that we will be *wanting* to go to China', implying that today we do not *want* to go to China (i.e. by tomorrow we will have changed our mind) is not available.

If the 要 *yào* of (28) is in fact future (or epistemic) rather than deontic, then according to van Gelderen (2004: 155–178), it should occupy the head of an MP rather that the head of an AspP, as I've implied. But is there any evidence for this? Other than the semantic notions covered in Section 3 above, it is very difficult to prove that 要 *yào* can or has existed in Asp. However, recent work on sentence final particles (SFPs) (Erlewine to appear) in Modern Mandarin demonstrates that 要 *yào* in fact currently occupies M. Since modern 要 *yào* is future, earlier 要 *yào* is deontic and verbal before that, we can infer a grammaticalization course of V > Asp > M. Nothing in this grammaticalization course implies that the other forms of 要 *yào* (deontic/full verb) cannot contemporaneously exist in Modern Chinese, and as mentinoed before, their usage is still widespread.

---

17.   It remains somewhat of a mystery as to why 洗澡 *xǐzǎo* could not raise to occupy that position and attach to 了-*le*. If it did, however, it would be identical with a completely separate semantic meaning, given that there is a separate change-of-state 了 *le* that can appear at the end of sentences. See Section 4.2 below.

18.   As a reviewer points out, 要 *yào* here and in similar sentences can have a deontic reading. I agree, and am hestitant to call 要 *yào* in any case a full-fledged epistemic. It may be the case that 要 *yào* in Modern Mandarin has become a sort of 'deontic future'. In any case, the use of 要 *yào* appears to be more grammaticalized than (14) and (15).

4.2　要 *Yào* as the head of a mood phrase

Modern Mandarin has two separate Aspect markers with the form 了 *le*. The first one, which I designated as "了 *-le*", (the hyphen indicating its ability to attach to a verb) is a telic marker- it indicates whether or not an event has been completed. The second 了 *le* is a change of state/inchoative marker, and indicates that a new event has come about. Rather than appearing attached to the verb, it appears as an SFP.

SFPs in Mandarin have traditionally been considered to be part of the extended CP, appearing in head-final position with respect to the rest of the clause. Erlewine (to appear) suggests that this analysis is incorrect, at least for a subset of SFPs that includes 了 *le*. He places them instead below TP but above VP, and also in a head-final configuration. (29) compares the traditional analysis with Erlewine's:

(29)　a.

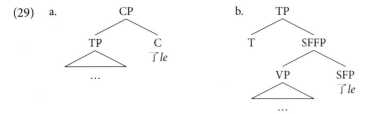

I identify Erlewine's SFPP category as AspP (akin to Grano, 2012). Adding MP to the spine gives us the following:

(30)

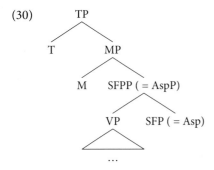

Returning the SFP analysis, Erlewine (p. 5) asserts that the SFPs under question cannot be in CP, or else they would scope over all TP-internal operators. What the evidence shows is that TP operators scope over SFPs, and SFPs scope over VP-internal operators. I reproduce his schematic below, with some modification:

(31)　a.　$[_{TP} [_{SFPP} [_{VP} \dots Op \dots] \text{ SFP }]]$　　　　SFP > Op, #Op > SFP

　　　b.　$[_{TP} \dots Op \dots [_{SFPP} [\text{ VP SFP }]]$　　　#SFP > Op, Op > SFP

Erlewine shows that in the case of modals, the circumstantial ability modal 能 *néng* 'able to' scopes under 了 *le*, while the epistemic modal 可能 *kěnéng* 'may' scopes over 了 *le* (his Example (18), p. 9):

(32) a. 張　三　能　去　台北　了　　　　　*le* > ABLE TO, #ABLE TO > *le*
　　　 Zhāng Sān néng qù Táiběi le
　　　 Zhang San able go Taibei SFP
　　　 'It has become the case that Zhang San is able to go to Taibei'.

　　 b. 張　三　可能　去　台北　了　　　　#*le* > MAY, MAY > *le*
　　　 Zhāng Sān kěnéng qù Táiběi le
　　　 Zhang San may　go Taibei SFP
　　　 # 'It has become possible that Zhang San goes to Taibei'.
　　　 ok 'Zhang San may have gone to Taibei'.[19]

In other words, (32a) asserts that Zhang San can now, as a change of state, go to Taibei (perhaps Zhang San raised enough money for a plane ticket, got over his fear of flying, was able to find a pet-sitter in time, etc.). It does *not* mean something like 'Zhang San is able *to have gone* to Taibei'. Hence, the change of state 了 *le* scopes over the entire phrase. Conversely, (32b) does not mean that Zhang San, may now, as a change of state, go to Taibei. Instead, it means that it may be the case, that he has in fact, as a new state, gone to Taibei.

Using Erlewine's method, we can see that a future marker like 要 *yào* can not only appear with SFP 了 *le* (meaning they occupy different categories), but scopes over SFP 了 *le* (meaning that 要 *yào* is in a phrase higher):

(33) 我　明天　　　要　去　成都　　　了　　　#*le* > WILL, WILL > *le*
　　 wǒ míngtiān yào qù Chéngdū le
　　 I　tomorrow will go Chengdu SFP
　　 # 'It is now the case [change of state] that tomorrow, I will go to Chengdu'.[20]
　　 ok 'Tomorrow, I will be going to Chengdu [as a new state]'.

Conversely, one lexical item that has begun to renew the formerly deontic 要 *yào*, 須要 *xūyào* 'must', scopes under 了 *le*:

(34) 我　明天　　　須要　去　成都　　　了　　　*le* > MUST, #MUST>*le*
　　 wǒ míngtiān xūyào qù Chéngdū le
　　 I　tomorrow must go Chengdu SFP

　　 ok 'It is now the case [change of state] that tomorrow, I must go to Chengdu'. (Ex: an employee comes home to tell her husband that her boss is unexpectedly sending her on assignment to Chengdu the next day)[21]
　　 # 'It will be the case that tomorrow, I must go to Chengdu'. (Ex: an employee predicts that her employer will send her to Chengdu, even though she is currently not assigned to go).

---

19. It is possible that 可能 *kěnéng* is an adverb and not an auxiliary, given that 可能 *kěnéng* can appear in the far left periphery, while 能 *néng* alone cannot.

20. The 'deontic future' reading is relevant here too. See Note 19.

21. At least one native speaker consulted considers both scopes (*le* > MUST and MUST > *le*) possible in this case.

This supports the idea that there are in fact at least two separate positions for modals in Chinese, MP for epistemics or future and AspP for deontics. The cyclical renewal of the formerly deontic 要 *yào* by 須要 *xūyào* (through the support of an additional morpheme) shows that 要 *yào* has climbed steadily 'up the tree', V > ASP > M, where it currently resides.

This brings us to two final important problems. The first is with regards to the headedness issue of (29) and (30) – why would Chinese have phrases that are not consistently head-initial? Erlewine attempts to solve this by appealing to certain notions of phase theory – i.e. since his SFP head is at the edge of a dynamic phase (Bošković 2013), it appears at the end of the higher spell-out domain, and therefore doesn't violate the Final-over-Final Constraint (FOFC) of Holmberg (2000), and thus allows a head-final phrase to take a head-initial phrase as its complement. I put aside any further analysis of dynamic phases and the FOFC, but note that even if this works for SFPs, this would still pose a problem for the thesis that deontics occupy Asp if Asp is head-final.

Since 須要 *xūyào* scopes under 了 *le*, the solution appears to lie in creating a new phrasal category for 須要 *xūyào* and the Ancient Chinese deontic 要 *yào*. Call it Asp$_2$P, and assume it is directly below the Asp$_1$P of 了 *le* and other aspectual SFPs, and directly above VP:

(35)

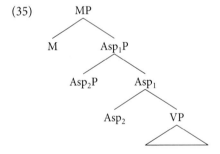

Under this analysis, we are still left with a number of questions, including why 要 *yào* 'skips' Asp$_1$ in the course of its grammaticalization whereas other verbs, such as the one which became the SFP 了 *le* clearly did not, and how this might alter Erlewine's analysis. I leave these problems open for further research.

4.3   Verbal renewal

Above, I looked briefly at the fact that a deontic form clearly related to 要 *yào*, namely 須要 *xūyào*, has entered into Mandarin. Hence, any deontic reading of 要 *yào* has been largely overshadowed by the future reading. Similar replacements are happening with the verbal usage.

As mentioned, the verbal use of 要 *yào* still exists in Modern Chinese, and behaves especially so when taking an NP complement, as in (28a). But this appears to be falling out of favor – speakers (of Mandarin, at least) tend to report that using the full verb

要 *yào* alone feels too terse and direct, and therefore impolite. Grammars, textbooks, and online usage guides tend to follow suit, recommending that 想 *xiǎng* 'to want', 'to think' or 想要 *xiǎngyào* 'to wish', 'to want', is preferred in most instances to 要 *yào*. I suspect that this feeling of (im)politeness by native speakers is epiphenomenal to the grammaticalization process, there being a positive correlation between grammaticalized words and informal usage generally (as in English *wanna* and *gonna*, etc., as well as the replacement of *want* with *would like*). Some of the differences between the older forms and their renewed versions are given below (scenario: buying bread from a clerk or shopkeeper):

Modern Mandarin

(35) a. 我   想   買   面包
           wǒ   xiǎng mǎi miànbāo
           I   think buy bread
           'I would like to buy (some) bread' (more polite)

      b. 我   _{VP}要 買   面包
           wǒ   yào   mǎi miànbāo
           I   want buy bread
           'I want to buy (some) bread' (less polite)

Furthermore, the negative 不要 *búyào* appears to be strongly dispreferred over the politer 不想 *bù xiǎng* when a speaker wishes to show unwillingness (although the difference is not one of grammaticality). 不要 *Búyào* has in fact 'fused' into the negative imperative 別 *bié*, so any other negative modal reading may simply not be available (Huang 1988), and 不想 *bù xiǎng* has renewed it as well.

Overall, it appears that the full verb form of 要 *yào* is being renewed by 想 *xiǎng*. While native speakers reason that this is simply because 想 *xiǎng* is more polite and less direct, we may note that grammaticalized forms in general tend to be the opposite. But is 要 *yào* primed for grammaticalization *because* it's more direct, or is it more direct because it has undergone grammaticalization? I suspect that the latter is true, but leave this to be determined by further research.

5.   Conclusion

Over the course of this chapter I have investigated the diachronic changes of the Chinese word 要 *yāo/yào*, from the Archaic and Ancient periods to the Modern period. The development of the word 要 *yāo/yào* parallels the development of English *will*, which has itself grammaticalized from a full verb into a future modal auxiliary, only to be renewed again by the full verb *want*. This process constitutes a grammaticalization cycle.

The future cycle in Chinese has seen 要 *yāo/yào* develop from a full verb into a deontic modal and finally into a future time marker. This diachronic change has moved 要 *yāo/yào* 'up the tree' from V to Asp to M, as shown by M's scopal relations to sentence final particles. True deontic uses are increasingly rare, and tend to be substituted by renewed forms such as 須要 *xūyào*. The full verb version of 要 *yào* in Modern Mandarin is being renewed as well, with speakers preferring 想 *xiǎng* or 想要 *xiǎngyào*, citing issues of politeness that may in fact be rooted in grammaticalization.

要 *Yào*'s status in Modern Chinese remains ambiguous, and researchers such as Li and Thompson (1981) argue that 要 *yào* ought *not* to be considered a full-fledged auxiliary. Hopefully, the research presented here sheds some light on that controversy, with two conclusions being apparent: (a) certain uses of 要 *yào* are indeed auxiliary, and (b) the nature of the ambiguous status of 要 *yào* has to do with how grammaticalization works generally. Although step-wise incremental grammaticalization leads to the formation of new syntactic categories, the old category does not automatically disappear (a parallel to biological evolution). The cycle approach predicts that such older forms will eventually be renewed or replaced, but this takes time, and an intermediary stage must always exist in which newer forms are emerging while older forms remain. Despite its long history, this is the space that 要 *yāo/yào* occupies – the cycle has yet to fully complete, and the tension remains. And so we may fully expect that the grammars of Mandarin to be written far in the future will not make any mention of 要 *yào* as a full verb, just as modern English grammars do not for *will*, except perhaps as a historical curiosity.

References

Aijmer, Karin. 1985. The semantic development of *will*. In *Historical Semantics, Historical Word-formation,* Jacek Fisiak (ed.). Berlin: Mouton de Gruyter.

Beekes, Robert S.P. 1995. *Comparative Indo-European Linguistics: An Introduction*. Amsterdam: John Benjamins. doi:10.1075/z.72

Bošković, Žjelko. 2013. Now I'm a phase, now I'm not a phase: On the variability of phases with extraction and ellipsis. *Linguistic Inquiry* 45: 27–89. doi:10.1162/LING_a_00148

Boye, Kasper. 2012. *Epistemic Meaning: A Crosslinguistic and Functional-cognitive Study*. Berlin: De Gruyter Mouton. doi:10.1515/9783110219036

Bybee, Joan. 1985. *Morphology: A Study of the Relation between Form and Meaning* [Typological Studies in Language 9]. Amsterdam: John Benjamins. doi:10.1075/tsl.9

Bybee, Joan & Pagliuca, William. 1985. Cross-linguistic comparison and the development of grammatical meaning. In *Historical Semantics, Historical Word-formation*, Jacek Fisiak (ed.). Berlin: Mouton de Gruyter.

Bybee, Joan & Pagliuca, William. 1987. The evolution of future meaning. In *Papers from the Seventh International Conference on Historical Linguistics* [Current Issues in Linguistic Theory 48], Anna Giacalone Ramat, Onofrio Carruba & Giuliano Bernini (eds),. Amsterdam: John Benjamins. doi:10.1075/cilt.48

Chomsky, Noam. 2013. Problems of projection. *Lingua* 130: 33–49. doi:10.1016/j.lingua.2012.12.003

Chomsky, Noam. 2014. Problems of projection: Extensions. Ms, MIT.

Cinque, Guillermo. 1999. *Adverbs and Functional Heads*. Oxford: OUP.

Coates, Jennifer. 1983. *The Semantics of Modal Auxiliaries*. London: Croom Helm. doi:10.1075/cilt.48

Dobson, William A.C.H. 1974. *A Dictionary of the Chinese Particles*. Toronto: University of Toronto Press.

Erlewine, Michael Yoshitaka. To appear. Sentence final particles at the vP phase edge. *Proceedings of the 25th North American Conference on Chinese Linguistics*.

Folli, Raffaela & Harley, Heidi. 2004. Flavors of v: Consuming results in Italian and English. In *Aspectual Inquiries*, Roumyana Slabakova & Paula Kempchinsky (eds), Dordrecht: Kluwer.

van Gelderen, Elly. 1993. *The Rise of Functional Categories* [Linguistik Aktuell/Linguistics Today 9] Amsterdam: John Benjamins. doi:10.1075/la.9

van Gelderen, Elly. 2004. *Grammaticalization as Economy* [Linguistik Aktuell/Linguistics Today 71]. Amsterdam: John Benjamins. doi:10.1075/la.71

van Gelderen, Elly. (ed.). 2009. *Cyclical Change* [Linguistik Aktuell/Linguistics Today 146]. Amsterdam: John Benjamins. doi:10.1075/la.146

van Gelderen, Elly. 2011. *The Linguistic Cycle: Language Change and the Language Faculty*. Oxford: OUP. doi:10.1093/acprof:oso/9780199756056.001.0001

Grano, Thomas. A. 2012. Control and Restructuring at the Syntax-semantics Interface. Ph.D. dissertation, University of Chicago.

Grimshaw, Jane. 1979. Complement selection and the lexicon. *Linguistic Inquiry* 10: 279–326.

Haegeman, Liliane M.V. 1983. *The Semantics of* will *in Present-day British English: A Unified Account*. Brussels: Paleis der Academiën.

Holmberg, Anders. 2000. Deriving OV order in Finnish. In *The Derivation of VO and OV* [Linguisik Aktuell/Linguistics Today 31], Peter Svenonius (ed.), 131–152. Amsterdam: John Benjamins. doi:10.1075/la.31.06hol

Huang, Cheng-Teh James. 1988. *Wǒ pǎo de kuài* and Chinese phrase structure. *Language* 64: 274–311. doi:10.2307/415435

Kratzer, Angelika. 1977. What 'must' and 'can' must and can mean. *Linguistics and Philosophy* 1: 337–355. doi:10.1007/BF00353453

Legge, James. 1966. *The Four Books*: Confucian Analects, the Great Learning, the Doctrine of the Mean, and the Works of Mencius. New York NY: Paragon Book Reprint Corp.

Li, Charles N. & Thompson, Sandra A. 1981. *Mandarin Chinese: A Functional Reference Grammar*. Berkeley CA: University of California Press.

Lightfoot, David W. 1979. *Principles of Diachronic Syntax*. Cambridge: CUP.

Lyons, John. 1977. *Semantics*. Cambridge: CUP.

Lyons, John. 1982. Deixis and subjectivity: *Loquor, ergo sum?* In *Speech, Place and Action: Studies in Deixis and Related Topics,* Robert Jarvella & Wolfgang Klein (eds). New York NY: John Wiley and Sons.

Palmer, Frank R. 2001. *Mood and Modality,* 2nd edn. Cambridge: CUP. doi:10.1017/CBO9781139167178

Sarkar, Anoop. 1998. The conflict between future tense and modality: The case of will in English. *University of Pennsylvania Working Papers in Linguistics* 5(2): 91–117.

Shepherd, Susan C. 1982. From deontic to epistemic: An analysis of modals in the history of English, creoles, and language acquisition. In *Papers from the Fifth International Conference on Historical Linguistics* [Current Issues in Linguistic Theory 21], Anders Ahlqvist (ed.),. 316–323. Amsterdam: John Benjamins. doi:10.1075/cilt.21.36she

Traugott, Elizabeth Closs. 1989. On the rise of epistemic meanings in English: An example of subjectification in semantic change. *Language* 65: 31–55. doi:10.2307/414841

Ulving, Tor. 1997. *Dictionary of Old and Middle Chinese: Bernhard Karlgren's* Grammata serica recensa *Alphabetically Arranged*. Gothenburg: Acta Universitatis Gothoburgensis.

Visser, Fredericus Theodorus. 1969. *An Historical Syntax of the English Language*. Leiden: E.J. Brill.

You, H.Y. (尤雪瑛) 1998. Some speculations on the semantic change of Chinese modal verb "yao". 文山評論 1(2): 161–175.

Author Index

Subject and Language Index